The Individual, Marriage, and the Family

EIGHTH EDITION

LLOYD SAXTON

College of San Mateo

Wadsworth Publishing Company ❖ Belmont, California ❖ A Division of Wadsworth, Inc.

Editor: Serina Beauparlant
Editorial Assistant: Marla Nowick
Production Editor: Sandra Craig
Designer: Andrew H. Ogus
Print Buyer: Randy Hurst
Art Editor: Donna Kalal
Permissions Editor: Peggy Meehan
Photo Researchers: Deborah Bull and Susan
    Wechsler/Photosearch
Technical Illustrator: Kathryn W. Werhane
Cover: Andrew H. Ogus
Cover Images: Detail from *The Family,* sculpture
    by Gustav Vigeland. Reproduced by
    permission of the Municipality of Oslo and
    the Vigeland Museum. Background image
    from *Art Forms from Plant Life: 122 Photographs
    by William M. Harlow,* Dover Publications,
    Inc., New York.
Compositor: Thompson Type, San Diego
Printer: R. R. Donnelley & Sons Company,
    Crawfordsville, Indiana

Printed in the United States of America
1 2 3 4 5 6 7 8 9 10 — 97 96 95 94 93

Library of Congress Cataloging-in-Publication Data

Saxton, Lloyd.
    The individual, marriage, and the family / Lloyd
Saxton. — 8th ed.
        p.   cm.
    Includes bibliographical references and index.
    ISBN 0-534-19728-0
    1. Family life education — United States.
2. Marriage — United States.   3. Family — United
States.   I. Title.
HQ10.5.U6S39   1993
306.8'0973 — dc20   92-38448

FOR NANCY

CONTENTS IN BRIEF

CONTENTS

CHAPTER 3
The Many Faces of Love   51

CHAPTER 4
Fundamentals of Sexuality and Eroticism 83

CHAPTER 8
The Changing Family in a Changing Society   219

CHAPTER 9
Women, Work, and the Family   257

CHAPTER 10
Parenting and the Development of Children 295

PART IV
CONFLICT, DIVORCE, AND REMARRIAGE

CHAPTER 11
Couples in Conflict: Problems of Communication   333

PREFACE

While teaching marriage-and-family courses at the College of San Mateo and counseling troubled couples in San Francisco, I began to see a pattern in the characteristic problems of intimate couple interaction. The "before" and "after" experiences did not follow the romanticized image commonly projected in our popular culture: The students I taught looked upon marriage with romantic idealism, but the couples who came to my counseling office were disillusioned and bitter. I began to realize that despite the preoccupation in our society not only with love and sexuality but with nearly all male-female interactions, most of my students and virtually all of the troubled couples in the counseling office were astonishingly unaware of the extraordinary dimensions of love, of the physiological, psychological, and societal patterns of their sexuality, and of the many other forces that are involved in establishing and maintaining a sound relationship.

This book was conceived as a response to these informational gaps. It describes key discoveries made by researchers in a wide range of disciplines — biology, sexology, psychology, sociology, political science, history, economics, and demography, as well as the arts, philosophy, and theology. One by one, pieces of the fascinating mystery of the relationship between the sexes are put into place, yielding a picture of the wide scope of male-female behavior in dating, marriage, and the family in our unique contemporary society.

In assembling this broad array of inquiry and knowledge, I have sought clarity without over-simplification, so that accurate, unbiased, interesting, and practical information becomes readily available to readers. This book should thus prove a useful tool for instructors who are faced with the task of helping students develop their understanding and appreciation of the complexity and richness of intimate relationships.

Important topics covered in the book are such universals as gender, love, sexuality, intimacy, communication, commitment, power, conflict, work, money, singlehood, courtship, cohabitation, marriage, family, divorce, remarriage, child development, and family violence. Gender, of course, colors virtually all aspects of male-female interaction. Love is of critical importance not only in the bonding of a couple but in almost all aspects of intimate and familial interaction, such as the bonding between a mother and child. Sexuality is almost always an important aspect of intimate couple interaction and bonding, although its meaning varies from individual to individual and from couple to couple. Communication is, of course, basic to all interaction, while work and money form a persistent thread woven through the fabric of most individual and family concerns.

What Is New in This Edition

In response to the changing face of the American family and to suggestions from many professors, a new chapter, "Women, Work, and the Family" (Chapter 9), is now included in the book.

In addition, all demographic data has been thoroughly updated, and new material reflecting recent research has been added to the following topics:

- The importance of communication; the differences between the meaning and intent of women's and men's conversation.

- The increased need for intimacy and commitment in our society; the effect of loneliness on physical health and well-being.

- Theories of mutual attraction and mate selection; the impact of shyness; methods of successfully treating shyness.

- The relation between religion and marriage; the rising incidence of interfaith marriage.

- The growing population of racial-ethnic groups in our society, such as Hispanics and Asian Americans; the changing economic status of racial-ethnic groups; patterns of dating, marriage, divorce, and family structure in these groups.

- Male and female sexuality; communication and sexual interaction; sexual desire and sexual aversion; the significance of lovemaps as an explanation for attraction or aversion between potential lovers; sexual compatibility and incompatibility; sexual problems and sexual dysfunction; sex and aging; extramarital sex; patterns of sexuality in straight, gay, and lesbian couples; paraphilia (abnormal patterns of sexuality).

- The high rate of teenage pregnancy; poor fetal development, low birth weight, and high infant mortality for babies with teenage mothers; the likelihood of lifelong poverty for teenage mothers; the controversy over whether high schools should provide contraceptive information and devices (such as condoms) to their students; the position of right-to-life groups and freedom-of-choice groups regarding this issue; the position of these groups regarding abortion.

- The impact of AIDS and other STDs on individuals and society.

- The sexual abuse of women, including unwanted sexual innuendo, unwanted sexual aggression, sexual harassment, rape, and date rape.

- Family violence; the battering of women; reasons why women stay in violent relationships; child battering; child molestation; parent battering; the effects of alcohol and drug abuse on families.

- Communication and conflict between couples; the relationship among power, sex, and money in cohabitation and marriage; the complex interaction between relationship satisfaction and sexual satisfaction for men and women.

- Delayed marriage and the rising incidence of never-married singles; types of never-married singles; the correlation between increased education and delayed marriage for women; the decrease in marriage prospects for women over age thirty; black women's relatively lower prospects for marriage; delayed parenthood; the increased incidence of child-free marriages.

- The rising incidence of cohabitation; cohabiting families; commitment in cohabitation; what men and women expect from cohabitation; the advantages and disadvantages of cohabitation; the relatively higher divorce rate of couples who have cohabited before marriage (or remarriage).

- The changing American family; the fragmentation of the traditional family through higher divorce rates and rising out-of-wedlock births; the single-parent family; the two-earner family; the fivefold increase (since the 1960s) of employed mothers of preschool children; the problems of mothers who work a second shift at home after completing a first shift at their workplace; the rising poverty rate of single parents; role strain and work overload in single-parent and two-earner families; stresses on family members; "supermoms" and "superdads"; the lack of leisure time and the lack of time with children in single-parent and two-earner families; latchkey children; near-homeless and homeless families; remarriages and stepfamilies.

- Unemployment, lower-paying jobs, part-time jobs, job insecurity, and the deteriorating economic situation of middle- and low-income families.

- Discrimination against women; the "glass ceiling."

- Falling levels of educational attainment; the increasing cost of higher education; deteriorating standards of health care for children; increasing levels of depression and anxiety among children; the increase in childhood obesity; the increasing number of developmental and behavioral disorders of children; the rising rate of teenage suicide.

- Divorce and separation; consequences and effects of no-fault divorce on children, on women, and on men; noncaring divorced fathers; nonpayment of child support; the continuing effect of marital disruption following a divorce; the increase in annulments granted by the Catholic church; issues of child custody for working parents.

- Authoritative, authoritarian, and permissive parenting; parental stress; male and female roles in nurturing children; maximizing the potential of children; the importance of fathers in child development; the importance of peer friendships in child development.

Three new features have been added to the Eighth Edition. A boxed feature, "What Do You Know?" now opens each chapter, providing readers with an intriguing glimpse of the chapter's contents and challenging their knowledge of the topic. Key Terms are now supplied at the end of each chapter, followed by a list of Suggestions for Further Reading.

In addition, the Glossary has been expanded, and the Subject Index is more detailed.

Acknowledgments

No textbook is written alone, and I should like to express my gratitude to the following instructors of marriage-and-family courses, who have made their own special insights available to me, generously giving their time and interest and providing me with advice and suggestions during the preparation of this edition: Doug A. Abbott, University of Nebraska; Brent Barlow, Brigham Young University; Laurie Lane Goldberg, Arizona State University; Michael Goslin, Tallahassee Community College; Mary June Impson, Texas Woman's University; Keith Kimble, Catawba Valley Community College; Gary Luft, University of Akron; Shirley McCorkell, Saddleback College; T. Robert Moseley, Rockland Community College; William Polich, Rochester Community College; Thomas W. Roberts, Western Kentucky University; Roger H. Rubin, University of Maryland, College Park; Charles F. Seidel, Mansfield University; Tom Sibley, Bossier Parish Community College; and Karen Cole Smith, Santa Fe Community College.

I must also acknowledge a debt of gratitude to the numerous researchers and writers in the field (more than nine hundred references are listed in this edition). Any shortcomings are mine, not theirs.

I should also like to thank my colleagues and students, who were a rich source of stimulating challenges and queries—a wellspring of inspiration for many of the concepts in the book.

I also wish to express my appreciation for the encouragement and help provided by the skilled professionals at Wadsworth — the editors, artists, designers, and researchers who saw this book through the process from its inception through the many stages of development and production. Special thanks are merited by the sociology editor, Serina Beauparlant, and the production editor, Sandra Craig.

And finally, I wish to acknowledge the collaboration of my wife, Nancy, who not only actively participated in much of the research and contributed many of the ideas but also forced me to think through many of my initial ideas before I could put them in sensible form. The vision of this book is as much hers as mine.

Lloyd Saxton
Larkspur, California, 1993

PART I

Introduction

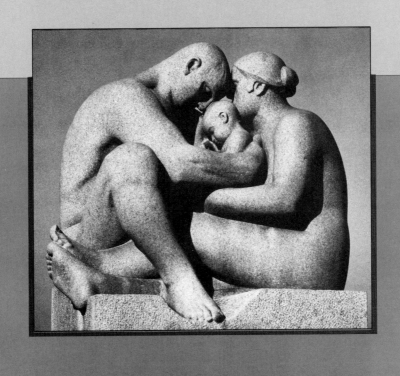

CHAPTER 1

An Overview

Jack and Jill went up the hill . . .
Nursery Rhyme (Anonymous)

The Nature of Relationships
Societal Patterns of Relating
Sexuality and the Family in Today's America

What Do You Know?

Some of the following statements are true and some are false.
Can you tell which are which?

T/F   1. Wanting to be part of a couple is of relatively little importance in our society.

T/F   2. Most people in our society feel that their happiness is based chiefly on the quality of their close relationships.

T/F   3. A bond within a couple is always based on sex.

T/F   4. Maintaining closeness with another person can be the most important aspect of one's life.

T/F   5. Everyone has about the same need for intimacy.

T/F   6. Given one wish in life, most Americans would wish to be loved.

T/F   7. Dating and romantic love are characteristic of most of the world's societies.

T/F   8. A young black woman has about the same likelihood of marriage as a young white woman.

T/F   9. The divorce rate among blacks in the United States is about twice as high as it is among whites.

Answers: 1-F, 2-T, 3-F, 4-T, 5-F, 6-T, 7-F, 8-F, 9-T.

Every human being has certain basic needs. We seek first to fulfill our basic physical needs for such things as food, shelter, safety, and reasonable comfort.[1] When these needs are partially satisfied, we seek to fulfill our basic social needs for direct, intrinsically rewarding interactions with others — who will receive and return the essential satisfactions of companionship, emotional support, affection, and, in some relationships, sex. We seek a place in our immediate society (whatever it may be) where we may achieve some measure of acceptance, recognition, and respect. And we seek to acquire meaning and purpose in our lives.

In traditional America, we would seek to fulfill these basic physical and social needs by dating, courting, and marrying. We would attempt to earn a living for ourselves and our families, rear our children, and find some satisfactions and meaning in the personal interactions of marriage and family, and in the group interactions of vocational and leisure-time affiliations and activities. In present-day America, with its high divorce rate, high remarriage rate, and high incidence of single parents, the family has been redefined. The same needs and the same values still apply, but they are now taking different forms, with new manifestations.

How we seek to obtain basic satisfactions in both the physical world (of objects and things) and the social world (of other people) depends on two interacting functions: (1) our genetic makeup — the individual anatomical, physiological, and psychological factors that are unique to each person, and (2) our socialization — the way we have learned through interaction with our society to view our environment and ourselves, the expectations we have developed though this interaction, and the ways we have learned to interact with others to satisfy our needs. Together, these two functions (genetic and learned) form our individuation, our own distinctive personality. In other words, although each of us is uniquely ourselves, an individual differentiated from every other person, we discover and experience our existence and individuality within the group — the society and culture into which we are born. We internalize the societal norms and experiences to form our own unmatched personality;[2] yet we inevitably come to be indistinguishable in many respects from the other persons who are products of the same society and culture. We are socialized individuals.

It is the societal aspect of human behavior that makes a book such as this possible; for we may examine the society and its culture and determine with reasonable accuracy the general behavioral patterns of persons in that society and its subsocieties as they seek to fulfill their individual needs. It is the individualistic aspect of human behavior that makes a book such as this practicable; for we will find that the quality and success of an intimate relationship (whether in dating, cohabitation, or marriage) depend not so much on cultural similarities of the two people as on their individual differences and their awareness and appreciation of each other's qualities, needs, and responses. Such awareness and appreciation are the chief purposes of this book; the dynamics, the success, and the failure of an intimate relationship in our differentiated and complex society are the subjects.

In this chapter we will look first at the nature of relationships and then at the nature of the society in which we are all immersed.

---

[1] In some situations, of course, a social need will take precedence over physical needs — for example, the mother who will do without food in order to feed her children.

[2] The values, attitudes, and expectations of a society that become a part of a person's own code of behavior are said to be internalized.

Loneliness is a very common experience in our contemporary mass society.
George Tooker: The Subway, *1950.*

The Nature of Relationships

We have all experienced an enormously wide range of relationships in our lives. For most of us, these relationships form the very core of our existence. The relationship between the sexes is especially fascinating — artists, lyricists, and scientists alike have speculated endlessly about its meaning and its ramifications. Philosophers, theologians, psychologists, sociologists, historians, and demographers have not been immune to its mystery.

As complex and varied, and sometimes puzzling, as our relationships are, they may be conceptualized as falling into just two major types: (1) secondary relationships and (2) primary relationships. These have quite different characteristics from one another, and both are essential for the survival and well-being of the individual in today's America.

Secondary and Primary Relationships

Except for the rare few who manage to live as isolates, away from all human contact, we all relate to one another in a continual series of encounters from birth. Most of these interactions are secondary relationships.

A **secondary relationship** is an interaction with someone whom we either do not know at all or know very little. Each person in a secondary relationship is important to the other only because of the *function* each fulfills for the other. This function — the provision or exchange of goods or services — is the basis of most social interactions in our society.

Secondary relationships are relatively brief, formal, and impersonal. They are generally based on a mutually agreed-upon reciprocity of exchange, or ***quid pro quo*** ("something for something").

For example, a shopper who goes into a supermarket to buy a pint of milk has a secondary relationship with the checker. Neither the shopper nor the checker is important to the other as a unique individual; each is interchangeable. The shopper could be replaced by another shopper or the checker by another checker without making any meaningful difference to the transaction. Moreover, the value of the exchange is precisely determined beforehand — "not a penny more nor a penny less." If either person in the transaction deviated too much from the role behavior expected in the exchange,[3] their relationship would collapse. The role behavior of the person in the position "shopper" and that of the person in the position "checker" are confined within fairly narrow limits, in much the same way that a classic *pas de deux* is precisely choreographed.

In contrast, a **primary relationship** is relatively enduring, informal, and personal. The values that each person provides for the other and receives from the other are not precisely fixed and may be intangible. The exchange of satisfactions depends on the unique qualities each has as an individual. The human values of affection, acceptance, compassion, and understanding are not only important but essential to the transaction in a primary relationship. Because the unique quality of each person is crucial, individuals are not interchangeable in primary relationships. (See Table 1-1.)

Extrinsic and Intrinsic Satisfactions

The satisfactions exchanged in a secondary relationship are **extrinsic** (external, or derived

---

[3]Role behavior is the behavior expected of a person who is occupying a socially recognized position — for example, "shopper," "checker," or more complex positions such as "parent." Positions (in the sociological sense) always carry expected and prescribed role behaviors appropriate to the position.

TABLE 1-1

Characteristics of Primary and Secondary Relationships

Characteristics of Secondary Relationships	Characteristics of Primary Relationships
Impersonal	Personal
Formal	Informal
Precise	Spontaneous
Deliberate	Intimate
Quid pro quo specified	*Quid pro quo* unspecified
Human qualities of affection, compassion, etc., relatively unimportant	Human qualities of affection, compassion, etc., very important
Personal characteristics relatively unimportant	Personal characteristics very important
Emphasis on the function, or service, each is fulfilling	Emphasis on the interaction of the couple
Satisfactions usually extrinsic	Satisfactions usually intrinsic

---

from without). Thus the pint of milk for the shopper and the money for the checker are examples of extrinsic satisfactions. The satisfaction obtained from a primary relationship, on the other hand, is chiefly **intrinsic** (pleasurable in and of itself); that is, the satisfaction in a primary relationship is provided by the nature of the interaction, not by giving or receiving goods or services that are external to the relationship.

It is possible, of course, for a given transaction to have overtones of a primary relationship for one person while being purely a secondary relationship for the other person. For example, one person may receive personal (intrinsic) satisfaction while the other receives money (extrinsic satisfaction). If a couple in a primary relationship are dancing with each other, each is receiving intrinsic satisfaction. Compare this with the situation in a taxi dance club of the 1930s: A hostess (a "taxi dancer") would dance with a patron in exchange for a token costing ten cents. The dancing gave the hostess no intrinsic satisfaction; for her, this was a secondary relationship, and most of her satisfaction was extrinsic (in the form of being paid). The patron, however, received intrinsic satisfaction from dancing with the hostess; otherwise he would not have been willing to pay her. In this relationship, the *quid pro quo* is intrinsic for one person and extrinsic for the other. There is usually an overlap, however, between intrinsic and extrinsic satisfactions. In most interactions each person experiences some elements of each.

A relationship that starts out as secondary may move, either gradually or quickly, toward the primary end of the continuum.

Continuum of Secondary and Primary Relationships

In the real world of human experience, just as any transaction usually has some elements of intrinsic and extrinsic satisfaction for both participants, so does the relationship normally fall between the two extremes of secondary and primary (see Figure 1-1). Virtually all relationships start at the secondary end of the continuum. The pattern of progression is usually from strangers, to acquaintances, to companions, to friends — and then perhaps to lovers. For example, suppose a man walks into his favorite coffee shop after an absence of several weeks and finds that a new waitress has been hired. Initially, his interaction with this waitress is clearly second-ary. Her function is to provide him with the extrinsic satisfaction of food and service, while he provides her with the extrinsic satisfaction of paying the check and leaving a tip. If the man becomes interested in her as an individual with unique personal qualities, his relationship with her might begin to move away from the secondary and toward the primary end of the continuum. If she reciprocates his interest and responds positively to his overtures of friendliness, the relationship may continue to move toward the primary end of the scale.

A relationship may also move in the opposite direction, from the primary end of the continuum toward the secondary end. Thus, a young woman may begin to refuse dates if she loses

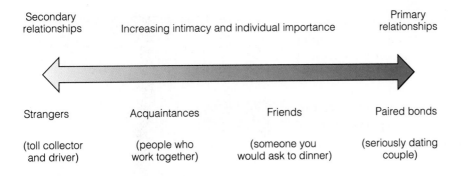

FIGURE 1-1

The continuum of secondary and primary relationships.

interest in a young man. Or a married couple may "fall out of love" to the point at which they are very formal, impersonal, and perhaps hostile toward each other in any necessary interaction (such as meeting in a divorce lawyer's office to discuss a property settlement).

The closer a relationship is to the primary end of the continuum, the more complex it becomes, the more subtle are the satisfactions exchanged, and the more difficult it is to assess the relative value of each person's satisfactions. Fulfilling expectations in a primary relationship must depend chiefly on each person wanting to please the other and deriving intrinsic satisfaction from doing so.

Primary Relationships and Paired Bonds

A couple in a primary relationship may form a paired bond. A **bond** is anything that ties, binds, or fastens together. Emotional forces of love, affection, self-disclosure, and commitment form the bond that ties or binds a couple together. A bond between two people may form quickly (so-called love at first sight) or it may have mutual liking and respect as a basis and build gradually through a series of shared activities, experiences, interests, and ideas.

Types of Paired Bonds A **paired bond** may be either sexual (erotic), such as the bond between lovers, or asexual (not erotic), such as the bond between family members or between companions or friends. An asexual bond may be just as intense as a sexual bond. For example, the bond between a mother and child is very intense, but it is asexual.[4] Adults may also form asexual paired bonds with friends or companions. With dating couples, pair bonding often depends initially on physical appearance or on **limerence**—a strongly compulsive, overwhelming attraction to another person. If this limerent attraction is mutual (reciprocated), each of the couple seems unique to the other and the bonding is especially strong (see Chapter 3). In early adolescence, such a bond may be asexual, forged from elements of romantic love and attraction. In later adolescence and adulthood, the bond may be

---

[4]The pair bonding between mother and infant seems to depend initially upon skin-to-skin and eye-to-eye contact during the first few hours and days following birth (see Chapter 10).

BOX 1-1

Pair Bonding with an Animal

A paired bond can form between a person and an animal, and such a bond can rival in intensity the paired bonds that form between two people. Pet owners often so love their animals that they regard them as close members of the family.

Since the days of the ancient Egyptians, pets have been loved by their owners. In return, pets have responded with nonjudgmental loyalty and love. "Like children, pets depend upon us, but unlike children they never grow up, never ask for the car, and seldom cry, fuss, or say *no*" (Meer 1984, p. 60).

In a classic study of pets and their owners, 80 percent of the owners often felt that their pets were their closest companions. Virtually all pet owners talk to their pets, and about 40 percent talk to their pets as confidants. More than half of all people who own dogs or cats sleep with them in the same bed, and an additional one-third sleep with them in the same room (Meer 1984). One out of two pet owners keep pictures of their pets in their wallets or display such pictures at home or in the office, and one out of four pet owners have a formal drawing or portrait of their pet (Horn and Meer 1984).

Pet-food products are the single largest category of supermarket items. Pet food takes up an average of 240 linear feet of supermarket shelf space; this is more space than is taken up by baby food or by any other category (Horn and Meer 1984).

Nearly all (97 percent) pet owners over age 50 are so grief stricken at the death of a family pet that their lives are severely disrupted. It is not unusual for a bereaved pet owner to hold a funeral service for the dead animal and to have the body interred in a pet cemetery (Horn and Meer 1984).

sexual (see Chapters 3, 4, and 5). An asexual paired bond may also be forged between a person and an animal. This human-animal bond may be extraordinarily intense (see Box 1-1).

Pair Bonding and Love   Love can take many different forms and is a very difficult concept to define. For a detailed analysis of the various aspects of love in a paired bond, see Chapter 3. Briefly, when a couple are in love, each values the other and is preoccupied with feelings, thoughts, dreams, and fantasies about the other. Being in love is perhaps the ultimate experience of bonding. Given one wish, most people would wish to be loved (Avery 1989).

Pair Bonding, Commitment, and Exclusivity   Each member of a couple who are romantically in love feels committed to the other, and expects the other to feel committed in return. Commit-

Bonding may occur between a person and an animal.

side attraction occurs, persists, and is acted upon, the initial bond is likely to be destroyed. Exclusivity is usually regarded as essential to success in a committed relationship. It should be noted, however, that there are people who have no compunctions, or feel no guilt, about being in love with more than one person at a time—for them, this is a normal aspect of romantic love.[5]

Pair Bonding and Intimacy One of the characteristics of a paired bond is **intimacy**. The need to achieve pair bonding and intimacy has been recognized as a basic drive by many researchers.[6] Achieving and maintaining intimacy in a paired bond can be the center of one's life, for maintaining an intimate relationship may provide a validation of one's identity and place in the world. Because of the crucial function that intimacy plays in a person's life—and because of the difficulties that may occur in its absence—the importance of establishing and maintaining intimate relationships can scarcely be overemphasized. The need for intimacy, and the search for it, are often driving forces that initiate or motivate dating and then impel a person to cohabit or to marry (see Chapter 5).

The major components of intimacy are feelings of closeness, warmth, affection, mutual trust, interdependence, and self-disclosure (Avery 1989; Perlman and Duck 1987). Each person in an intimate relationship has an effect on the other; that is, a change in one person brings about a change in the other (Berscheid and Peplau 1983).

ment implies stability, duration, and consistency. Thus neither of the couple anticipates becoming romantically attracted to anyone outside the relationship, and typically only one paired bond is formed at a time.

If one of the couple in a paired bond is romantically attracted to someone else, the person being attracted in this way typically feels guilty or disloyal (such an attraction usually carries the onus of cheating in our society). If such an out-

---

[5]A **ludus** person may be in love with two or more persons at a time. On the other hand, an **eros** person is especially devoted to exclusivity in a romantically paired bond. As we will see (Chapter 3), most people are a blend of personality types, so that—along with most human traits—the emphasis on exclusivity occurs along a range that extends from low to high.

[6]See, for example, Kieffer 1977, Maslow 1971, Berger and Kellner 1970, Fromm 1970, and Angyal 1965.

Some couples consistently value a particular kind of closeness — either physical, intellectual, or emotional closeness — in their relationships. More commonly, couples may especially value emotional closeness at one time, intellectual closeness at another time, and physical closeness at still other times. Intimate couples usually experience a blend of emotional, physical, and intellectual closeness (Perlman and Duck 1987).

Not all intimacy is the same; intimacy may be sexual or asexual, as we have seen. In addition to the presence or absence of sexuality, intimacy varies in intensity across the continuum of relationships. We may have a low degree of intimacy with a casual acquaintance or friend or a high degree of intimacy with a best friend or a lover. The degree of intensity in a relationship depends on three factors: breadth, openness, and depth (Kieffer 1977).

- **Breadth** of intimacy is measured by the number of activities, beliefs, and interests a couple share.

- **Openness** in intimacy is measured by the extent of self-disclosure in the relationship. The more we are able and willing to disclose our innermost thoughts and feelings to another person, the greater the openness. Because openness leaves us vulnerable to rejection, we may find this aspect of intimacy very threatening. However, if we remain guarded or cautious, keeping the normal social safeguards in place, we cannot achieve openness in an intimate relationship, whatever its breadth.

- **Depth** is a measure of how important each of the couple is to the other — how committed they are. When depth is a major characteristic of an intimate relationship, just being together results in both people feeling a sense of well-being, often described as a sense of wholeness or completeness. When the depth of intimacy is very great,

each member of the couple experiences a sense of uniting with the other (Kieffer 1977).

People with a Low Need for Intimacy

All human characteristics vary in intensity from one person to another, and the need for intimacy is no exception. Some people have a lower need for intimacy than others and may prefer privacy and independence. These people may live alone and work alone by choice (see Chapter 6).

People with a low need for intimacy are of three types: preintimates, pseudo-intimates, and isolates:[7]

- **Preintimates** are capable of closeness but are in no hurry to achieve intimacy. Perhaps they feel ambivalent about commitment. In the meantime, preintimates proceed at their own pace.

- **Pseudo-intimates** appear to be in an intimate relationship, but they are not. Pseudo-intimates may date, cohabit, or marry, but their relationships never attain any openness or depth but instead remain superficial and shallow social interactions with little emotional involvement and little commitment. Pseudo-intimates are usually storge (pronounced STORE-gay) personality types (see Chapter 3).

- **Isolates** have very little need for any social interaction. They tend to be recluses, avoiding human contact as much as possible. An isolate may be a saint pursuing self-enlightenment, a social misfit, or anything in between.

None of these three personality types exists in pure form. As with all human traits, the need

---

[7]This discussion is drawn from Orlofsky, quoted in Perlman and Fehr 1987, pp. 17–18.

for solitude and for being intensely involved in the pursuit of knowledge, work, art, or religion varies by degree and may change with circumstances.

Societal Patterns of Relating

We all live within our society, which has certain patterns to which we must conform. We must seek to satisfy our basic needs for pair bonding, intimacy, and commitment within the confines of our own particular society. Whenever we pursue the attainment of love, sex, marriage, and a family of our own (in whatever form it may take), we do so within a societal setting.

Society and Culture

A **society** is an aggregate of people in a relatively large associational group that has some sort of permanence.[8] All societies must provide for humans' fundamental needs: finding food, protecting themselves from enemies, reproducing, and nurturing and socializing their children. The way people accomplish these fundamentals — the specific tools they use and the values and attitudes they learn — is termed **culture** and varies considerably from society to society.

Culture comprises all the thoughts, beliefs, customs, laws, mores, values, religious observances, festivals, food preferences, languages, art, entertainment, songs, dramas, literature, tools, implements, artifacts, and social institutions[9] that are current in a society.

Patterns of dating, romantic love, sexual behavior, and male-female roles in marriage are all culturally determined and differ markedly not only from society to society but also within each subsociety of the society at large. All societies, however, make some provision for sexuality, without which there would be no children to perpetuate the society's existence into the next generation. All societies have developed elaborate rules, laws, customs, and procedures for channeling sexuality, and societies differ enormously in the ways in which they have done this (see Chapter 7).

Members of a society are indoctrinated into its culture by a process of **cultural conditioning** or **socialization**. Cultural conditioning is ubiquitous, inescapable, and essential for survival in any society. The process of cultural conditioning starts in infancy and is normally well established by the time a child is about five years old (see Chapters 2 and 10).

Subsocieties and Subcultures

Most societies — certainly our own — are made up of a number of different **subsocieties**, each with its own characteristic **subculture**. Although much of what we do is virtually identical throughout our society, some patterns of behavior differ significantly from one subsociety to another. Thus, patterns of dating, incidence of teenage pregnancy, birth-control methods, birthrates, incidence of cohabitation, marriage

---

[8] The concept of society has been defined in various ways, including "a relatively self-sufficient and self-sustaining group of people who are united by social relationships and who live in a particular territory" (Stark 1989), "a population that occupies the same territory, is subject to the same political authority, and participates in a common culture" (Robertson 1987), "a group of individuals competing for conventional prizes by conventional means" (Wynne-Edwards 1964), and "an aggregate of people who live and work together, and who share a common body of meanings and a common sense of values" (Brown 1963).

---

[9] A social institution is a collective solution to a need. A social institution may consist of no more than two people (such as marriage), or it may consist of millions of people (such as the military). Schools, churches, insurance companies, banks, health clubs, and bowling leagues, as well as baptism, *bar mitzvah*, marriage, and divorce, are all examples of social institutions.

rates, incidence of divorce, incidence of remarriage, and characteristics of family interaction differ markedly among our various subsocieties. To lump together all the members of our society can therefore be very misleading. For example, although about half of all first marriages in our society end in divorce, some subsocieties have only a fraction of this rate (see Chapter 12).

We will pay special attention to subsocieties based on social class, religion, and racial-ethnic groups. When appropriate and when information in available, we will also note divergences among other demographic groups that are not usually regarded as subsocieties, such as groups based on gender, educational level, occupation, marital status, or age.

Social Class   Many aspects of how we date, marry, relate to spouses, divorce, and remarry differ significantly from one social class to another. **Social class** is a convenient, though imperfect, measure of a person's position in the hierarchy of a society (see Box 1-2). Social class is based chiefly on such factors as a person's amount of income, source of income, occupation, level of education, nature of residence, and location of residence. Family name, which is a basic determinant of position in a caste system, contributes to one's position in our social class system only indirectly — in terms of such factors as occupation, amount and source of income, level of education, and nature and location of residence.

Using these measures, sociologists construct an index that places individuals in the upper, middle, or lower social class. They then further divide these classes into upper-upper, lower-upper, upper-middle, lower-middle, upper-lower, and lower-lower classes. Together, the lower-middle and upper-lower classes constitute the "working class" — the backbone of the subsociety that produces goods and renders services. The upper class includes the truly powerful,

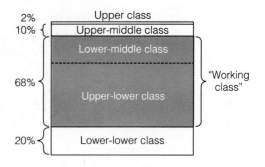

FIGURE 1-2
Stratification of social classes in the United States.

wealthy decision makers of our society. The upper-middle class includes professionals, managers, and small-business owners. Lower-middle class people are "white-collar" workers, such as salespeople, bank tellers, file clerks, typists, and secretaries. The upper-lower class is composed of "blue-collar" workers, such as carpenters, electricians, truckers, and other skilled workers. The lower-lower class includes those who do menial unskilled work, transients, and those who chronically remain unemployed.

The percentages of our population in these social classes vary from area to area, from community to community, and with one's definition of social class. In general, nationwide, sociologists consider about 2 percent of our society to be upper class, about 10 percent to be upper-middle class, about 68 percent to be "working class," and about 20 percent to be lower-lower class (see Figure 1-2).

Certain problems exist with the concept of social class. Precise definitions are difficult to establish and even more difficult to apply, exceptions abound, cross-class characteristics occur (only a high school education but relatively high income), and some people — such as sports stars, entertainers, and other celebrities — don't seem to fit into the classification system at all. Moreover, in our society it is possible to move from

All Societies Are Stratified

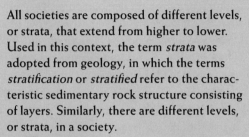

All societies are composed of different levels, or strata, that extend from higher to lower. Used in this context, the term *strata* was adopted from geology, in which the terms *stratification* or *stratified* refer to the characteristic sedimentary rock structure consisting of layers. Similarly, there are different levels, or strata, in a society.

The members of a society in the upper strata have more wealth, power, influence, and status and obtain more of the wanted goods of the society than those in lower levels. Those in the lower levels have relatively less wealth, power, influence, and status and obtain fewer of the wanted goods of the society. The higher-status members generally are more admired, are healthier, and live longer than lower-status members.

Some societies are rigidly stratified into a *caste system*. In these societies, a person's position in the hierarchy of the society is fixed at birth. Moving from one caste to another after birth is forbidden.

In our society, a person's position in the hierarchy of the society is measured by *social class* (sometimes called *socioeconomic class*). A person is born into a social class but is not restricted to that class for life. A person in our society is relatively free to move from one level of our social hierarchy to another—either up or down.

The social classes of our society constitute subsocieties with subcultures that are significantly different from one another. For example, different social classes have different demographic patterns of being educated, dating, marrying, giving birth, divorcing, receiving health care, and dying. Sociologists construct an index of a person's place in the hierarchical structure of our society so that they are better able to identify and study different demographic patterns.

The stratification of our society is a reality, but the concept of social class is not always an accurate reflection of this stratification.

---

one class to another—usually through education—so that one might be in a different social class from one's parents or from one's brothers or sisters.

Race and Ethnicity Racial-ethnic groups constitute other important subsocieties in the United States. Different racial-ethnic groups

have different marriage rates, birthrates, and divorce rates; they also have different rates of violence and different death rates, which in turn affect their patterns of dating and marital and familial interactions (see Chapters 5, 7, 8, 12, and 13).

Race and ethnicity are not the same. The concept of **race** is very difficult to define and is by no means agreed upon by either biologists or anthropologists. Some anthropologists deny that race exists, while others recognize from two to more than a hundred different races — using pigmentation, hair, facial features and bone structure, teeth, and blood type to arrive at a classification system (Montagu 1964). **Ethnicity** refers to a group of people with common customs, language, or cultural origin or background.

The U.S. Census Bureau does not profess to use a scientific definition of race but obtains information on race through self-identification of respondents; the data represent self-classification by people according to the race with which they identify. The 1990 census recognized four racial groups:[10] (1) white, (2) black, (3), American Indian, Aleut, or Eskimo, and (4) Asian or Pacific Islander. A person who chose not to identify with any of these races was instructed to mark "other." According to this classification system, as of 1990, 1 percent of our population were American Indians, Aleuts, or Eskimos; 3 percent were Asians and Pacific Islanders; 12 percent were blacks; 80 percent were whites; and 4 percent were "other" (Riche 1991b).

"Hispanic" was not offered as a choice on the 1990 census. Hispanic denotes an ethnic group, not a race. The term "Hispanic" refers to Spanish or Latin heritage, or ethnicity. Most Hispanics — 22.4 million people, or 9 percent of our population (Bodovitz 1991b) — identified themselves as "white" on the 1990 census form and reported their origin variously as "Mexican American, Chicano, Mexican, Puerto Rican, Cuban, Central or South American, or other Hispanic origin" (*Statistical Abstract of the United States* 1991, p. 4).

If current trends continue, by the end of the twentieth century more than one-third of our population will be composed of Hispanics, blacks, and Asian-Americans.[11] The number of Hispanics may virtually triple to 64 million sometime in the first decade of the twenty-first century, surpassing blacks as our nation's largest minority group (Crispell 1992).

Religion The various religions in the United States constitute other important subsocieties. Many of the religious groups in America have cultural patterns and demographic characteristics that are significantly different from other groups.

Although religious convictions and beliefs often affect our behavior in dating, marriage, and the family, these differences are much less significant in our society than they are in many others (see Chapter 7). For example, in Northern Ireland cross-dating between Catholics and Protestants is absolutely forbidden, and intermarriage is virtually unknown.

The most prevalent religion in our society is Protestantism (56 percent). Within Protestantism are more than 500 different denominations, many of which differ significantly from one another in terms of their cultural patterns.[12] Roman Catholics account for about 28 percent of our population, and 2 percent are Jews — Orthodox, Conservative, and Reformed (see Chapter 7). Islam, Buddhism, Taoism, and Confucianism are just some of the other major religions in our society; they account for about 4 percent of our population. About 10 percent have no religious preference (see Chapter 7).

---

[10]The 1980 census recognized 15 racial groups. See U.S. Bureau of the Census, 1980 Census Questionnaire on Race (1991).

[11]See U.S. Bureau of the Census, "Projections of the Hispanic Population by Age and Sex: 1989–2010" (1990); and "Projections of the Total Population by Age, Sex, and Race: 1989–2010" (1990).

[12]The Amish church, for example, is among the most culturally conservative Protestant denominations in the United States. The Amish, a Mennonite sect, settled chiefly in Pennsylvania and Ohio during the eighteenth century. Their distinct subculture prohibits the use of most modern technologies (automobiles, electricity), encourages the wearing of staid clothing, and permits no intermarriage with other sects.

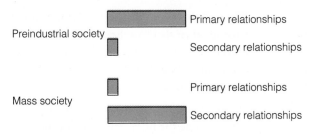

Preindustrial society — Primary relationships / Secondary relationships

Mass society — Primary relationships / Secondary relationships

A mass society is characterized by a greater dependence on secondary relationships and less dependence on primary relationships, whereas the opposite is true of a preindustrial society.

FIGURE 1-3
Secondary and primary relationships in preindustrial and mass societies.

Primary and Secondary Relationships in a Mass Society

There are relatively more secondary relationships than primary relationships in a mass society[13] as compared to a preindustrial society. In a preindustrial society nearly everyone is regarded as an individual with unique qualities, as someone who has some sort of effect on others in the society. There is no lack of intimacy.

In a mass society such as ours, on the other hand, there are relatively few primary relationships, often limited to one's family and friends. In the "outside" world in a mass society, almost all relationships are secondary (see Figure 1-3).

In our society it is quite possible for an adult who is single and living alone to go through an entire day — day after day — without experiencing a single primary relationship. More than 12 percent of our population lives alone (see Chapter 6). A single person can ride to work on a bus

(secondary relationship with the bus driver and with other passengers), be relatively isolated in an office (secondary relationships with coworkers and supervisors), eat lunch in a coffee shop (secondary relationships with the server, cashier, and other patrons), keep a doctor's appointment (secondary relationship with the receptionist, nurse, and doctor), and go to a movie in the evening (secondary relationship with the cashier and other patrons).

This relative lack of primary relationships, and the consequent reliance on secondary relationships, can lead to loneliness and depersonalization. In a world of depersonalized relationships, each person is regarded chiefly as an interchangeable commodity valued only for the functions and the services he or she provides. Qualities of intimacy and personal fulfillment are notably lacking in the depersonalized formal world of secondary relationships.

It has been known for some time that loneliness can cause physical illness as well as chronic depression. Loneliness is correlated with a high incidence of such diseases as cirrhosis of the liver, tuberculosis, pneumonia, diabetes, rheumatic fever, and cancer.

When matched for age, occupation, and other characteristics, nearly twice as many single

---

[13]A **mass society** has five notable characteristics: (1) mass production, (2) mass manipulation of tastes by advertising, promotion, and public relations, (3) a highly urbanized community structure, (4) highly specialized functions for many of the society's members — functions that require a long period of education and training, and (5) a relative scarcity of primary relationships.

men as married men die of heart disease. A person who is living alone is twice as likely to have a second heart attack, and to die from it, than a person living with family or friends. Loneliness is apparently as much a part of ill health as high cholesterol levels in the bloodstream; Americans are dying from isolation (Case et al. 1992; Lynch 1977). In short, physicians are not just talking about the pain of loneliness — a subject also discussed in the media and addressed in drama and music; they are reporting a life-threatening condition.

Sexuality and the Family in Today's America

Changes During the Gender-Role Revolution: 1960s–1990s

Americans' behavior in matters relating to sexuality, dating, marriage, and the family has changed so dramatically since the late 1950s that the period had been called a "gender-role revolution" (see Chapter 9). Consider these changes:

- Among teenage college women, the proportion who are sexually active on a casual date has increased fivefold — from 10 percent to 50 percent (see Chapter 5).

- Among the total population of teenage women, the proportion who have experienced nonmarital sex has increased nearly fourfold — from 20 percent to 75 percent (see Chapter 5).

- The number of illegitimate births to teenagers is now the highest of any industrialized nation on earth (see Chapter 5).

- The marriage rate has dropped. The likelihood that teenagers or young adults will never marry is higher than it was a generation ago (see Chapter 6).

- Women who marry are likely to marry at a later age than their mothers or grandmothers did. The proportion of unmarried women ages twenty to thirty-four has doubled (see Chapter 6).

- Women have increasingly sought employment outside the home, creating for themselves economic, social, and political opportunities. Young women are now much more likely to support themselves; they feel free not only to delay marriage but also to live singly in their own households. Very few young women had these options in previous generations (see Chapter 9).

- People who choose to delay marriage may also choose to cohabit and have the benefits of intimacy, love, and sexuality without the commitment and responsibilities of marriage. Cohabitation, long regarded as unacceptable by middle-class standards, is now so commonplace that the odds of a single person cohabiting before marriage are about 50–50 (see Chapter 6).

- Married women are likely to be working outside the home even if they have preschool children. In the late 1950s, only one in five young married women worked outside the home (see Chapter 9).

- People are more likely to have no children or fewer children compared with earlier generations. In 1990, for the first time in our history, married-couple households with no children outnumbered married-couple households with children under age eighteen (see Chapter 8).

- In 1960, the national statistical expectation that a first marriage would end in divorce was about one in four; today, it is at least one in two (see Chapter 12).

- Following the doubled divorce rate, the incidence of remarriage has climbed. Fully 80 percent of divorced men and 75 percent of divorced women remarry. More than 50 percent of recent marriages were remarriages for at least one of the couple (see Chapter 13).

- With the rising incidence of remarriage, the incidence of stepfamilies has tripled. More than two-thirds of remarriages involve children. Stepparents put problems with stepchildren first when listing difficulties in the remarriage (see Chapters 8 and 13).

- Remarriages have a significantly higher rate of divorce than do first marriages (see Chapters 12 and 13).

- With the rising divorce rate and the skyrocketing incidence of teenage pregnancies, the single-parent family is our fastest-growing family form. One out of four young children in the United States now lives in a single-parent family. Too often a single income cannot meet the cost of essentials in these families (see Chapters 8 and 9).

- A generation ago, the cohabiting family was virtually unknown, and the term hadn't yet been coined. With the postponement of marriage and the high divorce rate, the cohabiting family is now rising in incidence. More than one in three cohabiting couples have children under age eighteen living in the household (see Chapter 6).

- Homeless families were virtually unknown a generation ago. Today, families with children constitute about one-third of our homeless population. These homeless families are usually a single mother with one or two children (see Chapters 8 and 9).

- Finally, as the United States becomes increasingly multicultural, American patterns of sexuality, dating, marriage, and family forms and interaction are likely to continue to change (see Chapter 8).

Despite these sweeping changes in our society, the importance of bonding, intimacy, love, and sexuality has not changed. Research in the 1970s and 1980s found that most people believed that being in love and being loved in return were the most highly valued things in life — valued more highly than wealth, power, knowledge, or religion (Kelley et al. 1983; Campbell, Converse, and Rodgers 1976). There is no reason to believe that this evaluation has changed. As we have noted, given one wish in life, most people would wish to be loved. Nor has the importance of the family diminished; it has simply evolved into new forms (see Chapter 8).

Individual Variations in the Social Pattern

The preceding list describes average, nationwide expectations that are virtually meaningless when applied to any particular individual. For example, a person's actuarial life expectancy might be age 72, but she or he might be killed at any time in an auto accident, regardless of current age.

Moreover, demographic expectations vary significantly from group to group. A person's actuarial expectations will not only vary from nationwide average data but will vary with membership in a particular group, or cohort. (A **cohort** is a group of individuals having in common some statistical factor such as age, marital status, social class, or race.) The following expectations relate to one or more cohorts:

- A white female is much more likely to get married than is a black female (see Chapters 7 and 8).

- The divorce rate among whites is half of the divorce rate among blacks (see Chapter 12).

- The divorce rate for people who marry for the first time in their twenties and thirties is half that of those who marry in their teens (see Chapter 12).

- The divorce rate for people who get a college degree and enter a profession is significantly lower than that for people who do not graduate from college and get a blue-collar job (see Chapter 12).

- Unmarried teenagers who become pregnant and have a child are likely to obtain much less education, earn much less money, and live below the poverty line (see Chapter 5).

It is important to realize that even within these demographic categories (race, age at marriage, amount of education, occupational status), each individual's pattern in dating, sexuality, and love is unique. Whom we date, whom we fall in love with, who falls in love with us, and whom we marry depend upon our own *individual* characteristics.

Why then look at the overall statistics if they are meaningless when applied to an individual? Researchers examine these statistics because they reveal the *probability* of what will happen within a cohort. Once we become aware of group behavior, we can understand more about the society in which we live and the culture of which we are a part. We can then have greater perspective about our own behavior and about the behavior of our family and friends.

In short, fundamental human needs will likely drive each of us to become part of a couple, form a paired bond, find love, find sexual pleasure, have children, and seek out stability and commitment in a family. This is a basic, nearly universal pattern in our society. However, the way each of us fits into this pattern depends upon just who we are. And for some, the pattern doesn't apply at all. For example, a Roman Catholic priest or a nun takes a vow of celibacy, and many of us choose not to marry at all (see Chapter 6).

Throughout this text we will examine the differences — the uniqueness of individual experience — within the framework of this "universal" pattern.

SUMMARY

Relationships vary enormously, from very close and intimate to very distant and casual. A close intimate interaction with another person is called a primary relationship, and a more distant formal interaction is called a secondary relationship. All interactions can be conceptualized as falling somewhere on a continuum stretching from the extremely intimate to the extremely distant. A relationship usually begins at the secondary end of this continuum and then moves toward the primary end. A relationship may also move in the other direction — from the primary end toward the secondary end — as friendships break up or as lovers quarrel and separate. Secondary relationships are relatively more common in our own mass society than they are in preindustrial societies. This makes the intimacy achieved by couples especially valuable.

There are three aspects of intimacy: breadth, openness, and depth. Breadth of intimacy is measured by the number of activities and interests the couple share; openness in intimacy is a function of how candid and nondefensive the couple are with each other; and depth refers to how important each is to the other — how deeply committed they are to each other as a couple.

A close relationship between two people can be called a paired bond. Each person in a paired bond feels comfortable, self-assured, and contented when the other person is present or is felt to be accessible, and uncomfortable and restless when the other is absent or is felt to be unaccessible. A paired bond may be asexual (such as the bond between family members or friends), or it may have a strong romantic and sexual element (such as the bond between lovers).

Love is a complex and difficult concept to define, but in our culture being in love encompasses bonding, intimacy, and commitment. The major religions prevalent in our society traditionally consider commitment to be the most important ingredient of marriage.

We can form relationships and become part of a paired bond only within the cultural framework of our society. Our society, however, contains many different subsocieties, each with its own characteristic subculture. It is therefore misleading to analyze cultural patterns as though our society were homogeneous, for it is not. Three major determinants of the subcultures in our society are social class, race-ethnicity, and religion.

As we enter the twenty-first century, the face of America is changing. Not only have our patterns of sexuality, dating, marriage, and family structure changed over the last generation, but we are moving from being a society largely composed of whites of European cultural origin to an increasingly multicultural society. By the end of the twentieth century, a third of our population will be composed of racial-ethnic minorities—Hispanics, blacks, and Asian-Americans. The cultural impact of this change will result in increased diversity in our dating, marital, and familial patterns.

Enormous changes have taken place in our society over the last generation. The incidence of nonmarital sexual relations has increased; the number of births to unmarried teenage mothers has skyrocketed; the divorce rate has doubled; women have surged into the world of outside employment and have gained a rising measure of economic, social, and political equality; the birthrate has declined; and the traditional nuclear family has become a minority family form. Meanwhile, the incidence of single-parent families, stepfamilies, cohabiting families, and other nontraditional family forms has climbed.

KEY TERMS

The following is a list of key terms in this chapter.
These terms are defined in context within the chapter, and many may also be found in the glossary.

bond	ethnicity	mass society	race
breadth in intimacy	extrinsic satisfactions	openness in intimacy	secondary relationship
cohort	intimacy	paired bond	social class
cultural conditioning	intrinsic satisfactions	preintimates	socialization
culture	isolates	primary relationship	society
depth in intimacy	limerence	pseudo-intimates	subculture
eros	ludus	*quid pro quo*	subsociety

QUESTIONS

1. What are the characteristics of a secondary relationship?

2. What are the characteristics of a primary relationship? Discuss the importance of primary relationships in our society.

3. Discuss the meaning of *bonding* in a close relationship.

4. What is meant by *breadth* in intimacy? By *openness*? By *depth*? Discuss the importance of each in a paired bond.

5. What is meant by *commitment*? Discuss its importance in dating and in marriage.

6. Define the concepts of *society* and *culture*. Give examples.

7. Name three important subsocieties in America. Discuss the subculture of each of these subsocieties.

8. What is the role of individual differences in the pattern of shared experience?

9. Describe the changes that have taken place in American patterns of sexuality, dating, marriage, and family interaction during the last generation.

10. Define the terms *race* and *ethnicity*. Give examples to illustrate your definitions.

11. What is happening to the racial-ethnic composition of our society? Discuss the effect that these demographic changes may have on cultural patterns in our society.

SUGGESTIONS FOR FURTHER READING

Brehm, S. *Intimate Relationships*, 2nd ed. New York: Random House, 1990.

Crosby, John F. *Reply to Myth: Perspectives in Intimacy*. New York: John Wiley, 1985.

Holmes, J. G., and Rempel, J. K. "Trust in Close Relationships." In Clyde Hendrick (ed.), *Close Relationships*, pp. 187–220. Newbury Park, Calif.: Sage Publications, 1989.

Landry, Bart. *The New Black Middle Class*. Berkeley: University of California Press, 1987.

Langman, Lauren. "Social Stratification." In Marvin B. Sussman and Suzanne K. Steinmetz (eds.), *Handbook of Marriage and the Family*, pp. 211–49. New York: Plenum Press, 1987.

Lynch, James J. *The Broken Heart: The Medical Consequences of Loneliness*. New York: Basic Books, 1977.

Perlman, Daniel, and Duck, Steve, eds. *Intimate Relationships*. Newbury Park, Calif.: Sage Publications, 1987.

Rubin, Lillian Breslow. *Just Friends: The Role of Friendship in Our Lives*. New York: Harper & Row, 1985.

Skolnick, Arlene. *Embattled Paradise*. New York: Basic Books, 1991.

PART II

Gender, Love, and Sex

CHAPTER 2

Gender: Maleness and Femaleness in Our Society

I am a man and you are a woman.
I can't think of a better arrangement.

Groucho Marx

The Three Interacting Parts of Gender

Gender and Biology

Gender and Socialization

Gender Identity/Role

Gender Anomalies: When the
Components of Gender Go Awry

Gender and Life-Style

What Do You Know?

Some of the following statements are true and some are false.
Can you tell which are which?

T/F   1. Every single cell in your body is normally either a male cell or a female cell.

T/F   2. Gender refers chiefly to the physical characteristics of males and females.

T/F   3. Gender identity is the most important part of gender.

T/F   4. In our society, the average man's life expectancy is about seven years longer than the average woman's.

T/F   5. Men have only one primary gender characteristic.

T/F   6. The various aspects of gender are always concordant, or in accordance with one another.

T/F   7. In most societies, females are treated about the same as males and are granted about the same opportunities as males.

T/F   8. Most parents in our society treat little girls about the same as they treat little boys.

T/F   9. Men and women use language so differently that it amounts to cross-cultural communication.

T/F   10. Men are usually more confident than women and have little difficulty in asking for directions.

Answers: 1-T, 2-T, 3-T, 4-F, 5-T, 6-F, 7-F, 8-F, 9-T, 10-F

Gender is the concept of maleness or femaleness. Whenever we meet anyone, however briefly or casually, we notice that person's gender. If we remember the person at all, whatever else we may forget we never forget that person's gender.

Although there are many types of social interactions in which gender is not important, it is a significant part of many others. If a relationship between two people is erotic or romantic, gender is of central importance. If reproduction is involved, gender is essential.

Gender underlies the basis of dating, courtship, marriage, and the production and nurturance of children. It is an integral part of erotic attraction and satisfaction and a significant aspect of many forms of love. In short, the manifestations of gender underlie most topics in this book.

The Three Interacting Parts of Gender

When asked "What is maleness and femaleness?" most people would reply in terms of the biological differences between males and females because such differences are so obvious. By the time children are about three years old, for example, they are able to point to the physical differences between boys and girls and to identify themselves correctly as either a boy or a girl. However, as important as it is, biology alone does not determine maleness or femaleness. The three interacting aspects of maleness or femaleness are *biology, gender role,* and *gender identity.* We will examine each of these in turn.

The biological aspects of gender are physical characteristics—the anatomical and physiological[1] differences between males and females. These are the most obvious and most easily understood components of gender.

Gender role is the behavior one performs as an aspect of his or her gender. It is not a biological imperative; rather, it varies to some extent from society to society and within subsocieties of the society at large. However, all known societies regard some behavior as more appropriate for one gender than the other, and in all known societies males and females are socialized differently. Put another way, males and females are indoctrinated with different behavioral expectations, are granted different opportunities, and have different expectations from birth throughout life (Brown 1986; Hartmann 1976; Gough 1971). Gender-role behavior develops in response to gender-role socialization; it is the product of the interaction between the biological and the gender-identity aspects of gender.

Gender identity is one's sense of self as a male or female. Gender identity is the core of one's self-image, or one's perception of oneself as a unique individual. Gender identity, not biology, is the most important aspect of gender, although gender identity is based on and to some extent is inseparable from biology. Gender identity is also virtually inseparable from gender role. Whereas gender role is the outward *expression* of gender identity, gender identity is the inward *experience* of gender role (Money and Tucker 1975).

Together, these three interacting parts of gender direct and identify the maleness or femaleness of a person as he or she interacts or interrelates with others in society. It is important to emphasize that the three concomitants of gender are, in reality, inseparable. They always function together, interacting as an indivisible whole.

This does not mean that the three aspects of gender are always concordant, or in accordance

---

[1]Anatomy is related to structure; physiology is related to function or the way structures work.

with one another—that all three aspects of gender are always male or female. When the three parts of gender are not concordant, the result is called a gender anomaly. An **anomaly** is something that differs from expectation. (See "Gender Anomalies: When the Components of Gender Go Awry" later in this chapter.)

Although the three components of gender cannot be separated in reality, they can be separated *conceptually*, so that each may be studied in turn. Examining each component of gender in this way makes it easier to understand both their interactions and their functioning together as a whole. We will start by examining the biology of gender.

Gender and Biology

The initial basis of gender is biological. Males and females have significantly different biological characteristics. (It is equally true, of course, that most of their biologies are identical.) Biological differentiation into male or female begins with the sex chromosomes.

The Sex Chromosomes

Chromosomes are ribbonlike strands of genetic material.[2] There are forty-six chromosomes (twenty-three pairs) within each cell of the human body.[3] Two (one pair) of these are *sex chromosomes*.

There are two kinds of sex chromosomes: the **Y chromosome** (so-called because it looked like the letter Y under the microscope to the biologist who first identified it) and the **X chromosome** (which contains an extra "arm" and looks like the letter X). The X and Y chromosomes determine all the gender-related characteristics of the developing embryo and fetus; the other chromosomes determine other genetic characteristics. Every **egg cell** contains an X chromosome, but a **sperm cell** may have either an X chromosome or a Y chromosome (in addition to one chromosome from each of the other twenty-two chromosome pairs). Each human egg cell and sperm cell thus contains a total of twenty-three chromosomes instead of the forty-six chromosomes present in all body (somatic) cells. (Egg and sperm cells are not considered part of the human body.)

Thus, the initial determination of gender begins as part of the complex interaction of conception, which occurs when a sperm cell reaches, penetrates, and fuses with an egg cell, mingling the genetic material of the sperm with that of the egg. When this happens, a fertilized egg results. This single cell—the fertilized egg—contains all the information necessary for it to develop into a human being.

If the sperm that first reached and fertilized an egg was an X-bearing sperm, an **XX chromosomal pattern** (plus forty-four other chromosomes) is present in each body cell, and the person is a biological female. On the other hand, if a Y-bearing sperm first reached and fertilized an egg, an **XY chromosomal pattern** is present in

---

[2]They are called chromosomes because they looked like tiny, highly colored ribbons (*chroma* means color in Greek) to biologists peering through the first microscopes.

[3]Chromosomes are built from **genes**. Each human cell has a total of 100,000 genes in its forty-six chromosomes. These genes are, in turn, composed of *DNA molecules*. DNA molecules are built from a series of paired molecules called nucleotides.

These nucleotides form the treads of a structure that looks like a winding staircase (a helix). A DNA molecule is made of two such helixes (a double helix) and looks something like two spiral staircases wrapped around each other. The sequence of the nucleotides in the DNA molecule contains the instructions that enable the cell to function.

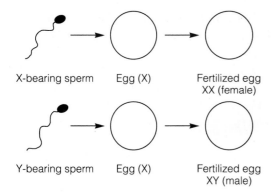

FIGURE 2-1
Gender is determined by the sperm.

each body cell, and the person is a biological male[4] (see Figure 2-1).

Because each of the 10 trillion body cells in humans has the same chromosomal pattern, a person is an XY male or an XX female in every body cell, unless a chromosomal anomaly occurred (more on this later).

Many more fertilized eggs are male (XY) than female (XX). There are an estimated 140 XY conceptions for every 100 XX conceptions (Money and Tucker 1975). However, male zygotes, embryos, and fetuses all have much higher death rates than those of females, so the ratio at birth is about 105 boys to 100 girls.[5] This higher death rate for males continues after birth. At age twenty-five, there is one woman for every man

in the United States, and by age eighty there are nearly two women for every man.[6] In other words, women are a numerical minority only until age twenty-five. After that age, women are a steadily increasing majority, until they outnumber men by more than two to one. The average white woman's life expectancy at birth is 6.6 years longer than the average white man's; the average black woman's life expectancy at birth is 8.5 years longer than the average black man's[7] (see Box 2-1).

The Sex Hormones

Hormones are chemical messengers that help regulate the body's physiological behavior. Acting as "the body's chemical couriers, they carry coded messages between sending organs and target cells. The glands resemble radio stations broadcasting signals into the surrounding air. The target cells resemble listeners, tuning into the programs they want to hear" (Benderly 1987, p. 14).

Sex Hormones and Prenatal Development of Gender Anatomy   For the first six weeks after conception, the embryo is all-purpose, with *growth buds* that can develop into either male or female organs. The embryo has a pair of **gonads**, which can develop into either testicles or ovaries. There are *wolffian tubes* that are capable of developing into the internal genitalia of the male, and *mullerian tubes* that can develop into the internal genitalia of the female. A tiny protruding bud of tissue called a *genital tubercle* will develop into either a penis or a clitoris (again,

---

[4]There is a very simple way to determine a person's chromosomal pattern. Because every body cell may be expected to have an identical chromosomal pattern, cells obtained by lightly scraping the inside of the cheek may be placed on a microscope slide, stained, and examined for a distinctive spot of color (the Barr body) that indicates an X chromosome. The Y chromosome may be just as readily seen by utilizing another stain that produces a fluorescent patch on a Y chromosome.

[5]U.S. Bureau of the Census, "Ratio of Males to Females by Age Group: 1940 to 1989" (1991).

[6]U.S. Bureau of the Census, "Total Population, by Sex, Race, and Age: 1989" (1991).

[7]U.S. National Center for Health Statistics, "Expectations of Life and Expected Deaths, by Race, Sex, and Age: 1988" (1991).

BOX 2-1

Why Do Women Live Longer?

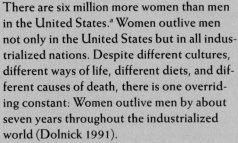

There are six million more women than men in the United States.[a] Women outlive men not only in the United States but in all industrialized nations. Despite different cultures, different ways of life, different diets, and different causes of death, there is one overriding constant: Women outlive men by about seven years throughout the industrialized world (Dolnick 1991).

Differential survival rates begin at conception, and at all life stages thereafter mortality rates are higher for males than for females. Male infants die in larger numbers than do female infants. Throughout childhood and adolescence, males continue to have higher death rates. As adults, every one of the leading causes of death—heart disease, lung cancer, homicide, cirrhosis of the liver, and pneumonia—kills men at a rate about twice that of women.[b] More male disorders are inherited, predisposing men to have lower life expectancies (Renzetti and Curran 1989; Sorensen et al. 1985).

Part of the damage that leads to men's higher death rates is self-inflicted. About a third of the longevity gap can be traced to the ways men act. Men smoke more than

---

[a]U.S. Bureau of the Census, "Total Population, by Sex, Race, and Age: 1989" (1991).

[b]U.S. National Center for Health Statistics, "Death Rates by Selected Causes and Selected Characteristics: 1978 to 1989" (1991).

---

depending on the hormone mix). Below this genital tubercle is an opening that either fuses together in the male (forming the scrotal sac that contains the testicles) or stays open in the female (forming the labia).

During the first six weeks following conception, the XX and XY embryos proceed along the same neutral pathway of sex development. But by the end of the sixth week, a "fork in the road" is reached. At that time, the Y chromosomes of a male embryo send a message in some as yet undetermined way to the two gonads, and they respond by becoming **testicles**.

Once the gonad has differentiated into a testicle, it starts to manufacture **sex hormones**— **androgen** (the male sex hormone) and **estrogen** (the female sex hormone)—but the mix contains much more androgen than estrogen. Influenced by this androgen-dominated hormone mix, the wolffian structures develop while the mullerian structures wither away.

The wolffian structures become the *seminal vesicles*, the *prostate gland*, and the long tubes called the *vas deferens*, whereas the genital tubercle forms the **scrotum**, which receives the testicles when they descend about seven months after

women, drink more, and take more life-threatening chances. Men are murdered (usually by other men) three times as often as women are, and men commit suicide two or three times as often as women do.[c] Male drivers are more likely to drive through a red light, more likely to drive after drinking, and less likely to signal a turn. Men have twice as many fatal accidents per mile driven as women do (Dolnick 1991).

But behavior doesn't explain all of the longevity gap. Even among nonsmokers, for example, death rates from heart disease, lung cancer, and emphysema are two to four times higher for men than they are for women.[d]

During the 1950s stress was commonly blamed for men's higher mortality rates. It was hypothesized that men were subject to significantly more stress in the workplace than women experienced at home. However, from the 1950s to the 1990s the proportion of women employed outside the home more than doubled. Women who work away from home were found to be just as healthy as women who work at home (Dolnick 1991).

Researchers have suggested that one reason for females' lower mortality rate from infancy on may be a result of the production of immunogenic agents in the genes of the X chromosome. Researchers have also hypothesized that females have a higher ability than males to fight infections because of the action of female hormones (estrogen and progesterone) on certain blood cells (Lips 1988).

It should be noted, however, that despite their lower mortality rate, women have higher levels of stress than men and higher rates of exhaustion, headaches, dermatology problems, mental illness, and chronic illnesses (Berkow et al. 1987; Sheldrake, Cromack, and McGuire 1976).

---

[c]U.S. National Center for Health Statistics, "Death Rates . . . 1978 to 1989."

[d]"Death Rates . . . 1978 to 1989."

conception. The genital tubercle becomes the **penis**. (For further definitions and descriptions of these biological structures, see Chapter 4.)

If no Y chromosome is present, another six weeks go by before the primitive, undifferentiated gonads begin to develop into ovaries, packed with enough egg cells to last a lifetime. In the absence of testicles, the prenatal hormone mix is not predominantly androgen, and the wolffian structures begin to wither away. The remaining mullerian structures will then develop into a **uterus, fallopian tubes**, and upper **vagina**. The genital tubercle becomes a **clitoris**, and the opening below the genital tubercle becomes the **labia**.

In the chronology of prenatal sexual differentiation, the external organs are finished last. The development of the external genitalia begins during the third or fourth month after conception and is usually complete by the fifth month (see Figure 2-2).

Adolescence and the Onset of Adulthood In people's early teens the sex hormones normally make another dramatic difference in the biology of males and females. At this time the blood-

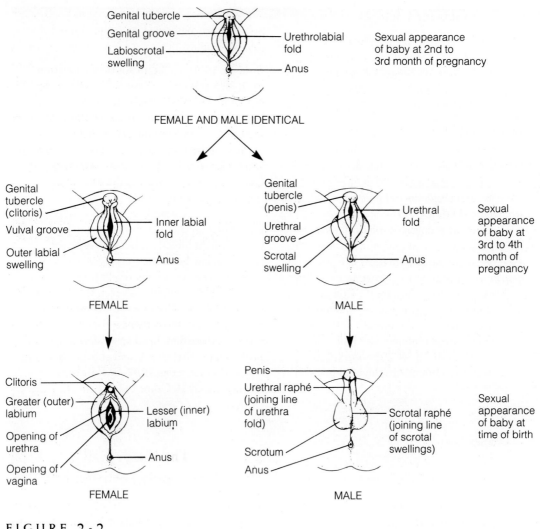

Genital tubercle
Genital groove
Labioscrotal swelling
Urethrolabial fold
Anus

Sexual appearance of baby at 2nd to 3rd month of pregnancy

FEMALE AND MALE IDENTICAL

Genital tubercle (clitoris)
Vulval groove
Outer labial swelling
Inner labial fold
Anus

FEMALE

Genital tubercle (penis)
Urethral groove
Scrotal swelling
Urethral fold
Anus

Sexual appearance of baby at 3rd to 4th month of pregnancy

MALE

Clitoris
Greater (outer) labium
Lesser (inner) labium
Opening of urethra
Anus
Opening of vagina

FEMALE

Penis
Urethral raphé (joining line of urethra fold)
Scrotum
Anus
Scrotal raphé (joining line of scrotal swellings)

Sexual appearance of baby at time of birth

MALE

FIGURE 2-2
Differentiation of external genitalia.

stream is normally flooded with a mixture of sex hormones (androgen and estrogen). If the person is male, the mixture of hormones, released from his testicles, primarily contains androgen, which normally causes the primary and secondary gender characteristics of the male to develop. If the person is female, the mixture of hormones, re-

leased from her ovaries, primarily contains estrogen, which normally causes the primary and secondary gender characteristics of the female to develop. This period in a person's life — when sex hormones flood the bloodstream with profound physical and psychological results — is called **puberty** and is the beginning of adolescence.

Primary Gender Characteristics

Men have only one **primary gender characteristic**: sperm production (ejaculation). Women have three primary gender characteristics: **ovulation (menstruation)**, **gestation**[8] (if she becomes pregnant), and **lactation,** which is the production of milk in her breasts to feed the baby after it is born.

Each of these primary gender characteristics is biologically assigned exclusively to one gender. Primary gender characteristics are not available to the opposite gender and cannot be made available by any known method: No woman can produce sperm, and no man can menstruate, gestate, or lactate.

As fundamental as the primary gender characteristics are, however, they do not necessarily *determine* gender. A man is considered a male, with the cultural and gender identity of a male, even if he is sterile (does not produce sperm). In fact, whether or not a man produces sperm has very little to do with his identification as a male. Similarly, many women never gestate or lactate, and a few do not even menstruate. They are, nonetheless, women. For example, ballerinas, gymnasts, and other athletes may not menstruate.[9]

Secondary Gender Characteristics

Although **secondary gender characteristics** have nothing to do with reproduction, they are very important aspects of our self-perception.

They are also important determinants of both how we are perceived by others and how we relate to others; that is, the way we see ourselves and the ways in which we interact socially with others are profoundly influenced by our secondary gender characteristics.

Secondary gender characteristics for males include a relatively larger skeletal structure, stronger muscles, thicker skin, and a different hair distribution[10] than those of females. Postpubertal males also have relatively deeper voices than females.[11] The secondary gender characteristics for females include an extra layer of fat beneath the skin, which makes the average woman's body softer and more rounded than the average man's.

Secondary gender characteristics are extremely important to each individual. A person is likely to experience a severe identity crisis if secondary gender characteristics fail to develop on schedule. Such a crisis may be so severe that it results in panic (Money and Tucker 1975). (For a summary of the development of adult gender identity, see Figure 2-3.)

The Concept of Overlapping Distributions

Unlike primary gender characteristics, secondary gender characteristics are available to either gender. Secondary gender characteristics differentiate men and women only in terms of *averages*

---

[8]*Gestation* refers to the period from conception until birth. Complex biological processes turn a fertilized egg into a new human being during gestation. (See Appendix C for a detailed account of the process of gestation.)

[9]The reason for this is that such active women have a relatively low percentage of body fat. In adolescents, a body fat level of less than 17 percent delays the onset of puberty; when the level of body fat in adult women drops below 22 percent (as opposed to 26–28 percent for the average twenty-five-year-old woman), menstruation may cease (O'Herlihy 1982).

[10]Although hair is distributed differently on the bodies and faces of men and women, the pattern of scalp hair is similar in both genders, except for a greater tendency toward baldness in men, which is partially caused by the male sex hormone testosterone. (Another cause is genetic.)

[11]If a boy is **castrated** before puberty, he will never develop secondary gender characteristics; for example, his voice will not deepen.

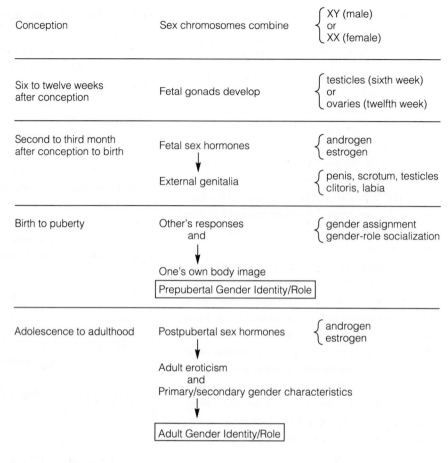

Conception	Sex chromosomes combine	$\begin{cases} \text{XY (male)} \\ \text{or} \\ \text{XX (female)} \end{cases}$
Six to twelve weeks after conception	Fetal gonads develop	$\begin{cases} \text{testicles (sixth week)} \\ \text{or} \\ \text{ovaries (twelfth week)} \end{cases}$
Second to third month after conception to birth	Fetal sex hormones ↓ External genitalia	$\begin{cases} \text{androgen} \\ \text{estrogen} \end{cases}$ $\begin{cases} \text{penis, scrotum, testicles} \\ \text{clitoris, labia} \end{cases}$
Birth to puberty	Other's responses and ↓ One's own body image Prepubertal Gender Identity/Role	$\begin{cases} \text{gender assignment} \\ \text{gender-role socialization} \end{cases}$
Adolescence to adulthood	Postpubertal sex hormones ↓ Adult eroticism and Primary/secondary gender characteristics ↓ Adult Gender Identity/Role	$\begin{cases} \text{androgen} \\ \text{estrogen} \end{cases}$

FIGURE 2-3

The development of gender identity from conception to adulthood.

of *populations* of men and women. For example, a man may have more female secondary gender characteristics than most women. Thus, such a man is smaller, weaker, or has more rounded contours or a higher voice than the average woman. Similarly, some women are taller, stronger, or have more angular contours or deeper voices than the average man.

In other words, there are *overlapping distributions* of many secondary gender traits. If the numbers of men and women at various heights are plotted for each of those heights, for example,

the two resulting frequency distributions will overlap (see Figure 2-4).

This concept of overlapping distributions is very important in understanding gender-related differences. It applies not only to such obvious physical traits as height, but to many psychological traits as well. For example, nurturant behavior has been observed to be a female trait in nonhuman mammals and is thought to be so in human beings as well (although this has yet to be proved). However, some men are more nurturant than some women. Thus nurturance in

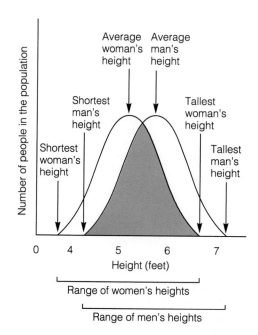

Average woman's height

Average man's height

Shortest man's height

Tallest woman's height

Shortest woman's height

Tallest man's height

Number of people in the population

0   4   5   6   7

Height (feet)

Range of women's heights

Range of men's heights

FIGURE 2-4
An example of overlapping distributions.

male and female mammals is an example of overlapping distributions with regard to a psychological trait. (See Chapter 9 for elaboration of this topic.)

Role of Sex Hormones in Behavior

Although the effects of the sex hormones on the behavior of other mammals is quite pronounced (see Box 2-2), it is controversial for humans. Current theory suggests that although sex hormones probably *predispose* men and women to behave in certain ways, social factors determine whether the behavior actually develops. For example, it is commonly accepted that although the flood of sex hormones into the bloodstream that occurs at puberty is probably responsible for the increasingly urgent romantic interest that typically emerges in adolescence and early adult-

hood, social factors are involved as well (Money and Tucker 1975).

Some observers have suggested that women's greater commitment to child care may be influenced by sex hormones. If so, this would be an example of overlapping distributions because some men are more nurturant than most women (Money and Tucker 1975).

Gender and Socialization

From birth on, all known societies indoctrinate boys and girls into the role behaviors expected of them as men and women. One of the fundamental patterns of all societies has been to indoctrinate and direct males into the roles of protector, provider, husband, and father, and females into roles of homemaker, wife, and mother (Fuchs 1988). The indoctrination of an individual into a pattern of gender-linked expectations, attitudes, and behavior is called **gender-role socialization**.

Traditional Patterns of Gender-Role Socialization

When a baby is born, one of the first things the person assisting the delivery does is to inspect the external genitalia and then announce the newborn's gender ("It's a girl!" or "It's a boy!"). Little girls and little boys are treated differently, and different behavior is expected from them, *from this moment on.*

Research indicates that most parents talk to little girls significantly more than they do to little boys and that they treat little girls more gently. They also encourage girls to be neat and clean and to play quietly — in short, to be "feminine" as our culture defines it. In contrast, parents usually encourage boys to be rougher in play, to be more independent and aggressive than girls,

BOX 2-2

Effects of Sex Hormones on the Behavior of Domesticated Mammals

In nonhuman mammals the behavioral effects of the sex hormones are quite obvious. A postpubertal male with testosterone (a component of the male sex hormone androgen) in his bloodstream is normally much more aggressive than castrated males (who have had their testicles removed). This characteristic aggression is especially noteworthy in male territorial defense behavior and in competition for available females. Bulls, for example, are typically aggressive, dominant, and fierce. They must be handled carefully, cannot be kept in an enclosure with other bulls, and are usually too intractable to be used for labor. In contrast, steers — bulls that are castrated before they reach puberty — are typically docile and submissive. They can be kept in an enclosure with other steers and can be used as draft animals to pull plows or carts. In short, bulls and steers have significantly different behavioral characteristics that result from the presence or absence of testosterone in their bloodstreams.

Among cats, tomcats are notably aggressive and are apt to fight with other male cats to protect their territory and compete for available females. If a tomcat is castrated early enough in life, these aggressive tendencies either do not emerge at all or are considerably diminished. If a tomcat is neutered after his aggressive behavior has been established, however, it may persist — though usually to a somewhat lesser degree. This persistence of aggressive behavior after castration illustrates the complexity of gender-related behavior, even in nonhuman mammals. (See "Nature Versus Nurture" later in this chapter.)

In female cats the release of the female sex hormones into the bloodstream brings about the normal "presenting behavior," with the female crouching before the male with her hindquarters elevated. The presence of female sex hormones also causes the release of pheromones — scents that cause the male to become sexually aroused. After a female cat has given birth, the female sex hormones impel her to nurse and protect her kittens.

and to "act like a man" — in general, to be "masculine" as our culture defines it. Indeed, if a little boy does not conform to these standards, he is likely to be teased or ridiculed — first by his parents and perhaps later by his friends (Campbell 1989; Richardson 1988; Culp, Cook, and Housley 1983).

Parents typically perceive girls to be more vulnerable and fragile than boys and usually assign girls household tasks related to the tradi-

PART II ♣ GENDER, LOVE, AND SEX

tional mother's role (helping to cook and clean). Parents typically perceive boys as stronger and more aggressive and encourage them to help their father in performing yard work or making minor repairs. Parents both praise and punish boys more and give them more intense socialization than they do girls. Girls become aware very early in life that more attention is paid to boys and interpret this to mean that boys are therefore more important than girls (Basow 1986; Hoffman 1977; Maccoby and Jacklin 1974).

Parents dress girls and boys differently, provide them with different toys, and discourage them from pursuing other-sex interests. Thus, parents usually give children toys that encourage quiet, nurturant behavior in girls (toy dishes and nurses' outfits, for example) and active, aggressive behavior in boys (toy trucks, weapons, and cowboy suits, for instance). By the time children are five years old and start school, they normally have the gender-role identity of their biological gender and are well indoctrinated into the differential role behavior expected of girls and boys (Fuchs 1988; Lott 1987; Stoneman, Brody, and MacKinnon 1986).

It should be noted that race and social class have an important influence on gender socialization and that the stereotype for black girls is quite different from the traditional female role for white girls (Cazenave 1984; Canter and Ageton 1984; Weitzman 1975). Black girls are taught to be independent and strong (Malson 1983; Smith 1982). White girls are encouraged to pursue an education as well as to be capable homemakers and mothers. Subtle pressure is put on white, but not black, girls from puberty on to find an appropriate mate (Basow 1986; Katz 1979).

Experiences in school continue the initial gender-role socialization begun by parents. Research shows that teachers usually reward girls for being quieter, less physically active, and less aggressive in the classroom than boys, and many teachers also encourage boys to dominate girls in the classroom (Lockheed 1986; Sadker and Sadker 1985). Twenty years after the federal government officially banned discrimination against girls in public schools, studies find that girls still receive less attention from teachers, are often steered into lower-paying professions, and graduate with an education inferior to that of boys. In short, these studies find that little has changed since the antibias law of 1972. Teachers call on boys 80 percent more often than they call on girls. There is a 50 percent difference between boys' and girls' scores in the math and science section of the Scholastic Aptitude Test. Only 18 percent of girls taking high school physics and calculus plan to major in science or engineering in college, as compared with 64 percent of boys (Asimov 1992).

Current Patterns of Gender-Role Socialization

The traditional patterns of gender-role socialization are slowly giving way to a more egalitarian treatment of boys and girls. Many parents and schools are encouraging girls to take subjects that traditionally were regarded as chiefly male (such as science and math), and authors and publishers are trying to give a more balanced treatment of females and males in textbooks from early primers on.

Girls are being increasingly encouraged by parents and educators not only to take the same classes and participate in the same educational and recreational activities as boys do, but also to aspire to careers in professions previously available either predominately or exclusively to men. Most women now enter the work force, remain single much longer than they did even a decade ago, have only one or two children when they do bear children, and return to work while the children are very young, combining in the process family and work outside the home. And, in marriages that end in divorce (as about half do), the mother often must support herself and her children with little help from the father (Fuchs 1988). Therefore, emphasis on career training is now an important aspect of anyone's education. For a detailed analysis of these very important issues for women and their meaning for men, children, and our society at large, see Chapter 9.

Another important aspect of anyone's education is physical activity in sports and recreation, and active team sports for girls are now organized and promoted in most schools; in fact, in many schools girls and boys play on the same team. There are apparently no significant differences in athletic abilities between boys and girls under age twelve, except those that can be attributed to expectation and training (Douglas and Miller 1977).

Training and experience have been found to eliminate sex differences in many physical and athletic events. After as little as one year in a unified physical educational program, prepubescent boys and girls performed at similar levels on most physical fitness tests. Improvement by girls was significant, and by the last year of testing, girls performed better than same-age boys from the previous two years. Similarly, the U.S. Army found in 1977 that, when women were given regular basic training and then compared with men, there was little difference in relative performance. Between 1970 and 1982, women's best performance in the marathon run improved by a little over 20 percent, whereas the men's record improved a scant 0.1 percent. In the 1983 Boston Marathon, Joan Benoit's world-record time would have beaten the 1961 male winner in the race (Basow 1986).

Although women were virtually barred from competitive sports in our society until the twentieth century, they now play most competitive sports just as well as men except at the uppermost levels, and even there women are surpassing men in some events. For example, swimmer

Although women are virtually barred from sports in our society until the present century, they now play most competitive sports. Most schools now offer equal opportunities in sports and physical education programs.

Diana Nyad, who swam around Manhattan Island in 1976, beat the men's fastest time by about two hours (Douglas and Miller 1977).

"Nature Versus Nurture" in Gender Characteristics

It is difficult to determine whether "**nature**" (biology) is more important than "**nurture**" (social factors such as expectations, training, and opportunity). Moreover, societal factors are so inextricably interrelated with biological factors that it is difficult to measure their relative influences.

Certainly, nature predisposes, or makes more likely, the occurrence of a behavior. A behavior's actual occurrence, however, is usually related to social factors.

In addition, small differences in biological gender characteristics may be magnified by the effects of socialization. For example, women may be genetically predisposed to be more nurturant than men, as already noted. If this biologically based tendency does in fact exist as a predominately female characteristic, it may be magnified by the societal expectation that females display nurturant behavior. A woman who does not display nurturant behavior is under considerable pressure to conform to the societal expectation. Thus, most women may be more nurturant than most men as a result of the interaction of a small biological component magnified by the effect of societal expectations (Fuchs 1988).

An interesting example of biosocial interaction is the pronounced tendency of children to choose same-sex playmates: Boys tend to play with boys, and girls tend to play with girls. This self-segregation is very widespread and seems unrelated to parental encouragement. There may be a genetically programmed tendency toward gender segregation that stems from "the simple fact that a child is, and is known to be, a boy or a girl" (Maccoby and Jacklin 1987, p. 283).

Gender-Related Language Differences

Men and women often find it very difficult to communicate. Many women feel that men won't really talk to them but instead only lecture or criticize. On the other hand, many men feel that women don't stick to the point in a discussion and often wind up nagging them. In her pioneering work on sociolinguistics, *You Just Don't Understand* (1990), Deborah Tannen (a professor of linguistics at Georgetown University) finds that men and women live in different worlds and use conversation so differently from each other that it amounts to **cross-cultural communication**. These differences are so great that men and women often leave a discussion with sharply different conclusions, and, if questioned, each would report a completely different conversation.

Is this "cross-cultural communication problem" between men and women genetically programmed, cultural, or a combination of both? When does it begin? We will consider these questions in the following sections.

Language and Relating in Girls   The essential differences between males and females in the use of language in our society begin very early in life. Many researchers have found that boys and girls as young as three or four years old have quite consistently different ways of talking and relating to one another (Sheldon 1990; Tannen 1990; Maltz and Borker 1982).

Girls typically spend much of their time simply sitting together and talking—achieving harmony, forming alliances, and exchanging confidences. Friendships are often made and maintained by telling secrets, and the center of a girl's social life often is a best friend. Girls use conversation chiefly to establish connections—to maintain intimacy in relationships. Girls typically monitor their relationships continually for subtly shifting alliances (Sheldon 1990; Tannen 1990).

Girls do not usually try to dominate a conversation; instead they try not to give offense and to be liked. Girls rarely give one another orders but instead tend to make suggestions. This enables girls to influence others to do something without telling them what to do. "As early as ages 2–5, girls typically initiate action by saying 'lets' or 'we.'" When a girl does this, it not only influences others without appearing to dominate them but also establishes her identity as a member of the group (Tannen 1990, p. 97).

Girls typically play with others in pairs or in small groups. Everyone gets a turn in many of the games they commonly play, such as hopscotch, jump rope, and playing house. Games that girls typically play do not have winners or losers, and in these games girls only infrequently try to be superior or seek attention or status. Although some girls are more skilled than others, they do not emphasize such differences. They are reluctant to exhibit their skills at the expense of a playmate and typically do not boast about their prowess. Girls rarely challenge other girls directly but instead tend to keep one another at equal rank. From childhood on, girls criticize playmates who try to stand out or to appear better than others (Tannen 1990).

Language and Relating in Boys   Boys rarely focus on simply talking with one another, and they rarely emphasize achieving harmony, exchanging confidences, or forming alliances. Boys typically tend to communicate chiefly through activities rather than conversation; the focus in these activities is competition, not connection. Boy's conversations often consist of arguing about who is the most skillful or superior in their games and activities. They often boast about their skills. Unlike girls—who typically live in a world that emphasizes connection, mutual concern, and equality—boys typically live in a world that is hierarchically structured and emphasizes competition (Tannen 1990).

In a boy's world, status, not connection, is the most important element. A boy with relatively low status will find himself dominated by the others in the group, whereas a boy with high status will command respect and prestige. Whereas girls continually monitor their relationships by looking for subtle shifts in alliance, boys continually monitor their relationships by looking for subtle shifts in status (Tannen 1990).

Boys typically achieve and maintain status by giving orders and having them followed. Instead of striving for consensus and making suggestions, as girls do, after ages two to five boys relate by giving one another commands. Their groups usually have a leader who tells others what to do and how to do it (Tannen 1990).

Instead of playing together in pairs or small groups in noncompetitive games, as girls tend to do, boys tend to relate to one another in large groups in which they are ranked in terms of power, status, and prestige. Boys' games usually have complex rules that the players often argue about, and normally these games have winners and losers. Moreover, it is very important who wins and who loses in these games (Tannen 1990).

Language and Relating in Women   As girls mature and become women, they continue to speak and hear a language of connection and intimacy, seeing themselves as part of a world that is primarily a network of connections. In this world of connections, conversation is used to match experiences and explore similarities, to find rapport and achieve consensus, to establish intimacy and avoid isolation. For women, telling others what they're thinking and feeling, and what happened that day and how they felt about it, is a way to show involvement; listening is a way to show interest and caring (Tannen 1990). Getting together and talking about their feelings and what is happening in their lives is at the heart of friendship for women:

> Women's lives have historically been
> hemmed in . . . by the demands of others—
> their family's, their husband's—and women
> expect their actions to be influenced by oth-
> ers. . . . Their struggle is to keep the ties
> strong, keep everyone in the community,
> and accommodate to others' needs—while
> making what efforts they can at damage
> control with respect to their own needs and
> preferences. (Tannen 1990, p. 152)

Women are well aware of **hierarchies** in the world, but their focus is on hierarchies of friendship rather than on hierarchies of power and accomplishment, and their speech reflects this. In common with girls, women rarely try to dominate a conversation, appear better than others, or boast about their accomplishments. Nor do most understand why men are so prone to talk about things that women usually avoid. They usually don't identify with men's talk because it violates so many of their own codes. Women would rather hear conversation about feelings and relationships (Tannen 1990).

Language and Relating in Men   Men seldom sit and talk about what they're thinking or feeling. As they did as boys, men like to relate to one another through activities — playing games, attending sports events, watching TV, or discussing what they are doing or seeing. Men's speech commonly reports, imparts information, exhibits knowledge, displays skills, boasts of accomplishments, or holds the center of attention through the telling of stories or jokes. Unlike women, men are inclined to focus on achieving and maintaining independence in a conversation while they jockey for status.

As boys grow to be men, they typically continue to experience life as a contest and see themselves as living in a world characterized by a hierarchical social order in which talking with others puts them either one-up or one-down. Conversations are chiefly designed to preserve independence and avoid failure (Tannen 1990).

Language and Relating Between Men and Women   The most frequent complaint women have about men is "He doesn't talk to me." Women often regard men as taciturn and perceive a man's failure to talk to them as a failure in intimacy. However, just as women have had practice expressing their thoughts and feelings, men have had practice in keeping their thoughts

"Because my genetic programming prevents me from stopping to ask directions—<u>that's why!</u>"

and feelings to themselves. A man may regard a woman's insistence that he talk about his feelings as a violation of his independence (Tannen 1990).

The second most frequent complaint women have about men is "He doesn't listen to me." Women are likely to talk about the events of the day in terms of their thoughts and feelings, and to share or "connect" with the other person in the conversation. Thus whereas women typically focus on establishing rapport in a conversation, men usually focus on giving a report rather than on establishing rapport. If a man feels uncomfortable or is not interested in a conversation that focuses on establishing rapport, the woman quite properly feels that she is not being listened to (Tannen 1990).

Consider another difference. Men generally hate to ask for directions; most women, on the other hand, have no hesitancy in asking for directions and can't understand why men are so reluctant to do so. The explanation is simply that men and women perceive the world differently. For a woman to ask for directions is simply an extension of the way she normally relates to others; she is seeking cooperation, harmony, and connection. For a man to ask for directions is to put himself in a position of deferring to another, of admitting that the other knows more than he does. This puts the other person in a position of power — a situation that males have been conditioned to avoid since early childhood.

Women may be labeled "nags" by men because of these differences in their worldviews and the consequent differences in the way they talk and relate to others. Men often resent the slightest hint that they are being told what to do by someone who is not an acknowledged authority figure (such as a person in a position of command). From childhood on, males have learned that to follow a command places them in a lower status position. When a woman asks a man to do something and then asks him again, she is probably doing so because she feels that he would comply if he only understood what she wanted. But a man who wants to avoid the feeling that he is following orders ("Don't tell me what to do!") is deeply conditioned not to do what he is asked because this lowers his status. Nagging is the result, because each time she repeats the request he again neglects to fulfill it.

Gender Identity/Role

Gender identity is one's sense of one's self as a male or female and is "the anchor of one's emotional health." Gender role is everything a person does that indicates that he or she is a male or female. As we have seen, gender identity is the inward experience of gender role, and gender role is the outward expression of gender identity. Gender identity and gender role are therefore inseparable. "The term *gender identity/role* emphasizes this unity" (Money and Tucker 1975, p. 9).

Gender identity/role develops during infancy and early childhood from a child's growing awareness that there are two different categories of people: one group called girls or women and one group called boys or men. Obviously a child cannot verbalize these concepts; he or she simply acquires these principles experientially as a function of his or her genetically programmed development combined with exposure to the environment in which he or she is immersed from birth. In other words, the child is forming the concept of gender — without, of course, being aware that this is what he or she is doing.

Second, the child is told that he or she is a boy or girl, is treated like a boy or girl, and is expected to behave like a boy or girl. As a result, the child gradually learns to identify himself or herself as a boy or girl. To put it another way, a template is developing in the child's awareness that there are males and there are females, and that he or she is one or the other (Money and Tucker 1975).[12]

"If you were a boy you acted like a boy and did boy things because your parents, and others, approved of this behavior." If you were a girl, you learned to act like a girl, both from the role models around you and approval for fulfilling the expected role behavior. "When the gender identity gate closed behind you it locked tight. You knew in the very core of your consciousness that you were male or female. Nothing short of dis-

---

[12]Boys learn very early in childhood that they have a penis (by whatever name it is called) and identify their boyhood (or maleness) with the presence of a penis; children initially identify girls with the absence of a penis rather than with the presence of a vagina, and still later with the presence of a clitoris (Brazelton 1990; Money and Tucker 1975). Sigmund Freud hypothesized that girls developed a pervasive sense of loss, that persisted in their consciousness, believing that they had once had a penis but it had been amputated. He called this phenomenon "penis envy." The discovery of the clitoris only comes much later in a girl's development, and may not necessarily reassure her that she has something that the boy does not have, that is equivalent in value to the penis. This is an interesting and controversial theory (Mullahy 1952; Thompson 1951; and Freud 1938).

PART II ♣ GENDER, LOVE, AND SEX

aster could ever again shake that conviction, and this happened before you got three, or at most four, candles on your birthday cake" (Money and Tucker 1975, p. 119).

Thus, both biology and social factors affect how parents and other people relate to a child, and this treatment (along with the child's perception of his or her own differential physical characteristics) gradually leads to the establishment of gender identity/role. The initial fixing of gender identity/role is usually complete before age three; however, the process normally continues throughout childhood, adolescence, and into adulthood (see Figure 2-3).

Evidence indicates that gender identity is usually more important than biology in determining gender identity/role. This conclusion comes from two areas of research: (1) studies of matched pairs of hermaphrodites,[13] one of whom received the gender assignment of male at birth while the other received the gender assignment of female, and (2) studies of identical twins, one of whom was given the gender-role socialization of a male and the other the gender-role socialization of a female.

First let us look at the evidence for the importance of socialization in studies of matched pairs of hermaphrodites. Suppose that we find a pair of hermaphrodites who have the same chromosomal gender (XX or XY) and essentially the same biology but who have external genitalia that are difficult to identify. (A large clitoris may be identified as a small penis, or a small penis

may be identified as a large clitoris.) If one of this pair was identified as a male at birth and the other was identified as a female, they are a biologically **matched pair**. The child who is given the gender assignment of "female" will receive the gender-role socialization of a female, whereas the child who is given the gender assignment "male" will receive the gender-role socialization of a male. Then the importance of socialization and gender identity may be compared with the importance of the underlying biology — which is the same for both.

An example will make this clearer. Suppose two babies each have a penislike clitoris and fused labia that resemble a scrotum. If one is (mistakenly) identified as a male at birth, she will be given a boy's name and will be treated as a boy from then on (receiving the gender-role socialization of a male). If the other is (correctly) identified as a female, she will receive the gender-role socialization of a female. When the female who has been mistakenly identified as a male reaches puberty, her ovaries will begin to release a hormonal mix that is predominantly estrogen, and she will develop a feminized body. Money and Tucker (1975) have found that despite the overwhelming evidence that she is a biological female, the person in such a predicament will continue to identify "himself" as a male and will regard the developing female characteristics as deformities.

These researchers found the same results in other types of hermaphrodites. In each case, the person was found to have a gender identity consistent with upbringing and socialization, despite the underlying biology. This research provides a clear-cut illustration of the overriding importance of gender identity — even when it conflicts with biology — in determining adult gender characteristics. Clearly gender identity is the chief factor in determining gender and will override biology if there is a conflict. In this interaction, "nurture" triumphs over "nature."

---

[13]A **hermaphrodite** is a person with both male and female biological characteristics. For example, a chromosomal female fetus (XX) may be exposed to a prenatal overdose of androgen (or synthetic progestin) that does not interfere with the differentiation of internal female reproductive organs but does masculinize the molding of the external genitalia. At birth, the baby may look like either a girl or a boy, depending on the strength and timing of the sex hormone exposure.

What happens to the other half of this matched pair, the one who was correctly identified as a female at birth and was then raised as a female? What effect does the prenatal androgenization have on her life? Money and Tucker found virtually no effect. They found that she will grow up behaving as other girls do, except for a tendency toward "tomboyism," and may marry and have children. She will have the gender-identity behavior of a female as an adult and will be indistinguishable from other women, despite her prenatal androgenization.

The second type of research that we will consider here comes from studies of **identical twins**, one of whom is reared as a female and the other as a male. Because identical twins develop from a single fertilized egg, they have exactly the same chromosomal patterns and their biologies are essentially identical.[14] If one member of a pair of identical twins is reared as a female and the other as a male, the relative importance of gender-role socialization and biology can be compared.

Such an experiment could not rightfully be conducted by a researcher who deliberately chooses to misassign the gender of one twin, of course; such an intentional manipulation would be highly unethical. However, many studies of identical twins, one of whom had already been assigned a different gender from the other, have been done. Because these studies provide important data regarding the relative importance of biology as compared to gender-role socialization and gender identity, we will consider one such case in some detail.

A young couple took their identical twin boys to a physician to be circumcised when the boys were seven months old. The physician used an electric cauterizing needle to remove the foreskin of the first twin who was brought into the operating room. When this baby's foreskin didn't give on the first try, or the second, the physician increased the current. On the third try, the surge of heat literally cooked the baby's penis, which dried up and in a few days fell off completely like the stub of an umbilical cord. When the baby was about fifteen months old, the parents decided to reassign his gender as female. The parents began using a girl's name and dressing and treating "her" as a girl. At the age of twenty-one months, the child was taken to the hospital for removal of the testicles and feminization of the external genitalia (Money and Tucker 1975).

Although "she" had been the dominant twin in infancy, by early childhood her behavior was quite different from that of her twin brother. She preferred dresses to pants, enjoyed wearing hair ribbons, bracelets, and frilly blouses, and interacted playfully with her father. Quite unlike her brother, she was neat and dainty, experimented happily with different styles for her long hair, and often tried to help in the kitchen. Her history offers convincing evidence that gender-role socialization and gender identity may override the underlying biology of gender (Money and Tucker 1975). (See Figure 2-5.)

Gender Anomalies: When the Components of Gender Go Awry

The various aspects of gender are usually *concordant* (in accordance with one another). In that case, the chromosomal (XY) male has a hormone mix with a preponderance of male sex hormones,

[14]Even identical twins are not necessarily exposed to the same prenatal hormones, of course, because individual differences may represent different barriers to these hormones. The presumption, however, is that the biologies of identical twins are essentially identical and that any differences in gender-role behavior are a function of social influences.

BIOLOGICAL SOURCES

Genetics (XX or XY chromosomes).

Primitive gonadal tissues differentiate into prenatal ovaries or testicles.

Prenatal ovaries or testicles produce sex hormones.

At puberty, sex hormones cause emergence of primary and secondary gender characteristics.

Sex hormones continue to act throughout lifetime.

CULTURAL SOURCES

Gender-role socialization begins at birth with the identification of the baby as a boy or girl (according to appearance of external genitalia).

Gender-role socialization continues throughout infancy, childhood, and adulthood through agencies of the family, friends and acquaintances, schools, the mass media (magazines, newspapers, television, and movies), and the public in general.

GENDER-IDENTITY SOURCES

Gender identity is the identification of oneself as a male or female and is an important component of each person's self-identity (or self-image).

Gender identity begins to take definite forms at about age three, occurring as a function of the interaction of the biological and cultural factors just mentioned.

Gender identity then has a continuing and significant effect on a person's gender-linked physical characteristics, psychological tendencies, and gender-role behavior.

Evidence from matched pairs of hermaphrodites and other sources indicates that although the bases of gender characteristics are highly complex and interrelated, the overriding factor seems to be one's gender identity.

FIGURE 2-5

Sources of adult gender characteristics.

the gender-role socialization of a male, and the gender identity of a male; similarly, the chromosomal (XX) female has a hormone mix with a preponderance of female sex hormones, the gender-role socialization of a female, and the gender identity of a female.

However, the various aspects of gender may be *discordant* (not in accordance with one another). For example, it is quite possible for a

chromosomal (XY) male to have body tissue that does not respond to the masculinizing male hormones so that he has the secondary gender characteristics of a female. Or a chromosomal (XX) female may have a preponderance of female sex hormones and the gender identity of a female but have received the gender-role socialization of a male. In either case, the three aspects of gender — biology, socialization (or culture), and gender identity — are not concordant, and gender confusion results.

Although there are countless possibilities for such confusion, they fall into four general categories: chromosomal anomalies, hermaphroditism, transsexualism, and transvestitism. The incidences of these gender anomalies are unknown.

Chromosomal Anomalies

Gender anomalies may begin at conception if the fertilized egg does not have a normal XX or XY chromosomal structure. For example, the fertilized egg may have an XO chromosomal pattern, in which one chromosome is missing. Because male gender characteristics develop only when the Y chromosome is present, an adult with this pattern is always a female but usually has a deficient reproductive system. Or the fertilized egg may have an extra X chromosome (XXX). An adult with this chromosomal structure is very definitely a female but is often mentally deficient.

Males with an extra Y chromosome (XYY) tend to be taller than average, and research indicates that they are also more aggressive and impulsive and slower to develop self-control. Although XYY males are "supermasculine" in terms of size and aggression, they are often sterile.

A male with an extra X chromosome (XYX) typically has a low level of androgen and underdeveloped primary and secondary gender characteristics, commonly suffers from gender-identity confusion, has a low sex drive, and is often sterile (Money and Tucker 1975).

Hermaphroditism

A hermaphrodite is broadly defined as a person with physical characteristics of both genders. One type of hermaphrodite is born with a male (XY) chromosomal pattern, testicles, and a preponderance of male hormones in his hormone mix but has imperfectly formed genitalia: a small, open-ended penis, undescended testicles, and an incompletely fused scrotum. He may be identified at birth as a female with a large clitoris. Similarly, a female baby with XX chromosomes, ovaries, and a preponderance of female hormones in her hormone mix may be born with an unusually large clitoris and partially fused labia so that the external genitalia resemble those of a male; she may be identified as a male with a small penis.

Such gender misassignment may not be discovered until the person reaches puberty and unexpected secondary gender characteristics begin to develop. At that time, the genetic female who has been raised as a male and has the gender identity of a male begins to develop breasts and other secondary gender characteristics of a female. The genetic male who has been raised as a female and has the gender identity of a female begins to develop a deeper voice, a beard, and other secondary gender characteristics of a male.

In such cases the person's gender may be redefined in accordance with his or her newly developing physical characteristics, or the physical characteristics may be altered by administration of synthetic hormones so that they conform to the person's gender identity. As we have seen, gender identity almost invariably overrides biology, so the usual choice is to alter the physical structure.

Transsexualism

Occasionally, one's gender identity conflicts with both one's biology and one's gender-role socialization. For example, an XY male who has a normal male hormone mix, whose body tissue responds normally to these hormones, and who has experienced the gender-role socialization of a male may nevertheless feel that he really is a woman trapped in a man's body. Similarly, an XX female with a normal female hormone mix and the gender-role socialization of a female may feel that she really is a man trapped in a woman's body. The person who feels such a discordance between gender identity on the one hand and biological and gender-role aspects of gender on the other is called a **transsexual**. In short, transsexuals have gender identities that are not in accordance with their biologies or their gender roles. They feel uncomfortable with their bodies and with the social ramifications of their gender-related places in society.

Medical science can now help transsexuals change their bodies to conform to their gender identities. A man can have his penis, scrotum, and testicles surgically removed and replaced with a functioning vagina. With sex hormone therapy, he can then develop the breasts, body contours, and hair distribution of a normal female. Similarly, a woman can undergo treatment to become a man by having her breasts surgically removed and male genitalia constructed. Hormone therapy can then give her the typical male secondary gender characteristics. Such operations have their limits, however. Science has not yet found a way to construct an erectile penis for the new man, and the new woman's body cannot become pregnant.

Sex-change surgery is lengthy, painful, and expensive. That so many transsexuals go through the process indicates how strongly gender identity is felt—even when it conflicts with the biological reality and a lifetime of gender-role socialization.

Transvestism

A **transvestite** is a person who periodically feels compelled to impersonate and wear the clothes of the opposite gender (to cross-dress) and to be accepted in a social situation as a member of the opposite gender (to "pass"). Most transvestites are men. The male transvestite is not usually ef-

feminate (as our culture defines the term) and is usually heterosexual. On the contrary, he is often very masculine in appearance, manner, and dress, and often works in an occupation that is characteristically considered "macho," such as truck driver, stevedore, or construction worker (Money and Tucker 1975).

Gender and Life-Style

What does gender mean in terms of the life each of us leads in today's society? How are our expectations and opportunities controlled by the accident of gender—by the fact that either an X-bearing sperm or a Y-bearing sperm fertilized the egg from which each of us developed? Whatever the sources of gender-role behavior and the relative importance of biological factors and cultural conditioning, it is certainly inescapable that gender has enormous consequences for the individual.

Women in all societies have always worked as hard as men to produce economic goods and services, but they have typically done this in or near the home, and they have combined this work with child production and child care. In short, as far back as we have recorded history, women in all known societies have always been assigned gender-role behavior that could be performed without interfering with their primary responsibilities for bearing and raising children (Hochschild 1989; Brown 1986; Hartmann 1976; Gough 1971).[15]

Further, political and economic power has always rested chiefly in the hands of men. No

---

[15] This is not to say that mothers in these societies always had the exclusive responsibility for child care. They often had some help, usually from other female relatives or older children (Margolis 1984; Minge-Klevana 1980; Lambert 1979; Weisner and Gallimore 1977; Brown 1970).

society has ever been discovered in which females have had a dominant share of power.[16] Legends of Amazon tribes in which women ruled over men are simply that: legends with no basis in historical fact (Schlegel 1977; Aronoff and Krano 1975; Hammond and Jablow 1975).

Sweeping changes that have come about in our own society are now in the process of changing these age-old patterns, as we will see. Most mothers with young children now work outside the home — while still maintaining the chief responsibility for housework and child care. And

---

[16]Individual women have held positions of great power, of course, even in patrilineal societies. Queen Elizabeth I gave her name to an age during the lusty period of the Renaissance, as Queen Victoria did during the nineteenth century in England. In more recent times, Golda Meir in Israel, Indira Gandhi in India, and Margaret Thatcher in Great Britain have provided vigorous leadership.

women are increasingly entering the portals of power. What have these revolutionary changes meant for women's life-style? What has been the effect on men? And what have been the consequences for children? These very important aspects of gender as they relate to the individual's experience in marriage will be explored in Chapter 9.

Gender differences in the manifestations of love and commitment are examined in Chapter 3. The differences between male and female expressions of sexuality are detailed in Chapter 4. The gender differences in dating, single, and cohabiting people are examined in Chapters 5 and 6. The issue of violence against women is explored in Chapter 8. And the very considerable gender differences in the effects of divorce and remarriage on the individual are examined in Chapters 12 and 13.

SUMMARY

Gender — maleness or femaleness — comes from the three interacting forces of biology, culture, and gender identity. The biological factors of gender are the anatomical and physiological differences between males and females. These differences begin at conception. If an X-bearing sperm unites with an egg, the fertilized egg will have an XX chromosomal pattern and be female. If a Y-bearing sperm fuses with an egg, the fertilized egg will have an XY chromosomal pattern and be male.

If the Y chromosome is present (and if it is, XY is the chromosomal pattern of each cell of the embryo), differentiation of tissue into male genitalia begins under the direction of prenatal hormones. If the Y chromosome is *not* present, differentiation of tissue into female genitalia begins to occur about eight weeks after conception.

The sex hormones — androgen (male) and estrogen (female) — play an important role again at puberty, when the hormonal mix in the bloodstream becomes predominately estrogen in females and predominately androgen in males. This hormonal mix contributes to the development of the primary gender characteristics: sperm production in the male, and menstruation, gestation, and lactation in the female.

This hormonal mix also contributes to the development of secondary gender characteristics, which for men include relatively greater physical size and strength, deeper voice, thicker skin, and a particular distribution pattern of body hair, and which for women include a layer of fat just under the skin, broader hips, and a different pattern of distribution for body hair. The primary gender characteristics are biological imperatives; no male can menstruate, gestate, or lactate, and no female can produce sperm. The secondary gender characteristics are not biological imperatives, however; instead, they differentiate men and women only in terms of averages for populations of males and females.

The cultural source of gender is gender-role socialization. From birth on, boys and girls are treated differently, and different patterns of behavior are expected from boys and girls. The patterns of behavior expected of females and males as a function of their gender are called gender-role behaviors and are different for females and males in all known societies.

KEY TERMS

The following is a list of key terms in this chapter.
These terms are defined in context within the chapter, and many may also be found in the glossary.

androgen	gestation	puberty
anomaly	gonads	scrotum
castration	hermaphrodite	secondary gender characteristics
chromosome	hierarchy	sex hormones
clitoris	hormones	sperm cell
cross-cultural communication	identical twin	testicle
egg cell	labia	transsexual
estrogen	lactation	transvestite
fallopian tubes	matched pair	uterus
gender	menstruation	vagina
gender identity	"nature vs. nurture"	X chromosome
gender identity/role	overlapping distributions	Y chromosome
gender role	ovulation	XX chromosome structure
gender-role socialization	penis	XY chromosome structure
genes	primary gender characteristics	

QUESTIONS

1. What are the three basic sources of gender? Discuss the importance of each in our society.

2. What is a gender anomaly? Give an example of each of the four general types of gender anomalies and discuss each example briefly.

3. What are primary and secondary gender characteristics of men and women?

4. What is the concept of overlapping distributions as it refers to secondary gender traits? How is this concept important in understanding gender-related differences?

5. What is meant by gender-role socialization? Discuss current patterns of gender-role socialization.

6. Discuss the communication problems between men and women; give examples.

SUGGESTIONS FOR FURTHER READING

Astrachan, Anthony. *How Men Feel: Their Response to Women's Demands for Equality and Power.* New York: Anchor Press/Doubleday, 1988.

Balswick, Jack. *The Inexpressive Male.* Lexington, Mass.: Lexington Books, 1988.

Basow, Susan A. *Gender Stereotypes: Traditions and Alternatives,* 2nd ed. Belmont, Calif.: Wadsworth, 1986.

Epstein, Cynthia Fuchs. *Deceptive Distinctions: Sex, Gender, and the Social Order.* New Haven, Conn.: Yale University Press, 1988.

Fausto-Sterling, Anne. *Myths of Gender: Biological Theories About Women and Men.* New York: Basic Books, 1985.

Kimmel, Michael S., ed. *Changing Men: New Directions on Men and Masculinity.* Newbury Park, Calif.: Sage Publications, 1987.

Risman, B. J., and Schwartz, Pepper, eds. *Gender in Intimate Relationships: A Microstructural Approach.* Belmont, Calif.: Wadsworth, 1989.

Stump, Jane Barr. *What's the Difference? How Men and Women Compare.* New York: Morrow, 1985.

Tannen, Deborah. *You Just Don't Understand.* New York: Morrow, 1990.

CHAPTER 3

The Many Faces of Love

Being deeply loved by someone gives you strength,
while loving someone deeply gives you courage.

Lao Tzu

Love as an Emotion

Love from Infancy to Maturity

Liking, Loving, and the Passion Cluster

Love and Limerence

Romantic Love

Sexual Love

Companionate Love

Altruistic Love

Love and Commitment

Love and Jealousy

Types of Lovers

What Do You Know?

Some of the following statements are true and some are false.
Can you tell which are which?

T/F   1. *Love* is a relatively simple term to define because it is so commonly experienced.

T/F   2. Love is one of the most important aspects of most people's lives.

T/F   3. Love is essentially an extreme example of *like*.

T/F   4. Men are able to distinguish between their feelings of liking and loving much more accurately than are women.

T/F   5. *Limerence* means an extreme, compulsive attraction for another person.

T/F   6. Romantic love may continue after marriage.

T/F   7. Women are much more vulnerable to falling in love than men, fall in love much more quickly than men, and cling more tenaciously to a dying love affair.

T/F   8. Women are much more likely than men to express jealousy through rage or violence.

T/F   9. Anthropologists have found no society in which sexual jealousy is absent.

Answers: 1-F, 2-T, 3-F, 4-F, 5-T, 6-T, 7-F, 8-F, 9-T.

Love is a difficult term to define because the word is used to mean so many different things. One may speak of love as an abstraction or a concept, such as love of country, love of liberty, or love of God. The word *love* may also be used to mean an intense interest in an activity such as music, dancing, or sports. Thus one may say, "I love ballet" or "I love baseball." The meaning of love that we are interested in here, of course, is interpersonal love, especially within a couple. This aspect of love can be of enormous importance for individuals:

> Love is one of the most important things in life. People have been known to lie, cheat, steal and kill for it. Even in the most materialistic of societies, it remains one of the few things that cannot be bought. And it has puzzled poets, philosophers, writers, psychologists and practically everyone else who has tried to understand it. (Sternberg 1985, p. 60)

For a sample of students' thoughts on the importance of love, see Box 3-1.

Love as an Emotion

The complexity of the meaning of love is illustrated by the fact that the language of classical Greece differentiated three aspects of love within a couple: **philos,** which referred to an attraction characterized by deep, enduring friendship; **eros,** which referred to a passionate, sexual attraction; and **agape,** which referred to the self-sacrificing, nondemanding spiritual satisfaction a person feels when providing for the other. There was no single word for love in classical Greece.

One reason why love is such a complex phenomenon is that it is an *emotion,* and emotions have four different components: physical acts, physiological changes, subjective feelings, and motivation. A person who identifies an emotion as just one of these components has only a partial understanding of the phenomenon. Thus although a person may describe love as the subjective feelings of attraction or need, the emotion of love also includes physical acts, physiological changes, and motivation.

The physical acts that reflect or are identified as love are support, acceptance, giving, nurturing, caring, kindness, generosity, unselfishness, and affection. Thus providing either physical or emotional support for another may be an act of love, as may a gift or a hug.

The physiological changes that occur as part of the emotion of love may include tension, trembling, and a sensation of "butterflies in the stomach." Even such extreme reactions as changes in hormone levels, blood sugar levels, and pulse rate may occur.

The subjective feelings that are part of the emotion of love are the most difficult to identify and define objectively. They are, nonetheless, very real, very intense, and very obvious to anyone experiencing them: the sense of awareness of the other, the emotional involvement with the other, and the sense of need and dependence on the other.

The motivational component of love can be central in giving direction to a person's activities, thoughts, perceptions, and feelings, virtually taking over nearly all aspects of the person's life while all other motivations take on secondary importance. It is no accident that the words *emotion* and *motivation* have the same root.

Love from Infancy to Maturity

The need to experience demonstrations of love is apparently innate, inborn, or genetically programmed in human beings, for it is essential to survival in infancy and to well-being in adulthood. However, the abilities to feel the emotion

BOX 3-1

Students' Experiences of Love

The following are students' replies to the question, "What is love?"

- "Love is the feeling that your special person is the most important thing in the world to you. It means wanting to be with that person all the time whether in person or in spirit. It means feeling like you have something so powerful inside you that you are going to explode. Love is a very special closeness and caring. For me love also means that when I'm being held by the one I love that nothing can hurt me, that I am safe and secure."

- "Love is caring for another person as much or even more than you care for yourself. Security. Warmth. Sharing everything. Looked upon as eternal. Self-enhancing. Life has more meaning and fulfillment. Love causes all the good qualities to come out in people."

- "When you feel an emptiness when the other person is gone, then you are experiencing love. When you're with each other, you feel fulfilled and complete. It can make you feel secure within yourself knowing someone loves you. When you are 'in love' you feel better when you are with the other person. The other person makes you feel whole."

- "Love is sharing, caring, living for, and helping another person or persons with whom you enjoy life. It is the ultimate in life — it's what you live each day for. Love is a kind of fondness for a person. Emotional feelings and respect for someone. Being able to give a little of yourself and not expect anything back. A brightening of the senses when you are together. It's the security of knowing that someone cares. Needing someone emotionally."

- "Love is when you feel like you're part of your loved one. It's when you feel like your world will break if your lover leaves you. Love is when you think of someone you love and you feel warm or you tingle in your spine."

- "Love is a warmth you feel when you see and touch that special person. That person is your best friend, sexual partner, or just someone you would be willing to do anything, including starving, for. Love is giving of your mind and body totally to that special person."

- "Love is a very important requirement for wholeness. Without love I feel incomplete as a person."

of love, to express it through actions, and to accept it from another person are apparently learned behaviors that are acquired through early experience in infancy and childhood (Fromm 1970).

The Importance of Self-Love

The emotion of love is first experienced in infancy as a result of receiving nurturance from one's mother (who is the usual primary care giver). Infants who are held, caressed, hugged, fondled, and otherwise given tactile demonstrations of love and caring come to value themselves, to perceive themselves as having importance and worth, and to love themselves. Infants must apparently have this experience of themselves as the recipients of love before they can experience love for others. This idea is reflected in the biblical injunction that calls on us to "love one another as thyself" (Fromm 1970).

People who lack this initial experience of self-love typically will, as they mature, try to compensate through an attitude of greedy self-interest—by perceiving others chiefly in terms of their usefulness and by manipulating them for personal gain. This attitude is called *selfishness*, which is the antithesis (or opposite) of self-love:

> Close observation shows that while the selfish person is always concerned with himself, he is never satisfied, is always restless, always driven by a fear of not getting enough, of missing something, of being deprived of something. If we observe (him) still closer . . . we find that this person is basically not fond of himself, but deeply dislikes himself. (Fromm 1970, p. 115)

By contrast, a person operating from a firm base of self-regard and self-love extends this sense of self-acceptance to the acceptance and regard of others. He or she is able to love others, to "fall in love" as an adolescent or adult, and to provide love for and accept love from others. A person lacking this basic self-love feels unworthy of being loved by another; as a result she or he is unable to believe that another's love is genuine, needs constant reassurance, and ultimately is unable to participate in the mutually interdependent love of which the emotionally mature adult is capable.

The infant who experiences self-love is then able to direct this emotion toward another person—usually the mother, from whom an infant normally receives the most nurturance and demonstrations of love. Other members of the immediate family and other people who actively nurture the infant also become objects of its love. As the child grows older, animals may well be recipients of its early feelings of love. Children also learn to feel love for inanimate objects such as dolls or stuffed animals, whose presence provides tactile comfort and a sense of security and emotional support (Fromm 1970).

Dependence, Independence, and Interdependence

Infants are characteristically *dependent* in relating to others; they take everything they need from others and supply nothing they need for themselves. In an adult-infant pattern of nurturance, the infant derives satisfaction in receiving nurturance while the adult derives satisfaction in providing it (see Figure 3-1).

By ages three to five, children normally begin to demonstrate increasing *independence*, insisting on being allowed to tie their own shoes, button their own clothes, and feed themselves with a spoon. Needs for independence usually reach a peak in adolescence. Dependence needs remain, of course, but normally decrease in relative importance after adolescence (see Chapter 10). In the fully mature adult, the focus has shifted to the need for *interdependence*, in which people

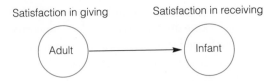

Satisfaction in giving   Satisfaction in receiving

Adult → Infant

FIGURE 3-1
Pattern of adult-infant nurturance.

provide as well as receive emotional support and love. In adulthood we are expected to provide our offspring with the love we received as infants, thus completing a full cycle from dependence to independence to interdependence — from receiving love, nurturance, and support in infancy to providing it to an infant in adulthood.[1] "Infantile love follows the principle: 'I love you because I need you.' Mature love says: 'I need you because I love you'" (Fromm 1970, p. 34).

All three needs — dependence, independence, and interdependence — are present in a person from early childhood on, but the emphasis shifts from dependence to independence to interdependence as the person proceeds through the corresponding developmental stages in infancy, adolescence, and maturity.

The Transition from Adult-Infant Love to Mature Love

With adult-infant love, the adult provides love for the infant and receives satisfaction in doing so. This is the prototype of **altruistic love** — love

[1] There are, of course, great individual differences to this generalization — "the course of true love never runs smooth." In some families the children provide more love to the parents than they receive from them (the classic example of this occurs in chronic child abuse), and in some families there is little love exchanged (or provided) by either the parents or the child (see Chapter 10).

In marriage, alternate provision of love is probably more characteristic than simultaneous love, but much satisfaction may also be simultaneous.

that is characterized by giving and providing. Mature love, in contrast, involves a reciprocity in which each person both provides and receives love. This is not to say that adult-infant love and mature love are completely different experiences or mutually exclusive but rather that they are two different manifestations of love. Certain aspects of adult-infant love are probably present from time to time in any adult-adult relationship. Moreover, there is no abrupt shift that occurs between the end of adult-infant love and the beginning of mature love; the transition is gradual. Children begin to provide love at a very early age, and some children eventually provide more love than they receive.

There are two patterns of mature love: *simultaneous mutuality,* in which both people provide

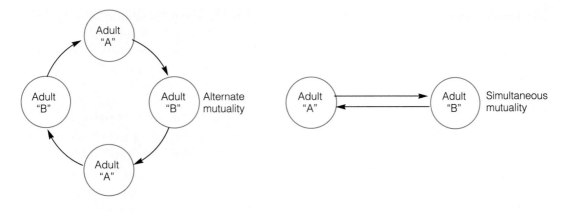

FIGURE 3-2
The two patterns of mature love: alternate mutuality and simultaneous mutuality.

and receive demonstrations of love at the same time, and *alternate mutuality,* in which each person provides love at one time and receives it at another (see Figure 3-2).

An important characteristic of emotional maturity is the ability to *postpone gratification* by providing for another person's needs without expecting (or demanding) immediate reciprocation. Thus an emotionally mature person, characterized by the ability to express mature love, is able to provide nurturance when another person needs it. In an ideal adult-adult relationship, the other person will reciprocate when needed at some later time. If the provision of nurturance and demonstrations of love and affection always go in one direction, the relationship will probably be threatened. Overall, the providing and the receiving should more or less balance out, although in any relationship one person usually provides somewhat more than the other.

Simultaneous love is probably more characteristic of dating and courtship than it is of marriage because two people will probably continue to date each other only so long as each is receiving demonstrations of love at the same time that he or she is providing them. On the other hand,

alternate provision of love is probably more characteristic of marriage, for it is not realistic to expect that both spouses will always want the same thing at the same time. Thus it is important for a pattern of alternate need provision to emerge, even though much of the satisfaction in the interaction may also be simultaneous (see Chapter 7).

Liking, Loving, and the Passion Cluster

One obvious component of loving is liking. However, loving is not simply an extreme manifestation of liking. One of the first scientific studies of love found that both liking and loving are characterized by respect, attraction, affection, need, care, trust, and tolerance. However, *liking* emphasizes respect, attraction, and affection, whereas *loving* emphasizes need, care, trust, and tolerance (Rubin 1973, p. 216):

- A person in love *needs* the other's presence or to feel that the other is accessible. A person in love feels desolated, isolated, and lonely when the other is not present or is felt to be inaccessible.

- A person in love wants to take *care* of the other — to provide nurturing, protection, and support.
- A person in love typically *trusts* the other and feels free to confide innermost feelings.
- A person in love will *tolerate* disappointments, faults, and shortcomings in the other and will forgive practically anything.

These qualities of love — need, care, trust, and tolerance — occur on a continuum from little to great. They also differ in degree from one couple to another and from one time to another within the same couple. Thus need might be relatively stronger at one time and care relatively stronger at another time, or need might be greater in one couple and care in another couple (Rubin 1973).

Studies indicate that in the United States, caring is the most prominent component of love — more important than needing or trusting. Caring is usually believed to be the central component of love in our society, and when we use the word *love*, we are usually talking about caring (Kelley et al. 1983; Steck et al. 1982).

Women are able to distinguish between their feelings of liking and their feelings of loving much more accurately than men are. A woman usually knows whether she just likes a man or whether she loves him; a man might not be sure. "Whereas men may often blur such fine distinctions as the one between liking and loving, women may be more likely to experience and express the two sentiments as being distinct from one another (Rubin 1973, p. 220).

Love within a couple — romantic love — has the additional *passion cluster* of fascination, exclusiveness, and sexual desire (Davis 1985):

- *Fascination.* Lovers tend to be fascinated with each other and to be preoccupied with

thoughts about the other, even when they should be involved in other activities. Lovers tend to think about, look at, and want to talk to or merely be with the other: "I would go to bed thinking about what we would do together, dream about it, and wake up ready to be with him again." "I have trouble concentrating; she just seems to be in my head no matter what I am doing" (p. 24).

- *Exclusiveness.* Lovers tend to exclude all others from their special relationship with each other. This relationship is given priority over all other friendships that each may have, and no one else is admitted to their special, shared intimacy.
- *Sexual Desire.* Lovers want, need, and expect physical intimacy with each other. Each wants to touch, fondle, and caress the other. Young lovers may not proceed to sexual intercourse, however; the element of sexual desire may remain idealized or romanticized.

In summary, lovers both share the aspects of friendship and possess the attributes of the passion cluster (see Figure 3-3).

Love and Limerence

The "passion cluster" is a manifestation of **limerence** — a compulsive attraction for another person, or an inability to get another person out of one's mind. This limerent aspect of falling in love — the idealization, the daydreaming, the compulsive fascination — has been portrayed in countless song lyrics, poems, novels, plays, operas, and ballets. Tennov's (1979) research indicates that experience of limerence is not limited to the imagination of artists but is a significant experience for a large proportion of our population, men and women alike.

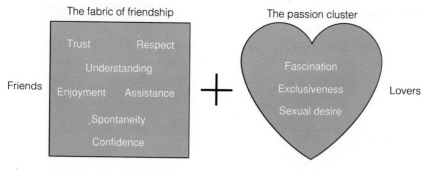

The fabric of friendship

The passion cluster

Trust   Respect

Understanding

Friends   Enjoyment   Assistance   Lovers

Spontaneity

Confidence

Fascination

Exclusiveness

Sexual desire

Lovers share the characteristics of friendship but also possess the characteristics of the passion cluster: sexual desire (which they may or may not act upon), exclusiveness, and fascination.

FIGURE 3-3
Friends and lovers.
Source: K. E. Davis (1985).

Tennov also found, however, that the significance of limerence can vary extremely from one person to another. For the eros lover, for example, limerence may be of overwhelming importance; for the storge lover, limerence may seem incomprehensible and silly (see the section "Types of Lovers").

Although many people are nonlimerent and cannot imagine what a limerent experience would be like, limerent people outnumber nonlimerent people. The exact percentage of the population that falls into each category is unknown (Tennov 1979).

The Characteristics of Limerence

Limerent people imagine what the other person would think of the scene they are witnessing, the experience they are having, or the fortune or misfortune that is befalling them. They visualize how they will tell about it, how the other will respond, and what will be said between them. When limerence is mutual, two people have an almost obsessive compulsion to review shared experiences or events: "There is the park bench we sat on" or "That was the song we danced to last year" (Tennov 1979).

The limerent person has an emotional reliance on the other's actions, an acute sensitivity to any reaction or response from the other that could be interpreted favorably:

> Limerence is marked by preoccupation with thoughts of the loved one and the certain knowledge that only this person can satisfy your needs. The limerent lover's mood depends almost totally on the actions of the loved one; that person's every gesture and word is doted on in hope of approval and fear of rejection. (Masters, Johnson, and Kolodny 1988, p. 217)

A favorable response from the other brings ecstatic emotional highs; rejection brings despondent emotional lows (Tennov 1979). Any opposition to the fulfillment of the limerent person's need for the other has the effect of intensifying his or her compulsive attraction (Tennov 1979).

Limerence may build gradually after a long acquaintance: "Someone takes on a special meaning. It may be an old friend unexpectedly seen in a new way" (Tennov 1979, p. 17). Or limerence may begin suddenly and dramatically, with "love at first sight" (Money 1980; Tennov 1979).

When limerence does begin suddenly, confusion, fear of rejection, and almost incapacitating shyness in the other's presence are common. Physical correlates often include a pounding heart, trembling, pallor, flushing, awkwardness, and stammering; an aching in the center of the chest just below the sternum; and a sense of buoyancy — a feeling of "walking on air" — when reciprocation seems evident (Money 1986; Tennov 1979).

The choice of limerent partner seems to depend on the presence of a person who matches one's lovemap. A *lovemap* is "an idealized and highly idiosyncratic image." It depicts an idealized lover and "what, as a pair, you do together in an idealized, romantic, erotic, and sexualized relationship. A lovemap exists in mental imagery first, in dreams and fantasies, and then maybe translates into action with a partner" (Money 1986, p. xvi).

Limerence and Infatuation

Limerence is often regarded by some with tolerant amusement, as simply an infatuation or a "crush." Whether the emotion being experienced is "true" love or not is chiefly a point of view, however. The emotion that an onlooker may refer to as simply infatuation (a sort of counterfeit love) may well be regarded as love by the person involved.

Because of our society's emphasis on the importance of romantic love, adolescents or young adults may dream of the fulfillment of love. They may then "fall in love" to fulfill this culturally conditioned need, and these experiences may be called infatuation. For the people involved, however, the experience can be intense. And if a person discovers that the limerence is not mutual, the pain and disappointment can be devastating.

The Phenomenon of Crystallization

For a limerent person, the other's traits become "crystallized"; that is, attractive characteristics are exaggerated and seen as remarkably beautiful, whereas unattractive ones are given little or no attention. Popular tradition has attributed this process to a disinclination to see defects or shortcomings in the other ("love is blind"), but it is really a matter of emphasis. The limerent bias brings forth the positive and downplays the unfavorable. In Tennov's (1979) study of 2,000 couples, two-thirds of the men and three-fourths of the women were able to indicate their partner's character defects, physical defects, and bad habits. But perception of these defects did not impede the development of limerence.

Crystallization proceeds through two stages. During the first stage, as much as 30 percent of the limerent person's time is preoccupied with thoughts of the other. During the second stage the limerent person may think of the other as much as 90 percent of the time — almost constantly.

Positive and Negative Limerence

During the stage of limerence in which someone thinks of another almost constantly, the experience of limerence can be felt either as ecstasy or as keen despair, depending on whether or not the limerence is mutual. When the emotion is mutual, it is called *positive limerence*; when the emotion is not mutual — when the other person rejects all overtures — the resultant emotion is called *negative limerence* (Tennov 1979).

Positive limerence brings extreme joy, delight, happiness, and contentment. Negative limerence can be agonizing and can plunge the limerent person into depths of anguish and despair. Negative limerence has been described as being lovesick, lovelorn, or heartbroken: "Lovelorn suffering is intense. It is like the grief of bereavement" (Money 1980, p. 64).

The Duration of Limerence

Tennov discovered that as important as limerence is in the lives of many people in our society, the period of time during which it occurs in full intensity is usually about two years. Its duration may be much shorter than this, however, especially for ludus lovers, for whom it may last only weeks or months (see the section "Types of Lovers"). However, limerence may also last much longer than the average of two years, and it may endure for a lifetime.

In a fascinating footnote to history, the extraordinary limerent attraction of Nicholas II (the last czar of Russia) to Alexandra (a young German princess) had a profound effect on global affairs. Nicholas II was a powerful figure with autocratic domination over one-sixth of the world. But his limerent attraction to Alexandra became so all-absorbing that, according to some historians, he neglected affairs of state, which led to the fall of czarist Russia and the rise of communism (Massie 1967). He remained almost totally absorbed by his relationship with Alexandra throughout their marriage (which began in 1894) until he was executed along with Alexandra and their children (in 1918). An entry in Nicholas II's diary expresses the depth of his feeling for Alexandra:

I dreamed that I was loved, I woke and found it to be true and thanked God on my knees for it. True love is the gift which God has given, daily, stronger, deeper, fuller, purer. (Massie 1967, p. 38)

The Replacement of Limerence with Commitment

If limerence fades and lessens for a couple in a long-term relationship, emphasis then shifts to other aspects of bonding. Each may think of the other when they are apart, but not with the same intense, compulsive preoccupation and idealization characteristic of limerence. Mutual commitment becomes more central in their awareness, as do altruism and shared emotional support. If the couple has one or more children, mutual love for them, as well as a shared commitment and concern for their well-being, provides additional bonds for the couple. (See the section "Love and Commitment".)

Romantic Love

Modern romantic love is visionary, idyllic, imaginative, and adventurous. It is the idealization of beauty, grace, and charm in the woman and strength, courage, and sacrifice in the man. Romantic love also has a large component of limerence, and although romantic love was initially asexual, it may now be combined with sexual or erotic fulfillment (see Box 3-2).

The principal role of each person in romantic love is to fulfill the other person's idealistic expectations, so that as a pair they conform to the romantic ideals learned from countless role models in the books, comic strips, television shows, and motion pictures to which most of us have been exposed since early childhood. The couple label their emotions as "romantic" and then feel and behave in accordance with

BOX 3-2

A Brief History of Romantic Love, Sex, and Marriage

Our modern concept of romantic love originated in the twelfth century as **courtly love**, which was embodied in the devotion of an errant knight who swore eternal fealty (intense and compelling fidelity, loyalty, or devotion) to his lady. However, courtly love was always asexual. Sex was regarded as ignoble, degrading, and animalistic. Proper chivalrous conduct demanded that there be no sexual relations between a courtly lover and his lady.

A knight's love for his lady was expected to exemplify the Platonic ideal[a] of selfless

courage and sacrifice without any physical contact—and often without any communication whatsoever. Any communication between courtly lovers was usually very brief—only a few lines (perhaps of verse). Sometimes a token, such as a flower or a handkerchief, would be granted to the knight by his lady. In the prototypical story of romantic love, Sir Lancelot loved Guinevere, who was King Arthur's wife and—in the original version—totally beyond Lancelot's reach.

Marriage, on the other hand, was a frankly sexual relationship that was concerned with practical matters, such as the "joining of lands, the cementing of loyalties, and the production of heirs and future defenders." It had nothing to do with love or romance: "What had love for an ideal woman

---

[a]Platonic love transcends physical desire to emphasize the purely spiritual or ideal relation between a man and a woman—a relation in which all yearning and aspiration for sexual fulfillment have been either suppressed or sublimated.

"romantic" expectations. Not only does each person idealize the other, but each also tries to fulfill the ideal of the other.

Romantic Love and Marriage Today

The modern concept of romantic love has assumed enormous importance in dating and courtship, and it has now become the major rea-

son for marrying. Two people are expected to fall romantically in love and then to marry because they are in love. Modern-day American society makes romantic love a primary basis for marriage and sets up the expectation that a married person will derive all romantic satisfaction within the framework of marriage. If extramarital romantic involvement does occur, our cultural expectation is that it must either be discontin-

to do with details of crops and cattle, fleas and fireplaces, serfs and swamp drainage?" (Hunt 1959, p. 137). Romantic love was not blended with marriage until the Victorian Era (1837–1901).

Even though romantic love was first blended with marriage in the nineteenth century, romantic love was not blended with sex until well into the twentieth century. Sex was thought of as crude and vulgar by the Victorians. Romantic love was tender and idealistic—almost the antithesis of sex. "The female ideal in the nineteenth century was a sweet girl-mother, in whom sexual desire was considered pathological." The ardent young male was expected to fall romantically in love yet remain sexually restrained (Biegel 1951).

Until World War II, the hero in popular fiction was usually portrayed as sentimental and sexless, and books that represented sex realistically (such as *Lady Chatterley's Lover*) were banned as pornographic. In all stories in the *Saturday Evening Post*—one of the most popular publications in the United States during the period before World War II—both the hero and the heroine were to be portrayed (in the words of an editor) as "solid from the waist down."

A U.S. Supreme Court decision in the 1950s held that if a publication were to be judged obscene according to various standards, it must be considered in its entirety — not in reference to its sexual content alone. This ruling in effect struck down all prohibitions against pornography, and long-banned books became available in bookstores and libraries throughout the United States. By the 1960s, new social attitudes toward sex were signaled in the mass media by a frank acceptance of sexuality, not only in popular fiction, but also in song lyrics, motion pictures, and Broadway plays and musicals. Heroes and heroines were portrayed as openly sexual as well as romantic. By the end of the 1960s romantic love had become compatible with sex, and a blend of romantic love, sex, and marriage had become the ideal. This would have profoundly shocked the Victorians, whose queen advised young women, when submitting to sex in the marriage bed, to "close your eyes and think of England."

ued or institutionalized through divorce and remarriage.

The social setting of medieval Europe, in which the modern concept of romantic love developed, clearly separated romance from the institution of marriage. Marriage was arranged by the families involved and was based on practical considerations unrelated to whatever personal attraction the man and woman might feel for

each other. Marriage was not regarded as an institution designed to fulfill personal desires, but rather as a sober relationship that provided for societal and economic needs and for the establishment and maintenance of a family.

Even though the ideal in our society now combines romantic love with marriage, many of the values of romantic love contradict those of marriage. For example, the emphasis in romance is on freedom, whereas the emphasis in marriage is on responsibility. Values in romantic love are personal, whereas values in marriage are familial. And romance is private, tumultuous, idiosyncratic, and characterized by an intensity of experience and heightened awareness, whereas marriage is public, seeks stability, and is routine and often mundane.

Romantic love, which may lead to marriage, often ends after the marriage has begun. Disillusion, misunderstanding, and conflict may begin shortly after (and sometimes during) the honeymoon (see Chapters 4 and 12). Of those marriages (about half of them) that do not end in divorce, many are chronically unhappy. Even when two people are no longer romantically in love, they may remain married because of some sense of commitment.

On the other hand, romantic love can continue after marriage. If a person identifies with the other as a real person rather than as a projection of idealized needs, then marital interaction can deepen and mature the romantic love of dating and courtship. Although in the early stages of any couple's relationship the limerent, sexual, and romantic components are probably more prominent than in the later stages — which are more often characterized by the companionate, altruistic, and commitment elements of love — there are certainly great individual differences in this regard. Some couples retain elements of romance in their marriage throughout middle and old age (see Chapter 8).

Who Are More Romantic — Men or Women?

Women are usually portrayed as being more romantic than men, as dreaming more often about romantic fulfillment. Women are considered to be more interested in discussing affairs of the heart, whereas men are traditionally expected to talk about such things as sports, cars, and business. But do young women really spend more time immersed in fantasies about meeting a daring, dashing, handsome, and ardent admirer (the knight on the white charger) than young men spend daydreaming about their feminine ideal (the princess in the tower)? The anecdotal evidence is contradictory.

On the one hand, nearly all love songs are written by men, as are virtually all ballets, operas, and ballads — although a notable exception is Elizabeth Barrett Browning's sonnet on the meaning of love (see Box 3-3). On the other hand, romantic novels are usually written by women and are almost exclusively *read* by women — an estimated eight million "dedicated" readers in the United States alone. And although women are "increasingly forsaking kitchens and laundry rooms for law offices and board rooms, the market for romance has only grown stronger" (Furillo 1990, p. 18).

In country-western songs — another reflection of popular culture — it is usually the woman who is portrayed as sacrificing everything for the man she loves. The man, on the other hand, is usually portrayed as having less urgent and more muted feelings. Moreover, the men in these songs are often drifters who brush aside passionate or tender emotions ("Baby, baby, don't get hooked on me").

In *Women Who Love Too Much* (1985), Robin Norwood provides a ten-point recovery program that offers women a "sure way to free themselves from destructive loving." That there was a need and a demand for such a book is indicated by its enormous success. *Women Who Love Too Much* became a No. 1 best-seller on the *New York Times* list, with more than a million copies in print. Apparently a large number of American women identified with the concept of the book and purchased it. There is no comparable book titled *Men Who Love Too Much*.

What about scientific research that addresses the question of whether women or men are more

BOX 3-3

A Vision of Idealized Love

The love affair between Elizabeth Barrett and Robert Browning was limerent, romantic, and altruistic and included strong elements of commitment and attachment, although for many months no physical contact took place between them. Occasional visits were under the very close surveillance of Elizabeth's family. (She was a virtually bedridden invalid at the time and was carefully guarded by a tyrannical Victorian father.) They nevertheless managed courtship — chiefly through letters — and were married in 1846.

Elizabeth Barrett Browning's sonnet (XLIII from *Sonnets from the Portuguese*) celebrating her feelings for Robert Browning is regarded as one of the most notable in our language:

How do I love thee? Let me count the ways.
I love thee to the depth and breadth and
    height
My soul can reach, when feeling out of sight
For the ends of Being and Ideal Grace.
I love thee to the level of every day's
Most quiet need, by sun and candle-light.
I love thee freely, as men strive for Right;
I love thee purely, as they turn from Praise.
I love thee with the passion put to use
In my old griefs, and with my childhood's
    faith.
I love thee with a love I seemed to lose
With my lost saints, — I love thee with the
    breath,
Smiles, tears of all my life! — and, if God
    choose,
I shall but love thee better after death.

romantic? Contrary to the anecdotal evidence just presented, the limited amount of research available suggests that more often men are more vulnerable to falling romantically in love. Moreover, men are likely to fall in love more quickly. In one classic study in which men and women were asked how early in the affair they had become aware that they were in love, 20 percent of the men said they had fallen in love before the fourth date, as compared with 15 percent of the women. Nearly half (45 percent) of the women were still not sure whether they were in love by the twentieth date, as compared with less than a third (30 percent) of the men (Kanin et al. 1970).

Not only do men fall romantically in love more quickly than women; they also cling more tenaciously to a dying love affair. Men find it more difficult to accept the fact that they are no longer loved — that the affair is over and there is nothing they can do about it. Women tend to be more philosophical and more practical in taking steps to meet new people and make new friends. Moreover, men are more depressed, lonelier, and function less effectively than women once a relationship ends. Three times as many men as women commit suicide after a disastrous love affair (Walster and Walster 1978; Hill et al. 1976).

It may be speculated that, since women have much more to gain or lose from a serious love affair, they have been genetically programmed over millions of years of genetic heritage to be wary about falling in love. It is, of course, a biological imperative that women — not men — are the ones who become pregnant, with all the responsibilities that this implies. To fall in love is therefore a far more serious commitment for a woman than it is for a man. She is placed in a precarious situation if she falls in love without first securing the emotional bonds that will ensure protection and support if she becomes pregnant.

Sexual Love

Sexual love is love in which there is a strong sexual or erotic component; that is, people who experience this type of love desire each other sexually. The model of sexual love emphasizes providing sexual satisfaction for each other. If the provision and receiving of sexual satisfaction is mutual, then both the need-related and the care-related aspects of sexual love are fulfilled.

Obviously, it is possible to love another person without having any sexual feelings at all. Parents' love for their children, for example, does not normally include a sexual component. It is also possible for a person to desire another person sexually without being in love. Thus, sexual desire and sexual fulfillment can occur without love, and love can occur without sex. When both occur at the same time with the same person, it is called sexual love.

Sexual love can perhaps best be defined in psychological terms. Before we proceed, however, it is important to understand the derivation of the terms *love object* and *sex object*, which are specific examples of the more general term *goal object*. To a psychologist, a goal object is anything that brings satisfaction to the person that acquires it, achieves it, or consumes it. Psychologists recognize two general categories of needs: physical needs and psychological needs. Thus if a person is hungry and eats a hamburger, the hamburger is the goal object — it satisfies the hunger (a physical need). Similarly, if a person is lonely, the need is companionship, and a person who satisfies this psychological need becomes the goal object. Whereas physical needs are satisfied by physical objects (such as a hamburger), psychological needs are often satisfied by interactions with other people.

When the motive (need) is love, the other person becomes the goal object and in this case is called a love object. Similarly, when the motive is sex, the person who is the goal object is called a sex object. When a person's needs for sex and love are being satisfied by one person — when a person's love object and sex object are the same person — he or she is experiencing sexual love.

How important sexual love is for the contemporary couple varies considerably. It may be of no importance, have moderate importance, or be of central importance. For some young romantically involved couples it may not be a factor at all, for romantic love need not include sex. Many young contemporary couples focus on the idealistic factors of romantic love and may be totally involved with each other emotionally without having sexual relations.[2]

A study that specifically addressed the question of the relation between love and sex among contemporary college students found that the student respondents clearly distinguished be-

---

[2]For example, a clear majority (62 percent) of young women ages fifteen through seventeen have not experienced sexual intercourse. At age eighteen, about one-fourth (26 percent) of young women are still virgins (Forrest and Singh 1990).

tween a relationship that involves "love and commitment" and one that involves "sexuality." Whereas these students characterized "sexual relationships" as those involving brief flirtatious or sexual interactions, they characterized "love and commitment relationships" as long-lasting and intense (Forgas and Dobosz 1980; see also Kelley et al. 1983, pp. 266–67). Kelley et al. (1983) reported that

> undergraduates believe that two persons can interact sexually without there being any love between them and, moreover, that there can be long-lasting, close relationships between sexually mature males and females without any overt sexual activity. (p. 277)

Clearly, sex can play a very important role in a couple's long-term relationship when it is fused with love and commitment. And although the Forgas and Dobosz (1980) study found that college students distinguished between love and sex, it also found that students were aware that love and sex could be combined and that sexuality for pleasure (without love or commitment) could also be important in a couple's experience.

Sex can have many meanings for individuals and for couples. Sex can be a very powerful motive in its own right, or it may be of negligible importance. Not only is there a wide range in the strength of individuals' sex drive; there is also a wide range in individuals' attitudes toward sex. For no other significant human experience do people have such an extreme range of degrees of motivation. Other basic needs — for sleep or food, for example — are more important to some people than to others, but none have anywhere near the wide range of importance that sex does. Attitudes toward sex range from viewing it as being extremely pleasurable to being extremely unpleasant, disgusting, or painful — with considering it to be mildly pleasurable or boring, irritating, and annoying falling in between. As we will see in Chapter 4, **erotophiles** are those who

view eroticism positively, whereas **erotophobes** are those who view it negatively.

When love and sex — each a powerful emotion in its own right — occur together, directed toward the same person at the same time, these two powerful forces are fused into one, and each reinforces the other. When sexual love occurs between two erotophiles, each may be virtually transported into another dimension of experience. Erotophobes, on the other hand, typically discount the importance of sexuality as a life experience, as a significant aspect of male-female interaction, or as an important part of marriage.

How common are the idyllic, tumultuous, compelling experiences of erotophiles and the very different experiences of erotophobes? There are simply no data available. For everyday people in everyday life, the experience of sexual love is likely to fall somewhere between the two extremes on the erotophilic-erotophobic continuum (see Chapter 4).

Companionate Love

Whereas limerence, romantic love, and sexual love emphasize primarily the needing (and, to some extent, the caring) aspects of love, **companionate love** emphasizes the aspects of trust and tolerance. Companionate love develops from an interaction that both people find satisfying and from which they gain mutual trust. The couple "learn to tolerate each other's idiosyncrasies in order to sustain the relationship and the need gratification it provides" (Kelley et al. 1983, p. 283). Companionate love also has strong overtones of liking: respect, admiration, and affection.

Companionate love usually develops slowly and gradually. It may begin with limerence and then continue after limerence has lessened. Or a couple may simply be drawn together without experiencing any limerent attraction at all; that is, their interaction may be companionate from the beginning. Companionate love provides a sense of satisfaction in simply being with the other person. It is sensible, calm, and relaxed.

Successfully married couples typically spend much more of their time together at the comfortable and rewarding level of companionate love than at the exalted heights of limerent, romantic, or sexual involvement. Thus companionate love is clearly an important type of love.

Altruistic Love

Altruism is the emotional satisfaction that a person receives from providing nurturance for another. When altruism is foremost in a loving relationship, that relationship is considered altruistic love. The prototype of altruistic love is the love a mother has for her child. The ability of the mother to receive satisfaction from providing such nurturance is an essential characteristic of mammals, who give birth to live, helpless young who must be nurtured and cared for if they are to survive.[3] Because altruistic love embodies, almost exclusively, the caring component of love, altruistic love is close to the Greek concept of agape.

With couples, mutual altruistic love, in which each cares deeply for the other, is obviously a very strong element of bonding—although, as with virtually all human experience, it exists on a continuum from little to great. In fact, altruistic love is probably a necessary ingredient for any combination of lasting love in a couple.

Altruistic love may even be the dominant characteristic of a relationship, as it was for Sid-ney Carton in Charles Dickens's *A Tale of Two Cities*. Carton loved Lucie so much that he sacrificed his life so that she might be happy, even though her happiness was derived from an intense attraction to another man. This example of altruistic love in its ultimate form also contains strong elements of romance (Carton idealizes Lucie) and limerence (thoughts of Lucie overwhelm most of Carton's waking hours). Elements of sexual love, however, are virtually absent. Thus Carton's devotion is an example of "pure" altruism because his only gain is the satisfaction he derives from providing for Lucie's happiness.

Love and Commitment

Commitment in a relationship involves consistency and an intention to maintain the relationship over time. It reflects the stable conditions that in part attracted two people to each other and keeps them together; indeed, the central component of commitment is *stability* (Kelley et al. 1983). According to Lauer and Lauer (1986),

> commitment involves a promise of dedication to a relationship in which there is an emotional attachment to another person who has made the same promise. . . . Commitment means the willingness and determination to work through troubled times. (pp. 50, 57)

Whereas limerence often serves as the initial impetus that first brings a couple together to form a bonded pair, commitment is more likely to hold them together after limerence diminishes and is no longer a powerful force that is central to the relationship.

Although commitment is very closely related to love, Kelley et al. (1983), in their extensive research on the nature of commitment, found that love and commitment are different: Love may occur without commitment, and com-

---

[3]This aspect of caring is not limited to mammals; it is also characteristic of birds. (Some species of fish and reptiles also protect their eggs until they hatch, although most fish and reptiles simply abandon the eggs once they are laid.)

"What's your policy regarding love?"

mitment may occur without love. These researchers observed that although love may include commitment — that is, that commitment may stem from love — commitment may also stem from outside forces such as social pressures and obligations that hold a couple together even though they have never been or are no longer in love. Kelley and coworkers also found that commitment in a relationship will continue only as long as the factors promoting commitment outweigh the negative aspects of commitment.

Impetus for maintaining commitment can be internal (such as affection, liking, shared interests and activities, or love) or external (such as a formal declaration of engagement, the signing of the marriage license, the persistent pressure of religious beliefs, or the expectations of family, friends, or coworkers). Also working to maintain a sense of commitment may be the costs of abandoning the marriage (such as the pain of betraying the trust of someone with whom one has made a significant emotional investment and the emotional problems of dealing with the disap-

proval of family and friends) and the practical problems that arise when filing for divorce, dividing property, deciding on child custody, and providing economic support for children after divorce.

The negative aspects of maintaining commitment can include the emotional difficulty of trying to maintain a relationship after affection, liking, respect, and attraction have waned and the need to abandon the possibility of finding an attractive alternate relationship (Kelley et al. 1983).

The major religions place a good deal of emphasis on the importance of commitment in marriage. At least one (Roman Catholicism) views it as the most important aspect of the relationship; once married, Catholics are obligated to maintain their commitment to each other and to the marriage even if their attraction for each other is no longer significant or if one or both are significantly attracted to someone else.

Love and Jealousy

Jealousy is the emotion we feel when we perceive that a satisfaction we have been receiving from someone is withdrawn from us and given to someone else. Our perception need not be accurate; the emotion may be just as painful and the outcome just as tragic when the jealousy is without foundation.[4] We are jealous of the satisfactions given to the other that we regard as rightfully ours.

Jealousy and grief are closely related in that when we experience either, we have lost something and do not expect to get it back. Jealousy

---

[4]One of the best-known examples of jealousy in all literature, for example, is that felt by Othello toward his wife, Desdemona (in Shakespeare's drama and Verdi's opera). Othello strangles Desdemona to death in a jealous rage, acting on the mistaken belief that she has been unfaithful to him.

and envy are also closely related and often occur together, but they stem from different sources. Envy is the result of a desire to have something that is possessed by another, whereas jealousy stems from a desire to maintain in the face of an apparent challenge something we already have.

Patterns of Jealousy

Expressions of jealousy include recriminations and charges of unfairness ("How can you do this to me after all we've meant to each other?"); verbal cruelty and threats of getting even ("What's sauce for the goose is sauce for the gander"); and appeals to duty or marital vows (appeals to the "commitment" aspect of the couple's relationship). Jealousy may also be expressed by long sieges of silence—the jealous one remaining quiet and uncommunicative—while the atmosphere is filled with unstated charges of aggrieved innocence and wounded trust. This pattern of stony silence may succeed in punishing the other (without being overtly aggressive) by encouraging the guilt feelings the other is presumed to have.

On the other hand, jealousy may not be expressed outwardly at all. Instead, the jealous person may turn inward in self-blame and self-recrimination; that is, instead of directing aggression (whether overt or covert) toward the other person, the jealous person may engage in self-accusation and self-degradation. The "wronged" person may even derive a measure of satisfaction from an orgy of self-pity, becoming in the process morose and dejected. This behavior may lead to feelings of inferiority and even to tendencies toward self-destruction (whether slowly through abuse of alcohol or drugs or swiftly through suicide). In its extreme form the behavior becomes *masochism*—deriving satisfaction from self-degradation—and the masochist may regress to a state of almost total helplessness, misery, and submission (Coleman 1984).

A tendency toward self-pity may be reinforced by satisfactions called *secondary gains*. One important secondary gain may be the feelings of self-righteousness a person might generate by condemning another's betrayal of the trust of intimacy as disloyalty, dishonesty, or "cheating." Another secondary gain may be the solicitous attention that might be secured from others, for a person who is tortured by self-pity over a lover's infidelity often receives sympathy and comfort from friends and relatives. This solicitous attention and emotional support, combined with feelings of self-righteous indignation, can be a very powerful reinforcer in sustaining the sufferer's jealousy.

Whether the jealous person's response is recrimination, verbal attack, or periods of icy silence, it usually includes alternating demands and pleas that the withdrawn intimacy and love be returned. If this combination of pressures is successful, the "guilty" one—the one who has withdrawn love from the other—may try to put the relationship back on its former footing by asking for understanding and forgiveness ("It's you I really love"). This will occur, however, only if the one who has withdrawn love really wants to return the relationship to its former level of intimacy and trust. If he or she has fallen out of love and prefers to end the relationship, the jealous person ultimately must deal with the reality of being rejected. This process, of course, can be extremely painful and may have long-lasting consequences, as we will see in the section on the aftermath of divorce in Chapter 12.

In the case of a person who is unjustly accused, protesting one's innocence should be easier since it means simply establishing the truth. However, a jealous person may be beyond reason, may see betrayal at every hand, and may refuse (or be unable) to accept declarations of innocence—even when they are true. This was the situation with Othello and Desdemona, for example, as noted earlier.

Paul Robeson and Uta Hagen appear in a 1943 production of Shakespeare's Othello, *one of literature's greatest studies of jealousy.*

Even if the person who has in fact withdrawn love tries to make amends, attempts at restoring the relationship to its former level of intimacy may not always be successful. The person who was jealous and felt betrayed may still be hurt, suspicious, and mistrustful, whereas the one who "strayed" or "cheated" might feel abused or manipulated by the other's pleas and demands. This lingering resentment on the part of one or both of the couple may prevent their relationship from ever regaining its former closeness, even though separation or divorce may be avoided.

Male-Female Differences in Jealousy

Although little research has been conducted on jealousy and research samples have been small, the available evidence indicates that men are more likely to deny feelings of jealousy and women are more likely to acknowledge them.

Men are more likely, however, to express jealousy through rage or violence, although such outbursts are often followed by feelings of depression, gloom, and despondency. Men are also more likely to blame the other person, the third party, or the circumstances, whereas women are more likely to blame themselves. And whereas jealous men are more likely to focus on the sexual component of the betrayal, women are more likely to focus on the emotional involvement between the other person and the third party (Corzine 1974; Reik 1949; Gottschalk 1936).

Both men and women report feeling jealous when their spouses had an extramarital affair (Buunk 1982). However, a person who has relatively high self-esteem is less likely to continue to feel jealous (Stewart and Beatty 1985; Pines and Aronson 1983).

The data among college students suggest that women are more jealous than men. Women are more likely than men to feel jealous when their dating partner spends time away from them — whether with friends, family, hobbies, or sports (Hansen 1985; James 1988). Among both male and female students, those who have unrealistic romantic perceptions of their dating partner are the most likely to be jealous (Lester et al. 1985).

The Nature of Sexual Jealousy

To love sexually is to risk losing that love, and jealousy is most often experienced in relation to sexual love, which involves heightened degrees of trust and intimacy. Sexual jealousy is often the most insidious form of jealousy because potentially powerful feelings and needs are at stake; further, sexual fidelity in our society is often considered an index of being cared for and is therefore closely associated with feelings of self-worth. A person may feel that the person with whom he or she is in love and who is no longer returning this love is betraying the most intimate and vulnerable trust. If the person giving love, affection, and emotional support threatens to withdraw these satisfactions and give them to someone else, the resultant feelings of jealousy can be powerful, painful, and compulsive.

Clanton and Smith (1977) point out, however, that sexual jealousy results chiefly from the fear of losing intimacy, not just from the fear of losing the opportunity for copulation. In a close sexual relationship, the couple share intimate experiences that may be quite intense, and either person may well feel jealous when threatened by the loss of this intimacy and trust.

Reiss (1986) finds that the self-disclosure aspect of sexuality — the "revelations to others of intimate aspects of the self" — is one of its key elements. As noted in Chapter 1, this self-disclosure, or openness, is an important dimension of intimacy. Another key element of sexuality is physical pleasure, which can be quite intense. Because pleasure and self-disclosure "are the nucleus of almost all valued human relationships" (p. 235), it follows that a threatened withdrawal of sexuality by the other and its redirection toward a third person may well be perceived as catastrophic. Not only is a significant physical pleasure no longer available, but the loss of intimacy can only be construed as a betrayal of the most devastating dimensions, for one's innermost trust in the very vulnerable area of self-disclosure is involved. It is not surprising, then, that feelings of jealousy can be extremely powerful and excruciatingly painful.

Reiss (1986) views jealousy as a "boundary-maintenance mechanism that aims at protecting those relationships socially viewed as important" — and all societies view sexuality as important. From Reiss's point of view, jealousy is seen as a significant regulatory factor in all intimate couple relationships (which in our society means dating, cohabitation, and marriage):

> On a social-psychological . . . level, jealousy is a negative emotional response to a felt threat from an outsider to a valued relationship. The society we live in informs us as to which relationships are supposed to have the boundary mechanism of jealousy. Some forms of sexual relationships are always among those relationships that societies choose to protect. (p. 236)

How Common Is Sexual Jealousy?

Anthropologists have found no society in which sexual jealousy is absent. Sexual jealousy occurs in highly sexist societies and in relatively nonsexist societies, as well as in both sexually restrictive societies and sexually permissive societies (Clanton and Smith 1977).

Reiss (1986) found that marital jealousy occurs even in cultures such as the Lepcha and Greenland Eskimos, found by some studies to be relatively free of jealousy (O'Kelly 1980; Gorer 1967). Moreover, individual examples of jealousy in these societies can be quite intense (Stephens 1982).

Impersonal Jealousy

Although jealousy most often occurs when a person withdraws attention, affection, intimacy, or love and then directs those attentions toward another person, it is quite possible for a person to be jealous of an activity or physical object. Thus one might be jealous of another person's work, hobbies or sports, or anything that takes the attention of that person away from oneself and directs it elsewhere (Clanton and Smith 1977).

Destructive or Pathological Jealousy

Jealousy can arouse fear and anxiety, insecurity and self-doubt, depression and despair—or it can arouse anger, rage, violence, and a desire for retribution or vengeance to redress the perceived betrayal of one's trust (Clanton and Smith 1977). Given its explosive potential and its capacity for compulsively dominating a person's awareness, jealousy can make a normally calm, sensible, intelligent person act in a totally unreasonable way—seething with anger, resentment, and rage that can erupt into violence. Jealousy may even be seen by some as legitimizing, as giving the jealous person the right to be violent, even to murder. Jealousy is responsible for a large proportion of what police call "crimes of passion," in which one partner beats, stabs, or shoots the other—the "love me or I'll kill you" syndrome (Pagelow 1984).

Handling Jealousy Constructively

Can jealousy be dealt with constructively? The answer seems to be that, in general, jealousy can be handled constructively if the following are true:

- The jealous person understands the dynamics of jealousy.
- The jealous person values the well-being of the other person.
- The jealous person is able to give up the temptation to enjoy the secondary gains: moral indignation, self-righteousness, and the support of sympathetic friends and relatives.
- The jealous person is able to gain perspective on the overall situation instead of focusing exclusively on his or her own pain.

For example, suppose a husband and wife are at a party, and she is spending a good deal of time in animated conversation with an attractive man. The husband finds himself becoming more and more agitated and uncomfortable and begins to feel undeniable twinges of jealousy. He might handle the situation constructively, as reported by Lobsenz (1977):

I asked myself some questions. For example, why is she animated? Obviously, she is having a good talk. Perhaps I don't discuss things that interest her much—maybe I should work a bit harder, be less conversationally predictable. Do I love her? Yes. (If I didn't, why would it matter how animatedly she talked to someone else?) Since I do love her, why shouldn't I be pleased that she is enjoying herself? Don't I want her to have a good time at the party? Or do I think because she is enjoying a good conversation she is arranging a tryst with a good-looking fellow? Obviously not.

Once I realized that my wife's conversation with someone else took nothing away from me—in fact, it pointed to a way I could improve our relationship—I also realized there was no reason for jealousy. (pp. 30–31)

This is not to say, of course, that one can always deal with the problem of jealousy solely by self-examination and a change in one's behavior. On the contrary, jealousy can rarely be treated in isolation because it usually involves an interaction between oneself and others. Thus dealing with jealousy constructively usually means acknowledging the feelings of the other person (and perhaps those of the third person), as well as one's own feelings:

> Your jealousy is not your problem alone. It is also a problem for your partner and for the person whose interest in your partner sparks your jealousy. . . . Typically, three or more persons are involved in the production of jealous feelings and behaviors. Ideally, all three should take on part of the responsibility for minimizing its negative consequences. (Clanton and Smith 1977, p. 163)

Finally, the jealous person must be prepared to acknowledge the reality of the situation and the reality of the other person's feelings. Perhaps the relationship cannot be salvaged. Love can be earned to a certain extent ("To be loved, be lovable"), but it cannot be forced. It must be given or granted freely by the other person; it cannot be coerced by appeals for justice and through accusations of betrayal.

Is it advisable to repress feelings of jealousy — to shut them out of awareness with an "I don't care" attitude — rather than to acknowledge them? Probably not, because this response only drives jealousy underground. Such repressed jealousy will continue its corrosive influence, manifesting itself in such forms as irritability and aggressiveness, coldness, or feigned indifference, all of which can only be counted on to push the other person away — perhaps into the arms of the third person. Moreover, driving jealousy underground or refusing to acknowledge it makes it unavailable to conscious awareness, where dealing with it constructively is at least a possibility.

Types of Lovers

Because love is such a complex emotion that involves so many different components, it is not surprising that there are different types of lovers. Certainly, the experience of loving and of being loved varies greatly from one person to another.

In exhaustive and definitive research, Canadian psychologist John Alan Lee (1973) analyzed some 4,000 accounts of love — from classical Greek times to the present — and then compared them with accounts of modernday love experiences. By using the statistical technique of factor analysis, Lee demonstrated that there are just three basic experiences of love within a couple. All the countless variations of love — whether recounted in the mainstream of literature for the past 2,500 years or described by Lee's sample of modernday lovers — occur because of the virtually infinite number of ways it is possible to combine the variations within these three basic types.

Lee labeled the three basic types of love within a couple as follows:

- **Eros** ("AIR-ose") — passionate, all-enveloping love
- **Ludus** ("LOO-doos") — playful, flirtatious love
- **Storge** ("STOR-gay") — calm, compassionate love

Lee found that these three major categories of love never occur in their pure form but rather in a bewildering array of combinations. Nevertheless, one or the other of the basic types predominate with each lover.

In addition, Lee found that a person's typology of love is not necessarily fixed, even for the duration of a specific love affair, but may change from an emphasis on eros to an emphasis on ludus or storge. Moreover, a person may experience love with one person quite differently from love with another.

One important contribution of this research is the recognition that "true love" is simply what a person thinks it is; that is, each person defines the concept of "true love" in terms of his or her own personal experience and individual style of loving. Lee concludes that each unique type of love is equally valid and that no one type is necessarily "truer" than another.

Given the bewildering varieties of love that may occur when elements of the three major categories are combined, it is not surprising that disappointments in love occur frequently. Moreover, a person who regards his or her own definition of love as the only "true" or valid one may be puzzled or impatient when attempting to relate to someone whose approach to love does not fit those preconceptions. These insights regarding the nature of love help explain the pain and puzzlement that may occur when a person characterized by one style of loving attempts to relate to a person characterized by a different style of loving. People may become devastated by their failure to understand someone else who has a completely different concept of the meaning of love.

What are the characteristics of the three major styles of loving described by Lee? Are you predominantly a storge, ludus, or eros lover? Let us examine each in turn.

Eros Lovers

The eros lover is very susceptible to a limerent experience; in fact, limerence is a very important aspect of the eros person's consciousness. The eros lover characteristically feels an immediate, powerful limerent attraction to the other person, accompanied by various physiological reactions (a sensation of a tight band across the chest or a fluttering in the stomach, increased pulse rate, shortness of breath, and trembling). It is not unusual for an eros person to seem struck dumb when first encountering an ideal other and to be unable to make any sensible conversation. Looking into the other's eyes can cause a sensation approaching shock, so that sustained eye contact becomes virtually impossible (Lee 1973). MacDonald (1971) gives an intriguing description of this phenomenon:

> Something moved somehow behind her eyes, maybe like a pair of eyes behind them, suddenly opening to look out at me. It is something happening, like the world turning over and stopping at an angle you didn't know about . . . like being trapped there, like our eyes got caught somehow, and I couldn't move away. (p. 17)

The type of beauty that each eros person holds as a vision or the embodiment of an ideal is so specific that he or she can sort through a number of photographs very quickly and select the ones that best portray this idealized concept of beauty. (Other types of lovers cannot do this.) It is thus not surprising that an eros person experiences intense feelings of excitement, anticipation, and hope at the first sight of someone who represents the physical embodiment of an ideal — especially since the specifications are so precise that they can be fulfilled by only a very few people (Lee 1973).

Parker (1983) gives the following description of this embodiment of an ideal:

> I had loved her since I saw her. Loved her, or the imagined her, before I'd met her. Loved her before I was able to understand what love meant, before I knew of sex, loved her since I could feel and had spent my life

waiting to meet her and then waiting to have her love me. (pp. 55–56)

This phenomenon of being "lovestruck" does not mean that the eros person is interested only in physical beauty. "Love at first sight" is merely a shorthand expression for the kind of love that begins with a powerful visual attraction. The eros lover will establish a sustained relationship, however, only if this visual attraction is followed by emotional, intellectual, and sexual rapport.

More than any other kind of love, eros is characterized by an active and imaginative interest in sexual fulfillment. Eros people typically press for a sexual relationship early on and usually become lovers shortly after meeting. Nothing is more deadly to eros people than lack of sexual enthusiasm. If the eros person is attracted to someone who is not freely erotic, the joy and wonder are short-lived, and the relationship is likely to be doomed to wistful disappointment (Lee 1973).

Ludus Lovers

In contrast to eros lovers, ludus lovers experience a love affair as essentially a game to be played for amusement, pleasure, and excitement without deep or lasting emotional involvement or commitment. Flattery, coyness, coquetry, and gallantry are all part of the ludus strategy of love and add spice and pleasurable tension to the couple's interaction.

The ludus person does not have a specific vision of ideal beauty as does the eros person but instead has a wide range of physical tastes, and anyone who falls within that range may be considered a desirable partner. This is exemplified by the lyrics of Stephen Stills: "But if you can't be with the one you love, love the one you're with."

Ludus love is most easily played with several partners at once. Not telling each partner about the other is part of the fun and is completely acceptable. Unlike eros lovers, ludus lovers are quite content with their detachment from the intense feelings of love and so are rarely possessive or jealous.

A ludus lover engages in sex for fun, not for emotional closeness, and is much more willing to delay sexual satisfaction than is the eros lover, for whom sex is an integral part of the fascination.

When the game of ludus love is played by two lovers who understand the rules and expectations, the relationship can be ended quite gracefully, especially because each usually has at least one other lover at the same time. With a ludus couple, neither expects to obtain lasting satisfaction from a love affair, but only an interlude of adventure, excitement, fun, and perhaps sexual satisfaction.

However, when an eros lover has the misfortune to fall in love with a ludus lover who is anticipating a ludus adventure, the ludus lover's attempts to keep the relationship pleasantly causal are usually unsuccessful because of the eros person's limerent characteristics. The ensuing, almost inevitable breakup can be quite painful for the eros lover (Lee 1973).

Storge Lovers

Storge love is based on practical considerations. Storge love is an unexciting, uneventful, unpassionate, companionate form of love in which the relationship is characterized by quiet affection and commitment. The goals of the storge lover are marriage, children, and an established place in the community.

Whereas eros lovers study each other's faces, talk endlessly about each other's past lives and current feelings, and are intensely aware of the fact of being in love, storge lovers tend to take each other casually for granted. In fact, storge love may be difficult to distinguish from a close, enduring friendship.

A storge person is definitely nonlimerent and cannot imagine the intensity of feeling and impulsive involvement of a limerent attraction. To the storge person, the ecstasy of eros love is an illusion — it may occur in drama but is not to be taken seriously in real life. And for a storge lover, the playfulness of ludus love is a mockery of serious love. On the other hand, for the eros lover, storge love is not really love at all; and for the ludus lover, storge love seems dull, pedestrian, and uneventful.

Storge people do not have any ideals of physical beauty, and there is no dramatic beginning to storge love. Storge people either drift into marriage with someone who enjoys the same interests and activities, or they deliberately plan to marry a compatible person. The storge person would be puzzled by an eros or ludus lover who expects a more dramatic experience. Once married, storge people are relatively undemanding and nonpossessive. They are not upset, for example, by lengthy physical absences.

Classic examples of storge love occur among people who grow up together as neighbors or meet as schoolmates, but storge love can also develop between people who meet as adults, especially if they have such similar backgrounds that they might have grown up together.

Sexual intimacy comes late in the slow development of a storge relationship, not because the storge person is necessarily asexual, antisexual, or erotophobic but because rapid progress toward sexual intimacy is considered inappropriate. Sex is not all that important and does not become a factor until after intellectual and emotional understanding and rapport have been achieved, and even then the storge person does not anticipate emotional intensity. The concept of extreme pleasure or ecstasy in relating to the other is completely beyond the range of the storge lover's expectations. It is therefore not surprising that sexual disappointment is far less likely to break up the storge pair than it is an eros pair.

Although storge love is rarely hectic or urgent, it is not without its disagreements and conflicts, and storge relationships do not always survive. If a breakup does occur, storge lovers are very likely to remain good friends. It would be inconceivable to a storge person that two people who had truly loved each other at one time could hate each other simply because they had ceased to be lovers (Lee 1973).

Manic Lovers

Of all the possible combinations of the three basic types of love within a couple, one of the most interesting is *manic love,* which is a combination of eros and ludus. Manic love is the theme of innumerable song lyrics, plays, and romantic novels, with their familiar characteristics of helpless obsession, extreme jealousy, and a tragic ending. This literature of love portrays the manic lover as a person whose feelings are beyond rational control and who struggles continually with the agony of recrimination and self-doubt, tortured with questions about the other's faithfulness and sincerity.

A manic lover is characteristically limerent. Usually the limerence is negative, and the manic lover is racked by yearning and moodiness and alternates between highs of irrational joy and lows of anxiety and despair. The slightest lack of response from the other person causes pain and resentment, whereas any sign of warmth brings relief and encouragement. The manic lover's pleasure is always short-lived, however, because the need for attention and for demonstrations of caring and affection are virtually insatiable.

Manic lovers see difficulties as challenges to their devotion. If there are no difficulties, they invent them, seeing rivals everywhere and distrusting the other person's sincerity. From the manic lover's point of view, extreme jealousy is perfectly reasonable because it is a "proof" of love. Manic lovers seem almost possessed by some strange demon or gripped by a sort of madness that seizes them and produces a torment of unsatisfied desire and repeated humiliation.

Sexual intimacy only brings new problems to the manic lover. Uncertain of his or her attractiveness and lacking a genuine rapport with the other person, the manic lover is unable to participate in a mutually compatible sexual interaction.

Manic love rarely ends happily, and most manic lovers remain troubled by the experience for months or even years. A period of hatred of the former partner is almost essential if the manic lover is finally to achieve an attitude of indifference. During the recovery period, the manic lover is often in a condition popularly known as "on the rebound." This period can be very dangerous for any new partner because the unrequited manic lover is likely to act in quite a luduslike way. Once a successful relationship has been achieved, he or she will very probably drop the new partner, thus getting even for the previous disappointment. If the new partner is a ludus person there is no problem, but if he or she is an eros or manic lover, the cycle of getting a broken heart and then in turn being a heartbreaker begins another round.

It is theoretically possible for a manic attachment to develop into a lasting love, but Lee (1973) found only rare instances of this. For the relationship to endure, the other person must have the patience and strength of ego to ride out the possessiveness, the recriminations, and the stormy emotions. Only an eros person is likely to do this. A ludus person would never tolerate the manic lover's extremes, and although a storge person may try to be kind, he or she would be unable to reciprocate the manic lover's intensity.

Interestingly, most of the manic lovers in Lee's study believed that despite the pain and the anguish, the experience of falling in love had been profitable because the extremes of their emotion had brought them to the realization of how much they could care for another person.

To determine what type of lover you are according to Lee's formulation, answer the questions in Table 3-1.

SUMMARY

Love is a complex emotion with many interacting components. The ancient Greeks had no single word for love but distinguished among *philos* (the love of friendship), *eros* (a passionate sexual love), and *agape* (a self-sacrificing, altruistic love).

Like all emotions, love has four components: physical actions, physiological changes, subjective feelings, and motivation. Love is a very important phenomenon in human experience, and the need to receive love is apparently inborn. Infants and children who do not receive adequate love are seriously disadvantaged, and adults need love to lead fulfilled, creative lives.

The ability to love is learned by social experience that begins at infancy. The bond between an infant and his or her mother (or other care giver) provides a firm basis for self-love. Infants who learn to love themselves can then love others and will become adults who are able to give love to their own children.

Adult-infant love is unidirectional only; adult-adult love is reciprocal, with each person both providing and receiving love. As people develop from infancy to adulthood, the focus of their needs normally moves from dependency to independency to interdependency. An individ-

TABLE 3-1

The Love Chart

To find out what type of lover you are, respond to each statement as it applies to a current boyfriend or girlfriend, lover or spouse.

A = almost always, U = usually, R = rarely, N = never (or almost never)

1. You have a clearly defined image of your desired partner.
2. You felt a strong emotional reaction to him or her on the first encounter.
3. You are preoccupied with thoughts about him or her.
4. You are eager to see him or her every day.
5. You discuss future plans and a wide range of interests and experiences.
6. Tactile, sensual contact is important to the relationship.
7. Sexual intimacy was achieved early in the relationship.
8. You feel that success in love is more important than success in other areas of your life.
9. You want to be in love or have love as security.
10. You try to force him or her to show more feeling and commitment.
11. You declared your love first.
12. You are willing to suffer neglect and abuse from him or her.
13. You deliberately restrain frequency of contact with him or her.
14. You restrict discussion and display of your feelings with him or her.
15. If a breakup is coming, you feel it is better to drop the other person before being dropped.
16. You play the field and have several persons who could love you.
17. You are more interested in pleasure than in emotional attachment.
18. You feel the need to love someone you have grown accustomed to.
19. You believe that the test of time is the only sure way to find real love.
20. You don't believe that true love happens suddenly or dramatically.

If you responded A or U to statements 1–8, you are probably an eros lover. If you responded A or U to statements 3–4 and 8–12, your love style tends to be manic. If you responded A or U to statements 13–17 and R or N to the other statements, you are probably a ludus lover. If you responded A or U to statements 17–20, together with R or N for the other statements, your love style tends to be storge. (Remember, there are many intermediate styles of love, and a person's love style may shift from time to time or from partner to partner.)

Source: Adapted from Lee (1974, p. 45).

ual thus progresses from infant love to the fully mature love of the emotionally secure adult who receives satisfaction in providing nurturing, care, and protection to others. One of the characteristics of emotional maturity is the ability to postpone gratification, and adult-adult love includes both simultaneous and alternate manifestations of love; an emotionally mature person can be content to provide love for another person without expecting immediate reciprocation.

Contemporary analyses of the emotion of love indicate that it is not just an extreme version of liking. Liking emphasizes respect, attraction, and affection. Love includes these feelings but emphasizes need, care, trust, and tolerance. Love within a couple also includes a passion cluster of fascination, exclusiveness, and sexual desire.

Limerence is an overwhelming, compulsive attraction for another person. Romantic love is visionary and idyllic—the idealization of beauty, grace, and charm in the woman and strength, courage, and sacrifice in the man. It is closely related to limerence. Modern-day romantic love may be sexual or nonsexual, but initially—in its origins as courtly love in the twelfth century—romantic love was asexual. Sexual love has a strong erotic component. Although it has gained increasing recognition as a legitimate aspect of modernday romantic love, it may have great importance, negligible importance, or no importance for an individual couple. Companionate love is sensible, calm, and relaxed and emphasizes trust, tolerance, and commitment in the relationship. Companionate love is probably more frequently experienced by married couples in long-term relationships than are the passionate, tumultuous components of love. Altruistic love is unselfish, caring, self-sacrificing love that puts the other's well-being ahead of one's own. It is close to the Greek concept of agape.

Commitment is closely related to love. However, love may occur without commitment, and commitment may occur without love. The central aspects of commitment—an intention to maintain the relationship—are stability, consistency, and duration.

Jealousy is a painful emotion that may result from potentially lost love—that is, the perception that the other person is withdrawing love and giving it to someone else. Jealousy may be turned outward so that blame is directed toward the other person for being disloyal or for betraying trust and intimacy, or it may be directed inward so that it is expressed as self-blame, depression, and despondency. Whereas men are more likely to direct jealous feelings outward, expressing them through rage or violence, women are more likely to blame themselves. Men are also more likely to focus on the sexual activity of the betrayal, whereas women are more likely to focus on the emotional involvement threatened.

Current theory finds three basic types of love within a couple: eros love (passionate, sexual), ludus love (playful, flirtatious), and storge love (calm, companionate). Each person's characteristic experience of love is a mixture of these three types, but usually one type predominates. The number of possible mixtures is infinite, and "true love" is defined by each individual according to his or her unique mixture of these types. Over time, a person may shift from being predominately characterized by one type of love to being predominately characterized by another.

KEY TERMS

The following is a list of key terms in this chapter.
These terms are defined in context within the chapter, and many may also be found in the Glossary.

adult-infant love	commitment	crystallization	erotophile
agape love	companionate love	dependence	erotophobe
altruistic love	courtly love	eros love	independence

interdependence	manic love	perception	self-love
jealousy	masochism	philos love	sexual love
limerence	mature love	romantic love	storge love
ludus love	nurturance	self-disclosure	

QUESTIONS

1. Describe the differences between adult-infant love and mature love.

2. Discuss the differences between loving and liking.

3. Discuss the characteristics of limerence as an aspect of love.

4. What is romantic love? How important is it in our society?

5. What are the major characteristics of sexual love? Companionate love? Altruistic love?

6. What are the major characteristics of the eros lover? The ludus lover? The storge lover? The manic lover?

7. Discuss the importance of commitment in marriage.

8. Describe an example of destructive or pathological jealousy.

9. How can jealousy be handled constructively?

SUGGESTIONS FOR FURTHER READING

Cancian, Francesca M. *Love in America: Gender and Self-Development*. New York: Cambridge University Press, 1987.

Ehrenreich, Barbara; Hess, Elizabeth; and Jacobs, Gloria. *Re-Making Love: The Feminization of Sex*. New York: Doubleday, 1986.

Douglas, Jack D., and Atwell, Freda Cruise. *Love, Intimacy and Sex*. Newbury Park, Calif.: Sage, 1988.

Fromm, Erich. *The Art of Loving*. New York: Bantam, 1970.

Gardella, Peter. *Innocent Ecstasy: How Christianity Gave America an Ethic of Sexual Pleasure*. New York: Oxford University Press, 1985.

Hatfield, Elaine. "Passionate and Companionate Love." In Robert Sternberg and Michael Barnes (eds.), *The Psychology of Love*. New Haven, Conn.: Yale University Press, 1988.

Kelley, Harold H., et al. *Close Relationships*. New York: Freeman, 1983.

May, Rollo. *Cry for Myth*. New York: Norton, 1990.

Tennov, Dorothy. *Love and Limerence*. New York: Stein & Day, 1979.

CHAPTER 4

Fundamentals of Sexuality and Eroticism

And sweet, reluctant, amorous delay.
John Milton, "Paradise Lost"

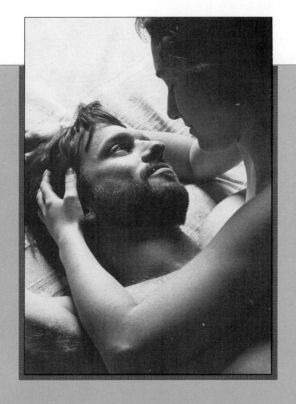

Male Sexuality

Female Sexuality

Complexity of Erotic Interaction

Heterosexuality, Homosexuality, and Bisexuality

What Do You Know?

Some of the following statements are true and some are false.
Can you tell which are which?

T/F   1. There are two sources of penile erection, with extremely important differences.

T/F   2. Males do not experience orgasm until puberty.

T/F   3. Men who are very active sexually, with a high frequency of ejaculation, are usually less creative, less productive, and less successful than other men.

T/F   4. Males may learn to experience a series of orgasms without ejaculation.

T/F   5. Some men in their nineties have the same hormonal levels as those under age fifty.

T/F   6. The vagina is the homologue of the penis.

T/F   7. Vaginal lubrication is the counterpart of penile erection in the male.

T/F   8. The average orgasm in females lasts three to four seconds but may last as long as twenty to sixty seconds.

T/F   9. The subjective experience of orgasm is virtually the same for women and men.

T/F   10. An estimated half of all married couples in our society are sexually incompatible.

Answers: 1-T, 2-F, 3-F, 4-T, 5-T, 6-F, 7-T, 8-T, 9-T, 10-T.

The most obvious manifestation of gender is sexual behavior. *Sexual behavior, which is any behavior that is based on gender,* may vary from mild flirtation to the all-consuming passion of Romeo and Juliet.

Sex is arguably one of the most important of all human activities. It is the process by which the individuals of a species reproduce; it is the central behavior that forms families; and it is a key component of the emotional lives of individuals. The emotion that results when sexual behavior is fused with love may reach an intensity that is nothing short of astonishing (see Chapter 3). Sexual behavior is also central to a number of social and medical problems, such as marital difficulties and divorce, rape, incest and child abuse, unwanted pregnancy, abortion, and sexually transmitted diseases (Smith 1991).

In all known societies, sexuality is believed to be of critical importance. This is true whether the society is relatively permissive and approving of a wide range of erotic behavior or is very confining and restrictive (Reiss 1986).

In this chapter we will examine the basic elements of sexuality — male sexuality, female sexuality, and the complexity of erotic and romantic interactions between males and females.

Male Sexuality

Males have some erotic[1] characteristics that are very similar to those of females and others that are quite different. Erotic characteristics of both males and females are based first on their sexual anatomy and physiology.

---

[1]**Erotic** means having to do with sexual excitement, pleasure, or desire. An erotic sensation can occur in reaction to psychological stimuli (such as imagination or fantasy) or in reaction to stimuli from any of the five senses: sight, smell, taste, hearing, or touch.

Male Anatomy and Physiology

The **penis,** which is located at the base of the abdomen, consists of a shaft and a cone-shaped head, or **glans.** The shaft is about three-fourths of the length of the penis, and the glans is about one-fourth. The glans is covered with very thin, sensitive tissue and, unless the male has been circumcised,[2] a heavier retractable foreskin, which is an extension of the loose skin covering the shaft. When flaccid (soft), the penis lies on the **scrotum,** a sac that contains two testicles, within which the sperm cells develop. When the penis becomes erect, the skin covering the shaft expands and, in uncircumcised men, slides back to uncover the glans.

Normal flaccid penis length varies from less than two inches to a little longer than four inches, with the average about four inches long and a little less than an inch in diameter (Reinisch 1990). Many men worry that their penis is too small. The second most frequently asked question men pose at The Kinsey Institute[3] is about penis size and how it can be increased. (The most frequently asked question is about the problem of getting and keeping an erection, but more on this later.) There is no known way of increasing penis size. However, differences in

---

[2]**Circumcision** consists of trimming away the foreskin to expose the glans of the penis. Among Jews and Muslims this has religious significance; in some societies it may be an initiation rite; in our own society it is performed on about 60 percent of male babies for medical reasons. Since the American Academy of Pediatrics stated in 1975 that there was no medical reason for routine circumcision (Money 1985), and since many insurance carriers now classify it as unnecessary surgery, and refuse to pay for it, the incidence may be expected to decline (Lightfoot-Kline 1989; Wallerstein 1986).

[3]The Kinsey Institute for Research in Sex, Gender, and Reproduction at Indiana University is one of the foremost organizations of its kind in the United States. It is currently directed by June M. Reinisch, a leading researcher in human sexuality and psychosexual development.

length of the flaccid penis are relatively unimportant because during erection, shorter than average penises increase proportionately more than longer than average penises. And most erect penises are within a typical size range: between five and seven inches long and about an inch and a half in diameter (Reinisch 1990).

The shaft of the penis consists chiefly of three spongy cylinders surrounding the **urethra,** a tube that carries urine and semen from inside the body.[4] Typically, a male reacts to erotic stimulation in part by a flow of blood into the spongy tissue of the penile cylinders. If blood flows into this spongy tissue faster than it flows out, the cylinders become engorged with blood, and the penis becomes larger, stiffens, and starts to stand out from the body. This process of **erection** may take anywhere from a few seconds to several minutes or longer. As the penis becomes erect, stiffening, hardening, and projecting out from the body, it pulls the now taut scrotum upward. In the erect stage, the penis is able to penetrate the *vagina* of the female. (See Figure 4-1.)

Spontaneous erection may occur in response to erotic stimuli — whether input from any of the five senses or from a dream, fantasy, or memory. An erotic spontaneous erection may occur at an inopportune time or may fail to occur at an opportune time — for example, when a male is intent upon copulating[5] with an attractive and willing partner. When this happens, fear of erectile failure may itself cause the failure to occur, and this can become a persistent problem for a male.

---

[4]The cylinder on the underside of the penis is called the **corpus spongiosum.** The two cylinders that fill the sides and top of the penis are called the **corpus cavernosa** (Seeley, Stephens, and Tate 1989).

[5]The terms **copulate** and **copulation** mean insertion of a penis into a vagina. (Oral copulation means inserting the penis into the mouth, and anal copulation means inserting it into the anus.)

Failure of the erotic spontaneous erection need not be a problem, however, since tactile (touch) stimulation of a primary erogenous zone will normally cause the penis to become erect — a tactile erection. (An **erogenous zone** is a part of the body that responds to tactile stimulation with pleasure and erotic arousal.) In young males (under age twenty-five), a few seconds to a few minutes of appropriate tactile stimulation of an erogenous zone will usually cause a tactile erection; with older males, the penis may not become erect for several minutes or more (see the section "Aging and Sexuality in the Male"). Whatever his age, however, tactile stimulation will not cause the penis to become erect unless the male is both physiologically and psychologically prepared to be erotically aroused; erotic response is not simply automatic (see the section "Problems with Sexual Functioning").

A spontaneous erection may also occur with no erotic meaning. It is quite common for a male (especially a young male) to awaken with an erection, and these "morning erections" may be unrelated to erotic arousal. Spontaneous erections may also occur during the sleep cycle, usually during the REM (rapid eye movement) phase of sleep, and these erections are not usually related to erotic arousal or associated with erotic dreams. Spontaneous erections with no erotic content may also occur when a male is awake and may last for a few minutes or, in the young male, for an hour or longer. As with erotic spontaneous erection, a nonerotic erection may occur at such inopportune times as sitting in class or in church or riding on a bus and may be awkward and embarrassing. The male normally has no control over spontaneous erections (whether erotic or nonerotic), and there is nothing he can do except wait for the turgid penis to subside.

Both the glans and the shaft of the penis are primary erogenous zones in the male. The glans

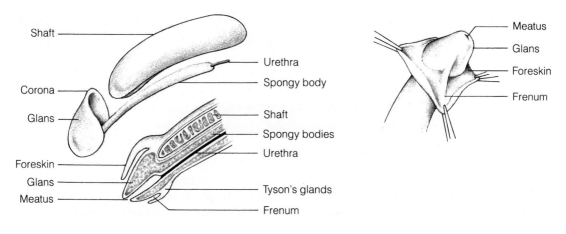

Shaft

Corona

Glans

Foreskin

Glans

Meatus

Urethra

Spongy body

Shaft

Spongy bodies

Urethra

Tyson's glands

Frenum

Meatus

Glans

Foreskin

Frenum

FIGURE 4-1
The penis.

is typically the most erotically sensitive part of a male's body. The most erotically sensitive part of the glans is the corona, and the most sensitive part of the corona is the *frenum*, which is on the lower surface of the glans where the foreskin is attached. The *meatus*, the opening to the urethra at the tip of the penis (see Figure 4-1), is also erotically sensitive in most males. Many males nevertheless prefer stimulation of the shaft — or alternate stimulation of the shaft and various areas of the glans. The nipple is a primary erogenous zone for about half of all males, who may respond to tactile stimulation of their nipples with erection and even with orgasm. The anus is also richly supplied with nerve endings and is a primary erogenous zone for about half of all males. Another primary erogenous zone for many males is the perineum, the area between the base of the scrotum and the anus; for these males, pressure on the perineum can cause erection (Reinisch 1990; Starr and Weiner 1981; Kinsey et al. 1948, 1953).

A penis may have a slight curve to one side when erect. About a third of men (30 percent)

say that their erections point to the left, and about one in twenty (6 percent) say that they point to the right; the rest say that their erections point straight ahead (Reinisch 1990).

Because the glans is also filled with spongy tissue, it also enlarges during erection, and the **corona,** the crownlike ridge at the back of the glans, swells and becomes more prominent.

A male normally has two testicles (the male **gonads**) within the scrotum. Testicles are oval and are normally about an inch and a half long and about an inch in diameter, although one testicle may be slightly larger than the other. One testicle usually hangs lower than the other, which helps prevent the testicles from being squeezed when a man's legs are together. (Testicles are extremely sensitive to pain, whether from a blow or from being squeezed.) The left testicle usually hangs lower in right-handed men; in left-handed men the right testicle usually hangs lower (Reinisch 1990).

Testicles have two important functions: producing testosterone, a hormone that is necessary for male development and sexual functioning

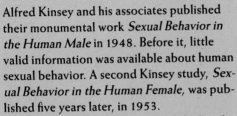
Alfred Kinsey and his associates published their monumental work *Sexual Behavior in the Human Male* in 1948. Before it, little valid information was available about human sexual behavior. A second Kinsey study, *Sexual Behavior in the Human Female*, was published five years later, in 1953.

The classic Kinsey interview asked each subject 350 questions covering every conceivable aspect of erotic activity. Kinsey interviewers went everywhere — into manufacturing plants, colleges, churches, and prisons. More than 17,000 interviews were conducted, and the statistical theory through which conclusions were drawn was exhaustively checked and reviewed. A system of cross-checks was devised that involved,

for example, taking histories from both a husband and wife so that their statements could be compared. The researchers also conducted follow-up interviews after two years and after four years.

Kinsey and his group did not, however, observe sexual behavior directly; they simply cataloged it. *Taxonomy* is the branch of science that names, describes, and classifies — and Kinsey was a taxonomist. Kinsey and his associates named, described, and classified the type, extent, and frequency of various sexual activities in our society.

A full decade was to pass before researchers William Masters and Virginia Johnson took the step of directly observing men and women performing a variety of sexual ac-

---

(see Chapter 2) and producing sperm cells, which are the basic reproductive cells in the male. The average man normally produces four to five billion sperm cells each month. Sperm cells are only about one five-hundredth of an inch in length and thousands of times smaller than egg cells; they are not visible to the unaided eye. (See Figure 4-2.)

Beginning with puberty, the seminal vesicles and the prostate gland produce semen, which is normally ejaculated with orgasm (see the section "Orgasm Phase"). Semen contains the sperm cells, which, when ejaculated into the vagina, propel themselves through the cervix, into the

uterus, and then into the fallopian tubes, where, if an egg is present, conception may occur (see Appendix C). In our society, boys usually begin to undergo genital development at eleven to twelve years of age, with their genitals reaching adult size and shape at ages fourteen to fifteen (Masters, Johnson, and Kolodny 1988).

Erotic Response Cycle in the Male

One of the most important discoveries of sex researchers William Masters and Virginia Johnson (see Box 4-1) was that males and females go through the same four phases of erotic response.

tivities under rigorous laboratory conditions. Hundreds of subjects participated, ranging in age from eighteen to eighty-nine. Scientific observation of human sexual behavior in this way would not have been acceptable at the time of Kinsey's studies.

The researchers noted and recorded the subjects' physiological responses to the various activities. They measured these responses precisely with electronic instruments, many of which had been specially devised for the study. For example, Masters and Johnson developed a camera that could be housed (together with the required illumination) in a plastic penis, so that the interior of the vagina could be photographed during simulated copulation.

Masters and Johnson's research detected the four phases of erotic response. It documented such phenomena as the ballooning of the vagina, the lubricating fluid that was exuded from the vaginal walls, and the extrusion (opening) of the labia during the excitement phase. The study identified precisely the physiological responses that occurred during orgasm and pinpointed the similarities and differences in male and female erotic characteristics.

In 1966, Masters and Johnson published their trailblazing *Human Sexual Response,* a report of their systematic and painstaking research on specific sexual activities directly observed, measured, and recorded in the laboratory. Their study has been criticized for ignoring the role of emotions in erotic response. They did not deny the importance of emotion (whether love, affection, fear, or dread) but instead chose to focus in their initial research on the physiological correlates of erotic arousal. In subsequent work they turned to the study of the psychological and social factors of sexuality, as have other researchers.

According to Masters and Johnson (1966), these four phases are excitement, plateau, orgasm, and resolution.

Excitement Phase   The most notable signal that a male is in the excitement phase of erotic response is penile erection (although the penis may be erect without being in the excitement phase, as we have seen). Other significant changes during the excitement phase typically include rising blood pressure and increasing pulse rate; in addition, involuntary muscles may contract and nipples may be erect (Masters, Johnson, and Kolodny 1988).

Males experience erection from early infancy, and most discover that rubbing or stroking their erection causes a pleasurable sensation. However, most boys learn how to masturbate to orgasm from another boy. By the time they reach puberty, 80 percent of boys in our society have experienced several hundred orgasms (see the section "Orgasm Phase" for a description of orgasm). Most males masturbate to orgasm rather quickly by stroking the penis in an up-and-down motion that simulates the thrusting of copulation. (As we have seen, prepubertal males do not ejaculate with orgasm.) Unlike females, males are very predictable in their masturbatory

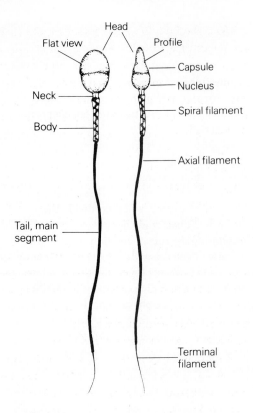

Head
Flat view
Profile
Neck
Body
Capsule
Nucleus
Spiral filament
Axial filament
Tail, main segment
Terminal filament

FIGURE 4-2
The sperm.

techniques, with little variation, unless they have learned to acquire ejaculatory control (see the section "Acquiring Ejaculatory Control") (Masters, Johnson, and Kolodny 1988; Reinisch 1990). Kinsey (1948) and his coworkers believed that one of their most important discoveries regarding male sexuality was that most males begin a pattern of frequency of orgasm at puberty and then maintain this pattern into old age whatever their social circumstances — never-married, married, separated, divorced, or widowed.

Plateau Phase With continued stimulation, the male enters the *plateau phase*, which may last for several minutes to an hour or more. During this phase all physiological characteristics of the excitement phase continue; in addition, the coronal ridge of the glans enlarges further and the color deepens.

Beginning a year or two before puberty, which usually begins between ages eleven and twelve in our society, a few drops of **pre-ejaculatory fluid** may be exuded from the meatus during the plateau stage. This clear, slippery fluid is produced in two, pea-sized *Cowper's glands* (Reinisch 1990). After puberty, sperm may be present in this pre-ejaculatory fluid in sufficient quantity to impregnate a female, even if the male never ejaculates within her vagina.

Orgasm Phase With continued stimulation, the male enters the *orgasm phase*, which begins with a sensation of suspension, or inevitability. The sensation of suspension that precedes orgasm is usually followed immediately by a sense of tension. Facial expressions may become tortured. Pulse rate may more than double and blood pressure may double, while breathing may become deeper and faster. Orgasm is often accompanied by increasing *hypoxia* — shortage of oxygen — which causes a person to gasp and gulp for air. The senses of smell, taste, hearing, sight, and touch are typically greatly diminished. Brain-wave patterns change, reflecting the altered state of consciousness during orgasm. The orgasm itself normally lasts for three to four seconds (Masters, Johnson, and Kolodny 1988).

As with all human experience, there are great individual differences in the experience of orgasm. Some males typically experience reactions that are very extreme, whereas others typically have relatively mild sensations. Moreover, the experience of orgasm may differ significantly for the same person from one orgasm to another. Some males make no sound at all and show no visible muscular tension; others scream or have violent, uncontrollable muscle spasms, and a few even lose consciousness for a brief time. Most males fall somewhere between these extremes. The physical reactions of a person during orgasm do not necessarily reflect the depth of pleasure being experienced; the subjective experience of orgasm is usually extremely pleasurable for most males (Masters, Johnson, and Kolodny 1988).

Orgasm is normally followed by *euphoria* — a profound sense of well-being and contentment — and a man often drops into a brief, deep, relaxing sleep. The feeling of euphoria often remains for several hours and may remain for a day or longer. One reason for the subjective feelings of well-being and contentment that normally follow orgasm may be the increased level in the bloodstream of two hormones: testosterone and oxytocin (see Box 4-2).

Although it is unusual, instead of feeling a profound pleasure, a man may feel a sense of shame, sadness, or dejection following orgasm. This experience is called *postcoital depression*. A person who feels postcoital depression may associate sexuality with feelings of guilt or fear (Masters and Johnson 1966; Kinsey et al. 1948, 1953).

As we have seen, a postpubertal male normally ejaculates with orgasm. Typically semen is ejaculated in a series of jets that may spurt several feet. The total volume of semen ejaculated is normally about one teaspoon: About two-thirds is fluid from the seminal vesicles, and about one-third is fluid from the prostate gland. This amount of semen usually contains from 200 to 500 million sperm cells but may contain as many as a billion (Seeley, Stephens, and Tate 1989). The color of semen may be various shades of white, yellow, or gray. The texture is usually creamy and thick immediately after ejaculation, but then the semen becomes more liquid. Semen soon dries after exposure to air (Reinisch 1990).

As with all physiological responses, the characteristics of ejaculation and the ejaculate (semen) vary among men and from one time to another for any one man. Semen is typically viscous (thick) and milky but varies from being almost gelatinous to being thin and watery. Although semen usually spurts forcibly from the penis in a series of jets, it may spurt just once or twice or may simply seep out. And although the amount of semen in each ejaculation is usually about a teaspoonful, it may be just a few drops (Masters, Johnson, and Kolodny 1988; Starr and Weiner 1981).

The seminal vesicles and the prostate gland typically produce semen continually from puberty until death. The adult male usually ejaculates this semen two or three times a week — although this ejaculatory schedule may vary widely from one man to another. One of the key findings of Kinsey's research was the wide range of frequency of ejaculation in males, extending from several times a day from puberty on to once a year or less. About one male in a hundred goes for as long as five years without ejaculating. All of these frequencies of ejaculation are considered to be normal (Masters, Johnson, and Kolodny 1988; Kinsey et al. 1948).

Another key finding by Kinsey and his colleagues (1948, 1953) was that males who have a higher than average frequency of ejaculation during adolescence continue to have a higher than average frequency of ejaculation throughout middle and old age. This finding was supported by Masters and Johnson's studies in 1966 and by subsequent research (Reinisch 1990). These researchers agree that the more sexually active a boy is in adolescence, the more sexually active he will be throughout his lifetime. The researchers also found that, in general, men who had a high frequency of ejaculation were also more active, creative, and productive in nonsexual activities. Conversely, men who had a

BOX 4-2

Orgasm and Feelings of Well-Being

When a male becomes erotically aroused, two powerful hormones are released into his bloodstream: *testosterone* and *oxytocin*. Testosterone is produced chiefly in the testicles, whereas oxytocin is secreted by the pituitary gland (at the base of the brain) in both men and women.

The level of testosterone in the bloodstream rises (or falls) as anabolism rises (or falls). *Anabolism* is characterized by the building of proteins, tissues, and cells; by increased bodily defenses against infection; by good health; and by a rise in generalized feelings of well-being. Put another way, testosterone levels in the blood and anabolism are positively correlated (Brecher and Brecher 1976). In contrast, the level of testosterone in the bloodstream is negatively correlated with catabolism; as one rises, the other falls. *Catabolism* is characterized by breakdown of proteins, wasting away of tissues, death of body cells, loss of calcium from bones, lowered bodily defenses against infection, poor health, and a drop in generalized feelings of well-being (Brecher and Brecher 1976).

Testosterone levels in the bloodstream of males increase significantly with erotic stimulation. For example, when male subjects viewed a film showing petting and copulation, their testosterone levels rose an average of 35 percent and remained relatively high for several hours. A matched control group of men who did not see the film did not experience a rise in testosterone (Brecher and Brecher 1976).

Oxytocin — the "pleasure hormone" — acts on many regions of the brain known to be involved in sexual behavior in nonhuman mammals. Evidence suggests a link between oxytocin and sexual and social behaviors in humans as well. Oxytocin is associated with many of life's more pleasurable social and sexual exchanges. In the moments preceding and during orgasm in men, the levels of oxytocin in the bloodstream rise dramatically, surging to three to five times the normal level (Angier 1991).

Comparable research on the levels of testosterone and oxytocin in the bloodstream of women during erotic arousal and orgasm has not yet been done. It may be that the characteristic rise of these powerful hormones that accompanies erotic arousal is not unique to men. However, women's subjective experience of orgasm, and their subsequent feelings of well-being, have been found to be indistinguishable from those of men.

relatively low frequency of ejaculation tended to be less active in other areas of their lives as well.

Resolution Phase   Following orgasm, a male returns to normal physiological functioning during the *resolution phase*. During this phase muscle tension, pulse rate, blood pressure, and breathing return to their pre-excitement norms, and the penis returns to its flaccid state.

As part of the resolution phase, most males must go through a *refractory period*, when the body is incapable of responding to stimulation that is normally experienced as erotic. The refractory period may last for only a few minutes, with an erection being maintained between one orgasm and the next, or the refractory period may last for an hour, for several hours, or even for several days. The length of the refractory period gradually increases as men grow older, from five to fifteen minutes in an eighteen-year-old to eighteen to twenty-four hours in a sixty-year-old. The more often a male ejaculates as part of his normal pattern, the shorter the refractory period (Hatcher et al. 1990; Reinisch 1990; Masters, Johnson, and Kolodny 1988).

Acquiring Ejaculatory Control

The most frequent sexual complaint of the young adult male is ejaculating too soon (before his partner has reached orgasm), although premature ejaculation is not limited to young males.

Interest, arousal, erection, orgasm, and ejaculation are separate processes. A man may be erotically interested and aroused, may have an erection and several satisfying orgasms close together, but may ejaculate only during the final orgasm. Or he may choose not to ejaculate — a man can learn to have entirely satisfactory orgasms without ejaculating at all (Reinisch 1990).

Sexologists have discovered two techniques that enable a man to acquire ejaculatory control. In one method, the *stop-start technique*, a man stim-

ulates one of his own primary erogenous zones (usually the penis) until he senses that ejaculation is imminent (but not yet inevitable). He then stops the stimulation before ejaculating; he may or may not experience orgasm. Once the urge to ejaculate has subsided, he resumes the stimulation until he again nears the onset of ejaculation, at which time he again ceases the stimulation. In this way, he acquires the ability to detect the difference between the sensation of imminent orgasm and the sensation of imminent ejaculation. He may then delay ejaculation almost indefinitely if he wishes, perhaps experiencing a series of orgasms (Reinisch 1992; Kaplan 1989; Brauer and Brauer 1984).

A second method that helps recondition the ejaculatory reflex is the *squeeze technique*. This method involves placing the thumb on the coronal ridge and the index finger on the frenum, applying a firm pressure for about four seconds, and then abruptly releasing the pressure. Pressure is always applied from the top of the coronal ridge to the frenum, never from side to side (Masters, Johnson, and Kolodny 1988).

For as yet unknown reasons, the squeeze technique reduces the urgency to ejaculate. It should be used earlier rather than at the moment of ejaculatory inevitability and should be repeated periodically, every few minutes, whenever ejaculation is imminent. The squeeze technique will cause partial loss of erection; however, tactile stimulation may be resumed immediately and the erection regained (Masters, Johnson, and Kolodny 1988).

Aging and Sexuality in the Male

It is commonly believed that most people have little or no sexual life after age sixty — that they live in some kind of sexual wasteland with declining interest, responsiveness, and performance. However, research finds that aging does not necessarily bring about a change in the average man's interests, appreciation, or enjoyment of erotic activity. A man's sex life usually depends chiefly on the availability of a willing and cooperative partner. Men who are sexually active during youth and middle age will usually continue to be sexually active in old age (Starr and Weiner 1981; Money 1980; Kinsey et al. 1948, 1953).

Aging in men is a very gradual psychoendocrine[6] and psychosexual process, with great individual differences in both its onset and its progress. Men do not experience a *climacteric* ("change of life")[7] as women do (Starr and Weiner 1981; Money 1980).

Psychoendocrine aging in the male is a product of many events, one of which is a decrease in the testosterone level in the bloodstream. This rarely happens before age fifty and often does not happen until ages seventy, eighty, or older. Some men in their nineties have the same hormonal levels as the average man in his forties or younger (Money 1980). In their study of sexuality in men between ages sixty and ninety-one, Starr and Weiner (1981) found that 80 percent of older men were still sexually active.

Starr and Weiner (1981) did observe changes in older men's sexuality. Their erections did not last as long, their ejaculations were not as forceful and had less volume, and their refractory periods lasted longer. The study also found, however, that older men can usually copulate without ejaculating much longer than younger men and that the importance of ejaculation is greatly decreased for older men. Whereas younger men feel a compulsion to ejaculate, older men may derive great pleasure and satisfaction from petting, fellatio, and copulation without ejaculation.

Older men have a broader appreciation of sexuality, in contrast to younger men's focus on penile response (Starr and Weiner 1981).

That males copulate less frequently at age seventy-five than they do at age twenty-five does not mean that they find sexuality is less meaningful or less satisfying. For older men, quality of orgasm is far more important than frequency of orgasm, and two-thirds of the sexually active older men experienced stronger, more profound orgasms than they did when they were younger (Starr and Weiner 1981).

A man may fail to achieve an erection whatever his age, and erectile failure may become more common after age forty. However, most men — whatever their age — will continue to respond with an erection when a primary erogenous zone is stimulated persistently and appropriately (Reinisch 1990; Starr and Weiner 1981; Masters and Johnson 1966).

Female Sexuality

As with male sexuality, the bases of female sexuality are the anatomical and physiological features characteristic of the female gender. These features form the fundamentals of women's reproductive and erotic behavior.

Female Anatomy and Physiology

As in the male, the external genitalia of the female (collectively called the **vulva**) are located at the base of the abdomen between the legs. They consist of *labia majora* (outer lips) and *labia minora* (inner lips), which close the entrance to the **vagina**. The labia are the homologue[8] of the scrotum. The **clitoris**, which is the homologue

---

[6]**Psychoendocrine** refers to the effect of hormones from the endocrine glands on physiological responses, emotions, and behavior.

[7]The female climacteric denotes the end of regular ovulation (see the section "Female Anatomy and Physiology").

[8]The term *homologue* means developed from the same prenatal structure (see Chapter 2).

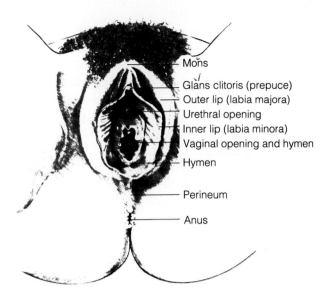

Mons
Glans clitoris (prepuce)
Outer lip (labia majora)
Urethral opening
Inner lip (labia minora)
Vaginal opening and hymen

Hymen

Perineum

Anus

FIGURE 4-3
External genitalia of the female.

of the penis, is situated just below the point where the labia join, near the top of the vulva (see Figure 4-3).

Although the clitoris plays no role in reproduction, clitoral stimulation is the chief source of erotic arousal and orgasm in most women (Reinisch 1990; Masters, Johnson, and Kolodny 1988). The clitoris consists of a shaft and a glans, but unlike the penis, the shaft does not hang free, and only the glans may be felt. The glans of the clitoris is usually about the size of a pea. As the homologue of the penis, the clitoris has an equivalent number of nerve endings but in a much smaller area and is thus exquisitely erotically sensitive. When erotically aroused (usually by tactile stimulation), the shaft of the clitoris extends in length and the glans grows larger and harder. The glans also extends out from the clitoral prepuce, which is the homologue of the foreskin (Reinisch 1990).

A membrane called the *hymen* is located at the entrance to the vagina, or *vestibule*. The hy-

men (sometimes called "maidenhead" in slang) plays no role in reproduction or in erotic arousal or pleasure. The hymen may partially close off the entrance to the vagina or it may be totally absent. It may be absent from birth or it may be ruptured by insertion of tampons or by active participation in sports. Thus it is quite possible for a female to be a virgin and still have little or no hymen. A hymen that does partially close off the entrance to the vagina may be ruptured by the thrusting of an erect penis during a woman's first copulation. Rupturing the hymen in this way may cause some discomfort and minor bleeding or (rarely) pain and heavy bleeding.[9]

The *vagina* is normally about six inches long, extending from its entrance (between the labia minora) to just beyond the *cervix*, which is the

---

[9]An unusually thick hymen with only a very small perforation can be opened easily by a simple and painless procedure in a physician's office.

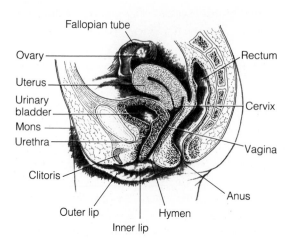

FIGURE 4-4
Female urogenital system.

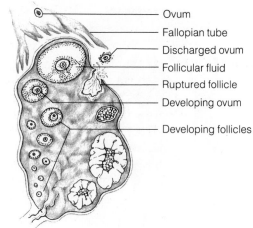

FIGURE 4-5
Ovulation.

opening at the top rear of the vagina that leads to the uterus (see Figure 4-4).

The female gonads that produce the human egg cells (*female gametes* or *ova*) are the *ovaries*, which are the homologues of the testicles.[10] Just as males have two testicles, females have two ovaries. However, unlike the testicles, the ovaries are situated deep within the body—in the pelvis, below and to each side of the navel. Each ovary, which is ovoid and about an inch and a half in diameter, is made up of glandular tissue and *egg sacs* (*follicles*). At birth a female has all the follicles she will ever have—about two million in each ovary—but only about 250 of them will ever become active and produce an egg (Martin and Reeder 1991).

[10]As noted in Chapter 2, the growth buds present in the embryo for the first six weeks after conception will develop into either ovaries or testicles, labia or scrotum, and clitoris or penis, depending on the prenatal hormone mix, which in turn depends on chromosomal pattern (XX in the female and XY in the male).

Once each lunar month (twenty-eight days or so), from puberty to menopause, approximately twenty follicles will be activated. However, only one will ripen and eject an ovum. This is quite a different pattern from men's production of sperm cells, as many as ten billion of which may be ejaculated each month (Martin and Reeder 1991).

Girls usually reach puberty anytime between ages ten and sixteen in our society. One-third now reach puberty at or before age eleven, but most girls enter puberty between the ages of twelve and thirteen (Martin and Reeder 1991).

The release of an egg from an erupting follicle is called **ovulation** (see Figure 4-5), which is the first step of the **menstrual cycle**. One end of a *fallopian tube* opens to partially enclose an ovary, and when an egg erupts from a follicle, it is swept into that ovary's fallopian tube through the slow movement of fluid and the action of cilia (tiny hairlike structures that line the walls of the tube). The other end of the fallopian tube leads into the *uterus* (also called the **womb**), a thick-walled, expandable organ within which the fetus[11] will develop during the *gestation* period, or pregnancy. (For further discussion of pregnancy and reproduction, see Appendix C.)

If no sperm are present in the fallopian tube, the egg will disintegrate, and the part of the uterine wall that has thickened in preparation for the fertilized egg is sloughed off with blood and other material in a process called *menstruation*.

The time at which a young woman first begins to menstruate is called the **menarche**; the cessation of menstruation is called **menopause**. Women in our society reach menopause at the average age of fifty-one, but it can begin as early as forty-five or as late as fifty-five (Hatcher et al. 1990).

Menstruation usually lasts about four days but can last for a longer or shorter period of time. Many women experience discomfort during menstruation; some women experience discomfort just before they menstruate, a phenomenon called *premenstrual syndrome* (PMS).

The cycle of ovulation, engorgement of the uterine wall with blood, menstruation, and subsequent ovulation complete the *menstrual cycle*. Although this cycle normally repeats itself about every twenty-eight days, many women experience longer or shorter cycles, and in some women cycles may be irregular. Moreover, such factors as emotional stress, fatigue, hormonal changes, and diet may interrupt the cycle. Pregnancy always interrupts the cycle; when a woman becomes pregnant, ovulation and men-

struation cease, and the menstrual cycle does not resume until she is no longer pregnant.

Erotic Response Cycle in the Female

In common with males, females react to appropriate stimuli by a progression through four phases of erotic response: excitement, plateau, orgasm, and resolution. There is no refractory period for the female; a woman may proceed immediately from one orgasm to another. With continuing tactile stimulation (usually of the clitoris) she may experience a series of orgasms, each of increasing intensity, before she is erotically satiated (Masters and Johnson 1966).

Excitement Phase A primary erogenous zone in most females is the clitoris, although the *mons* (the fleshy mound just above the vulva) and the vulva (especially the labia minora) are also important erogenous zones. The *G spot*[12] may also be an important erogenous zone in some women. The G spot is on the anterior (front) wall of the vagina, from one to three inches from the vaginal opening. Intravaginal massage in this area may lead to high levels of sexual excitement (Hatcher et al. 1990). (See Box 4-3.)

The nipple is a primary erogenous zone for about half of all women. Many women react to nipple stimulation with a very strong erotic response and even orgasm, and for many women the entire breast is an erogenous zone. Other women do not like breast or nipple stimulation, and some find it disturbing or annoying (see the section "Having Sex with Another Person").

The *perineum* (the area between the anus and the vulva) is a primary erogenous zone for many women, as is the anus, which contains a rich

---

[11]When a fertilized egg begins to divide, which usually happens almost immediately after fertilization, it is called a **zygote**. It continues to divide as it is swept down the fallopian tube to the uterus. When it implants in the lining of the uterus (*endometrium*), it is called a **blastocyst**. It then develops into a **germinal disc**, an **embryo**, and finally a **fetus**. (See Appendix C.)

[12]The *G spot* is named for the German physician (Ernst Grafenburg) who first suggested its presence in 1950 (Masters, Johnson, and Kolodny 1986).

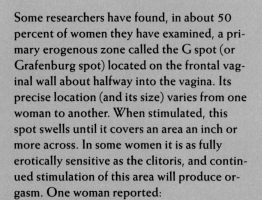
Some researchers have found, in about 50 percent of women they have examined, a primary erogenous zone called the G spot (or Grafenburg spot) located on the frontal vaginal wall about halfway into the vagina. Its precise location (and its size) varies from one woman to another. When stimulated, this spot swells until it covers an area an inch or more across. In some women it is as fully erotically sensitive as the clitoris, and continued stimulation of this area will produce orgasm. One woman reported:

> I have always had orgasms, but I have never had much stimulation when the penis was completely inside my vagina. In fact, sometimes my excitement and arousal would end abruptly when the penis entered me completely. I have always been most excitable when the penis was only one-half or one-third its way into my vagina. Now I know why—at that point it hit my "magic spot." (Ladas et al. 1982, p. 40)

Some women even report that when orgasm follows stimulation of the G spot, they release fluid as if they were ejaculating (Hatcher et al. 1990; Zilbergeld 1982; Ladas et al. 1982).

supply of nerve endings. Indeed, almost any area of the body may be a source of erotic arousal, with great individual differences in this regard. Virtually any portion of her skin may yield pleasurable and exciting sensations when caressed, providing she is willing and prepared to be touched (Hatcher et al. 1990; Kinsey et al. 1953).

When a woman responds to tactile stimulation of an erogenous zone she enters the excitement phase, signaled by vaginal lubrication. A very slick lubricating fluid is exuded from the walls of the vagina, perhaps within ten to thirty seconds of erotic stimulation. Vaginal lubrication is not only the female counterpart of penile erection (Masters and Johnson 1966) but an important component of male-female erotic interaction.

The inner two-thirds of the vagina "balloon" in the excitement phase, while the outer one-third contracts, or tightens. Both the inner and outer lips of the vulva (the labia minora and the labia majora) swell, protrude, and become increasingly sensitized to erotic stimulation. The color of the labia minora deepens from pink to red. Other physiological changes include a rising pulse rate, rising blood pressure, nipple erection, and involuntary muscle contraction. In some women, the excitement phase is accompanied by a flushing of the skin (Masters and Johnson 1966).

Many females first experience erotic arousal through masturbation. Unlike males, who usually learn to masturbate from a companion, females generally learn to masturbate though their own experimentation. Females are more likely than males to feel inhibition about masturbating and usually begin masturbating at a much later age than males do. Many females do not begin masturbation until they reach their dating or even their early married years (Reinisch 1990).

Physiologically, women and men are equally erotically responsive; they react equally quickly to adequate erotic stimulation — given that they are receptive to such stimulation. (Erotic response is not simply mechanical, as we have seen.) Women usually masturbate to orgasm rather quickly (the median figure is just under four minutes), and those who masturbate longer do so deliberately — to prolong erotic pleasure (Masters, Johnson, and Kolodny 1988).

Female masturbatory methods (unlike the masturbatory techniques of males) are characterized by great individual differences. Masters and Johnson (1966) observed that no two women masturbated in precisely the same way and that even a slight variation from a woman's preferred pattern may be anti-erotic or even annoying.

Plateau Phase When a woman enters the plateau phase of erotic response, vaginal lubrication increases, the inner two-thirds of the vagina balloon further, the outer one-third contracts (tightens) even more, the glans of the clitoris grows larger and harder, the labia minora change to a deeper red, the nipples become more erect, pulse rate and blood pressure continue to rise, and involuntary muscle contraction increases (Masters and Johnson 1966).

Orgasm Phase Orgasm in the female is signaled by dramatic physiological responses: Heart rate and blood pressure double; muscles

rhythmically tense and relax; breath comes in gasps; various areas of the skin flush; the senses of smell, hearing, sight, and touch are temporarily diminished; and the facial expression typically becomes tortured. The average female orgasm lasts from three to four seconds (as it does for the male), but some women experience longer orgasms — from twenty to sixty seconds.

Kinsey and coworkers (1953) found that about one in four females had experienced orgasm by puberty (as compared with about four in five males). Thus most (three-fourths) prepubescent females have no sense of the meaning of orgasm from their own experience (Kinsey et al. 1953).

The subjective experience of orgasm is the same for women and men, except that women do not ejaculate. This similarity was demonstrated in a study in which men and women were asked to write descriptions of how orgasm felt. The researchers then changed to gender-neutral terms any words that revealed the gender of the writer ("clitoris" and "penis" were changed to "genitals," for example) and gave the descriptions to a panel of evaluators (male and female gynecologists, clinical psychologists, and medical students). The evaluators could not tell which of the descriptions of orgasm were written by men and which were written by women; their rate of successful identification was no better than would be expected by chance alone (Proctor et al. 1974). For a sample of descriptions of orgasms, see Box 4-4.

There are different patterns of male-female erotic responses that pertain to the timing of the couple's orgasms (see Figure 4-6). In two of these patterns the female is left sexually unfulfilled (either still not aroused or in the plateau phase) after her partner's ejaculation. While he may drift into sleep, she may feel frustrated, irritated, annoyed, restless, or disturbed instead of feeling the euphoria, contentment, and deep relaxation

BOX 4-4

The Similarity of Male and Female Orgasm

Which of the following descriptions of orgasm were written by males and which were written by females? (Correct answers are given at the bottom of this box.)

M _____ 1. Just before I reach orgasm, I
F _____   feel warmth in my genital area. The warmth turns into a heat which spreads up my back and all the way into my fingers and toes. Although I am usually fairly quiet during most of love-making, at orgasm I often moan quite loudly.

M _____ 2. Basically, I feel a glow that
F _____   starts in my genitals, and then spreads through my whole body. Sometimes one orgasm is enough, and other times, it is not completely satisfying.

M _____ 3. For me, orgasm feels like a
F _____   building wave of emotion. First, I notice a pulsing sensation that is quite localized, then it spreads through my whole body. Afterwards, I feel tired but also superrelaxed.

M _____ 4. I concentrate all my attention
F _____   on the sensations in the genitals, and when I come, I completely lose contact with everything around me. My body feels incredibly alive and seems to vibrate. Afterwards, I just want to hold my lover and be very still.

M _____ 5. Sexual orgasm just seems to
F _____   happen to me. I can't explain how or why, but I suddenly experience an intense rush of feeling, and then it's gone, just as suddenly. Often, I want to experience it more than once.

M _____ 6. Just before orgasm, I am mostly
F _____   aware of the muscle contractions. When the orgasm comes, I feel my whole body sort of explode, and then slip into a deep relaxation, so that I feel I can hardly move.

M _____ 7. My anxiety about sex definitely
F _____   inhibits my orgasm. There are times that I feel some intense sensations, but usually I am too inhibited to let myself go. If I am not very comfortable with my partner, it is very difficult to come. I have orgasms most easily when I masturbate.

M _____ 8. I think orgasm is overrated. I
F _____   sometimes spend over an hour getting turned on, and then the orgasm takes only a few seconds. I'd like to learn how to make the feeling of orgasm last longer.

Answers: 1-F, 2-F, 3-M, 4-M, 5-F, 6-F, 7-M, 8-M.

Source: Proctor et al. (1974). Reprinted with permission of Human Sciences Press.

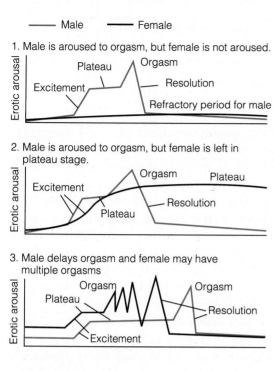

— Male   — Female

1. Male is aroused to orgasm, but female is not aroused.

Erotic arousal

Plateau   Orgasm

Excitement   Resolution

Refractory period for male

2. Male is aroused to orgasm, but female is left in plateau stage.

Erotic arousal

Orgasm   Plateau

Excitement

Resolution

Plateau

3. Male delays orgasm and female may have multiple orgasms

Erotic arousal

Orgasm   Orgasm

Plateau   Resolution

Excitement

FIGURE 4-6
Patterns of male-female erotic responses.

characteristic of the aftermath of orgasm. If these patterns (male satisfaction, female dissatisfaction) become routine, severe repercussions (sexual incompatibility) can occur.

A third pattern of male-female erotic response relates to a delay in ejaculation and the absence of a refractory period in women (see Figure 4-6). Because women do not experience a refractory period, they may quickly have a second, a third, or additional orgasms, each of increasing intensity (Masters, Johnson, and Kolodny 1988).

Resolution Phase In the fourth phase of erotic response — the *resolution* phase — the female returns to normal physiological functioning. Pulse rate, blood pressure, breathing, and muscle tension all revert to their pre-excitement levels. The labia, clitoris, vagina, and uterus return to their unstimulated size and position as the congestion of the blood vessels subsides.

Individual Differences in Female Sexuality

As we have noted, men begin a pattern of frequency of orgasm at puberty and maintain that pattern into old age. Kinsey and coworkers (1953) regarded the absence of such a pattern for women as among their most important findings. Women may change the frequency of orgasms and the characteristics of their erotic responses from situation to situation and over the stages of their lives. Indeed, the variations in erotic behavior among women are so great that one woman may be incapable of understanding the meaning of sexuality for another woman (Kinsey et al. 1953).

Aging and Sexuality in the Female

Earlier beliefs that menopause is an extremely traumatic period in a woman's life have not been borne out by research. On the contrary, most women do not experience menopause as a critical event but instead feel an increased sense of serenity and well-being and report fewer complaints after menopause than before (McKinlay 1988; Brock 1979).

Menopause is normally characterized by lowered levels of estrogen, which may cause vaginal dryness, and a physician may prescribe hormone treatment that restores vaginal lubrication. Calcium supplements are usually advised, with or without hormone treatment (Hatcher et al. 1990).

Although menopause marks a decline in fertility, it does not signal a decline in erotic response. In fact, many women experience an increase in erotic interest and response after the beginning of menopause (Brock 1979). In their definitive research on older Americans, Starr and Weiner (1981) found that women's erotic responses may remain essentially unchanged long after menopause is completed. Sexually active women in their sixties, seventies, and even eighties enjoyed erotic stimulation just as much as they did when younger and usually experienced orgasm. The following comment is typical of those Starr and Weiner (1981) reported:

> I want you to know that I am eighty-three years old. He was eighty-five. We had sex right up until the end. We loved it and it was wonderful. (p. 52)

Among Starr and Weiner's (1981) respondents who were not sexually active (about one in five), nearly all (96 percent) said that they desired sexual relations but lacked the opportunity. More older women than men lacked the opportunity for sexual relations simply because in the pertinent age groups women clearly outnumber men.[13] Starr and Weiner (1981) also found that because three out of four wives eventually become widows, many women over age sixty are simply without sex partners. The report concludes that the most crucial reason for lack of sexuality in older women was the nonavailability of men.

Complexity of Erotic Interaction

Even though the physical aspects of erotic response are clearly extraordinarily complex, the psychological and social aspects of sexual interaction are even more complex:

> People are incorrigibly themselves. They are shy, cheerful, dissatisfied. They like

one another, and are mysteries to one another . . . and the seesaw of their erotic interests rarely balances. (Updike 1979, p. 10)

Erotophiles and Erotophobes

Part of the complexity of sexual interaction comes from the fact that individuals vary enormously in their attitudes toward sexuality. Some people find sex compulsively pleasurable; others are indifferent to sex; still others are "turned off" by sex and find it boring or distasteful. If a couple are mismatched in their sexual orientations or expectations, they will be sexually incompatible; if they are matched, whether they both find sex to be pleasurable or to be boring or disgusting, they will be sexually compatible.

Sexologists call a person who finds sex pleasurable an **erotophile**; a person who is disinterested or aversive to sex is called an **erotophobe**[14] (Byrne 1977).

Erotophiles experience sexuality as an extremely significant part of their consciousness and life-styles. They are often preoccupied with sexual themes, have rich fantasy lives relating to erotic activity, and are interested in exploring variations of sexual behavior. Erotophobes feel that sexual behavior is relatively unimportant (except for reproduction). They feel uncomfortable about sexual matters and are very conservative about any variation of sexual behavior that is not strictly related to reproduction.

Erotophilic and erotophobic people do not constitute two separate groups; rather, these people occupy places on a continuum of sexual attitudes. Some individuals are pronounced erotophiles, whereas others are only mildly erotophilic; others are pronounced erotophobes, and still others are only mildly erotophobic.

---

[13]U.S. Bureau of the Census, "Persons Living Alone, by Sex and Age: 1970 to 1989" (1991).

[14]The combining form *-phile* means having an affinity for or a strong attraction to; *-phobe* means fearing of or averse to.

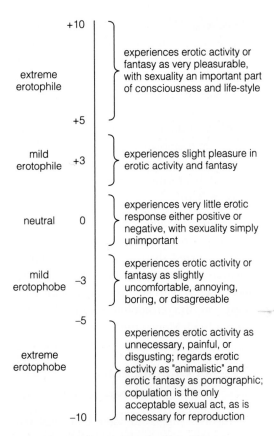

+10	experiences erotic activity or fantasy as very pleasurable, with sexuality an important part of consciousness and life-style
extreme erotophile	
+5	
mild erotophile +3	experiences slight pleasure in erotic activity and fantasy
neutral 0	experiences very little erotic response either positive or negative, with sexuality simply unimportant
mild erotophobe −3	experiences erotic activity or fantasy as slightly uncomfortable, annoying, boring, or disagreeable
−5	
extreme erotophobe	experiences erotic activity as unnecessary, painful, or disgusting; regards erotic activity as "animalistic" and erotic fantasy as pornographic; copulation is the only acceptable sexual act, as is
−10	necessary for reproduction

Human behavior is enormously diverse from one individual to another and does not fit precisely into any scheme or categorization. Moreover, a person may move from one characteristic to another from time to time, depending on many factors. In general, however, our population may be represented along a continuum that extends from very positive erotic characteristics through neutral to very negative. There is probably no other important human potential with such a wide range of response.

FIGURE 4-7
The erotophile-erotophobe scale.

We can thus construct an erotophile-erotophobe scale (see Figure 4-7). A most extreme erotophile would be assigned a + 10 on the scale, and a most extreme erotophobe would be assigned a − 10. A mild erotophile would fall at about + 3, whereas a mild erotophobe would

fall at about − 3. A person who is relatively neutral regarding sexuality would be between + 3 and − 3.

Other terms can be used to describe attitudes to sexuality. Money (1986, 1988) uses the term *hyperphilia* to describe the outlook of an erotophile and the term *hypophilia*[15] to describe that of an erotophobe. The phrases "Don Juan complex," "Casanova complex," or "satyriasis" are sometimes used to describe a pronounced erotophile who is male; "nymphomaniac" has been used to describe a pronounced erotophile who is female.

Most people are neither extreme erotophiles nor extreme erotophobes but fall somewhere in between, usually on a relatively neutral position on the scale. In one study, married couples were asked to pick (from a list) the five activities they enjoyed most. They were then asked to rate these five enjoyable activities from "most enjoyed" to "least enjoyed." "Reading books" came in first for wives, being selected by more than a third (37 percent) as their most enjoyable activity. "Sexual/affectional activities" was chosen by almost one-fourth (23 percent) of the wives. "Sewing for pleasure" was chosen next, by 22 percent. Most husbands chose various other activities before "sexual/affectional." However, this activity was chosen by more husbands (45 percent) than any other single activity. "Attending athletic events" was the second most popular activity for husbands, and "reading books" was third (Mancini and Orthner 1978). Other research has also found that nearly half (45 percent) of our population—men and women alike—are either "sexually conservative" or "nonsexual" (Flax 1984).

Men are usually assumed to be more hyperphilic (highly sexed) than women, although the

---

[15] The prefix *hyper-* means above or behind, whereas the prefix *hypo-* means under or beneath.

two populations overlap in this regard, and some women are more hyperphilic than most men (Masters, Johnson, and Kolodny 1988). There is considerable anecdotal evidence to support this assumption concerning male sexuality. Certainly, more magazines are devoted to nude or partially clad women than are devoted to nude or partially clad men. Heterosexual men patronize female prostitutes far more than heterosexual women use male prostitutes. Gay men commonly use male prostitutes but lesbians rarely patronize female prostitutes.

To address this issue of male and female attitudes toward sexuality, Blumstein and Schwartz (1983) asked heterosexual, gay, and lesbian couples how often they had sex. They found that 67 percent of gay couples had sex three or more times a week, compared with 45 percent of heterosexual married couples and 33 percent of lesbian couples. Put another way, sexual interaction was most frequent when both partners were male, least frequent when they were both female, and intermediate when one partner was male and the other was female. Moreover, both the married and gay men stated that they were dissatisfied with a relationship in which the incidence of sexuality is low and satisfied when the incidence of sexuality is high. The lesbians and heterosexual females stated that they did not need a high level of sexuality before they were satisfied with the relationship. Fifty-nine percent of the gay males reported that it was important for a partner to look sexy, as did 57 percent of the husbands; only 31 percent of the wives and 35 percent of the lesbians reported that this was important. Finally, 84 percent of the wives believed that sexual fidelity (monogamy) was important, compared with 75 percent of the husbands, 71 percent of the lesbians, and 36 percent of the gays (Blumstein and Schwartz 1983). Other investigators have reported similar findings. Concluded Collins and Coltrane (1991):

In general, then, it appears that sexual activity remains more a male than a female province in our society. Left to themselves, men have more sex, women less. Each group has corresponding levels of concern about sex as a basis for relationships. Females are more concerned about emotional ties, possessiveness, and their own fidelity, although when men are married to women, the possessiveness of that relationship affects them too. (p. 350)

Thus researchers agree rather closely on two points: (1) In our society, most men are more sexually oriented than most women, although women are potentially as erotically responsive as men, and (2) both men and women are about midway on the erotophile-erotophobe scale (Reinisch 1990; Money 1986, 1988).

Cultural Impact on Women's Sexuality

Early theories suggested some biological tendency for women to be less erotically oriented than men in our society (see, for example, Kinsey et al. 1953). Subsequent research, however, has thrown doubt on such a biological hypothesis and points to cultural reasons for the relatively high incidence of erotophobic or only mildly erotophilic women in our society. We will cite three studies that support this cultural hypothesis, the first of which was conducted in West Germany in 1970.

This landmark study found that female students at the University of Hamburg were no different from male students in their responses to viewing erotic material. After male and female students were shown films that graphically depicted masturbation, fellatio, cunnilingus, and copulation, they were asked to rate their subjective reactions to these films, ranging from strongly aroused, to mildly aroused, to not aroused, to repelled or disgusted. The study found no significant differences in the self-reported arousal levels of these men and women; however, a large percentage of the women (about 40 percent) reported a slightly *more* intense erotic arousal than did the average male respondent. In a similar study American women reported significantly less arousal than the average male respondent (Schmidt and Sigusch 1970).

If the biological hypothesis were true, German women should show the same indifference or repugnance to sexuality (relative to men) as American women. That they did not cast grave doubts on the biological hypothesis.

In 1971, a definitive study in Mangaia, an island of the Polynesian group in the South Pacific, specifically addressed the question of orgasmic experience of women compared with men. This study found that Mangaian women almost invariably experience orgasm during copulation, just as men do. Moreover, both men and women in Mangaia expect the woman to have at least three orgasms before the man ejaculates. In short, the study found that Mangaian women are just as erotically oriented as Mangaian men. The concept of hypophilia is unknown there, and no word for the concept exists in the Mangaian language (Marshall 1971).

The conclusion seems inescapable. The reason for American women's relative indifference to sexuality and relatively high level of hypophilia must be cultural — unless American women are biologically different from Mangaian women, and no such biological difference has been found.

Julia Heiman (1975) reviewed these two studies and then hypothesized that American women are just as erotically responsive as women in other cultures but do not realize it. The possibility that American women do not recognize their own sexuality would explain why American women, with the same biology as other women, are less responsive to erotic stimuli and are less orgasmic. To test her hypothesis Heiman repeated the Hamburg study, but with one major difference: Instead of asking for a subjective appraisal of their erotic response, Heiman devised an objective method of measuring the erotic response of her subjects indirectly.

It had been known since Masters and Johnson's (1966) experiments that a direct physiological reaction to erotic stimulation was **vasocongestion** (congestion in the blood vessels) in the penis and vagina. This vasocongestion results in either partial or full penile erection and increased blood volume and blood pressure in the vagina. (It also resulted in extrusion of the labia and extension of the clitoris.)

Heiman measured erotic response in male subjects by placing a ring around the base of the penile shaft. As vasocongestion occurred, the penile shaft enlarged, putting pressure on the ring and providing a measure of the degree of penile engorgement. She measured the degree of erotic response in female subjects by placing a **photoplethysmograph** just inside the entrance to the vagina to measure the degree of vasocongestion there.

What Heiman found was that when the male and female college students in her study listened to audiotapes of descriptions of sexual behavior, the degree of vaginal vasocongestion in the women was the same as the degree of penile vasocongestion in the men. She also found that vaginal vasocongestion was greatest among women when they were listening to descriptions of explicitly graphic sexual behavior — masturbation, cunnilingus, fellatio, and copulation.

Interestingly, most of the women in Heiman's study denied having any erotic sensations. Further, nearly half (42 percent) of the women who had the greatest physiological responses insisted that they felt no response at all. Heiman concluded that American women were not aware of their own sexuality because they had been culturally conditioned to deny it. Put another way, she concluded that women's minds were unaware of what their bodies were doing.

Having Sex with Another Person

Individual sexual response is extraordinarily complex, as we have noted. When two individuals are interacting, each must have regard for the responses of the other. Communication, sensitivity, acceptance, and understanding are key ingredients of a satisfactory sexual relationship — as they are in almost any type of relationship. It is important that each person communicate to the other — verbally and non-verbally — what is expected, what is liked, and what is disliked.

Self-disclosure in erotic interaction may represent the ultimate of communication in a relationship. Physical pleasure and self-disclosure form "the nucleus of almost all valued intimate interactions" (Reiss 1986, p. 235).

In order to experience orgasm, people must feel comfortable in telling their partners what they like and what they do not like. In order to do this, they must first learn for themselves what arouses them to orgasm. They must then be able to trust their partners enough to be able to reveal such personal information.

For example, from one-half to three-fourths of women cannot reach orgasm through penile thrusting alone; these women will reach orgasm only with manual or oral stimulation of the clitoris or adjacent areas. Moreover, many women who *do* reach orgasm through penile thrusting nevertheless prefer oral or manual stimulation (Reinisch 1990).

Many men assume that women prefer a man to have a large penis. However, women report that they do not care about penis size. The va-

Auguste Rodin, The Kiss, *1886.*

gina is most sensitive to stimulation in the two inches nearest the labia, and even a very short penis will reach this area. Moreover, the clitoris is typically much more sensitive to erotic stimulation than the vagina, and is more readily responsive to manual or oral stimuli than it is to penile thrusting (Reinisch 1990).

Although women do not experience a refractory period, many do not like erotic stimulation following orgasm; finding any movement annoying or distracting, they prefer to be quiet. Other women enjoy a resumption of stimulation following orgasm and may not be sexually satiated until they have experienced sequential orgasms. Moreover, a woman who does not experience sequential orgasms may not be satiated before having additional, subsequent orgasms after a time (Reinisch 1991).

Most of our population prefers to copulate in the dark; 55 percent of men and 83 percent of women prefer no light at all. Sexologists suggest that men may prefer light because they are more erotically responsive to visual stimuli, whereas women are more responsive to touch. In addition, many women dislike some aspects of their bodies and feel self-conscious and reluctant to be viewed intimately (Reinisch 1990).

Most men find that their sexual responsiveness is highest in the morning, when their hormone levels are at their peak. Some women find that their sexual desire fluctuates with their menstrual cycle, and different women experience peak desire at different times of the cycle. Other women experience heightened desire on certain days of the week, such as Fridays or Saturdays, that are unrelated to the menstrual cycle (Reinisch 1990).

Most men (90 percent) assume that women like breast stimulation, but they are correct in this assumption only about half the time. Many women find breast stimulation distracting or annoying; some women always dislike it, whereas others dislike it only part of the time — usually at about the time when their menstrual flow begins. Other women are very erotically responsive to breast stimulation and may experience orgasm in this way. A woman may enjoy stimulation of the entire breast, not just the nipple and the *areola* (the area surrounding the nipple). About one woman in ten stimulates her breasts as a masturbation technique (Reinisch 1990).

About the same proportion of men (50 percent) enjoy breast stimulation, usually that focusing on the nipple and the areola. A man who thoroughly enjoys nipple stimulation may also use it as a masturbation technique and will experience strongly erotic sensations when his partner stimulates his nipples (Reinisch 1990; Masters and Johnson 1966; Kinsey 1948, 1953).

A little fewer than half of both men and women enjoy receiving suction kisses or being bitten gently. Slightly more than half don't like being sucked or bitten in this way and find it annoying or anti-erotic. These kisses and bites may leave reddish discolorations on the skin ("love bites," or hickeys) that often last for a day or more. If one person likes the sensation of sucking and biting on the other's skin while the other person doesn't like it, there may be a problem (Reinisch 1990). If a person enjoys biting so hard that it causes pain or injury (or enjoys being bitten this hard), this behavior is called a **paraphilia** — a behavior that goes beyond the usual bounds of erotic pleasure (see the section "Paraphilias").

From 50 to 80 percent of married women under age 25 have performed fellatio, with one-third to two-thirds saying that they enjoyed it; other women fellate their partner solely for his enjoyment. Most men (56 percent) report that they have performed cunnilingus, and nearly all (95 percent) enjoyed it (Reinisch 1990).

The Kama Sutra, "the classic Hindu treatise on love and social conduct," published about 200 A.D., describes 529 different positions for copulation. An excellent current sex manual is *The New Joy of Sex* by Alex Comfort (1991). The positions preferred vary among individuals. Maximum penile penetration occurs with the woman on her back, her thighs compressed against her chest, and her calves over her partner's shoulders. Minimal penetration occurs when she is on her back with her legs extended flat and close together, while her partner's legs straddle hers. In this position, vaginal penetration is shallow, but her thighs tend to press her labia together so that they clasp the penis (Hatcher et al. 1990).

A frequent question received by The Kinsey Institute is how often do the "average" couple of a particular age group have sex? The answer to this question is virtually meaningless because there is no such thing as an "average couple." There are great individual differences in sexuality, as we have learned. Some couples copulate two or three times every day, whereas others do not copulate at all. Sexologists consider all of these frequencies of copulation "normal" so long as each partner in the couple is satisfied with the level of sexual activity.

Problems with Sexual Functioning

The problems of a couple that fall at different places on the erotophile-erotophobe scale may be significant — depending on just how far apart the partners are. The problem is significant enough to be termed *sexual incompatibility* in about half of all marriages (Masters and Johnson 1966; Reinisch 1990).

When there is a problem of incompatibility, it is counterproductive for the more hyperphilic partner (usually the male) simply to pressure the other to submit to unwanted sex. It is also counterproductive for one partner to ignore the differences in personal or cultural values of the other. What is productive is to acknowledge one's own needs, to communicate these needs to the other, and to acknowledge and attempt to fulfill the other's needs Of course, this is not possible if the couple are too far apart in their needs and expectations.

Low Sexual Desire About half of all sexual problems have to do with the first part of a sexual interaction — sexual desire. If sexual desire is low or absent, sexual arousal is unlikely. As we have seen, sexologists now conclude that contrary to earlier evidence, men and women are equally likely to have low sexual desire.

A person's place on the erotophile-erotophobe scale is shaped partly by prenatal events, such as the various hormonal mixes that influ-

enced fetal development. Events that occurred during childhood are also important factors in a person's sexual attitude, and adolescent experiences are often critical in shaping a person's developing sexuality. Thus sexual attitude is rooted very deeply in each person's consciousness. Some people perceive sex as a driving force, others have only a slight sexual awareness, while for others sex carries negative implications (Money 1986).

Low desire can affect all sexual interaction for some people, whereas for others, low desire may occur only at a specific time or place or with a specific situation, activity, or partner (Reinisch 1990).

The psychological causes of lowered sexual desire are many. One cause may be unrealistic expectations about sex, which are usually based on faulty knowledge of sexual physiology. Another cause is dislike of one's own body (low self-esteem). Fear of not being able to meet a partner's expectations lowers sexual desire in some people. Lack of trust of one's partner or pressure from a more hyperphilic partner to copulate more frequently may lower desire. Suppressed anger about nonsexual conflicts within the relationship is a major cause of low or inhibited sexual desire. Chronic depression is a classic cause of sexual disinterest. Grief can inhibit sexual desire. Fear of pregnancy may block or inhibit sexual desire, as may fear of STDs (Hatcher et al. 1990).

Low sexual desire may also be caused by physical factors, such as chronic fatigue, poor nutrition or fasting, substance abuse (drugs or alcohol), tranquilizers, and some prescription medications (such as those for high blood pressure). Birth control pills may decrease sexual desire in some women. Hormonal imbalances such as estrogen deficiency in women or testosterone deficiency in men may lower sexual desire. If there is a possibility that low sexual desire has a physical cause, a physician who specializes in sexual problems should be consulted for diagnosis and possible treatment (Hatcher et al. 1990; Reinisch 1990).

Some people have an aversion to sex that may be specific or general. A person with a specific sexual aversion may reject only some particular ideas, beliefs, or practices (for example, oral sex). A person with a strong general aversion to sex will avoid all sexual interaction; this is the pronounced erotophobe, who regards sexuality with distaste. A pronounced erotophobe may even dislike and avoid, whenever possible, any genital contact, whether with a sexual partner or with his or her own genitals. (A male erotophobe, for example, may urinate without touching his penis, as though such touching would somehow contaminate him.) A person who persists in attempting to copulate with a sufficiently erotophobic partner may precipitate a full-scale panic attack in that partner (Reinisch 1990).

Spectatoring   Most sexually dysfunctional men and women are self-consciously aware of what they are doing; they are thinking rather than feeling. Masters and Johnson (1966) called this *spectatoring*. Spectatoring can result in a continual inner dialogue, perhaps even critical self-analysis, that interferes with the spontaneous enjoyment of sex and blocks the sensations necessary for arousal and orgasm.

Sexologists emphasize that men and women alike should be immersed in the sensory experience of the moment — sights, sounds, smells, tastes, and touch; they should not allow themselves to be distracted by thinking (Hatcher et al. 1990; Reinisch 1990).

With men, spectatoring can retard or prevent erection, a phenomenon called *performance anxiety*. Sexologists may treat performance anxiety by temporarily forbidding the couple to copulate while they practice touching, caressing, and kissing. Forbidding copulation relieves the anxiety about erection (or about "performing") and

reduces spectatoring. When the man stops thinking and starts feeling, erection usually becomes the inevitable result of tactile stimulation (Hatcher et al. 1990; Masters and Johnson 1966).

Once erection occurs, spectatoring can lead to rapid ejaculation. Ejaculatory control can normally be acquired by training in such techniques as the stop-start method, as already noted. Once in the excitement phase, most men proceed through the plateau phase to orgasm; failure to achieve orgasm is rare for males.

Women, in contrast, may not initially experience orgasm during copulation. Women gain sexual responsiveness only gradually and must learn to experience orgasm. Spectatoring can interfere with this process of learning. Sexologists emphasize that this learning experience should be enjoyable, not goal-oriented. A woman should focus on the sensations she is experiencing and the pleasure she is feeling; she should *not* focus on striving for orgasm. Once she focuses on the flood of erotic sensations, orgasm becomes inevitable (Masters, Johnson, and Kolodny 1988).

Special Problems of the Male   A man who fails to have an erection cannot copulate and is often spoken of as being "impotent." Failure of erection may simply mean that he is ignorant of the tactile erection; when spontaneous erection does not occur, he thinks that he is incapable of erection. Fear of failure may, in itself, cause erectile failure, as we have noted.

Another possibility is that he experiences orgasm and ejaculation — but without erection. As we have noted, there are several processes, each with different mechanisms, involved in male sexuality: desire, erection, orgasm, and ejaculation. Any one or more of these processes can be disrupted by psychological or physical causes or by a combination of both. Not having an erection, or not ejaculating, doesn't necessarily mean that he has lost his sexual desire or his ability to experience orgasm. Another possibility is that a man's limited interest in sex, or perhaps even his aversion to sex, may impede the occurrence of erection.

The term *impotence* is therefore a very vague, inexact term with limited usefulness. It may mean lack of erection in a sexually oriented male, or it may be used in reference to a man who experiences orgasm or ejaculation without erection, or it may mean low sexual desire. For this reason, sexologists prefer the more precise descriptive terms *low sexual desire* and *erectile difficulty* (Reinisch 1990).

Erectile failure can be caused by the same factors that cause low sexual drive: nervousness, tension, insecurity, low self-esteem, fear of not meeting a partner's expectations, fear of rejection, fear of STDs, or fear of getting his partner pregnant. In common with low sexual desire, erectile failure may be caused by such physical factors as fatigue, poor nutrition, substance abuse, tranquilizers, diabetes, and some medications.

Smoking may also cause erectile failure. A study at Boston University School of Medicine that examined the penile X rays of 195 men (average age: thirty-five) found smokers to have significant blockage of their penile arteries. The heavier the smoking, the greater the blockage (Azadzoi 1992).

Erectile failure can occur at one time and place and not at another, or with one partner and not another. It may be occasional or chronic. And, as we have noted, it may result simply from ignorance of the tactile erection when a spontaneous erection fails to occur.

A man who repeatedly attempts penetration of a woman who has *vaginismus* (an involuntary tightening of the vaginal muscles) may develop difficulties. He may be reluctant to cause her pain or may doubt his abilities as an erotic partner. In consequence, he may lose his sexual desire or his erection (Reinisch 1990).

A man may experience *dyspareunia* (painful copulation). Physical problems, including infections of the prostate, urinary tract, or seminal vesicles, cause about half of all cases of dyspareunia in men. Some medications may cause dyspareunia in both men and women (Reinisch 1990). Sexologists find that tension and fear about sexuality are also major causes of dyspareunia. These emotions impede the physical processes of arousal. Nonsexual problems in the relationship are another major cause of dyspareunia (Reinisch 1990).

Special Problems of the Female   A woman who has difficulty in experiencing orgasm is called *anorgasmic*. If she has not yet learned how to have orgasm, her anorgasmia is primary; if she has lost her ability to become orgasmic after having experienced orgasm in the past, her anorgasmia is secondary.

Primary anorgasmia is very common in our society. At least 10 percent of women over age twenty-five have not yet learned how to have orgasm (Hatcher et al. 1990).

Various psychological factors may cause *secondary anorgasmia*, including too little trust, love, respect, warmth, and understanding both for and from her partner. She may feel pressured to have intercourse when she doesn't wish to. She may feel anger, hostility, or resentment toward her partner but be unable to express these feelings directly. Her partner may be sexually dysfunctional or unaware of her needs related to orgasm. As we have noted, perhaps as many as 75 percent of women do not experience orgasm from penile thrusting alone and need tactile or oral stimulation. Secondary anorgasmia may also be caused by grief or depression.

Physical factors such as fatigue, alcoholism (or other substance abuse), dieting, poor nutrition, medication, illness, or estrogen deprivation may also cause secondary anorgasmia.

A woman may be sexually dysfunctional because of vaginismus, either because she has a distaste for sex or fears copulation. She may also have vaginismus if she isn't yet familiar with her erotic physiological processes and hasn't learned to experience orgasm. Sexologists estimate that about one woman in ten in our society has vaginismus (Hatcher et al. 1990).

A woman with chronic vaginismus may need professional help. Fortunately, treatment for vaginismus has virtually a 100 percent success rate. Such treatment combines education (information about erotic functioning), counseling, and gradual dilation of the vagina. Intercourse is deemed "out of bounds" until she is confident that her vagina will be perfectly comfortable accommodating an erection (Hatcher et al. 1990).

Some sexually dysfunctional women experience penetration as painful. Psychological causes of dyspareunia may include feelings of shame or guilt about copulating, fear of pregnancy, fear of disease (especially AIDS), or nonsexual problems in the relationship (such as lack of tenderness, poor communication, or resentment). Often the cause simply is inadequate erotic arousal. In such cases, receiving information about the fundamentals of erotic anatomy and physiology and learning how to increase arousal may solve the problem.

A woman who has experienced painful copulation may involuntarily tighten her vaginal muscles whenever penetration is imminent. The situation then becomes a self-fulfilling prophecy: A woman who fears intercourse may involuntarily tighten her vaginal muscles, which causes her to experience painful intercourse, which increases her fear. Thus, dyspareunia may cause vaginismus, and vice versa. (Hatcher et al. 1990).

The initial causes of painful intercourse are usually physical. They include vaginal infection, scar tissue, urinary-tract infections, and menopausal changes in vaginal tissue. These problems normally yield quite readily to proper treatment (Reinisch 1990).

Once all physical causes have been ruled out or corrected, a woman should be open and free in communicating with her partner about her fears and erotic needs. Dyspareunia and vaginismus may be symptoms of a problem in communication. Ideally, she should avoid performance anxiety (spectatoring) by focusing on pleasant physical sensations (Hatcher et al. 1990).

Women who have been victims of rape may suffer from both vaginismus and dyspareunia and may be unable to have an intimate relationship for years following the attack. They may have little or no sexual desire and may have difficulty with the nonsexual aspects of an intimate relationship as well. A rape victim may have lowered self-esteem, doubt her self-worth, and be afraid of letting herself be vulnerable in emotional or erotic intimacy with another. A woman who is suffering from the chronic effects of rape may find it necessary to seek professional help from someone who is trained and experienced in treating such problems (Reinisch 1990).

Aphrodisiacs   Humans have searched for a magic drug or potion that will kindle sexual desire since earliest recorded history. Much of our classical literature rests on this theme of a "love potion." In our own times, the concept of such a potion is generally discounted as superstitious. Nevertheless, the search continues for a chemical or drug that will either enhance sexual desire or cause the penis to erect. Such a drug is called an *aphrodisiac*, after Aphrodite, the Greek goddess of love and beauty. To date, no such drug has been discovered, and advertisements claiming a product has such properties are fraudulent. There is as yet no known way to bring about sexual desire by any kind of drug, and no oral drug that will cause penile erection is currently known (Reinisch 1990).

"Spanish fly" (cantharis) is widely believed to be an aphrodisiac, but it is not. Similarly ginseng, yohimbine, and mandrake root have long been thought to be aphrodisiacs, although to date scientific evidence for such properties is lacking. Rhinoceros have been hunted virtually to extinction because their horns, when dried and powdered, are sold as an aphrodisiac, although the powder has no such property. Various foods, such as oysters and asparagus, are believed without proof to be aphrodisiacs, usually on the basis of a superficial resemblance to the genitalia. However, such beliefs can provide readiness to respond, and a person who believes oysters are an aphrodisiac and eats them with this expectation may be sexually aroused, a phenomenon called a "placebo effect." Good health, good nutrition, pleasant surroundings, and a receptive partner are conducive to sexual arousal but may not properly be called aphrodisiacs.

Paraphilias

A **paraphilia** is an erotic behavior that goes beyond what is usually recognized as "normal" or generally acceptable. (The term comes from the Greek *para*, which means "beyond," and *philia*, which means "love.") In legal terminology, a paraphilia is called a "perversion." In the vernacular (or everyday language), a paraphilia is called "bizarre" or "kinky." A paraphiliac (the person with the paraphilia) is usually male (Money 1988).

A person will be driven to satisfy erotic needs that are not usually recognized as acceptable if his *lovemap* — a "template" of an idealized sexual partner — is paraphilic. Paraphiliacs are demanding, insistent, and compulsive and will not be governed by punishment or imprisonment. On the other hand, paraphilias are not socially contagious; they cannot be acquired by reading about them, by looking at movies or videotapes of paraphilic activity, or by associating with a paraphiliac. The incidence of para-

philia is on the rise in the United States, with each generation producing more paraphiliacs than the one before it. The causes for this are unknown (Money 1988).

The definition of an act as a paraphilia is usually a social one; that is, an act that may be regarded as perfectly normal (a *normophilia*) by one group may be regarded by another group as a paraphilia. Thus various sexual activities that are considered normal and are legal in some states are considered abnormal and are illegal in others. A 1986 U.S. Supreme Court ruling upheld the right of states to have such laws. For example, in most states oral sex between consenting adults is regarded as a normophilia and is legal. In Maryland, however, oral sex between consenting adults, even if they are married to each other, is regarded as a paraphilia and is illegal; a perpetrator, if convicted, may be sentenced to ten years in the state penitentiary (Money 1988).

However, some sexual activities are universally regarded as paraphilias. About forty activities are currently recognized as paraphilias by sexologists (not just by political, religious, legal, social, or other special interest groups) and may be subdivided into six paraphilia categories: marauding and predation, fetishes, mercantile or venal, sacrifice and expiation, eligibility, and allurement (Money 1988, pp. 181–84).

- *Marauding and Predation.* The marauding and predation paraphilia requires that the paraphiliac kidnap, force, or violently attack the other in order to be sexually satisfied and reach orgasm. Rapes fall into this category of Money's classification scheme. (It should be noted that many authorities — rape counselors and therapists and members of the legal community, for example — consider rape an act of violence, not a sexual act.)

- *Fetishes.* In the fetish paraphilia, lust is directed toward an object, token, or talisman.

A *fetish* is an object associated with the human body that is considered to have magical powers; it may derive its power from any of the senses. Common fetishes are women's panties, bras, stockings, or shoes. Parts of the body that are commonly fetishes are hair, breasts, legs, hands, or feet. Photographs, drawings or paintings, or other representations of these features may also be fetishes. As a paraphilia, a fetish is not just a preferred erotic stimuli but is *necessary* for erotic arousal, erection, and orgasm. However, the term *fetish* is often used simply to mean an aspect of a person that holds special interest or fascination for another person.

- *Mercantile or Venal.* The mercantile or venal paraphilia requires that the paraphiliac either pay for sexual activities or be paid for them. The paraphiliac cannot be sexually aroused or satisfied without bargaining with a partner and paying what the partner demands to perform the sexual activities (such as fellatio or copulation) required. Apparently, the lovemap rationale is that no decent person would consent to the defilement of lust for pleasure or enjoyment but would perform these acts only for money (or other compensation).

- *Sacrifice and Expiation.* The sacrifice and expiation paraphilia requires that one of the partners makes a sacrifice to expiate the guilt of lust. This is manifested as an act of extreme *sadism* (sexual pleasure in hurting another) or *masochism* (sexual pleasure in being hurt). Commercial establishments (houses of prostitution) that charge for providing sexual services to their patrons have standardized charges for bondage, spanking, and whipping. A sadistic patron may pay to bind, spank, or whip a prostitute, whereas a masochistic patron may pay to be bound,

spanked, or whipped. (Mild forms of bondage, whipping, or spanking are considered to be normophilias and are not unusual practices between consenting partners. If the whipping, beating, or spanking is severe, however, it is deemed a paraphilia.) The extreme sacrifice (in the sense that pertains to paraphilias) is sadistic murder. Such "lust" murders are not uncommon in our society.

- *Eligibility.* Eligibility paraphilias require that the partner must have certain marks or features (stigmas) that arouse the paraphiliac. There are two classes of stigmas: morphophilic and chronophilic. In *morphophilia*, such features as body build, appearance, or race may make the partner an eligible object of lust. In one type of morphophilia (acrotomophilia) the partner must have an amputated stump; in another type of morphophilia (zoophilia) the partner must be an animal. The most bizarre example of morphophilia (necrophilia) requires the partner to be dead.[16] (A prostitute may pretend to be a corpse to satisfy a necrophiliac patron.) In *chronophilia*, a partner must be of a certain age to be eligible as an object of lust. For example, a chronophiliac may be erotically aroused only by a partner in her twenties or thirties. He may thus go through a series of divorces, always marrying a woman in the necessary age group. With some chronophilias the partner must be an infant (infantophilia), a child (pedophilia), or pubescent (ephebophobia). These three paraphilias are classified as criminal in all states. The opposite paraphilia, needing an older partner (gerontophilia), is not classified as criminal.

---

[16] In the most bizarre form of morphophilia — necrophilia — the partner must be dead. In a widely followed case in 1992, Jeffrey Dahmer was convicted in Milwaukee of murdering fifteen boys and young men in order to have corpses he could use as sexual partners.

Again, a paraphilia is not just a preference; it is a compulsion. A paraphiliac is not capable of being erotically aroused and is unable to have an erection or reach orgasm unless the partner meets the eligibility requirements demanded by his paraphilia.

- *Allurement.* The allurement paraphilia requires that the partner not progress from the preliminaries of erotic interaction to genital contact. A person with this paraphilia has a phobic aversion to genital contact. This is the one paraphilia that is just as common (or perhaps more common) among women as among men. "An unwary lover . . . who fails to recognize the phobia and retreat from it is at risk of being accused of date rape or spouse rape" (Money 1988, p. 183). One allurement paraphilia is evident in an *exhibitionist,* who obtains erotic pleasure by exposing his genitals to a stranger with no expectation of genital contact. The allurement paraphilia may also be evident in a *voyeur,* who illicitly spies on nudity or copulation. (This does not mean that the enjoyment of viewing nudity and sexuality is a paraphilia; sexologists regard receiving pleasure from viewing nudity or copulation as perfectly normal. It becomes a paraphilia only if it is illicit and is an essential requirement for sexual arousal.)

Heterosexuality, Homosexuality, and Bisexuality

A person whose romantic and erotic orientation is directed toward someone of the opposite gender is termed a **heterosexual.** If the orientation is toward someone of the same gender, the person is termed a **homosexual.** And if the orientation may be directed toward a person of either gender, the person is termed a **bisexual.** What-

ever the orientation, the fear of rejection, the intensity of emotional involvement, the importance of esthetic details, and the romantic fantasies and dreams regarding the other person may be the same.

The Heterosexual-Homosexual Continuum

Although a person may be spoken of as heterosexual, homosexual, or bisexual, sexual orientation occurs on a continuum. Heterosexuals and homosexuals do not exist in separate and distinct populations, for each individual has some aspects of both. To illustrate this principle, Kinsey and coworkers (1948) devised a heterosexual-homosexual rating scale that indicates seven ratings or degrees of sexuality (see Figure 4-8).

Clearly, a wide range of experiences falls within this continuum. Moreover, a person's sexual orientation may change with age, the passage of time, experience, the situation, and the availability of a sexual partner.

What, then, is a homosexual? Someone who has lifelong, exclusively homosexual experiences and is incapable of erotic interest in or response to a person of the opposite gender? Someone who has predominantly homosexual experiences? Someone who has occasional homosexual experiences?

In their attempts to answer these questions, Money and Tucker (1975) developed the concepts of obligative and episodic homosexuality:

- *Obligative homosexuals* are people who are exclusively homosexual throughout their lifetimes. Obligative homosexuals are erotically, aesthetically, and romantically attracted solely to members of their own gender and are not attracted to members of the opposite gender.
- *Episodic homosexuals* are people who are essentially heterosexual but engage in homo-

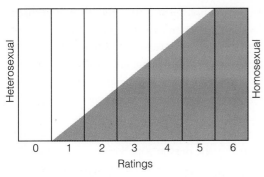

0   exclusively heterosexual with no homosexual
    experience
1   predominantly heterosexual, only incidental
    homosexual experience
2   predominantly heterosexual, but more than
    incidental homosexual experience
3   equal heterosexual and homosexual experience
4   predominantly homosexual, but more than
    incidental heterosexual experience
5   predominantly homosexual, only incidental
    heterosexual experience
6   exclusively homosexual

FIGURE 4-8

Heterosexual-homosexual rating scale.

Source: From *Sexual Behavior in the Human Male* by Alfred Kinsey et al. (1948). Reprinted by permission of the Kinsey Institute for Research in Sex, Gender, and Reproduction, Inc.

---

sexual behavior occasionally or for limited times. Bisexuals are episodic homosexuals.

Incidence of Homosexuality

Determining the incidence of homosexuality in our society is difficult because there are so many degrees of homosexuality. Moreover, the incidence of homosexuality varies with age, marital status, education, occupation, religious affiliation, and whether the setting is urban or rural (Kinsey et al. 1948). Consider the following information (also from Kinsey et al. 1948):

- Over all age groups, single men have a higher incidence of homosexual experience than married men of the same age.

- Incidence of homosexual experience *increases* with age among unmarried men but *decreases* with age among the total male population (after a peak in adolescence and early adulthood).

- Men who go through high school (but do not attend college) have the highest incidence of homosexual experience; men who go to college have the lowest incidence of homosexual experience.

- Men in lower occupational levels have a higher incidence of homosexual experience than men in higher occupational levels.

- Men who have a Protestant affiliation have a higher incidence of homosexual experience than men with a Roman Catholic affiliation (nearly double for some age cohorts[17]). Men who have no active religious affiliation have a much higher incidence of homosexual experience than men who have an active affiliation with a religious group.

- Men who live in an urban setting have a higher incidence of homosexual experience than men who live in a rural setting (nearly double for some age cohorts).

- Incidence of homosexuality among blacks is about twice the incidence among whites (Pietropinto and Simenauer 1977; Hunt 1974).[18] (Incidence of homosexuality among Hispanics, Native Americans, and Asian-Americans in our society is unknown.)

- Incidence of homosexuality among females is about half the incidence among males (Reinisch 1990; Tavris and Sadd 1977; Hunt 1974; Kinsey et al. 1948, 1953).

---

[17]A *cohort* in a demographic study is a group of individuals that have some statistical factor (such as age) in common.

[18]Kinsey et al. (1948) did not include blacks or other minority groups in their research.

Given this varying incidence of homosexuality among different groups, researchers can only estimate the incidences of homosexuality in our society. For example, approximately 2–8 percent of men have exclusively homosexual experiences for at least three years; 10–25 percent have "more than incidental" homosexual experiences for at least three years. Approximately 1–4 percent of males in our society are obligative homosexuals, having exclusively homosexual experiences throughout their lifetimes.[19] For a summary of information on the incidence of homosexuality among males in our society, see Table 4-1.

Characteristics of Homosexual Relationships

Homosexuality cuts across all boundaries of race, religion, occupation, age, and social class. Studies have consistently found that homosexuals are indistinguishable from heterosexuals except for their sexual orientation. Put another way, the only significant discernible difference between homosexuals and heterosexuals seems to be that homosexuals prefer, in varying degrees, to relate affectionately, aesthetically, romantically, and erotically to members of their own gender. Homosexuals are no more apt to

have psychological difficulties than heterosexuals, except when they are under the pressure of social rejection (Reinisch 1990; Kurdek and Schmitt 1986; Blumstein and Schwartz 1983).

Falling in love and being compulsively attracted to another person can be either a homosexual or a heterosexual experience. The only difference is that in homosexuality the love-object — the person with whom one forms a loving paired bond — is someone of the same (rather than the opposite) gender. Both homosexual and heterosexual couples have the same fears of rejection, the same relationship problems, and the same problems with sexual functioning (Money 1988; Reinisch 1990).

Not quite half of all gays live in a long-term relationship that endures for an average of two to three years (Harry 1983; Peplau and Amaro 1982), and the incidence of long-term relationships is somewhat higher among lesbians than it is among gays (Buunk and van Driel 1989). Because homosexual couples are not pressured by society to stay together (as married couples are), and because many societal pressures tend to force homosexual couples apart, the fact that nearly half of all homosexual relationships last for two or three years is a demonstration of the potential strength of a homosexual bond. A homosexual couple in a long-term relationship experiences about the same degree of love and emotional satisfaction as a married couple (Kurdek and Schmitt 1986).

What Do Homosexuals Do?

One of the most common questions received by The Kinsey Institute is "What do homosexuals do?" (Reinisch 1990).

The only difference between heterosexual and homosexual erotic activities is that homosexuals cannot perform penile-vaginal insertion together. Except for this, homosexuals and het-

---

[19]Researchers agree rather closely on this range of 1–4 percent for obligative homosexuals. Kinsey et al. (1948) estimated the figure to be 4 percent; the study by Bieber et al. (1962), perhaps the most ambitious and best-known work of its type, estimated the figure to be 1–2 percent; Hunt (1974) reported that 1 percent of males rated themselves as "mainly or totally" homosexual; Pietropinto and Simenauer (1977) estimated the figure to be 1.3 percent for adult males; the Mattachine Society, one of the oldest homophile organizations in the United States, estimates that 1 percent of the adult males in the country are exclusively homosexual and belong to the openly homosexual community in their cities. Perhaps another 1–2 percent who are exclusively homosexual and are part of the homosexual "underground" avoid the openly homosexual community.

TABLE 4-1

Incidence of Male Homosexuality in Our Society

	Percentage
Exclusive (obligative) homosexuality	1–4
Exclusively homosexual for at least three years	2–8
"More or less exclusively" homosexual for at least three years	2–10
At least as much homosexual as heterosexual experience for at least three years	4–18
"More than incidental" homosexual experience for at least three years	10–25
Any overt homosexual contact to orgasm	20–37

Figures given are for white males; incidence among black males is about twice that of whites.

The high figures are from Kinsey et al.'s (1948) total sample; the low figures are from Pietropinto and Simenauer (1977), Hunt (1974), Karlen (1971), Bieber et al. (1962), and Kinsey's 100 percent samples of men's clubs, schools, classes, and other groups.

The high figures are interesting because they have long been quoted as an accurate representation of our population; the low figures are probably a closer approximation of the demographic reality. (For discussion and more detail, see text.)

The incidence of homosexuality is higher among unmarried males than among married males, among urban groups than rural groups, among the less educated than the more educated, among low-status occupations than high-status occupations, among Protestant denominations than Roman Catholics, among religiously nondevout than devout, and among younger males than older males (except among unmarried males, for whom the rate increases with age).

Because of these interrelated factors, any statement regarding the overall incidence of homosexuality is of limited value.

erosexuals can do the same things and have the same erotic experiences of interest, arousal, erection (for males), orgasm, ejaculation (for postpubertal males), and resolution. Gays usually experience orgasm through mutual masturbation or through fellatio. Relatively few practice anal intercourse (Reinisch 1990).

Lesbians are much more relationship-centered than gays, place more emphasis upon car-ing and total involvement, and are much less promiscuous. Whereas gays tend to be genitally oriented, a lesbian's sensate focus is more on the whole body. Many lesbians limit their erotic involvement to hugging, embracing, and kissing. It is not known whether these lesbian characteristics are male-female differences or gay-lesbian differences (Buunk and van Driel 1989; Blumstein and Schwartz 1983).

The ancient Greeks extolled homosexuality in certain contexts.

When lesbians engage in direct erotic stimulation, it is usually through caressing each other's breasts and nipples. The most commonly used method to reach orgasm is mutual masturbation. The second most commonly used method to reach orgasm is oral-genital stimulation (Reinish 1990).

Attitudes Toward Homosexuality

Attitudes toward homosexuality have varied through the ages and from culture to culture, but generally they have been negative. The ancient Greeks extolled homosexuality as an ideal in certain cultural and spiritual contexts (such as warrior pairs). However, the Greeks rejected homosexual acts when their sole reason was sexual gratification (Conrad and Schneider 1980). The ancient Hebrews treated homosexuality as a capital offense: "If a man lies with a man as with a woman, both have committed an abomination; they shall be put to death" (Leviticus 20:13). The Romans accepted homosexual behavior in classical times but increasingly condemned it with the spread of Christianity. By the sixth century A.D., the Roman Justinian Code condemned homosexuals to torture and mutilation until death. During the Middle Ages, homosexuals were simply burned at the stake (Buunk and van Driel 1989).

Homosexuality was a crime throughout the United States until 1961 — when some states began to decriminalize homosexuality — and is still a crime in about half of all states.[20] Until recently, a person convicted of *sodomy*[21] in Nevada could be sentenced to life imprisonment.

Until 1973, homosexuality was classified as an illness or an abnormality by both the psychiatric and psychological establishments. Defense attorneys in sodomy trials used medical disability as grounds for leniency. An attorney defending a client accused of sodomy would call physicians as expert witnesses to testify that a homosexual needed not punishment or incarceration but medical treatment — that a homosexual was not a criminal but was ill and deserved compassion.

In 1973, the American Psychiatric Association removed homosexuality from its list of abnormal behavior and reclassified it as a *variant* or *alternate* form of sexuality. The American Psychological Association followed suit two years later. (See Box 4-5.)

[20]Homosexual acts between consenting adults was a crime in twenty-four states, with a maximum sentence of twenty years in Rhode Island, fifteen years in Michigan, and ten years in Washington, D.C., and a *minimum* sentence of five years in Idaho, as of 1986 (Buunk and van Driel 1989).

[21]*Sodomy* is the most commonly used term for an illegal sexual activity. (Other terms sometimes used by state legislatures are "buggery" and "a crime against nature.") Fellatio, cunnilingus, and anal copulation between consenting adults are examples of activities that may be defined as illegal. As previously noted, psychiatrists, psychologists, and sexologists regard these acts as normal when performed between consenting adults, whatever the gender. (The term *sodomy* comes from Sodom, a city in ancient Palestine; because of the depravity of their populations, God destroyed Sodom and its twin city Gomorrah; see Genesis 19:24.)

BOX 4-5

The Declassification of Homosexuality

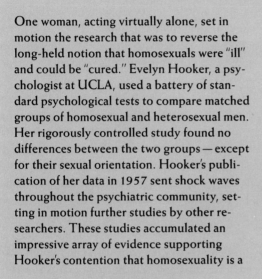

One woman, acting virtually alone, set in motion the research that was to reverse the long-held notion that homosexuals were "ill" and could be "cured." Evelyn Hooker, a psychologist at UCLA, used a battery of standard psychological tests to compare matched groups of homosexual and heterosexual men. Her rigorously controlled study found no differences between the two groups — except for their sexual orientation. Hooker's publication of her data in 1957 sent shock waves throughout the psychiatric community, setting in motion further studies by other researchers. These studies accumulated an impressive array of evidence supporting Hooker's contention that homosexuality is a function of the total personality, and is not an aberration, an illness, or an abnormality. Thus, her initial publication in 1957 set off a chain reaction that ultimately led to the removal of homosexuality from the American Psychiatric Association's list of mental illnesses in 1973 (Harvey 1992).

Before the declassification of homosexuality as an illness, homosexuals were routinely subjected to medical treatments designed to effect a cure. These therapies included estrogen and testosterone injections, castration, hysterectomy, electric shock treatment (EST), and lobotomy (Harvey 1992).

Even before the psychiatric and psychological establishments declared homosexuality a normal, alternate form of sexuality, a number of religious groups had taken the lead in calling for church reforms. As long ago as 1963, for example, the organization of British Quakers stated that "homosexual affection can be as selfless as heterosexual affection" and that therefore it is not necessarily a sin. At a 1967 symposium on homosexuality, a group of Episcopalian clergy agreed that the church should classify homosexual acts between consenting adults as morally neutral and that homosexual acts should be judged by the results, which may be good. The Reverend Walter D. Dennis, Canon of St. John's the Divine in New York City, stated that "a homosexual relationship should be judged by the same criteria as a heterosexual marriage — that is, whether it is intended to foster a . . . relationship of love" (Auchincloss 1968, p. 74).

Meanwhile, a number of Roman Catholic theologians began to challenge that religion's position that homosexual activity is morally wrong. These theologians argued that a committed relationship between two members of the same gender is better than no marriage at all and certainly better than promiscuity. Some priests began advising sexually active homosexuals to take communion and offered a special mass for members of Dignity, a nationwide organization of Roman Catholic homosexuals (Sciolino 1984). As part of a wide-ranging statement on human sexuality, the national Conference of Catholic Bishops declared in 1990 that homosexuality is not freely chosen and therefore is not sinful.[22]

As the legal, medical, and religious establishments began to modify their positions toward an acceptance of homosexuality as an alternate form of sexual expression, the attitude of our general population also began to change. Homosexuals have become more socially and politically visible since the 1960s. A few celebrities (Truman Capote, Tennessee Williams) began to proclaim their homosexuality openly, and a gay subculture began to emerge, especially in large coastal cities. A nationwide Gay Rights movement developed. At least 600 gay student groups have emerged on university and college campuses since the 1960s, and more than forty of these groups have programs in gay and lesbian studies. In some places (such as San Francisco) homosexuals have become politically effective, with a significant power base (Milbank 1992; Shilts 1987).

By the 1990s, more than a hundred universities had formalized rules that specifically prohibited discrimination based on sexual orientation. Regulations were enacted to protect minority groups, including homosexuals, from slurs and epithets. Violators were subject to punishment by campus authorities. At Rutgers University, one of the more active institutions in advancing gay and lesbian rights, students can request and be assigned a homosexual roommate as casually as they might request a nonsmoker (Milbank 1992).

Nevertheless, homosexuals are very cautious about "coming out of the closet." Even though

Rutgers University is virtually a model of formal acceptance of variant life-styles, only about 150 of an estimated 5,000 gay and lesbian students are open about their sexual orientation. (The total student population is about 50,000.) Of those who have come out, only about fifty could be called "activists" in the gay or lesbian subcultures. Thus, only about 3 percent of homosexuals come out at Rutgers, and about 1 percent are activists. The national figure is certainly no larger and may well be smaller. The vast majority of gays and lesbians, perhaps 97 percent or more, prefer to conceal their sexual orientation (Milbank 1992).

The low incidence of gays and lesbians who openly proclaim their sexual orientation can probably be traced to realistic fears that they will be rejected (or discriminated against) by family, friends, acquaintances, employers, and landlords — even though such discrimination may be illegal in their state. Although homosexuals are *not* free to choose their sexual orientation, they *are* free to be "invisible" — to blend into our predominantly heterosexual, homophobic society. Blending into the heterosexual majority in this way is a viable option that may be seen as much safer than coming out and risking all-but-inevitable and perhaps devastating discrimination (Milbank 1992).

People tend to be less tolerant of homosexuals of their own gender; men are less tolerant of gays and more tolerant of lesbians, whereas women are less tolerant of lesbians and more tolerant of gays (Whitley 1987).

Society in general is more indifferent to female homosexuality than it is to male homosexuality; lesbians arouse much less hostility than gays do. Most of our population have confused and ambiguous feelings about lesbianism, rather than the strongly negative feelings they have about gays. Thus legal prosecution of lesbians is virtually unknown (Buunk and van Driel 1989).

---

[22]U.S. Conference of Catholic Bishops, *Human Sexuality — A Catholic Perspective for Education and Lifelong Learning*, 1990.

What "Causes" Homosexuality?

The "causes" of homosexuality are very complex, involving physical, social, and self-identity factors. They are not well understood, but then neither are the "causes" of heterosexuality. The Kinsey Institute has found no evidence to support the theory that boys who grew up with dominant mothers and weak, inadequate fathers are likely to become homosexual. Nor is there evidence that homosexuality is socially contagious; studies have found that children of homosexual parents have no higher incidence of homosexuality than children of heterosexual parents. Similarly, there is no evidence to suggest that an older person can seduce a younger one into becoming homosexual. And there is no evidence that traumatic heterosexual experiences in adolescence may cause a person to develop homosexuality (Reinisch 1990).

The Kinsey Institute finds that a homosexual orientation seems to stem from a deep-seated predisposition, possibly a biological one, that first appears in childhood. For males in particular, sexual orientation seems to develop early in life, often before the teenage years. Homosexual feelings almost always precede homosexual activity by several years (Reinisch 1990).

Two studies have found significant anatomical differences between the brains of homosexual and heterosexual men. In one study, Simon LeVay, a neurobiologist at the Salk Institute in San Diego, found that an oval cluster of neurons in the hypothalamus known to influence sexual behavior is about half the size in gay men as it is in straight men, and in some gay men the cluster does not occur at all. On average, the cluster is about half the size in women as it is in men (Grady 1992; Barinaga 1991; Winslow 1991).

In a second study, Laura Allen and Roger Gorsky (researchers at UCLA Medical School) concluded that the *anterior commissure* (a bundle of nerves connecting the left and right sides of the brain) is larger on average in gay men than in straight men. It is also larger than it is in women, although on average the anterior commissure is significantly larger in women than it is in men. On average, the anterior commissure nerve bundle in gay men was 18 percent larger than in women and 34 percent larger than in the presumably heterosexual men. The exact function of these nerve fibers is unclear, but it appears to be related to "lateralization," or the degree to which the two sides of the brain perform different functions. Women tend to have better language skills than men, for instance, which may be due in part to better communications between sides of their brains (Allen and Gorsky 1992).

Although the findings show a great deal of overlap in the size of brain structures among men and women, gay or straight, and it is impossible to determine sexual orientation from studying a single brain, if consistent average differences are confirmed by further studies, this would support the growing conviction among many scientists that most gay men, and presumably lesbian women, do not consciously choose their sexual preferences but are naturally born with them (Allen and Gorsky 1992).

According to John Money of Johns Hopkins University, one of the foremost investigators of human sexuality, sexual orientation — whether heterosexual, homosexual, or bisexual — is beyond deliberate control. After extensive research, Money developed the theory that each person has a *lovemap* that acts as a very powerful force in directing a person's sexual behavior. A lovemap, which develops from a number of interacting prenatal and postnatal factors, depicts an idealized lover, and a person compulsively dreams and imagines relating to that lover romantically, sensually, and erotically. Money (1986, 1988) finds that a homosexual or bisexual person has a homophilic love map. Whatever its exact basis, the capacity for lovemap formation is present at birth — perhaps with certain predispositions — and the lovemap then develops within the early years of childhood.

Lovemaps usually develop with heterosexual imagery, but they may develop with homosexual or bisexual imagery. A person with a homophilic lovemap can fall in love and find romantic and erotic satisfaction only with a person of the same gender. Similarly, a person with a heterophilic lovemap can fall in love and find romantic and erotic satisfaction only with a person of the opposite gender. A lovemap is highly individualistic or idiosyncratic, however, and the degree of homophilia or heterophilia varies from one person to another. (Thus a person may be an obli-

gative homosexual, an episodic homosexual, or a heterosexual.) Once a lovemap develops, however, a person is no longer free to *choose* his or her sexual orientation; a lovemap may change during the course of a person's lifetime from a heterophilic orientation to a homophilic one and then back to a heterophilic one, but this apparently is something a person cannot normally control through will (Money 1986, 1988).

People with a heterophilic lovemap often feel very strongly about their sexual orientation. If this were not so, "decent people would not persecute their homosexual fellow citizens nor tolerate their persecution. Instead, they would live and let live those who are destined to have a different way of being human in love and sex" (Money 1988, p. 110).

SUMMARY

An erotic sensation can arise from fantasy, dreams, or imagination, or it can arise from physical stimulation of any of the five senses — sight, smell, hearing, taste, or touch. Men are usually more responsive to sight than women, who are usually more responsive to touch.

Any part of the body can act as an erogenous zone, but the primary erogenous zones in men are the frenum, corona, meatus, and shaft of the penis. Primary erogenous zones in women are the clitoris and adjacent areas, the labia, the vestibule of the vagina, and the first third of the vagina. Many women have a primary erogenous zone about halfway into the vagina, on the upper wall; this G spot is just as erotically responsive as the clitoris in some women.

Some people respond to an object, a specific part of the body or a representation of the body, or clothing. This object is called a fetish if it is necessary for an erotic response. Fetishism is a paraphilia — an erotic behavior that goes beyond what is generally considered "acceptable." Other

paraphilias include exhibitionism, voyeurism, pedophilia, sadism, and masochism.

If psychologically prepared to do so, men and women alike respond to appropriate erotic stimuli by proceeding through four phases of erotic response: excitement, plateau, orgasm, and resolution. A prepubertal male experiences orgasm without ejaculation; a postpubertal male usually ejaculates with orgasm. Men usually go through a refractory period following ejaculation, a period during which they are physiologically incapable of reentering the excitement phase. The length of the refractory period varies from just a few minutes to several hours or more.

The primary signal that a man is in the excitement phase is penile erection; a woman signals her entry into the excitement phase with vaginal lubrication. Because a man must have at least a partial erection in order to copulate, he is in the excitement phase, and copulation is automatically pleasurable. In contrast, because a woman can copulate without vaginal lubrication, she may copulate before reaching the excitement phase; thus copulation is not automatically pleasurable for a woman and may be uncomfortable or even painful.

Rapid ejaculation is often a problem for men, whereas not reaching orgasm is often a problem for women. It may therefore be advantageous to delay ejaculation. Men may do this by following a training procedure that consists of learning to distinguish the difference between the sensations of imminent orgasm and imminent ejaculation. He may then delay ejaculation almost indefinitely, perhaps experiencing an orgasm or a series of orgasms. One training procedure to accomplish this is the "stop-start" method; another method is the "squeeze technique."

From 50 to 75 percent of women in our society do not experience orgasm by penile thrusting alone during copulation. These women require oral or digital stimulation of the clitoris (or adjacent areas) before, during, or following copulation.

An erotophile, or hyperphiliac, is a person who is erotically oriented and responsive. An erotophobe, or hypophiliac, is a person who is indifferent or aversive to sex. Most of our population, men and women alike, are about midway on the erotophile-erotophobe scale, either mildly erotophilic or mildly erotophobic. So long as both partners are at about the same place on the scale, they will be sexually compatible. If they are too far apart on the scale they are likely to have sexual difficulties and misunderstandings.

The most common sexual dysfunction in our society is lack of sexual desire, which sometimes extends to sexual aversion.

Heterosexuality and homosexuality lie along a single continuum, with most individuals having some aspects of each. Homosexuality has not been classified by psychiatrists as "abnormal" since 1973, and homosexuals are indistinguishable by any known test — except for their sexual orientation. Causes of sexual orientation are unknown, but researchers agree that one's sexual orientation is not a matter of choice.

KEY TERMS

The following is a list of key terms in this chapter.
These terms are defined in context within the chapter, and many may also be found in the glossary.

anabolism	Cowper's glands	erotic
anorgasmic	cunnilingus	erotic response cycle
aphrodisiac	Don Juan complex	erotophile
bisexual	dyspareunia	erotophobe
Casanova complex	ejaculate	euphoria
circumcision	ejaculation	excitement phase
climateric	ejaculatory control	exhibitionist
clitoris	episodic homosexual	fallopian tube
copulation	erection	fellatio
corona	erogenous zone	fetish

follicles	menopause	refractory period
foreskin	menstrual cycle	resolution phase
frenum	menstruation	sadism
gestation	mons	satyriasis
glans	morning erection	scrotum
G spot	nymphomaniac	spectatoring
heterosexual	obligative homosexual	sperm cells
homosexual	orgasm phase	squeeze technique
hymen	ovulation	stop-start technique
hyperphilia	oxytocin	tactile stimulation
hypophilia	paraphilia	taxonomy
hypoxia	penis	testicle
impotence	perineum	testosterone
incompatibility	phobia	urogenital system
labia (minora and majora)	plateau phase	uterus
lesbian	post-coital depression	vagina
lovemap	premenstrual syndrome (PMS)	vaginismus
masochism	pre-ejaculatory fluid	vasocongestion
masturbation	psychoendocrine aging	voyeur
meatus	psychosexual process	vulva
menarche	puberty	zygote

QUESTIONS

1. What are the four phases of erotic response?

2. What is the most notable characteristic of the excitement phase in the male? In the female? Discuss the importance of these differences in male-female sexual interaction.

3. What is the refractory period? Discuss its importance in terms of male-female sexual interaction.

4. Discuss the attitudes toward homosexuality in our society.

5. Discuss the effects of aging on the sexuality of males and females.

6. What are the characteristics of an erotophile? Of an erotophobe? Describe the possible consequences in a marriage in which each of the couple is on a different position on the erotophile-erotophobe scale.

Buunk, Bram P., and van Driel, Barry. *Variant Lifestyles and Relationships*. Newbury Park, Calif.: Sage, 1989.

Comfort, Alex. *The New Joy of Sex: A Gourmet Guide to Lovemaking for the Nineties*. New York: Crown Publishing, 1991.

D'Emilio, John, and Freedman, Estelle B. *Intimate Matters: A History of Sexuality in America*. New York: Harper & Row, 1988.

Lightfoot-Klein, Hanny. *Prisoners of Ritual: An Odyssey into Female Circumcision in Africa*. New York: Harrington Park Press, 1989.

Masters, William H.; Johnson, Virginia E.; and Kolodny, R. C. *Human Sexuality*, 3rd ed. Glenview, Ill.: Scott Foresman, 1988.

Money, John. *Gay, Straight, & In-Between: The Sexology of Erotic Orientation*. New York: Oxford University Press, 1988.

Money, John. *Lovemaps*. New York: Irvington Publishers, 1986.

Reinisch, June M. *The Kinsey Institute New Report on Sex*. New York: St. Martin's Press, 1990.

Reiss, Ira L. *Journey into Sexuality: An Exploratory Voyage*. Englewood Cliffs, N.J.: Prentice-Hall, 1986.

Schur, Edwin M. *The Americanization of Sex*. Philadelphia: Temple University Press, 1988.

Weg, Ruth B., ed. *Sexuality in the Later Years: Roles and Behavior*. New York: Academic Press, 1983.

PART III

Courtship, Marriage, and the Family

CHAPTER 5

Dating and Courtship

To be loved, be loveable.

Montaigne, "Essays I," Ch. 31

Courtship and Marriage by Parental Arrangement
Courtship and Marriage by Mutual Choice
Dating as a Method of Courtship by Mutual Choice
The Field of Eligibles in Dating
The Mystery of Personal Attraction in Dating
Dating and Sexuality
Dating and Teenage Pregnancy

What Do You Know?

Some of the following statements are true and some are false.
Can you tell which are which?

T/F   1. Responsibility for marital choice rests with the parents in only a very few of the world's societies.

T/F   2. Undating and unmarried women tend to be of relatively high status, whereas undating and unmarried men tend to be of relatively low status.

T/F   3. The aphorism "Familiarity breeds contempt" is usually accurate.

T/F   4. The setting in which an initial meeting takes place is one of the key elements of attraction between two people.

T/F   5. When we look at someone we find attractive, the pupils of our eyes become larger.

T/F   6. A mistake that many shy people make is to role-play the behavior of a bold person.

T/F   7. A woman can become pregnant the first time she has sexual intercourse.

T/F   8. More than four out of five teenage unwed mothers are themselves daughters of teenage unwed mothers.

T/F   9. Dating is commonplace in most of the world's societies.

Answers: 1-F, 2-T, 3-F, 4-T, 5-T, 6-F, 7-T, 8-T, 9-F

*C*ourtship is a nearly universal behavior among higher animals; its function is attraction for the purpose of mating. In order for sexual reproduction to take place, it is essential that males and females of a species cooperate so that sperm reach eggs and a new generation is produced. A great variety of animals — from insects to humans — have evolved complex courtship procedures. Courtship is not simply a hit-or-miss procedure. The male must approach the female in a highly ritualized pattern of behavior if he is to be accepted as a mate.

In some species, courtship can be very dangerous. For example, the male black widow spider is only a fraction of the size of the female, and if he does not approach her carefully, he will be killed and eaten. He must first pluck the web in a certain rhythm before moving next to her. He then strokes her abdomen before depositing the sperm. His departure must then be precipitous or he will still be seized and devoured. If the female is disturbed by any deviation from the courtship ritual, the penalty to the male is death.

Among some aquatic animals, fertilization takes place outside the body (without copulation), but courtship rituals can still be complex. Among sticklebacks (a kind of scaleless fish), for example, the male makes a vivid display of color to attract a female and attacks and drives away other male rivals. He remains close by while she deposits her eggs in a hollow prepared in the streambed; then he covers the eggs with his milt (sperm).

Among wild horses, males conduct courtship by fighting and defeating other stallions in the presence of the mares. In this highly formalized courtship ritual, the dominant stallion earns the opportunity to mate with as many mares as he can collect. He must then keep vigilant watch over his harem and his territory and drive away any male challengers to either.

The existence of a family system is universal among humans. In all societies ever discovered there has always been some form of courtship, some form of marriage, and some form of the family, which together make up the family system of the society. Dating, the preferred form of courtship in our society, is very rare among societies worldwide. Most societies use a system of courtship and marriage that is based on parental arrangement rather than mutual choice (Reiss 1980).

FIGURE 5-1
The family system.

In human societies, courtship procedures vary enormously from one culture to another. In some societies courtship is solely the responsibility of the two sets of parents, who participate in a series of carefully orchestrated interactions designed to acquire the best possible match for their son or daughter. In such situations the young people themselves have very little choice, and their personalities are not considered to be of primary importance. In other societies it is the responsibility of each young adult to find her or his own mate, and personal considerations are thought to be *very* important. In these societies, courtship consists of a process in which one person tentatively approaches another person regarded as uniquely attractive, and if the attraction is mutual the two people may ultimately form a paired bond.

Whatever the form, courtship is universal in human experience and has institutional status in all societies. It constitutes the first stage of the **family system** — the interlocking institutions of courtship, marriage, and the family — that ensures the production and nurturance of children and thus ensures the continued existence of the society (see Figure 5-1).

Courtship and Marriage by Parental Arrangement

In most of the world's societies the responsibility for marital choice rests with the parents. In courtship by parental arrangement, each family is looking for a union that will be economically advantageous. Each tries to pair their son or daughter with someone who is healthy and well educated and has a respected family name with a good genetic line. Ideally, the potential bridegroom should have economic, professional, or political "prospects," and the potential bride should be healthy, beautiful, and intelligent. Ideally, too, each should have money or property. Both must also be members of the community and belong to the same social class.

Marriage in these societies is seen chiefly as a means of providing for the continuity of each line, of ensuring each family's economic and political well-being and growth. After marriage, title to property is usually held by the bride's or bridegroom's family. Marriage contracts are often made in the names of both families; sometimes the signatures of the bride and groom are not even required. In mate selection by parental arrangement, romantic considerations and the compatibility of the couple are regarded as relatively unimportant and are given little attention. Love is presumed to follow marriage, not precede it. In most societies, however, the prospective bride and bridegroom are consulted and their inclinations respected. Each has veto power if the parents' choice is totally unacceptable (Mace and Mace 1974).

A go-between is used to approach the family of a prospective bride or bridegroom—to exchange information and perhaps photographs and to check into the family's background. The go-between may be a professional *marriage broker.* The marriage broker's knowledge, skills, and resources are often regarded as indispensable, and a family that does not use a broker is often at a serious disadvantage and may even be misled. When two professionals negotiate, both families are protected. The marriage broker seeks out and approaches the parents of a marriageable son or daughter who might be acceptable to her or his client. The broker assesses the potential bride or bridegroom's appearance, age, health, education, skills, training, and social status. If the client (the parents) is interested, very cautious formal exchanges begin, but no commitment is implied at this point. If both families wish to pursue the negotiations after these initial exchanges, additional conferences are arranged; these conferences may lead to a formal engagement.

The institution of dowry is used in societies in which women are considered economic liabilities who are supported by their families before marriage and will be supported by their husbands after marriage. A **dowry** is either money or property given to the bridegroom by the bride's family; it either becomes solely his or is shared by him though legal ownership by his wife.

In many of these societies the dowry is indispensable. In contemporary Greece, for example, it is usually not possible for a young woman to marry without sufficient dowry, and her father and brothers traditionally assume the responsibility of providing her with a suitable one. It is a cardinal rule in these families that no brother may marry until every sister has been provided with a husband. Moreover, family honor demands a lavish wedding feast. If the bridegroom comes from out of town, the cost of boarding him and his family and guests must be borne by the bride's family. In countries where dowries are the custom, a father with several daughters faces financial ruin unless he is relatively wealthy.

The institution of **bride price** is the opposite of dowry and is used in societies in which women are considered economic assets because they contribute to their families' income through their skills and labor. In these societies, instead of being offered a dowry the groom's family is asked to pay a bride price. In many African communities, elaborate techniques and precise property evaluation (usually involving livestock) have long been used to determine bride price. In contemporary Japan, bridegrooms usually must provide a bride price chiefly as an expression of status and good intentions. After the marriage, most of the money is returned to the bridegroom and is used to purchase household furnishings.

In societies that require parental arrangement for marital choice, an engaged couple is usually regarded as firmly committed to marriage. If a woman's fiance attempts to break the engagement in contemporary Spain or Sicily, it is customary for him to be hunted down by her father and brothers and brought forcibly to the wedding. If he still refuses to marry, he may be killed. In these societies, engagements are clearly regarded as exceedingly serious, and the celebrations accompanying an engagement may be more elaborate and extensive than wedding ceremonies and receptions in our society.

Very few data exist concerning the success or failure of parentally arranged marriages, mainly because "failure" (that is, termination of the marriage) is seldom considered a possibility. Nor is personal happiness a factor in "successful" marriages. Marriage is regarded primarily as an institution that fulfills important social, economic, and political needs. The husband and wife are expected to meet certain minimum standards for duties (usually income provision for the husband and homemaking, childbearing, and child care for the wife). So long as each fulfills these minimal expectations, the marriage is considered successful.

When, on rare occasions, these standards are not met — for example, when a husband deserts his wife or fails to provide a minimum income, or, in some societies, when a wife cannot bear children — the only recourse for the injured spouse is generally to have his or her family assess the problem and decide whether the marriage contract has been breached. If personal unhappiness is the cause of marital problems, usually the couple must simply try to adjust to the circumstances. In India, an unhappy wife often must make a serious suicide attempt before her family is moved to intervene on her behalf. In all such cases the marriage can be terminated, but only with great shame to both families, particularly to the family of the irresponsible, inadequate, or unhappy spouse.

Courtship and Marriage by Mutual Choice

In societies that have courtship by mutual choice, the prospective bride and bridegroom choose each other, usually on the basis of each's personal attraction for the other and with little regard for the factors that are so important in courtship and mate selection by parental arrangement. Courtship and marriage by mutual choice began to replace courtship by parental arrangement in our society in the late nineteenth century and was firmly established as **dating** by the 1920s (Mead 1959).[1]

This change to courtship by mutual choice began in the United States in the latter part of the nineteenth century when young, unmarried working-class women entered the workplace expanded by mass-production industries. Working outside the home brought young women into

---

[1]In some groups in the United States marital choice is still characterized by rigorous control and parental approval. One such group is the Amish.

casual contact with young men without the formality of introductions.

The first women to move into the world of work outside the home were lower-class women employed in factories and mills. Beginning about 1915, young middle-class women, who had previously been limited chiefly to such occupations as teacher, governess, or "lady's companion," began increasingly to find employment in offices and stores. A major movement of women into the work force occurred during World War I, when the mass shifting of men from civilian employment into the armed forces suddenly created job openings for women as secretaries, clerks, and sales personnel — positions that previously had been occupied solely by men. Use of the typewriter and the telephone, both of which were invented near the close of the nineteenth century, expanded rapidly, and scores of young women became typists and telephone operators as business firms grew and multiplied.

The influx of young women in the business world was accompanied by the growth of coeducation, as young women were admitted to high schools and colleges in ever-growing numbers. Although young women were by no means completely free of courtship supervision, these changes in their working and educational environments made it possible for women to associate with men on an increasingly casual basis.

Another significant development — the invention of the automobile and its rapidly expanding use in the 1920s — greatly increased mobility and provided transportation to the roadhouses and nightclubs that were beginning to spring up. Automobiles also served as small, intimate, mobile parlors where couples could easily obtain privacy.

Meanwhile, the newly invented telephone provided a means of close personal communication that reached right inside the home. A young man could now communicate directly with a young woman without going through the formality of being greeted by her family. The cinema (or motion pictures) was another invention of the period that provided young couples with a dark and relatively secluded place to go, as well as with matinee idols whose romantic behavior they could emulate. Newspapers, magazines, and the newly invented radio further popularized the romantic ideal so that young couples were presented role models at every turn.

By the 1920s — the Roaring Twenties or the "jazz age" — the "old-fashioned girl" was regarded as a "flat tire." The idealized version of femininity became the flapper, a thoroughly urbanized and industrialized transformation of the Gibson Girl.[2] The Gibson Girl wore ankle-length skirts, squeezed her waist down to a fourteen-inch circumference with a whalebone corset, and ideally had hair that reached to her waist. The flapper wore skirts above the knee, "bobbed" (cut off) her hair (which she then shingled and marcelled), and replaced her corset with a girdle. (By the 1960s, the girdle was in turn replaced by pantyhose.) The flapper also "went out" with young men whom she met at work or at parties. Within one generation, age-old rituals of courtship by parental arrangement[3] began to seem old-fashioned and even quaint.

---

[2]The Gibson Girl, the creation of artist Charles Gibson, was widely admired as the ideal of feminine beauty during the late nineteenth and early twentieth centuries.

[3]Until the twentieth century, parental supervision of daughters remained very strict, not only in the middle and upper classes but in the lower classes as well. It was virtually impossible for a young woman to meet a young man unless she was introduced by a member of her family; if the young man was interested, he asked permission to "call" on her. When a young man asked for such permission, he was in effect declaring his intention to court her with an eye toward marriage. By the latter part of the nineteenth century, this convention had relaxed somewhat, but the first call was still considered a public indication of interest in marriage.

Financial Status and Dating

Although the topic of financial resources is now usually avoided during courtship in our society, this was not always the case. Before the advent of dating around 1920, parents regarded money as one of the chief factors in a marriage arrangement. The prospective husband's financial worth was an important consideration because he alone was expected to provide the income for the family. The man was expected to ask for the woman's hand in marriage, and the father would grant this permission only if he thought there was reason to believe that his daughter (and his subsequent grandchildren) would be ade-

quately provided for. In working-class families, the prospective husband was expected to be employed at a steady job and to have a wage that was at least the equivalent of that earned by the prospective bride's father.

Today, a couple may begin courtship (serious dating) with little awareness or regard for the other's financial status. Because parents have largely lost control over marital choice, the father's right to inquire into the prospective groom's earning ability is largely a part of the past, nearly as archaic as bargaining over the bride's dowry.

Dating as a Method of Courtship by Mutual Choice

Beginning in the late nineteenth century, then, a pattern of courtship by mutual choice developed in which a young man could ask a young woman to share an afternoon or evening with him socially without having been introduced by a member of the family, without parental supervision, and with no commitment beyond the social intercourse itself. As we have seen, this new pattern of courtship—a sharp departure from previous methods of courtship by parental choice—was firmly established by the 1920s, when it became known as dating (Mead 1959).

Dating did not necessarily imply a serious courtship, and it served other purposes in our changing society as well. Couples would date simply for fun, for relaxation, for recreation, or just to be part of the group—to do what others were doing. Because his daughter's acceptance of a young man's request for a date did not necessarily imply serious courtship, it was not imperative that the young woman's father approve of the young man's "prospects" (see Box 5-1).

Within a decade—by the 1930s—young people of all social classes were very impatient with parents who regarded casual meetings as "pickups"—a stigma associated with the lower class. By the 1950s and 1960s, the young people of the 1930s and 1940s had become parents, and

For some young people in the 1990s, hanging out in large or small groups is as popular as dating.

serious misgivings regarding the practice of dating were limited largely to the grandparents' generation, who were thought to be long out of touch with the modern scene. By the 1970s and 1980s, dating was so taken for granted that the time-honored method of careful supervision and marital choice by parental arrangement seemed archaic, buried in the mists of history.

Dating has undergone many changes since its inception in the 1920s. It was initially rather formal: Both people were carefully and sometimes elaborately dressed, and the young man was expected to request a date well in advance. It was not considered proper for a woman to initiate a date except under very unusual circumstances. By the early 1960s, dating had become more relaxed, casual, and spontaneous, and dress codes were less stringent. During the 1960s it became increasingly acceptable for a woman to ask a man for a date. By the late 1960s sexuality had become more acceptable in dating. During the 1970s many colleges and universities aban-

doned curfews and lockout regulations for female students, and many established mixed dormitories. By the 1980s cohabitation had become commonplace as the logical extension of dating, and by the late 1980s significantly more than half (58 percent) of married couples had lived together first (Bumpass and Sweet 1989b). (For a more detailed discussion of cohabitation, see Chapter 6.)

Although dating has become a commonplace means in our society by which young people pair off, court by mutual choice, and perhaps marry, it is still rare throughout most of the world's societies. It is virtually unknown in China (which has one-fourth of the world's population); it is almost unknown in India (which has one-sixth of the world's population); it is still relatively rare in most areas of Africa, South America, and Mexico and in the rural Mediterranean areas of Greece, Sicily, Spain, and Portugal; and it is usually prohibited in Egypt, Saudi Arabia, Iran, Iraq, Libya, and Ethiopia. Most areas of western Eu-

"You're not at all like your answering machine."

The Experience of Dating

rope now accept dating, but not to the extent that it is accepted in the United States, Great Britain, Canada, Australia, New Zealand, and other English-speaking countries and in the Pacific islands of Oceania such as Polynesia and Melanesia.

The Experience of Dating

A date is a special event in that it always implies a certain amount of intimacy between the couple, although the degree of closeness may vary from very slight to very intimate. No matter how casual the date, the implication of a special caring or choosing always exists. If one or the other does not feel comfortable with this closeness on a first date, subsequent requests for dates are usually refused.

A date is not the same as an appointment, even though both are agreements to meet at a specific time and to share a certain activity. An appointment with the dentist is not a date, nor is a business lunch a date. The differences between an appointment and a date are clearly understood in our culture.

A request for a date, as well as its acceptance or refusal, usually involves heightened awareness of the other person. The couple is established (to some extent) in a relationship or interaction that is different from a casual encounter or a business appointment. For the duration of the date, however casual, each assumes a special significance for the other and is consciously aware of this significance. In the intimacy of serious dating, a person often explores his or her innermost feelings, ideals, and convictions, finding new depths in old emotions and experiencing new ones.

Although dating is usually considered the province of teenagers and young adults, people of all ages may date. A date may even occur between a single person and a married person or between two people who are already married to others, although both situations are usually considered illicit in our society. A date is still called a "date" even if there is no possibility for courtship or marriage and regardless of whether the couple is heterosexual or homosexual.

The adolescent usually enters the dating world gradually, after first relating to the opposite gender in casual groupings that may occur almost anywhere—school playgrounds, churches, one another's homes, coffee shops, bowling alleys, skating rinks, tennis courts, beaches, or shopping malls. Initial dating often includes two couples (double dating), a custom in which the presence of another person of the same gender provides some mutual security and enables the sharing of an unfamiliar (and often scary) situation. When one person (usually the boy) takes the plunge and risks rejection by asking the other for a date, a significant event that marks a change in sociosexual development has taken place. Even for a person who has grown up in a family with brothers and sisters in the household, relating on a one-to-one basis with a non-family member of the opposite gender can at first be uncomfortable at least. Still, most adolescents make the transition into dating despite some painful experiences (even some memories that may haunt them for years). Disasters in early dating may even be helpful because they provide concrete experience about acceptable dating expectations. Gradually, with experience, adolescents gain dating skills and become increasingly at ease.

Random, casual dating usually develops into dating one person more or less exclusively, a practice sometimes called "going steady." Such exclusive dating is often a prelude to courtship or may in itself constitute courtship. Each person's decision about whether he or she wishes to marry the other usually occurs during this final stage of serious, intimate dating. If young people did not follow this process in a society in which parentally arranged marriages are no longer the norm, they would never marry.

Breaking off an intimate relationship is usually more serious for men than it is for women. Men are more reluctant to break off a relationship and they suffer more and longer after a breakup, as we have seen (see Chapter 3). After a period of recovery, each usually starts dating again, with casual dates with different people leading once more to dating one person exclusively. After a series of such affairs, over 90 percent of our population eventually become part of a relationship that is strong enough and persistent enough to survive an engagement (formal or informal) that leads to marriage (see Chapter 7).

As part of this phase of serious, intensive commitment, the couple may decide to live together (cohabit). Because 90–95 percent of our population eventually marry, cohabitation is apparently an extension of the dating and courtship phase of marital choice, rather than a replacement for marriage (Wilson 1991). Although cohabitation was not considered socially acceptable until the 1970s and was usually limited to the lower class, it is now approaching institutional status and is very common in all classes of our society (see Chapter 6).

The Field of Eligibles in Dating

Although we use the system of marital choice by mutual selection in our society, the belief that the selection is completely free is an illusion. Although a young person might appear to be free to date, court, and then marry anyone he or she pleases, in actuality this apparent freedom of choice is restricted by many cultural factors, both conscious and unconscious.

In choosing a mate, everyone is inexorably bound by two opposing forces that create what sociologists call the *field of eligibles*—the population within which marital choice may be made (see Figure 5-2). These opposing forces are ex-

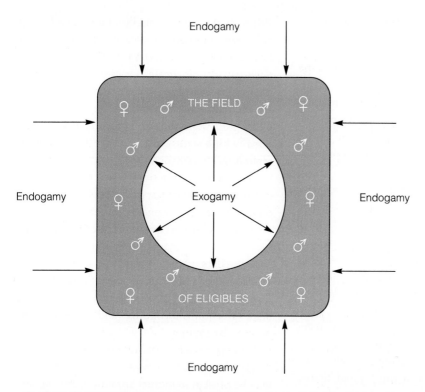

The field of eligibles (for marriage) is limited in all known societies by the two opposing forces of *endogamy* (fear and mistrust of outsiders) and *exogamy* (prohibition against marrying a close relative).

FIGURE 5-2
The field of eligibles.

---

ogamy (the pressure to marry outside the family group) and endogamy (the pressure to avoid marrying outsiders).

Exogamy

Exogamy is the pressure to marry outside the family, although the definition of what constitutes a family varies from one society to another. During the T'ang Dynasty in China (A.D. 618–907), for example, it was prohibited for a person to marry anyone with the same surname, even if there was no blood relation — an extreme example of exogamy.

All societies forbid marriage of mother to son, father to daughter, grandparent to grandchild, uncle to niece, or aunt to nephew, and virtually all societies forbid marriage of brother to sister or half brother to half sister.[4] In our society, some states also prohibit marriage of first cousins and the marriage of a woman to a brother-in-law or a man to a sister-in-law (even though there is no blood relation).

---

[4]There have been exceptions to this prohibition. For example, in the Middle Kingdom of ancient Egypt, brother-sister marriages were not only permitted but preferred. Such marriages also took place in the royal family of early Hawaii.

Endogamy and Homogamy

Endogamy, which opposes exogamy and is the pressure to marry within a group, is based on the human tendency to fear, distrust, or hate outsiders. This characteristic is found to some extent and in varying degrees among all people, although some individuals, some groups within a society, and some societies are far more distrustful than others.

In our society, an important aspect of endogamy is **homogamy** — the force that impels a person to marry someone of the same race, religion, ethnic group, age, intelligence, social class, family background, and educational level.[5] Marriage that brings together two people from different races, religions, ethnic groups, or social classes is called *intermarriage.*

Whereas only about 1.5 percent of marriages in our society are interracial (see Chapter 7), interfaith marriages now account for about 40 percent of all marriages in the United States. Thus religion does not seem to be as strong a homogamous force as race. Belonging to a particular ethnic group (so that couples share many of the same traditions and interests) may act as a force for homogamy, but its influence is difficult to measure. Similarly, it is difficult to measure the degree of influence of social class as a homogamous factor. Certainly, social class is related to such factors as place of residence, schooling, church affiliation, speech pattern, vocational level, educational level, and income, so social class obviously acts as a homogamous force to some degree.

Age also acts as a very significant force for homogamy. People usually date and marry someone who is within a few years of their own age, although the man is usually older.[6] The highly publicized marriages between men in their sixties or seventies and women in their teens or twenties are statistically insignificant, and marriages between older women and younger men are even rarer. Such marriages are usually noted in the press when the older person has an exceptionally high status (related to wealth, power, or reputation) in our society.

The mutual attraction of two people by opposite or complementary factors is called **heterogamy.** It seems reasonable, for example, to expect that opposites would attract in relation to such traits as dominance and submission, nurturance and dependence, masochism and sadism, or vicariousness and achievement. However, even though the notion of heterogamy in dating and mate selection is intriguing (and acknowledged by popular sayings such as "opposites attract"), its effect has not been substantiated by research. Although some heterogamous characteristics may be present in mutual attraction, they apparently occur in a complex blending with homogamous factors, and thus their effects are difficult to substantiate (Eshleman 1991; Buss and Barnes 1986; Murstein and Brust 1985).

The Dating Differential

The **dating differential** — the idea that men tend to date "down" and women to date "up" with respect to age, height, intelligence, educational level, and social class — violates (to some extent) the principle of homogamy. In all societies, men prefer youthful, physically attractive women, whereas women are attracted to men who are somewhat older, have good financial prospects, and are ambitious and industrious. These preferences are found in samples of people ranging

---

[5]Homogamy may be less influential in mate selection among some black women, who tend to marry men who are less educated than themselves and have been previously married (Taylor et al. 1990).

[6]U.S. National Center for Health Statistics, "Marriages — Age Differences of Bride and Groom, by Age: 1987" (1991).

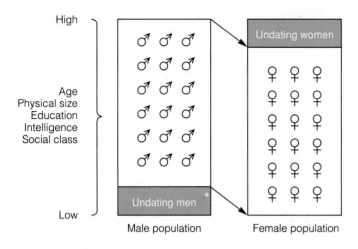

High

Age
Physical size
Education
Intelligence
Social class

Low

Undating women

Undating men

Male population

Female population

Males tend to date "down" and females to date "up" in terms of such factors as age, size, education, intelligence, and social class. This leaves a residue of undating women of relatively high status, whereas the undating men are of relatively low status. It also means that from about age twenty-five on, women have far fewer eligible men who are available for dating or marrying, whereas men who are twenty-five or older are not handicapped in this regard.

FIGURE 5-3
The dating differential.

from coast-dwelling Australians to urban Brazilians to rural Zulus in South Africa (Buss 1985).

The dating differential can have very serious effects for women. After a single woman reaches her twenty-fifth birthday, her prospects for dating (and marrying) dwindle — if she is looking for men in the thirty-and-over age group, which contains relatively few eligible men. (There are nearly two-and-a-half times as many single women ages twenty to twenty-four as there are single men ages thirty to thirty-four.[7]) In consequence, women may find that beginning in their early twenties, they meet fewer eligible men each year; once unmarried women reach their thirties, the age aspect of the dating differential

makes it even less likely that they will meet eligible prospects (see Chapter 7).

Men, however, are in a completely different position because of the demographic realities. In general, men in their mid-twenties tend to date women in their late teens or early twenties, an age range that contains a large pool of unmarried women. When men reach their thirties, they may now date women between their late teens and their late twenties, so that the population of available women may even have increased.

The phenomenon of the dating differential also helps explain why unmarried women are often from relatively higher-status populations than are unmarried men of the same age (see Figure 5-3). Overall, there are about equal numbers of young men and young women. But because men tend to date and marry women with lower statuses with respect to age, physical size,

[7]U.S. Bureau of the Census, "Marital Status of the Population, by Sex and Age: 1989" (1991).

education, intelligence, and social class, the women who get left out ("undating women") are those with high status with respect to these factors. (For the same reason, men of low status become "undating men.")

The Mystery of Personal Attraction in Dating

Within the field of eligibles (which is formed by the opposing forces of endogamy and exogamy), people in our society may exercise freedom of choice as to whom to date and whom to marry. Can the mystery of unique attraction — the strong feelings of admiration and desire that one person may feel for another — be explained? Why are these feelings sometimes reciprocated and sometimes rejected?

Much remains unknown about this mystery of attraction (and its opposite, rejection), but much of the mystery has yielded to research. Because our process of mate selection is based on mutual choice, the question of how such mutual attraction comes about has drawn a good deal of attention from sociologists and psychologists.

Physical Attraction and the First Impression

Most people assume that physical appearance is an important ingredient of attraction, especially in first impressions, and research has borne this out. Physically attractive people are assumed to be more sociable, sensitive, interesting, poised, and warmer than less attractive people; they are also assumed to be more dependable, trustworthy, and moral (Hatfield and Sprecher 1986; Patzer 1985; Cash and Janda 1984).

Research begun in the early 1970s has shown that not only do good looks influ-

ence such things as choice of friends, lovers, and mates, but that they can also affect school grades, selection for jobs, and even the outcome of a trial. (Cash and Janda 1984, p. 47)

First impressions may also be based on a person's social or conversational skills, of course, or upon his or her possession of special abilities such as dancing, singing, or sports, or upon possession of one or more highly visible status symbols such as obvious manifestations of wealth or power. A first impression may also be based upon none of these things but upon a reputation that has preceded the initial meeting, such as the person's status as a sports star, entertainer, or professional. However, most first impressions are based upon physical appearance. "The characteristic that impresses people the most, when meeting anyone from a job application to a blind date, is appearance" (Cash and Janda 1984, p. 47).

Of course, considerable individual differences exist in what is regarded as physically attractive. Some women are attracted to tall men and others to short men, although research indicates that most women like men of about medium height (Graziano et al. 1978). Some men prefer plump women, and other men like slim women. And whereas the popular ideal in our society favors slim women, the ideal in most societies favors plump women (Ford and Beach 1970).

Propinquity

Although first impressions are often very important and physical appearance is often the basis of the first impression, it is surprising how often simple **propinquity** — closeness in time and space — determines whom one dates and marries (Morgan 1981). Most people marry someone they have met in the neighborhood, or someone who has attended the same school or church, played tennis on the same courts, or worked in the same office.

Sheer exposure to each other usually causes two people to like each other better. This growing appreciation of the other person's good qualities apparently occurs because repeated exposure makes the other person more familiar. And whereas we tend to evaluate people we have not seen before or do not know well as potentially dangerous, familiarity tends to breed liking. Thus the aphorism "Familiarity breeds contempt" is not usually accurate (Zajonc 1968).

A classic study that dramatically illustrates the importance of propinquity (Festinger 1951) examined the interaction of residents in a housing unit in which the apartments were arranged around U-shaped grassy courts, with two end apartments in each court facing the street. The study found that the likelihood of two people becoming friends was directly related to how far apart their apartments were. Friendships sprung up most frequently between next-door neighbors, less frequently between people whose apartments were separated by two units, and still less frequently between people whose apartments were separated by three or more units. As the distance between apartments increased, the number of friendships declined, so that it was rare to find a friendship between people who lived in apartments more than four or five units apart.

The same study also found that any architectural feature that caused a resident to encounter others frequently tended to increase that person's popularity. Thus a person whose apartment was near a mailbox or a stairwell had significantly more friends than other residents. In contrast, any architectural feature that took a resident out of the mainstream of traffic flow had a chilling effect on that person's popularity. People who lived in the end apartments that faced the street (rather than the court) had fewer than half as many friends as anyone else in the unit. Thus the architects had unwittingly shaped the social lives of the building's residents.

The practical implications of such research seem to be that if we arrange our lives so that we increase the opportunities to associate with a variety of potential acquaintances, companions, or friends, we maximize the probability of finding someone to whom we will be especially attracted — and who will be attracted to us as well.

Associated Circumstances

Researchers find that one of the key aspects of attraction is simply the setting in which a meeting takes place and that these *associated circumstances* can have surprising force. Apparently, we are attracted to people with whom we associate in pleasant surroundings and tend to dislike those with whom we associate in unpleasant surroundings.

Psychologists have gathered considerable evidence for the idea that attraction is related to the situation in which an interaction takes place. In one study, half the subjects (men and women) met in a comfortable, pleasant room, whereas the other half met in an uncomfortable, unpleasant room. Both groups were subsequently given a questionnaire designed to ascertain how much the subjects liked the people in their group. Those who had met in the comfortable surroundings liked one another significantly more than those who had met in the unpleasant room (Griffitt 1970).

In another classic study, subjects were asked to give their impressions of photographs of some different men and women. One group of evaluators viewed the photographs in a very pleasant room with beautiful draperies, elegant paintings, and comfortable chairs. The other group evaluated the same photographs in a shabbily furnished room with dirty walls and uncomfortable chairs. Viewers in the pleasant room (both men and women) rated the photographs as significantly more attractive than did viewers in the unpleasant room (Maslow and Mintz 1956).

The implications are obvious: If we want to maximize the possibility that someone will be attracted to us, it is important to meet that person in pleasing surroundings and under pleasant circumstances.

Body Language

When two people meet they communicate nonverbally as well as verbally, and the nonverbal aspect of their interaction may be more important than verbal interaction in terms of the degree of attraction each feels for the other. Feelings of friendliness, indifference, or hostility are clearly revealed by *body language* — posture, stance, gestures, and facial expression (Malandro and Barker 1983). In some situations, 90 percent or more of communication between two people is nonverbal (Hall 1973, 1976; Mehrabian 1971).

Gestures, Stance, and Eye Contact When people like one another, they tend to look at one another, lean toward one another as they talk, and have an open stance in which their arms are hanging loosely or spread apart. Conversely, people who do not like one another (or are angry at the moment) tend not to look at one another, lean apart or away from one another, and have a closed stance in which their arms are folded, their legs are crossed, and/or their bodies are turned away or their faces are averted. This nonverbal communication is received (usually unconsciously) and prompts a response. Thus if one person leans away from another and averts his or her face, the other person will (perhaps unconsciously) sense the rejection or hostility — even though the verbal content of the communication may be friendly (Stevens, Rice, and Johnson 1986; Hall 1973, 1976).

Two people who are attracted to each other also maintain more eye contact than people who are not. Whereas people who like one another tend to spend most of the time looking into one another's eyes, strangers or casual acquaintances have eye contact only about a third of the time when they are talking together, glancing away most of the time and then glancing back again (Malandro and Barker 1983; Rubin 1973).

Pupillary Response Hess (1975) found that when we look at something we find attractive, the pupils of our eyes enlarge; when we look at something we find unattractive, they contract. Thus when someone looks at you and is attracted to you, the pupils of that person's eyes will become larger; if the person doesn't like you, the pupils will become smaller. And if the dislike is intense, the pupils may even shrink to virtual pinpoints.

Hess also found that when we relate to other people we unconsciously check out this *pupillary response*. If the pupils are large, we unconsciously interpret this to mean that a person likes us; if the pupils are small, we interpret this to mean that a person dislikes us. Because we like to be liked, we react more favorably to a person who looks at us with large pupils than we do to one who looks at us with small pupils. The nonverbal communication of pupillary size is a significant factor in whether one person responds to another with attraction or aversion (see Box 5-2).

The pupillary response described here occurs unconsciously and cannot be controlled deliberately. Thus individuals' true feelings are revealed by their pupillary response. Any dissembling, masking, or camouflaging of true feelings must be done verbally or by nonverbal body language that can be consciously controlled. The aphorism "The eyes are the windows of the soul" appears to have some real truth.

The "Personal Space Bubble" All of us maintain a *"personal space bubble"* around ourselves, and we let only a few people penetrate this bubble.

BOX 5-2

Attractiveness and Pupil Size

One of the experiments conducted by Hess (1975) involved retouching a photograph of an attractive woman so that her pupils appear to be larger. When this photograph and the original were shown to a large group of subjects who were asked to select the photograph in which the woman seemed to be more sympathetic, warmer, happier, or more attractive, the respondents picked the one in which the woman had larger pupils. Moreover, the subjects' own pupils grew larger when they looked at the retouched photo and smaller when they looked at the original.

In another experiment, Hess used a drug to dilate a woman's pupils for one encounter and then a different drug to make the same woman's pupils smaller for another encounter. When the subjects encountered the woman whose pupils had been artificially dilated, they described her as "soft, "gentle," and "open." In contrast, when the same subjects encountered the same woman when her pupils were artificially small, they described her as "harsh," "brassy," and "cold." Apparently, then, pupillary size not only reflects emotional states but also serves as a clue that all of us use in assessing how other people feel about us and how we feel about them. We seem to be aware, unconsciously, that large pupils indicate interest and therefore warmth and acceptance.

This phenomenon has been used in some societies to enhance the attractiveness of young women. For example, in southern Italy and in the antebellum South of our own country, young women used a substance called belladonna to dilate their pupils as part of their standard cosmetic practice. They believed that putting drops of the belladonna into their eyes before a ball or other social occasion would make them more attractive. (The word *belladonna* means "beautiful lady.")

The size of the bubble depends on how well we know the other person and whether or not we are attracted to him or her. In our society, the preferred distance is between four and seven feet for a stranger, a casual acquaintance, or someone to whom we are not attracted. If a person comes closer than this, we grow uncomfortable and uneasy. Indeed, if a person moves within a three-foot space, we move away. If it is not possible to back off—if, for example, we are in a corner of the room at a party—we may begin to feel threatened and respond either by becoming hostile and aggressive or by becoming tense, depressed, and withdrawn (Cromie 1978; Hall 1976).

Only people we are attracted to are freely permitted to come within the zone that extends from about eighteen inches to three or four feet from us. And the innermost zone, which extends out to about eighteen inches, is open only to those we feel close to, trust, and like. If someone we are not attracted to or do not know intimately moves within this eighteen-inch space, we usually react swiftly with alarm, becoming either angry or defensive. Exceptions to this reaction, of course, occur in situations such as crowded elevators, buses, or two adjoining stools at a counter in a coffee shop. In such situations we accept the intrusion with stiffness and ritualized procedure. In the elevator, for example, we usually stand with our arms pressed against our sides and look straight ahead. In the coffee shop, we generally ignore a stranger sitting on an adjacent stool (Cromie 1978; Hall 1976). Of course, in some other social situations — dancing or contact sports, for example — we expect physical proximity and even touching.

One interesting experiment designed to explore the importance of this eighteen-inch zone was conducted in a library. In this experiment a research assistant would enter the library and take a seat next to a young woman sitting alone at a study table. When the research assistant would move into the woman's eighteen-inch zone, the women would react by drawing in their bodies, turning away, or marking off their personal territory with books, a purse, or articles of clothing (Cromie 1978).

In another study, graduate students played the role of police officers. When the bogus police officers moved within the eighteen-inch zone of students they were questioning, the students' speech would become unsteady and jerky, the students would glance away frequently, and they would fidget and give other obvious signs of being uncomfortable and either defensive or hostile (Cromie 1978).

It is obviously important that we observe others' eighteen-inch zone when making their acquaintance because penetrating this personal space bubble too quickly is liable to bring rejection. Generally, when two people penetrate each other's eighteen-inch zone with mutual acceptance, this signals a readiness for intimacy and that each person finds the other attractive.

The characteristic size of the personal space bubble is different from one culture to another. In Latin America and the Middle East, strangers comfortably converse at a distance that people in our society reserve for personal friends (closer than eighteen inches). In Mediterranean countries businesspeople do not place a desk between themselves and visitors but instead prefer close, even physical, contact. These differences can sometimes cause cross-cultural misunderstandings. If, for example, an American and an Arab are talking and the American steps back when he or she feels that the Arab is too close, the Arab may conclude that the American is cold and unfriendly (Hall 1976).

Equivalent Status Matching

Research indicates that we are usually attracted to someone of about our social desirability; that is, we do not expect to date someone who exactly matches our "perfect ideal" but instead hope to find someone whose relative desirability is about the same as ours (Patzer 1985; Murstein and Christy 1976). "We all tend to end up with partners of approximately our own social value. Thus, our selection of a mate appears to be a delicate compromise between our desire to capture an ideal partner and our realization that we must eventually settle for what we deserve" (Walster and Walster 1978, p. 141).

This inclination to be attracted to someone of about the same desirability status can be seen very clearly with respect to physical appearance. In one classic research project, dating couples were observed in various places (theater lobbies, parties, and so on) and rated according to their physical appearances on a scale from 1 to 5 (in half-point intervals). The study found that 60 percent of the couples were separated by only half a point on the scale, 86 percent were separated by one point or less, and no couples were separated by more than two and a half points (Silverman 1971). The study also found that the more similarly rated two people were, the more likely they were to touch (allow each other within their eighteen-inch zones). Sixty percent of the "highly similar" couples touched, as compared with 46 percent of the "moderately similar" couples and only 22 percent of the "dissimilar couples" (Silverman 1971).

More important, perhaps, is the finding that couples are often matched in terms of psychological characteristics. Research suggests that two emotionally immature people are likely to find each other attractive, as are two emotionally mature people. When a person who is relatively mature emotionally is attracted to someone who is emotionally immature, the tendency is for the emotionally mature person to become relatively more immature to match the characteristics of the other person (Coleman 1984).

What happens, then, when someone "beats the odds" — when someone ends up dating (or marrying) a person who clearly has superior (or inferior) status in terms of important physical, psychological, or social qualities? There are three possibilities: The person with the more desirable traits and characteristics will become more like the other person (so that a match is obtained); the relationship will be characterized by disharmony and unhappiness as the higher-status person feels angry, cheated, and resentful and the lower-status person feels uneasy and guilty; or the relationship will fail and the couple will separate (Coleman 1984). Walster and Walster (1978) pose this question in this way:

What happens when the Prince marries Cinderella? It's obvious, of course, why the Prince might be dissatisfied: he can never

really forget that he could have married a princess. But, Cinderella . . . might have cause for unhappiness too. . . . On the one hand, she is eager to keep the prince's love. After all, what are her chances for attracting so desirable a partner a second time? On the other hand, she is painfully aware that the prince has little reason to stay with her. Thus, both the "superior" and the "inferior" partner in an inequitable relation might feel uneasy. (p. 142)

Trade-offs: Attraction Compromises

Although it seems clear that people are attracted to others who have about the same status in various important physical, psychological, and social qualities, it is also clear that this matching does not usually occur for every quality. Generally, people must compromise — that is, accept someone they consider high in one quality but low in another so that the lower-ranked quality is "traded off" for the higher one. Such *trade-offs* are not necessarily made deliberately; they are very likely made unconsciously.

A few examples may help make this clear. A woman may find a man physically unattractive, but if he is wealthy or powerful (has high status), she may trade off his physical appearance for his wealth and success. This facet of male-female interaction is captured beautifully by P. D. James in her novel *Unnatural Causes* (1967):

Without being the least attracted to him physically she was beginning to find him interesting, even a little intriguing. It was surprising what the possession of two hundred thousand pounds could do for a man. Already she could detect the subtle patina of success, the assurance and complacency that the possession of power or money invariably gives. (p. 114)

Or perhaps a man is attracted to the physical appearance of a woman but feels that she is emotionally immature. He may compromise, accepting her emotional immaturity while seeking her beauty. And consider the situation presented by Walster and Walster (1978):

> An aging politician who proposes marriage to a young, attractive woman may be trading his prestige and power for her beauty and youth. There is compelling evidence that men and women do engage in such complicated balancing and counterbalancing in selecting mates. (p. 139)

These examples, of course, describe the most common stereotypes of seemingly unmatched couples.

Each of us has limits, of course, to the degree that we will accept in others a relatively low level of a specific trait we regard as important. Put another way, no matter what other attractive qualities others might have, if we decide that another person is too low in some other, more important quality, then we will not find that person attractive. As noted earlier, such trade-offs are often made unconsciously. People do not usually consciously "add up points" but instead simply feel some emotional response based on the combination of wanted and unwanted qualities that the other person has.

An interesting illustration of this trading off phenomenon was found in the results of a research study that asked, "Who is better looking—you or your partner?" The research subjects were asked to describe specifically their partners' physical attractiveness by checking one of the following five choices:

- Much more attractive than I
- Slightly more attractive than I
- As attractive as I
- Slightly less attractive than I
- Much less attractive than I

The men and women who thought they were physically more attractive than their partners stated that their partners' other assets balanced things out—that their partners were, for example, especially loving, self-sacrificing, or wealthy. Similarly, those who regarded themselves as physically less attractive felt they possessed other valuable assets that balanced things (Berscheid, Walster, and Bohrnstedt 1972).

Of course, successful relationships may occur even when people pursue someone initially regarded as beyond their reach. For example, in Leo Tolstoy's *War and Peace* Pierre in effect says to Natasha that although he cannot imagine her accepting him, he must try because he could not bear to lose so desirable a person without an attempt, however futile. To his great delight Natasha does accept him; it was a long shot that paid off. (This aspect of attraction is reflected in such sayings as "Nothing ventured, nothing gained" and "Faint heart ne'er won fair lady.")

Attraction and Reciprocal Interaction

It is obvious, of course, that a relationship cannot develop unless there is reciprocal attraction. Usually one person is more attracted than the other, and for teenagers and young adults, especially (but also for older adults), the attempt to have this attraction reciprocated by the other can be a major preoccupation. The person who is most attracted will often court the other with diligence, trying to provide rewards that might be deemed sufficiently attractive to bring the relationship into balance. In fact, complete reciprocity seems to be rare; most relationships are somewhat unbalanced in that one person loves more while the other permits himself or herself to be loved.

"I must confess I've noticed your stopping by for a drink, but I never dreamed you'd noticed me."

Trying to attract another person can be especially difficult in the initial interaction. Some people are very adept at this — they are confident, un-self-conscious, mildly self-deprecating, and amusing — and may have a large number of acquaintances, companions, and friends. Most people, however, often find this process uncomfortable, confusing, and painful, and they stumble through their initial encounters as best they can. One way or another, most people make it through this initial period of *reciprocal interaction* (although some are haunted for years by lost opportunities and visions of what might have been if only they had been successful in approaching that especially attractive person so long ago).

People often wonder whether it is better to play "hard to get" or to admit frankly that one likes another person. A classic study designed to test this question found that it makes no difference. In this research an attractive female experimenter played "hard to get" for half the male subjects (either refusing a date or accepting very reluctantly) and accepted dates eagerly for the other half. In a series of five experiments, the same results were obtained. The male subjects liked the "easy-to-get" woman and the "hard-to-get" woman equally well. The best answer, then, to the question of how to behave in order to attract someone seems to be "Be yourself" (Walster et al. 1973).

During the period of initial interaction, the person being pursued may be concerned about what he or she thinks are the motivations of the pursuer. If an heiress believes that she is liked "for herself" (that is, for her personal qualities), she may respond differently than if she suspects that her pursuer's behavior is designed to get his hands on her money. Our behavior may thus be perceived as either charming or offensive, depending on how others perceive our motivation.

Sometimes, of course, reciprocal attraction is immediate, and each person is spontaneously drawn to the other. Such "love at first sight" (the eros type of love discussed in Chapter 3) has been presented in many famous passages in literature. In Shakespeare's *Romeo and Juliet*, for example, Romeo gets a glimpse of Juliet across a crowded dance floor and is transfixed. Even though their families are sworn enemies and Romeo has crashed the masked ball uninvited, Juliet immediately responds with a very strong reciprocal attraction (act 1, scene 5).

Anticipation of the Other's Response

Our willingness to act on an attraction we feel for another person is modified by our expectations of that person's response to us. Thus even though we might perceive someone as highly attractive, if we think that he or she is beyond our reach we may decide to modify our feelings and "worship from afar."

Suppose a young woman is invited to a party and finds that she knows virtually no one there. Then she looks around the room and sees a very attractive young man. On a scale of 1 to 10, he clearly rates a 10 in her value system. Does she immediately move toward him, engage him in conversation, and try to win his interest? Not necessarily, for on the heels of her initial attraction comes a (probably unconscious) appraisal of her chances. Suppose she regards the probability of his reciprocating as very low — perhaps 4 on a scale of 10. Suppose we assume that the *attraction factor* (the degree of attraction that she feels and that she will act on) is the product of the initial attraction (10 in this example) multiplied by the perceived possibility for success in approaching the other (4 in this example). In this situation, then, the attraction factor would be 10

times 4, or 40 — not very high on a scale of 100. She will probably not make the approach.

Continuing the example, suppose the woman looks around the room and spots another guest quietly standing by himself. He is relatively attractive — perhaps an 8. She evaluates (again unconsciously) her perceived chance for reciprocation as relatively high — perhaps a 9. The attraction factor in this situation would be 8 times 9, or 72, which is relatively high on a scale of 100 and certainly higher than the attraction factor of 40 for the first person. It could be predicted then, with relative certainty, that the woman would approach the second man.

Shyness

One of the factors that affects our anticipation of another person's response to an overture of friendship is shyness. A shy person is much less likely to make the approach than a self-confident person who is not shy. Surprisingly, many self-confident, successful people are quite shy (Zimbardo 1977).

Shyness — shrinking from human contact — is one of the most prevalent characteristics of people in our society. In a random survey of more than 5,000 people, Zimbardo (1977) and his colleagues found that 40 percent had been shy for most of their lives and that 60 percent of these people considered it a serious personal handicap. Some of these men and women lived in virtual isolation, without friends and without a sex life.

A person who suffers from shyness anticipates rejection and is thus unable to make an initial approach to another person. Because shy people regard others as their "judges" and are very concerned about being negatively evaluated, they have excessive fear of taking social risks or venturing an approach that has an uncertain outcome.

Extreme shyness can result in loneliness, anxiety, and depression. A shy person is prevented from realizing his or her full potential and from enjoying the company of other people. Shy people lose out by not venturing out in life and by letting other people and situations control their reactions.

Psychologists have found that the origins of extreme shyness may be present at birth. This inborn tendency, or "temperamental shyness," is apparent in young children who are predisposed to shyness as teenagers and adults. To date, this research has been limited to middle-class white American children. Researchers find that 20 percent of these children are born "temperamentally shy" (Kagan 1991).

Fortunately, shyness can be conquered if one takes deliberate steps to do so. Zimbardo (1977) found that the simple exercise of greeting everyone you pass in your normal environment (neighborhood, school, office, and so on) brings immediate and gratifying results. Most people greeted in this way want to make contact with another person but are often too shy themselves to open up and make the initial overture.

Zimbardo (1977) advises shy students to make an agreement with themselves to speak at least once in every one of their class sessions or groups so that their shyness can be gradually overcome. Very shy people can start by doing relatively simple things, such as saying hello to three strangers, and then build from there, controlling their anxieties by imagining desired outcomes rather than feared consequences.

Zimbardo (1977) also finds that shy people can make deliberate attempts to overcome shyness through **active listening**—listening completely and attentively, assuming an attentive posture, smiling, nodding occasional approval, and looking interested. This behavior shifts a person's focus of attention from oneself to the other person, which can help lessen shyness. Moreover, because it is very flattering to be listened to in this way, the speaker usually becomes receptive to further acquaintance, which often

is not the case for a person who is not really listened to and thus experiences a feeling of rejection.

Coleman (1984) describes another solution to the problem of shyness: Simply role-play the behavior of a bold person. Coleman's research indicates that people who deliberately act self-assured may come to feel genuinely self-assured and thus may become much less shy. Moreover, people who role-play self-assurance in this way typically receive the immediate reward of getting positive responses from others, which reinforces the role playing and makes it easier. Thus self-assurance is gradually raised until it starts to feel natural and eventually becomes the reality.

The Reward Theory of Attraction

We are attracted, then, to what we find rewarding. All organisms are genetically programmed to avoid punishments and seek rewards, both of which psychologists call *reinforcers*. The initial attraction that inexorably draws us into dating, courtship, and marriage is based on an equation in which the punishments are deemed to be significantly outweighed by the rewards.

In other words, being provided with psychological, social, and physical satisfactions is rewarding, and being denied these satisfactions (or being deprived of them) is punishing. Thus according to the *reward theory of attraction*, two people will be drawn to each other if they find each other rewarding. If the rewards are not present for one person, the attraction will be one-sided. If the negative aspects of the relationship—the punishments—increase until they outweigh the rewards, the couple will no longer find each other attractive. If punishments emanate from one person, that person will become less attractive to the other and will perhaps be rejected.

The problem, of course, in analyzing and explaining attraction in terms of the reward theory is that there are so many complications within this fairly basic formulation because attraction is an emotion, and emotions are extremely complex (see Chapter 3). Moreover, there are great individual differences among people, so that a quality found extremely rewarding by one person may be regarded with indifference by another. Thus even though one person might find being with a particular individual extremely satisfying and rewarding, someone else might find the same person's company dull or disagreeable.

In addition, there is much about personal attraction that remains mysterious and defies logical analysis. For example, no one has as yet explained the limerent attraction that can transform an individual's life when another person becomes so desirable that nothing else can be considered of comparable worth (see Chapter 3).

Another problem in assessing the reward theory in practice is that because we will probably never find all the qualities we want in one person (except in an extreme limerent initial attraction), we must usually compromise by trading off a disappointing quality that brings little or no satisfaction for an especially valued quality that brings a great deal of satisfaction.

Despite these (and other) complications, it nonetheless seems abundantly clear that we find a person attractive if that person can provide us with sufficient rewards — whatever this means to us — and that we find a person exceptionally attractive if that person can provide us with exceptional rewards. Social scientists have succeeded in isolating many of the variables that are rewarding: homogamy, positive associated circumstances, propinquity, relatively equivalent status, and reciprocity of attraction.

Much of what we find attractive in another person is obvious. Certainly we will be attracted to a person who is noncritical and nonjudgmental, who is physically desirable, who provides us with material benefits such as subsistence, comfort, and security and with psychological satisfactions such as warmth, kindness, compassion, generosity, humor, emotional support, emotional security, understanding, acceptance, and appreciation.

The flip side of attraction involves punishers, which are the opposites of rewards. Thus criticism, fault-finding, judgmental remarks or observations, rudeness, discourtesy, unkindness, lack of awareness, insensitivity, callousness, lack of humor, lack of warmth, an absence of appreciation, and failure to provide significant satisfactions are experienced as punishers — to varying degrees, of course, because of the important factor of individual differences.

Although the reward theory of attraction seems to be a simple matter of common sense, it is, surprisingly, often overlooked. And if we lose sight of it and begin to withhold important satisfactions from someone else or provide punishers, the degree to which we will be considered attractive will diminish accordingly. Ironically, people sometimes apply punishers deliberately in an effort to "improve" the other person by trying to motivate change in a desired direction. It makes little difference whether punishers are well-meaning or mean-spirited, however, for they still have the same effect of unbalancing the equation that led to the initial attraction.

Although we may sometimes tolerate punishers as part of a trade-off, we can do so only up to a point — the point at which they are no longer outweighed by significant rewards. We also tolerate punishers briefly or intermittently, so long as we can anticipate significant rewards in the not-so-distant future. Again, we do not add up a balance sheet or check off wanted qualities before deciding to feel a sense of attraction. The balancing of trade-offs is not logical or rational, but is simply something we do as part of being human.

There are times, too, when we may stay in a relationship with someone who is no longer providing us with as many satisfactions as before because of other factors that have entered the equation since the initial attraction. The binding force may come from a sense of responsibility for children, altruistic love, a strong sense of commitment, social pressures, or simply reluctance or disinclination to change (see Chapter 3).

Dating and Sexuality

In the following sections we will examine the changing roles of sexuality in dating since dating became firmly established as a method of courtship and marital choice around 1920. First we consider the decades before 1960.

The Kinsey Era: Before 1960

Initially, copulation was not commonly accepted as a part of dating, especially for youths in their early or middle teens. During the Kinsey era only 3 percent of white females had experienced sexual intercourse by age fifteen (Kinsey et al. 1953).[8] About one white woman in four was sexually experienced by age twenty, and about two women in four copulated before marriage. However, for many the experience occurred only once (at most just five or six times), usually with their fiance just before the wedding (Kinsey et al. 1953).

If a couple had sex while dating and the woman became pregnant, the man responsible was expected to marry her in a so-called shotgun wedding.[9] Failing this, her parents were

---

[8]As noted earlier (Chapter 4), Kinsey's sample included whites only.

[9]The term *shotgun wedding* stems from the frontier era, when the bride's father or brother would literally stand watch over the wedding ceremony with a shotgun. The man responsible for the woman's pregnancy would either go through with the marriage or be shot. The term became a metaphor to describe any wedding in which the groom was under duress to marry a pregnant woman.

likely to send her out of town to live with a relative until the child was born and could be placed for adoption, keeping her disgrace a secret from all but immediate family members. The young unmarried mother would return home only when her appearance had returned to normal. School authorities, neighbors, and friends would not be told the true reason she had been away.

Rising Incidence of Sexuality in Dating: 1960–1990

Sexual attitudes, expectations, and behavior began to change in the 1960s with the advent of the pill, which gave a woman considerably more control of her reproductive system. According to Cunningham (1990), nothing else in this century—perhaps not even winning the right to vote—made such an immediate difference in women's lives:

> The Pill provoked profound social change. It helped lower the birth rate and end America's baby boom in 1964. It spurred sexual frankness and experimentation. It allowed women to think seriously about careers because they could postpone childbirth. And it sparked the feminist and pro-choice movements; once women felt they were in charge of their own bodies, they began to question the authority of their husbands, their bosses, their doctors and their churches. (p. 15)

The U.S. Food and Drug Administration approved the sale of the pill in our society in 1960 (see Appendix B). Beginning in the 1960s, the incidence of premarital copulation began to climb.

Compared to the Kinsey era, women under age twenty have had much more sexual experience in the last three decades (see Table 5-1). By 1988, over 38 percent of women ages fifteen to

TABLE 5-1

Percentage of U.S. Women Ages 15–19 Who Have Had Sexual Intercourse — by Age and Race/Ethnicity: 1988

	Ages	
	15–17	18–19
All groups	38.4	74.4
Blacks	50.5	78.0
Non-Hispanic whites	36.2	74.3
Hispanics	36.1	70.0

Source: Forrest, Jacqueline Darroch, and Singh, Susheela, "The Sexual and Reproductive Behavior of American Women, 1982–1988." *Family Planning Perspectives* 22 (September/October 1990): 208.

seventeen and over 74 percent of women ages eighteen and nineteen had experienced sexual intercourse. Even though direct comparison of these data and the Kinsey data is not possible because the cohorts examined were not always the same, the trend is clear.

The incidence of teenage males having sex on dates has also increased, although much less dramatically. Kinsey (1948) reported that 71 percent of never-married white males had experienced sexual intercourse by age nineteen; in 1988 the proportion had increased to 76 percent (see Table 5-2). Among blacks and Hispanics, 96 percent and 81 percent, respectively, had experienced sexual intercourse. (Comparable figures for blacks and Hispanics are not available from the Kinsey era, as previously noted.)

The trend among college students reflected the national averages. The proportion of teenage college women having sex on dates rose from about 19 percent in 1958 to 29 percent in the mid-1960s. By 1980, 64 percent of teenage college women students were having sex on dates (Robinson and Jedlicka 1982; Kinsey et al. 1948, 1953).

The incidence of premarital sexual intercourse among college women who were past their teens rose to even higher levels. By 1978 some 83 percent of unmarried college women over age twenty-two were having sex on dates (see Figure 5-4).

A rise in the proportion of college women having sexual intercourse on dates has occurred for casual dates, for dates with a steady boy-

TABLE 5-2

Percentage of Never-Married U.S. Men Ages 13–19 Who Have Had Sexual Intercourse — by Age and Race/Ethnicity: 1988

Ages	All Groups	Blacks	Non-Hispanic Whites	Hispanics
13 and under	5.4	19.8	2.9	3.9
14	11.0	34.6	7.1	6.3
15	21.1	47.8	16.2	19.4
16	37.8	63.5	33.0	37.7
17	57.5	78.4	53.0	63.2
18	67.4	84.7	69.8	60.9
19	79.0	95.8	75.9	80.5

Source: Sonenstein, Freya L., Pleck, Joseph H., and Ku, Leighton C., "Levels of Sexual Activity Among Adolescent Males in the United States." *Family Planning Perspectives* 23 (July/August 1991): 163.

friend, and for dates with a fiance (see Figure 5-5). In 1978, fully one-half of college women were having sexual intercourse on casual dates, a fivefold rise from the 1958 incidence of about 10 percent. In 1978, fully two-thirds (67 percent) of college women were copulating on dates with their steady boyfriends, compared with only about 15 percent in 1958. And whereas only 31 percent of college women were copulating with their fiance in 1958, 76 percent were doing so in 1978.

Meanwhile, as of 1978 almost half (43 percent) of college women were experiencing cunnilingus or performing fellatio on casual dates. Nearly two out of three college women (63 percent) participated in oral-genital sex with a steady date; 74 percent participated in oral-

genital sex on dates with a fiance. Comparison with previous years is not possible because earlier researchers did not ask the question regarding incidence of these activities on dates (Bell and Coughey 1980).

Research designed to compare the sexual practices of college women before and after the onset of AIDS, studied college women who had come to the college health service to consult a gynecologist (DeBuono et al. 1990). The age range of these women was seventeen to thirty-seven, their average age was about twenty-one, and 80 percent of them were undergraduates. The proportion of these women who were sexually active had not changed during the three periods checked: 1975 (88 percent), 1986 (87 percent), and 1989 (87 percent).

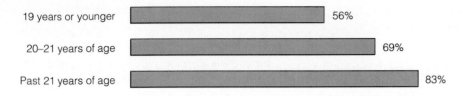

FIGURE 5-4

Incidence of premarital copulation among college women for three age cohorts.

Source: Data from Bell and Coughey (1980), p. 356.

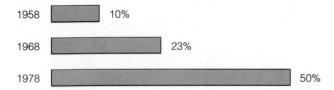

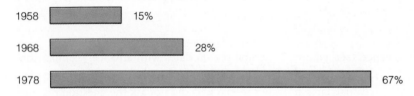

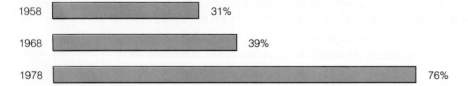

FIGURE 5-5

Incidence of premarital copulation among college women by dating category, 1958, 1968, and 1978.

Source: Data from Bell and Coughey (1980), p. 355.

The proportion who had experienced sexual intercourse with six or more men (about 21 percent) was the same in the three surveys, as was the proportion who had experienced sexual intercourse with three or more men during the year before the survey (about 21 percent), as was the proportion who had practiced fellatio (86 percent), cunnilingus (29 percent), or anal intercourse (9 percent).

The study concluded that, despite the widespread publicity about the dangers of AIDS (and other STDs), and the risk of multiple partners and oral or anal sex, there was little change in the sexual behavior of American college women from 1975 to 1989. The one exception was that the proportion who regularly used condoms during sexual intercourse rose from about 12 percent in 1975, to 21 percent in 1986, and 41 percent in 1989 (DeBuono et al. 1990).

On the other hand, other research (McNally and Mosher 1991) found that nearly one-third (31 percent) of sexually active, unmarried American women have changed their sexual behavior in response to the threat of AIDS; the most common change is limiting their sexual encounters to one man (about 16 percent of respondents). Other changes reported were restricting copulation to someone whom the woman knows well (11 percent), reducing the frequency of copulation (9 percent), and refusing to have sexual intercourse at all (5 percent).

Before the 1960s, female students at colleges and universities were under the strict control of campus authorities. Administrators assumed responsibility for supervising them under the doctrine of *in locus parentis* ("in place of parents"). Female undergraduates were required to live in campus housing facilities, where they could be subject to rigorous control. They could not stay out past a certain hour — often 10 P.M. on weeknights and midnight on weekends — after which the facilities' doors were locked. Men were not permitted above the first floor. Residents could

entertain men in the public lounge area, where a chaperone was usually present. Displays of affection (such as hugging, kissing, and sometimes even holding hands) were prohibited, and residents were subject to disciplinary action if they persisted in flaunting regulations. Sexual contact between a couple was usually possible only in an auto — and it was relatively limited even there.

As part of the dramatic changes of the 1960s, the *in locus parentis* doctrine was gradually abandoned. Many colleges established coed dormitories, with men and women living in the same residence hall. Campus authorities placed almost no restrictions on people's freedom to visit in one another's rooms, and supervision of sexual activity was virtually nonexistent. Meanwhile, college health services began to dispense birth control information and equipment.

Effect of Premarital Copulation on Happiness in Marriage

Do young women who experience premarital copulation have happier marriages or unhappier marriages than women who are virgins on their wedding day? Does sexual experience before marriage help resolve problems of sexuality beforehand, or does it lead to more problems?

According to one study (Tavris and Sadd, 1977), premarital copulation has no effect on happiness in a subsequent marriage. (The one exception involved girls who copulate before age sixteen and who have a relatively high incidence of copulation with many different boys; these girls subsequently have a higher divorce rate than other women.) Concluded Tavris and Sadd:

> This means that of all the many factors that go into a good marriage and a good sex life, premarital sex is not one of them. It means that some women have perfectly happy marriages although they were virgins on

their wedding day, and that others are perfectly happy to have experimented to their heart's and body's content. (pp. 53–54)

The finding that young women age sixteen and over who copulate before marriage have neither a greater nor lower probability of a happy marriage does not extend to cohabitation, however. Cohabiting couples — those who live together before they marry — have a higher divorce rate than other couples (see Chapter 6).

Unwanted Sexual Aggression: The Issues of Rape and Date Rape

Long smoldering as an individual and a societal issue, unwanted sexual aggression assumed unprecedented political importance for the 1990s when it was polarized by the Clarence Thomas Senate confirmation hearing in 1991. Americans (and much of the world) were glued to their televisions as Anita Hill's allegations of sexual harassment were scrutinized.

Unwanted sexual aggression can range from sexual innuendo to sexual harassment to rape. All of these forms can occur with a stranger, an acquaintance, a date, or a member of the victim's family. The aggressor may be male or female and the victim may be male or female, but usually the aggressor is male and the victim female (although homosexual rape, in which both the aggressor and the victim are male, is not uncommon, especially in such situations as prison).

Rape is most commonly understood to mean forcing a woman to have sex against her wishes by using physical or psychological force, the threat of force, drugs, deception, or any combination of these. Rape is a serious crime, punishable by up to thirty years in prison in some states and by the death penalty in others.

Statutory rape has a clear-cut legal definition; it means that the victim was below the legal age of consent and is automatically a crime. If the rapist is a relative of the victim, this is incest; if the victim is a child, this is pedophilia. Both are crimes (see Chapter 4).

If the rapist is a stranger, it is usually simply called *rape*; if he is an acquaintance, it is *acquaintance rape*; if he is a date, it is *date rape*. The legal issue in all these rapes is that of *nonconsent*. It is easier to establish nonconsent if the rapist is a stranger. If he is an acquaintance or a date, the issue of nonconsent becomes more difficult to establish, and a woman may be reluctant to bring formal charges because of the necessity of proving that force was used — especially if the force was psychological or deceptive.

Because our culture expects males to be sexually aggressive and females to be relatively submissive, establishing nonconsent is often the issue upon which rape trials turn. The jury must be convinced that the alleged victim did not give tacit consent. For example, the jurors in the William Kennedy Smith trial in 1991 in Florida decided that, even though Smith copulated with the woman, she was not raped — despite her contention that she had not consented. The jurors decided that, given community standards of expectation, she had tacitly consented. The jurors in the Mike Tyson trial the following year in Indiana decided that the woman was raped. Given the same community standards, she was deceived and had not tacitly consented.

Date rape is an issue of grave concern on today's college campuses. Education programs have proliferated in American colleges and universities during the past decade, with educational videos, pamphlets, training manuals, and posters alerting students to the dangers of date and acquaintance rape. Rape Awareness Weeks have become annual events, and many schools have appointed special deans to deal with charges of sexual assault.

What constitutes date rape? The FBI defines rape as "carnal knowledge of a female forcibly and without her consent." Statutory Law of New

York City defines rape as "sexual intercourse compelled by the use of physical force, or threat of physical force, which places a person in fear of immediate death or physical injury." Using these definitions, date rape would simply be rape that occurred on a date or with an acquaintance rather than with a stranger or a relative. However, many campus groups extend the meaning of rape to include an absence of mutual desire, verbally aggressive behavior, or unwanted sexual innuendo on a date. For example, the Department of Human Services at Cornell University defines rape as "any sexual intercourse without mutual desire" (Parrot 1990). The Acquaintance Rape Prevention Workshop at Swarthmore College includes "verbal harassment and inappropriate innuendo" in its definition of rape (Gutmann 1990). Verbal harassment or inappropriate sexual innuendo are not legally considered rape, but leaving the legal issues aside, if the harassment or the sexual innuendo is embarrassing, disagreeable, shocking, or painful to the victim, it is unwanted sexual aggression and is unconscionable. Sexual innuendo may legally be considered sexual harassment (if not rape), which is illegal in certain situations — for example, if the aggressor is in a position of authority and is using this position to harass the victim. The incidence of sexual harassment is not known, but more cases are being reported since the Anita Hill–Clarence Thomas controversy mentioned earlier (Abramson 1992).

It is difficult to evaluate the estimated incidence of date rape because researchers have used different definitions of rape in their studies, such as "verbal attack," "verbal persuasion," and "attempted" rape (Koss et al. 1989; Struckman-Johnson 1988; Carlson 1987).[10] For example, an ambitious study of more than 6,000 students on thirty-two college campuses reported that about one woman student in eight had experienced either an "actual" or an "attempted" date rape (Moss 1987). This figure tells us very little about the sexual experiences of these women on dates; the term "actual" rape seems clear, but the report fails to specify what it means by "attempted" rape. It thus fails to distinguish between a wide range of behavior — from an unpleasant experience that a young woman felt bad about to one in which an attacker callously, brutally, and persistently tried to force her to submit to vaginal, anal, or oral copulation (Gutmann 1990). Another widely cited study (Koss, Gidycz, and Wisniewski 1987) reported that one woman student in four had been a victim of rape or "attempted" rape. Again, however, the study does not specify what it means by "attempted" rape (Gutmann 1990). Put another way, a study that used the Cornell University definition or the Swarthmore College definition of rape would yield significantly different figures than a study that used the FBI definition or the New York City definition.

Another problem with ascertaining the incidence of date rape is that such assaults are consistently underreported. Even when the sexual encounter is undeniably a rape — when the woman has struggled unsuccessfully to avoid penetration — an estimated nine in ten are not reported (Moss 1987).

Whatever the incidence of date rape, and however it is defined, it is unquestionably of serious concern. It may resolve itself, however, into an issue of self-awareness, self-respect, and communication: Ideally, if both a young man and young woman on a date know what they want and don't want and communicate these feelings and wants to the other, they will promote mutual understanding and respect. Relating in this way may or may not include sexual intercourse — that becomes a mutual decision.

---

[10]See also Moss 1987; McKinney 1986; Lane and Gwartney-Gibbs 1985.

Consider the following: Jill, nineteen years old and sexually experienced, is studying alone in her dorm room at about 10 P.M. She hears a knock, opens the door, and finds Jack, looking morose and disheveled. Since Jack is an acquaintance from one of her classes, she asks him in. He sits on the bed while she sits on the chair by her desk. After sitting silently for a few minutes, Jack blurts out that he is failing his exams and is going to drop out of premed and go to work driving a truck for his uncle. Jill moves over to the bed beside him and says that would be a mistake. She wants to give him comfort and understanding but has no thought of sex. He puts his arm around her and hugs her. She empathizes with him and doesn't want to add rejection to his problems, so she hugs him back. After a short time he begins to caress her sexually. She protests but doesn't forcibly resist. When he insists on having sexual intercourse despite her protests, she complies, although it is not what she wishes. A few minutes later she asks him to leave and he does. Was Jill raped?

Dating and Teenage Pregnancy

The increased incidence and frequency of copulation by dating teenagers has been accompanied by an alarming rise in teenage pregnancies. Pregnancy usually locks teenagers into poverty, and teenagers' babies are often ill. Public costs for caring for pregnant teenagers and for young mothers and their babies are enormous. Establishing birth control clinics in high schools has been shown to lower the rate of pregnancy among the students, but many powerful groups regard these clinics as improper and immoral and vigorously oppose their use.

We will examine the extraordinarily complex issues of teenage pregnancy in the following sections.

Incidence of Teenage Pregnancy

The United States has the highest rate of teenage pregnancy of any industrialized nation in the world.[11] One out of every ten American women ages fifteen to nineteen becomes pregnant every year (see Figure 5-6); by comparison, European nations average about 3.5 percent and Japan averages 1 percent.[12] Blacks have the highest rate of teenage pregnancy (23 percent) in the United States (see Figure 5-7), followed by Hispanics (16 percent), whites (11 percent), and Asian and Pacific Islander Americans (6 percent). The likelihood of a teenager becoming pregnant is negatively correlated with her level of education: The lower her level of education, the higher the likelihood of pregnancy (Abrahamse et al. 1988).

Teenage Pregnancy and Contraception

One reason for this high rate of teenage pregnancy and unmarried motherhood is the high incidence of premarital copulation, but another reason is that three out of four teenagers who are having sexual intercourse do not regularly use a condom or other method of contraception (Hatcher et al. 1990; Westoff 1988a). Poor teenagers (those below the poverty line) are the least likely to use contraceptives (Forrest and Singh 1990).

Teenagers do not use contraceptives for many reasons, the two most common of which are believing that the risk of pregnancy is small and failing to anticipate that intercourse might occur. Other reasons cited are inconvenience, dislike of condoms, thoughtlessness, simple carelessness,

---

[11]U.N. Population Studies, "Adolescent Reproductive Behavior: Evidence from Developed Countries" (1988).

[12]U.N. Population Studies, "Adolescent Reproductive Behavior."

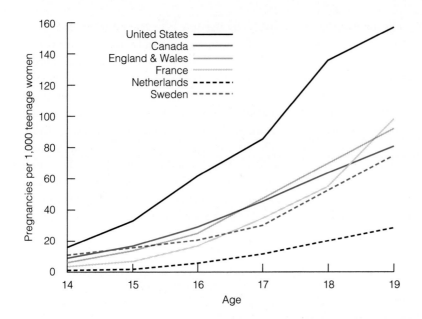

FIGURE 5 - 6

Pregnancies per 1,000 women under age twenty by single year of age, 1980, in six countries.

Note: Pregnancies are calculated as the simple sum of abortions and births and are therefore underestimated.

Source: Hatcher et al. (1990), Figure 25:2, p. 520.

FIGURE 5 - 7

Births to American teenage mothers, by race/ethnicity, as percent of all births: 1988.

Source: U.S. National Center for Health Statistics, "Live Births, by Race and Type of Hispanic Origin — Selected Characteristics: 1988." *Vital Statistics of the United States,* annual. Washington, D.C.: Government Printing Office, 1991.

or even a desire to become pregnant (Hatcher et al. 1990; Katrowitz et al. 1987). It is also likely that failure to use contraceptives is due in part to the widespread belief among teenagers of the following false myths (Katrowitz et al. 1987):

- A woman cannot become pregnant the first time she copulates. (This is not true.)

- A woman cannot become pregnant from occasional copulation. (This is not true.)

- A woman cannot become pregnant if she copulates while standing up. (This is not true.)

Teenage Pregnancy and Abortion

A teenager who becomes pregnant rarely marries the father of her child; she either becomes a single parent or she has an abortion. About one-fourth of all abortions in our society are performed on teenage girls — 11 percent for those ages fifteen to seventeen and 14 percent for those ages eighteen to nineteen (Henshaw and Van Vort 1989). American teenagers abort about half of their pregnancies (Westoff 1988b). Nearly 400,000 teenagers obtained abortions in 1990 (Hatcher et al. 1990).

Most abortions are performed on socially advantaged white women who can afford to pay for them (Hatcher et al. 1990; Jones et al. 1986). Relatively few abortions are performed on the poor, who cannot afford to pay for them. Federal funding of most abortions for low-income women was banned by Congress in 1976; only nine states have acted on their own to fund abortion programs.

Teenage Pregnancy and Poverty

There is a strong correlation between early childbearing and poverty. The women most likely to become teenage mothers are black, poorly educated, and head a single-parent family with income below the poverty line. Three-fourths of all births to teenagers occur among poor women, many of whom drop out of school and go on welfare. As adults they earn, on the average, about one-half as much money as those who have completed high school. Thus becoming a teenage mother often puts the young woman into a lifelong pattern of poverty and dependency (Hatcher et al. 1990; Wallis 1985).

There is a very high likelihood that girls of teenage mothers will also become teenage mothers; about 82 percent of teenage unwed mothers are themselves daughters of teenage unwed mothers (Wallis 1985; Makinson 1985).

Teenage Pregnancy and Health

Because a sizable number of pregnant teenagers are poor, ignorant of medical needs, or careless about making medical appointments, few receive adequate prenatal care. In fact, four of every five pregnant teenagers receive *no* prenatal care during the critical first trimester of pregnancy.[13] Poor teenagers usually have inadequate nutrition as well, a combination that can have serious health effects for both mothers and their babies (Hatcher et al. 1990; Wallis 1985).

Teenage mothers have twice the incidence of low birth-weight babies (compared with mothers over age twenty), and 70 percent of deaths of newborn babies in the United States are due to low birth weight.[14] Newborns who do survive are in a high-risk category, for infants of teenage

---

[13]U.S. National Center for Health Statistics, "Advance Report of Final Natality Statistics, 1986" (1988).

[14]U.S. National Center for Health Statistics, "Live Births, by Place of Delivery; Median and Low-Birth Weight; and Prenatal Care: 1960 to 1988" (1991).

mothers are three times more likely to die in the first year of life than children born to older women. Those who survive until their first birthday often have high incidences of mental and emotional handicaps. More babies of unwed teenage mothers are born with birth defects than babies of other women.[15]

In 1984, the public spent some $8.6 billion to provide prenatal care for pregnant teenagers (Katrowitz et al. 1987). After a teenage mother's child is born, the costs rise even higher. In 1985, for example, $17 billion was paid through AFDC (Aid to Families with Dependent Children), food stamps, and Medicaid to women who first gave birth as teenagers (Burt 1986).

Teenage Pregnancy and Fathers

Although relatively few studies have explored the problems of teenage fathers, the limited research available finds (not surprisingly) that they are much less adversely affected than teenage mothers by the pregnancy and the birth of a child — although high school dropout rates are higher for teenage fathers than they are for other male students (Elster and Lamb 1986; Marsiglio and Mott 1986).

Teenage fathers often deny paternity. When they do admit paternity, they often doubt their capability for providing either economic or emotional support for the mother or the child. The father usually simply withdraws from a difficult situation, leaving the mother to deal with the problems of child care and child support as best she can. Ultimately the teenage mother is usually left with the responsibility for the child, and the teenage father's concern can best be described as limited (Furstenberg et al. 1989).

---

[15]U.S. National Center for Health Statistics, "Infant Deaths and Infant Mortality Rates by Cause of Death: 1980 to 1988" (1991).

A Search for Solutions to the Problems of Teenage Pregnancy

Several studies have concluded that establishing birth-control clinics in high schools has been effective in lowering teenage pregnancy rates (Kenney 1986; Zabin et al. 1986; Dryfoos 1985). In these clinics, students are counseled both by health professionals and by peer counselors, who are students trained to discuss sexual concerns. Research indicates that peer counselors are more likely to change a student's attitude and behavior than are professional counselors (Hatcher et al. 1990).

Contraceptives (especially condoms and the pill), together with instructions for their use, are dispensed at these clinics. Making contraceptives available seems to be important, for research indicates that not even high-quality sex education programs are as effective as actually providing contraceptive devices (Trussell 1988). Studies also find that establishing a birth-control clinic in a high school can cut its students' birth rate in half (Katrowitz et al. 1987).

For this reason, advocates of clinics maintain that students should be provided with contraceptives and instructions on how to use them (Wallis 1985). They believe that what was once a matter of morality has become a matter of public health. Those who advocate birth-control clinics in high schools take the position that our society must face reality. They emphasize that the statistics speak for themselves — that teenagers are sexually active and girls are getting pregnant at a shockingly high rate, and that something must be done (Katrowitz et al. 1987). In 1988, about 120 birth-control clinics had been established in American high schools, and more are being planned (Read 1988).

Persistent opposition to these clinics has developed, however. Many well-organized and highly vocal groups believe that "the problem is premarital sexual activity" and that "reducing the risk of pregnancy will both legitimize adolescent sex and increase its prevalence" (Trussell 1988, p. 262). The politically powerful Right to Life movement and the Roman Catholic Church are two groups that vehemently oppose the clinics on the grounds that they are morally unacceptable — that they implicitly condone students' illicit sexual activities. A coalition of religious leaders, politicians, and school board members vigorously oppose the entire concept of high school clinics; they passionately believe that the only ethical answer to the problem of teenage pregnancy is to return to the moral standards of our past (Read 1988).

Traditional American moral and ethical standards considered sexuality to be legitimate only when it took place within the context of love and marriage. Such standards emphasized that love,

commitment, and responsibility were essential prerequisites to sexual intercourse, and until the 1960s sexuality was sanctified only within marriage. Opponents of high school clinics believe that schools should once again accept and emphasize these values as being basic to our life-style. They fervently believe that any other solution to the problem of teenage sexuality, pregnancy, and parenthood is morally bankrupt — that accepting the legitimacy of teenage sexuality and providing students with birth control devices will only accelerate moral decay (Read 1988).

It is a sign of the times that whereas as recently as the 1920s all birth-control clinics were illegal in the United States and laws against contraception were rigorously enforced (see Chapter 2), condoms are now available in automatic vending machines in many high schools and most colleges.

SUMMARY

Courtship is one of the universals found in all known human societies. It is the first stage of the family system that also includes marriage and the family. In most of the world's societies, courtship and marital choice are dictated by parental arrangement. In our society, courtship by mutual choice began emerging as women entered the work force and was firmly established by the 1920s.

With this change, dating was not limited to courtship but also provided fun, relaxation, and recreation. Dates could be instigated by the couple rather than just by parents (an introduction by a family member was not required), and it became perfectly appropriate for a young couple to meet casually, with little supervision and relative freedom. Moreover, there was no commitment to continue the relationship beyond the duration of the date.

Although people in our society can choose their own dating and marriage partners, each person's selection is bounded by the opposing forces of exogamy (the pressure to marry outside the family) and endogamy (the pressure to marry within a group). One aspect of endogamy is homogamy, which impels a person to date someone who is of the same race or ethnic group and religion and who is of about the same age, educational level, intelligence, social class, and family background; however, the dating differential — the principle that men tend to date "down" whereas women tend to date "up" — violates this principle to some extent.

When two people are attracted to each other, the initial impression is often based on physical appearance, but propinquity (closeness in time and space) can also have an important effect on whom one dates and marries. Repeated exposure to another person usually causes us to like that person better simply because of increased familiarity. Associated circumstances can also be a key aspect of mutual attraction because people tend to like one another better if they interact in pleasant surroundings.

In terms of the attraction each person feels for the other, the nonverbal aspect of a couple's interaction may be more important than their verbal interaction.

People are usually attracted to others whom they perceive to have about the same status, although if there is a pronounced disparity, one quality may be traded off for another. For a relationship to develop the attraction between two people must be reciprocal. If one person is more attracted than the other, he or she may have to court that person diligently.

In general, people are attracted to those whom they find rewarding. Being provided with physical, psychological, or societal satisfactions are rewarding, whereas being denied them is punishing. Two people are drawn to each other if both people find the other rewarding. If the rewards are present for one but not for the other, the attraction will not be reciprocated.

Although much about attraction (such as the compulsive characteristics of limerence) has not yet yielded to logical analysis or scientific investigation, it nonetheless remains an important force in people's lives, one that can lead to a determined effort at courtship and ultimately to marriage.

The incidence of premarital sexuality has risen in our society since the 1960s, when the contraceptive pill became available. The incidence of teenage pregnancy in America is now the highest of any industrialized nation in the world. The problems of teenage pregnancy are exacerbated by poverty and poor health and are taking a toll on both teenage mothers and their babies.

KEY TERMS

The following is a list of key terms in this chapter.
These terms are defined in context within the chapter, and many may also be found in the Glossary.

active listening	endogamy	propinquity
associated circumstances	exogamy	pupillary response
attraction factor	family system	reciprocal interaction
body language	field of eligibles	reinforcers
bride price	heterogamy	reward theory of attraction
courtship	homogamy	shotgun wedding
date rape	*in locus parentis*	shyness
dating	intermarriage	trade-offs
dating differential	marriage broker	
dowry	personal space bubble	

QUESTIONS

1. Describe the changes in our society that led to the shift from courtship by parental arrangement to courtship by mutual choice.

2. What is meant by the field of eligibles in dating? Define exogamy, endogamy, and homogamy, and give examples of each.

3. What is the dating differential? How does the dating differential have different meaning for men and women in our society?

4. Describe the importance of physical attraction, propinquity, and associated circumstances in dating.

5. What is meant by body language? What is the pupillary response? What is the importance of the "personal space bubble"?

6. Give an example of a trade-off in reciprocal attraction in a dating couple.

7. What function does anticipating another person's responses have in initiating interaction with that person? What function does shyness have in anticipating another person's response?

8. What is the reward theory of attraction? How may it help explain the degree of attraction one person feels for another?

SUGGESTIONS FOR FURTHER READING

Buchmann, Marlis. *The Script of Life in Modern Society: Entry Into Adulthood in a Changing World.* Chicago: University of Chicago Press, 1989.

Chilman, Catherine S. *Adolescent Sexuality in a Changing American Society.* New York: Wiley, 1983.

Coles, Robert, and Stokes, Geoffrey. *Sex and the American Teenager.* New York: Harper & Row, 1985.

Hayes, Cheryl D., ed. *Risking the Future: Adolescent Sexuality, Pregnancy and Childbearing.* Washington, D.C.: National Academy Press, 1987.

Rothman, Ellen K. *Hands and Hearts: A History of Courtship in America.* New York: Basic Books, 1984.

CHAPTER 6

Singlehood and Cohabitation

Come live with me and be my love, . . .

Christopher Marlowe, "The Passionate Shepherd to His Love"

Singles and Independence
Attitudes Toward Singles
Rising Incidence of Singles
Staying Single or Marrying
Life-styles of Singles
Cohabiting Singles

What Do You Know?

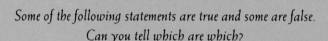

Some of the following statements are true and some are false.
Can you tell which are which?

T/F   1. From the colonial period until well into the twentieth century in the United States, most singles lived with their own families or as servants or boarders with other families.

T/F   2. Freedom for singles was initially achieved by women.

T/F   3. A single woman's prospects for marriage increase from about age thirty-five on.

T/F   4. Singles tend to have fewer psychological and medical problems than married people.

T/F   5. It is easier for a single man to find a companion, friend, or lover than it is for a woman.

T/F   6. Few singles are able to find a companion for the night in a singles bar.

T/F   7. At least half of all recently married couples have cohabited first.

T/F   8. In cohabitation, the person with the least commitment has the most power.

T/F   9. Couples who cohabit before marriage have a higher divorce rate than couples who do not cohabit first.

T/F 10. There is a direct correlation between education and cohabitation: The higher the level of education, the higher the incidence of cohabitation.

Answers: 1-T, 2-F, 3-F, 4-F, 5-F, 6-T, 7-T, 8-T, 9-T, 10-F

All of us start our adult lives as a single.[1] It is during this time of singlehood that we learn the meaning of sexuality and romantic love. Nearly all of us date, court, and marry, although many postpone marriage for a time by remaining single in the living arrangement called **cohabitation** — living together in a sexual relationship without marrying.

Of those who ultimately marry (90–95 percent of us),[2] about one-half return to singlehood through divorce (see Chapter 12). Among those who remain married, half return to singlehood when their spouse dies.

Singlehood is thus a very important part of the average person's experience, whether during adolescence, young adulthood, middle age, old age, or any combination of these life stages. In this chapter we will examine the nature of singlehood — in all its various categories — and explore its relation to marriage.

Singles and Independence

Until well into the twentieth century singles of all ages had very little independence. Singles usually lived with a family, either their own or as a servant or a boarder with another family. Living in such a setting, they were constrained by the family's expectations and were expected to abide by its rules. Singles achieved independence and freedom from restrictions only by marrying and

"*I'm a bachelor myself.*"

establishing their own family and household (Thornton and Freedman 1982).

As our economy began to change from agricultural to industrial in the second half of the nineteenth century, single men began to leave farms for jobs in towns and cities. As boarding houses began to spring up, single men began to stay in them instead of with families. Although the proprietors of these houses typically exercised familylike control over their boarders, constraints, rules, and supervision were not as stringent as they were within a family setting. Still, single men did not have the freedom of married men until well into the twentieth century (Thornton and Freedman 1982).

Single women lagged well behind men in their attainment of independence and freedom.[3]

---

[1] Demographers use the term *single* to mean adults who are not legally married — whether never-married, divorced, separated, widowed, or cohabiting (Stein 1983).

[2] According to Arthur Norton, assistant chief of the U.S. Census Bureau's population division, historically only 5 percent of Americans have remained never-married singles throughout their lives; he estimates, however, that among Americans alive today, this percentage has at least doubled to 10 percent (Norton and Miller 1991).

[3] For a fascinating study of the emergence of socially and economically independent young women, see Ruth Freeman and Patricia Klaus, "Blessed or Not? The New Spinster in England and the United States in the Late Nineteenth and Early Twentieth Centuries," *Journal of Family History* 9 (Winter 1984): 394–414.

In fact, the emancipation of single women has occurred so recently in our society that language has not yet caught up with social reality: There is no word in our language for the female equivalent of a bachelor. The term *female bachelor* would be a contradiction in terms because a bachelor is by definition an unmarried man. (In feudal times, the term *bachelor* referred to a young knight who was in the service of another knight.) *Bachelorette* has sexist overtones (a mini-bachelor?), and the term *spinster* (which was originally used in the twelfth century to refer to a woman who earned her living with a spinning wheel) is archaic. The term *old maid* was widely used until fairly recently but is now archaic (and probably inaccurate, for originally a "maid" or "maiden" was a virgin). An unmarried, independent woman today is usually neither old nor a "maiden."

Attitudes Toward Singles

Americans have long regarded singles—men and women alike—with a mixture of scorn, tolerance, and condescension. During the colonial period, singles were penalized by higher taxes, presumably to encourage marriage and the production of children (Murstein 1974).

In 1960, four out of five adults believed that a never-married woman over age thirty was likely to be sick, neurotic, or immoral; only one in four adults believed this in 1978. A widely held stereotype portrayed never-married women over age thirty, and never-married men over age forty, as homosexual, asexual, or otherwise abnormal (Yankelovitch 1981).

Social science professionals also believed that never-married middle-aged singles were abnormal. Psychologists and sociologists typically regarded middle-aged singlehood as an aberration that needed to be explained. These pro-

fessionals focused on factors that supposedly interrupted the normal process leading to marriage, citing physical disability, illness, mental incompetence, social ineptness, selfishness, or prolonged immaturity as explanations for middle-aged, never-married singlehood. Some professionals also cited such less-judgmental explanations as religion, military service, or prison. Others pointed out that a man might be unable to marry because he was responsible for aged parents; the death of a parent might be a turning point in a bachelor's life—a watershed event that allowed him to consider marriage seriously for the first time (Buunk and van Driel 1989).

Present-day psychologists and sociologists no longer regard never-married singlehood in middle age as an *aberration* but as a *variant*—a variation in life-style that does not imply some sort of physical, emotional, or social pathology. (Buunk and van Driel 1989).

Rising Incidence of Singles

About forty-nine million Americans twenty-five years of age and older are never-married, divorced, or widowed. Some of these are cohabiting but are nonetheless considered to be single by demographers, as noted. The number of married people in our society has increased only 19 percent since 1970, whereas the number of singles has increased by 85 percent. Thus the number of singles has grown more than four times as fast as the number of married people—a truly dramatic change in the composition of America (DeWitt 1992).

Nearly three-fourths of young women (eighteen to twenty-four years of age) were single in 1990, compared with just half of women of this age in 1970. Among women in their late twenties (twenty-five to twenty-nine), nearly 40 percent were single in 1990, compared with just

15 percent in 1970. Similar increases took place in other age groups.[4]

Nearly half of all men in their twenties were single in 1990, whereas only about one in five were single in 1970. More than one in three men in their early thirties (thirty to thirty-four) were single in 1990; only slightly more than one in ten were single in 1970.[5]

The rapid rise in the incidence of singlehood as a life-style in the United States has had a considerable effect on family structure and function, as we will see (Chapter 8).

Never-Married Singles

Never-married singles have contributed the most to the rapid rise in singlehood as a life-style, although the incidence of divorced singles has been rising almost as rapidly (see the later section). In 1990, nearly two-thirds of young women (twenty to twenty-four years of age) had never married, compared with only one-third in 1970. In 1990, one in three women in their late twenties (twenty-five to twenty-nine) had never married, compared with only one in ten in 1970.[6]

In 1990, three-fourths of young men (ages twenty to twenty-four) had never married, compared with just one-half in 1970. Nearly half (45 percent) of those in their late twenties (twenty-five to twenty-nine) had never married, compared with just one in ten in 1970. In their early thirties (ages thirty to thirty-four) 27 percent had never married, compared with just 9 percent in 1970.[7]

Effects of Higher Education on Singlehood Among Women

Increasing numbers of young women have been entering college since the mid-twentieth century; the proportion of college students who are women has been steadily rising. In 1985 — for the first time in history — there were more women than men in four-year colleges.[8]

The rising number of young women going to college is directly related to the rising number of young single women: When women go to college they usually marry later. Women who graduate from college generally postpone marriage even longer.[9] As college graduates they have earned the chance of entry into interesting and well-paying jobs. These young women often wish to remain unmarried and live independently for a time while they pursue a career. Studies find that women who remain single through graduate school are more successful in their careers than other women (Houseknecht, Vaughan, and Statham 1987).

Many reasons have been suggested why highly educated women are more likely to remain never-married than other women. Many professional women and executives may be choosing career over marriage. Perhaps these women have difficulty finding suitable marriage partners because men tend to avoid marrying women with more education or more status than themselves (see the section "The Dating Differential" in Chapter 5). It has also been suggested that highly educated women may be

[4]U.S. Bureau of the Census, *Current Population Reports*, P-20, No. 450, March 1990; *Current Population Reports*, 1970 revised. Washington, D.C.: Government Printing Office, 1991.

[5]U.S. Bureau of the Census, *Current Population Reports*.

[6]U.S. Bureau of the Census, "Marital Status and Living Arrangements: March 1990" (1991).

[7]U.S. Bureau of the Census, "Marital Status."

[8]U.S. Department of Education, Center for Education Statistics, "Enrollment in Institutions of Higher Education, by Sex, Age, and Attendance, 1970 to 1985, and Projections, 1995" (1988).

[9]"Marital Status."

more selective and thus meet fewer marriage prospects (Sweet and Bumpass 1987).

Age at First Marriage

The rapidly increasing numbers of never-married singles do not necessarily mean that fewer people are marrying (Bumpass, Sweet, and Cherlin 1991). One explanation for the rising incidence of never-married singles is simply that the age at first marriage has been rising—for both men and women. In 1960, when the uptrend in singlehood started, the median age at first marriage for women was 20.3; in 1990, it was 23.9, an increase of nearly four years. For men, the median age at first marriage increased approximately proportionately, from 22.8 to 26.1.[10] This uptrend in median age at first marriage reversed a long-term downtrend since 1890 (see Table 6-1).

It is not clear what proportion of people now in their twenties and thirties will never marry. Historically this proportion has remained close to 5 percent (Sweet and Bumpass 1987). Some demographers project that if present trends continue, one white woman in ten (10 percent) and four black women in ten (40 percent) will never marry (Norton and Miller 1991). Other demographers have used the same data to predict that we will return to the previous pattern, at least for whites—that 5 percent of whites will remain never-married while the proportion will be much higher for blacks (Wilson 1991).

Minority Groups and Singlehood

Never-Married Blacks More than one-third as many blacks as whites have never been married at ages thirty-five to forty. This growing difference between white and black women has been

[10] "Marital Status."

TABLE 6-1

Median Age at First Marriage, 1890–1990

Year	Females	Males
1990	23.9	26.1
1980	22.0	24.7
1970	20.8	23.2
1960	20.3	22.8
1950	20.3	22.8
1940	21.5	24.3
1930	21.3	24.3
1920	21.2	24.6
1910	21.6	25.1
1900	21.9	25.9
1890	22.0	26.1

Source: U.S. Bureau of the Census, "Marital Status and Living Arrangements: March 1990," by Arlene F. Saluter, Current Population Reports, Series P-20, No. 450, Table A, p. 1 (Washington, D.C.: Government Printing Office, May 1991).

emphasized by researchers, who point out that whereas historically black women have generally married later than white women, by 1975 almost the same proportion of women of both groups had married by their forties. In that year about 96 percent of white women and 90 percent of black women had been married by their late thirties; fifteen years later—in 1990—these figures were 91 percent for white women and 75 percent for black women (Norton and Miller 1991).

Other demographers predict that if current trends continue, by the end of the century the *majority* of adult blacks will never have married

(Stein 1981; Staples 1981). With the current population, the proportion of never-married blacks past age sixty-five is about the same as the proportion of never-married whites of this age group (Buunk and van Driel 1989).

Other Racial-Ethnic Groups Asian-Americans are even more likely than black women to be never-married in their early twenties. Hispanic-Americans are less likely to be single than white women in their early twenties; among Hispanics, Mexican-American marriage rates are similar to those of whites (Sweet and Bumpass 1987). Japanese, Hawaiian, and Puerto Rican men and Filipino and Puerto Rican women have higher than average rates of never-married singles compared with our overall population (Sweet and Bumpass 1987). On the other hand, among Vietnamese, Filipino, Chinese, and Indian men and Chinese-American women, the proportion of never-married singles is lower than it is among our overall population. Korean-Americans have an especially low proportion of never-married singles (Sweet and Bumpass 1987).

Divorced Singles

The numbers of divorced singles has increased sharply in the United States, with the divorce rate doubling from the 1960s to the 1980s (see Chapter 12). More than one million people were divorced each year during the 1980s.[11] In addition to the rising numbers of divorced people, the remarriage rate of divorced singles has been shrinking, and the number of divorced people who never remarry has been growing. Also, for those who do remarry, the length of time between divorce and remarriage has been length-

ening (Wilson 1991). Moreover, the incidence of divorce in remarriages is about 50 percent higher than it is for a first marriage, as we will see. All of these trends have resulted in a sharp increase in the number of divorced singles (Wilson 1991; Norton and Moorman 1987).

Widowed Singles

There was no increase in the incidence of widowed singles in our society from the 1960s to the 1980s. There are, however, more widows than widowers — about five times as many.[12] There are two reasons why widows outnumber widowers by a ratio of about five to one. First, women live about seven years longer than men.[13] Second, the average wife in our society is nearly three years younger than her husband (see Chapter 5). For these two reasons, the average wife can expect to be a widow for about ten years (seven plus three). Because there are about five widows for every widower, widows have a far lower statistical expectation for remarriage than widowers do.

Staying Single or Marrying

Some singles are actively dating in expectation of marriage in the immediate future. Others expect to be married sometime but are not anticipating marriage in the near future. Others would like to be married but have no realistic expectation for marriage. Still other singles are perfectly content with their life-style and have

---

[11]U.S. National Center for Health Statistics, "Marriages and Divorces — Number and Rate, by State: 1980 to 1988" (1990).

[12]In 1988, 12.2 percent of women in our society were widows, compared with 2.7 percent of men. U.S. Bureau of the Census, "Marital Status of the Population, by Sex and Age, 1989" (1991).

[13]In 1988, women in the United States could expect to live an average of 78.5 years, compared with 71.8 years for men. U.S. National Center for Health Statistics, "Expectation for Life at Birth: 1960 to 1989, and Projections, 1990 to 2010" (1991).

no intention of ever marrying. In other words, some people are temporary singles — either voluntarily or involuntarily — whereas other people are permanent singles, either voluntarily or involuntarily.

Temporary Singles

Temporary singles view singlehood as an interim period preceding eventual marriage. For many of these singles, serious dating may be the central focus of their lives.

Other singles may be actively dating but do not view marriage as an immediate concern. Some may be postponing marriage because they are absorbed with other interests (such as education or career). Others may feel that they are not yet ready to limit their experiences of intimacy, commitment, and involvement to just one person. Still others may not wish to exchange their freedom for the responsibilities and constraints of marriage. Others may simply be waiting for the "right one" and feel no urgency; in the meantime, while waiting to fall in love they are enjoying singlehood and dating.

Singles Past Age Thirty-Five Singles who are past age thirty-five are usually regarded as "late-marrying." Because there are significant differences between the characteristics and the opportunities of late-marrying women and late-marrying men, we will consider each in turn.

Late-Marrying Women Women past age thirty-five who wish to marry have only a 60 percent chance of doing so, and this percentage drops sharply with each passing year.[14] One reason is simply the demographic realities. At age thirty-five, women outnumber men by a ratio of 5 to 4;

at age forty-five, the ratio is 2 to 1, and at age sixty, it is 4 to 1. These ratios indicate a relatively low statistical probability of marriage for women simply because there are relatively few available prospects.[15]

Although women over age thirty-five may feel that eligible men prefer younger women, this is not always the case. Most men prefer a woman who is just slightly younger, for they often find these women more sexually, intellectually, and emotionally interesting than much younger women. Men who marry after age forty-five, for example, usually marry women who are about forty-one (Lovenheim 1987).

The mid-thirties can be an uncomfortable period for a single woman as she sees more and more of her friends get married. This is also a critical period for a single woman because the biological deadline for bearing children is nearing. She may feel that if she is to ever become a mother, it is a case of "now or never." Because of the demographics that limit the number of available men, this period can be a very trying and difficult one for many single women (Buunk and van Driel 1989).

One of the characteristics of women who marry for the first time after age thirty-five is that they typically have a high level of self-confidence. These women are usually "persistent, self-confident, clever about creating opportunities, focused, and willing to endure rejection" (Lovenheim 1987, p. 14).

Late-Marrying Men Men past age thirty-five have fewer problems finding marriage prospects because they typically date and marry relatively more abundant younger women. Thus, the demographics work in men's favor, just as they work against women.

---

[14]U.S. Bureau of the Census, "Resident Population by Age, Sex, and Race: 1970 to 1989" (1991).

[15]U.S. Bureau of the Census, "Marital Status of the Population, by Sex and Age: 1989" (1991).

Moreover, studies find that late-marrying bachelors are not under the pressure to marry that women are. For men, peer pressure to marry is more characteristic of their adolescent and early adult years. Thus a late-marrying bachelor can, if he wishes, enjoy his freedom from the responsibilities of marriage with little peer pressure and with the knowledge that he will have plenty of available prospects if and when he chooses to marry (Buunk and van Driel 1989). In addition, men are under less pressure from a biological deadline for having children than women are (see Chapter 4).

Middle-aged bachelors are often more committed to their career than are women, and they are also more often committed to a responsibility for aging parents. As we have seen, the death of a parent is often a turning point in a late-marrying bachelor's life, allowing him to consider marriage seriously for the first time (Buunk and van Driel 1989).

A study (Waehler 1991) of never-married heterosexual men in their forties found three characteristic personality types:

- Men who are able to form significant relationships but do not wish to. These men are satisfied with their life-style and prefer to remain unattached and single for the time being. These single men, who might be classified as satisfied and flexible, constitute 20 percent of all never-married heterosexual men in their forties.

- Men who are satisfied with their life-style but are rigid. These men lack warm feelings for others, want to avoid commitment, and prefer to limit their relationships to shared activities (tennis, squash, golf) rather than risk intimacy. These men make up about 30 percent of the total group.

- Men who are dissatisfied with their life-style and their emotional lives. These men crave close relationships but are unable to form

them. They retreat from intimacy because it is too demanding and restrictive. About half (50 percent) of the total group may be classified as dissatisfied.

Thus, about half of all single heterosexual men in their forties are satisfied and happy with their life-style — whether "satisfied but rigid" (30 percent) or "satisfied and flexible" (20 percent). These men feel no pressure to marry, are successful and reasonably content, and exhibit no physical, emotional, or social pathology. The other half are dissatisfied with their life-style and fear intimacy and the risk of vulnerability in a close relationship (Waehler 1991).

Permanent Singles

Some permanent singles may not be interested in marriage either because they have a relatively low sex drive or because they may be erotophobic and have an antipathy toward sex (see Chapter 4). Others cannot imagine themselves ever falling in love (see Chapter 3). Still others may never marry because they are obligative homosexuals (see Chapter 4).[16] Some permanent singles would like to be married but have only marginal prospects for marriage because of physical, psychological, or social handicaps.

It would be fatuous, however, to suggest that never-married singles are necessarily deficient or inadequate. Our world has benefited enormously from people who voluntarily remained single throughout their lives; a few notable examples are Plato, Isaac Newton, Leonardo da Vinci, Jonathan Swift, John Keats, Henry David Thoreau, Edward Albee, Elizabeth I of England, Florence Nightingale, Emily Dickinson, Willa Cather, and Marian Anderson.

---

[16]Even though some religious orders will perform homosexual marriages, demographers still classify the two people in such marriages as single.

Some singles may choose to remain unmarried (*celibate*) for religious reasons. Roman Catholic priests, monks, and nuns *must* remain celibate. Other singles have only a scant chance for marriage because demographics are against them; thus large numbers of widowed women remain single simply because there are relatively few available men. Some divorced singles may be so disillusioned by a first marriage that they do not want to try again.

There are disproportionately large numbers of single black women compared with white women. This disparity can be traced, in part, to the relatively high mortality among black men, the large numbers of black men in prison, the relatively higher rates of homosexuality among black men compared with whites, and the fact that more black men marry white women than black women marry white men. Moreover, black women tend to be more highly educated than black men and don't wish to marry "down"—an example of the dating differential (Buunk and van Driel 1989). Black women are more likely to be committed to upward mobility than are black men and see upward mobility as incompatible with marriage (Higgenbotham 1981). Black college women often prefer to stay single, whereas black college men do not (Rao and Rao 1980).

Life-styles of Singles

Singles cannot be stereotyped and are as different from each other as people who are married. Next we will consider some aspects of singles' life-styles.

Living Arrangements

A single person's living arrangement is one of the key determinants of his or her life-style. It makes a big difference whether a single is living with family, is sharing an apartment, is living alone in a single-person household, or is living in group quarters.

The most significant determinant of a single's living arrangement is age. Demographers have identified some critical ages as they relate to living arrangements (Sweet and Bumpass 1987).

At age eighteen, 75 percent of singles live with their parents and are under their parents' supervision. Only 5 percent of men and 8 percent of women are living on their own in nonfamily households. Many singles are still in high school; some are in college and are living in dorms or rooming houses; others have graduated from high school or dropped out of school and are working or are unemployed; still others are in the army or in prison.

At age twenty-one about half of all singles are living with their parents, about 10 percent are in college dorms or rooming houses, about 25 percent of men and nearly 30 percent of women are living on their own in nonfamily households, and about 8 percent are living alone in one-person households. About 5 percent of women are "family heads," many of whom are unmarried mothers living with their children.

At age twenty-four about 40 percent of singles are living with their parents.

At age twenty-nine about 25 percent of singles still live with their parents.[17] About 60 percent of single men and 50 percent of single women live on their own in nonfamily households, most living by themselves in single-person households. About 17 percent of single women are family heads living with their children.

Consider the following information concerning living arrangements among racial-ethnic groups (Sweet and Bumpass 1987):

---

[17]Among women ages twenty-five to thirty-four, nearly three in ten who had children of their own were living with their children in their parents' household. U.S. Bureau of the Census, "Marital Status and Living Arrangements: March 1989" (1990).

- Single black women of all ages are more likely to be a family head and are much more likely to have their own children in the household.

- Single black men of all ages are more likely to be living in group quarters, such as army barracks or prisons.

- Single black men and women of all ages are more likely to be living in the household of a relative, are less likely to be living alone or with roommates, and are less likely to be living in college dorms or rooming houses.

- A significantly higher proportion of Mexican-Americans (64 percent) and Cubans (78 percent) ages eighteen to twenty-four live with their parents.

- Among college students ages eighteen to twenty-two, about 45 percent of whites and 50 percent of blacks live with their parents.

Movement into Cities

Singles who are not living with their parents, in college dorms or rooming houses, in army barracks, or in prison tend to drift to large metropolitan areas (Carter and Glick 1976). During the mid-1980s, singles accounted for more than a fourth of home sales and more than half of condominium sales in New York, San Francisco, and Los Angeles, cities that had the most populous single communities (Syrzycki and Walsh 1986).

Singles tend to congregate in urban areas to join a community of other singles — those with similar interests and life-styles. Large metropolitan areas offer more opportunities for finding congenial companions, making friends, and seeking sexual conquests, and perhaps for falling in love. Socializing in small towns usually takes place in private homes and is dominated by married couples.

Loneliness

Among the best aspects of being single is the freedom it provides. Freedom and lack of responsibility or commitment are often the aspects of singlehood that a person misses most after marriage. Singles have freedom to search for adventure and romance, and the uncertainty of the search adds zest to the chase. This search for romantic adventure is expected to end with marriage.

Paradoxically, however, this search for adventure and romance can also be a source of emotional pain, discouragement, loneliness, and depression. The worst aspect of singlehood can be a lack of significant relationships.

A lack of friendship, companionship, and intimacy can lead to profound loneliness. About one-fourth of singles — men and women alike — report loneliness as their chief problem (Simenauer and Carroll 1982). The late teenage years are often the loneliest part of a person's life; however, singles in their twenties, thirties, and forties are also often chronically lonely (Simenauer and Carroll 1982; Lopata 1979).

The foundation of successful socializing and relating to the opposite gender is normally established during adolescence. An adolescent who dates only rarely and misses the opportunity to acquire the social skills of listening, responding, and flirting is likely to be chronically lonely as an adult, for these skills are more difficult to acquire later in life (Burns 1986; Peplau 1986; Weiss 1981).

Close, caring friendships can provide social continuity and the basic satisfactions of sharing. Friendships may not only be a major source of emotional support but may even mean emotional survival for singles — not only during difficult times but during trouble-free times as well (Stein 1981).

Because of the problem of loneliness, one of the chief preoccupations for singles — especially

The single life may appear full of adventure and romance, but for many singles the reality is occasional or persistent loneliness.

those who are living alone — is to develop and maintain close ties and significant friendships. A person's self-concept largely depends on the responses of friends. A single who has only secondary relationships with other people may feel anonymous and fragmented (Case et al. 1992; Avery 1989; Perlman and Duck 1987).

Our society mistakenly considers loneliness to be primarily a women's problem. This may be because women are more apt to admit feeling lonely, whereas men are more apt to deny it (Weiss 1981). Studies indicate that the proportions of single people who are severely lonely are about the same for men and women. It is apparently no easier for a man to find a companion, friend, or lover than it is for a woman (Weiss 1981).

Although it has long been traditional in our society for men to initiate relationships (to "make the first move"), this male prerogative apparently is no advantage in finding companionship or establishing a relationship and avoiding loneliness.

Loneliness cannot be ended merely by ending *aloneness*; loneliness will not yield to just any sort of social interaction. In fact, random socializing may actually increase loneliness. Thus a lonely person might feel excruciatingly alone in the midst of a group. Loneliness may be ended only by establishing an intimate relationship (Stein 1981).

One of the major problems of loneliness is that it normally leads to severe, chronic depression. Divorced singles are usually more prone to depression than never-married singles. Divorced singles find that their level of depression usually increases for about four years following a divorce, unless they establish a new close relationship or remarry (Menaghan and Lieberman 1986).

It is interesting to note that a divorced single parent with custody of several children is usually more depressed than a divorced single parent who has custody of only one child. In general, the level of depression increases as the number of children in the household increases. Exactly the opposite is true for married couples with children: As the number of children in the household increases, the level of depression decreases. These opposite experiences of depression between singles with children and married couples with children is quite marked (Pearlin and Johnson 1981).

In addition to depression, loneliness is often associated with chronic illness. Singles tend to have more physical and psychological complaints and ailments than married people and have a shorter life expectancy. Singles living alone have a relatively higher incidence of diabetes, pneumonia, rheumatic fever, cirrhosis of the liver, and cancer. Social isolation, the lack of companionship, and loneliness are significant contributors to premature death. When matched for age, occupation, and other characteristics, nearly twice as many single men die of heart disease as do married men. Heart attack survivors who live alone are almost twice as likely as those who live with other people to have a second heart attack and to die from it (Case et al. 1992; Lynch 1977).

Looking for Sex

Unless they are cohabiting, singles do not have ready access to sex. Not surprisingly, then, many singles are preoccupied with the search for sexual encounters.

Sex can be a powerful drive, although the degree to which individuals are driven by sexual urgencies varies according to where they are on the erotophile-erotophobe scale. A person very low on the scale would have a low sexual drive and would be mainly preoccupied with such things as studies, thoughts of career, or religion (this is not to say that a religious person is necessarily asexual). On the other hand, a person high on the erotophile-erotophobe scale might find sexual needs so pressing that sexual matters color virtually all thoughts, dreams, plans, and activities.

Singles are often thought of as having a constant stream of encounters with interesting, fascinating people, believed not only to lead exciting social lives but also to have a wide variety of encounters with attractive, glamorous, romantic, and willing sexual partners. Although undoubtedly some singles match this stereotype, research reveals that swinging singleness is enjoyed by relatively few. Most singles in a popular "body-exchange hangout" end up going home without a sexual companion for the night. For single women who are sexually active but not cohabiting, sexual encounters are rarely the result of a pickup at a singles bar or meeting place but instead usually occur within in the context of friendship, trust, affection, and intimacy. This fact severely limits the opportunities of the sexually driven male who is searching for quick sex with no commitment (Tanfer 1987).

A national study (Tanfer 1987) found that a majority (58 percent) of single women in their twenties were not sexually active at the time of the interview (unless they were cohabiting; most single women in their twenties who are sexually active are cohabiting). Moreover, women who were sexually active had copulated with a lifetime total of just four or five different men; about half of these affairs had been with a long-term boyfriend (Tanfer 1987). According to this study, then, most single women in their twenties who are not cohabiting have few sexual encounters, and a sizable number have no sexual encounters at all.

Cohabiting Singles

Cohabitation is defined as living together in a sexual relationship without being married. Few singles deliberately decide to cohabit; instead, they usually drift into a pattern of staying together at one or the other's place more and more often, until they find that most of their belongings have accumulated at one person's place. They are now essentially living together at the same residence, and because it doesn't make much sense to keep paying rent on two places, it becomes more economical to cohabit (Macklin 1988).

Some couples do deliberately decide to cohabit. For some of these couples, the proposition "Will you live with me?" may replace the traditional proposal "Will you marry me?" (Others deliberately cohabit as a kind of "trial marriage" and eventually do marry.) Presumably the suggestion to cohabit would be preceded by a declaration of love, unless the proposed cohabitation is to be very casual. In such a very casual relationship, convenience, affection, and sexual compatibility may be the basis for the cohabitation rather than love, which usually implies commitment.

Changes in Attitudes and Incidence of Cohabitation

As recently as 1968, middle-class cohabitation was so rare that when a female student at Barnard College was discovered living off campus with a male student from Columbia University, the story made the front pages of major newspapers throughout the United States and was featured

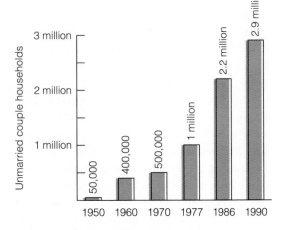

As currently defined by the Census Bureau, an unmarried couple is two people of the opposite sex who share living quarters.

F I G U R E   6 - 1

The rise in cohabitation in the United States,
1950–1990.

Source: Data from U.S. Bureau of the Census, "Marital Status and Living Arrangements: March 1990" (1991) and from Glick (1988).

in a lead article in *Time* magazine. The incidence of cohabitation in the United States has been steadily rising from a negligible 50,000 households in 1950 to 2.9 million households in 1990 (see Figure 6-1).

Before 1960, cohabitation was rare and was virtually limited to the lower class. Our society seemed committed to the belief that sexual relations were illicit outside the sanctity of marriage. Religious and lay establishments alike viewed cohabitation as a violation of fundamental ethical and moral principles.

A parent who discovered that a daughter was living with a young man to whom she was not married might well have been shocked, appalled, outraged, and ashamed. When faced with the reality of a cohabiting daughter (see Box 6-1),

BOX 6-1

Demographic Characteristics of Cohabiting Women[a]

- The lower a woman's education level is, the more likely she will be to cohabit. Women who have less than a high school education are three times as likely to cohabit as college-educated women — 23 percent vs. 7 percent.

- Cohabitation is more common among women in the lower and lower-middle classes.

- Women who grow up in single-parent families are more likely to cohabit than women who grow up in intact families.

- Women who become sexually experienced early in their teens are more likely to cohabit than are other women.

- Never-married women who have had children are twice as likely to be cohabit-

ing or to have cohabited than are never-married women who have not had children.

- Women who are unemployed are much more likely to cohabit than are employed women.

- Catholic and non-Catholic women are equally likely to cohabit, but women who indicate no religious preference are more likely to cohabit (48 percent) than women who have a religious affiliation (28 percent). Frequency of church attendance is negatively correlated with incidence of cohabitation: The higher the frequency of attendance, the lower the incidence of cohabitation.

- Birth of a child to a cohabiting woman usually precipitates either marriage or the breakup of the relationship.

[a]Bumpass, Sweet, and Cherlin 1991; Tanfer 1987.

parents often refused to acknowledge the situation. When ultimately forced to confront it, many refused to meet the young man; some parents even refused to continue a relationship with their daughter. These parental attitudes often remained unmollified until after the couple married, when a grandchild would usually bring about a reconciliation. Because of the double standard in our society (see Chapter 4), parents were more likely to accept a cohabiting son than a cohabiting daughter. Parents were more apt to

view a cohabiting son with sorrow rather than grief.

Cohabitation was not only considered illicit and immoral; it was illegal in most states. In these states, copulation between an unmarried couple was formally defined by statutory law as *fornication*, which is a felony. (Cohabitation is still illegal in some states, although these states rarely enforce such laws; a couple might be well advised to check the current law in their own state before deciding to cohabit.)

The condemnation of cohabitation as illicit and unacceptable began to soften after 1960 (as part of the changes of the Gender-Role Revolution; see Chapter 9). In 1970, 11 percent of never-married people cohabited before marrying (Bumpass and Sweet 1989a). By the early 1980s a national survey found that only slightly more than half of our population (52 percent) still felt that it was morally wrong for unmarried couples to live together in a sexual relationship (Yankelovich 1981). In the late 1980s, about a fourth (23 percent) of those interviewed in a Gallup poll said they would object to having cohabitors as neighbors (Gallup 1989b). By 1990 nearly half of never-married people, and about 60 percent of previously-married people, cohabited first (Bumpass, Sweet, and Cherlin 1991; Bumpass 1990).

Nearly 60 percent of cohabiting couples are never-married singles. Nearly 40 percent are separated or divorced singles, and a few (about 3 percent) are widowed.[18]

Despite the rise in incidence of cohabitation, there are many more married couples than cohabiting couples. In 1988, 95 percent of couples sharing a household in a sexual relationship were married; just 5 percent were cohabiting.[19] This is a fivefold increase from 1960, when only 1 percent of couples sharing a household in a sexual relationship were cohabiting (Nord and Zill 1991).

Cohabiting couples are, on the average, some six to seven years older than most couples at first marriage (Macklin 1988). Most cohabitors (about 60 percent) are between twenty-five and forty-four years of age, about 20 percent are under age 25, and about 20 percent are older than forty-four.[20]

The most common image of cohabiting couples — college students or young couples — does not usually include a family with children. Yet in 1990 about 40 percent of cohabiting couples had children living in the household. One-third of those couples had never married, and nearly half included previously married cohabitors. About one in six (17 percent) never-married cohabiting couples has a child that was born since they began living together. "In cohabitation, issues of parenting (and stepparenting) are very much a part of the picture" (Bumpass, Sweet, and Cherlin 1991, pp. 919–20).

Cohabitation tends to be a short-lived state. Rarely does a couple cohabit for more than about three years. By this time, a decision is usually made to either marry or separate. Very rarely does a couple continue to cohabit as a semipermanent or even permanent alternative to marriage (Bumpass 1989; Macklin 1988; Tanfer 1987). "Only about one in 10 remain cohabiting after 5 years without either marrying or breaking up." Duration of cohabitation is longest among previously married people (Bumpass, Sweet, and Cherlin 1991, p. 919).

Most cohabitors expect to marry, although never-married cohabitors are more inclined to marry than previously married cohabitors. About four of five (81 percent) never-married cohabitors and three of five (61 percent) previously married cohabitors plan to marry their cohabitor. Although only about 13 percent of never-married cohabitors expect never to marry, nearly a third (30 percent) of previously married cohabitors never expect to remarry (Bumpass, Sweet, and Cherlin 1991).

When cohabitors separate, the impact of the break is proportional to the extent of the emo-

---

[18]"Marital Status."

[19]Census data indicate that some 2.6 million unmarried heterosexual couples were cohabiting in 1988, as compared to 54.4 million married couples ("Marital Status").

[20]"Marital Status"; U.S. Bureau of the Census, "Unmarried Couples, by Selected Characteristics, 1970 to 1989, and by Marital Status of Partners" (1991).

tional investment each person has in the relationship. The trauma may be minimal for casual cohabitors, but for those who are deeply involved the trauma of separation may be as great as that in divorce, including denial, anger, and grief (Macklin 1988).

Marriages preceded by cohabitation have a 50 percent higher divorce rate than other marriages (Bumpass and Sweet 1989b). One reason for the high divorce rate for cohabitors who subsequently marry may be that they represent a population that holds less traditional family values than those who do not cohabit before marrying. In one study, three-fourths of couples who did not cohabit before marrying said that they regarded marriage as a lifelong commitment, whereas only 55 percent of those who cohabited before marrying viewed marriage this seriously (Bumpass 1989).

Forces Underlying the Emergence of Cohabitation

Reasons for the emergence of widespread cohabitation are many and complex. Some of the reasons are societal and may be traced to fundamental shifts in our culture, whereas others involve the preferences of individuals who choose to cohabit rather than marry. We will describe these factors in the three lists that follow.

Cultural Changes That Favor Cohabitation

- Sexuality outside of marriage has become increasingly acceptable. There is greater acceptance of sexuality simply for physical pleasure and as an expression of affection and intimacy not necessarily related to reproduction.
- The women's movement has sought for women the same rights and privileges as those enjoyed by men.

- More women are postponing marriage to acquire the education and training necessary to establish themselves in a career.
- Working, career-oriented, professional women may cohabit as a realistic compromise that avoids the loneliness of the unattached single while retaining freedom to build their careers. This is a quasi-marriage without the commitment or the legal responsibilities of marriage (Osius 1991).
- Reliable, effective, and easy-to-use contraception is now available. It is no coincidence that societal acceptance of cohabitation has followed the development of the contraceptive pill in the 1960s (Makepeace 1975).

Reasons Women and Men Give for Cohabiting[21]

- To test compatibility before marriage (56 percent of women, 51 percent of men).
- To share living expenses (26 percent of women, 28 percent of men).
- Is more sexually satisfying than dating (18 percent of women, 17 percent of men).
- Allows more independence than marriage (19 percent of women, 17 percent of men).
- Requires less commitment than marriage (18 percent of women, 14 percent of men).
- Requires less sexual faithfulness than marriage (10 percent of women, 12 percent of men).

Reasons Women and Men Give for *Not* Cohabiting[21]

- Requires more sexual faithfulness than dating (28 percent of women, 24 percent of men).

---

[21]Data from Bumpass, Sweet, and Cherlin 1991, p. 920.

- Requires more commitment than dating (25 percent of women, 19 percent of men).
- Is emotionally risky (18 percent of women, 13 percent of men).
- Parents disapprove (11 percent of women, 8 percent of men).
- Is morally wrong (9 percent of women, 6 percent of men).
- Is financially risky (7 percent of women, 7 percent of men).
- Friends disapprove (4 percent of women, 4 percent of men).

A couple may decide to cohabit to avoid paying a higher income tax, although there are no data on how often this occurs. This "marriage tax" may be a significant sum, depending on each partner's income.[22]

Finally, seniors may decide to cohabit for the same reasons that younger people do or to avoid the complications of merging their financial assets.

Problems Cohabitors Commonly Face

Cohabiting couples have some problems that married couples do not have. Chief among these problems are lack of norms, violence, legal problems, and dealing with children in a family structure that is not sanctified by marriage.

Lack of Norms   Cohabitation is such a recently widespread life-style that societal norms have not yet had time to develop. For example, there is still no word that is commonly used in our language to describe people who live together outside of marriage. (The term *cohabitor* is accurate and precise but is rarely used in everyday speech.) The absence of a commonly accepted term for a cohabitor underlines the ambiguous nature of cohabitation in our society.

This ambiguity is dramatized virtually every time a cohabitor introduces his or her partner — what does one call a person with whom one is cohabiting? Cohabitors often use the terms "girlfriend" or "boyfriend," but these terms are neither accurate nor appropriate because they do not express (or even imply) a live-in relationship. Thus, girlfriend and boyfriend are not only imprecise but misleading.

A cohabitor may introduce his or her partner as a "friend," but this also fails to define the relationship accurately. Cohabitors rarely use the term "housemate," which is accurate but imprecise. The U.S. Bureau of the Census has adopted the acronym POSSLQ (Persons of the Opposite Sex Sharing Living Quarters) to designate cohabitors, but this is too clumsy to achieve popular usage. LIL (live-in lover) is both precise and accurate but has never achieved popular usage.

A cohabitor may avoid the issue simply by introducing his or her partner by name or by neglecting to introduce the partner at all. However, refusing to acknowledge a relationship in this way could imply that it is illicit or shameful, and the partner who is not acknowledged may feel hurt, angry, and rejected.

Common issues with respect to cohabitation that currently have no normative society-wide solutions include the following (Macklin 1988):

- What happens if a woman gets pregnant?
- What happens to assets if the couple separate, or if one of the couple dies?
- What is to be the attitude toward sharing the rent, household costs, food, eating out, and vacations?
- To what extent will decisions be made jointly?

---

[22]A married couple filing jointly will pay a higher income tax than the same couple who are unmarried and file separate returns (see Chapter 14).

- What is to be the attitude toward relatives?
- If children are involved, what is to be the attitude toward them?

A cohabiting person may feel uncomfortable bringing up any of these issues because to do so would imply a permanent relationship, which might be presumptuous and might well introduce still further problems (Macklin 1988).

Violence in Cohabitation A survey of 6,000 couples found that violence occurs more than twice as often among cohabiting couples as among married couples (35 percent compared with 14 percent). These incidents of violence include everything from slaps to homicide (Straus 1988).

Studies find that the chief sources for violence between cohabitors are a lack of emotional investment in the relationship and a greater isolation from family and friends than is common among married couples. Another source of the greater incidence of violence between cohabitors is poverty, for the pressures of poverty can lead to violence (Straus 1988). Poverty is more characteristic of cohabitation than it is of marriage because most cohabitors are in the lower classes, as we have seen.

This is not to say that violence within couples does not occur in the middle class; violence within couples cuts across all social classes, as we will see in Chapter 8.

Legal Ramifications of Cohabitation Legal implications of cohabitation vary widely from state to state; in some states it is illegal for an unmarried couple to live together as husband and wife. As noted earlier, these states define copulation between unmarried people as fornication, which is a statutory crime.

If a cohabiting woman becomes pregnant and bears the child, the child is born out of wedlock and is legally classified as illegitimate (a bastard). Illegitimate children are subject to many legal and social difficulties in all states. The U.S. Supreme Court ruled in 1977 that a state may not totally bar an illegitimate child's inheritance if the father dies intestate (without leaving a will), but this ruling does not mean that illegitimate children must be given the same rights of inheritance as legitimate children.

Although the legal ramifications of cohabitation are still being worked out by the courts, a cohabiting couple deny themselves protections provided by law even in states in which cohabitation is not illegal. If a cohabiting couple break up, there may be serious problems dividing the assets. In all states, if one of the cohabiting couple dies intestate, all of the deceased person's property will be inherited by relatives.

In some states one cohabitor may sue the other for an equal share of all property acquired during the cohabitation (*Marvin v. Marvin*, 18 Cal. 3d 660, 1976). In other states, if one cohabitor moves out, takes all the assets, and leaves the other destitute, the abandoned person has little recourse to the law—unless he or she can prove in court (which can be costly) precisely who paid what for which items.

Children and Cohabitation A cohabiting couple living in a household with children constitutes a *cohabiting family*. This family may contain her children, his children, their children, or a combination of his, hers, and theirs. A cohabiting family may be very stable and may endure for years, or it may be transient. (The cohabiting family form is discussed in Chapter 8.)

Noncustodial parents may object to their children living with a custodial parent who is sharing the household with a live-in lover. The children's grandparents may also object to their grandchildren living in this situation, particularly if there are several successive cohabitors (Macklin 1988).

Although some children accept their parent's live-in lover (perhaps to restore a sense of stability that was lost with the divorce), many children do not and are troubled, upset, or resentful about the situation. They resent the live-in lover as an undesirable intruder who threatens to shatter the exclusivity, intimacy, and closeness they have with their parent. They are uneasy about the implications of a sexual relationship between their parent and a live-in lover. Children often wish for reconciliation of their divorced parents — even though this is unlikely — and they may believe that a live-in lover diminishes this possibility. Serious problems may emerge if sexual overtones develop between an older child and a live-in lover.

Meanwhile, most live-in lovers have difficulty relating to a cohabitor's children. A live-in lover is in much the same position as a stepparent but has more difficulty in fulfilling these roles because his or her status is ambiguous: The live-in lover is neither a parent nor a stepparent but is only occupying a position in the household that would normally be filled by one or the other. There are few norms for this situation, and those that do exist are poorly defined and provide little guidance or authority; the live-in lover does not have the social, ethical, legal, or religious status or backing accorded a parent or a stepparent. Although the role of parent is difficult and the role of stepparent is more difficult, the role of live-in lover is the most difficult of all (Macklin 1988). (For a discussion of the difficult role of stepparent, see Chapter 13).

Cohabitation and Love

There are various types of cohabitation and reasons for cohabiting, as we have seen. Some cohabitations undoubtedly involve love, and others do not.

A couple may casually cohabit for convenience, affection, sexual satisfaction, and economic benefits, so long as this is what they both wish. Other couples may fall in love and decide to cohabit because they are not yet ready for the formal, legal commitment of marriage. For still others a relationship that starts out as casual may deepen, commitment may grow, and the couple may fall in love. Cohabiting couples who do fall in love in this way normally marry.

Cohabitation and Sex

Sexual access to each other in the privacy, comfort, and convenience of their own household is certainly one of the driving forces for cohabitation. Cohabiting couples typically copulate at least three or four times a week. Studies find that sex is a major bond for nearly all (85 to 99 percent) cohabiting couples (Blumstein and Schwartz 1983).

Sexual Satisfaction and Relationship Satisfaction Sex is not only of essential importance in its own right; it is also important because of its influence on almost every aspect of a couple's relationship. A sexual relationship of high quality usually enhances the quality of all of the couple's interactions, but a sexual life of lower quality tends to put a blight on their whole relationship (Blumstein and Schwartz 1983).

There are, of course, great individual differences in the importance of sex for the individual and for the relationship, as we have seen (Chapter 4). If each of the couple is on the low end of the erotophile-erotophobe scale, sex will be of much less importance to them than if they are on the high end of the scale.

In addition, there is a complex interaction between sexual satisfaction and relationship satisfaction for a cohabiting couple, and men and women typically have different priorities for sexual satisfaction and relationship satisfaction: Relationship satisfaction comes first for women; sexual satisfaction comes first for men. In other words, a woman must usually be satisfied with the relationship before she can be satisfied with sex, whereas a man must usually be satisfied with sex before he can be satisfied with the relationship (Blumstein and Schwartz 1983). (See also "Sexual Satisfaction and Relationship Satisfaction" with respect to marriage in Chapter 7.)

Sexual Initiating and Complying   A man is traditionally socialized to initiate sexual activity, whereas a woman is socialized to respond to him. If she is the more hyperphilic, this can be a problem. Studies find that it may be risky for a woman to be too aggressive in initiating sex because a man may feel that she is usurping his role, and he may become alarmed if he is not the sexual aggressor most of the time. A woman is more hyperphilic — more ardent and more passionate — in about one-fifth of couples (Pietropinto 1990; Rubin 1976).

Couples are happiest when either feels free to initiate sex. Cohabiting couples are typically more egalitarian than married couples in the freedom of either to initiate sex or play the aggressive role in their sexual interaction (Blumstein and Schwartz 1983).

Sex as Power in Cohabitation   One of the important aspects of sexuality is that it can be used as an instrument of power or manipulation. The one who is lower on the erotophile-erotophobe scale (usually the woman) can use sex as a means of wielding control by providing sex as a reward or withholding it as punishment. (This is an example of the *principle of least interest:* The person who has the least to lose has the most power in an interaction.)

A cohabiting woman must be more careful than a married woman in wielding power in this way, however, because it is much easier for a cohabiting couple to break up. The cohabiting man may simply walk away if he is not satisfied with the relationship, and for men relationship satisfaction is usually based on sexual satisfaction, as we have seen. A wife is safer in wielding her sexual power because a married couple are held together by social and legal bonds not present in cohabitation. (See Chapter 7 for a further discussion of the ramifications of sex as power.)

Cohabitation and Money

As pervasive as the influence of sex is on cohabiting couples, money is the single most commonly discussed topic. According to Blumstein and Schwartz (1983), who analyzed data from 12,000 subjects, couples fight more about how to spend money than they do about any other issue.

Money as Power in Cohabitation   Cohabiting women usually have less power in the relationship than men because women generally earn less money. A women who earns less money is also granted less status and less respect (Blumstein and Schwartz 1983). A national study in 1991 found that a significant proportion (32 percent) of cohabiting women believed that their emotional security would be better if they were married (Bumpass, Sweet, and Cherlin 1991).

A cohabitor who believes that he or she does not have an equal say in the couple's use of available funds — what they buy and when they buy it — will typically feel devalued, depressed, angry, and frustrated. This appears to hold true no matter who has earned the money (Blumstein and Schwartz 1983). (The issue of money as power in marriage is addressed in Chapters 8 and 9.)

Pooling Money or Keeping Separate Accounts Studies indicate that each of a cohabiting couple usually pays an approximately equal share of household expenses, even though one almost always earns more than the other. This principle of "paying one's own way" is felt by most cohabitors to be an important statement of independence (Blumstein and Schwartz 1983). The one earning less (usually the woman) pays a price for this independence, however, by having to allow the other (usually the man) to spend more on personal pleasures — clothes, hobbies, sports, entertainment — or to put it in an individual savings account or investment (Blumstein and Schwartz 1983).

Most cohabiting couples keep their money separate. Thus each might have a separate checking account to pay for an agreed-upon share of the household expenses. The practice of keeping separate accounts in this way is in sharp contrast to the pattern followed by most married couples, who simply pool their money.

Traditionally, a couple did not share a household until they were married, and after marriage the husband had the responsibility for providing for his wife. A husband who fulfilled the provider role usually assumed that money he earned would go into a common fund to be used by the couple jointly. Such husbands assumed that if their wife went to work, the money she earned would also wind up in the same fund. In marriage, the presumption tends to be one of "not your money and my money but rather *our* money." A husband or wife who objects to pooling financial resources is likely to put his or her commitment in doubt and raise serious questions about mutual trust (Blumstein and Schwartz 1983, p. 100).

Thus a key issue emerges — whether to continue to keep their money in separate accounts or to pool it — when a cohabiting couple becomes more than casually committed to each other. Their decision with respect to this issue becomes fundamental to their continuing relationship (Blumstein and Schwartz 1983). Cohabitation always involves tension between independence on the one hand and commitment on the other; a decision to pool resources is a signal that this tension between independence and commitment is being resolved in favor of commitment. Deciding to pool financial assets is thus the single most important indicator that a couple has become "solidified as a unit" (Macklin 1988; Blumstein and Schwartz 1983).

SUMMARY

Before the twentieth century, single people in our society had very little independence or freedom. They usually lived with a family and were subject to the family's supervision. As our society moved from a reliance on agriculture to increasing industrialization in the late nineteenth and early twentieth centuries, boarding houses became more popular, and single people acquired somewhat more freedom. However, single men did not begin to have the freedom of married men until well into the twentieth century, and single women achieved this freedom only with their entry into the world of work outside the household. Young women now form a new class of economically and socially independent singles.

Single people now constitute a large and growing segment of the population. The increase in the proportion of never-married singles does not mean that fewer people are marrying — only that they are marrying later. From 90 to 95 percent of our population marry at some time in their lives. The number of divorced singles is also increasing because of a rising divorce rate, a longer interval between divorce and remarriage, and the high incidence of second divorces following a remarriage. The number of widowed singles is increasing due to a longer life expectancy for women.

Single people tend to drift from small towns to suburban or urban areas, probably because there are more things to do in these areas and more singles with whom to associate. One of the greatest preoccupations for single people can be to find companions and friends to create a social network that can serve as their major source of emotional support. Unfortunately, loneliness and depression can be a problem for singles, and despite common beliefs that suggest otherwise, men are just as subject to loneliness as women. Loneliness is often a source of depression, which is correlated with both physical and psychological problems.

The incidence of cohabitation as a life-style for singles increased sharply in the 1970s and the 1980s. More than half of recently married couples now cohabit before marriage. Even though some people enter cohabitation with the idea of testing their chances for successful marriage without divorce, research indicates that cohabitation before marriage is in fact correlated with higher divorce rates.

The rapid increase in the incidence of cohabitation has been traced to many sources: the women's movement's efforts to secure more freedom for women, the increasing number of women postponing marriage, an increased acceptance of sexuality not related to reproduction, the rising divorce rate (which may have prompted previously married singles to be wary of marriage), and the development of effective and readily available contraceptives.

There is evidence of an inverse relation between education and cohabitation: The lower the level of education, the higher the likelihood of cohabitation. And although there is no correlation between religious affiliation and cohabitation, there is a correlation between the depth of religious commitment and the incidence of cohabitation: The greater the depth of religious commitment, the lower the likelihood of cohabitation.

The popularity of cohabitation has occurred so recently that there are few norms established that reduce the ambiguous nature of the relationship. This ambiguity can be a source of conflict when couples must work out patterns that are not established by custom and tradition. There is similar ambiguity regarding the interaction of a parent's live-in lover with children.

The legal implications of cohabitation vary widely from state to state, but it is still associated with the seldom-prosecuted crime of fornication in some states. Children born to unmarried couples are considered illegitimate in all states, which can cause them many legal and social difficulties. When cohabiting couples break up, they may experience problems dividing their assets, and if one person dies without leaving a will, all property may go to the family of the deceased.

KEY TERMS

The following is a list of key terms in this chapter.
These terms are defined in context within the chapter, and many may also be found in the Glossary.

aberration	cohabiting family	LIL (live-in lover)	variant
celibate	cohabitation	principle of least interest	

QUESTIONS

1. Compare the status of single people in our colonial period and in the nineteenth century with the status of single people in our society today.

2. Discuss the rise of a new class of singles — never-married women who are economically and socially independent.

3. What are the four versions of singlehood? Define and describe each one.

4. Discuss the problems of loneliness and depression in relation to singlehood.

5. Discuss the rising incidence of cohabitation in the United States. When did the increase in cohabitation start to occur? What were the reasons for the increase?

6. Discuss the issue of cohabitation and the expectation for marriage, especially with regard to women.

7. What is the relationship between cohabitation and likelihood of success in the cohabiting couple's eventual marriage? Is the incidence of divorce higher or lower for cohabiting couples who later marry? Suggest possible reasons for this relationship between cohabitation and successful or unsuccessful marriage.

SUGGESTIONS FOR FURTHER READING

Blumstein, Philip, and Schwartz, Pepper. *American Couples*. New York: Pocket Books, 1983.

Chilman, Catherine; Nunnally, Elam W.; and Cox, Fred M. *Variant Family Forms*. Newbury Park, Calif.: Sage, 1988.

Cargan, Leonard, and Melko, Matthew. *Singles: Myths and Realities*. Beverly Hills, Calif.: Sage, 1982.

Kephart, William M. *Extraordinary Groups: An Examination of Unconventional Life-Styles*, 3rd ed. New York: St. Martin's Press, 1987.

Macklin, Eleanor. "Nontraditional Family Forms." In Marvin B. Sussman and Suzanne K. Steinmetz (eds.), *Handbook of Marriage and the Family*, pp. 317–67. New York: Plenum, 1987.

Simenauer, Jacqueline, and Carroll, David. *Singles: The New Americans*. New York: Simon & Schuster, 1982.

Simon, Barbara Levy. *Never Married Women*. Philadelphia: Temple University Press, 1987.

Stein, Peter J., ed. *Single Life: Unmarried Adults in Social Context*. New York: St. Martin's Press, 1981.

CHAPTER 7

Marriage:
The Married Couple

*Therefore shall a man leave his father and his mother, and shall
cleave unto his wife, and they shall be one flesh.*

Genesis 2:24

From Singlehood to Marriage

Sex in Marriage

Sex Outside of Marriage: Adultery

Child-Free Marriages

Marriage While in College

Intermarriage

The Meaning of Marriage for Society

What Do You Know?

*Some of the following statements are true and some are false.
Can you tell which are which?*

T/F   1. Only a few states have incest laws prohibiting marriage between blood relations.

T/F   2. Being married to more than one person at a time is illegal in the United States and is called *bigamy*.

T/F   3. Few societies throughout the world, and few religions, make provisions for divorce.

T/F   4. Most women in executive positions do not have children.

T/F   5. If a woman has been married for more than five years and does not have a child, she is very likely to remain childless.

T/F   6. The more education a woman has, the less likely she is to remain childless.

T/F   7. Before the separation of church and state in the eighteenth and nineteenth centuries, interfaith marriages were illegal in Western societies.

T/F   8. Interfaith marriages have about a 50 percent higher rate of failure than other marriages.

T/F   9. Sex is relatively unimportant in most American marriages.

T/F   10. Adultery is more common among wives than among husbands.

Answers: 1-F, 2-T, 3-F, 4-T, 5-T, 6-F, 7-T, 8-F, 9-F, 10-F

Marriage is very popular in our society. Between 90 and 95 percent of Americans marry at some point in their lives (see Figure 7-1). In this chapter we will examine the meaning of marriage both from the individual's point of view and for society.

From Singlehood to Marriage

Deciding to marry is a decision that has far-reaching consequences, for it will irrevocably change the rest of the person's life. Even if the marriage is dissolved by divorce, as about half are, a significant number of important social, emotional, and economic ties still remain. These ties continue to have a pervasive influence that persists long after the divorce (see Chapters 12 and 13).

Why should a person choose to take the step of marrying? Why choose to marry when it is quite possible simply to cohabit — an arrangement that provides many of the benefits of marriage without all of the responsibilities?

The Meaning of Marriage for the Individual

Marriage as a Sacrament One reason why almost all of our population marry, rather than simply cohabiting, is the prevalent belief in our society that living with another person in a sexual relationship without being married is morally wrong. Many people believe that cohabitation violates their deepest moral, ethical, and religious principles. Thus, a good many couples in our society marry in order to sanctify a sexual relationship.

From the Christian point of view, for example, marriage is seen as an institution of divine significance. This conception of marriage emphasizes the sacred tie between the couple and God, with the marriage regarded as "Holy Matrimony," the "Holy Estate," or "God's Holy Ordinance." Once established, marriage is under the jurisdiction of God.

Most marriage ceremonies in our society take place under the auspices of a minister, priest, or rabbi, and in religious terms marriage is regarded as a *sacrament*, an outward and visible sign of inward and spiritual grace. Three-fourths of couples who are entering a first marriage choose to have a religious ceremony. Nearly two-thirds of divorced people who are entering a second marriage choose to have a religious ceremony, as do most widows and widowers who are entering a second marriage.[1]

Marriage as Commitment A person in love usually wants commitment, and marriage is a public affirmation of commitment — a statement that each anticipates that their relationship will be permanent.

Mutual commitment is formalized by the wedding ceremony. The ceremony is a celebration of each person's free choice of and commitment to the other. A couple may choose to marry because they feel that it is important to make this public statement. The couple who marry feel that the reassurance of love and commitment that each receives from, and grants to, the other is worth the loss of freedom that goes with marriage.

In all societies, marriage is regarded as a relatively permanent bond, and in some societies marriage is virtually irrevocable. Thus in countries in which Roman Catholicism is the dominant religion (such as Northern Ireland, Italy, and Brazil), divorce is nearly impossible to obtain.

Divorce was very rare throughout Western civilization until the eighteenth century. Although it was possible to have a marriage annulled by

---

[1]U.S. National Center for Health Statistics, "Weddings Performed in Religious Ceremonies" (1988).

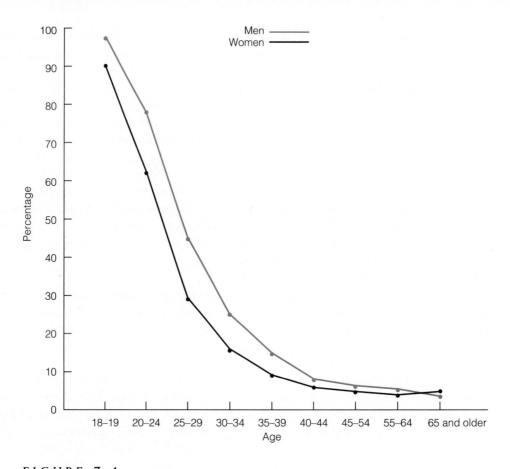

FIGURE 7-1

Percentage of never-married singles in the United States, by age and sex: 1989.

Source: U.S. Bureau of the Census, "Single (Never-Married) Persons as Percent of Total Population, by Sex and Age: 1970 to 1989." *Current Population Reports*, Series P-20, No. 445. Washington, D.C.: Government Printing Office, 1991.

the church, which meant that it was formally and officially regarded as never having existed in the first place, annulment required a papal decree. Civil divorce began to be granted by legislative action in the eighteenth century and came under the jurisdiction of the courts in the nineteenth century. Divorce was still relatively uncommon in our society, however, until well into the twentieth century. The Roman Catholic Church still does not recognize civil divorce and regards marriage as a divine institution not to be tampered with by humans (see Chapter 12).[2]

---

[2]Protestants and Jews take the position that marital vows for lifelong fidelity are expressions of solemn intent made with all sincerity at the time of the wedding. However, they believe that although marriages should not fail, they sometimes do. They also maintain that when a marriage does fail, the couple should not be punished for their fallibility. Thus Protestants and Jews reluctantly accept divorce as a valid way to end a

TABLE 7-1

Marriage Terms

Term	Definition
Monogamy	One husband with one wife
Polygyny	One husband with two or more wives
Polyandry	One wife with two or more husbands
Polygamy	Either polygyny, polyandry, or group marriage
Bigamy	Illegal polygamy
Group marriage	Several husbands with several wives

Unfortunately, marriage cannot guarantee commitment, and about half of all couples who affirm their commitment through marriage end their relationship with divorce.

Marrying to Have Children   Many couples marry because they expect to have children and want their children to be legitimatized by marriage. This is not to say that cohabiting couples never bear children, or that trust, commitment, and reliability are never present in cohabitation, but rather that marriage affirms the expected permanence of the relationship. As we will see, the one universal characteristic of marriage in all known societies is that marriage legitimatizes children.

Marrying for Economic Security   At one time in our history it was difficult for people (especially women) to survive without the economic partnership provided by marriage. Although some people still marry for economic security, this reason for marrying is not nearly as important as it was in the preindustrial age. Industrialization provided both men and women the opportunity to be economically independent of each other (see Chapter 9).

Monogamy and Polygamy   *Monogamy* — one man and one woman married to each other at any one time — is the only form of marriage that is permitted in our society; any form of multiple marriage is considered *bigamy* in the United States and is illegal (see Table 7-1).

Polygyny (one husband with two or more wives) is the preferred form of marriage throughout most (75 percent) of the world's societies. However, most of the marriages in those societies are monogamous because the number

---

marriage and open the way for a remarriage. It should be noted that even though the Roman Catholic Church does not recognize civil divorce, Catholics divorce at about the same rate as Protestants and Jews (see Chapter 12).

of marriageable men in each society is usually about equal to the number of marriageable women. (Thus if one man has two or more wives, it means that another man or other men must have none.) Only the most powerful and wealthy men in such societies can usually afford to have more than one wife (Murdock 1957). In the United States, members of the Church of Jesus Christ of Latter-day Saints (Mormons) practiced polygyny until the 1870s, when Congress passed legislation outlawing multiple marriage. There are still some communities of Mormons in Nevada that practice polygyny in defiance of the law.

Polyandry (one wife with two or more husbands) is a very rare form of marriage, preferred by less than 1 percent of the world's societies. *Group marriage* (two or more husbands married to two or more wives) has never occurred in any society as a cultural norm (Murdock 1957).

Polygamy means any kind of multiple marriage: polygyny, polyandry, or group marriage.

The Shift in the Meaning of Marriage from Medieval Times to Today From the Middle Ages until the nineteenth century in Western societies, the emphasis on marriage as a sacred institution was much greater than it is now. During the nineteenth century the emphasis shifted toward a view of marriage as a civil institution, and during the twentieth century the emphasis has shifted again, this time toward a view of marriage as an institution that primarily provides personal satisfaction (see Figure 7-2). Contributing to this latest shift in the meaning of marriage is the depersonalization of modern mass society, which makes any intimate relationship especially important (see Chapter 1).

This growing emphasis on the importance of individual satisfaction in marriage is also related, of course, to the emergence of mutual selection as a method of courtship and marital choice, which replaced such practical considerations as status, wealth, property, and family name with the personal considerations of limerence and romantic love. It is also related to the increasing economic and social independence of women. Because women are no longer dependent on marriage for economic security, men and women alike are able to focus on personal satisfaction as the most significant aspect of marriage. And if satisfaction is lacking, either has the option of ending the marriage by obtaining a divorce. (It is true, however, that a woman's standard of living tends to fall after a divorce, whereas a man's tends to rise; see Chapter 12.)

Getting Married

Before two people may marry in our society they must fill out an application for a marriage license at an appropriate government agency. Most states require a blood test (to detect evidence of syphilis[3]) before they will issue a license. Most states also specify a delay between the blood test and the issuance of the license, thereby giving people an opportunity to change their minds about getting married. Marriage licenses are issued by the individual states and must be used within the issuing state.

A state will issue a marriage license once the necessary legal requirements have been met, and then the couple may be married by anyone authorized by the state to perform a marriage ceremony. Although most states require witnesses to be present at the marriage, the actual form of the ceremony is often unregulated.

When the official who performs the ceremony signs the marriage license, it becomes a *marriage certificate*, which serves as proof of marriage in the eyes of the state. Once the ceremony is completed, a copy of the marriage certificate is sent to the state board of health's vital statistics

---

[3]For a discussion of syphilis, see Appendix A.

From the Middle Ages until the nineteenth century, the sacred aspect of marriage was emphasized.

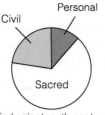

Early nineteenth century

The nineteenth century ushered in an emphasis on the civil aspect of marriage.

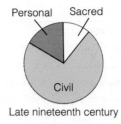

Late nineteenth century

The twentieth century ushered in an emphasis on the personal satisfactions in marriage.

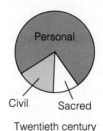

Twentieth century

FIGURE 7-2
Historical changes in the meaning of marriage.

division, where it becomes a matter of public record. Such proof of marriage is often invaluable in terms of such issues as inheritance rights, social security, insurance, and legitimacy of children.

A person cannot obtain a marriage license without being older than a certain minimum age, which varies from state to state. In most states, the age of eligibility is eighteen for males and sixteen for females (if they have parental consent) or twenty-one for males and eighteen for females (if they do not have parental consent). Some states do not require parental consent for minors who have previously been married; other states allow female minors to marry if they are pregnant or already have children.

All states have incest laws prohibiting marriage between blood relations, although the degree of relatedness that prohibits marriage varies from state to state. No state will issue a marriage license to a father and daughter, mother and son, brother and sister, uncle and niece, aunt and nephew, or grandparent and grandchild. Most states do not allow marriage between half brother and half sister or between first cousins, and some states prohibit marriage between second cousins. Other states prohibit the marriage of in-laws even when there is no blood relation, such as a marriage between a woman and her brother-in-law or between a man and his sister-in-law.

Common-Law Marriage

Originally marriage was neither civil nor religious but was solely a matter between the two people or the two families involved. During the Middle Ages the Roman Catholic Church gradually assumed control over marriage in western Europe. Private marriages continued to occur, but the church refused to recognize them as valid.

In the United States, marriage became regulated by civil laws in the nineteenth century, and state after state took the position that private marriages were valid so long as they were not expressly forbidden by statute. Such unions were called "common-law marriages." Today only a few states still recognize these common-law marriages — a heritage from earlier times — as legal (see Box 7-1).

Legal Rights and Obligations in Marriage

The legal rights and obligations of married couples in our society are very complicated and vary from state to state. Property may be held in joint tenancy, be considered community property, or be owned by either the husband or the wife alone. Even if a husband or a wife owns property outright, however, he or she may not dispose of it without regard to the spouse's rights if the spouse contests this act of disposal.

For these reasons, premarital contracts have long been used by wealthy people in their estate planning. These contracts supersede both inheritance laws and wills. People who are not necessarily wealthy may also use premarital contracts, especially in the case of second marriages, to safeguard the inheritance rights of children. Men, especially when remarrying, may ask a woman to waive the right of spousal support in the event of divorce; this is legal in some states but not in others (Dullea 1988).

The Creation of Kinship Relations

When two people are married, kinship relations are automatically established. Thus a marriage joins not only two individuals but also two families, and the precise relationship between the in-laws is specified by both tradition and law. In many societies these in-law relationships are significant in everyday interaction. In our society they have two important legal functions: They establish incest prohibitions, and they set up stable lines of inheritance in the absence of a will.

It should be noted, however, that the family's kinship structure is not necessarily one of blood, and that adopting a child has the same kinship force as giving birth to the child. It is the social definition — not biological ties — that determines who is kin (Reiss 1980).

Sex in Marriage

Among the most important parts of marriage are companionship; intimacy; shared thoughts, plans, and dreams; enjoyable leisure time together; high-quality communication with each other; and (for many) shared satisfactions involving children and shared religious fulfillment. There is no question that these things are of central concern and undeniable importance (Blumstein and Schwartz 1983).

Despite the importance of these matters, the three key aspects of most American marriages are those related to money, work, and sex. These

BOX 7-1

Marriage with No License: Common-Law Marriage

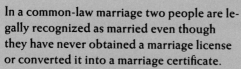

In a common-law marriage two people are legally recognized as married even though they have never obtained a marriage license or converted it into a marriage certificate.

Common-law marriage was more prevalent in our society during the pioneer period, when many communities did not have a judge or a clergyman who was authorized to perform marriages. The convention developed that if two people declared themselves to be married before the community and lived together as husband and wife, they were married by common law. Sometimes couples who were thus married by common law would later have a formal ceremony when a clergyman or judge was available (the so-called circuit-rider clergyman or judge). Other couples would postpone a formal ceremony until after they had children, sometimes even until the children were grown.

Today most states do not recognize a common-law marriage unless it has already been accepted as legal in another state. Although the question of legality most often arises with reference to inheritance rights and the legitimacy of offspring, the growing incidence of cohabitation has made the legal ramifications of common-law marriage more complex.

three key aspects are not only important in themselves, but they are also related to other important aspects of the marriage. Certainly, almost all aspects of a couple's interaction are involved, to some extent, with questions relating to money and work: How much money do we have, and how should we spend it? After working, how much energy and free time do we have to spend together? And, as we will see, almost all aspects of marriage are crucially influenced by the quality of a couple's sex life (Blumstein and Schwartz 1983).

We will focus on issues relating to work and marriage in Chapter 9 and on issues relating to money and marriage in Chapter 14. In the following sections we will examine issues specifically related to sex and marriage. (For discussions of fundamental issues of sexuality and eroticism, see Chapter 4.)

Sex as a Major Bond

Blumstein and Schwartz (1983) concluded that sex is a major bond for 85 to 99 percent of American marriages. Because sex affects almost every aspect of the couple's interaction, for most marriages "a good sex life is central to a good overall relationship" (p. 281). A good sex life depends on the couple's matched interest and pleasure and on each's perception that the other is content.

As we saw in Chapter 4, it is not so much the extent of sexual activity that is important, but rather that each has about the same level of sexual interest and responsiveness. Whereas sex may be of central concern to an erotophile, it may have negative implications for an erotophobe; for someone who is about midway between the erotophobic and erotophilic ends of the scale, sex may simply be of little interest. (This explains the 1 to 15 percent of marriages in which sex is *not* a major bond.)

Blumstein and Schwartz (1983) found that nearly half of married couples (45 percent) copulated three or more times a week during the first ten years of marriage.[4] After ten or more years, they copulated two or three times a week. For most couples, frequency and regularity of copulation were positively correlated with the level of happiness in the marriage (Blumstein and Schwartz 1983).

Although the husband is more frequently the one who is more interested in sex, in fully 20 to 25 percent of marriages the wife is relatively higher on the erotophile-erotophobe scale (Pietropinto 1990; Rubin 1976).

Sexual Satisfaction and Relationship Satisfaction

There are significant differences between men and women in the connection between sexual satisfaction and relationship satisfaction. A classic study by Udry (1968) found that for women,

relationship satisfaction comes first; it must precede sexual satisfaction. Put another way, most women will not experience sexual satisfaction unless they are first satisfied with the quality of the relationship. With men, it is just the opposite: Sexual satisfaction comes first and forms the basis for relationship satisfaction. Because for most marriages sex is a major cornerstone upon which happiness in marriage rests, recognizing this difference between men and women can be crucial for marital harmony.

If there is a problem with either the couple's overall relationship or their sexual relationship, one spouse must take the first step (see Figure 7-3). Perhaps the husband may attempt to make the quality of the relationship more satisfactory for his wife; she is then more likely to be sexually responsive and in turn to provide him with greater sexual satisfaction. As a result it is more likely that he will be satisfied with the overall quality of the relationship. Or perhaps the wife may take the first step by providing her husband with sexual satisfaction, making it more likely that he will be happy with the quality of the relationship. He is then more apt to demonstrate those qualities that will make her more satisfied with the relationship, which in turn makes it more likely that she will be happy sexually.

Sex as Power in Marriage

When sex becomes an exercise in power in a marriage, both sexual satisfaction and relationship satisfaction are in jeopardy.

As we have seen, the principle of least interest states that the person who is less interested in any matter has more power in that matter. Thus one spouse who is significantly lower than the other spouse on the erotophile-erotophobe scale may use sex as an instrument of power, gaining control of the marriage by providing sexual pleasure as a reward or withholding it as a

---

[4]Masters, Johnson, and Kolodny (1988) found that the "average" married couple copulated two to three times a week in their twenties and thirties; by age fifty this had declined to about once a week. "Average" means very little, however, because there is such a wide divergence of frequency from one couple to another (see Chapter 4).

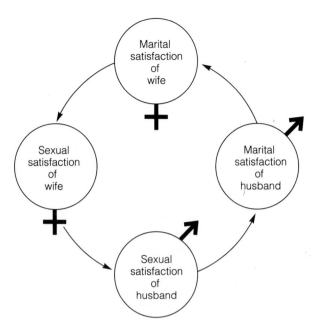

FIGURE 7-3

The interactions between sexual satisfaction and marital satisfaction.

Source: Data from Udry (1968).

punishment. In contrast, a spouse who is higher on the erotophile-erotophobe scale may use sex as a demonstration of power by demanding sexual compliance from the other spouse.

Sexual Initiating and Complying

For a wife to demand sexual compliance from her husband is much less common than for a husband to demand sexual compliance from his wife. This pattern results from the long-held tradition in our society that men initiate sexual activity whereas women comply. Because of this expectation, it may be risky for a wife to demand sexual compliance from her husband. Our culture socializes people to expect that a wife will wait for her husband to take the lead in initiating

sexual activity, and many American women feel that they must be careful not to initiate sex (Blumstein and Schwartz 1983):

> [Women] do not want to usurp what they know are historic male prerogatives and they fear bruising the male ego. . . . As the woman initiates more, the issue of her having the bigger appetite emerges and with it a challenge to the man's sense of worth. (pp. 209–12)

A marriage is usually more harmonious when each member of the couple has an equivalent say in initiating sex. These egalitarian couples copulate more frequently than couples in which the male is usually the sole initiator. Married couples are usually less egalitarian in this regard than cohabiting couples (Blumstein and Schwartz 1983).

Sex Outside of Marriage: Adultery

A married person who has sex with someone outside the marriage is committing *adultery*. Adultery is usually associated with deceit and secrecy, or "cheating." It may involve only a single transgression, a few occasional, brief sexual liaisons with little or no emotional involvement, or a deep emotional attachment and persistent commitment that lasts for years.[5]

The term *adultery* comes from the verb to *adulterate*, which means to add an inferior substance that contaminates, debases, or makes the original substance impure. One example would be diluting a valuable ingredient (such as milk) with a less valuable one (such as water). Adultery originally applied only to wives, for a husband might consider his bloodline to be "adulterated" if his wife copulated with another man because the paternity of a child subsequently born to the woman could be called into question. In biblical times, a wife who was judged to be guilty of adultery was liable to be stoned to death.

Taboos forbidding married people to have sex outside of marriage are common among most societies throughout the world (although the penalty is rarely death). For example, Murdock's classic study (1949) found that a taboo against adultery was present in 81 percent of the 148 societies studied. Only 5 percent of these societies allowed adultery to be practiced freely, and only 13 percent permitted adultery conditionally, with various restrictions. A small proportion of married couples in our society practices *consensual adultery* (see Box 7-2).

Americans have traditionally condemned adultery as a serious threat to marriage — as a source of distrust, disillusionment, and marital unhappiness (Greeley, Michael, and Smith 1990). Adultery was the principal ground for divorce in most states before the advent of no-fault divorce (see Chapter 12). There has been, however, a traditional double standard that condemns extramarital sex for women more than it does for men (Masters, Johnson, and Kolodny 1988).

Until the 1960s, adultery was a criminal offense in all states, and today it remains a criminal offense in most states (although adultery laws are rarely enforced). All three prominent religions in our society — Roman Catholicism, Protestantism, and Judaism — classify adultery as a sin (Segraves 1989).

Incidence of Adultery

Some past studies (Kinsey et al. 1948; Hunt 1974) found that from the turn of the century to the early 1970s, about one husband in two had committed adultery, as had one wife in four. More recent studies find that the overall incidence of adultery has remained relatively constant for both husbands and wives (Smith 1990; Greeley, Michael, and Smith 1990). However, among some groups of wives, the incidence of adultery has reached the same incidence as that among husbands. For example, among young wives (under age twenty-five) the incidence is about one in two. Incidence among wives of all age groups who work outside the home is also about one in two — double the incidence among homemakers (Segraves 1989; Wyatt, Peters, and

---

[5]When in some societies a man is having such an extended affair and assumes some financial responsibility for the woman, she is called his mistress. Having a mistress is quite common in many European countries, where it is regarded as a privilege of wealthy married men, but it is relatively rare in the United States (Masters, Johnson, and Kolodny 1988).

BOX 7-2

Consensual Adultery

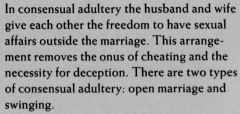

In consensual adultery the husband and wife give each other the freedom to have sexual affairs outside the marriage. This arrangement removes the onus of cheating and the necessity for deception. There are two types of consensual adultery: open marriage and swinging.

In *open marriage*, both the husband and wife may pursue sexual liaisons separately and independently from the other, and they may or may not reveal various details to the other. There are no data on the extent of open marriage in our society.

In *swinging*, the husband and wife are sexually intimate with another couple (or individual) together—at the same time and in the same place. Surveys find that 2—4 percent of married couples have engaged in swinging; less than half of these have done so on a regular basis (Masters, Johnson, and Kolodny 1988).

Proponents of consensual adultery feel that no one person is always the preferred sexual partner in all situations; they seek enjoyment in a variety of sexual experiences, even though their primary loyalty is to their marriage. They regard a limitation on their freedom to explore various sexual relationships as a serious infringement on their freedom and feel that the benefits of open marriage are increased self-awareness and zest for living.

Opponents to consensual adultery believe that it violates the Judeo-Christian religious precept that forbids sexual relations with anyone other than one's spouse and emphasizes the sanctity of marriage and the importance of sexual fidelity. Our culture is based on this precept, which is absorbed from early childhood and is very deeply embedded in the consciousness of most people. Moreover, the danger of contracting an STD can be a very practical risk in consensual adultery (see Appendix A).

Guthrie 1988; Clement, Schmidt, and Kruse 1984). However, not all studies agree with these figures. For example, in their nationwide study Blumstein and Schwartz (1983) found that only 26 percent of husbands and 21 percent of wives admitted to any extramarital sexual adventures.

Husbands usually have affairs with women who are about their own age; wives, on the other hand, are just as likely to have an affair with a younger man as with an older man (Segraves 1989; Forsyth and Fournet 1987).

The rate of infidelity is negatively correlated with education—the lower the level of education, the higher the rate of infidelity. Those who live in large suburbs have a higher rate of infidelity than those who live in small towns. Blacks have a higher rate of infidelity than whites (Smith 1991).

Age-specific incidences of adultery differ between husbands and wives. Among husbands the incidence of adultery *decreases* with age, whereas among wives it *increases* with age (Segraves 1989).

Opportunity is an important factor in determining whether people commit adultery. Many homemakers, for example, say that if they had the opportunity, they would have an affair. Some return to school or evening classes in order to meet partners for this purpose (Segraves 1989).

A casual sexual adventure with no strings attached, no emotional involvement, and no commitment contrasts sharply with a long-term extramarital affair in which there is deep emotional involvement, intimacy, commitment, and love (Masters, Johnson, and Kolodny 1988). Not surprisingly, a happily married person is less likely to commit adultery than one who is not. Most marriages have cycles: Some periods are marked by intense satisfaction and closeness, whereas other periods are marked by unhappiness, emptiness, or conflict. Stresses and dissatisfactions at these points in a marriage can influence the likelihood that one spouse or the other will look for a sexual adventure outside the marriage (Brecher et al. 1984).

Motivation for Adultery

The reasons people cite for committing adultery are many and typically differ for husbands and wives. Men usually mention novelty and sexuality as the chief attractions for an extramarital affair; in general, women are more attracted to sensitivity, tenderness, and caring — qualities that override physical attraction or financial status (Segraves 1989).

Wives under age thirty-five are likely to commit adultery because they seek more sexual diversity — a motivation similar to that expressed by husbands. Wives older than thirty-five are more likely to have an extramarital affair because

they are discontented with the marriage (Petersen et al. 1983; Glass and Wright 1977).

Women also typically perceive the meaning of adultery differently than do men. When wives commit adultery, they tend to describe it in emotional rather than sexual terms. They tend to see the affair as a significant, serious, and even momentous event — not simply as an isolated sexual adventure. Wives tend to view their affairs in the context of the marriage and of the overall pattern of their lives. Husbands, on the other hand, tend both to view their affairs as relatively casual, isolated sexual adventures and to describe them in sexual terms (Brecher et al. 1984).

Wives who commit adultery are likely to associate it with a progressive decrease in marital satisfaction or with deterioration of the marriage. Husbands, on the other hand, are more likely to feel that extramarital sex will increase marital satisfaction by decreasing tension and boredom within the marriage (Brecher et al. 1984).

Problems concerning sexuality within a marriage often provide either spouse the motivation for having an extramarital affair. If, for example, a wife wants to "make love" but her husband only wants to "have sex," she may seek satisfaction in an extramarital affair. Husbands may also turn to romantic affairs outside marriage if their wives are willing to engage only in quick, perfunctory genital encounters. Brecher et al. (1984) cite a sixty-eight-year-old man who had been married for thirty-nine years to a woman who disliked any sexual encounter that was not brief and occasional:

> "She is unwilling to engage in sexual variations or extended foreplay, and is often reluctant to have sex at all. Consequently, I seek variety from two widows of about fifty years old — and from young prostitutes. . . . The widows are anxious for sex, want vari-

ety, no inhibitions. The young prostitutes give me the variety of youth, beautiful bodies — but the experienced widows give me much better sex." (p. 122)

Summarized, then, motivation for adultery may include one or more of the following reasons (Brecher et al. 1984):

- *Hedonism.* A person may have an extramarital affair simply because it is pleasurable.

- *Variety of sexual experience.* The prospect of a new sexual partner may hold promise of a different, new, and exciting experience.

- *Search for emotional satisfaction.* A person may feel that his or her emotional needs are not being met within the marriage.

- *Yearning for romance.* A person may feel that his or her life is passing by devoid of romance and that a new love affair will counteract these feelings of stagnation and futility.

- *Curiosity.* A person may just want to see what it would be like to be sexually intimate with someone else.

- *Attraction.* Romantic and sexual intimacy outside of marriage may emerge as a person discovers increased interest and emotional compatibility with another person. The sexual encounter that may then occur is neither deliberate nor planned.

- *Rebellion.* A person may consider the expectation of monogamy to be an undesirable restriction in marriage and may seek extramarital affairs as a gesture of independence.

Child-Free Marriages

Although the one universal function of marriage is the legitimization of children, *child-free marriages* are now one of the most rapidly growing forms of marriage in our society.

Incidence of Child-Free Marriages

Until the mid-1970s, only about one married couple in ten in our society did not have children. Their marriages were called "childless" and the woman was usually pitied as "barren," even though the infertility might well be traced to the husband rather than the wife. Very few of these marriages were childless by choice (Mosher 1982).

As we have seen, the development of the contraceptive pill in the 1960s made voluntary childlessness a realistic option. (The other methods of birth control then available were not nearly so effective.) Then, in 1973, the U.S. Supreme Court legalized abortion (see Appendix B). Before these changes, married couples simply took it for granted that, short of sexual abstinence, they would become parents.

The decline in fertility has been pervasive in our society; women of all ages, races, and educational levels are having fewer children than they did a generation ago (see Figure 7-4). In 1960 the general fertility rate (births per 1,000 women of childbearing age) was 118, well above the replacement rate of 70.[6] By 1973 the rate had dropped below the replacement level, and it has remained below it ever since (Fuchs 1988). Part of this drop can be explained by women having fewer children, but it also reflects a growing tendency toward childlessness. In 1960, for example, 18 percent of all women ages twenty-five to thirty-nine did not have a child; by 1986, 28 percent of all women in this age group were childless, as were more than 40 percent of white women in their late twenties (Fuchs 1988). This

---

[6] This rate would yield an average of 2.1 births per woman over thirty years of potential childbearing. Deaths in infancy and childhood would result in two children reaching adulthood, thus just replacing their parents (Fuchs 1988).

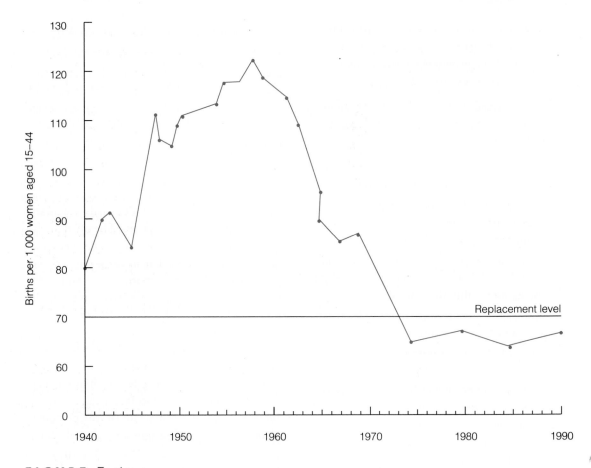

FIGURE 7-4

General fertility rates in the United States: 1940–1990. *

*The baby boom occurred from 1946 to 1964, when as many as 4.3 million babies were born each year. After more than two decades, births began to rise again in the early 1980s and again in 1990, when 4.1 million babies were born. Early data for 1991 show a 1–3 percent decline compared with 1990, and demographers predict the decline will continue through the 1990s. (U.S. National Center for Health Statistics, "Live Births per 1,000 Population," *Monthly Vital Statistics Report*, December 1991, and unpublished data.)

Source: U.S. National Center for Health Statistics, "Annual Summary of Births, Marriages, Divorces, and Deaths: 1989." In *Monthly Vital Statistics Report* 38 (13): 3, 1990. DHHS Publication No. PHS 90-1120

rise in childlessness may be occurring because many women are simply postponing having children, but some demographers predict a continuing trend. A repeat of the baby boom is not expected by demographers of the Population Reference Bureau, partly because of long-term changes in the economy that make supporting large families increasingly difficult (De Vita and Bouvier 1992).

If a woman has been married for five years and has not had a child, it is very likely that she will remain childless; 90 percent of all births occur within the first five years of marriage. After age thirty, the odds for permanent childlessness increase further. Among child-free wives ages thirty to thirty-four, it has been estimated that more than 93 percent will not have a child (Baldwin and Nord 1984).

Women who neither belong to a church or synagogue nor have strong traditional religious beliefs have a much higher incidence of childlessness than do women who do belong to a religious institution or hold strong traditional religious beliefs (Veevers 1979). And the more education a woman has, the more likely she is to remain childless, especially if she has had four or more years of college.[7]

With regard to geography, married women who live in urban areas are much more likely to be childless than those who live in rural farming areas; the incidence of childless women in rural nonfarming areas is about halfway between that in urban areas and rural farming areas.[8] Urban areas may have a higher incidence of voluntary childlessness because they offer young wives a wider variety of acceptable social roles, because they are less traditionally oriented, and because of selective migration of childless couples from rural areas (Veevers 1979).

Among women who marry more than once, rates of childlessness are substantially higher. Women are twice as likely to remain childless during their second marriage as during their first marriage (Glick and Lin 1987). Finally, wives who are employed outside the home have substantially higher rates of childlessness than do homemakers, although it is not clear whether

---

[7]U.S. Bureau of the Census, "Social and Economic Characteristics of Women, 18–44 Years Old, Who Have Had a Child in the Last Year: 1988" (1991).

[8]U.S. National Center for Health Statistics, *Vital and Health Statistics*, Series 10 (1984).

career involvement is the cause or the consequence of not having children (Baldwin and Nord 1984).

Motivations for Child-Free Marriages

The dramatic increase in the number of married couples remaining voluntarily child-free, which reflects extraordinary modifications in personal life-style, is occurring because of many interrelated factors.

From the point of view of economic determinism, it is not simply a coincidence that the drop in the fertility rate is correlated with the rising number of women entering the world of outside employment and the rising cost of bearing and raising children (see Chapter 9). Not only have children been transformed from economic assets into economic liabilities, but the choice to have a child may be the most financially costly decision a couple can make. If the wife works outside the home (and most with young children do), child care can cost several thousand dollars a year. And if the wife doesn't work so that she can take care of the children, the cost is whatever her income could have been. If a couple choose to send their children to private school, this can also cost several thousand dollars a year. And the annual cost of sending a child to college can be even more. In addition, there are the costs for food, clothing, medical and dental needs, and other expenses (see Chapter 14).

If a woman has a successful career, she may be reluctant to risk jeopardizing it by having children and may decide to postpone having them. With attitudes toward sex roles and childbearing changing, motherhood is becoming more a choice than an obligation (Nord and Zill 1991; Ryder 1990). Later a woman may decide to remain permanently childless or may find that she is no longer able to conceive. Most women continue to want children, but by deferring childbearing they are running the risk of having fewer children or of remaining childless (Nord and Zill 1991). Most women in executive positions do not have children (see Chapter 9).

Few couples plan at the beginning of their marriages to remain child-free; instead, they reach this decision progressively, with a series of postponements that occur in four stages (Cutright and Polanto 1977; Lindenmayer et al. 1977):

- Couples may initially put off childbearing until a definite objective, such as being out of debt, is achieved.

- Subsequently, couples may still intend to have children but become increasingly vague about when.

- Later, couples begin to debate the specific pros and cons of parenthood.

- Finally, couples make the definite decision not to have children.

Success Rate of Child-Free Marriages

Research reveals a positive correlation between childlessness and marital satisfaction and reports that child-free couples are more likely to report being happily married than are couples with children (Baldwin and Nord 1984).

Perhaps one reason for this finding is that communication can be more effective within child-free couples than it is between marriage partners who are also parents. In a child-free marriage, each person may pay more attention to the other and thus attend to the other with greater intensity. Certainly, once a child is born, all parents — except the very indifferent, the very rich, or the very innovative — must modify their preferences, desires, interests, and concerns to accommodate the demands and needs of that child. Many studies find that the life-styles of most parents revolve around the interests and needs of the infant or growing child, rather than around adult interests, so that their life-styles become child-centered rather than adult-centered (Hartup 1989).

Other studies have found that child-free couples tend to have more egalitarian relationships than do couples who have children and that their marriages are less likely to be characterized by authoritarian patterns of male dominance. Thus child-free couples are more likely to work out disagreements and conflicts more easily and democratically than are couples who are parents. Whereas gender roles in child-free marriages tend to be relatively interchangeable or androgynous, even couples who profess a liberal ideology with regard to gender roles typically find that a gender-related division of labor is part of their daily lives when they have children. These findings are not really surprising because the arrival of a child tends to accentuate biological gender differences and reinforce traditional gender roles — at least for the first years of childhood (Callan 1984; Veevers 1980).

On the other hand, children obviously bring some couples joys and delights as well as problems. Undoubtedly, some couples who initially begin by postponing children regret their decision when it is no longer biologically possible for them to have a child. Couples in such circumstances may even decide to adopt a child.

It is impossible to determine whether child-free marriage is more satisfying than parenthood; there simply are too many variables. And only the future will tell whether we will return to the norms of the past (when 90 percent of married couples had children) or find that the current incidence of child-free marriages will persist or even increase.

Marriage While in College

Marriage while in college was an anomaly until the late 1940s. Indeed, it used to be that such marriages had to be kept secret because colleges and universities expelled students who married. It was not until the late 1940s, with the enrollment of thousands of veterans of World War II, that married college students ceased to be so unusual. Married students are still relatively rare, however; only about 10 percent of male college students and 14 percent of female college students were married and living with their spouses in 1987.[9]

Perhaps the greatest danger of an early marriage is that intellectual inquiry may be stifled for both partners, so that their educational goals become oriented chiefly toward career training rather than toward inquiry for its own sake — for knowledge, wisdom, and self-development.

Even with the recent developments in contraceptive techniques, a surprising number of unwanted pregnancies still occur among young married couples. (See the discussion on birth control and unwanted pregnancies in Appendix B.) Thus a substantial number of student couples must deal with the expenses and complications of children who are not expected and may not be wanted.

Obviously, childbirth is followed by problems of crowding, increased expenses, and the logistics of child care. In fact, because of its importance in providing women the same opportunity that men have to engage in educational pursuits, child care is one of the key issues on many campuses today.

Another problem faced by many students who marry while in college is finding enough money to continue school, which can be a problem even in the absence of pregnancy. For some students, one source of income is parental subsidy. Some parents continue to provide financial support for their children if they marry because they consider it vital that their children complete their educations. Other parents choose not to subsidize their married children's education because they consider marriage to be a statement of economic independence.[10]

If parents withdraw their financial support following a marriage, the couple experience sustained economic pressure. A much larger percentage of married students, as compared with single students, work part-time and attend college part-time.[11] Unfortunately, a common problem of students who work part-time while going to school is that they don't have enough time to study. The consequences of insufficient study time and subsequent poor grades may be substantial — a substandard income and an unwanted occupation for the remainder of that person's working life.

When two students marry, one may drop out of school and work full-time so that the other has the freedom to study. Although this solution may solve the problem for the person who stays in school (usually the husband), it curtails the other person's intellectual growth and limits his or her capacity to enter a profession or land a well-paying job. Moreover, when one person surpasses the other in intellectual and social development, the marriage may be jeopardized.

It is important to note that the effects of marriages between students vary considerably

---

[9]U.S. Bureau of the Census, "Households, Families, Subfamilies, Married Couples, and Unrelated Individuals: 1960–1987" (1988); U.S. Department of Education, Center for Education Statistics, "Higher Education — Summary: 1970 to 1988" (1991).

[10]U.S. Department of Education, "Higher Education."

[11]U.S. Bureau of Labor Statistics, "Workers on Flexible Schedules, by Selected Characteristics: 1989" (1991).

from one person to another. Students differ significantly in terms of emotional maturity, intellectual maturity, self-knowledge, motivation, and ability to earn money to subsidize their own educations — as well as in their abilities to resolve the conflicts of marriage.

Intermarriage

A marriage between people of different races or religions is called *intermarriage*.

A substantial minority of our population intermarry. Intermarriages often have personal and social characteristics that are different from those of homogamous marriages. In this section we will explore the kinds of intermarriage, the attitudes of people in our society toward these marriages, what motivates people to enter them, and how their success rates compare with those for homogamous marriages.

Interracial Marriages

The incidence of *interracial marriage* in the United States is statistically negligible. In 1986, just 1.5 percent of all existing marriages were classified by the Census Bureau as interracial. As low as it is, the incidence of interracial marriage has increased markedly since a 1967 U.S. Supreme Court ruling that invalidated laws that prohibited them.[12] The number of interracial marriages increased 600 percent between the 1960 and the 1980 censuses (Glick 1988).

Black-white intermarriages in our society account for almost one in four (23 percent) interracial marriages, or 0.4 percent of all marriages. Three times as many black men marry white women as white men marry black women.[13]

In 1987, 3 percent of all births in the United States were children of interracial marriages. About 39 percent of these were black-white, 36 percent were Asian-white, 18 percent were Native American-white, and 7 percent were Asian-black or black-Native American (McCubbin 1990).

Most interracial couples probably marry for the same reasons as racially homogamous couples — they fall in love. But because people entering interracial marriages are likely to be aware of the unusual problems involved, other factors may also contribute. White people may marry interracially for idealistic reasons — to defy the prevalent cultural prejudice of our society and demonstrate that he or she refuses to identify with racial bigotry. Or interracial marriage may occur as a rebellion against parental authority. (This presumes, of course, that the parents are racially prejudiced.) And finally, the lure of the exotic may induce a person to be attracted to someone from another race. Attractions based on such differences are described in the literature for many societies, both ancient and modern.

The factors that motivate interracial marriage may, in many cases, counterbalance the social pressures against it. The very fact that interracial couples decide to get married, despite difficulties of which most are aware, indicates their high motivation for marrying. And although many sociologists indicate that interracial marriages are riskier than homogamous marriages, there is very little statistical evidence to either support or refute this belief. Indeed, no

---

[12]Until 1967 many states prohibited interracial marriage by law. In that year the U.S. Supreme Court handed down a decision ruling that all such discriminatory statutes were unconstitutional, and interracial marriage became legal throughout the United States. Before that time a couple who had been legally married in one state might find that their marriage was declared illegal and void in another state, and that their children were regarded as illegitimate.

[13]U.S. Bureau of the Census, "Black-White Married Couples: 1970 to 1989" (1991).

national figures are available on the success rate for interracial marriages, and what data are available do not indicate the racial composition of the marriages (Reiss 1980). In general, however, recent data suggest that interracial marriages — often because of difficulties in finding acceptance and a social network of support in times of difficulty — may contribute more than their share to the high incidence of marital dissolution in our society (Reiss and Lee 1988).

An interracial couple in our society is often a target for bigotry and a cause of irrational fear. The degree of difficulty faced by interracial couples varies, of course, with such factors as social status, economic level, geographic area, and the specific races involved.

Although sociologists have found no evidence of any special discrimination against children of marriages between a white person and a black person, these marriages are more likely than homogamous marriages to be child-free because of the couple's concerns about how having interracial parentage would affect their children. Sociologists find that offspring of these marriages are generally considered to be blacks by both the white and the black communities, so that they are neither more nor less acceptable to either racial community than other black children. Because this acceptance level is not very high in our society, an interracial couple's concern about the well-being of their children is realistic (Reiss 1980).

Interfaith Marriages

In the United States, the term *interfaith marriage* usually refers to a marriage that "mixes" a Protestant, a Roman Catholic, or a Jew (the three prominent religions in this country) with someone from one of the other two faiths.

It is important to note, however, that there are at least 250 denominations of Protestants in the United States, and there are more differences between some of them than there are between Protestantism and Catholicism (National Council of the Churches of Christ in the United States of America 1991). The marriage of a Mormon to an Episcopalian, then, might be considered an intermarriage by the families involved.

There are two denominations of Catholics — Greek Orthodox and Roman Catholics — and there are major differences between them. For example, priests in the Greek Orthodox church may marry. (Although many countries are chiefly Greek Orthodox, most of the people referred to as "Catholics" in the United States are Roman Catholics.)

There are three major denominations of Jews: Orthodox, Conservative, and Reform, with truly major differences among them. The marriage of an Orthodox Jew to a Reform Jew may be considered an intermarriage by the families involved (American Jewish Yearbook 1991).

Protestants, at 56 percent of the population, are the largest religious group in the United States. Roman Catholics are next (28 percent), whereas Jews are only a very small minority of about 2 percent.[14]

Before the separation of church and state in the eighteenth and nineteenth centuries, interfaith marriages were illegal in Western societies. In some countries, such as Northern Ireland, marriages between Catholics and Protestants are still illegal today. Although interfaith marriages are now legal in this country, they are still rigorously opposed by many Protestants, Catholics, and Jews alike. This opposition is apparently

---

[14]Gallup Organization, "Religious Preference, Church Membership, and Attendance: 1957 to 1989 (1991). The Jewish population in the United States is a good deal larger than 2 percent if nonreligious Jews are included. The Council of Jewish Federations identifies a broader category called "Jews by association" — a group that lives in households with at least one Jew (Kosmin 1991).

based on the fears that the couple's family life may be disrupted if they do not belong to the same faith and that each person's religious affiliation may be weakened or dissolved.

Incidence of Interfaith Marriage

In the 1950s, only 4 percent of Protestants, 12 percent of Roman Catholics, and 4 percent of Jews married outside their faith (Glenn 1982). In the 1970s, the incidence of intermarriage had nearly doubled for Protestants to 7 percent, had increased to 18 percent for Roman Catholics, and had tripled to 12 percent for Jews. This is a remarkable increase in the incidence of interfaith marriage in our society (Glenn 1982).

More recently, a 1990 survey found that an astonishing 52 percent of Jews were marrying outside their faith, an extraordinary rise from 4 percent in the 1950s and 12 percent in the 1970s (Kosmin 1991). Not only are 52 percent of Jews marrying outside their faith, but 72 percent of children in these interfaith families are being raised in a non-Judaic religion (or in no religion at all). Fully 90 percent of these children of Jewish-Gentile marriages are, themselves, marrying non-Jews (Kosmin 1991). "We have a phenomenon here that will have a great impact upon the viability of the Jewish community in the twenty-first century" (Davis 1992, p. 1).

There are several possible reasons for the increasing incidence of interfaith marriage in our society, including the trend of cultural assimilation of many minority groups, the merging of cultural values (particularly those of the middle class) that has tended to diminish religious differences, and the weakening of institutional controls that forbid interfaith marriage (Barlow 1977).

According to Rabbi David Davis, Chair of Judaic Studies at the University of San Francisco, the sharp rise in incidence of Jews marrying outside their faith can be attributed to "the breakdown of the family structure, the lack of a ghetto mentality, the mobility of the modern generation, and the fact that families are often geographically dislocated" (Davis 1992, p. 1).

From an individual point of view, a couple may decide to enter an interfaith marriage because they have complementary needs and interests and because they fell in love. Given the widespread opposition to interfaith marriage, however, other factors may be operant. One such factor may be a smaller number of prospects within members of a person's own religion than among members of other religions. It is quite possible that two people of different faiths may not consider their religious differences to be of great importance. Moreover, a marriage that is statistically classified as an interfaith marriage may, in reality, be no such thing, as when both people are agnostic or have little commitment to any religion and simply accept nominal identification as either "Protestant," "Roman Catholic," or "Jew."

Institutional Opposition to Interfaith Marriage

Interfaith marriage is actively discouraged, and sometimes forbidden, by official religious doctrines of all three prominent faiths in our society.

The various Protestant denominations all oppose mixed marriage, although to various degrees; Jehovah's Witnesses, for example, are vehement in their opposition, whereas Unitarians are much more accepting.

The Roman Catholic Church is much more unified and much more militant than most Protestant denominations in opposing interfaith marriages, requiring that its members be married in the church if they wish their marriage to be sanctioned and if they wish to remain in a state of grace so that they can receive communion.

Roman Catholic participation in a marriage before a civil official or non-Catholic clergy is expressly forbidden, and such a marriage, although legal in the view of non-Catholic clergy and civil authorities, is invalid in the view of the

Catholic church. A Catholic who wishes to marry a non-Catholic and remain in a state of grace must first receive dispensation from a priest and must make a "sincere promise" to remain steadfast in the Catholic faith and to do "all in his or her power" to have all children baptized and brought up in the Catholic church. The non-Catholic person must be informed of the promises that the Catholic person makes, and both people are to be "clearly instructed on the ends and essential properties" of marriage as they are perceived by the church (Pope Paul VI 1970).[15]

Among the most militant of all in its opposition to mixed marriages is Orthodox Judaism, which has from its inception regarded interfaith marriage as a sin. Both the Talmud and the Rabbinical Codes state unequivocally that intermarriage is punishable by banishment, the Judaic equivalent of excommunication. Moreover, Orthodox Judaism does not recognize the legitimacy of civil marriage for its members and believes that a Jew is properly married only when a rabbi has officiated (Mayer 1985).

Almost no Orthodox and very few Conservative rabbis will agree to officiate at weddings for mixed couples. Some Reform rabbis are more lenient, however, and many perform such weddings without insisting on the conversion of the non-Jewish partner — as long as that partner agrees to respect the other person's faith and to raise the children as Jews. Although Judaism does not proselytize, any person who undertakes to study the history and theology of Judaism may become a Jew and may then be accepted as a proper mate for a Jew (Davis 1992).

Although the figures vary somewhat with the faiths involved, interfaith marriages seem to have about a 10 percent higher failure rate than homogamous marriages. There is no evidence, however, that marriages between people of different Protestant denominations have any less stability than marriages between people of the same denomination (Heaton 1984; Glenn 1982; Bumpass and Sweet 1972). Nonetheless, divorce seems more likely among Protestants of different denominations than it is among nonmixed Catholic and Jewish couples (Glenn and Supancic 1984).

It is conceivable, of course, that examining divorce statistics may not reveal the true level of tension in interfaith marriages. Even when the two people in an interfaith marriage do not openly disagree about their separate faiths or engage in discussions of comparative theology, one or both may feel resentment or uneasiness over such issues as birth control, the children's indoctrination into the other's religion, or any religious practices that may interfere with the daily routine of their marriage. Depending on the circumstances, these disagreements need not necessarily lead to divorce.

No one really knows whether differences in the husband's and wife's religions are more or less significant than other differences. Religious leaders and counselors issue dire warnings about the risks of interfaith marriages, but these opinions represent an unavoidable bias and are not really substantiated with statistical evidence of marital failure.

The Meaning of Marriage for Society

Anthropologists have not discovered a society that lacked the institution of marriage. It is conceivable that a society could perpetuate itself from one generation to another without the institution of marriage, but no such society has ever been found. Apparently marriage serves

---

[15]Since 1970, a mass may be included as part of the marriage ceremony, subject to the local priest's approval (Johnson 1980).

some essential functions for the survival of the group.

Marriage as the Basis for the Nuclear Family

Sociologists believe that the reason marriage is necessary for the survival of the group is that it is the basis for the *nuclear family*—the married couple and their offspring. The nuclear family is found in some form in all known societies. Despite the many family forms and variations that have appeared throughout the world's societies, there has never been any widespread departure from some form of the nuclear family based on some form of marriage (Reiss 1980). For a further discussion of the countless forms that the family may take and the numerous essential functions that the family performs as a social institution, see Chapter 8.

Marriage as an Institution for Producing and Nurturing Children

In his definitive study of the forms and functions of marriage, Reiss (1980) found that only one function was universal in all known societies:

legitimatizing children. The society places the children with the couple that produced them and identifies them with this couple. The society then typically assigns the responsibility for the care of these children to this couple. Society licenses the married couple to produce children via the marriage license (Reiss 1980). Thus the society defines the married couple's rights and obligations with regard to their children and to each other. The parents are expected to remain together and provide a stable environment for the children they have produced.

This is a universal ideal for all societies, but one that is not always achieved, of course. In our society, for example, only about half of all married couples remain together to provide a stable environment for their children (see Chapter 12). Also, unmarried couples have children; about one child in four in the United States is born to a single mother (see Chapter 8). Moreover, many married couples do not have children but remain together in a child-free marriage. Despite these shortcomings in actual practice, the institution of marriage nevertheless provides a *societally preferred* method for producing and nurturing children. For further discussion of the nature and meaning of the family in our society see Chapter 8.

SUMMARY

Marriage is the second phase of the interlocking family system that consists of courtship, marriage, and the family. Some form of marriage is found in all known societies, as are some form of courtship and some form of the family. The key function of marriage in all known societies is to legitimatize children. All societies typically assign responsibility for the care and socialization of children to the married couple that produced them.

The decision to marry a particular person is one of the most important decisions of one's life. Even if the marriage is dissolved by divorce, many important psychological, societal, and economic ties remain and will continue to have persistent and significant effects throughout one's life.

The decision to marry may stem from a multiplicity of interrelated emotional, psychological, religious, and societal factors. Many people choose to marry as an avowal of anticipated permanence, trust, reliability, and commitment — a public statement that one loves and is loved by the other person. Other couples may opt for marriage because they feel that cohabitation is morally unacceptable and violates their religious or ethical principles. Many couples marry because they expect to have children and feel that their children should be legitimatized by marriage. Others marry because of parental or peer pressure. Although some people still marry for economic security, this reason is not nearly as important today as it once was, when it was very difficult for a person to survive economically without the partnership of marriage. Perhaps the most important reason for marrying in our society today is that one is in love.

All states require couples who plan to get married to apply for a marriage license. Different states have different requirements for issuing this license, but all states have a minimum age requirement and prohibit the marriage of close relatives (although the degree of closeness varies from state to state). Most states require a blood test before issuing a marriage license, and there is usually a "cooling off" period of a few days before the final marriage contract can be signed.

Throughout most of the world's societies, the preferred form of marriage is polygyny (multiple wives), whereas only a few societies have ever permitted polyandry (multiple husbands). The term *polygamy* refers to either polygyny or polyandry. *Bigamy* refers to illegal polygamy.

All societies regard marriage as a relatively permanent bond or commitment; the expectation is that marriage will be permanent, although most societies also make provision for divorce. From a religious point of view, marriage is regarded as a sacrament by all three prominent religions in our society (Protestantism, Roman Catholicism, and Judaism), and three-fourths of the people who are marrying for the first time have religious ceremonies, as do 60 percent of divorced people who remarry.

Marriage was viewed chiefly as an institution of divine significance until the nineteenth century. During the nineteenth century, however, the emphasis shifted toward a view of marriage as a civil institution. And during the twentieth century, the emphasis has shifted again toward a view of marriage as a vehicle for personal satisfaction. These shifts reflect a change in emphasis only, as all three aspects of marriage continue to be important.

Sexuality provides a major bond for most married couples, although the importance of sex varies significantly from individual to individual and from couple to couple. So long as each member of the couple is at about the same position on the erotophile-erotophobe scale, they are likely to be sexually compatible. If they are at different positions on the scale, their sexual interaction may become an exercise in power and manipulation. Moreover, there is complex interaction between sexual satisfaction and relationship satisfaction. If a husband is sexually satisfied, he will usually be satisfied with the relationship. With wives, relationship satisfaction must usually precede sexual satisfaction.

The incidence of adultery ranges from 30 to 60 percent in our society; adultery is usually about twice as likely to be committed by men as by women. However, in some groups and at some ages, the incidence of adultery among wives may be as high as, or higher than, it is among husbands.

Although one of the universal functions of marriage is the legitimatization of children, child-free marriage is now one of the most rapidly growing forms of marriage in our society.

Marriage among students, which was very unusual until the present generation, is still relatively uncommon today. Perhaps the greatest danger of marriage before college graduation is that intellectual inquiry will be stifled when educational goals become replaced by an emphasis on career training.

Interracial couples in our society are often victims of bigotry, with the degree of discrimination varying with such factors as geographic area, economic level, social status, and the specific races involved. In black-white marriages, children are usually considered to be members of the black community. There is no evidence that interracial marriages have a higher incidence of marital difficulty than do homogamous marriages. The incidence of interracial marriage is very low in our society, involving fewer than 2 percent of all marriages.

Interfaith marriages are actively discouraged, and in some cases forbidden, by all three prominent religions in our society because of the fear that they would disrupt family life. Interfaith marriages seem to have about a 10 percent higher failure rate than do homogamous marriages, although data are limited.

Since all known societies have some form of marriage, the institution is apparently essential for a society's survival. The reason, according to sociologists, is that marriage forms the basis for the nuclear family, which is also universal. Although marriage serves many functions, the one common to all societies is that of legitimizing children. All societies also expect that a married couple will care for the children they produce.

KEY TERMS

The following is a list of key terms in this chapter.
These terms are defined in context within the chapter, and many may also be found in the Glossary.

adultery	fertility rate	interracial	polyandry
bigamy	group marriage	marriage	polygamy
child-free marriage	hedonism	monogamy	polygyny
common-law marriage	interfaith marriage	nuclear family	sacrament
consensual adultery	intermarriage	open marriage	swinging

QUESTIONS

1. Discuss the reasons why some people choose to marry rather than cohabit. Why may some people choose cohabitation over marriage?

2. Define each of the following terms: *polygyny, polyandry, polygamy, monogamy, bigamy.*

3. Discuss the shifts in the meaning of marriage from medieval times to today.

4. What is the incidence of child-free marriages in our society? What are the characteristics of women who are likely to remain childless?

5. What are the pros and cons of marriage while in college? Discuss the effects of marriages between students on grades and subsequent employment options.

6. What is the incidence of interracial marriage in the United States today? For what reasons do people marry interracially?

7. What is the incidence of interfaith marriage in our society? Discuss the implications of the rise in incidence of interfaith marriages.

8. Discuss the interaction between sexual satisfaction and relationship satisfaction for husbands and wives.

SUGGESTIONS FOR FURTHER READING

Bellah, Robert, et al. *Habits of the Heart: Individuation and Commitment in American Life.* New York: Harper & Row, 1985.

Gilder, George. *Men and Marriage.* Gretna, La.: Pelican, 1986.

Lawson, Annette. *Adultery: An Analysis of Love and Betrayal.* New York: Basic Books, 1988.

Mayer, Egon. *Love and Tradition: Marriages Between Jews and Christians.* New York: Plenum Press, 1985.

Puttman, Frank. *Private Lives: Infidelity and the Betrayal of Intimacy.* New York: Norton, 1989.

Rubin, Lillian Breslow. *Erotic Wars.* New York: Farrar, Straus & Giroux, 1990.

Scarf, Maggie. *Intimate Partners: Patterns in Love and Marriage.* New York: Random House, 1987.

Vannoy-Hiller, Dana, and Philliber, William H. *Successful Women in Marriage.* Newbury Park, Calif.: Sage, 1989.

Whitbourne, Susan, and Ebmeyer, Joyce. *Identity and Intimacy in Marriage: A Study of Couples.* New York: Springer-Verlag, 1990.

The Changing Family in a Changing Society

It is easier to rule a kingdom than to regulate a family.

Chinese proverb

The Importance of the Family

Family Forms Among Human Societies

Family Forms in America

Racial-Ethnic Families in America

The Life Cycle of the Family

Violence in the American Family

What Do You Know?

Some of the following statements are true and some are false.
Can you tell which are which?

T/F   1. Most Americans regard family life as the most important element of their lives.

T/F   2. A good family life ranks first in importance for nearly 90 percent of Americans.

T/F   3. The incidence of single-parent families has been dropping gradually during the past two decades.

T/F   4. More than half of all children who live in single-parent households with their mothers live below the poverty line.

T/F   5. Researchers find that in general, the child-rearing years are the happiest of all stages in the life cycle of the family.

T/F   6. For the wife, the level of marital satisfaction usually drops when children are born.

T/F   7. Mothers typically respond to the departure of their children with an "empty nest syndrome," a period characterized by depression and a sense of uselessness.

T/F   8. Researchers have been unable to verify the existence of a "mid-life crisis."

T/F   9. Most older people have little interest in sexuality.

T/F   10. Older people tend to be lonelier or more depressed than younger people.

Answers: 1-T, 2-T, 3-F, 4-T, 5-F, 6-T, 7-F, 8-T, 9-F, 10-F

There is no question that the family is a fundamental social grouping. Despite its built-in strife and imperfections (and even violence), the family is the oldest and toughest of all human institutions and has outlasted much that seemed eternal — gods, empires, and economic or political systems.

The term *family* is one of the most commonly used words in our language; it is known to every child. Yet, as commonly as the word is used, the concept of "family" is difficult to define precisely. Anthropologists and historians have identified between 2,000 and 3,000 distinct societies — groups of people with ways of life so different from one another that they are regarded as having separate cultures, and each of them has evolved a different functioning version of marriage and the family (Gordon 1978).

In this chapter we will explore the meaning of the concept of family. We will examine both the changing family in today's America and the typical life cycle through which our families move. And we will also explore the paradox that, although families normally provide nurturance, warmth, and emotional support in our impersonal mass society, many families bring abuse, despair, and violence into the lives of one or more of their members.

The Importance of the Family

The family is one of the basic units of society, and its importance can scarcely be overemphasized. It is important both from a sociological perspective and in the perception of individuals — most of whom grow up in some form of family, as we will see.

Sociological Importance of the Family

The family plays such a vital role in the organization of any society that, even with the great diversity among societies, none has ever been discovered that did not have some form of the family (Reiss 1980).

Because aging and death are inevitable, a society would cease to exist after only one generation without the continued infusion of children — unless, of course, it could depend on perpetual immigration, which has never occurred in any known society.[1] The family not only serves the vital function of producing the next generation of children; it plays the single most important role of any social institution in the socialization of these children. Although other social institutions are important in instilling cultural norms in children (thereby shaping the character of the society in subsequent generations), the family plays a crucial role in socializing children. The family is especially important because it is the first agency to instill social rules and cultural conventions in children during the critical early years before children are exposed to the formal educational system.

The early values and codes of behavior that children first learn continue to play a key role in shaping their codes of conduct as they grow into adults. Modes of thought and action, systems of values, and ethical standards are more likely to become habitual when they are instilled in childhood, at which time they become the foundation for subsequent attitudes and behavior. Other important social organizations such as schools, churches, athletic organizations, community groups, and even street gangs and cliques are of great importance in the socialization process but can only build on what has already been established by the family (Reiss 1980).

---

[1]There have been small societies (usually religious cults) that have banned marriage, copulation, and family groups, and so have had to depend on continual recruitment of new members for their continuing existence. Although these societies have sometimes grown initially, they have never lasted very long, usually disintegrating with the death of the leader.

If the family—in whatever form it may take—is inoperative or is ineffectual in socializing its children, the consequences may be serious, for both the society and the children. At best, the negative consequences may simply deprive youths of the opportunities for a satisfactory life-style; at worst, the consequences may include dropping out of school, poverty, discouragement, desperation, alcohol or drug abuse, teenage pregnancy, gang violence, murder, Youth Authority detention, or prison (Reiss 1980).

The Importance of the Family to Individuals

Most people get the essential physical satisfactions of food, clothing, and shelter within a family. They also get a myriad of interpersonal satisfactions that make up the fabric of life. They expect family to provide stability, nurturance, loyalty, protection, and support. Most people form their deepest and most lasting emotional ties within their family. In a relatively impersonal mass society such as ours, the family performs an "affectional" function, serving as a source of emotional support, providing a sense of belonging, and giving a certain amount of emotional security from the dangers and threats of the outside world. Some families are more successful than others in providing these qualities, of course, and families may even be a source of pain and sorrow—but more on this later.

The family is central in the consciousness of virtually everyone in our society. Each family develops its own unique characteristics that distinguish it from other families. Each family has its own private jokes, myths, and rituals. Most families are bound together emotionally by a sense of shared experiences and understanding.

Because practically all of us are born and raised within some form of family, our initial experiences, which form the basis for our view of ourselves and of the world around us, are chiefly derived from a family setting.

What People *Say* About the Importance of the Family If we can believe what Americans say, family ties are the most important part of their lives—more important than work, money, recreation, friendships, religion, or anything else. The evidence for this comes from surveys conducted over half a century by more than a dozen research organizations (Glenn 1991).

A 1989 Gallup poll found that "a good family life" ranked first in importance for nearly nine out of ten Americans (89 percent), coming in ahead of "self-respect" (84 percent), "sense of accomplishment" (69 percent), "an exciting life" (58 percent), and "having a good time" (41 percent) (Gallup 1989a). In 1989, the Massachusetts Mutual American Family Value Study found that most respondents rated such values as "having a happy marriage" far above "being financially secure." Each year since 1976 the Monitoring the Futures Project at the University of Michigan has asked a sample of high school seniors to rate fourteen life goals. "Having a good marriage and family life" has consistently ranked first (Glenn 1991).

In one of the most definitive studies to date, the White House Conference on Families found in 1980 that 80 percent of the respondents ranked family life as either "the most important element in my life" (61 percent) or "one of the most important elements in my life" (19 percent). (See Figure 8-1.)

All of these data reflect what Americans *say* about the importance of the family to them. Additional supporting evidence is provided by many studies[2] conducted between 1970 and 1988 that found correlations between having a satisfactory family life and having a satisfactory life

---

[2]See Glenn (1991) for a bibliography of these studies.

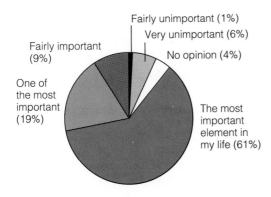

Fairly unimportant (1%)

Very unimportant (6%)

Fairly important (9%)

No opinion (4%)

One of the most important (19%)

The most important element in my life (61%)

How important is family life to you?

FIGURE 8-1
How Americans look at family life.

Source: White House Conference on Families (1980).

in general. The implication is that people who are satisfied with their family life are likely to be satisfied with their personal lives as a whole. (Conversely, people with a low level of satisfaction with family life are likely to have a relatively low level of personal satisfaction.) Thus it is apparently better to be unmarried than unhappily married, but to be happily married is the single most important predictor of overall personal happiness (Glenn 1991).

What People *Do*: The Increasing Legitimacy of Self-Interest   Although Americans say that they place a high value on family life, and although having a satisfactory life-style is correlated with having a satisfactory family life, it is not unusual for a person to sacrifice a good family life in order to obtain other values. Materialistic goals, such as money or career success, have grown increasingly important in recent years, even when these goals are in direct competition with having a happy family life. These days a growing proportion of college freshmen say that an important (or even essential) goal in

life is be "very well off financially." The proportion of college freshmen who embrace this goal has increased from 40 percent in the early 1970s to 70 percent in 1985 (Glenn 1991; Astin, Green, and Korn 1987). One of the dominant themes running through much of current marriage and family literature is that self-interest is replacing family interest and commitment (Sweet and Bumpass 1987; Hochschild 1989).

Over the decades the emphasis has shifted from a focus on the interests and needs of a broad group of extended kin, to those of the nuclear family, to those of the individual. Today, when self-interest competes with family values and parenting, Americans increasingly acknowledge the legitimacy of self-interest (Sweet and Bumpass 1987). In the matter of what Americans really think about the family, perhaps actions speak louder than words.

Family and Nonfamily Households in America

About 70 percent of people live in *family households* with the members related by either blood, marriage, or adoption: 56 percent of these live in married-couple households, 10 percent in single-parent households, and 5 percent in households containing two or more family members (such as siblings, grandmother and grandchild, or aunt with her niece or nephew) (Crispell 1991a).

About 30 percent of people live in *nonfamily* households: 25 percent live alone (Nord and Zill 1991) and 5 percent live in "other nonfamily households" that include roommates and unmarried couples (Crispell 1991a).[3] If a cohabitor has children sharing the household, it obviously contains relatives; nevertheless the Census Bureau classifies it as "nonfamily" unless the

---

[3]Numbers do not add up to 100 because of rounding.

cohabitor with children is the head of the household.[4] As we have seen (Chapter 6), the Census Bureau estimates that 95 percent of couples sharing a household in a sexual relationship are married, while 5 percent are cohabiting.[5]

There have been many significant changes in the structure and function of American households during this century. Consider the following:

- The proportion of married-couple households in our society has dropped sharply since 1919, from about 80 percent to today's 56 percent (Nord and Zill 1991).

- Fewer than one in ten of today's husbands provide the sole support for their families (Crispell 1991a), yet this was the norm until about mid-century when wives began to enter the work force (see Chapter 9).

- The proportion of married-couple families living with their own children (biological or adopted) under age eighteen[6] has dropped to an all-time low of 26 percent; 43 percent of married-couple families lived with their minor children in 1940 (Nord and Zill 1991).

- Finally, perhaps the most dramatic change of all is the rise in numbers of people living

alone as singles in our society. At the beginning of the century, only about 5 percent of people lived by themselves; this proportion has multiplied fivefold to reach the 25 percent who live alone today (Nord and Zill 1991; Kobrin 1976).

Homeless Families   Demographers estimate that in the United States there are from 600,000 to three million homeless people — people who have no housing unit in which to live. They sleep in doorways, under bridges, in bus stops, in subways, or in temporary shelters. About one-third of these homeless people are families — usually one parent with two or three children (Hutton 1991; Kozell 1988). (See Chapter 9 for a further discussion of families living in poverty and children in homeless families.)

Family Forms Among Human Societies

The classic definition of the term *family*, and the one most often cited as definitive, is the straightforward statement of Murdock (1949):

> The family is a social group characterized by common residence, economic cooperation and reproduction. It includes adults of both sexes, at least two of whom maintain a socially approved sexual relationship, and one or more children, own or adopted, of the sexually cohabiting adults. (p. 1)

Murdock classified the family into three types: (1) the nuclear family, consisting of a married man and woman and their offspring; (2) the extended family, consisting of two or more nuclear families living together (with various relatives) in one household; and (3) the polygamous

---

[4]This sounds confusing but is really very straightforward. The Census Bureau classifies a cohabiting couple as a "nonfamily household" if (1) neither cohabitor has children in the household or (2) the parent of children in the household is not the head of the household. If the parent of children *is* the head of the household, the Census Bureau classifies it as a "family" household (Crispell 1991a).

[5]U.S. Bureau of the Census, "Marital Status and Living Arrangements: March 1990" (1991).

[6]The term *children* can be used simply as a synonym of "offspring" to mean people of any age. It is interesting to note that more than half of all eighteen- to twenty-four-year-old "children" live with their parents (Crispell 1991a).

family, consisting of two or more nuclear families joined by multiple marriage.

The Nuclear Family

The nuclear family is the source of children and thus provides the foundation for the next generation. The traditional nuclear family also nurtures and socializes the children it produces. The parents are, in a sense, "licensed" to produce children (via the marriage license), and the children remain and are identified with the couple.

The married couple's rights and obligations are defined not only with regard to each other, but also with regard to their children. The parents are expected to remain together and provide a stable environment for the children. That these functions are so essential is thought to explain why the nuclear family occurs in some form in all known societies (Stephens 1982).

The monogamous nuclear family is now thought to have occurred as a basic family form since early human history. It was once thought that early in human history, group marriage was the norm, with several adult men relating sexually to several adult women, forming an interdependent and relatively permanent group that was a basis for a family structure (Murdock 1949). Sociologists now doubt that group marriage ever occurred as a dominant form; rather, the monogamous nuclear family was probably the basis of social structure from earliest time and existed in even the most primitive societies. Each time a primitive society has been discovered, it has turned out that its social structure was based on the monogamous nuclear family (Reiss 1980).

An interesting development in this regard was the 1971 discovery of a surviving Stone Age tribe in the mountains of the Philippine island of Mindanao. This tribe (the Tassidy) had no permanent dwellings, no crops, and only the crudest tools of stone and bamboo. They made fire by the friction of wood against wood and kept no domestic animals. Nevertheless, the Tassidy lived in basic nuclear family units consisting of a husband, wife, and unmarried children.

An even more primitive society was the pygmies of the Andaman Island forests, who were discovered by European explorers two centuries ago. The Andaman Island pygmies were so primitive that they did not know how to make fire. Yet the basis of their social structure was the nuclear family based on a monogamous marriage.

The Extended Family

Very elaborate versions of the extended family have emerged in some human societies. For example, the *corporate family* (which reached its greatest development during the Ch'ing Dynasty in China, 1644–1912) often contained as many as seventy or eighty people living together in a walled compound of several buildings. The oldest man exercised patriarchal domination over his wife and concubines, their unmarried sons and daughters, their married sons and their wives and children, and even married grandsons and their wives and children. The ideal was to have six generations of the family living in the compound and for the family to go to nine generations without a division of property.[7]

An interesting version of the extended family occurs among the Mentawei of western Sumatra. Here, couples are committed to each other but do not marry until middle age. Meanwhile, the woman continues to live in her father's

---

[7] The most frequently occurring family form, however, even in societies that idealize the extended family, has always been the nuclear family; the average household size in these societies has never been more than three to five people (Reiss 1980; Gordon 1978; Shorter 1975).

household while the man lives apart in *his* father's household. Children are adopted at birth by their mother's father (their maternal grandfather) and are supported by her brothers (their maternal uncles). When the couple reaches middle age, they marry and establish their own household. The husband then formally adopts his now fully grown children. A typical household among the Mentawei, then, consists of a set of grandparents, their sons and daughters, and their daughter's children. In other words, adult sons live with their parents and sisters and support their sister's children rather than their own children — who live in their grandparent's household with their mother, aunts, and uncles (Shorter 1975).

Another interesting version of the extended family, and one that occurs much closer to home, is the *stem family* of rural Ireland. (This version of the family also occurs in other societies.) In the stem family, a son inherits the farm (which is usually too small to be subdivided) from his father. However, instead of the eldest son automatically inheriting, the father can designate any son he wishes as heir. (When the eldest son automatically inherits property from his father, the system is called *primogeniture* — a system found in many societies.) Because the father in a stem family can designate any son he wishes as his heir, sons who do not move to jobs in cities (emigrate) must work on the family farm in virtually total subordination to their father. They can only hope to be the one chosen to inherit the property. Even after the sons are in their thirties or forties, any wages from side jobs they may have (such as working on another farm) traditionally go to the father. Because marriage involves a property settlement and the sons do not have any property until an heir is named, they may not marry until the father is ready to reveal his heir and retire. The son who is named heir then marries and moves his wife into the household, turning over one of the rooms in the house to his parents, for whom he provides food, fuel, and other provisions. Thus the household in a stem family consists of the parents and their children until the father retires, after which it consists of the old couple, the son who has been named heir, his wife and children, and any other unmarried sons or daughters who remain (Gordon 1983).

Polygamous Families

The polygamous family, the third category of Murdock's (1949) classification scheme, is the preferred family form for a solid majority of the world's societies (see Chapter 7).

Clearly, polygyny (one husband with two or more wives) has an advantage over monogamy in societies in which the ratio of marriageable men to marriageable women is low due to any number of factors. In these societies, polygyny makes it possible for more women to marry and to have children. In societies in which women do most of the productive work, having more than one wife would be an economic advantage for the husband. In societies in which women are not expected to do so much productive work, having more than one wife may be regarded as a sign of status, affluence, and power. A household containing multiple wives and their children would be expensive to maintain and could be afforded only by a wealthy, powerful man.

One example of an existing polygynous culture is the Bogand tribe in central Africa. To minimize jealousy among wives in this society, husbands and wives live apart. The husband provides each wife with a house and garden of her own and invites the women, one at a time, to come to his house for visits. Conflict is further reduced by a system of clearly defined responsibilities. The first wife, outranking all her successors, looks after the couple's religious fetishes — objects such as water buffalo horns filled with herbs and clay and presumably inhabited by powerful spirits. The second wife is charged with shaving her husband's head, cutting his nails, and then protecting the trimmings from enemies who might use them in potentially lethal magic ceremonies. Additional duties are assigned to other wives (Wernick 1974).

Polyandry, in which one wife has two or more husbands, has been permitted by only a tiny percentage of the world's societies and has nearly vanished today. Nevertheless, it is perfectly logical under certain conditions. For example, among the Nayar of the Malabar coast in southern India, a girl is married at puberty to a young man who is chosen by an astrologer and preferably has higher social position than she does. The bridegroom might or might not consummate the marriage, but he is subsequently expected to have nothing more to do with his wife. She then takes a succession of several husbands who visit her at night but have no legal commitment except to bring a suitable gift of cloth if the union results in a baby whose paternity he chooses to recognize. All the children by this succession of fathers are brought up by the mother and her sisters in a large house that is ruled by the mother's eldest brother (Reiss 1980).

The Nayar polyandrous family startled early anthropologists and sociologists, who debated whether the arrangement even fitted into the concept of "marriage." The Nayar, however, certainly thought so, and they took their rules very seriously — strangling any girl who broke them (if, for example, she copulated with a man of a lower caste). Viewed in the context of the Nayar society, the rules of marriage made sense: The Nayar were a caste of professional soldiers, and all the young men were away from the community for most of the year, fighting or training. Nayar family arrangements allowed them access to women when they returned on leave and at the same time provided a stable home for the children (Reiss 1980).

Family Forms in America

The Industrial Revolution in the eighteenth and nineteenth centuries and the Gender-Role Revolution in the twentieth century have had an enormous impact on the face of the American family, changing it almost beyond recognition. There is no one "American family" today; instead, there are many American families, or alternate family forms. Indeed, declines in the prevalence of the nuclear family have been observed in developed countries around the world, not just in the United States. Before we consider the various family forms found in America today, we must first trace the history of the traditional American family.

Decline of the Traditional American Family

From colonial days until the 1950s, the traditional American family consisted of two parents living with their biological (or adopted) children (and perhaps other relatives or paid workers) in one household. When necessary (because of injury, illness, death, or economic hardship), children would be "farmed out"[8] to a relative in another household, who would assume responsibility for their care. Generations of rural American children were brought up in this way.

---

[8]The term *farmed out* has an interesting origin. In our agricultural past, if a family could not take care of all its children, one (or more) would be placed in another farming household, where children would be expected to earn their keep. Girls would typically help with the housework, cooking, and child care; boys would typically help with the outside work of planting, plowing, and animal husbandry. Both boys and girls would help with the "truck" garden (which produced vegetables for the family's table), and both boys and girls would feed chickens, ducks, and geese, gather eggs, and milk cows or goats. Any money that farmed-out children earned was, both by custom and by law, the property of their father.

BOX 8-1

Complex Family Groupings

Consider the following situation: Jill lived with her parents (a nuclear family) until she was eight, at which time her parents divorced. Her mother was granted custody, but Jill always felt closer to her father and spent many afternoons, weekends, and summers with him. Then her father remarried. Even though her mother remained her custodial parent, Jill considered herself to be equally a part of the family grouping composed of her father and stepmother. She continued to spend afternoons, weekends, and summers with her father and his second wife — her stepmother.

She exchanged cards, greetings, and gifts with her father and stepmother at Christmas and on birthdays, had a key to their house,

and kept many of her clothes and belongings there. When she entered college recently, she listed her father as her major source of support because he is paying her tuition and other expenses.

Meanwhile, her mother has remarried, and Jill then became a member of a family that consisted of her mother and stepfather. In one household she has a mother and stepfather; in the other household she has a father and stepmother.

Now, suppose her mother and stepfather had a son — who is her half-brother — and then got divorced. Her stepfather obtained custody of his son, Jill's half-brother, and then remarried, too. Jill and her half-brother remain very close, and she now spends a

---

Even as our society began shifting from agriculture to industry in the mid-nineteenth century, this traditional family form persisted, except that growing numbers of fathers worked outside the home (see Chapter 9 for a more detailed description of this period). Until the late 1950s, four out of five families still consisted of an employed father and a mother who concentrated her efforts on housework and child care.

Monumental forces were again set in motion in the late 1950s with the massive movement of married women into the work force, a plunge in the birthrate, a rapid rise in the divorce rate, postponement of marriage, postponement of childbearing, and economic and political results

of the women's liberation movement. These forces of change amount to a gender-role revolution (Exter 1991; Fuchs 1988; Sweet and Bumpass 1987) that has transformed the American family. By the late 1980s, the traditional nuclear family was no longer the dominant family form in America; it had been replaced as a dominant family form by alternate family forms: the *stepfamily*, the *single-parent family*, the *cohabiting family*, and the *two-earner family*. In a two-earner family, both parents are employed outside the home. (The movement of mothers of young children into the world of outside employment will be examined in Chapter 9.) Next we examine in turn each of these alternate family forms.

good deal of time in her ex-stepfather's home with his second wife and her half-brother; she considers this household to be a part of her immediate family. Moreover, they welcome her into their home and consider her a part of their family. This family form, then, consists of Jill, her ex-stepfather, her half-brother — who is Jill's blood relation — and her ex-stepfather's second wife (who has no kin name in our family system but whom Jill probably regards as a kind of functional stepmother).

Jill's mother now marries for the third time. Jill doesn't like her mother's third husband (her second stepfather) very much. She feels more at home with her ex-stepfather's family and feels a special intimacy with her half-brother, with whom she has a blood tie. Moreover, this family grouping still considers her a part of their family and continues to welcome her into their home.

Meanwhile, Jill continues to identify with the family grouping composed of her father and her stepmother, spends a good deal of time at their home, and continues to be supported financially by her father.

Although Jill has no nuclear family, she has quite an extensive extended family — if all the kin of her mother, father, stepmother, stepfather, and ex-stepfather are included. She identifies with three immediate families: two stepfamilies (one containing her mother and second stepfather and one containing her father and stepmother) and an unclassified family containing her ex-stepfather, his second wife, and Jill's half-brother.

This example may be extended still further, with any number of possible permutations and combinations. With multiple divorces, remarriages, cohabitations, and offspring of different pairs of parents combined in various family groupings, there are so many possible variations of the family form that only a few have been given names. These various functional family groupings are usually simply lumped together as "stepfamilies."

The Stepfamily

Sociologists commonly recognize three forms of stepfamilies: the reconstituted family, the blended family, and the binuclear family.

A *reconstituted family*, which consists of a parent, his or her children, and a stepparent, is created when a widowed or divorced parent with custody of children is remarried to someone who does not have children. A *blended family* is created when two divorced (or widowed) people who have children marry each other (Ihinger-Tallman and Pasley 1987). A *binuclear family* consists of two families formed when two previously married couples with children remarry, forming two new nuclear families. Each of these families consists of a parent, a stepparent, and the parent's children (Ahrons 1979). All of these families (reconstituted, blended, and binuclear) have specific and distinguishing structural and functional characteristics that have merited study by sociologists. They all have one overriding characteristic: Each family consists of stepparents and stepchildren in various configurations (see Box 8-1). For simplicity, then, all of them can be considered *stepfamilies*, and that is the term we will use in the remainder of this book.

Demographers estimate that 44 percent of all marriages are now a remarriage for one or both spouses (Pasley and Ihinger-Tallman 1988).

"Well, my mommy kept her name."

Most of these remarriages involve children. Seventeen percent of married-couple families with children are stepfamilies (Glick 1990). More than half of the people in the United States have been, are now, or will be a member of a stepfamily at some point in their lives (Glick 1992). (For a further discussion of remarriage and stepparenting, see Chapter 13.)

A high incidence of remarriages and stepfamilies is not new to our society. In colonial Plymouth, Massachusetts, nearly half of husbands and one wife in four were in a remarriage. These remarriages, however, followed the death of a spouse, not a divorce (Demos 1970). What is new today is that remarriage is likely to follow divorce rather than death.

Today's stepchildren typically have a noncustodial father in addition to a stepfather (who lives in the household). This is a significantly different configuration from the stepfamily of Plymouth Colony, in which one of the child's parents had usually died. The difficult and complex role interactions among parents (custodial and absent), stepparents, children, and stepchildren are explored in Chapter 13.

The Single-Parent Family

A single-parent family can occur in any one of four ways: (1) when a child's parents are divorced or separated, (2) when one of the child's parents has died, (3) when the mother has never been married and is living alone, or (4) when the courts have approved the adoption of a child by a single person. The incidence of single-parent families has been increasing rapidly during the past two decades. Consider the following statistics concerning single-parent families:

- About 10 percent of all American households are now single-parent families.[9]

---

[9]U.S. Bureau of the Census, "Changing American Households and Families: 1980–1990" (1991).

TABLE 8-1

Births to Unmarried American Women as Percent of All Births, by Race: 1970–1988

	1970	1980	1985	1987	1988
Total	10.7	18.4	22.0	24.5	25.7
White	5.7	11.0	14.5	16.7	17.7
Black	37.6	55.2	60.1	62.2	63.5

Source: U.S. National Center for Health Statistics, "Births to Unmarried Women, by Race of Child and Age of Mother: 1970 to 1988" (1991).

- About one baby in four is born to an unwed mother; of these births, 64 percent are black and 18 percent are white (see Table 8-1).

- As a result of the high birthrate of illegitimate children and the high divorce rate, one American child in four now lives in a single-parent family.[10] In 1990, 61 percent of black children, 29 percent of Hispanic children, and 17 percent of white children lived in single-parent families (McNeil 1992).[11]

- Nine out of ten black children and four out of ten white children born to unmarried mothers are kept by the mother. Grandmothers are often very helpful in raising black children (Spanier 1989).

- More than half (54 percent) of all mothers in single-parent households live in poverty.

Nearly one in five single-parent, male-headed families also live in poverty. Seventy-five percent of black, 46 percent of Hispanic, and 43 percent of white single parents live in poverty.[12]

It should be noted, however, that just as a two-parent family does not automatically guarantee well-adjusted, adequately socialized, creative, productive children, neither does a single-parent family automatically guarantee the opposite. Undoubtedly, some children in single-parent families receive better care than other children in two-parent families receive.

Toni Morrison, winner of the 1988 Pulitzer prize for her novel *Beloved*, speaks from her own experience as a black single mother:

> I don't think a female running a house is a problem. . . . It's perceived as one because of the notion that a head is a man. . . . The notion that the head is the one who brings in

[10]U.S. Bureau of the Census, "Children Under 18 Years Old, by Presence of Parents: 1970 to 1988" (1990).

[11]In 1990 there were nearly eight million single-parent families in the United States. Female-headed families numbered 6.8 million; male-headed families numbered 1.2 million. U.S. Bureau of the Census, "Changing American Households."

[12]U.S. National Center for Children in Poverty, "Distribution of All Children and of Poor Children, by Family Type and Race: 1987" (1991).

Some children in single-parent families receive better care than other children in two-parent families.

the most money is a patriarchal notion, that a woman — and I have raised two children alone — is somehow lesser than a male head. Or that I am incomplete without the male. This is not true. (Angelo 1989, p. 122)

The Cohabiting Family

The acceptance of cohabitation in our society has led to a form of the family that consists of a couple living in a sexual relationship together with her, his, or their children. As we have seen in Chapter 6, four out of ten cohabitations include children living in the household.

Consider, for example, the situation of a divorced father with custody of two children who is cohabiting with a divorced mother and her child. The cohabiting couple and their children share a household as a functioning family. They

have been in a stable relationship with shared responsibilities for eight years — a year longer than the average (median) length of marriage.

The couple regard themselves as committed to each other and to the children and consider themselves a family. Perhaps they have not married for any number of reasons, none of which necessarily means a lack of commitment. One reason might be that if they marry they may pay a much higher income tax, which they simply cannot afford (see Chapter 14). This "marriage tax" exacts significant economic penalties from a cohabiting couple if they decide to marry.

Functionally, then, this grouping is a family even though it does not fit the usual definition of "family" because the couple are not related either by blood or by marriage. This family is one example of a well-established, deeply committed cohabiting family.

Unmarried couples are gaining increasing social acceptance, as we have seen in Chapter 6. Cohabiting families are now being granted recognition as legal family units in some communities. In San Francisco, for example, cohabiting families are formally recognized as domestic partners and are eligible for such advantages as family leave. The emphasis in our society seems to be shifting away from defining a family strictly in terms of blood or legal ties and toward defining a family in terms of emotional bonds (Crispell 1991b).

Two-Earner Families

Regardless of whether the family is a nuclear family, a stepfamily, or a cohabiting family, it is now the norm for the mother to work outside the home. The resultant *two-earner family* is attracting increasing attention in part because of its growing prevalence. U.S. Census data show that both husband and wife have paying jobs in about two-thirds of families with one or more children under age eighteen.[13] In addition, dual employment can affect the couple's relationship and create child-care problems. (These issues are addressed in Chapter 9.) Demographers project that if present trends continue, more than three-fourths of mothers with preschool children will be in the work force within the next generation (Adams and Adams 1990).

Racial-Ethnic Families in America

Racial-ethnic families constitute a large and growing minority in our society, as we have seen (Chapter 1). If present trends continue, more than one-third of our population will be black, Hispanic, and Asian American by the end of the decade.[14]

The Black Family

With the decline in marriage rates among black women and the increase in black female-headed households, the family patterns of blacks and whites are moving farther apart than they have ever been in this century (Cherlin 1989; Spanier 1989:

- More than six out of ten black children are born out of wedlock. (Less than one in five white children are born out of wedlock.)

- Nine out of ten black children born to an unmarried mother are kept by the mother.

(Four out of ten white children born to an unmarried mother are kept by the mother.) (See Table 8-2.)

- Only about half of all black family households are married couples, as compared with more than three-quarters of white family households.

- Four out of ten black families are female-headed. (Less than one white family in ten is female-headed.)

- Fewer than four in ten black children live with both parents. (Eight out of ten white children live with both parents.)

- More than four in ten black children live below the poverty level, as compared with less than one in five white children.

These demographic facts, along with high unemployment, high rates of family disruption, increased welfare dependence, and violence in inner-city neighborhoods, are thought by some scholars to be a direct response to the economic upheavals in America in the 1980s and 1990s (Skolnick 1991; Newman 1988; Wilson 1987). Other scholars believe that the changes in black family life also stem from other, much more deep-seated social, cultural, and legal factors that have existed for decades (Nord and Zill 1991; Ellwood and Crane 1990; Farley and Allen 1987).

Only about 70 percent of adult black men work and contribute the major share of the family household income; thus nearly 30 percent are unemployed. In 1989, almost three out of four black families in which the husband was present had incomes below the national median.[15] Income continues to be lower for blacks with

---

[13]U.S. Bureau of Labor Statistics, "Labor Force Participation Rates for Wives, Husband Present, by Age of Own Youngest Child: 1975 to 1989" (1991).

[14]U.S. Bureau of the Census, "Projections of the Hispanic Population by Age and Sex: 1989–2010" (1990); and "Projections of the Total Population by Age, Sex, and Race: 1989–2010" (1990).

[15]U.S. Bureau of the Census, "Money Income of Families — Percent Distribution by Income Level, by Race, and Hispanic Origin of Householder, and Selected Characteristics: 1988 and 1989" (1991).

TABLE 8-2

Some Comparisons Between Black and White Family Households

	Black Family Households	White Family Households
Married-couple households	51.3%	83.2%
Female-headed households	43	9
Children living with both parents	39	79
Children born out of wedlock	64	15
Children living in poverty	44	15

Sources: U.S. Bureau of the Census, "Household and Family Characteristics: March 1990 and 1989" (1990); "Children Below the Poverty Level, by Race and Hispanic Origin: 1970 to 1989" (1991).

comparable education and occupations than for whites (Pettigrew 1989).

Blacks have higher rates of separation and divorce than any other racial-ethnic group in the United States (Cherlin 1989; Glenn and Supancic 1984).

As we have seen in Chapter 6, the high proportion of unemployed and unemployable black men reduces the availability of potential marriage partners to the extent that growing numbers of young black women are concerned that they will never find a husband able to support a family and thus "see no advantage to marriage" (Skolnick 1991, p. 16).

Several detailed studies of blacks in America have offered various economic explanations for the differences between white and black families, citing shortcomings in the welfare system and the relatively high unemployment and low wages of both black men and women. However, none of these economic explanations have been very successful. It is apparent that the differences between white and black families are not just

caused by economic forces but are much more complex, involving many interrelated, multifaceted issues that are deeply embedded in our culture (Nord and Zill 1991; Ellwood and Crane 1990; Farley and Allen 1987).

The Hispanic Family

The Hispanic population is growing at roughly five times the rate of the U.S. population as a whole (Valdés 1991). Demographers project that the number of Hispanics in our population may triple to sixty-four million in the first decade of the twenty-first century, surpassing blacks as America's largest minority group (Crispell 1991a). As we have noted, Hispanics are an ethnic group, not a race.

Hispanics in the United States are divided into the following four subgroups:

• Mexican Americans (Chicanos), who make up nearly two-thirds (63 percent) of the Hispanic population.

- Puerto Rican Americans (about 12 percent of American Hispanics).
- Cuban Americans (about 6 percent of American Hispanics).
- Hispanics from various Central and South American countries (about 19 percent of American Hispanics).[16]

In 1989, median family income of Hispanic families was $22,948, compared with $35,975 for whites and $20,209 for blacks.[17]

Hispanics do not assimilate as fast as other groups of immigrants to the United States but tend instead to marry within the subgroup of origin. Hispanics love their culture and prefer to associate with other Hispanics from within their own subgroup, with whom they share similar values and ease of communication (Valdés 1991).

Three-quarters of Hispanic Americans live in California, Texas, New York, Florida, or Illinois, with almost two-thirds living in metropolitan areas (Bodovitz 1991b).

Wages for Chicanos continue to be low for both men and women. More than one Chicano family in four lives below the poverty level.[18] Most Chicanos use English as their dominant language and steadily improve their job status from temporary to permanent jobs (Massey 1986).

In 1990, nearly 45 percent of Chicanos graduated from high school, and nearly 30 percent of these students enrolled in college. However, only 7 percent of Chicanos had four or more years of college in 1989.[19]

Traditionally, Chicano families have been male-dominated. Chicano women who are employed outside the home and see the more egalitarian attitude of other American women find that conflicts and tensions begin to emerge over the power structure in their own families (Zavella 1987).

Chicanos and Puerto Ricans tend to have large families, to be young (their median age is about twenty-four), to be relatively less educated than other Hispanics, and to be poor.

Female-headed households are highest among Puerto Rican families (44 percent) and lowest among Cuban American families. Puerto Ricans are slightly better educated than blacks, with just over half their population graduating from high school and nearly 10 percent having four or more years of college. Of all the subgroups of Hispanics, Puerto Ricans have the highest poverty level, with nearly four out of ten families living below the poverty level.[20]

Hispanics from Central and South American countries have a median age of twenty-eight; nearly two-thirds are high school graduates, and 17 percent have four or more years of college. One of these Hispanic families in four is female-headed, and nearly one in five families lives below the poverty level.[21]

Cuban Americans are generally from the middle and upper classes and identify closely with the white populations of these classes. They have higher incomes, smaller households, and are relatively older than other Hispanics (median age is thirty-nine), and nearly one in five has more than four years of college.[22]

---

[16]U.S. Bureau of the Census, "Social and Economic Aspects of the Hispanic Population: 1989" (1991).

[17]U.S. Bureau of the Census, "Money Income of Families."

[18]U.S. Bureau of the Census, "Social and Economic Aspects of the Hispanic Population."

[19]U.S. Bureau of the Census, *Tenth Annual Status Report on Minorities in Education*, January 20, 1992.

[20]"Social and Economic Aspects of the Hispanic Population."

[21]"Social and Economic Aspects of the Hispanic Population."

[22]U.S. Bureau of the Census, "White, Black, and Hispanic Households, by Type: 1970 to 1990" (1991).

Cuban Americans tend to use the Spanish language predominantly. For this reason they tend to distance themselves somewhat from non-Hispanic whites, even though they often share the same educational and occupational backgrounds as middle- and upper-class non-Hispanic whites.[23] Cuban Hispanics are increasingly being targeted by advertising markets because of their relative affluence (Bodovitz 1991b). In Miami, for example, numerous Spanish-language media options available to advertisers — ten radio stations, five magazines, and two daily newspapers — are vying to reach the large, affluent Cuban American population (Bodovitz 1991b).

Hispanics from Central and South America are intermediate between Cuban Americans and Mexican Americans in terms of education and income.[24]

The Asian American Family

Although Asian Americans represent a little less than 3 percent of our population, they are America's fastest-growing, most diverse, and most affluent minority group. Their influence on the economy is already quite significant. In 1989, the median household income of Asian Americans was $36,102, compared with $35,975 for non-Hispanic whites, $22,948 for Hispanics, and $20,209 for blacks.[25]

As of 1990, 70 percent of Asian Americans lived in metropolitan areas, with nearly 40 percent living in California. Three-fourths of them were relatively recent immigrants, coming from the Philippines, Vietnam, China, Korea, Iran, Taiwan, Cambodia, India, and Laos (Bodovitz and Edmonson 1991).

Traditionally, Asian families are patriarchal and have a clear-cut division of labor. The wife is expected to take care of the household and children, whereas the husband fulfills the role of breadwinner and expects to be obeyed by his wife and children (Kitano 1976).

The younger generation of Asian American women appear to be dissatisfied with the constraints of having an Asian husband, and intermarriage is high among the younger Japanese and Chinese Americans. A majority of third-generation Japanese American women now marry outside their race (Staples and Mirande 1980). Although divorce rates are low for first-generation Asian American immigrants, these rates are increasing among younger Asian Americans.[26]

Asian Americans normally achieve relatively high academic levels, with most graduating from high school and many graduating from college and then pursuing business or professional careers (Sue and Okazaki 1990). Researchers have yet to explain why this group has such a relatively high achievement pattern. Attributing their achievements either to genetic explanations (hereditary differences in intelligence between Asians and whites) or to cultural advantages based on familial patterns and expectations provokes intense controversy (Sue and Okazaki 1990). Despite the relatively high levels of academic achievement and business and professional success of many Asian Americans, they are nevertheless more likely to live in poverty than are whites — 11 percent versus 8 percent (Crispell 1992).

---

[23]"Social and Economic Aspects of the Hispanic Population."

[24]U.S. Bureau of the Census, "White, Black, and Hispanic Households."

[25]U.S. Bureau of the Census, "Money Income of Families"; Bodovitz and Edmonson (1991).

[26]U.S. National Center for Health Statistics," Marriages and Divorces — Number and Rate, by State: 1980 to 1988" (1990).

The Life Cycle of the Family

All people go through a life cycle that begins with conception and ends with death. The rhythms and cycles that govern our lives are fundamental, and their importance has long been recognized. Families also go through life cycles, whether they are traditional families, stepfamilies, cohabiting families, single-parent families, or child-free families. Although most research available on the life cycle of the family has been done on the traditional nuclear family, much of it can be applied to remarriages, to stepfamilies, and to cohabiting families. Even if a parental couple are not married, the dynamics may be essentially the same as for a married couple, if they remain together long enough. A single-parent family goes through the child-rearing stage, postchild state, and progression into old age and retirement, but the prechild stage is absent.

Although about one married couple in five has no children, very little is known about the life cycle of child-free families—except that they proceed through middle age to old age and retirement (see Chapter 7).

Because life cycles are inescapable and are generally parallel in most family forms, we will cite research conducted on the life cycle of the traditional American family even though this form is now a minority form. The life cycle of the family may be divided into the following stages:

- The prechild years as a married couple—before children are born (except for the single-parent family).

- The child-rearing years—from the birth of the first child until the last child leaves home.

- The postchild years—from the time the last child leaves home until the onset of old age.

- The retirement years.

- The return to singlehood (as a widow or widower)—when one of the couple dies.

The Prechild Years

For many couples, the prechild years are the happiest of all stages in the life cycle of the family. Apparently, for these people the best of all possible worlds is to be newly married and have no children.

A classic study published a generation ago (Blood and Wolfe 1960) summarized the prechild years of marriage:

> The first few years of marriage are a honeymoon, which continues the romance of the courtship. With the birth of the first baby, satisfaction with the standard of living and companionship declines. In subsequent years, love and understanding lag. . . . These trends do not involve all couples, but affect a very large proportion of the total. (pp. 87–88)

Most marriages never return to the happiness level of the prechild stage. However, the years after the children have left home are almost as happy as the prechild years. Thus the curve of marital satisfaction is generally U-shaped[27] (see Figure 8-2). This does not mean, of course, that all marriages follow this U-shaped curve. There are great individual differences in the effect that children have on a marriage; for many they bring great joy, satisfaction, and a sense of fulfillment

---

[27]Although there is a certain amount of controversy over the details of the curve and the problem of subjectivity in defining "marital satisfaction," the research of Rollins and Feldman (1970) that established the U-shaped curve of marital satisfaction over the marriage cycle has been supported by other studies, which are summarized in Spanier et al. (1975).

to a couple. Many couples who are richly rewarded by parenthood experience their children's accomplishments with pride and joy and find that the degree of marital satisfaction *rises* with each successive stage in the family cycle. These couples manage the difficulties and complications that children bring to a marriage with a minimum of conflict and a maximum of satisfaction.

The Child-Rearing Years

With the transition to parenthood, many changes occur in the couple's relationship and life-style. After an initial drop in the level of marital satisfaction for the average husband, his satisfaction may level off somewhat when the oldest child reaches age three. For the average wife, the level of marital satisfaction continues to fall until the oldest child reaches adolescence, at which time it rises sharply (see Figure 8-2). The rise in marital satisfaction for the wife at this time may occur because teenagers may require less time and attention than younger children do.

Lower-class parents do not commonly experience as high a level of marital satisfaction as do middle-class parents during the stage when their children are teenagers. These parents typically feel a severe financial squeeze during this stage, and teenagers are frequently pressured to move out of the home and be responsible for earning their own living. Middle-class parents, on the other hand, generally experience rising incomes during the period when their children are teenagers, and middle-class children are not usually expected to be economically independent. Rather, they are customarily sent to college while their parents continue to be financially responsible for them.[28]

---

[28]U.S. National Center for Education Statistics, *Undergraduate Financing of Postsecondary Education, May 1988* (1991).

The reported marital satisfaction level continues to rise for both parents during the so-called "launching stage" (stage 6 in Figure 8-2), which begins when the oldest child leaves home and ends when the youngest child leaves home. When the youngest child leaves, the postchild stage of the family cycle begins, and the typical couple are now middle-aged.

The Postchild Years

As a result of two trends — a longer life expectancy and a shorter childbearing period — contemporary couples spend about half their married lives in the postchild period of the family life cycle. The postchild period encompasses both middle age and old age. The marital satisfaction level during middle age can be nearly as high as the early prechild years of marriage (see Figure 8-2).

The media often describe the postchild stage of the family life cycle as the "empty nest syndrome." Although it is popularly supposed that mothers typically experience a lessened sense of usefulness and depression with the departure of their last child, researchers have been unable to verify the existence of the empty nest syndrome. They find that most mothers feel a sense of relief with the departure of their last child. These women enjoy having time for themselves and the others in their lives (Eastman 1992; Doress et al. 1984).

The "mid-life crisis" is another popular topic often described in the media. As with the empty nest syndrome, researchers have been unable to verify its existence (Skolnick 1991). In one study, for example, Skolnick (1987) studied eighty-four married couples and found only two who experienced anything that could be described as a mid-life crisis. In one, the husband reported that he was vaguely dissatisfied with his marriage but didn't know why; in the other, the husband thought that he might be homosexual (he later decided that he was not).

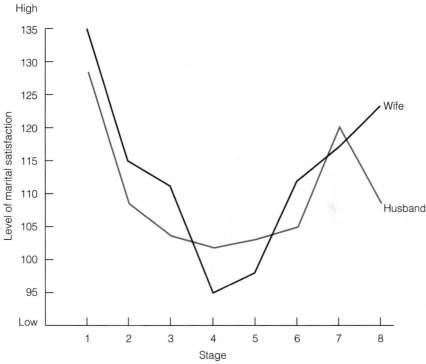

High

STAGE

1 Prechild years
2 Oldest child under three
3 Oldest child three to six
4 Oldest child six to thirteen

5 Oldest child thirteen to twenty-one
6 First child gone to last child gone—the "launching" years
7 Postchild years to retirement (middle-aged marriage)
8 Retirement to death of husband or wife (progression into old age)

FIGURE 8-2

Satisfaction over the life cycle of the family.

Source: Spanier et al. (1975), pp. 270–71. Copyright 1975 by the National Council on Family Relations. Reprinted by permission.

Changes do occur to everyone throughout the life cycle — biologically, socially, emotionally, and intellectually, and these changes are normally gradual. Although middle age is often regarded as a time of soul searching and preoccupation with one's diminishing biological capabilities, there is little or no research evidence to support the concept of a mid-life crisis (Skolnick 1991).

Although middle age brings about menopause in women, the purported difficulties of menopause are largely a cultural myth (McKinlay 1988; Starr and Weiner 1981; Brock 1979). Most women experience menopause as a stage of increasing tranquility, contentment, and (often) increased sexuality, as we have seen in Chapter 4. Men do not experience anything comparable to menopause in women. As men age they experience primarily a progression of gradual biological changes. Still, most men normally continue to function sexually until old age. Psychological crises can occur, of course, at any time, but there is no evidence that they are either more or less likely to occur in middle age (Skolnick 1991).

The Retirement Years

Old age occurs somewhere between ages sixty and eighty; very few people in their fifties are regarded as elderly, whereas very few in their eighties are not. The U.S. Census Bureau arbitrarily fixes the beginning of old age at age sixty-five. (Because federal legislation in 1978 moved the mandatory retirement age to seventy, the Census Bureau may someday follow suit.) People in their seventies often place the beginning of old age at eighty (Starr and Weiner 1981).

Like anyone, elderly people may feel younger or older than their chronological age. Moreover, one's biological or "vital" age may be a decade or more younger or older than one's chronological age. Medical experts agree that how a person functions is the important factor. The differences between a person's vital (biological) and chronological ages can be as much as thirty years. Reaction times in active people over age seventy can equal those of typical sedentary twenty-year-olds (Fries 1989).

One's psychological age may also be younger or older than one's chronological age. Many people retire well before age sixty-five or seventy, whereas others actively work into their seventies, eighties, or nineties (see Box 8-2). About one American in four returns to work after retiring.[29]

A white American male who survives to age sixty-five can, on the average, look forward to approximately another fifteen years of life. A white American female who reaches age sixty-five can anticipate another seventeen years of life.[30]

In 1989, thirty-one million people (nearly 13 percent of our population) were sixty-five years of age or older. One American in ten was eighty-five years of age or older in 1989, nearly double the proportion in 1960.[31]

Women over age sixty-five are the fastest growing segment of our population. Between 1970 and 1989, the population of women over age sixty-five increased twice as fast as the population of men over this age.[32]

Although many elderly people are not economically deprived, nearly one-third of those over age sixty-five live below the poverty line. Those who live in family households are much better off than those who live alone, with only about 6 percent below the poverty line. Elderly women are more often below the poverty line than are elderly men (39 percent as compared to 25 percent). The majority of the elderly poor are widows.[33]

To avoid financial problems, a retiree must not only have earned and saved enough to be financially secure during the initial years of retirement, but must also be prepared for subsequent years during which inflation can cause a fixed income to be increasingly inadequate with each passing year. Because of the shrinking value of the dollar, a person who is financially secure at retirement may be poverty stricken a few years later. At 5 percent inflation, $100,000 loses $64,151 of its purchasing power in twenty years (see Chapter 14).

---

[30]U.S. National Center for Health Statistics, "Expectation of Life and Expected Deaths, by Race, Sex, and Age: 1988" (1991).

[31]U.S. Bureau of the Census, "Population 65 Years and Over, by Age Group and Sex, 1900 to 1989, and Projections, 2020" (1991).

[32]U.S. Bureau of the Census, "Persons 65 Years Old and Over."

[33]"Persons 65 Years Old and Over."

---

[29]U.S. Bureau of the Census, "Persons 65 Years Old and Over— Characteristics, by Sex: 1970–1989" (1991).

BOX 8-2

Continuing Achievement After Age Sixty-Five

Money, health, and independence are certainly important factors influencing satisfaction after age sixty-five, but attitude and expectation are also of great importance. Some people start new hobbies; others begin actively pursuing some long-suppressed artistic or creative interest such as music, writing, or painting; still others start new businesses, accomplish a great feat, or achieve a position of power and influence. Consider these examples:

- Colonel Sanders started his Kentucky Fried Chicken franchise chain after age sixty-five.

- Golda Meir became the Prime Minister of Israel at age seventy-one.

- Katharine Hepburn starred in the award-winning *On Golden Pond* at age seventy-two.

- Konrad Adenauer assumed the leadership of postwar West Germany at age seventy-three, a position he maintained until age eighty-seven.

- Cardinal Angelo Roncalli became Pope John XXIII at age seventy-six and inaugurated major changes to begin a new era in Roman Catholicism.

- Grandma Moses (Anna Mary Robertson), who started painting in her late seventies, had her first one-woman exhibit at age eighty and was still working at age one hundred.

- Benjamin Franklin, at age eighty-one, made possible the adoption of the U.S. Constitution through skillful mediation among disagreeing convention delegates.

- Agatha Christie wrote the very successful last book of her famous Hercule Poirot series when she was eighty-three.

- Winston Churchill, having resigned from a second term as prime minister of Great Britain at age eighty, returned to the House of Commons as an ordinary Member of Parliament and won another Parliamentary election at age eighty-four.

- Pablo Casals, cellist and composer, was still giving concerts at age eighty-eight.

- Linus Pauling, winner of two Nobel prizes, was living alone, commuting several times a month to the Linus Pauling Institute of Science and Medicine, and working seven hours a day at age ninety (in 1992).

- George Burns starred in a Las Vegas nightclub act and performed in television specials in 1992 at age ninety-six.

- Eubie Blake, ragtime pianist and composer, was still actively working as a musician at age ninety-nine.

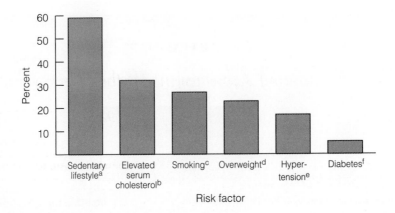

FIGURE 8-3

Six Factors Related to Coronary Heart Disease.

[a]Respondent self-reported no physical activity or irregular physical activity (i.e., fewer than three times per week and/or < 20 minutes per session).
[b]Measured ≥ 200 mg/dL by NHANES II.
[c]Respondent self-reported currently smoking.
[d]Based on body mass index ≥ 27.8 for men and ≥ 27.3 for women from self-reported height and weight of respondent.
[e]Respondent self-reported having been told by a physician that blood pressure is high on multiple checks, or respondent is on medication for high blood pressure.
[f]Respondent self-reported having been told by physician that respondent has diabetes.

Source: U.S. Centers for Disease Control, "Coronary Heart Disease Atrributable to Sedentary Life-style—Selected States: 1988." *Journal of the American Medical Association* 264, September 19, 1990, p. 1392.

Health has a major influence on a person's satisfaction throughout the life cycle of the family, but it is especially important in old age because of the inevitability of declining biological functioning with increasing years. On the average, people over sixty-five visit physicians 50 percent more often and have health care and medical expenses nearly four times costlier than those of younger people (Starr and Weiner 1981).

Nevertheless, despite the inevitable biological decline, the majority of elderly people in our society are healthy. Only 3 percent of the elderly studied by Starr and Weiner (1981) said that their health was "poor." Nearly three out of four (72 percent) of those aged sixty to ninety described their health as "excellent" or "good." Another 25 percent rated their health as "fair." Moreover, re-search finds that exercise can normally build cardiovascular strength and increase physical reserves to a striking degree at any age. Of the six factors most closely related to coronary heart disease, a sedentary life style is the most damaging, with about 60 percent of heart problems related to lack of exercise. About 30 percent of heart disease is related to a high cholesterol level, about 25 percent to smoking cigarettes, and about 22 percent to obesity (see Figure 8-3).

Not only are most older people healthy, but most live either with a spouse, or with someone other than a spouse, or independently (see Table 8-3). Only a very small percentage live in institutions.

Although it is widely believed that older people have little interest in sexuality, erotic in-

TABLE 8-3

Living Arrangements of the Elderly, by Sex and Age: 1989

	Living with Spouse	Living with Other Than Spouse	Living Alone	Living in Institutions
Women				
64–74 years old	51%	14%	34%	1%
75–84 years old	28	19	51	2
85 and older	9	33	54	4
Men				
65–84 years old	76%	7%	15%	2%
85 and older	48	18	33	1

Source: U.S. Bureau of the Census, "Marital Status and Living Arrangements: March 1989" (1991).

terest does not necessarily diminish significantly with age. Although there are great individual differences, in general sexuality does not change a great deal: Erotophiles remain interested in sexuality and erotophobes remain disinterested. (See Chapter 4 for a further discussion of this topic.)

Intergenerational ties continue to be important in our society despite the high incidence of divorce and remarriage. Not only are grandparents interested in and involved with their grandchildren and middle-aged offspring, but middle-aged people provide a great deal of care for dependent parents (Spanier 1989). Four out of five elderly people interact with their children and their grandchildren at least once a week. Elderly people usually enjoy these visits (Bengston 1986).

Grandparents play an important role in most families. When grandchildren live nearby there are usually regular visits, and grandmothers often become important caretakers for their grandchildren. With some families, divorce was found to strengthen ties between grandparents and grandchildren, especially for grandmothers whose daughters retained custody of the children. Given today's longer life expectancy, grandparents tend to be around longer, so that their role is extended as the grandchildren grow (Cherlin and Furstenberg 1986).

Grandparents of the 1990s thus have more time to influence the lives of their grandchildren. In 1991, almost half of all American grandparents were under age sixty, and one-third were under age fifty-five. Four in ten had gone to college, and their mean income was $29,000 per year (Schwartz and Waldrop 1992).

Despite the problems of poverty, the inevitability of aging, the increased needs for health care, and (for some) conflicts with adult children, most elderly people are happy. Some research contradicts the widely held assumption that old age is often a period of desolation and desperation and finds that satisfaction with one's life continues to rise in the postchild years and reaches nearly as high a level as in the prechild years (Butler 1985). This rise in satisfaction forms the top of the second leg of the U-shaped curve of reported marital satisfaction (see Figure 8-2). The satisfaction level drops off somewhat at retirement for husbands, but not for wives.

A nationwide survey in 1989 found that the older people get, the more satisfied they are with their lives. Nearly two-thirds of Americans over age sixty-five said that they were quite satisfied with their lives, compared with only about half of those between ages eighteen and forty-nine (Lewis 1989). The study also found that elderly people tend to be less lonely or depressed than younger people: Nearly three times as many young people as elderly people say they are depressed (Lewis 1989).

Finally, compared with young people, the elderly are less fearful of disease or death. In fact, the closer they come to the end of their lives, the less likely they are to think about death or to dread it. Nine out of ten people over age sixty-five said that they are not afraid to die, compared with eight out of ten middle-aged people and about seven out of ten young people (Lewis 1989).

Return to Singlehood: Widows and Widowers

Even if a marriage does not end in divorce, it must ultimately end with death. When one's spouse dies, emotions commonly evoked by the bereavement are regret and guilt ("If only I had . . ."), anger ("It's not fair!"), and denial — a psychoanalytic term that means "inability to accept the reality of a loss" (Kalish 1981).

These emotions are accompanied by a high degree of stress. On a scale of 1 to 100 stress units, the death of a spouse rates the maximum —

100 stress units. To put this in perspective, being convicted of a crime and put in jail rates 63 stress units, being fired from a job rates 47 stress units, and sexual problems rate 39 stress units (Bootzin et al. 1986).

High stress levels cause severe psychological problems such as clinical depression, which can render a person almost incapable of sleeping, eating, or being interested in any activity. High stress is also related to such bodily effects as high blood pressure, stroke, and heart disease. Moreover, the body's immune system is affected, so that people under stress are less resistant to a wide variety of illnesses. People under stress consequently have significantly higher mortality rates than average (Fries 1989).

The probability for remarriage is much lower for a widow than it is for a widower because in our population there are not as many elderly men as elderly women. The remarriage rate for widows over age sixty-five is one-fifth the rate for widowers.[34]

About three out of four elderly men (77 percent) are married. However, less than half (42 percent) of older women are married[35] (see Figure 8-4).

Violence in the American Family

Familial violence is a well-documented fact. Three children, three wives, and two husbands are killed every day in the United States by someone in their immediate family (Straus 1990). But familial violence is nothing new:

> Violence in the family is an ancient custom. The Roman husband was by law allowed to

---

[34]U.S. National Center for Health Statistics, "Marriage Rates and Median Age of Bride and Groom, by Previous Marital Status: 1970 to 1987" (1991).

[35]"Persons 65 Years Old and Over."

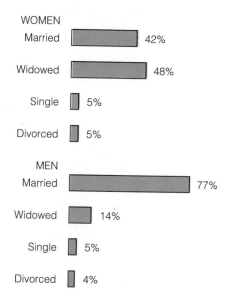

FIGURE 8-4

Marital status of people over age sixty-five in the United States, 1989.

Source: U.S. Bureau of the Census, "Persons 65 Years Old and Older—Characteristics, by Sex: 1970 to 1989" (1991).

kill any member of his family. The early records of the settlers in America indicate no lack of violence between all possible combinations of family members. Infanticide in history is common—with mothers being the usual persons to carry out the act. (Reiss 1980)

It is a curious paradox that the family, which traditionally is a fundamental source of emotional warmth, support, and security, may also be a hotbed of turmoil, strife, and pain. Ironically, the very factors that make family life appealing—"constant interaction, intimate relationships, emotional bonding, interdependency, and shared responsibilities—can create tensions that result in violent behavior between family members" (Kratcoski 1987, p. 47).

This dichotomy of strife, cruelty, and violence on the one hand and loyalty, commitment,

and interdependence on the other is characteristic of no other human institution. No matter how ugly or violent the internal strife, at the first hint of outside intervention families quickly close ranks, providing a united front to the outside world. Thus whenever neighbors call the police to the site of domestic violence, the family typically ceases attacking one another and may instead attack the police (Dunnigan 1992.)

At the core of our Judeo-Christian heritage is the prototypical first family—Adam and Eve. Adam and Eve experience what might be the ultimate in family disaster when their eldest son, Cain, murders his brother Abel:

> And Cain talked with Abel his brother. And it came to pass, when they were in the field, that Cain rose up against Abel his brother, and slew him. (Genesis, 4:8)

This portrayal of humanity's first family symbolizes deeply unconscious wellsprings of human nature, with the prototypical family both a cradle of violence and a source of nurturance. Violence in the family is not condoned in this biblical account, however. It is acknowledged as perhaps an inevitable part of human nature, but is vigorously condemned:

> And the Lord said unto Cain: "Where is Abel thy brother?" And he said: "I know not; am I my brother's keeper?" And He said: "What hast thou done? the voice of thy brother's blood cries unto Me from the ground.
>
> "And now cursed art thou from the ground, which hath opened her mouth to receive thy brother's blood from thy hand. When thou tillest the ground, it shall not henceforth yield unto thee her strength; a fugitive and a vagabond shalt thou be in the earth." (Genesis, 4:9–12)

In the following sections we will examine familial violence in its most common forms.

Wife Battering

Although no one knows the full extent of wife battering because most cases are not reported, specialists agree that it is now a social problem of major proportions. According to the surgeon general of the United States, domestic violence is the single largest cause of injury to women in our society—more common than automobile accidents, muggings, and rapes combined (Novello 1991). Consider the following information:

- A national study found that more than one couple in four (28 percent) reported domestic violence at some point in their marriage (Gelles and Straus 1988).

- Researchers estimate that severe, repeated violence occurs in one out of every fourteen (7 percent) American marriages (Dutton 1988).

- Husbands severely assault between 1.5 and two million wives each year (Straus and Gelles 1986). More than one-third of these women die from the effects of the beating (Novello 1991).

- Wives under age thirty experience twice as much violence as wives who are thirty to fifty years of age (Straus, Gelles, and Steinmetz 1980).

- Unemployed men commit double the rate of wife batterings as employed men, and men working part-time have an even higher rate of assault (Gelles and Cornell 1990).

- The median duration of a violent marriage is five years (Fagan, Stewart, and Stewart 1983).

Violence in affluent and middle-class families is often kept secret; neighbors do not usually call the police, and higher-income husbands are less likely to be arrested (Gelles and Cornell 1990). Nevertheless, wife battering is lodged in all segments of society, occurring in affluent, middle-class, and working-class families alike (Greaves, Heapy, and Wylie 1988; Lockhart 1987). Consider the following incidents of wife battering:

- An upper-class woman in Stamford, Connecticut, who was married to a Fortune 500 executive, routinely locked herself in their Lincoln Continental, where she would be safe from her husband's kicks and punches. She did not leave him because she feared he could sue for divorce on the basis of desertion, in which case she would not get any alimony and would be left relatively destitute (O'Reilly 1983).

- A middle-class housewife in South Hadley, Massachusetts, was first beaten by her husband when she was pregnant. Five years later he hurled a dinner plate at her in the kitchen. His aim was off and the plate shattered against the wall, sending a shard into their four-year-old daughter's eye—leaving her blind in that eye (O'Reilly 1983).

- A lower-class housewife in Atlanta, Georgia, was giving a birthday party for neighborhood children when her husband, a hospital worker, asked her to come into the bedroom. Here is how she reported the subsequent scene:

  He slapped me blind. He pulled the shotgun from the wall and dared me to move. I cried and asked him why he was bothering me. He just tore my clothes off. He said I was a bitch and used other ugly words. I asked him not to do that because the children and their parents were here but he just left the room and told everyone to leave. Then he told me to get back in bed and that we were going to make love. I said no. But he had the .38 and a knife and hit me. I got in and we did it. My nose was still bleeding. (O'Reilly 1983, p. 26)

It is not uncommon for a battered woman to stay with the man who has battered her, or even to return to him after having left the relationship. The reasons women do not end such relationships have been under scrutiny by researchers for some time.

A battered wife has often grown up with violence and accepts it as inevitable — or even as a form of caring. She may feel that the world is a dangerous place and that she needs a protector, even if it is a man who hits her. She may be both ashamed and afraid that any resistance will provoke new, even greater violence. She may be isolated from her family and friends and have no means of support other than her husband. She may be resigned to submission (O'Reilly 1983).

A battered wife may focus on positive aspects of the abusive relationship, viewing the love and affection she receives as more significant than the abuse. A battering husband may function well in others areas of the marriage and may even express sincere regret for abusing her (Walker 1979).

A battered wife may compare her situation to those of others she knows and be glad that she is "not married to a man who has affairs with other women; not being abused more severely or more frequently; not experiencing the financial and emotional difficulties associated with separation or divorce" (Andrews and Brewin 1990, p. 313). A woman who stays with her husband is able to see some positive aspects to their relationship, even if she sees little or no change in the frequency or severity of abuse or in the amount of affection expressed. She may feel that their relationship is "not as bad as it could be" (Andrews and Brewin 1990, p. 321).

Two decades ago, research found that women with low self-esteem are less likely to leave abusive husbands. Women are also less likely to leave abusive husbands if they believe that their husbands will stop the abusive behavior or if they fear economic hardship — especially if children are involved. The fewer the resources she has, the more she feels that she cannot escape (Gelles 1976).

Remaining with an abusive partner and continuing to experience abuse may ultimately be self-destructive no matter how "positively" the relationship is viewed compared to alternatives (Baumeister 1989). A battered wife's morale may be so low, and her despair and sense of helplessness so great, that she may resort to suicide as a final, desperate measure to escape an intolerable situation. One out of four suicide attempts by women is preceded by a prior history of battering (O'Reilly 1983).

Family, friends, and neighbors often blame a battered wife for not leaving her abusive husband. (They are blaming the victim.) In some cases she may even endorse this attitude and blame herself for the abuse; self-blame is undoubtedly related to the lack of support and sympathy from others to whom she turns for help (Herbert, Silver, and Ellard 1991). When a husband attacks his wife's self-esteem with psychological exploitation — for example, by telling her she is frigid, incompetent, and hysterical — this may cause her to blame herself for being battered (she can't really blame him for losing patience and battering such a person) (Walker 1979). A woman will be more likely to blame herself if she has been subjected to physical or sexual abuse in childhood (Andrews and Brewin 1990).

It is not uncommon for a woman who is living with a violent husband to blame herself for the battering she receives, but once she feels able to leave the situation, she usually changes from blaming herself to blaming her husband. This does not necessarily relieve her depression and anxiety, however; research finds that a woman who leaves an abusive situation often remains chronically depressed (Andrews and Brown 1988).

Before the early 1970s, wife battering was regarded as essentially a private matter and received little formal attention from social agencies. When a battered wife complained to her family, to friends, or to clergy, she was often not believed, or she might have been told that it was probably her fault for provoking her husband. She could expect little help from the police because wife-battering was not regarded as a criminal act.

Few shelters for battered wives existed in the United States before 1975, when the National Organization for Women created a task force to address the issue. Once shelters became available, demand for them proved to be enormous. By 1986, more than 1,000 had been built, all of which had long waiting lists (Gelles and Cornell 1990). Specialists in the field estimate that shelters for battered women accommodate only about one in five of those who need help (Straus and Gelles 1986; O'Reilly 1983).

The women's movement has been primarily responsible for funding these shelters, with little help received from the government. Legislation that would provide funds for them has been repeatedly defeated after being introduced into Congress (Straus and Gelles 1986). The National Domestic Violence Prevention and Treatment Act, introduced in 1979, was passed into law in the mid-1980s, but it has little funding. In 1991, the American Medical Association encouraged its members to join the Physicians Campaign Against Family Violence.

Wife battering is now regarded as a crime that should be acknowledged and remedied, rather than as a private matter that should be hidden and endured. States and municipalities have enacted legislation designed to give battered women a realistic chance of getting protection. Police departments now treat domestic violence as they do other assaults — as a criminal act (Straus and Gelles 1986; Sherman and Berk 1984).

Specialists in the problem of wife battering find that batterers are typically afflicted with severe degrees of insecurity, have low self-esteem, and may easily be slighted or feel challenged (Gelles and Cornell 1990). The picture presented by an abusive, violent man is consistent with the diagnosis of Borderline and Antisocial Personality Disorder (Hotaling and Sugarman 1986).

Men who experience childhood violence themselves, or observe parental violence, are much more likely to be abusive (O'Leary 1988). Men who have less education or a lower-status occupation are more likely to be abusive (Hornung, McCullough, and Sugimoto 1981). Stress associated with a large family size, poor housing, poor job satisfaction, and low income are all related to domestic violence, as is the family's power balance: Families in which decisions are shared are the least violent (Gelles and Cornell 1990).

Battering husbands may shout, scream, and explode into violence in performing what they see as the male's prerogative. They may demand not only acquiescence but also love and affection, believing that their wives are betraying them by not returning their love. Thus they may believe that they are simply (and reasonably) punishing their wives for outrageous and intolerable behavior (O'Reilly 1983).

Despite their displays of violence, some husbands who hit their wives are often afraid of losing the women they are punishing. This apparent contradiction between feelings and behavior is exemplified by the birthday party batterer whose actions were described earlier. The last time he saw his wife he beat her until he was exhausted from the effort. Here is his own report of the final episode, after which she left him:

When it was over, I picked her up off the floor and kissed her and told her I was sorry. I wanted to feel the pain that she felt. So I kissed her. Her nose was running and she was crying, and I loved her very much. (O'Reilly 1983, p. 26)

Such displays of belated remorse are not unusual for such batterers, who may even beat their victims to death. When such a man believes that his wife has failed to return his love, he may see this as betrayal and feel that punitive violence is the only answer. He may continue to beat his wife even as she proclaims her innocence — and her love — if he does not think he can believe what she says.

Some wife battering is simply a matter of wrongheaded brutality. Some batterers may beat a wife as a nineteenth century farmer beat his horse. This type of battering has neither overtones of punishment for betrayal nor overtones of fear of being deprived of love. This type of husband beats his wife simply because he is bigger, stronger, and more powerful, is annoyed with her, and wants to punish her perceived disobedience. With this type of battery, a wife is much more likely to leave her husband following the first episodes of violence (O'Reilly 1983).

Although alcohol does not in itself cause battering, most incidents of battering involve alcohol (Leonard and Jacob 1988). Thus among batterers, excessive use of alcohol and battering are positively correlated: As alcohol intake increases, so does the incidence of battering.[36] Similarly, although unemployment does not in itself cause battering, it can increase familial pressure and thus exacerbate conflicts. Not surprisingly, then, the incidence of battering is also positively correlated with the rate of unemployment: When the unemployment rate rises, so does the incidence of battering (Straus and Gelles 1986).

---

[36]U.S. National Center for Health Statistics, "Personal Health Practices, by Selected Characteristics: 1985" (1990).

Husband Battering

Husband battering is still regarded as essentially a private or family matter. Most domestic violence is directed toward the wife, as is clearly shown by police intervention reports (Berk, Newton, and Berk 1986).

Because a husband is usually larger and stronger than his wife, his physical injuries are usually less severe than a wife's, even when he is assaulted. Husbands rarely report being beaten by their wives, and professional agencies seem to show little interest in the problem (Dutton 1988).

With little research in this area, there are few reliable data regarding the incidence or extent of husband abuse. The Second National Family Violence Survey in 1986 did include data on violence toward husbands. According to this survey, about 4 percent of wives engaged in abusive behavior toward their husbands (Gelles and Straus 1988).

Presumably the causes of husband battering include breakdown of effective communication; feelings of injustice, outrage, or frustration on the part of the wife; or simple brutality. As yet there are no community-provided shelters for battered husbands in the United States, although some of the women's shelters are beginning to recognize the problem of husband abuse and are starting to offer services to men (Straus and Gelles 1986).

Child Abuse

There are three categories of child abuse: battering, sexual molestation, and psychological abuse. In the literature on child abuse, "abuse" is likely to refer to either battering or sexual abuse.

Abused youngsters are often either chronically depressed or overly aggressive and hostile. They usually have trouble relating to other children, have some kind of learning disability, and are often in trouble at school (Youngblade and Belsky 1989; Starr 1988).

Children who were not planned for are much more likely to be abused than other children. A child from a family with two unplanned births is nearly three times as likely to be abused as a child from a family with no unplanned births. And a child from a family with three unplanned births is nearly five times as likely to be abused as a child in a family with no unplanned births (Zuravin 1991).

Data from two national surveys on child abuse show that physical abuse toward children more than doubled, and sexual abuse more than tripled, between 1980 and 1986.[37] In addition to known cases of child abuse, there are an unknown number of cases that are not reported. Researchers estimate that only about one case in five of child abuse is ever reported (Faller 1990).

As of the end of 1991, the number of reports of child abuse was still growing. Severe budget cuts (combined with no national policy for aiding vulnerable children) and hard economic times (with the accompanying stress in families) make the reduction of child abuse in our society a formidable task (Liederman 1991).

Battered Children   The number of reported cases of child battering in the United States is rising sharply, more than tripling from 1976 to 1986 to reach more than two million reported cases.[38]

Researchers estimate that at least three out of every 100 American children have experienced a serious assault. A child who has ex-

perienced one known assault has probably experienced others that were not reported (Straus and Gelles 1986).

More women than men batter children. The most frequent victims of battering are children who are unwanted, physically handicapped, mentally retarded, or unusually brilliant. Teenage mothers batter their children more than do mothers over age twenty. Mothers who were themselves battered as children tend to be child batterers themselves (Widom 1989; Egeland, Jacobvitz, and Stroufe 1988).

A thirty-four-year-old mother who had severely battered her child reminisces about her own childhood:

> What I remember most about my mother was that she was always beating me. She'd beat me with high-heeled shoes, with my father's belt, with a potato masher. When I was eight, she black-and-blued my legs so badly I told her I'd go to the police. She said, "Go, they'll just put you into the darkest prison." So I stayed. When my breasts started growing at thirteen, she beat me across the chest until I fainted. Then she'd hug me and ask for forgiveness. When I turned sixteen, a day didn't pass without my mother calling me a whore, and saying that I'd end up in Potter's Field, dead, forgotten and damned for all eternity. (Magnuson 1983, p. 20)

Another mother who had battered her child recalls:

> I started abusing my boy because he was an accident and a screamer. When he was four months old, I hit him so hard my engagement ring carved a bloody furrow. . . . His screams shattered my heart. . . . Deep down, I knew he couldn't understand. But I also thought he was doing it on purpose. He'd start crying again and I'd hit him again, and I

[37]U.S. Department of Health and Human Services, *Executive Summary: National Study of the Incidence of Child Abuse and Neglect* (1981); *Study Findings: Study of the National Incidence and Prevalence of Child Abuse and Neglect* (1988).

[38]American Humane Association, "Child Maltreatment Cases Reported—Summary: 1976 to 1986" (1991).

felt so helpless when this happened. (Magnuson 1983, p. 20)

It is not clear whether poor and disadvantaged parents tend to batter their children more than do middle-class parents because there is a social-class bias in the tallying of cases of child abuse. Clinics and social welfare agencies, who are more likely to report suspected cases of child abuse, deal more frequently with the poor. Teachers and physicians may be less likely to accuse a middle-class parent of abusing a child, even when the evidence seems clear.

As with wife battering, child battering is positively correlated with excessive use of alcohol and with unemployment. Anything that increases a parent's stress level may contribute to battering, for a stressed-out parent is more likely to batter a child who cries persistently, is unruly, or is otherwise annoying.

Parents may tend to batter even very young children who are chronically ill and irritable (Magnuson 1983). Even with intensive care, their prognosis is poor, and they are irritable, cranky, and difficult to handle. They are not warmly responsive, cuddly, and lovable but instead stiffen and scream when they are held. Distraught mothers are likely to batter them in sheer desperation, making an already difficult (or impossible) situation even worse.

Sexually Abused Children   A *pedophile* is a person who sexually abuses (that is to say, performs any sexual acts with) a child. Pedophilia is universally classified as a paraphilia as we have seen (see Chapter 4). Pedophilia can range from stroking or fondling genital areas (masturbating a child); to licking or sucking the child's vulva, clitoris, or penis; to having the child suck the pedophile's penis; to vaginal or anal intercourse (Gelinas 1983). Most pedophiles begin while teenagers to molest children (McCall 1984). Pedophilia that occurs within a family is an example of *incest* — sexual activity between two people who are too closely related.

Incest, especially parent-child (or stepchild) pedophilia, is especially damaging because it violates the trust and safety that a child depends on and expects to receive in a family setting (Johnson 1989). Unfortunately, it is relatively easy to gain compliance of a young child by misrepresenting sex as affection or training, by using threats or bribes, or by exploiting the child's loyalty and desire to please and trust (Gelinas 1983).

Although victims as young as four months old have been identified, the average age at which sexual abuse begins is between eight and ten years; the average duration of sexual abuse is three to five years (Kempe and Kempe 1984). Until age eleven or twelve, sexual abuse of females is often restricted to fondling and stroking, oral-genital contact, and anal intercourse because of the difficulty of vaginal entry (Gelinas 1983). When children are older and more aware of the meaning of what is happening, pedophiles use increasing force to gain compliance (Greenfeld 1992).

There are at least four million pedophiles in the United States, most of whom (95 percent) are men. One pedophile in five molests both boys and girls. Most pedophiles start to molest children during adolescence, and by the time they are adults they are likely to have had dozens, or even hundreds, of victims (Faller 1990). Most pedophiles are not suspected by their wives, friends, or colleagues. Curiously enough, child molesters are often regarded as pillars of the community and are usually active in church work (McCall 1984).

Consider the following information about sexual abuse of children:

- Authorities estimate that at least one in three girls and one in six boys are sexually abused in our society. Girls are more likely to report sexual abuse than are boys (Wyatt and Powell 1988; Wyatt and Peters, 1986).

- About one-third of female molestations are by relatives; males are generally abused by nonfamily molesters (Emslie and Rosenfeld 1983).

- Incest occurs in an estimated 10 percent of American families (Russell 1986).

Sexual molestation of children by a family member occurs in all strata of society, cutting across socioeconomic, ethnic, educational, and cultural boundaries. It occurs in both urban and rural areas (Greenfeld 1992; Magnuson 1983). Sexual abuse can be just as physically and psychologically damaging to children as battering. Researchers agree that sexual abuse may affect children's development in all areas — cognitive, emotional, social, and psychological — and may seriously impair their overall functioning and coping ability (Boyer and Fine 1992; Iverson and Segal 1990).

The pain of growing up in incestuous families can be so overwhelming to children that at a very early age they make a choice between finding a way to cope or dying. As a result, behaviors that may appear antisocial, self-destructive, or bizarre may be perceived by them as crucial to their survival (Anderson 1992). Survival mechanisms usually involve attempts to avoid the hurt and pain, often through the use of alcohol or drugs. Self-blame and self-hatred are also common; it is less risky for them to blame themselves for the experience than it is to blame their abuser or their family for not protecting them (Greenfeld 1992).

Even after the incest is over, a child may continue to experience such signs of distress as nightmares, panic attacks, and recurrent weeping (Gelinas 1983). Adolescents tend to have additional problems, such as drug and alcohol abuse, hysterical seizures, promiscuity, early

pregnancy, hurting younger children, lying, stealing, engaging in prostitution, attempting suicide, and running away from home (Greenfeld 1992).

The destructive effects of incest often persist well into adult life, especially for women. The most prevalent and pervasive of these effects is an inability to trust others, which results in extreme ambivalence concerning intimacy and a sense of worthlessness (Greenfeld 1992). Other effects are sexual dysfunction in which intimacy and sexuality are associated with feelings of fear and memories of betrayal by a trusted protector (Greenfeld 1992; Johnson 1989). These damaging effects of incest can haunt a woman for the rest of her life, persisting long after she has married and has children of her own (Boyer and Fine 1992; Wyatt and Powell 1988).

Most incestuous sexual abuse involves a father (or stepfather) abusing a daughter (or stepdaughter) (Greenfeld 1992; Faller 1988; Sanford 1988). The most common pattern of incest begins when a daughter (or stepdaughter) is a preschooler, often when she is age two or younger. The abuse usually starts with genital fondling and proceeds over time to cunnilingus, then to fellatio, and finally to copulation. The father (or stepfather) may physically force his daughter (or stepdaughter) to do what he wishes, but he usually simply uses psychological persuasion (McCall 1984).

A woman who was the victim of incestuous assaults by her stepfather since she was nine years old recalls the following:

My brothers and sisters had been sent to bed; I was getting a special treat by being allowed to stay up and watch TV with my stepfather. I was reading our small-town newspaper and was puzzled about a word. "Daddy, what does assault mean? Is it like when the Three Stooges say 'I've never been so *assaulted* in my life'?" He had a strange expression on his face. "I'll show you what it means," he said. He took me into my parents' bedroom — mother was waitressing the evening shift. He removed my yellow pajamas and took off his clothes. Nothing was ever the same for me again. (McCall 1984, p. 35)

Father-daughter incest that begins in early childhood often persists for years, and it is not usually discovered unless the girl's parents divorce or she reaches adolescence and is old enough to leave home and avoid punishment for speaking out (Berliner 1988). It is not unusual for a girl to withdraw her accusation of sexual abuse, however. An adolescent will often feel intense guilt and fear about publicly revealing a pattern of sexual abuse by a parent. Her world, as she has known it, suddenly collapses. Her father is in jail and her mother is distraught. It is not uncommon for a girl to blame herself for the catastrophe that has suddenly hit her family. She may then repudiate her accusation in an attempt to put the family back together and regain some measure of peace (Faller 1990).

Psychological Abuse of Children The psychological or emotional abuse of children has received far less attention than either battering or sexual abuse. Experts disagree on a single definition, but the consensus is that constantly criticizing, humiliating, belittling, and threatening punishment constitutes psychological abuse. Psychological abuse occurs in all socioeconomic levels of our society (Wallerstein 1992).

The incidence and severity of psychological abuse increases when a parent's job is lost or must be replaced by a lower-paying job. Economic pressure usually results in a family becoming increasingly unstable (Garbarino 1986). Data suggest that the economic deterioration of families in the last fifteen years has produced more and more psychological abuse of children. As a result, the National Committee for Prevention of Child Abuse has been trying to raise public awareness of the seriousness of this issue. Children may be only marginally affected by psychological abuse or they may be emotionally crippled. Chronic, intense psychological abuse may cause a child to grow up full of rage and self-hatred (Garbarino 1986).

Parent Abuse

A national survey a decade ago found that one adolescent or young adult in ten in the United States had assaulted a parent at least once during the previous year (Straus, Gelles, and Steinmetz 1980). More recent studies have confirmed this figure (Gelles and Cornell 1990; Peek, Fischer, and Kidwell 1985; Cornell and Gelles 1982). This means that about 2.5 million parents were physically attacked, and about a million of these attacks were severe: Parents were punched, bitten, knifed, or shot by their children (Cornell and Gelles 1982).

Assaultive behavior obviously creates a great deal of stress in the household and causes further deterioration in the interactions between the parent and the children. Parents are reluctant to press charges because to do so would publicly acknowledge that they are being assaulted by their own children, and thus the behavior tends to persist (Agnew and Huguley 1989).

Data suggest that whites are more likely to batter parents than are blacks (Charles 1986; Casenave and Straus 1979). One study found no correlation between incidence or severity of assault and either socioeconomic level or the gender or size of the adolescent (Agnew and Huguley 1989).

Some middle-aged children also batter their elderly parents while they are living in the children's household. Concern over this social problem is growing because studies project that by 1996, 7.5 million Americans will be over age eighty, and being responsible for an elderly parent's care is increasingly becoming a reality of family life (Force 1990).

Children (who are themselves middle-aged) often feel stressed by the demands of career and of their own children, and they may feel unable to meet the needs of their aged parents as well, especially when the parents are living in the children's household. Many of these middle-aged children of elderly parents simply do not have the time, the energy, or the resources to take on these extra demands. Sometimes the stress of having an aged parent in the home leads to explosive violence (Force 1990).

Elderly people who are cared for by their families tend to be relatively isolated, and thus they are almost wholly dependent on those who abuse them. Understandably, they are reluctant to report incidents of mistreatment. Many victims who do report abuse subsequently withdraw their complaints because they are embarrassed to acknowledge the assault was from a member of their own family. Moreover, the alternative of institutionalization is immeasurably worse — it is one of their most nightmarish fears (Gelles and Cornell 1990).

SUMMARY

The family is the third component of the family system, preceded by courtship and marriage. The nuclear family consists of the married couple and their children. The extended family consists of the kin of each of the married couple. Single-parent families can occur if the parent is not married because of divorce or death. A stepfamily is created when a custodial parent remarries following a divorce or when a widowed parent remarries. Two-earner families are families with children in which both parents work outside the home.

Despite the many family types in the United States, all families have the core functions of producing and socializing children and providing stability, nurturance, loyalty, protection, and support for their members. In fact, although other social agencies such as churches and schools also play an important role, the family is the chief socializing agency of children. If the family is nonfunctional or ineffectual in socializing children, the consequences may be serious: school dropouts, poverty, discouragement, desperation, alcohol or drug abuse, teenage pregnancy, gang violence, prison.

Even though the American family is changing due to the growing proportion of single-parent families and the high incidence of family disruption by divorce, most Americans say that the family is the most important element in their lives and that a good family life ranks first in importance when compared with other highly valued experiences.

The life cycle of a family may be divided into the prechild years, the child-rearing years, the postchild years, and old age and progression into retirement. When graphed as a function of level of marital satisfaction, these stages create a U-shaped curve. The highest level of satisfaction occurs in the early years of the marriage, before children are born. Then the level of satisfaction drops until the children are teenagers, after which it begins to rise as the couple reaches the retirement years. For women the second highest level of reported marital satisfaction occurs after retirement. Men, on the other hand, reach the highest level of happiness in the postchild years that come before retirement.

Most elderly people are not economically deprived, are in good health, and are generally happy with their lives. In addition, most continue to live in their own households. Erotic interest does not necessarily diminish significantly with age.

When marriage is ended by the death of one of the spouses, the resultant stress for the survivor is rated as 100 on a scale of 1 to 100 stress units. Because high stress levels not only cause emotional problems but also affect the body's immune system so that the person is less resistant to a wide variety of illnesses, widows and widowers have a mortality rate that is much higher than average.

Paradoxically, the family is often a source of pain as well as a source of security and emotional satisfaction. Wife battering is widespread throughout all social classes of our society. Men who batter their wives may do so either because they believe that their wives have betrayed them by not returning their love or simply as an act of brutality. The incidence of battering tends to increase when unemployment rates rise, and in most instances of battering alcohol is involved. The incidence of husband battering is unknown.

The incidence of child abuse has also been rising in our society, whether the abuse is battering or sexual molestation. Mothers who themselves were battered as children tend to batter their own children, and a much higher percentage of teenage mothers abuse their babies than do mothers over age twenty.

Sexual molestation of children can be just as physically and psychologically damaging as battering. Although most child batterers are women, most pedophiles are men who begin as teenagers to molest children. A disproportionate number of child molesters are outwardly religious and are unsuspected by their wives, colleagues, and closest friends.

The most common form of incestual molestation involves fathers — whether biological fathers or stepfathers — abusing their daughters. This usually starts when the girls are of preschool age and gradually escalates over the years. This type of sexual abuse usually remains undiscovered until the girls are teenagers.

KEY TERMS

The following is a list of key terms in this chapter.
These terms are defined in context within the chapter, and many may also be found in the Glossary.

battering	gender-role revolution	patriarchal	psychological abuse
binuclear family	incest	pedophilia	racial-ethnic families
cohabiting family	Industrial Revolution	polyandrous family	single-parent family
corporate family	matriarchal	polyandry	socialization
extended family	monogamy	polygamous family	stem family
extended kin	nonfamily households	polygyny	stepfamily
family households	nuclear family	primogeniture	two-earner family

QUESTIONS

1. Name, define, describe, and give an example of the chief forms that the family may take.

2. Discuss the reasons that the family is considered by sociologists and psychologists to be the chief socializing agency of children in our society.

3. Discuss the degree of validity of the following statement: "Our family system is disintegrating."

4. What is the incidence of single-parent families in our society? Discuss the characteristics of the single-parent family.

5. Discuss the phenomena of wife battering and husband battering.

6. Discuss the problem of child abuse in our society.

7. Describe and discuss the U-shaped curve in the life cycle of the family.

8. What is the typical elderly person in our society like in terms of economic well-being, health, and sexuality?

SUGGESTIONS FOR FURTHER READING

Allen, Katherine. *Single Women/Family Ties.* Newbury Park, Calif.: Sage, 1989.

Blankenhorn, David; Bayne, Steven; and Elshtain, Jean Bethke, eds. *Rebuilding the Nest: A New Commitment to the American Family.* Milwaukee, Wisc.: Family Service America, 1990.

Booth, Alan, ed. *Contemporary Families: Looking Forward, Looking Back.* St. Paul, Minn.: National Council on Family Relations, 1991.

Brubaker, Timothy H. *Later-Life Families.* Beverly Hills, Calif.: Sage, 1986.

Cherlin, Andrew J., and Furstenberg, Frank F. Jr. *The New American Grandparent.* New York: Basic Books, 1986.

Finkelhor, David. *A Sourcebook on Child Sexual Abuse.* Beverly Hills, Calif.: Sage, 1986.

Gelles, Richard J. *Family Violence.* Newbury Park, Calif.: Sage, 1987.

Hutter, Mark. *The Changing Family: Comparative Perspectives.* New York: Macmillan, 1988.

Jackson, James S., ed. *Life in Black America: Findings from a National Survey.* Newbury Park, Calif.: Sage, 1991.

Levitan, Sar A.; Belous, Richard S.; and Gallo, Frank. *What's Happening to the American Family?* rev. ed. Baltimore: The Johns Hopkins University Press, 1988.

McAdoo, Harriet Pipes, ed. *Black Families*, 2nd ed. Newbury Park, Calif.: Sage, 1988.

CHAPTER 9

Women, Work, and the Family

Helmer: Before all else you are a wife and mother.
Nora: That I no longer believe. I believe that
before all else I am a human being.

Henrik Ibsen, "A Doll's House"

Women and Work in the Distant Past

Women and Work in Our Agrarian Past

Women and Work in Our Industrial Past

Women and Work in Our Recent Past:
The Gender-Role Revolution

Women and Work Today

The Plight of America's Children

What Do You Know?

Some of the following statements are true and some are false.
Can you tell which are which?

T/F   1. Throughout almost all history, men have been the chief producers of economic goods.

T/F   2. In the mid-nineteenth century, one-third of married women had at least seven children.

T/F   3. In general, women's economic well-being has dropped with the gender-role revolution that began in the 1960s.

T/F   4. The "glass ceiling" is a cultural myth; there is no research evidence that it exists.

T/F   5. Wives in two-earner families work a "second shift" at home that amounts to about four-and-a-half months of 40-hour work weeks each year.

T/F   6. Abortion was illegal in the United States from the colonial period until 1973.

T/F   7. Men's lives today are changing more than women's.

T/F   8. If a husband is unemployed or earns less than his wife, he usually does most of the housework.

T/F   9. In general, American children are better off today than their grandparents or their parents were at the same age.

T/F   10. When adjusted for inflation, wages have dropped significantly since the 1970s.

Answers: 1-F, 2-T, 3-T, 4-F, 5-T, 6-F, 7-F, 8-F, 9-F, 10-T.

Although the form that gender-role differentiation takes varies from one society to another, all known societies assign different roles to males and females. Moreover, all known societies socialize males and females differently, from infancy on, to fulfill these roles. Two basic imperatives underlie this differentiation of male-female roles:

- The economic imperative: that goods and services that are essential for the survival of the group must be produced.

- The biological imperative: that women bear children.

It is neither an economic nor a biological imperative that women be chiefly responsible for child care. Nevertheless, this responsibility has been an integral part of the role of females in all known societies; no society has ever assigned this role chiefly to males.

In preindustrial societies, a female (either the mother or a wet nurse) had to breast-feed a baby, so it was imperative that females have the chief responsibility for child care until the children were weaned (usually two to three years after birth). In these societies a mother was often pregnant again by this time, and so the cycle of pregnancy, childbirth, and child care would start again.

All societies have generally expected women to produce both economic goods and children first, and then to care for children. In order to fulfill these expectations, women have always been assigned work that could be done in or near the home, could be interrupted at any time, and was not dangerous (Gough 1971).

Thus women have typically specialized in inside work that was not inconsistent with child care, whereas men have specialized in outside work and have not had the chief responsibility for child care. In this way men and women have produced the economic goods necessary for the group's subsistence needs, as well as met the requirement, necessary for the group's survival,

that children be produced and then socialized (Gough 1971).

This pattern was interrupted (briefly in historical time) during the late nineteenth and early twentieth centuries, when women focused almost entirely on housekeeping and child care and men were virtually the sole economic providers. Gradually this imbalance—unique in human experience—yielded to the press of economic forces, and increasing numbers of wives began returning to their age-old function of producing economic goods while also retaining the chief responsibility for child care. The problem is that mothers could no longer work within or near the household to do this. In common with men, they were forced to leave the household (and their children) and work at outside, paid employment.

This development has put women in a dilemma of enormous proportions. If they stay at home and fulfill their role as child care providers (as they have for millennia), they cannot produce economic goods—and no society has permitted this pattern to persist for long. If they enter the work force to produce economic goods, they can neither look after their children nor supervise their care during the hours they are away from the household.

This predicament is apparently unique in human experience. To place this dilemma more clearly into perspective, let us briefly trace the history of women's and men's roles within the family and their shared responsibility in producing economic goods.

Women and Work in the Distant Past

Hunting and Gathering Societies

In by far the greater part of human history (fully 99 percent), hunting and gathering were the means of subsistence. Hunting and gathering

"I hunt and she gathers—otherwise, we couldn't make ends meet."

societies neither domesticate food animals nor plant and harvest grains, vegetables, and fruits; instead, they hunt and kill wild animals and pick wild plant foods as they become ripe and available.[1]

In hunting and gathering societies, childbearing began soon after the menarche (the initial menstruation) and continued until the menopause — a period of time that lasted most of the woman's lifetime.[2] A division of labor thus emerged in which women performed productive tasks that they could do while caring for infants and young children. Men performed tasks that could only be done away from the household (Gough 1971).

Because a mother would constantly be interrupted by children, her work emphasized tasks that did not require rapt attention but could frequently be stopped and then resumed, such as gathering and trading. No hunting and gathering society expected (or permitted) women to hunt large game or to fish deep waters because these activities were incompatible with the care of children (Gough 1971).

The men's efforts at hunting were not always successful, so the subsistence activities women performed provided most of the food for the group. Women were almost always able to bring home something edible. The family was therefore usually more dependent on the female's work than it was on the male's (Gough 1971).

Because men were bound neither by the biological imperative of childbearing nor the societal expectation for child care, they were typically free to roam at length, with extended

---

[1]Because these societies, which extend into the dim beginnings of human history, have left no written records, we must reconstruct their way of life from surviving hunting and gathering groups. About 175 of these have been studied in detail. The material in this and the following section is largely drawn from Kathleen Gough's article "The Origins of the Family" (1971).

[2]Hunting and gathering societies could not support many children. Because they knew little of birth control, they used abortion and infanticide to control the size of their families (Skolnick 1987; Tannahill 1980).

absences from the household, sometimes facing danger during hunting expeditions. Being skilled with weapons, men also protected the group from attack by predators and war parties of other men. In most of these societies, men did heavier physical labor than women (Gough 1971).

Within this pattern of gender-role differentiation, tasks were equally shared, and men and women had relatively equivalent status. Both were essential for the survival of the group, both knew what they were expected to do, and both were socialized in performing their gender-role functions from early childhood. Little girls copied the household tasks and the gathering and trading tasks of women, whereas little boys made toy weapons and played hunting games in imitation of the men (Gough 1971).

There was no emphasis on ownership in hunting and gathering societies; personal effects, weapons, and food were all shared (Lenski and Lenski 1974; Bronowski 1973).

Agricultural Societies

Small-scale hunting and gathering groups persisted from generation to generation for hundreds of thousands of years of human history. The plow, which was not developed until 10,000 B.C. in northern Africa, made large-scale agriculture possible.[3] Using plows, groups could plant and harvest more grain than they could consume, which made it not only possible but necessary for groups to settle in one place. Settlement, in turn, led to the concept of property ownership, which was followed by the concept of the hereditary transmission of property (Lenski and Lenski 1974; Bronowski 1973).

---

[3]Horticultural societies did plant and harvest foods and keep domestic animals, but they had not yet developed large-scale agriculture, which depended on the plow.

As a surplus of food led to a growth in population, larger social units began to appear, resulting in the establishment of cities and the emergence of centralized states ruled by kings and other hereditary monarchs. By about 4000 B.C., just 6,000 years after the invention of the plow, military conquests of one people by another became possible in the Near East, which contributed to the increasing stratification of society into different social classes (Lenski and Lenski 1974; Bronowski 1973).

Agricultural societies developed a sharper differentiation between gender roles than had hunting and gathering groups and had greater specialization of labor. As with the hunting and gathering societies, women performed tasks that could be done close to the home and were not incompatible with the nurturance and care of infants and children. Women's tasks consisted of planting, tending, and harvesting food plants; preserving produce; looking after small livestock (made possible by a settled way of life); producing such household items as candles and soap; making, mending, and laundering clothes; and producing, nursing, nurturing, and rearing children. Meanwhile, men's tasks centered chiefly around large-scale agriculture and the care and feeding of large livestock (Gough 1971).

With the development of the concept of property, males became relatively more dominant than they had been in hunting and gathering societies. This pattern of male dominance had its basis in the father's ownership and management of the farm, which was the source of subsistence and survival for the entire family. A peasant father could demand obedience from his children (and wife) because they had little choice about what they did or where they could live. Because crops and farm animals had to be tended regularly or they would die, disobedience could endanger the food supply and put the entire family in jeopardy. Responsibility, an essential quality for farmers and herders, was much less crucial in the preceding hunting and gathering societies (Cernea 1970).

In European peasant families of the eighteenth century (and earlier) the inequality between husband and wife was quite pronounced: Their difference in status was a fact of life both in the home and in the outside world. Cernea (1970) sums this up as follows:

> A wife should not walk beside her husband but follow behind him; when he stops to chat with another villager, she should stop at a definite distance behind him, not interfere with the conversation, wait and start again only after her husband starts walking. At home she is "the humble servant of her husband" for all his needs, under the penalty of being beaten. Out in the agricultural field she has to perform a considerable share of the hardest activities, side by side with her husband. Advanced pregnancy is not a reason to discontinue work, and giving birth to a child in the field is reported as a common occurrence. (p. 55)

Our own eighteenth to nineteenth century society stemmed chiefly from the agricultural societies of western Europe, where centuries of tradition had installed the husband and father as the dominant family figure.

Women and Work in Our Agrarian Past

In 1800, nearly 90 percent of our population were subsistence farmers.[4] Subsistence farm families either grew or made almost everything they

needed; whatever they could not grow or make they acquired by barter.

The Gender-Based Division of Labor on the Farm

In addition to bearing children and then having the chief responsibility for their care, farm wives produced a substantial amount of economic goods — services and products — that were essential for the family's continued subsistence and well-being. These goods were certainly the economic equivalent of everything produced by the husband (Kessler-Harris 1981; Brown 1970).

Farm wives produced economic goods and services through the unpaid work of cooking, baking, canning, and preserving food that they grew in a "truck garden" — a garden, usually near the kitchen, that provided all the produce (fruits and vegetables) needed by the family. This truck garden often produced more food than the family could use, and this surplus provided a "cash crop" that could be bartered or sold to obtain goods that farm wives could neither grow nor prepare, such as coffee, flour, farm animals, and agricultural tools. They also raised animals such as rabbits, pigs, goats, and dairy cows, and they raised ducks, turkeys, and chickens and collected their eggs. They also made most of the family's clothes, and washed and ironed them, too.

Often, farm wives would also produce large-scale economic goods and accumulate capital. It was not unusual, for example, for a subsistence farm wife to raise as much as ten acres of pumpkins, squashes, watermelons, and other produce in one season (Dick 1954).

Meanwhile, farm husbands specialized in outside work. They produced economic goods and services chiefly by the unpaid work of clearing the land, chopping down trees, pulling up stumps, digging post holes, making fences, mending fences, mending harnesses, handling the larger animals, and planting and harvesting

[4]U.S. Department of Agriculture, Economic Research Service (1988).

crops. A husband did not usually do housework; however, he hauled fuel and water for household use, split logs and chopped wood to feed the cookstove (until the boys were old enough to do this), and butchered animals to prepare them for the kitchen. He was also able, when necessary, to cook.

Farm husbands also had the responsibility, both by custom and by law, for making all major decisions. Often the wife was not even consulted (Margolis 1984; Beecher 1977; Ariès 1965).

Although husbands and wives focused on gender-role work, they did not perform such work exclusively, and there was much overlapping. Thus although heavy, outside work was chiefly the responsibility of husbands, wives, when necessary, would also do such work — picking up heavy stones to clear the fields, mending fences, assisting with harvesting, and plowing. In dire circumstances, wives were even known to act as draft animals, being harnessed to a plow. Farm folks did what was necessary to get the job done in order that the family might survive. And, although child care was chiefly the responsibility of wives, husbands supervised boys (and sometimes girls) who helped with the outside work and arbitrated disputes. And most farm husbands read the Bible to the family in the evenings and on Sundays (Margolis 1984).

This description, of course, is a generalized view of rural America in the nineteenth century; there were many exceptions. For example, the genteel white women on the plantations of the antebellum South did no "outside" work at all and very little "inside" work, which was done by the house slaves. These women bore children, of course, but much of the responsibility for child care was also assigned to slaves. Moreover, many middle-class urban wives did not follow the pattern typical of farm wives.

Children were an asset on the farm because they began to perform economically valuable tasks when they were just a few years old. As they grew older, their productivity increased. Little boys hoed weeds, chopped wood, herded farm animals, and made themselves useful in barns and fields. Little girls helped their mothers with the numerous household, truck garden, poultry, and small-animal chores. By law, boys and girls alike owed their labor to their father as long as they were minors. And if they worked outside the farm, such as for a neighbor, their wages were turned over to their father (Stratton 1981).

During the subsistence-farm period, men and women married to form an economically productive unit. Men's and women's tasks were inextricably interrelated, and children worked right along with their parents. Thus the family formed a cooperative unit in which all members were engaged in a life-style in which working and living were completely intertwined, and in which essential, economically productive tasks were performed by every member of the family.

The Production of Children

Although families in Europe had an average of only two or three children in the nineteenth century because the land simply could not support any more, our own frontier society of this period had seemingly boundless resources, and families averaged eight children. In 1850, one-third of all married women had at least seven children.[5]

As the nineteenth century progressed the birth rate dropped, but in 1900 the average (median) married woman was still producing five children. This meant that half of all married women had more than five children, and families of nine or ten children were not uncommon (Westoff and Parke 1972).

---

[5]U.S. Bureau of the Census, *Historical Statistics of the United States, Part I* (1975), p. 53.

During this period of our past, a wife was regarded as lazy or selfish if she did not have many children; a married woman was expected "to be fruitful and multiply." In an economic sense, children were a valuable commodity produced by the mother, and childbearing was one of the important unpaid services the farm wife performed.

So long as the societal expectation was that wives should have large families, and as long as wives fulfilled this expectation by giving birth to many children, women's horizons were pretty well limited to childbearing and child rearing. Children were the chief focus of their interest, energy, and time, and they essentially defined women's life-styles. A woman's identity was chiefly that of wife and mother, and her status was largely derived from that of her husband.

Women and Work in Our Industrial Past

The Effect of the Industrial Revolution

As the Industrial Revolution, which began in England in the mid-eighteenth century, progressed, our nineteenth-century society steadily evolved from a dependence on agriculture to a dependence on industrial production. This change — almost imperceptible at first — was to lead to the end of the family as an economically productive unit.

The first effect of the Industrial Revolution was that subsistence farmers began to leave the unpaid work on their farms and moved to urban and suburban areas to do paid work in factories, mills, and other commercial enterprises. When this happened, the husband's economic productivity in and around the household virtually ceased. The wife continued to grow and store what food she could so that her productivity at

home did not come to as abrupt a halt as her husband's had, but her economic productivity was curtailed more and more as the nineteenth century drew to a close and the twentieth century began.

The year 1850 is usually given as the transition point at which our society went from having a chiefly agricultural economy to a chiefly industrial economy. By 1850, more than half of all families were deriving their living from paid work performed by the husband, rather than from unpaid work performed by both the husband and the wife (and the children) on a subsistence farm.[6]

From the 1850s on, increasing numbers of families left farms and moved to urban or suburban areas. Instead of performing unpaid (but economically productive) work on a farm, husbands moved into paid labor outside the home to earn money that could be used to pay for the goods and services needed for the family's subsistence. By the beginning of the twentieth century, only about one American in five (19 percent) lived on a subsistence farm.[7]

Meanwhile, wives remained within the household, continuing to do housework and producing and caring for children. However, their role was now much less valuable than it had been in the past. A typical wife could no longer grow all the vegetables the family needed or produce chickens, eggs, milk, or butter. Instead, she shopped at stores to buy the food with money her husband was earning by performing paid work in the marketplace. In the parlance of the time, her husband "brought home the bacon"; more precisely, he brought home the income the wife used to buy the bacon. She then cooked it

---

[6]U.S. Department of Agriculture, Economic Research Service (1988).

[7]U.S. Department of Agriculture, Economic Research Service.

and served it to the family, in addition to performing all the other household chores.

Wives still produced children and had the chief responsibility for their care, but these functions had also dropped in economic value because children were not economically productive in urban and suburban areas. Indeed, the economic meaning of children became a drain, a cost, or a liability rather than the value or asset they had been on the farm. Thus at the same time that various social forces were eroding the wife's economic productivity, these same forces were causing children to become economic liabilities.

Although many children initially continued to contribute to the economic support of their families by working in mines, factories, and mills, such work was so arduous that it was resorted to only by very poor families. Then, during the late nineteenth and early twentieth centuries, this source of income was increasingly restricted by child labor laws. Other legislation was enacted that made children's attendance at school mandatory until a minimum age (usually sixteen). Thus for children, childhood and adolescence became long periods of economic dependence on the family.

The Criminalization of Contraception

Even though children had become a serious financial burden in the industrial economy of the late nineteenth and early twentieth centuries, our society still held the traditional view that it was a wife's duty to have as many children as possible — that her primary function was to submit to her husband's sexual needs, become pregnant, and bear and rear many children. This attitude was supported by custom, religion, and law (Mohr 1978; Smith 1974).

The need for family planning — for contraceptive information and techniques — became an urgent social issue of the times. Paradoxically, legislators responded to this need by *tightening* laws against contraception on the grounds that public morality was being threatened. Fourteen states enacted legislation that made it a crime for a physician to inform a patient about contraception. A physician convicted of violating this law could be sentenced to ten years at hard labor in a maximum security prison. The defense that the patient's life would be endangered by pregnancy carried no legal weight. At the federal level, Congress enacted the Comstock Law of 1873, which prohibited sending information about contraception through the mail (Gordon 1983; Gray 1979; Wilson 1979).

The Criminalization of Abortion

Abortion had been legal in the United States since the country's founding in 1776. In 1873, Congress enacted legislation that made it a criminal act for a woman to have an abortion — even if she were married, or had several children, or if giving birth to another child would threaten her life. With laws prohibiting contraception tightened and with abortion illegal, many wives with unwanted pregnancies resorted to using illegal abortionists, which was (and remains) very dangerous.

Historians estimate that after 1873 more than one million illegal abortions were performed in the United States each year. These abortions, which were performed by unqualified practitioners using dangerous techniques, caused an enormous toll: serious injury, sterility, and even death for countless women. Three-fourths of these illegal and dangerous operations were performed on married women who felt that they simply could not afford another child (Crawley et al. 1973).

Other women seriously and sometimes fatally injured themselves when, in desperation, they tried to terminate a pregnancy — by pounding themselves on the abdomen, hurling themselves down a flight of stairs, or drinking quinine or castor oil. When none of these methods worked, many desperate women sought to procure a mysterious black pill rumored to be effective in bringing about a "miscarriage." This black pill, ergot, is not effective unless a woman takes enough to cause her own death. Taking less will make her agonizingly ill but will not induce abortion. Ergot is an alkaline substance that may be used in very small doses to contract the uterus and abdomen after the fetus and afterbirth have emerged (Martin and Reeder 1991).

Many pregnant women resorted to inserting an object (such as a coat hanger) into the vagina, through the cervix, and into the uterus in an attempt to induce an abortion. This attempt commonly resulted in puncturing the uterine wall or in penetrating some other organ, causing severe pelvic infection and often accompanied by shock, kidney failure, and not infrequently death (Hatcher et al. 1990).

The search for an effective method of abortion has led to many unsound practices throughout history. Anthropologist George Devereux (1967) has identified nearly sixty ineffective or dangerous methods for attempting to induce abortion.[8] Despite this long search throughout history, no effective folk method has yet been discovered that will induce abortion without the risk of seriously injuring, incapacitating, or perhaps killing the woman.

Abortion can be safely induced, especially during the first trimester, but it must be done carefully by a properly trained practitioner under sterile conditions, using approved surgical or medical techniques. When done under these conditions, the mortality rate is practically zero (Martin and Reeder 1991; Hatcher et al. 1990). (See Appendix B for more details regarding abortion).

Abortion was illegal in the United States for 100 years — from 1873 to 1973. In 1973, the U.S. Supreme Court handed down a decision in *Roe v. Wade*, which states that laws prohibiting abortion are an invasion of a woman's privacy and are thus unconstitutional. The Court decided that women have the right to control their own bodies and thus are free to decide to abort an unwanted pregnancy, for any reason, during the first trimester.[9] To protect the woman's health, certain restrictions apply during the second trimester, but abortion during the third trimester is still illegal. For an overview of some of the issues surrounding abortion, see Box 9-1.

The Relegalization of Contraception

As women's needs for information concerning contraceptives increased because of the shift in economic and social conditions, public attitudes toward the desirability of controlling the size of families slowly responded. Although many men still proclaimed that "a woman's place is in the home," and that wives should be kept "barefoot and pregnant," public consciousness was gradually being changed.

In 1923, the first legal birth control clinic was established in New York City, chiefly because of the tireless, dedicated efforts of one woman: Margaret Sanger, a public health nurse, who virtually single-handedly opposed the combined

---

[8]Ineffective or dangerous methods of attempted abortion that have been used by various societies throughout history include application of skin irritants (such as black beetles or large ants) on the pregnant woman's abdomen; piling heavy weights on her abdomen; wrapping a belt around her abdomen and then cinching the belt tighter and tighter; punching and squeezing her abdomen; inserting a variety of pointed objects into her vagina, through her cervix, and into her uterus; starving her; and bleeding her (Devereux 1967).

---

[9]See *Jane Roe et al. v. Henry Wade,* Supreme Court of the United States, Opinion No. 70-40, January 1973.

might of the medical, political, legal, and religious establishments of the time (see Box 9-2). She had many powerful enemies and no allies — except the desperately poor women in the city's tenements who had already given birth to more children than they could possibly care for and had no way of preventing pregnancy except to refuse sex to their men. Given the prevailing attitudes, expectations, and power of the men of the times, this was not a very practical solution.

The establishment of a legal birth control clinic in New York City in 1923 marked a watershed in public opinion and societal attitudes about the advisability of contraception, and laws prohibiting family planning began to be repealed in jurisdiction after jurisdiction throughout the United States. As these laws were repealed, physicians were freed to advise patients regarding birth control without becoming vulnerable to criminal prosecution.

As information and contraceptive devices became more widely available and publicly acceptable, conditions were ripe for a further decline in the birth rate. The drop in the birth rate made the entry of married women into the world of outside employment possible while the drop in women's economic productivity within the home made their entry profitable. This situation provided evidence that supports *economic determinism* — the doctrine that holds that important cultural patterns — as well as individual behavior — stem from economic forces. According to this doctrine, a key factor in the falling birth rate was the decline in the economic importance of children (Fuchs 1988; Margolis 1984).

The Entry of Women into the Work Force

Unmarried women, especially those of the lower class, began to leave the household for paid jobs in the late nineteenth century, mainly to work at menial labor in factories and mills. At this time, little other work was available to women.

This movement of young unmarried women into the paid work force accelerated with World War I. By the 1920s, young unmarried women had begun to acquire office jobs as secretaries and telephone operators and became sales clerks in retail stores (Harris 1981).

It was still very unusual, however, for a married woman to work outside the household. In the late nineteenth or early twentieth centuries, having a working wife implied that a husband could not support his family. To avoid this stigma, a married woman did not leave the household for outside employment except by dire necessity.

Married women first began to move into the work force in the 1930s. By 1940 about one married woman in seven (15 percent) was working outside the home. Most of the working wives of the 1930s and 1940s were from the lower class (Harris 1981).

Women and Work in Our Recent Past: The Gender-Role Revolution

The 1960s brought a series of extraordinarily significant transformations in the life-styles of men and women that continue right up until today. These transformations have been so significant that they have amounted to a gender-role revolution (Fuchs 1988).

Social Change in the 1960s

The birth-control pill was first marketed in the United States in 1960, signaling a new era in women's ability to control their fertility (see Appendix B). Without fertility regulation, women's

BOX 9·1

The Emotion-Laden Arguments Regarding Abortion

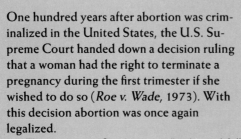

One hundred years after abortion was criminalized in the United States, the U.S. Supreme Court handed down a decision ruling that a woman had the right to terminate a pregnancy during the first trimester if she wished to do so (*Roe v. Wade*, 1973). With this decision abortion was once again legalized.

The bitter conflict between "right-to-life" groups and "pro-choice" groups only intensified with this Supreme Court decision. Prolifers believe that a human being comes into existence when the chromosomes of sperm and egg intermingle. They passionately believe that the new organism is a human being from the moment of conception, and that to destroy a human life is immoral. Very simply put, the right-to-life position is that abortion is murder.

Pro-choicers, on the other hand, passionately believe that a woman should have the

right to control her own body, and that a pregnant woman should have the freedom to choose whether to bear a baby or end a pregnancy if she wishes, for whatever reason. They further assert that a fertilized egg is not a human being, that it represents only a "blue print" of a human being — a complex single cell that, under proper circumstances, has the potential to *become* a human being. Both groups hold their convictions very deeply.

Because all "persons" are protected under the Constitution of the United States, the controversy necessarily focuses on the stage at which the unborn life form first becomes a person.

Interestingly, although a fetus is not legally a "person" until it is born, the unborn do have certain legal rights from the moment of conception. Courts have held, for example, that he or she can be the beneficiary of a

---

rights are mere words. A woman who has no control over her fertility cannot complete her education, cannot maintain gainful employment, and has very few real choices open to her (Fathalla 1992). Betty Friedan's *The Feminine Mystique*, published in 1963, both reported and instigated a new consciousness among women. It was so closely in tune with the times that it quickly became a national best-seller. Meanwhile, the Women's Liberation Movement developed a

unifying and politically significant groundswell that was to alter the consciousness of a nation.

In 1963, Congress enacted the Equal Pay Act, which asserted the principle that women should be paid the same as men for the same work. In 1964, Congress enacted the Civil Rights Act, which prohibited all forms of discrimination in employment. Thus "Help Wanted, Male" and "Help Wanted, Female" sections in newspaper want ads became illegal.

trust and inherit property from conception on. Moreover, when a pregnant woman puts an unborn life at risk by substance abuse, court rulings have held her to be guilty of *child* abuse and have forced her to enter rehabilitation programs during pregnancy (Martin and Reeder 1991).

From a scientific point of view, there is common agreement that a new life comes into existence at the moment of conception. Scientists do not agree, however, whether this new life form is a human being or only a potential human being.

If the new life form is not a human being at conception, when does it become human? As a zygote — at the point at which the fertilized egg begins to divide? At the blastocyst stage, when it implants in the uterine wall? At the embryo stage, when the human shape first begins to emerge? As a fetus, when it clearly begins to resemble human form? Or is the fetus considered human only after it is capable of independent life outside the woman's body?

This "age of viability" — the age at which it is possible for a fetus to survive outside the uterus — is currently regarded by the medical establishment to be about twenty-two or twenty-three weeks after conception, or at the borderline between the second and third trimesters (Martin and Reeder 1991). At this age it is possible — using the most advanced medical technology — that the fetus may survive outside the uterus.

With improving technology, however, it is possible to push back the age of viability — to what point can only be speculated. It is possible that the age of viability may be pushed all the way back to the fertilized egg, although at present this remains science fiction.

The current controversy between the proponents of the right-to-life for the unborn and the proponents of pro-choice for pregnant women continues to grow in scope and intensity. All interested parties will one day focus their attention on the Supreme Court to see whether it upholds or overturns *Roe v. Wade*.

The Civil Rights Act also prohibited gender discrimination in credit. For the first time, a married woman could now have a credit card in her own name (Jane Doe instead of Mrs. John Doe). Before the Civil Rights Act, only men could negotiate a mortgage, and bankers could not consider a wife's income as a factor in computing a married couple's eligibility for a loan. Now, not only can a wife's income be considered when a married couple apply for a loan, but a single woman can negotiate a mortgage on the same terms as a single man. (See Chapter 14 for a further discussion of women and credit.)

The Declining Birth Rate

Despite the significant drop in the birth rate since the nineteenth century, American women of childbearing age still had an average of 3.8 children in 1957 (the peak year of the baby

BOX 9-2

"Tell Jake to Sleep on the Roof"

Margaret Sanger was in New York City in 1912, working for the Visiting Nurses Association, a group of public health nurses dedicated to taking care of poverty-stricken women. These nurses went into the homes of women who lived in the tenements between 14th Street and East Broadway, where half a million people were crowded into an area designed for about one-fifth that many, living seven or eight to a room. The main task of the association was to help the women in this area through the ordeal of childbirth, which for many was a yearly event. These women were poor and malnourished, and many of them were ill. Many died in childbirth or from subsequent complications, and because they could not face still another child to care for, self-induced abortions were commonplace. The method frequently used was to insert a sharp instrument, such as a knitting needle, through the cervix to puncture the amniotic sac.

Something happened one hot summer afternoon in 1912 that was to change Margaret Sanger's life and that, in time, would have an enormous effect on the consciousness of our entire country. She was summoned to the room of a woman named Sadie Sachs, who was twenty-seven years old, had six children, and, in desperation, had tried to abort her current pregnancy. She was hemorrhaging so badly that Sanger was unable to stop the bleeding. She ran for a doctor, who was able to bring the hemorrhage under control but who warned Sachs that another such attempt might well be fatal. Sachs, who was barely conscious at the time, whispered to the doctor, "Tell me the secret, please! How can I prevent it?" The doctor, who was leaving the room, turned and said, "Oh, you want to have your cake and eat it, too, do you? I'll tell you the secret. Tell Jake to sleep on the roof" (Gray 1979, p. 54).

The attitude of the time was that conjugal relations were a husband's privilege and a wife's duty; if she became pregnant it was God's will. Condoms were available, but it was an unusual husband who could be per-

boom). The birth rate has continued to decline since then, dipping below the replacement level[10] in 1973 to an average of 1.8 children per woman of childbearing age. Reasons for the decline since 1957 include the continued rising

---

[10]As noted earlier, the *replacement level* is the birth rate that yields an average of 2.1 births per woman. At this rate, given the actuarial expectation for deaths in infancy and childhood, it is expected that two children will reach adulthood and thus replace their parents (Fuchs 1988).

suaded to use one. Withdrawal before ejaculation was also possible (if not uniformly effective), but it was even more difficult to persuade a husband to do that.

Jake chose not to sleep on the roof, use a condom, or withdraw, and Sadie Sachs was pregnant again a few months later. This time, when she tried to abort the fetus the hemorrhaging was fatal. Margaret Sanger arrived just a few minutes before Sadie Sachs died.

The callous (and typical) attitude of the medical establishment, as exemplified by this doctor, outraged Margaret Sanger. She was deeply moved by the plight of thousands of women who would risk death rather than remain pregnant.

The hopelessness of these women's attempts at birth control, their high mortality rate, the naked and hungry babies wrapped in newspapers to keep them from the cold, and the young children with pinched, wrinkled faces dressed in rags troubled Sanger so deeply that she became increasingly involved in a movement to provide women with birth control information. By 1916 she was dedicating herself completely to this cause (Sanger 1937).

Margaret Sanger was repeatedly arrested and thrown in jail, but she persevered in fighting, almost single-handedly, the American Medical Association and the federal government. By sheer determination and dogged persistence, she finally succeeded in having local, state, and then federal laws prohibiting birth control repealed, and in 1923 — eleven years after Sadie Sachs' death — she established the first legal birth control clinic in New York City.

The law against sending information about contraceptives through the mail was modified in the mid-1930s. During the 1940s and 1950s many states modified or repealed their laws prohibiting contraception, and finally, in 1965, the U.S. Supreme Court struck down all remaining state laws prohibiting the use of contraceptives.

Her crusade finally over, Margaret Sanger died a year later.

costs of having and raising children, a massive increase in women's employment, and delayed childbearing (Exter 1991).

A slight blip in the birth rate occurred in 1989, when it rose 0.1, to 1.9 births per woman of childbearing age. Demographers believe that this slight rise was caused by women who had delayed having children deciding to have a child before their "biological clock" ran down. Most demographers project that the birth rate will resume its decline in the 1990s (Exter 1991).

The low national birth rate does not mean that all women in the United States are having small families, however. On the contrary, many wives and many single mothers still have large families. In 1989, for example, 18 percent of Hispanic families had three or more children, as did 15 percent of black families and 9 percent of white families.[11]

The Declining Marriage Rate

Since the 1960s, the proportion of young women who postpone marriage has been rising dramatically. For example, in 1965 only one-third of twenty- to twenty-four-year-old women had never married (Fuchs 1988); in 1989, fully two-thirds of women of this age had never married — the highest proportion of young women remaining single to this age in our history.[12]

The Rising Divorce Rate

Between 1965 and 1975 the divorce rate in the United States doubled. It then grew more slowly to reach an all-time high in 1979, when demographers estimated that about one-half of all first marriages would end in divorce (Fuchs 1988). The overall divorce rate has decreased slightly since that time.[13] However, it is still rising for young married couples.

Demographers estimated in 1987 that 56 percent of all first marriages would end in divorce (Norton and Moorman 1987). Demographers also point out that another 6 percent of first marriages end in separation. Thus approximately 62 percent of first marriages are expected to end either in separation or divorce. The divorce rate for remarriages is about 25 percent higher than that for first marriages (Castro-Martin and Bumpass 1989; Furstenberg and Spanier 1987).

The Rising Proportion of Single Women

The declining marriage rate coupled with the rising divorce rate over the last thirty years has led to an unprecedented number of single women, whether never-married, divorced, or widowed. As we saw in Chapter 6, there has been a substantial increase in the proportion of single women in our society, especially young women. More than half of the increase in the proportion of women who were unmarried was the result of divorce (Fuchs 1988).

The Rising Proportion of Women in the Work Force

In 1960, only a little more than a third (38 percent) of women in our society were in the work force.[14] In 1986, the proportion of employed women passed the 50 percent mark;[15] by 1990, more than two-thirds (68 percent) of women were employed.[16]

In 1960, eight out of ten young wives and mothers specialized in housework and child care and depended on their husbands for the sole economic support of the family (Fuchs 1988). By 1989, more than half (54 percent) of mothers of children younger than one year, with a husband

---

[11]U.S. Bureau of the Census, "Families by Number of Own Children Under 18 Years Old: 1970 to 1989" (1991).

[12]U.S. Bureau of the Census, "Marital Status of the Population, by Sex and Age: 1989" (1991).

[13]U.S. National Center for Health Statistics, "Divorces and Annulments — Rate and Percent Distribution, by Age and Sex: 1987" (1991).

[14]U.S. Bureau of Labor Statistics, "Marital Status of Women in the Civilian Labor Force: 1960 to 1989" (1991); "Marital and Family Characteristics of the Labor Force, Current Population Survey, March 1990" (1991).

[15]U.S. Bureau of Labor Statistics, "Marital Status of Women."

[16]"Marital Status of Women"; "Marital and Family Characteristics of the Labor Force."

present in the household, were employed,[17] as were six out of ten mothers with children under six years of age.[18]

Moreover, working mothers are not primarily poor and lower class. Rather, the more affluent a family is, the greater will be the likelihood that the mother will work. College-educated wives are now more likely to work outside the home than are less well educated wives (Fuchs 1988).

The proportion of women entering the work force reached a peak in 1990 and began to level off, prompting some economists and sociologists to suggest that the proportion of women working outside the home might be approaching its upper limit. These observers see the leveling-off as a reflection of our societal expectation that women bear the chief responsibility for child care. They agree, however, that the ceiling — if one exists — will rise again, perhaps by the end of the 1990s, if the problems of child care for working mothers can be resolved (Uchitelle 1990).

Women and Work Today

Economists agree that women today are working longer hours, have less time to devote to child care, and have less leisure time than they did a generation ago. Only one group of women has not experienced a decline in their economic well-being:[19] women who are unmarried, have no children, are young (twenty-five to forty-four years of age), well educated (more than twelve years), and white (Fuchs 1988).

The wage differential (although slightly improved) persists; a "glass ceiling" often limits women's advancement; cultural stereotypes denigrating women remain, as does the myth of the importance of relative size and strength; unconscionable numbers of never-married or divorced mothers who head single-parent families are trapped in a cycle of poverty; and most mothers in two-earner families work a second shift at home of four-and-a-half months of forty-hour work weeks per year — a shift that relatively few husbands share. In the following sections we will examine these complex issues.

Women and the Wage Differential

Women have earned less than men for paid work throughout recorded history. Even when a woman — Cleopatra — was the absolute ruler in Egypt 5,000 years ago, women who worked in Egyptian workshops were paid less than half the wages paid to men (Pomeroy 1984).

In 1820, female workers in U.S. manufacturing firms earned about one-third as much as men (Goldin 1986). From 1890 to 1930 the *wage differential* (the amount of money women earn for every dollar a man earns) averaged about forty-five cents. By 1930, it was about sixty cents, the level at which it remained for the next fifty years (Fuchs 1988). In 1990, the wage differential was about seventy-two cents (Lewis 1991).[20]

---

[17]U.S. Bureau of Labor Statistics, "Labor Force Participation Rates for Wives, Husband Present, by Age of Own Youngest Child: 1975 to 1989" (1991).

[18]U.S. Bureau of Labor Statistics, "Married, Separated, and Divorced Women — Labor Force Status by Presence and Age of Children: 1960 to 1989" (1991).

[19]Economists define *economic well-being* as the quantity and quality of the economic goods one acquires by paid and unpaid work, and by one's access to leisure time (Fuchs 1988).

[20]In 1981 the U.S. Supreme Court established the principle that women must be paid the same as men for equivalent work and defined "equivalent work" as work that fulfills essentially the same function or requires the same amount of training or education. It does not have to be exactly the same work. Although some lawsuits have been successful in enforcing this principle, and although eventually the doctrine of equal pay for equivalent work may prevail, the wage differential has only increased twelve cents since 1981 — from sixty cents to seventy-two cents.

The seventy-two cents that women earn for every dollar that a man earns does not apply uniformly to all ages or to all occupations (see Figure 9-1). The income gap widens with age: After age fifty, women average only 64 percent of men's income, even among many higher-paid professional and managerial positions. Thus after age fifty, female managers average only 52 percent of male wages, and female accountants and auditors average only 60 percent. The wage differential, of course, also occurs within individual couples. Three-fourths of husbands earn more per hour than their wives.[21]

It should also be noted that, although the wage differential has closed slightly since 1960, any gain has been more than offset by the wages lost by women who only work part-time. If full-time work is defined to be at least thirty-five hours a week for forty-eight weeks each year, one-fourth of all employed women work only part-time (Lewis 1991). This is more than twice the number of men who work part-time.[22] Most women (three-fourths) who work part-time do so involuntarily—because they can't get full-time work. Many find it necessary to work at two or three part-time jobs to pay their bills.[23] Well-educated women are just as likely to work part-time as are less-educated women (Fuchs 1988). Finally, when a woman is laid off it takes her an average of nine months to find a new job; this is 38 percent longer than it takes a man (Lopez 1992).

Because retirement benefits are based on wages earned, the average lower pay for women extends into their retirement years. The average benefit for a woman retiring in 1985 was about 40 percent of the average benefit for a retiring man, and this figure has remained essentially the same since the 1960s.[24]

The Glass Ceiling

Although by law employers may not deny women advancement to top-level professional and executive positions, abundant research reveals the existence of a "glass ceiling"—an invisible, not openly acknowledged barrier above which it is very difficult for women to advance (Morrison and Von Glinow 1990; Thomas and Alderfer 1989; Hymowitz and Schellhardt 1986).

Extensive data show that less than 4 percent of board directorships and less than 2 percent of corporate officerships in Fortune 500 companies are held by women (Von Glinow and Knzyczowska 1988). Nor do women fare much better in government or in institutions of higher learning. Less than 9 percent of senior executive-level jobs in government offices are held by women (U.S. Office of Personnel Management 1989); and on average, each college and university nationwide employs just 1 percent of its female employees in positions of dean or higher (Sandler 1986). For an in-depth discussion of this very important topic of the glass ceiling see Kelly (1991) *The Gendered Economy* and Morrison, White, and Van Velson (1987) *Breaking the Glass Ceiling*.

It is interesting to note that most women who do manage to succeed in a professional career have sacrificed marriage and children to do so. More than half (52 percent) of women at the executive level are single, and 61 percent have

[21]U.S. Bureau of the Census, "Mean Earnings of Husbands and Wives in Married-Couple Families: 1981 and 1987" (1991).

[22]U.S. Bureau of Labor Statistics, "Employed and Unemployed Workers, by Work Schedules, Sex, and Age: 1980 to 1989" (1991).

[23]WOW (Wider Opportunities for Women) Report, "No Way Out: Working Poor Women in the United States" (1988).

[24]U.S. Social Security Administration, "Social Security (OASDI)—Retirement Benefits, by Sex: 1970–1985" (1987); "Social Security (OASDI)—Benefits, by Type of Beneficiary: 1970 to 1989" (1991).

a woman earns:

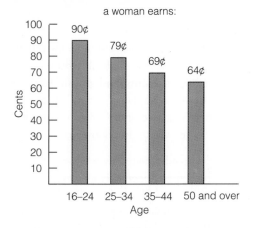

For every dollar earned by a man age 50 or older,
a woman of the same age earns:

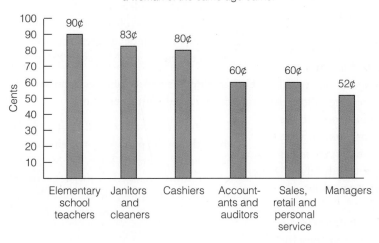

Median weekly earnings by occupation
for workers age 50 and older:

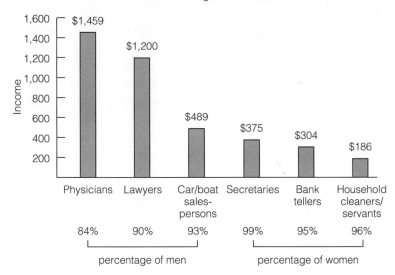

FIGURE 9-1

The income gap at a glance.

Source: Robert Lewis, "Equity
Eludes Women: Earnings Gap Is
Greatest After Age 50." *AARP*
Vol. 32, No. 10, November 1991,
p. 11. © 1991 AARP Bulletin. Re-
printed with permission.

no children. By contrast, 95 percent of male executives are married and 97 percent have children (Fraker 1984).

Stereotypical Views of Women

There is certainly less prejudice toward women at work today than there was in the late nineteenth century. Although Leo Tolstoy, a well-known novelist of that period highly regarded for his insight into cultural patterns, portrayed women very sympathetically, he nevertheless wrote in his diary (1891) that "to regard [women] as equals is cruelty." For a sampling of men's stereotypical views of women throughout history, see Box 9-3.

Until well into the twentieth century, women were believed to be less intelligent, less rational, and more prone to make illogical emotional judgments than men. Women were not allowed to vote, for example, because legislators and the public at large believed that most women were inherently incapable of understanding the issues at stake in an election. (The Nineteenth Amendment to the U.S. Constitution granted women the right to vote in 1920.)

Typical school boards in the United States in the 1920s expected female teachers to obey the following rules:

> Do not keep company with men; be home between the hours of 8 p.m. and 6 a.m.; do not loiter downtown in ice cream stores; do not get into a carriage with any man except your father or brother; do not dress in bright colors. (Zerfoss 1974)

Prejudice and discrimination against women in the workplace may not be so obvious in today's world, but they still exist. Frances K. Conley shocked both the academic and the medical communities nationwide when she abruptly resigned her prestigious position as full professor at Stanford Medical School in 1991. Dr. Conley took this admittedly drastic step to protest the rampant sexism in the medical school, where female medical students and physicians alike were discriminated against simply because of their gender. In a statement explaining her decision, Dr. Conley wrote the following:

> Those who administer my work environment have never been able to accept me as an equal person. Not because I lack professional competence, but because I use a different bathroom. I am minus the appropriate gender identification that permits full club membership. . . . I leave in place a validated legacy of sexism, a role model for all men, that women are, indeed, inferior and expected to remain so. (McCabe 1991, p. A-1)

Dr. Conley rescinded her resignation a few months later, but with reservations:

> Under no circumstances will I put up with what I did in the past. . . . If the environment there [Stanford University Medical School] is not changed by the steps they're taking now to improve things, I will be history once again. (McCabe 1991, p. A-1)

The Myth of the Importance of Size and Strength

Inequalities in opportunities for women, and the resultant economic disadvantage, have very little relation to women's relatively smaller size and lower physical strength compared with men. If size and strength were important sources of wealth or power in our society, then larger, stronger men would always be the wealthiest and most powerful, which obviously is not the case.

Some occupations, such as playing professional football, may always remain solely the province of males. Other occupations, such as

BOX 9-3

The "Inferior Sex": Men's Stereotypical Views of Women

It has long been traditional for men to regard women as "the inferior sex" (Starr 1991). The fact that most readers today would view the following quotes as outrageous or perhaps amusing illustrates how male-dominated societies' attitudes have changed — or have they?

I like them fluffy, I know it's bad taste,
With fluffy, soft looks and a flower at the
 waist. . . .
Not huffy, or stuffy, not tiny or tall,
But fluffy, just fluffy, with no brains at all.
(Sir Alan Patrick Herbert, 1927)

Eloquence in women shouldn't be praised; it is more fitting for them to lisp and stammer. (Martin Luther, 1538)

The wife ought not to have any feeling of her own but join with her husband. (Plutarch, A.D. 110)

Nature intended women to be our slaves. . . . What a mad idea to demand equality for women! (Napoleon, 1817)

I enjoy them as a breed, like a dog. . . . I don't mean that derogatorily. (Henry Miller, 1975)

Such is the stupidity of woman's character that it is incumbent upon her, in every particular, to distrust herself and obey her husband. (Confucius, ca. 500 B.C.)

Though destitute of virtue, or seeking pleasure elsewhere, or completely devoid of good qualities, a husband must be constantly worshiped as a god by the faithful wife. (Hindu scripture, ca. 100 B.C.)

Girls begin to talk and to stand on their feet sooner than boys because weeds always grow up more quickly than good crops. (Martin Luther, 1538)

Eighteen goddess-like daughters are not equal to one son with a hump. (Chinese proverb)

In law . . . a hundred women are equal to only one witness. (*Talmud, Yebamot* 88B)

Finally, to show that our point of view may not have changed all that much, after all:

Feminists and all these radical gals — most of them are failures. (The Reverend Jerry Falwell, 1989)

piano moving, oil rigging, and logging, may be difficult for most women because of the importance of size and strength. Still, many women are perfectly capable in these strength-related fields.

For the vast majority of occupations in our society, size and strength is simply not a factor. There is no reason why women cannot perform in these fields equally as well as men, for such factors as interest, expectation, aptitude, ability, training, and opportunity — all of which are cultural factors — are much more important than size.

Women in Single-Parent Families

Nearly 10 percent of family households are single-parent families.[25] About 25 percent of American children live in single-parent families:[26] 61 percent of black children, 19 percent of Hispanic children, and 17 percent of white children (McNeil 1992).

More than half of all mothers in single-parent families live below the poverty level — 75 percent of blacks, 46 percent of Hispanics, and 43 percent of whites.[27] (The federal government defines the *poverty level* as the minimum income necessary for bare survival.) Most single mothers must work at two jobs if they are to stay above the poverty level. The number of women working at two or more jobs increased fivefold between 1970 and 1989 (Kilborn 1990).

Single-Parent Families Headed by Never-Married Mothers   One out of four babies was born out of wedlock in 1988; this is a fivefold

increase from just one out of twenty babies born out of wedlock in 1960.[28]

Although the incidence of unwed motherhood is rising among whites, a disproportionate number of unwed mothers are Hispanic and black (see Chapter 5). One of every three black mothers is an unwed teenager. One black unwed teenage mother in three has a second illegitimate child while still in her teens (Hatcher et al. 1990).

Teenage mothers typically drop out of school, lack the education or training necessary to obtain a well-paying job, and have little hope for improving their financial situation (Hatcher et al. 1990). Their lifetime earnings are less than half those of women who bear their first child after age nineteen. These lower lifetime earnings extend to the second generation: The children of unmarried teenage mothers also tend to drop out of school and to have relatively low lifetime earnings.[29]

Single-Parent Families Headed by Divorced Mothers   The plight of a divorced mother with custody of her children can be just as burdensome as that of a never-married mother. A mother with dependent children customarily earns, on average, only 46 percent of the father's wage (Hewlett 1986). Nearly half (42 percent) of divorced fathers don't pay the amount of child support awarded by the court; about one divorced mother in four receives partial payment, and another one in four receives nothing at all (Peterson and Nord 1990). In 1987, the average amount of child support paid to a divorced

---

[25]U.S. Bureau of the Census, "Changing American Households and Families: 1980–1990" (1991).

[26]U.S. Bureau of the Census, "Children Under 18 Years Old, by Presence of Parents: 1970–1988" (1990).

[27]U.S. National Center for Children in Poverty, "Distribution of All Children and of Poor Children, by Family Type and Race: 1987" (1991).

[28]U.S. National Center for Health Statistics, "Babies Born Out-of-Wedlock in the U.S. by Race: 1970 to 1988" (1991); U.S. Bureau of the Census, *Studies in Marriage and the Family* (1989); U.S. National Center for Health Statistics, "Births to Unmarried Women, by Race and Age of Mother: 1950 to 1981" (1985).

[29]U.S. Center for Population Options, "Teenage Pregnancy and Too-Early Childbearing: Public Costs, Personal Consequences" (1989).

woman and her children was only $2,710 a year.[30] Even if this sum were paid regularly, it covers less than a quarter of the average costs of raising one child (Hewlett 1991). With inadequate child support payments and with her own wages less than half of her ex-husband's, the typical divorced mother heading a single-parent family slides into a life of poverty from which she is rarely able to escape (Danziger and Stern 1990).

Analysis of demographic data reveals that the average woman's standard of living drops a startling 73 percent following a divorce, according to Weitzman (1985); Hoffman and Duncan (1988) arrive at a more conservative drop of 30 percent. Meanwhile, the ex-husband's standard of living rises by 42 percent according to Weitzman (1985) and by 10–15 percent according to Hoffman (1987). (For further discussion of the divorce and its aftermath see Chapters 12 and 13).

Women in Two-Earner Families

Just how many women with young children worked outside the house in 1950 is not known; these women were so rare that the Bureau of Labor Statistics kept no records on them. Following the gender-role revolution that lasted from the 1960s to the 1990s, two-thirds of mothers had full-time jobs (thirty-five or more hours per week). More mothers than nonmothers had paid jobs (or were actively looking for one). Today more than 70 percent of wives and mothers are now working outside the home.[31]

Women in two-earner families generally do more unpaid work than men, especially housework and child care. Wives have increased their total hours of work each week by an average of

7 percent since 1960. Meanwhile, husbands have decreased their total hours of work by an equivalent 7 percent. Thus wives have less access to leisure time in the 1990s than they had in the 1960s (Fuchs 1988).

The Second Shift In most two-earner families, wives work at the second shift — unpaid work at home after a first shift in the workplace — for about fifteen hours a week more than their husbands work (Hochschild 1989). These fifteen hours a week amount to about four-and-a-half months of forty-hour work weeks each year. Men's strategies of resistance to doing second-shift work include waiting to be asked and hoping that they won't be. Once asked, many perform tasks reluctantly and poorly. Some men even protest that they weren't brought up to do housework. In landmark research (*The Second Shift*, 1989), Arlie Hochschild, professor of sociology at the University of California, Berkeley, intensively studied a group of two-earner families for ten years, even visiting them in their homes. Of the couples she studied, not a single husband thought that helping with the second shift would be a demonstration of love, and this was one of the wives' most common complaints (Hochschild 1989).

About one husband in five in two-earner families shares the second shift, and some of these families have a "superdad" that is the equivalent of a "supermom." Husbands who share the second shift work hours outside the home that are similar to those worked by nonsharing men, and they usually earn about the same as their wives (Hochschild 1989).

Working wives usually do the essential *daily* jobs at home — cleaning up, cooking, and child care — that tend to require a rather rigid, unalterable schedule. On weekends and holidays these women tend to feel compelled to do household chores. On the other hand, most of the functions of the second shift performed by

---

[30]U.S. Bureau of the Census, "Child Support and Alimony: Selected Characteristics of Women: 1987" (1991).

[31]U.S. Bureau of Labor Statistics, "Labor Force Participation."

husbands — such as repairing the house, changing the oil in the family car, straightening out the garage, mowing the lawn, or taking the children on an outing or to a fast-food restaurant — are discretionary and can be done on an elastic schedule if and when they wish. Husbands therefore have more freedom regarding the work of the second shift and are most likely to relieve their wives of those tasks that are easiest and most rewarding (Coleman 1991; Hochschild 1989).

Many families develop an "upstairs-downstairs" arrangement — a myth that the wife and the husband each do half of the second shift: She does the upstairs, and he does the downstairs. The "upstairs" consists of the bedrooms, bathrooms, living room, dining room, family room, and kitchen. The "downstairs" consists of the garage, workroom or hobby room, and outdoor areas. The husband's intermittent work in the "downstairs" area may be seen as an equivalent contribution to the workload that balances his wife's daily schedule of housekeeping, shopping, cooking, and caring for the children. According to this myth, gender roles have been equalized by this "upstairs-downstairs" arrangement, and as long as they both buy this, they can believe that the work of the second shift is shared. It may be important for the wife to believe this if she is to maintain her sense of liberation and independence. It may be important for the husband if he is to justify his life-style of greater leisure (Hochschild 1989).

The strain of working the extra four-and-a-half months of forty-hour weeks per year on the second shift affects many wives in obvious ways — fatigue, sickness, and emotional exhaustion. Working mothers are more likely than any other group to have symptoms of anxiety, such as dizziness, depression, and feelings of apprehension (Thoits 1986). The problems of the second shift inevitably affect husbands as well, especially if they don't do household work and child care directly: They can avoid the work, but they can't avoid the consequences of not doing the work. This is so because many wives feel deeply resentful toward their nonsharing husbands (Hochschild 1989).

In two-earner families, the constant pressure of work, the resultant exhaustion, and the lack of leisure time often leave both spouses with lowered interest in romantic interludes — as witness the bumperstickers that say "Working Parents Do It Less."

Economic Determinism, Gender Ideology, and Backstage Support   Many husbands who do not share the second shift point out that because men's work usually pays more than women's work, it makes sense to focus on the husband's work to maximize the family's income. According to this argument, relaxing at home makes it possible for him to do a better job at work. Many men believe that their chief responsibility is to be a good provider for the family and that their wife's chief responsibility is to take care of the household and the children. Many wives in two-earner families accept this premise and provide "backstage" support for their husband's work, which makes it easier for men to succeed in the workplace and contribute more toward the family's income (Hochschild 1989).

This situation is an example of the doctrine of economic determinism, which states that behavior is often determined by economic factors. Further, in this case, in which the wife provides the husband with backstage support so that he can earn money more efficiently for the entire family, the doctrine of economic determinism is in accord with the traditional gender ideology of male dominance and female submission.

However, in about one American two-earner family in five, the wife earns more than her husband. In this case, does the husband then provide backstage support for his wife's work and perform the second shift at home? Usually he does not. When economic determinism is not in accord with the traditional gender ideology of a dominant husband and a submissive wife, economic determinism has less influence than gender ideology. Thus a wife who is earning more than her husband and has greater career expectations cannot usually count on backstage support from her husband. In fact, a husband in this situation does even *less* of the second shift — and an unemployed husband does least of all (Hochschild 1989).

What is the reason for this apparent paradox? The explanation seems to be that in many cases a husband who earns less than his wife feels devalued because of the reversal of culturally expected roles. For a husband who already feels devalued to then assume the work of the second shift (in the process providing his wife with backstage support for her success) would (according to traditional gender ideology) further confirm his inadequacy as a male. Most successful wives apparently sense this threat to the male identity and respond by doing the work of the second shift — in addition to earning more income and holding the more prestigious position in the work world (Hochschild 1989).

In short, in most marriages gender ideology and economic determinism are in accord. Both tacitly support the wife's doing the second shift and providing backstage support for her husband. In marriages in which gender ideology and economic determinism are *not* in accord, gender ideology usually prevails.

It is also interesting to note that when a wife earns more than her husband, he may well develop problems with sexual functioning. Although a husband may deny any awareness of a connection between his wife's career success and his impotence, declaring that he is both proud of her abilities and good fortune and happy to have the additional income, he still may find himself in a doctor's office complaining of a disinterest in sex and difficulty in having an erec-

tion. In fact, the correlation between a relatively higher income for the wife and her husband's disinterest in sex is quite striking (Rosenberg 1992).

Women's Lives Today Are Changing More Than Men's As we have seen, before the Industrial Revolution in America most men and women lived out their lives on the family farm, where crops were grown and craft work was done mainly for domestic consumption. With industrialization came paying jobs outside the home, first for men and then for women. But industrialization did not affect men and women either at the same time or in the same way.

Initially, the most significant changes came for men. As men moved away from the farm and into factory work, their basic way of life changed. Although life changed for women too, most of them maintained their primary identity at home, and most wives remained involved primarily with housework and child care. Today, following the gender-role revolution, women's lives are changing faster than men's. It is now women who are leaving a home-oriented way of life as they move into the industrial economy (Hochschild 1989).

Most wives in two-earner marriages today believe that they should be equal to their husbands and should share with their husbands the job of earning money to support the family; in the 1950s these women's mothers did not hold such beliefs. Most wives today believe that a husband should share the work at home; before the gender-role revolution, the idea that such a thing was possible may not have occurred to many women (Hochschild 1989).

The average homemaker and mother of the 1950s has been transformed in the 1990s into a working wife and mother in a two-earner family, but husbands' lives remain pretty much the same. Thus a woman who is different from her mother is married to a man who is not much different from his father. He hasn't changed very much in his assumptions about gender ideology — except that he expects that his wife will want to work outside the household (Hochschild 1989).

Who Looks After the Relationship? When both the husband and wife work outside the household in a two-earner family, a problem of who looks after the relationship can arise. The conflict between work demands and maintaining the relationship is a chief source of conflict for many couples (Blumstein and Schwartz 1983).

Relationship-centered people consider their personal relationships more important than their work, and by providing care and nurturance in a relationship these people fulfill a *caretaker* role. Work-centered people focus on career, and by devoting most of their time, attention, interest, physical energy, and emotional strength to their jobs, these people fulfill a *provider* role.

People who fulfill the caretaker role are expected to be nurturing, compassionate, and understanding, traits traditionally regarded as "feminine" (or "expressive") in our society. Traditionally, wives have fulfilled the caretaker role. People who fulfill the provider role are expected to be forceful, aggressive, and work-centered, traits customarily regarded as "masculine" (or "instrumental") in our society (Shaver and Freedman 1976; Lunneborg and Rosenwood 1972; Bardwick 1971). Traditionally, men have fulfilled the provider role.

But what happens when both husband and wife have full-time obligations in the work world — when both are in the provider role? Who then fulfills the caretaker role?

Unless someone fulfills the caretaker role, the marriage is likely to be joyless, dreary, and strife-ridden. The happiest marriages are those in which both partners are relationship-centered and fulfill the caretaker role; about one-fourth of the couples in the study conducted by Blumstein and Schwartz (1983) fall into this category. The unhappiest marriages are those in which neither the wife nor the husband fulfills the caretaker role. Blumstein and Schwartz (1983) found that the husband fulfills the caretaker role in about 13 percent of marriages.

The Financial Consequences of Divorce in Two-Earner Families During the gender-role revolution the economic support that marriage provides for women and children has become increasingly less secure. The lower on the class ladder, the less stable marriage is, but divorce has increased in every social class. More and more working- and middle-class white women now face the situation black and Hispanic women have faced for some time: They cannot rely on marriage as a means of supporting themselves and their children.

Half of all marriages end in divorce, and divorced women typically experience a significant drop in their standard of living, whereas divorced men experience a substantial gain.

If the wife divorces the husband, perhaps to escape the pressures of a two-earner family — notably the equivalent of four-and-a-half months of forty-hour work weeks doing the second shift — she ceases to be a wife and becomes a divorced single mother who still has the responsibility for the household and child care but without the financial support of a husband. As we have seen, most single mothers, and most children of single mothers, live below the poverty line.

Most divorced men provide very little financial support for their children. Fully 80 percent of divorced fathers fail to fulfill their obligations to make court-ordered support payments. For most wives, then, a shaky marriage raises the prospect of economic insecurity if they leave it, and for many, leaving it can mean outright poverty. The frightening truth is that once pushed down the economic ladder, many divorced women (and their children) get stuck there because they have difficulty finding jobs with adequate pay and because most of them still have primary responsibility for the children (Hochschild 1989).

The growing instability of marriage today creates a new form of oppression that reduces the power of women inside marriage. They are reluctant to pressure their husbands to do more at home for fear of causing a family crisis. Wives look at their divorcing friends and ponder their own dilemmas: "Put up with an extra work of the second shift or divorce?" Most answer this question by saying, "I'll put up with it" (Hochschild 1989, p. 252).

Women's Choices Today

Although the realistic choices available to a young woman today are wider than they were in her grandmother's time, they are still quite limited. (Her grandmother simply hoped to marry a man who was a good provider, for very few women achieved success outside of marriage.) The typical young woman today is romantic and idealistic. She dreams of falling in love, marrying, and having children, or she dreams of having a profession or career. Or maybe both.

What are a young woman's realistic choices today?

- Marry a man who earns enough to provide for the family (have a traditional marriage) but give up on dreams of a profession or career.

- Marry and have a profession or career as well in a two-earner marriage with a husband who shares the second shift. Her odds are one in five of accomplishing this. As we have seen, one in five husbands do share the work load at home, and some are even "superdads."

- Marry and have a profession or career in a two-earner family—and work the second shift. Become a "supermom" and accept the extra work and lack of leisure time.

- Marry and have a profession or career in a two-earner family, and if the pressure becomes too much, divorce and become a single parent—even though most single mothers and their children are likely to experience severe financial hardship.

- Marry but expect to remain child-free in a two-earner, egalitarian marriage.

- Enter a cohabiting relationship, which provides companionship, love, and sex without the responsibilities of marriage, and remain child-free.

- Enter a cohabiting relationship, have a profession or career, and have children. Of course, cohabiting women usually do as much of the second shift work as married women (see Chapter 6).

- Remain single, have a profession or career, and have children.

- Remain single, unattached, and child-free, giving up on dreams of marriage and motherhood, and seek success in a profession or career.

Few young women contemplating their futures are clearly aware of all of these realistic possibilities. Instead, they have romantic dreams—of love, babies, and career—and fail to consider the implications of each option (Hochschild 1989).

The Plight of America's Children

Declining Incidence of Parental Contact with Children

Parents are spending much less time with their children today than parents did a generation ago. Since 1960, children have lost 10–12 hours of parental time per week (Fuchs 1988). The amount of "total contact time"—defined as time parents spend with children while doing other things—has dropped 40 percent during the last twenty-five years (Mattox 1990). Brazelton (1990) argues that much of the plight of today's children can be traced to this drop in incidence of parental contact, with a consequent lack of sufficient time for effective parenting.

There are many interrelated reasons for this drop in parental time spent with children. As we have noted, single parents and married parents in two-income families must often be absent from the household to earn money to support the family; these parents consequently have less time for parenting. In addition, as a result of the rising incidence of never-married mothers heading single-parent families and the escalating divorce rate, fathers are now much less likely to be a part of the household.

These changes have led to a drop in parental-contact time, and have made it necessary for parents to place children into various alternate child-care arrangements, many of which are inadequate at best and dangerous at worst. In addition, many school-age children are left to take care of themselves; studies find that these "latch-key children" are often troubled and disturbed (Richardson et al. 1989; Long and Long 1983).

In the preceding sections we have seen that single parents and married parents in two-earner families typically have less time for parenting than they would wish. In the following sections we will examine the issues of children's experiences concerning absentee fathers, inadequate day-care situations, and self-care.

Absent Fathers Given the higher incidences of divorce and out-of-wedlock births, twice as many children today have absent fathers as compared with children a generation ago. In 1988, nearly one out of four children lived with her or his mother alone, double the rate in 1970. As we will see in Chapter 12, many children never see their father after a divorce. More than four out of five children of divorce had not seen their fathers for more than a year (Furstenberg and Harris 1990). Most children who do see their divorced father see him only rarely (Furstenberg and Cherlin 1991; Seltzer and Bianchi 1988). In all, one child in four—fifteen million children— is growing up today with little or no contact with his or her father.[32]

Research has linked the absence of fathers to children's poor performance in school, psychological stress, and substance abuse (Hewlett 1991). Children with absent fathers get lower grades in school than other children (Krein and Beller 1988; Sweet and Bumpass 1987). Although adolescents from relatively affluent disrupted families do not usually drop out of school, relatively few go to college, so their educational attainment is usually below that of their parents' (Wallerstein and Blakeslee 1989).

Fathers play a particularly significant role in preventing substance abuse by their children. In a study at the University of California, Berkeley, for example, researchers found that adolescents who were close to their fathers were the least likely to abuse alcohol and drugs. More than a third of children from homes in which the father is absent abuse alcohol and drugs (Coombs and Landsverk 1988).

Wallerstein and Blakeslee (1989) found that for children with absent fathers, problems may lie dormant for years before surfacing in young adulthood, a phenomenon called the "sleeper" effect (see Chapter 12).

Inadequate Day Care Because most mothers of young children are employed, the majority of American families are now dependent on some

---

[32]U.S. Bureau of the Census, "Studies in Marriage and the Family" (1989).

form of alternate child care. Forty years ago just 12 percent of preschool children in America had employed mothers. Twenty years ago this figure had nearly tripled to 33 percent. Today, as we have seen, nearly three-fourths of preschool children in married-couple households have mothers who work outside the home. With black families, this figure is higher—more than 75 percent.[33]

Quality out-of-home child care is often too expensive for working-class and single parents. As a result, millions of American children suffer unsafe, low-quality care in poorly staffed, sometimes dangerous day-care centers—the only ones that many working single parents can afford (Zigler and Lang 1991). And with the need for day care increasing, the salaries of day-care teachers declined by more than 25 percent between 1977 and 1988 (Lewin 1989).

Although nearly half of the employers in our society are considering some form of child-care assistance for their employees, as yet such assistance is provided by only about 10 percent of employers (Offermann and Gowing 1990).

Rather than resorting to an inadequate day-care center that is affordable, many low-income families arrange for family day care—an arrangement in which a neighborhood woman (usually) cares for several children in her own home.[34] The cost of family day care is relatively low, averaging about fifty dollars a week.[35] However, not all family day-care facilities are licensed or regulated by public policy, and the standard of care can be very uneven. Some family day-care centers provide adequate care for children, but many do not, and it is very difficult to get reliable data because some operate informally as part of the "underground economy" (Blankenhorn and Sacks 1989).

Working parents sometimes put together a child-care "package" as a solution to their child-care problems. More than half of preschool-age children with working mothers were cared for in their own homes or in someone else's home during the fall of 1987. However, a smaller but growing proportion attended day care and group-care centers or nursery and preschool establishments (Turner 1991).

Child-care experts agree that although much out-of-home care is inadequate or worse, if the facilities, the caregivers, and the child-staff ratio[36] are all acceptable, a toddler may thrive on day care if the parent finds time to be with the child for a substantial amount of time each day. Most researchers agree, however, that infants belong with a parent for at least the first few months of life and that providing substitute care during this time is not normally advisable (Brazelton 1990; Morgan 1989).

Whatever type of day care is used, it is important that parents stay involved—that they observe the caretaker at mealtime and at playtime to see how she or he relates to the children and how nurturant, skilled, and patient she or he is (Brazelton 1990).

Latchkey Children As many as ten million schoolchildren ages six through thirteen are latchkey children who care for themselves. They return from school each day to an empty house because their parents are at work (Zigler and Lang 1991).

---

[33]"Labor Force Participation."

[34]About one out of three young children (ages three months to three years) of employed mothers are in family day care. U.S. Bureau of the Census, "Child Care Arrangements: Winter, 1986 to 1987" (1990).

[35]U.S. Survey of Income and Program Participation (1991).

---

[36]The child-staff ratio should allow for individual attention. The National Association for the Education of Young Children recommends a child-staff ratio of no more than 5:1 for toddlers (Morgan 1989). Brazelton (1990) recommends a ratio of 3:1 for babies and 4:1 for toddlers.

Sociologists and psychologists are concerned about the plight of latchkey children, who come home from school and let themselves into an empty house.

The latchkey children who spend the most time on their own each week are white children who live in affluent homes. Apparently, children from upper-income families frequently have parents who give careers a higher priority than family. Professional careers often mean that parents do not return home until long after the children's arrival from school. The children may be left on their own until seven or eight o'clock at night (Richardson et al. 1989), and many employers refuse to allow employees to either receive calls

from home or place calls to home except in case of emergency (Schellenbarger 1991).

Studies have found that many latchkey children are chronically frightened and lonely. About one in four suffers from insomnia and nightmares, has frequent feelings of depression and rejection, and is bitter, resentful, and angry (Long and Long 1983).[37] A 1987 survey of more than 1,000 teachers found that the isolation and lack of supervision caused severe problems for latchkey children, contributing in large measure to difficulties at school.[38] A 1989 study (of 5,000 eighth-grade students in the San Diego and Los Angeles areas) found that latchkey children, regardless of race, gender, or family income, were twice as likely to drink alcohol and take drugs as other children (Richardson et al. 1989).

Measures of Children's Declining Well-Being

There is much evidence that children's well-being has dropped substantially since the 1960s. Researchers agree that today's children are much more likely to be poor, homeless, and hungry; to have serious health problems; to underperform at school; to have a severe eating disorder or to take drugs; to bear a child out of wedlock; to be the victim of a violent crime; to need psychiatric help; or to commit suicide.[39]

For the first time in our history, America's children are less cared for, less prepared for life,

---

[37]A shortcoming of these studies is that they lack a control group. What percentage of other children suffer from sleeplessness and nightmares and are bitter, angry, and resentful? In the absence of this information, it is difficult to evaluate the findings regarding latchkey children.

[38]Children's Defense Fund, *A Vision of America's Future, An Agenda for the 1990s: A Children's Defense Budget* (1989).

[39]"Crisis in Adolescent Health." Report by the Office of Technological Assessment (1991); U.S. National Assessment of Educational Progress (October 1991); Waehler (1991).

and less healthy than their parents were at the same age.[40] Moreover, these problems are not confined to inner cities or to any one class but reach deep into the mainstream of American life.[41]

In the following sections we will examine the plight of America's children with respect to health care, education, psychological problems, poverty, and homelessness.

Health Care Increasing numbers of American children are not receiving even minimal health care. Fully half of all young American children are not being protected against polio,[42] and the number of reported cases of measles increased more than tenfold between 1983 and 1989, from 1,500 cases to more than 18,000 cases.[43]

America's world ranking in infant mortality rates has dropped from sixth lowest in the 1950s to twenty-fourth lowest in 1989. Black babies die at twice the rate of white babies in America. A black baby born in Washington, D.C., is now more likely to die in the first year of life than a black baby born in Jamaica or Trinidad.[44]

There is a direct relation between inadequate prenatal care and critically ill or deformed babies. More than 40,000 American babies die each year before they reach their first birthday, and half of these deaths occurred because their mothers received inadequate prenatal care.[45] Women who receive inadequate prenatal care are twice as likely to give birth to premature, low-birth-weight babies, and their mortality rate is *forty times* that of normal-weight babies in the first month of life.[46]

Babies who weigh under five pounds at birth frequently need a great deal of expensive medical attention. They are also much more likely than full-term babies to suffer lifelong disabilities, such as anemia, heart murmurs, cerebral palsy, seizure disorders, blindness, mental retardation, and susceptibility to infection (Martin and Reeder 1991).

The average cost of caring for one premature infant from birth until kindergarten is an estimated $100,000.[47] The average lifetime cost of care and treatment for just one of these babies is nearly $400,000, and their care costs Americans an estimated $2.4 billion annually. From a purely economic point of view, then, prenatal care is an excellent investment: Every dollar spent on prenatal care saves more than three dollars in medical costs during the first year of life alone.[48]

Prenatal care, on the other hand, is astonishingly inexpensive, costing approximately $400 (this is not a misprint) for the nine months of pregnancy.[49]

Finally, there has been an alarming rise in the use of crack (a form of cocaine) by pregnant

---

[40]U.S. National Commission on the Role of the School and the Community in Improving Adolescent Health (1990).

[41]U.S. National Commission on the Role of the School and the Community in Improving Adult Health. *Code Blue:* Uniting for Healthier Youths (1990).

[42]Select Committee on Children, Young and Families, "U.S. Children and Their Families" (1990).

[43]U.S. Centers for Disease Control, "Specified Reportable Diseases — Cases Reported: 1970 to 1989" (1991).

[44]U.S. National Center for Health Statistics, "Infant, Maternal, and Neonatal Mortality Rates, and Fetal Mortality Ratios, by Race: 1950 to 1989" (1992).

[45]"Fact Sheet," Select Committee on Children, Youth and Families (October 1989).

[46]U.S. National Commission to Prevent Infant Mortality, "Death Before Life: The Tragedy of Infant Mortality" (1988).

[47]U.S. National Commission to Prevent Infant Mortality, "Care for Children, Care for Our Future" (1988).

[48]U.S. National Commission to Prevent Infant Mortality, "Infant Mortality Fact Sheet" (1990); Select Committee on Children, Youth and Families, "Caring for New Mothers: Pressing Problems and New Solutions" (1989).

[49]U.S. National Commission to Prevent Infant Mortality, "Infant Mortality."

women, whose babies are born with severe physical disabilities. Experts estimate that from 75,000 to 375,000 babies who have been exposed to illicit drugs are born each year—from 2 to 11 percent of all births. These estimates would be much higher if alcohol (fetal alcohol syndrome) and nicotine were included (Cook, Petersen, and Moore 1990). (See Appendix C.)

The most common problems of drug-exposed babies are prematurity, low birth weight, neurological impairment, irritability, inability to sleep, muscle rigidity, high-pitched crying, convulsions, and permanent behavioral and learning disabilities, including short attention span and inability to concentrate. A disabling stroke often occurs prior to birth. Other babies suffer severe deformities of the heart, lungs, or digestive tract (Ehrlich and Finnegan 1988). Many crack babies—approximately 20,000 per year—also test positive for HIV (see Appendix A).

The Senate Finance Committee calculated that in 1988 the nation spent $2.5 billion on intensive care for drug-exposed babies and estimated that it will soon cost the United States at least fifteen billion dollars a year to prepare crack-exposed babies for kindergarten.[50]

Education Scholastic Aptitude Test (SAT) scores have declined in the United States since the mid-1960s in all types of schools, among all socioeconomic groups, and in all parts of the country (Fuchs 1988). Average SAT scores are now seventy points below where they were twenty-five years ago; for the first time in our history the educational attainment of one generation will be below that of their parents.[51]

___

[50]"Cost of Caring for 'Drug Babies,'" Senate Finance Committee (1989).

[51]U.S. National Center for Education Statistics, *Digest of Education Statistics* (December 1989).

In the early 1960s, the upper 5 percent of our mathematics students were unsurpassed by students anywhere in the world. By the late 1980s, American students consistently finished last, or nearly last, in international math and science proficiency tests (McKnight et al. 1987). In 1992, 90 percent of American students had test scores below international averages in math and science (Lapointe 1992).

Over the last thirty years the United States has dropped from eighteenth to forty-ninth place among nations in terms of the proportion of the population that is literate. Twenty percent—thirty-six million people—are functionally illiterate, which means that they cannot read or write at the eighth-grade level (Kirsch and Jungeblut 1985). Demographers estimate that as much as 40 percent of our minority student population is functionally illiterate (Hewlett 1991).

Students do much less homework today than they did in 1980. In the early 1980s, high school students averaged ten hours of homework a week; by the late 1980s this figure had been cut in half to five hours a week. At least one high school student in five does no homework at all (Zoglin 1990; Anderson, Mead, and Sullivan 1986).

According to a Nielsen survey, today's children watch twice as much television as their parents did. The average child now spends more time watching television than attending class. One school-age child in three is still watching TV at eleven o'clock at night (Nielsen Media Research 1991).

The level of general knowledge possessed by today's young people is indicated by the following, discussed in Hewlett (1991, pp. 65–67):

- Two out of five fourth graders today believe the world is flat (U.S. National Assessment of Educational Progress 1987).

- One out of five sixth graders cannot locate the United States on a world map (U.S. National Assessment of Educational Progress 1987).

- Four out of ten high school students in Boston, Massachusetts, cannot name the six New England states (Kilpatrick 1987).

- One out of four high school seniors in Dallas, Texas, cannot name the country that borders the United States on the south (Kilpatrick 1987).

- Almost half of all seventeen-year-olds cannot determine whether 87 percent of 10 is greater than, less than, or equal to 10 (U.S. National Assessment of Educational Progress 1987 and 1990).

Psychological Problems Researchers agree that today's children are having more trouble coping with stresses in their lives than did children a generation ago (Cherlin 1990; Furstenberg and Cherlin 1991; Emery 1988). Children who live in a single-parent family have three times as many emotional and behavioral problems as children living with both parents (Dawson 1991). Although the number of teenagers has decreased since the early 1970s, fifteen times as many were admitted to private psychiatric hospitals in the late 1980s (Kass 1989). A 1989 survey of psychologically disturbed teenagers who had been discharged from psychiatric hospitals found that nearly nine out of ten of these patients had been living in disrupted families at the time of their admission (Mersky and Swart 1989).

Suicide among adolescents has increased dramatically over the past twenty-five years (in contrast with suicide among adults, which has remained stable). The suicide rate for teenagers ages fifteen to nineteen tripled between 1960 and 1986. Researchers point out that a failed suicide attempt also reveals a depth of despair. In 1986, 10 percent of teenage boys and 18 percent of teenage girls made a failed attempt at sui-

cide. An even greater number of teenagers self-destruct slowly through substance abuse or violence (Fuchs 1988).

A very imprecise but suggestive measure of rising psychological stress among children is the increased incidence of obesity. National health surveys find that obesity is now a major disorder among American children, raising the risk of respiratory disease, diabetes, orthopedic problems, hypertension, and psychosocial disorders (Gortmaker et al. 1987). More than one out of four children ages six to eleven is obese,[52] an increase of 9 percent over the last twenty-five years. Severe obesity in this age group has doubled (from 6 to 12 percent). Among adolescents, severe obesity has increased by one-third (Fuchs 1988). A 1992 federal survey of almost 7,000 children found that poor children are nearly three times as likely to be overweight as children of middle-class or affluent families (Waldholtz 1992a).

Poverty People who started working during the 1950s or 1960s found their real earnings climbing at least 50 percent every decade; people who started working after 1973 saw their earnings drop every year (Hewlett 1991; Otten 1990; Gibbs 1989). A dramatic drop in wages and a rise in unemployment during the latter part of the 1980s have pushed many working families into poverty. The average wage (adjusted for inflation) plunged nearly 20 percent from 1973 to the late 1980s — from $24,021 in 1973 to $19,859 in the late 1980s (Hewlett 1991). The proportion of families that could buy a home on a single income was more than cut in half from 1976 to 1989, plummeting from 47 percent to 21 percent (Downey 1990).

---

[52]Obesity is defined as a body weight that is 20 percent over that in standard height-weight tables; severe obesity is defined as a weight that is at least twice that in standard height-weight tables (Berkow et al. 1987).

According to the Bureau of Labor Statistics, nearly twelve million Americans lost their jobs in the 1980s. About a third of these either remained unemployed or stopped looking for a job (left the work force). Of those who found new jobs, about half took either a pay cut, a lower-paying job in the service industry, or a part-time job; many blue-collar workers who lost a job had to settle for a service job, with a significant drop in pay (Hewlett 1991).

The incomes of blacks and Hispanics plunged even more than those of whites. Indeed, a significant number of minority men were and are unable to find any work at all. By 1990, many had stopped looking for a job, so they weren't included in the unemployment figures.[53] Young Hispanic and black men (under age twenty-five) are even more likely to be unemployed than older men, and in a typical month fully 50 percent of those under age twenty-five are unemployed (Crispell 1991a; Hewlett 1991). More than eight million working adults were below the poverty level in 1989, one-third more than there were in 1978 (Hewlett 1991).

The number of children under the age of sixteen in families that are below the poverty level is now more than twelve million, an increase of two and a quarter million since 1979. The poverty rate for children under age six was higher than for any other age group in the population.[54]

Consider the following statistics on the poor in America:

- One in five children of all ages lives below the poverty level.[55]

- One in four children under age six lives below the poverty level; more than half (54 percent) of children under age six who live with a single parent (mother only) live below the poverty level.[56]

- Nearly one family in three lives below the poverty level if the householder is under age twenty-five.[57]

- Nearly one in two black children lives below the poverty level.[58]

- More than one in three Hispanic children live below the poverty level.[59]

- The poor do not just live in ghettos, but are distributed throughout the United States (Hewlett 1991). Fewer than one American in ten classified as "poor" lives in the inner city (Ricketts and Sawhill 1988).

Family poverty is correlated with high rates of child neglect, infant mortality, childhood illnesses, school dropouts, teenage childbearing, drug abuse, violent crime, psychological distress, and diagnosable mental disorder (Hewlett 1991; Belle 1990).

Homelessness Although homelessness has always existed in the United States (estimates range from 200,000 to 1.5 million in the worst years of the Great Depression in the 1930s), today's homeless suffer from greater poverty and

---

[53]An "unemployed" person is someone who has no job and is looking for work; someone who has "left the work force" has no job but is not looking for work.

[54]U.S. Bureau of the Census, "Children Below the Poverty Level, by Race and Hispanic Origin: 1970 to 1989" (1991); U.S. National Center for Children in Poverty, "Distribution of All Children and of Poor Children, by Family Type and Race: 1987" (1991).

[55]U.S. Bureau of the Census, "Children Below the Poverty Level."

[56]U.S. National Center for Children in Poverty (1991).

[57]U.S. Bureau of the Census, "Families Below the Poverty Level — Selected Characteristics, by Race and Hispanic Origin: 1989" (1991).

[58]U.S. National Center for Children in Poverty.

[59]U.S. National Center for Children in Poverty.

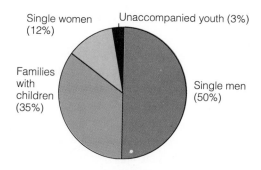

Single women (12%)

Unaccompanied youth (3%)

Families with children (35%)

Single men (50%)

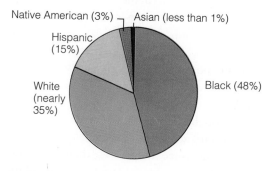

Native American (3%)

Asian (less than 1%)

Hispanic (15%)

White (nearly 35%)

Black (48%)

FIGURE 9-2

1991: Who are the homeless?

Source: U.S. Conference of Mayors, *The Continued Growth of Hunger, Homelessness, and Poverty in America's Cities.* Washington, D.C.: 1991.

include significant numbers of women and children (Rossi 1990; Monkkonen 1984). City and health officials estimate that from 600,000 to a million people were homeless in the United States in 1991 (Hutton 1991). More than one-third of our homeless (35 percent) are comprised of families, usually one parent with two or three children (see Figure 9-2). The average parent in a homeless family is twenty-seven years old, and the average child is six (Kozell 1988).

Health experts report that homeless children do not attend school regularly, develop chronic health problems because of poor sanitation and poor nutrition, and have high levels of stress and anxiety. These children usually receive no immunizations and have upper respiratory infections, skin disorders, diarrhea, and sleep disor-

ders (Rafferty and Shinn 1991). "Homelessness can be a devastating experience for a child. A home is much more than four walls and a roof. It provides warmth, security, and continuity. Homeless children quickly lose their emotional anchor—and their chance at an education" (Hewlett 1991, p. 45).

Is the Plight of Children a Women's or a Societal Issue?

Is a mother's working outside the household the chief cause of falling standards of child care? Should women be blamed for the plight of today's children?

Researchers have compiled evidence to support both sides of these issues, but the debate overlooks the central issue: For the most part, working mothers have no choice but to work if the family is to survive. Their choice is not between work and children but between work and economic collapse of the family (Hewlett 1991). The problem, then, is to provide optimal child care within the context of a mother's employment, and this is a societal problem. It must be solved at the societal level, just as it was created at the societal level (Hewlett 1991).

As we have seen, women have always worked to produce needed goods, but they once performed primarily work that could be done in or near the household and that was compatible with child care. The problem today is that most mothers of young children must seek employment outside the household—work that is usually incompatible with child care.

Resolving this dilemma is of paramount importance in the United States (Cherlin 1990; Fuchs 1988; Furstenberg 1988). It is perhaps the most significant challenge that America faces as we approach the twenty-first century (Spanier 1989). Our society needs to recognize that the worsening plight of our children places America's future at risk (Fuchs and Reklis 1992).

SUMMARY

The gender-related division of labor in our society has shifted since the time of subsistence farming. At that time both men and women chiefly did unpaid work to produce most of what they needed on the farm. Women bore many children, raised them, and worked long, hard hours performing household and farm chores. Men specialized in labor outside the household, mainly plowing, planting, and harvesting. Women were usually assisted by the older girls and men were assisted by the older boys.

About midway through the nineteenth century, families began to move off the farms and into urban and suburban areas, where the husband found work in industry. Men now did chiefly paid work in the marketplace away from the household, while women continued to work in the household and to care for children. During this transition, in the late nineteenth and early twentieth centuries, women's and children's work within the household became less economically valuable. Women produced fewer children, even though it was illegal for doctors to provide contraceptive information to women. Abortion, hitherto legal in the United States, was criminalized by an act of Congress in 1873. (It was legalized again a hundred years later, in 1973.)

During the late nineteenth and early twentieth centuries unmarried lower-class women began to move into paid employment outside the household, and this movement accelerated in the 1920s, following World War I. Laws against contraception began to be repealed in the 1920s, and having fewer children made it possible for married women to also seek employment outside the household. However, four out of five married women with young children were still specializing in housework and child care in the 1950s, while their husbands were earning the family's income.

Beginning in the 1960s, married middle-class women, including mothers of young children, increasingly entered the work force, and by the late 1980s most mothers of young children were employed outside the household. Additional changes since the 1960s included a precipitous drop in both the marriage rate and the birth rate to their lowest points in the history of our nation, a rise in the proportion of unmarried young women to an unprecedented peak, and an accelerating divorce rate. These changes have had such an enormous impact on the fabric of our society that they have been called a gender-role revolution.

Although women have made significant gains toward achieving economic and social independence since the 1950s, their economic well-being has dropped — largely because of the increased proportion of single-parent families headed by women. These women often live below the poverty level and often feel trapped in their situation with neither the time nor money to obtain the education or training that would enable them to better their lot. The proportion of single-parent families has grown rapidly since the 1950s because of two critical events: the rising incidence of never-married mothers and the rising incidence of divorced mothers.

Women in two-earner families are usually better off financially than women heading single-parent families, but they have much less leisure time and much less time to be with their children compared with women in married-couple families a generation ago. This is largely because 80 percent of women in two-earner families work a "second shift" that averages about fifteen hours each week, or about four-and-a-half months of forty-hour work weeks each year; only about 20 percent of husbands share the second shift.

Many women in single-parent families work outside the home because they wish to have a career, but most do so because of economic necessity. Similarly, many women in two-earner families work outside the home because they wish to have a career, but most married-couple families cannot survive without two incomes. Fathers now provide the sole support for only about 10 percent of American families, compared with 80 percent in the 1950s.

The rise in the numbers of single-parent families means that fewer households contain resident fathers. Thus children are receiving less parental contact with fathers as well as less parental contact from employed mothers; children have 40 percent less parental-contact hours today than they had prior to the 1960s. This has led to a situation in which alternate child-care arrangements have become the norm.

Although some alternate child-care arrangements are excellent, many are inadequate. Good child care is expensive, and single-parent families are usually less likely to be able to afford it than are two-earner families. In addition to placing children in alternate care, large numbers of children are left with no supervision at all after school—the so-called latchkey children.

For the first time in America's history, today's children are less well off than their parents. Children's well-being has dropped significantly in terms of their health care, educational attainment, prevalence of psychological problems, and the proportion living in poverty.

Child care specialists point out that the plight of today's children is a societal issue of grave import. Returning to the family of the recent past, with the father providing sole economic support while the mother devotes herself to homemaking and child care, is not a practicable solution for most families; nor is returning to the family of the distant past, with the mother caring for children while producing economic goods in or near the household. Individual families have found solutions, but without societal answers, significant numbers of women and most children will continue to be disadvantaged.

KEY TERMS

The following is a list of key terms in this chapter.
These terms are defined in context within the chapter, and many may also be found in the Glossary.

agrarian past

biological imperative

birth rate replacement level

caretaker role

criminalization of abortion

criminalization of contraception

economic determinism

economic goods and services

economic imperative

economic liability

economic well-being

economically productive

equivalent work

fertility control

functional illiteracy

gender ideology

gender-related division of labor

gender-role revolution

glass ceiling

Industrial Revolution

infanticide

latchkey children

preindustrial society

provider role

pro-choice groups

psychological stress

right-to-life groups

Scholastic Aptitude Test (SAT)

subsistence farm

substance abuse

| the "second shift" | truck garden | "sleeper" effect | "supermom" |
| trimester | wage differential | "superdad" | |

QUESTIONS

1. Describe the gender-related division of labor (men's work, women's work) on a subsistence farm of the nineteenth century.

2. Describe the gender-related division of labor in an industrial economy.

3. What major changes occurred in the gender-role revolution that began in the 1960s?

4. Discuss the reasons why women are currently at an economic disadvantage.

5. Describe the role of women in performing a "second shift" in two-earner families.

6. In what ways has children's well-being declined since the 1960s?

7. Why do today's children have significantly less parental contact time than children did prior to the 1960s?

SUGGESTIONS FOR FURTHER READING

Bergmann, Barbara. *The Economic Emergence of Women.* New York: Basic Books, 1986.

Brown, Clair, and Pechman, Joseph A. *Gender in the Workplace.* Washington, D.C.: Brookings Institution, 1987.

Davis, Kingsley. "Wives and Work: A Theory of the Sex-Role Revolution and Its Consequences." In Sanford M. Dornbusch and Myra H. Strober (eds.), *Feminism, Children, and the New Families.* New York: Guilford Press, 1988.

Garfinkel, Irwin, and McLanahan, Sara S. *Mothers and Their Children: A New American Dilemma.* Washington, D.C.: Urban Institute Press, 1986.

Golden, Stephanie. *The Women Outside: Meanings and Myths of Homelessness.* Berkeley: University of California Press, 1992.

Johnson, Miriam M. *Strong Mothers, Weak Wives: The Search for Gender Equality.* Berkeley: University of California Press, 1988.

Kelly, Rita Mae. *The Gendered Economy: Work, Careers, and Success.* Newbury Park, Calif.: Sage, 1991.

Mintz, Steven, and Kellogg, Susan. *Domestic Revolutions: A Social History of American Life.* New York: Free Press, 1988.

Newman, Katherine S. *Falling from Grace: The Experience of Downward Mobility in the American Middle Class.* New York: Free Press, 1988.

Schwartz, Felice. *Breaking with Tradition: Women, Work, and the New Facts of Life.* New York: Warner Books, 1992.

C H A P T E R 10

Parenting and the Development of Children

Children have more need of models than of critics.

Joseph Joubert, "Pensee"

The Developmental Sequence for Children

Components of Healthy Child Development

The Nature of Discipline

The Effects of a Child's Personality on the Family

What Do You Know?

Some of the following statements are true and some are false.
Can you tell which are which?

T/F   1. Whatever their race, almost all neonates (newborns) have smoky blue eyes and pinkish skin.

T/F   2. Ninety percent of all the neurons (brain cells) a person will ever have are present at birth.

T/F   3. If the fetus and infant are undernourished, the child's brain will have only about 60 percent of the normal number of neurons.

T/F   4. A crying child who is usually picked up and comforted will soon become "spoiled."

T/F   5. Children of poor families usually perform about as well in school as children of affluent families.

T/F   6. Compared with middle-class children, lower-class children are more likely to work harder in school.

T/F   7. It is a good idea to make the love we express to children conditional on good behavior.

T/F   8. Children have different personalities, temperaments, and abilities at birth.

T/F   9. Virtually all babies have about the same predisposition to cooing, gurgling, smiling, and making other expressions of contentment.

Answers: 1-T, 2-T, 3-T, 4-F, 5-F, 6-F, 7-F, 8-T, 9-F

After the birth of a child, a new and irrevocable life phase begins for the married couple, for with parenthood they assume responsibility for a new human being. The couple no longer relate just to each other; there is a third person to consider, a new, unique individual that initially places seemingly limitless demands on them. Because of the great importance of an infant's early years, this chapter will present a close look at child development processes and the needs of the infant and young child.

The Developmental Sequence for Children

The developmental sequence for children is the same in all societies. Children everywhere proceed from dependence to independence, from self-centeredness to an awareness of and a responsiveness to others, and from responding only to immediate satisfaction to an ability to delay gratification. This developmental process starts at birth, with the neonate.

The Neonate

A newborn baby is called a *neonate* for the first month of extrauterine life. During this first month, a complete transition must take place from fetal to postnatal modes of survival. Before birth the fetus is a waterborne, "water-breathing" creature completely secluded in a dark, warm environment that supports life. Oxygen, nutrients, antibodies, and hormones are fed directly into the bloodstream of the fetus through the umbilical cord, which also carries away waste products.

As soon as a baby is born and takes the first breath and the umbilical cord is clamped and cut, sudden cataclysmic changes occur in his or her environment and life support system. The neonate has left the warm, watery, secure environment within the mother, and now must adapt to the new situation immediately — or die.[1] Fortunately, babies are genetically programmed to do just this. Once the umbilical cord is cut — a few minutes after birth — neonates immediately begin to oxygenate their bodies by breathing air. Oxygenation of the body, which had previously been achieved via the maternal blood of the placenta, must now be achieved by the neonate, whose breathing mechanism requires that chest muscle groups be coordinated in complex, subtly balanced interactions. As the neonate becomes an air-breathing creature, the abdominal muscles surrounding the umbilical cord contract, circulation through the umbilical arteries and veins stops, and the shift from fetal to postnatal blood circulation begins. The shutting off of the umbilical arteries forces blood into the lungs, and the oxygen level of the blood (which drops when the umbilical cord is cut) reaches 90 percent of the normal level within about three hours. The acid-base balance of the blood is normal after about a week, and the blood pressure normalizes in about ten days (Behrman and Vaughan 1987).

Mechanisms for internal temperature control must also develop once the neonate is exposed to the external world. Until this happens, the neonate is at the mercy of changes in ambient temperature and may easily become overheated or chilled (Behrman and Vaughan 1987). The sweat glands do not operate for about a month, and the inability to sweat makes it difficult for neonates to adjust to heat. New parents often err on the side of keeping neonates too warm, which

---

[1] The highest risk to the newborn occurs during the first twenty-four hours (Cunningham et al. 1989).

not only makes them uncomfortable but may also interfere with the normal development of temperature-regulating mechanisms.

All neonates' first attempts at eating (which consist, of course, of sucking) are very unskilled, and they lose weight for the first few days.[2] When they are hungry, they root (pressing nose and mouth into the breast) and stop only when the nipple is placed the mouth. When they have found the nipple, they clasp and pump the breast with their hands, even though at all other times they usually keep their hands closed into fists and are unable to grasp things put into their hands.

The intestinal bacteria necessary for digestion must be taken in from the environment. These intestinal bacteria also produce vitamin K, which is important for blood clotting; thus until these bacteria are present, a cut or scratch presents a threat of serious hemorrhage for the neonate (Bucuvalas and Ballistreri 1987).

Neonates are also very susceptible to infections because they no longer are protected by the mother's immune system. The neonate's skin, gastrointestinal tract, and respiratory system are especially susceptible. However, overprotecting neonates from exposure to potentially infectious agents may have the paradoxical result of retarding the necessary formation of their own immune systems, thus making them even more vulnerable to infection (Bellanti et al. 1987).

Neonates spend about twenty hours a day sleeping. During the first few weeks, in fact, waking and sleeping are really only a matter of degree because neonates are rarely fully awake except when hungry, startled, or otherwise distressed. Asleep or awake, they are subject to fits and starts and tremors reflecting the spread of stimulation throughout their still immature nervous systems. When "awake," they are likely to stare fixedly and blankly at a face or spot of light that happens to fall within their field of vision.

Sleeping neonates produce the same brain wave patterns and rapid eye movement (REM) that accompany dreaming in adults. In fact, neonates have a higher proportion of REM sleep than adults do (Brazelton 1987). The purpose of REM sleep has not yet been discovered.

Not only can neonates see at birth, but they can track a moving object (Brazelton 1987). Neonates keep their eyes closed most of the time, however, and eye movements are usually random and uncoordinated until about the third week, when they can focus on things more accurately. Tear glands don't begin producing tears until the baby is about three months old; thus tears are absent when a neonate cries (Martin and Reeder 1991).

Brazelton (1987) points out that crying is a rich language for a baby. "Cries can mean hunger, pain, wet, mad, 'pick me up,' or 'just leave me alone.'... Parents begin to differentiate these cries and can usually tell if they are caused by pain, boredom, or hunger by the time the baby is three to four weeks old" (p. 132).

Individual differences are important from the very moment of birth. Neonates not only differ in their anatomical and physiological features (such as blood chemistry, hormonal balance, and size and shape of body organs) but also in their muscle tone, the vigor with which they root and suck,[3] and the forcefulness or sluggishness

---

[2]At birth, nearly 80 percent of the neonate's total body weight is water, more than one-third of which is extracellular fluid. It is the loss of this fluid during the first week of extrauterine life that accounts for the 10–15 percent weight loss (Behrman and Vaughan 1987).

[3]Sucking and swallowing reflexes are typically quite strong at birth. The rooting reflex (searching for the nipple) is also quite strong at birth and enables the neonate to find food by turning toward anything that touches the cheek or lips (Martin and Reeder 1991).

with which they act and move. Some neonates cry lustily and are lively, active, and squirmy, whereas others cry weakly and may be limp, passive, and unresponsive.

Neonates also differ greatly in such psychological factors as alertness, irritability, and sensitivity and responsiveness to the environment (such as light or noise). Whether these differences are genetic, are acquired during the first nine months of life in the uterus, or are a combination of these two factors is not known. It seems most likely that the neonate's personality and physical characteristics emerge from a combination of genetic and environmental factors — an interaction between "nature" and "nurture." Whatever the source, it is clear that the initial differences among neonates are quite pronounced and are obvious from birth (Green, Bax, and Tsitsikas 1989).

Because childbirth usually occurs in seclusion in our society, many people have never seen a neonate until they see their own, and they are frequently startled by its appearance. Neonates are surprisingly small — the average weight is about seven and a half pounds — and because they keep their legs drawn up, they look even smaller. Their heads make up a quarter of their length and seem to rest almost directly on their shoulders. Neither eye nor skin pigmentation is developed at birth, so virtually all neonates (even blacks) have smoky blue eyes and pinkish skin. Neonates seem almost chinless, and their noses are nearly flat. Their heads may be slightly misshapen as a result of the passage through the cervix and vagina. This *molding* of the head is caused by the overriding of the bones of the skull; it usually disappears within a week or two (Martin and Reeder 1991).

The genitals of the neonate are quite prominent, and both boys and girls have prominent breasts, which may temporarily secrete a milky substance ("witch's milk"). Girls may have a transient discharge that resembles a menstrual flow just after they are born. Both the breast secretions and the vaginal bleeding are caused by hormones absorbed from the mother's bloodstream and subside rapidly a few hours after birth (Martin and Reeder 1991).

The neonate's skull has six soft spots (*fontanels*) where certain structural bones have not yet grown together; the most conspicuous of these (at the very top of the head) may not close completely until the child is twelve to eighteen months of age (Martin and Reeder 1991).

The Infant

Infancy begins at the second month after birth and ends when the baby is walking and beginning to talk — at about twelve to fifteen months. During infancy, babies begin to look like people. They gain weight and develop a natural layer of fat, which fills out their scrawniness. Their hands and feet are chubby, and their abdomens are round. Their skin takes on a more typical color, and their heads and noses fill out to a normal shape. They now have large foreheads, small noses, small chins, plump cheeks, and large eyes. The irises of their eyes gradually change to their adult color, a process that may take as long as six months (Martin and Reeder 1991).

During the second month, infants are more awake than they were as neonates and show a more sustained response to an increasing variety of sights and sounds, including vacuum cleaners, television programs, and ringing telephones. They can usually raise their heads slightly to look at something. Although they still cannot really change position, they can usually arch their backs. Also during the second month, their crying stops at the sight of their mothers, and most infants respond to a human face by smiling. At this age, they still awaken for two or more night feedings.

Early in the third month, infants may reach out and bat at a dangling object, but they are not yet able to open their fingers to grasp it. Their eyes are now able to focus on near and far objects and can converge on an object as it approaches the nose. Infants are quite social at three months, gurgling and cooing in response to adult overtures and even to music. They recognize members of the family — smiling, wriggling, and gurgling at them — but may meet strangers with a solemn, reserved stare. They now usually sleep through the night (Brazelton 1987).

Infants first laugh when they are about four months old. They can now be propped in a sitting position for short periods of time and can half recline indefinitely in a baby carrier. They begin to eat semisolid, strained foods, although it will be months before they eat without spluttering, choking, coughing, and spitting. They are able to grasp things that interest them (until now they could just bat at them). However, they still cannot release anything; if they want to drop something they have grasped, they must rub it against their bodies until it is loosened from their grip.

By age five months infants can study their fingers, pick up something to examine or taste, show preference when given different colored patches, and remain in a sitting position for some time before their heads begin to loll and their bodies begin to slump (Behrman and Vaughan 1987).

By the time they are six months of age, they are able not only to grasp but also to manipulate and release something they are gripping. Between the ages of six and nine months, infants are usually able to roll completely over. They are now on our society's three-meal-a-day eating schedule, although they have occasional snacks throughout the day. They may sleep through the night. During this stage they begin to hold out their arms to be picked up, and they become highly responsive to the moods of those around them. Their vocalization becomes more differentiated, with consonants emerging to break up the vowel sounds and babbling replacing the gurgling and cooing (Behrman and Vaughan 1987).

Infants can usually sit up without support when they are six months old. They are now amused by noises, toys, and the movement of objects and are fascinated with repetition, discovery, experimentation, and imitation. Social games (and learning) evolve from the infant's imitating what parents do — and from the parents, in turn, imitating the infants (Brazelton 1987).

Usually by about seven months infants begin *creeping* for short distances, and by eight months they can *crawl*. (Creeping is achieving a forward locomotion when prone by pulling oneself forward with the arms and legs; when crawling, one is up on one's hands and knees.) They also begin to feed themselves with a spoon about this age, developing the muscle control necessary for contacting an object (their mouths) that they can feel but cannot see. The first two teeth appear by about the seventh month, though some babies are born with teeth (Behrman and Vaughan 1987).

By about eleven months infants can creep or crawl up and down stairs. They have also learned by this time that it is possible to detour around obstacles to get something they want. (In contrast, a chicken separated from food by a short length of wire fence may starve to death without ever discovering that it is possible to walk around the fence to get the food.)

Infants are quite active by the time they are eleven months old and no longer lie quietly while being dressed. They can now cooperate, holding their hands out for sleeves or raising their heads and shoulders to allow the shirt to pass behind their backs. They can now play pata-cake, work simple cupboard latches, turn electric lights off and on, regulate the volume on a television set, distinguish pictures of objects in books, and recognize themselves in a mirror (Brazelton 1987).

By the time they are twelve to fifteen months old, infants are actively relating to others, making eye contact, smiling, and laughing. Not only can they pull themselves up and stand alone, but they are well on the way to becoming highly active, self-directed, willful pedestrians. They can now not only imitate sounds and words but can understand much of the language of their culture, both verbal and nonverbal. They can engage in verbal as well as nonverbal social interaction, especially with their care givers (Brazelton 1987).

During the transition from the neonatal period to early childhood, one of the most important elements of socialization is established: the all-important sense of *basic trust*. Without this sense of trust, the sense of *autonomy*, which is fundamental to much future development, cannot be established (more on this later).

The Young Child

By the age of two years, babies are walking, running, climbing stairs, taking off their shoes and socks, and eating with a spoon. They now have a working vocabulary of about twenty-five words (Behrman and Vaughan 1987).

By three years of age they can play for short periods without supervision, color with crayons, dress dolls, and build with blocks. They can now get a glass of water from the kitchen faucet. They can eat safely with a fork. They are now relatively toilet trained, with only occasional daytime "accidents" (Chess and Thomas 1987).

Most four-year-olds can wash their hands and button their clothes. They show some sense of rhythm in running, skipping, and marching and are able to participate in simple group activities, such as kindergarten games. They can perform short errands and pick up after themselves if they are asked to (Brazelton 1987).

At five years of age, most children can dress themselves completely (except for tying and lacing), wash both face and hands, play in the immediate neighborhood unattended, and maintain unsupervised group games with their age-mates and with older children. They also can draw recognizable objects such as a house, a person, or a tree. By age five they are usually completely toilet trained (Chess and Thomas 1987).

From ages six to twelve, children are extremely busy acquiring information and mastery skills (the ability to manipulate objects). In the organized structure of the classroom they learn to read, write, and solve arithmetic problems. They absorb a very wide range of knowledge of many kinds—geographical, historical, grammatical, and scientific. They also develop physical skills, such as roller skating, bicycle riding, throwing and catching a ball, and jumping rope. And they acquire the skills of social behavior—group participation and interpersonal relating—that are important to functioning in society (Chess and Thomas 1987).

With more and more experience, children of this age achieve an increasingly realistic—that is, accurate—frame of reference in regard to their own natures and the nature of their environment. They develop physical, intellectual, and social competence in dealing with their culture. Finally, they learn, through handling specific problems, what kinds of problems they are likely to confront in the future and how they should prepare for and solve them (Coleman 1979).

As individuals develop from children into adults, their perception and discriminative abilities become successively more differentiated and precise. They first learn to differentiate between mother and father, to select one toy and not another, or to recognize a song or the difference between the sound of a clarinet and a trumpet. When they reach adulthood, they will have refined these early differentiations to an astonishing degree. They may be able to distinguish between the voices of two sopranos singing the same aria or tell a genuine van Gogh from an artful copy.

Similarly, behavioral skills and abilities are also progressively improved and refined — from putting one block on another to being able to build a tower of blocks, from rolling a ball back and forth to playing catch, from riding a tricycle to riding a bicycle, from driving a car to flying a jet airplane, from solving simple mechanical problems to building a radio, from taking a first-aid class to performing a delicate surgical operation, and from being on the debate team in high school to arguing a case before the Supreme Court.

This differential development takes place as part of the socialization process, for which the family is chiefly responsible in the early stages. The process of early socialization within the family lays the foundation for the continuing development of perceptual and manipulatory skills throughout childhood, adolescence, and adulthood — as well as for the continuing acquisition of information, knowledge, and wisdom. If this foundation is strong and well established, it is likely the child's full potential, as genetically programmed, will be developed.

Components of Healthy Child Development

Many components of healthy development are genetically programmed. Given this genetic programming, the development of the individual's potential is largely dependent on the parents. A primary physical component for the fulfill-ment of the child's potential is adequate nutrition, which provides the basic building blocks for all development. A primary psychological element is early bonding with the mother (or other primary care giver). It is also important that early parent-child relationships provide a sense of emotional security while avoiding "spoiling." Parent-child relationships should also promote the emergence of the child's self-esteem, promote intellectual development, and encourage the acquisition of mastery skills while acknowledging the concept of developmental readiness. Parent-child relationships should also maximize the probability that the child experiences more successes than failures, provide necessary tools and information as required, and foster the acquisition of accepted family and societal values. We will examine each of these in turn.

Nutrition and the Developing Brain

Because all experience is sensed by the brain and all behavior originates in the brain, it is basic to all development (see Box 10-1). The components contributing to the physical structure of the brain must be in place before intellectual abilities can develop, and the components necessary to the developing fetal brain are contained in the food that the woman eats during pregnancy.

For the brain there is only one chance for growth. All the other important organs of the body will continue to grow and will not achieve their full size until the person reaches the late teens or early twenties, but the brain is virtually complete in size and in the number of component parts at birth. Ninety percent of all the neurons a person will ever have are in place when the neonate emerges from the uterus (Jastrow 1981).

The second stage of brain development, during which the brain cells grow in size, occurs during infancy. By about twelve months after birth, cell division in the brain stops, and vir-

BOX 10 - 1

The Human Brain

The human brain is a moist, pulsing, jellylike organ that weighs about three pounds in the adult. These three pounds of brain tissue are built from more than ten billion neurons (nerve cells), each of which may interact with as many as 10,000 others. To get some idea of just how large a number ten billion is, imagine all these ten billion neurons dissected out of the brain and laid end to end. If this could be done they would reach from the earth to the moon — and back again! Because each of these ten billion neurons is connected to as many as 10,000 others, the circuitry of the brain is almost infinitely complex. There are perhaps 1,000 trillion circuit connections (or synapses) in the average human brain (Hooper and Teresi 1986). This number is larger than the number of stars in our galaxy or the number of grains of sand on all the beaches of the earth (Sagan 1980).

The complexity of the interactions between neurons gives rise to our awareness, our sense of self, and even our ability to examine the nature of our own brain (Jastrow 1981). And it is this interaction that yields all the aspects of awareness or consciousness — sight, hearing, hunger, thirst, sensuality, memory, creativity, thought, emotion — and the other components of being alive and aware. Moreover, the brain performs this miracle with dazzling speed. It is the most complex system in the entire known universe (Hooper and Teresi 1986).

tually all the brain cells a person will ever have are present. The third, and final, stage of brain development consists of forming communications connections (synapses) between neurons. This communicating network is largely complete by the time a child is about two years old, although connections continue to form throughout a person's lifetime as new information, skills, and memories are acquired. Because the brain develops its full physical potential by age two, the importance of adequate nutrition during this period cannot be overemphasized (Jastrow 1981).

If the fetus is undernourished (is not provided with the necessary nutritional elements), the neonate will have about 20 percent fewer brain cells than normal at birth. If the infant is undernourished during the first six months, cell division is slowed down by another 20 percent. If both the fetus and the infant are undernourished, the brain will have only about 60 percent of the number of neurons of a normal brain (Jastrow 1981).

In a classic example of the effect of nutrition on brain development, Chilean infants under six months of age who had been malnourished since birth were brought to a hospital, where they were put on a carefully balanced, nutritious diet. Two years later, these babies were evaluated and found to be severely mentally retarded.

Sixty-one percent were educable but needed special teaching; 36 percent were not educable and were trainable on simple tasks only; 3 percent could not even be trained and required custodial care (Wyden 1971).

To ensure that a child's intellectual potential is reached, it is necessary that the mother provide the embryo and fetus with nutritional elements from a variety of foods from the five basic food groups: (1) bread, cereal, rice, and pasta; (2) vegetables; (3) fruits; (4) milk, yogurt, and cheese; (5) meat, poultry, fish, dry beans, eggs, and nuts.[4] Vegetarians, who exclude fish, meat, and poultry from their diets, should be sure to include enough high-quality protein from other foods. The mother can continue to provide the neonate with the necessary building blocks for optimal development if she breast-feeds and continues to eat food from these five food groups. The infant will need to be provided these basic elements until full brain potential is reached at about age two. Adequate nutrition is also essential for continuing physical development — of bones, muscles, and other organs — into adulthood (Behrman and Vaughan 1987).

For a discussion of the effects on the brain of nonnutritious (and potentially harmful) substances pregnant women may ingest (aspirin, tobacco smoke, alcohol, illegal or prescription drugs) and the effects of diseases she may have during her pregnancy (measles, AIDS), see Appendixes A and C.

Early Bonding with a Care Giver

A second key component for optimal development is *bonding* — a close, intimate, mutual regard and attachment that begins between a care giver and a neonate immediately after birth. The first few hours after birth are apparently a critical period for bonding. In one study, mothers in one group were given their naked babies to hold for one hour immediately after birth and for five more hours during each of the next three days. Meanwhile, a control group of mothers was limited to holding their neonates for about a half hour a day every four hours (during feeding). A month later, the mothers given early contact with their babies fondled their babies more, spent more time soothing them when they cried during the pediatric examination, and maintained more eye contact during feeding than mothers in the control group. The mothers who had more and earlier contact were also more reluctant to leave their babies with someone else. A year later, their babies had been breast-fed longer, had gained more weight, smiled and laughed more, and cried less than babies from the control group. At five years of age, the children with early contact with mothers had significantly higher IQs and had advanced more in language tests than the control group children (Klaus and Kennell 1976).

In another study designed to determine the limits of the critical bonding period, one group of mothers had forty-five minutes of skin-to-skin contact with their babies immediately following delivery, whereas a second group had the same kind and amount of contact twelve hours after delivery. The study showed that when the babies were thirty-six hours old, the early contact mothers were significantly more attached to them than were the mothers who had contact twelve hours later. The early contact mothers held their babies face to face more often and fondled, kissed, caressed, talked to, and smiled at them more (Henig 1978). These and other studies indicate that the critical bonding period apparently occurs immediately after birth (Newton and Modahl 1978; Klaus and Kennell 1976).

Another study in the 1970s compared one group of mothers, who spent eight hours a day with their babies in a hospital room for the four

[4]U.S. Department of Agriculture, *Food Guide Pyramid*, (1992).

days after delivery, with another group of mothers who were with their babies only to feed them (which was standard hospital procedure at that time). When the babies of these two groups of mothers were compared two years later, significantly fewer instances of neglect, abuse, abandonment, or inadequate care were found among the early contact mothers (Spezzano and Waterman 1977).

These studies on bonding have had a significant effect on hospital policy. Before their publication, hospital policy had been to limit a mother's contact with her infant in order to minimize the danger of a baby's picking up an infection and to facilitate hospital routine. (It takes more staff, for example, to bring babies to their mothers frequently.) Fathers were banned from the delivery room and from early contact with a baby for the same reasons. Following the publication of these studies, hospitals changed their policy to allow mothers to handle their babies as soon and as much as possible and to allow fathers in the delivery room. (See the discussion on alternative birth centers in Appendix C.)

In the 1980s, however, the essential aspect of early bonding began to be questioned. Klaus and Kennell (1982), for example, out of concern that mothers who for whatever reasons missed this early bonding would feel discouraged and guilty, stated that "it seems unlikely that such a life-sustaining relationship would be dependent on a single process" (p. 70). Other studies as well — for example, Goldberg (1983), Chess and Thomas (1982), and Svejda, Pannabecker, and Emde (1982) — failed to confirm the critical nature of immediate bonding.

It must be emphasized that all researchers acknowledge both that bonding is important and that early, immediate bonding is desirable and optimal. Some point out, however, that under some circumstances (such as a caesarean section) the mother may not be able to hold the baby immediately. This does not mean that bonding will not take place; as Brazelton (1987) points out, bonding is a continuous process:

> Getting attached and getting to know one's baby — and yourself as a nurturer — is a long-term job. . . . Four months is a minimum amount of time for parents to attach to a new baby — emotionally and physically — and to relate to each other as a family. It takes months, not minutes, to be securely bonded to your baby and confident of oneself as a caring parent. (p. 228)

It is worth noting that the distance at which newborns see best is nine to twelve inches — which is also the distance between the mother's and neonate's eyes when the mother is breastfeeding or holding the baby in her arms. In addition to the importance of eye contact and being held in the mother's arms, interaction between a neonate and a mother occurs through sound. Neonates appear to move in rhythm with the mother's voice and pay more attention to high-pitched female voices than to male voices (Klaus and Kennell 1982; Macfarlane 1977).

Early Parent-Child Relationships: Attachment

One of the universals of child development found in all societies is the attachment of the infant to the mother (or care giver) during the second six months of a child's life. Beginning when they are about five or six months of age, all normal infants show distress and cry when they are separated from their mothers. This behavior becomes more and more pronounced during the next eighteen months and rises to a peak when the baby is about two years old. Beginning at about that age, children become increasingly comfortable relating to the mother (or primary care giver) at a distance, and physical contact is not always necessary as long as she is within sight (Hartup 1989).

If in this mother-child relationship the mother provides guidance, suggests activities just slightly advanced from the current stage, breaks the activities into substeps that the child can just manage to attain, and withdraws her help gradually as the child becomes more and more capable and independent, the child will develop a greater interest in exploring the world apart from the mother (Hartup 1989).

Among the most important aspects of early parent-child relationships are issues relating to emotional security and "spoiling," which are the two topics we will discuss next.

Providing Emotional Security All neonates, infants, and young children need to feel emotionally secure if optimal development of their genetic potential is to occur. Babies and children feel emotionally secure in an atmosphere characterized by parental affection, acceptance, understanding, and respect. The critical period for providing this need for emotional security seems to be from birth to about five years of age. If this need is met during the first five years, the probability is maximized that the child will regard the world as relatively good, stable, pleasant, and ultimately manageable. On the other hand, if a child's need for emotional security is not met during this critical five-year period, the child is likely to perceive the world as relatively unpleasant, unstable, dangerous, and threatening and will feel inadequate to cope with the demands of a hostile environment (Egeland 1989; Coleman 1979).

A child whose need for emotional security is met becomes increasingly easy to love, whereas a child whose need is not met becomes increasingly difficult to love, irritable, demanding, and petulant. Thus either an ascending or descending spiral is created: The child who is provided with ample demonstrations of love responds by becoming more lovable and receives even more love, and so on — an ascending spiral. Con-versely, the child who is insufficiently loved becomes less lovable and receives even less love — a descending spiral.

A child whose need for emotional security is fulfilled develops a sense of basic trust. Achieving this sense of basic trust is a very important developmental step for children because without it, children cannot establish the all-important autonomy (self-reliance) necessary if they are to develop their full potential as individuals (Erikson 1963).

Evidence for the importance of emotional security and the establishment of basic trust comes from several sources. One source is research comparing children reared in institutions with those reared within their families. All of these studies conclude that long separation from the mother (or other primary care giver) and from a secure home environment leads to intellectual, psychological, and social retardation. The consequences of being deprived of adequate emotional security are inconsolable distress, blunted responsiveness, incommunicability, impaired learning ability, ritualistic (and even bizarre) mannerisms, generalized apathy, and susceptibility to infection (see Coleman 1984; Bowlby 1973; and Wyden 1971).

The more isolated and deprived the child, the greater the deterioration. Moreover, adults who have experienced such deprivation in childhood are less able to care for their own children properly (Chess and Thomas 1987; Stroufe and Waters 1977).

Undeniably, parents are individuals and have different ways of expressing their affection; some parents are lavish with physical demonstrations of their feelings, whereas others are not but still manage to convey them. Some parents are soft and tender; some are bluff and hearty. Moreover, nobody can love a baby equally at all times and under all circumstances; both the parents' moods and the baby's moods vary over time. Babies are sometimes cranky and exasperating and other times winning and cheerful; parents are sometimes patient and caring and other times tired and impatient.

What is most important in terms of the child's developing sense of basic trust is the *reliability* of the parents' love throughout the inevitable mood swings, strains, problems, difficulties, and conflicts inherent in family life.

"Spoiling" a Child Children sometimes demonstrate behavior that some adults label "spoiled": frequent sulking, pouting, or temper tantrums. The crucial question is: What causes this behavior?

Most parents know that a crying child won't be spoiled by being picked up and comforted. On the contrary, babies who are comforted immediately feel more secure and ultimately cry less. However, parents sometimes feel that too much affection or attention will spoil a child and, with the best of intentions, may therefore deprive children of precisely the affection or attention they need.

Studies show that "spoiled" behavior is most likely to develop if the child experiences a lack of wholehearted interest and demonstrations of affection and love. This absence of genuine regard may cause the child to have comparatively low self-esteem and to feel relatively inadequate in dealing with the world. The child is then likely to manifest the behavior patterns termed "spoiled" (Brazelton 1987; Coleman 1979).

Of course, spoiled behavior may develop in children who are overprotected, who are smothered with inappropriate attention so that they do not get the independence they need in their stage of developmental readiness,[5] and who are improperly sheltered from experience (or from

reality testing). In other words, in order to avoid spoiling a child, it is important that parents be interested, affectionate, and supportive but not overprotective.

Finding this middle ground is not that difficult, for children usually do not ask for more emotional support and affection than they need at the moment. When infants cry, they may be seeking comfort or attention. When babies lift their arms, they may need either holding and emotional support or physical tending to (for example, they may be hungry or in pain). When children follow their parents around asking endless questions, they are not only looking for information; they are usually also seeking reassurance that they are valued and are regarded with affection and love. Conversely, when children struggle to get free of an embrace or want to go out to play, they have had all the parental nurturing they want or need for the moment; when they want more, they return for it (Brazelton 1987).

In short, if parents are sensitive and responsive to their child's behavior — which usually reveals the need that is paramount at the time — there is a good chance that the child will get a proper balance of love and affection on the one hand and freedom and independence on the other.

Parents also sometimes feel that an indulged child who has been showered with possessions is spoiled. However, an indulged child who is well behaved is not spoiled. No matter how many material things you provide them with, children who are also given limits and obey them will not be spoiled. A spoiled child is one who is "excessively self-centered, immature and manipulative, inconsiderate of others, prone to temper outbursts and unpleasant to be around. Such bratty behavior results from parents' failure to set and enforce guidelines for acceptable behavior consistent with the child's age" (McIntosh 1989, p. 28).

---

[5] The concept of developmental readiness is explored in the section "Mastery Skills" later in this chapter.

In other words, parents should set realistic, necessary limits on children's behavior and consistently enforce those limits. If parents do not teach children that some objects and some behaviors are out of bounds, they may not learn to respect other's possessions or recognize dangerous situations. The child who is then suddenly restrained might regard these limits as unreasonable. This may become a pattern: The parents fail to set reasonable boundaries and do not always reward expected behavior, and then they suddenly (and unreasonably, in the child's perception) insist on limits. The child is then confused about what is expected and may sulk, pout, or have a temper tantrum as a result. If this pattern of interaction between parents and the child becomes persistent, the child may be spoiled (Brazelton 1987; McIntosh 1989).

Certainly a razor blade is off limits for children because they could easily hurt themselves with it. Other objects, such as a valued, fragile plate, are equally off limits even though they are not dangerous. Riding a tricycle in the street is clearly off limits, as is throwing rocks at a neighbor's house (or at the neighbor). McIntosh (1989) suggests child-proofing the child's environment by putting hazardous or valuable objects out of the child's reach while firmly and consistently forbidding unacceptable behavior (and carefully explaining the reasons why). Meanwhile, acceptable behavior should be praised and rewarded. (See the section "Discipline and Setting Limits" later in this chapter.)

Apparently, then, in addition to providing appropriate attention and affection without overprotection, the rearing of well-adjusted, happy, competent, and unspoiled children requires that parents find a balance between encouraging them to explore the environment with as few restraints as possible, on the one hand, and setting and consistently enforcing necessary limits (which all children may be expected to test persistently) on the other.

Self-Esteem

The phenomenon of self is extraordinarily important to a child and continues to be of central importance throughout life, especially when manifested as self-respect, self-confidence, and self-esteem. Self-esteem is central to the development of a fully functioning, creative, productive, socially skilled, optimistic, and contented human being — whether an infant, a child, an adolescent, or an adult (Chess and Thomas 1987).

The concept of self is often referred to and is commonly considered to be readily understood. In general, when we use the words *I, me,* or *mine,* we are referring to our self. However, like the concepts of love and family, self is very difficult to define precisely. Chess and Thomas (1987) define the self as follows:

A simple and useful definition of the self is that it is made up of the identity, character, and essential qualities of a person, which tend to be enduring in nature. In essence, the self is one's own person or being who simultaneously remains the same and yet changes over time, who is similar to yet different from other people. We change as we cope with one life experience after another, yet a central core of our psychological being appears to us to remain the same and to endure. The sixty-year-old knows he is vastly different from the young adult he was at twenty; at the same time he feels deeply that he is the same person that he was at twenty. (p. 155)

Chess and Thomas take the position that a sense of self gradually emerges in a child from birth on and is well developed by age two. By this time, children can normally distinguish "I," "me," and "mine" from "you," "he," and "her." Chess and Thomas indicate that children are well aware of the difference between the inner world,

A child's self-esteem is fostered when care givers recognize his accomplishments.

as represented by the conceptualized self (as the actor, the doer, the feeler that provides a continuity of experience), and the outer world, which consists of all the nonself aspects of physical things, animals, and people. "With the crystallization of a definitive sense of self in the first two years, the stage is set for the development of self-esteem" (Chess and Thomas 1987, p. 166).

The sense of self that develops in children can be either a positive or a negative force. On the one hand, children may have the sense that they are fundamentally sound and effective; these children have self-esteem. Such children tend to function more effectively, which in turn contributes even more to their self-esteem. Their expectation that they will succeed increases the likelihood that they will in fact succeed. Thus their positive attitude toward themselves and toward the challenges in the world around them becomes a sort of self-fulfilling prophecy (Chess and Thomas 1987).

On the other hand, children who are characterized by self-doubt see difficulties everywhere and expect to fail. This expectation increases the likelihood that they will in fact fail because (in anticipation of failure) they don't try very hard. This cycle virtually guarantees failure and confirms their poor opinion of themselves — again, a self-fulfilling prophecy. These children may attempt to disguise feelings of self-doubt by bluster or bravado, all the while being concerned that this facade is transparent and will result in derision or contempt from others, thus further reinforcing the feelings of self-doubt.

Parents and others in the immediate family (and a care giver if the child is in a day-care center) play an essential part in the development of a child's self-esteem. If a child's growing achievement in everyday challenges — such as putting one block on another, rolling a ball back and forth with another person, tying shoelaces and buttoning clothes, using crayons in a coloring book, or riding a tricycle — is recognized and acknowledged, self-esteem will be built. This recognition and acknowledgment affirms to children that they are doing what they should be doing, and doing it well, which builds their self-esteem.

Parents can be too effusive, of course, and such praise can ring false; children can detect this falseness and become confused. Or parents may feel uncomfortable correcting a child, fearing that criticism may have a negative or stultifying effect on the child's emerging self-esteem. However, this denies children the opportunity to experience an honest reaction to their efforts. If parents respond with genuine feelings, whether admiring or critical, children are able to assess their own efforts accurately. This provides "reality testing"—feedback on the effects their actions are having—both in the world of physical objects and in the social world of other people. Without an honest reaction from parents, children are denied the information needed to achieve patterns of acceptable socialized behavior, and they don't have the opportunity to modify counterproductive behavior if such unacceptable behavior is not accurately identified by parents or other care givers. ("Don't take that crayon away from Tommy; that's his crayon," or "Don't hit Susan with that truck; you'll hurt her.") Children who are denied correction or criticism when it is warranted may become petty tyrants and are at a disadvantage in developing a healthy sense of self (Chess and Thomas 1987).

On the other hand, parents may hold unrealistically high standards for their children and feel uncomfortable giving them the praise they deserve. Or a parent may be psychologically disturbed and either not praise a child at all or offer praise in such a cold, stilted way that it fails to contribute to the child's self-esteem. If these children do not receive sufficient positive reactions from other people—either within or outside the family—their developing self-esteem may be stunted (Chess and Thomas 1987).

Finally, Chess and Thomas point out that normal children develop at different paces; some develop certain skills earlier than others and gain recognition easily, whereas others are "late bloomers." Moreover, although parents exercise important control over the measures that contribute to the development of their children's

self-esteem, they do not operate in a "social vacuum." Experiences and interactions with others outside the family may injure or diminish a child's self-esteem, perhaps seriously. In other instances outside events may have a beneficial effect, such as the interaction with a best friend or with an especially trusted teacher, coach, or counselor.

Intellectual Development

As we have seen, the prenatal period is a critical stage for intellectual development. If there is not adequate nutrition *in utero* — if the mother's diet is not balanced and sufficient — irreversible damage is done to the brain, and thus to the intellectual capacities, of the developing fetus. In addition, intellectual development can proceed to maximum potential only if children have continuing adequate nutrition as neonates and infants, when the brain is continuing its physical development.

However, another especially critical period for intellectual development was discovered by the Harvard Preschool Project in classic studies conducted in the mid-1970s (White 1975, 1976; Pines 1971). The researchers found that a critical period for intellectual development of the child is the eight-month period from ten to eighteen months of age. In this brief span of time the mother's actions (or those of another primary care giver) are extremely important in determining the child's future intellectual competence.

A child's intelligence is highly flexible before age four, but after this age it is unlikely that intelligence will change. The Harvard Preschool Project set out to find a procedure for raising the intellectual competence of children before this critical age of four.

First, it was first necessary to define what is meant by intellectual competence in small children. The researchers defined it in terms of children's readiness for first grade and their ability to deal with problems that came up in the school-yard and the classroom. Judgments were made by eighteen experienced observers — teachers and psychologists — who agreed very closely in their evaluations. On the basis of these judgments, the researchers were able to distinguish between two quite different groups of children: the A group, which rated exceptionally high in intellectual capacities, and the C group, which rated exceptionally low in intellectual capacities.

In sensory perception and motor skills, the two groups of children were virtually identical, but differences were clearly noted in seventeen specific intellectual and social skills. Children in the A group had these specific skills; children in the C group did not. Thus children in the A group were clearly superior in terms of anticipating consequences, planning and carrying out complicated projects, and understanding complex sentences.

In addition to these abilities, children in the A group knew how to get the attention of adults for information or help. The children in the C group were not able to do this and generally either disrupted the classroom or remained unnoticed.

The researchers then directed their attention to discovering the youngest age at which the two categories of children could be differentiated. They found that the youngest members of the A group, who were barely three years old, had exactly the same cluster of abilities as the six-year-old A's. Moreover, the three-year-old A's were already well ahead of the six-year-old C's in both social and intellectual skills. Whatever produced the differences between the A and C children must have occurred before the age of three.

When the project was extended to toddlers between the ages of one and three, the researchers found that the differences between the A's and C's were already clear by age eighteen months. The researchers were unable to find sufficient differences among children ten months old or younger, however, to divide them into A and C groups. Apparently, then, something very important must have happened between the ages of ten months and eighteen months that resulted in the highly significant differences between the two groups of children.

The researchers hypothesized that the differences in the children's behavior stemmed from interaction with their mothers. Attention was directed toward determining what differences, if any, occurred in the behavior of the mothers of A and C children.

After two years of painstaking work, differences in the mothers were pinpointed. The A mothers made available for play a rich variety of toys and household objects and allowed their children to roam all over the living area, placing dangerous objects beyond their reach. If a wandering one-year-old ran into something particularly exciting or encountered an insurmountable obstacle, the A mother would pause for a few seconds — interrupting whatever she was doing to deal with the problem — to encourage the child's curiosity or to suggest a related idea, thus transmitting (perhaps unwittingly) the important skill of using adults as a resource. The A mothers did this many times during the day in as short as ten- or twenty-second episodes. The initiative came from the children, but the A mothers encouraged the children to master the tasks they gave themselves.

The A mothers managed to turn even the dullest everyday situation (such as diaper changing) into an occasion for a game (such as peek-a-boo, which teaches the baby that things exist even when they are hidden from sight). The A mothers did not spend a great deal of time interacting with the child, however, nor did they do much deliberate teaching. It was estimated that an A mother seldom gave her undivided attention to her child for more than 10 percent of the child's waking time. For a baby who is awake twelve hours a day, this is only 1.2 hours.

The C mothers, on the other hand, protected their possessions and their children by ruling a large number of places out of bounds and restricting the child's tendency to explore. The C mothers also made themselves much less available. Although they might be patient, loving, and well-meaning, they talked to their babies less. The C mothers seldom encouraged their babies' attempts at making sense of the world, failed to stimulate them intellectually, and did not share their babies' excitement at making new discoveries and solving problems.

To become an A mother, then, it is important to fill the world of the ten- to eighteen-month-old child with small, manipulable, visually detailed objects (either toys or household items) and things to climb on, and to make these objects freely available. This freedom may conflict with a spotless home, but A mothers are not meticulous housekeepers. It is important to maximize interaction in the brief snatches of time available, to try first to understand what the child's activity means to the child and what he or she might be learning from it, and then to provide something new and interesting to think about or to do along those lines.

Although a mother need not always drop whatever she is doing to attend to her child's requests, she should respond with help or shared enthusiasm most of the time, stimulating in the process the child's desire to do things well and perhaps suggesting a related activity or game the child might try next. In every case, the mother should talk to the child a great deal, even before she is certain the child can understand, for research indicates that this will nourish the child's intellectual development.

Mastery Skills

Even as we emphasize the importance of fulfilling emotional needs and providing emotional security for children, we must not lose sight of the equal importance of providing them the opportunities for acquiring *mastery skills* — the ability to manipulate objects: to build and construct things, to play games, and to solve puzzles. Studies indicate that if mothers provide them appropriate stimulation, babies as young as two months of age develop greater cognitive abilities than a matched control group (Tamis-LeMonda and Bornstein 1990).

The Importance of Mastery Skills As neonates become infants and grow into young children, their early experiences with manipulating objects result either in increasing self-reliance and the eager pursuit of additional skills or in self-doubt, the perseverance of dependence, and the disinclination (or inability) to acquire skills and competency.

Although great individual differences in abilities and attitudes exist, some of which are genetically programmed, children who are not prepared for nursery school and who are unfamiliar and ill at ease with the objects they will be expected to manipulate there (blocks, balls, crayons, watercolors, picture books) will be at a disadvantage, and poor performance, anxiety, and lowered self-image are likely to result. Children who find themselves at a disadvantage in nursery school (and then in the first grade) tend to find their school experiences increasingly difficult from grade to grade because the skills and information acquired in later grades are usually based on abilities acquired in earlier grades (Chess and Thomas 1987; Coleman 1979).

On the other hand, children who are familiar beforehand with everything they will be expected to manipulate in nursery school have an advantage that helps to raise their self-images and increase their manipulative skills; these characteristics and attitudes will in turn carry over into subsequent schooling and ultimately contribute to the life-style they are likely to have as adults.

When adults take the time to accurately assess a child's developmental readiness, learning a new skill can be a successful, exciting experience that enhances the child's confidence.

Developmental Readiness *Developmental readiness* is a complex interaction of a child's maturing muscular and neurological capacities. Thus because children do not yet have the necessary sphincter muscle control to be toilet trained until they are between two and three years old, attempting to teach this (or any other ability or skill) before the child has the necessary developmental readiness is not only doomed to failure but will cause the child to experience feelings of frustration and defeat. The child who has too many experiences of failure will come to expect it, and the groundwork is laid for feelings of self-devaluation and a sense of inadequacy in coping with the world.

Teaching a child a skill just as the critical period of developmental readiness is reached is a happy experience for both parent and child. Timing the teaching effort to conform with de-velopmental readiness not only maximizes the possibility that the skill will be readily acquired but also avoids the emotional problems associated with failure. Repeated failures in trying to teach a child a skill frustrate both parent and child, and it is a rare parent that does not become discouraged or angry. If such failures occur too often and become characteristic, the atmosphere in the household becomes one of tension and fear for the child, disappointment for the parent, and frustration for both (Brazelton 1990; Coleman 1984).

Not only is it fruitless to try to teach mastery skills before the necessary muscular and neural control has been established, but introducing the challenge too late (after the critical period of developmental readiness is reached) may also result in failure because the child may then be disinterested, inattentive, or bored because the task is too simple. If the new activity or problem is not sufficiently intriguing or demanding for the child, succeeding at it will not be experienced as rewarding.

The ideal is to provide a child with a challenge just as he or she reaches developmental readiness for that activity. Then the task is neither so difficult that the child is doomed to fail nor so simple that it will not stimulate interest and attention.

Success Experiences Success experiences, as opposed to failure experiences, breed confidence, optimism, and a sense that the world is ultimately manageable. If most initial experiences are successful, subsequent occasional failures can be expected to act as stimuli to subsequent effort because the child anticipates ultimate success. However, too many failures will lead to expectations of failure, and as a result the world is experienced as unfriendly, cold, rejecting, and unmanageable. It is important, therefore, that the care giver maximize the probability for success experiences and minimize the probability for failure experiences by preparing the child adequately, by taking small preliminary steps to lay the groundwork for success, and by observing the crucial concept of developmental readiness.

Necessary Tools and Information Children cannot acquire mastery skills without having the necessary tools and information. For infants, the appropriate tools for acquiring mastery skills are such objects as rattles (for manipulative skills) and rag dolls (for relational skills). Small children can play with building blocks, large balls, pull toys, coloring books, and dolls.

As they grow older, children can use dull, round-tipped scissors, colored paper, paste, puzzles, and the thousand and one items of play that reflect our cultural preoccupations. Picture books encourage reading; building sets, balls and bats, and tricycles aid manipulative skills and foster neuromuscular coordination and a knowledge of spatial relations. All these skills contribute to a self-image of adequacy in controlling the environment and effectiveness in relating to others.

Information is just as important as tools in providing the basis for the development of appropriate mastery skills. In fact, information and mastery skills often go hand in hand. Children who have their questions answered promptly and candidly and as thoroughly as they are capable of understanding will not only acquire information but will also be self-assured intellectually. Children want to learn; they are as eager to acquire information as they are to acquire skills and abilities.

Cultural Values

A *value* is a measure of how much something— an object, an activity, information, or knowledge—is wanted or prized. Values are standards by which people measure the relative worth of everything from material objects to philosophical ideals.

The information and skills transmitted within the family in the process of initial socialization are those that are most valued by the family; that is, parental values initially determine what information is learned and what skills are acquired by a child. Thus through socialization within the family, a child acquires a pattern of values: what is respected or disdained, what is loved or hated, what is idealized or scorned. The values held by a family and transmitted to a child shape the type and extent of the information and skills the child acquires, the attitudes held, and the way he or she will relate as an adolescent or adult to the larger society (Spanier 1989).

What is valued by families in one society (or subsociety) is not necessarily valued by families in another society. Thus the information and activities valued by an urban family in our society may be quite different from the information or activities valued by a rural family in another country. Children in the United States learn how to ride tricycles, throw and catch balls, change stations on a television set, shop in grocery stores, and manipulate all the various tools and artifacts of our society because these activities are valued by our society. These activities would have no value in an African pygmy society, which might value instead the ability to track an animal or throw a spear accurately.

An interesting example of the pervasive influence of implicit values is revealed by how a child answers the question "Which do you think is more important in determining success — ability or luck?" Middle-class children are usually instilled with the value (or brought up to believe) that effort can be counted on to bring reward. These children reply "ability" when asked this question. The experiences of most economically deprived lower-class parents, on the other hand, have provided them little reason to anticipate success from their efforts alone; their children thus reply "luck" when asked this question. In other words, most middle-class children believe that effort leads to reward and tend to value effort; they have acquired this attitude from their parents. Most lower-class children come to believe that factors beyond their control (luck) play a major role in success and thus value luck much more than do middle-class children. The subtle values related to social class position are unintentionally handed down from parent to child and profoundly affect a child's attitudes, self-image, social behavior, and expectations (Wernick 1974).

Children of poor families usually do not perform as well in school as do more affluent children for many complex, interrelated reasons. One reason is that they apparently come to expect to gain little (or nothing) from hard work. Middle-class children, however, are more likely to be more attentive and to work harder because they have been indoctrinated with the value that "work pays off."

Importance of the Father to Children

As we have seen in Chapter 9, there have been three stages of American fatherhood, each a response to economic change. In the first (agrarian) stage, a father had the chief responsibility for training his sons to work on the farm. As better economic opportunities became available away from the farm in the second stage of economic development, fathers were absent from the household most of the day and had much less to do with the training of their sons. In both these stages, the father was often "distant and stern." Today, most families are in the third stage of economic development in which most mothers also work outside the household. However, most fathers still leave the chief responsibility for child care and training to the mother. "Most fathers have yet to embrace a notion of themselves as equally important as their wives at home" (Hochschild 1989, pp. 186–87).

Until the 1960s, few studies addressed the issue of a father's relationship with his children. "It was generally assumed that if the husband performed the instrumental tasks of his provider role, and the wife her expressive tasks as homemaker and mother, all would be well with the children, the nuclear family, and the larger society" (Collins and Coltrane 1991, p. 564).

Since the mid-1970s researchers have become increasingly interested in studying the role of fathers as caretakers of children. Studies have indicated that child care is typically an ongoing involvement for the mother, who continues to be immersed in essential household tasks. On the other hand, child care is customarily a transitory, intermittent, and fun activity for a father — if he participates in child care at all. Thus, a father may feel that he is making an important contribution to fulfilling household tasks by playing with the children, thereby freeing time for the mother to cook or clean. The mother, meanwhile, usually plays with the children *while* she is cooking or cleaning (Collins and Coltrane 1991; Hochschild 1989; Berk 1985).

Researchers have found considerable variation between men and women and among fathers in styles of relating to children. Fathers are more likely than mothers to play roughly, to be more directive or structured in their play, and to treat sons and daughters differently, favoring sons (Collins and Coltrane 1991; Lamb 1982). Black fathers seem to be more nurturant with their daughters than with their sons (Bradley 1985). Fathers talk to their sons more often, touch them more, and play with them more vigorously than they do with their daughters (Bronstein 1983). Working-class fathers tend to be stricter with their children than middle-class fathers (Bradley 1985; Lamb 1982). Mothers are usually less directive and offer verbal encouragement more frequently than fathers, and, as we have seen, generally perform various household tasks at the same time they are relating to their children (Collins and Coltrane 1991; Lamb 1982).

According to most current social theories, mothers and fathers treat children differently because as girls and boys they were socialized differently. As noted in Chapters 2 and 9, females are socialized from early childhood to demonstrate their competence through mothering, whereas males are socialized to demonstrate their competence through such thorough attention to work that inattention to children often results. This societal expectation for male and female gender-role differences has as its basis an unequal distribution of power and status between men and women.

Infants will bond with fathers as well as they do with mothers if the father spends enough time with them and gives them enough nurturing and attention (Brazelton 1987). As more and more mothers enter the world of outside employment, fathers, especially older fathers, are assuming more responsibility in caring for their children; being a successful parent is increasingly important to these fathers (Martin 1985). Many fathers want to become involved in caring for their children and can be competent in doing so — whatever the age of the child (Collins and Coltrane 1991; Lamb 1982; Pedersen 1980). Fathers who take an active role in parenting "think better of themselves, are more satisfied with their marriage, and view parenting as less stressful" (Cowan and Cowan 1983, p. 172). About one father in five shares the household work and child care (see Chapter 9).

A father's relationship with his children is an important aspect of family cohesion and harmony, and the amount and quality of comfort, affection, and stimulation provided by a father is a critical factor in the social, emotional, and physical development of children (Hanson and Bozett 1985; Jones and Lenz 1985; Lewis and Weinraub 1976).

Fathers who live in the household with their young children still typically spend very little time with them, however. Resident fathers of preschool-age children spend an average of about two hours per week on child care (Coltrane and Ishii-Kuntz 1990; Russell 1983). Although this is a fourfold increase from the thirty minutes per week spent in the mid-1970s, it is still a relatively small amount of time (Kotelchuck 1976).

Nonresident fathers, who are divorced and not a part of the household, see their children very rarely and take very little responsibility for them, as we have seen in Chapter 9 (see also Chapter 12).

In short, although a trend may be emerging in which fathers are becoming more involved in caring for their children, and even though some fathers (about one in five) are "superdads," most fathers still spend very little time with their children (Hochschild 1989; Jones 1985). As a result it remains difficult to assess the potential impact of fathers who play a more significant role in their children's lives (Collins and Coltrane 1991).

The Importance of Friendship

The essence of friendship is reciprocity and commitment between two people who regard themselves as essentially equal. Friendships are rare before age two, although children as young as ten months of age may choose special partners with whom they play for long periods (Howes 1992). Mothers sometimes are convinced that their infants have best friends, but this usually means that the infant has a regular playmate with whom he or she interacts harmoniously. Horizontal relationships (friendship with one's peers) are not usually formed before the child is about three years old (Hartup 1989).

Hartup identified two major kinds of relationships that are important for a child's development:

- vertical relationships with people who have greater power and more knowledge than the child does

- horizontal relationships with peers who have about the same amount of power and knowledge as the child does

Vertical relationships usually involve children and adults, and the child's role consists chiefly of demonstrations of submission and appeals for nurturance, whereas the adult's role involves providing nurturance and maintaining control. Children learn to acquire the basic social skills necessary for interacting with others in these vertical relationships. Children usually turn to their mothers for nurturance because they spend more time with them, but child-father relationships have many of the same essential qualities as child-mother relationships,

and fathers can provide the same comfort and support as mothers.

Horizontal relationships generally occur with other children and are characterized by mutual, egalitarian exchanges. In these interactions with others, children learn to elaborate the basic skills acquired in vertical relationships. In horizontal relationships, "the complexities of co-operation and competition are mastered and 'intimacy' in social relations is first achieved. . . . The construction of well-functioning relationships may be the most significant achievement in the child's socialization" (Hartup 1989, pp. 120, 125).

Friends relate to each other much more than do nonfriends; they smile at each other and laugh together more. As children grow older, mutual understanding, loyalty, and "the willingness to disclose one's secrets" are additional characteristics of friendship. Disagreements and conflicts are quite common between friends but the outcomes are often satisfactory to both, and friends are likely to remain close to and relate comfortably with each other after the disagreement has been resolved. During early adolescence, the emphasis on sharing and cooperation increases, indicating a growing awareness of the needs and wants of friends (Hartup 1989, p. 124).

A best friend becomes a type of paired bond that is more egalitarian than the paired bond between a mother and her child. It is with a best friend that children first have the experience of relating closely and unselfishly to another person, of providing as well as receiving in a reciprocal interchange. The experience of having a best friend is the basis for the successful interaction necessary for serious dating and courtship — and ultimately for the pair bonding that culminates in successful marriage (Hartup 1989).

From the preschool years through adolescence, children almost always form a friendship with someone of about the same age and of the same gender. Studies indicate that despite the gender-role revolution of the past thirty years, boys still prefer to "hang out" with boys, and girls with girls, probably because they find each other's styles of interaction compatible and speak essentially the same language. Female friendships tend to be closely knit and egalitarian, whereas male friendship groups tend to be loosely knit with clear status hierarchies (Maccoby 1992; Corsaro and Eder 1992; Tannen 1990).

From the preschool years through adolescence, only about 5 percent of children's friendships are cross-gender friendships. Siblings can be friends, but they generally have a more vertical relationship, with the older sibling providing nurturance for the younger one (Thorne 1986).

Children who do not develop a satisfactory vertical relationship with their mother (or other care giver) characteristically have low self-esteem and difficulty in forming friendships. They seem to lack the prerequisite skills for relating effectively with their peers and are apt to be "impulsive, mean, and disruptive" in relating to other children, who "immediately dislike and avoid them." These children seem to have an inadequate understanding of the reciprocities and intimacies involved in friendships, and any friendships they do form tend to be relatively unstable. "Probably the most important thing these children do is form friendships, break up friendships, and form new friendships" (Hartup 1989, pp. 5, 124).

Children who fail to develop satisfactory friendships are not only handicapped in relating to others from the outside, but as they grow older they have fewer opportunities for learning relational skills because others avoid them. They thus are liable to remain persistently disadvantaged in acquiring the requisite attitudes, expectations, and skills for succeeding in social interactions. Seriously deviant behavior may follow. Children who are regarded as hostile and aggressive (or simply as uncommunicative) by other children have a much higher incidence of referral to child guidance clinics (Hartup 1989; Achenbach and Edelbrock 1981; Selman 1980). Children who are unpopular and disliked by other children in early childhood continue to be rejected in adolescence and adulthood (Corsaro and Eder 1990; Coie et al. 1988). Moreover, a strong correlation exists between a child's inability to make friends in childhood and maladaptive behavior as an adult (Corsaro and Eder 1990; Parker and Asher 1987).

The Nature of Discipline

Discipline is conduct that sets limits on behavior and induces desired behaviors that eventually become self-perpetuating. Sociologists and psychologists agree that discipline is not only advisable but essential for happiness, security, accomplishment, and contentment. The undisciplined person, whether adult or child, is not only unsocialized but unfulfilled.

Discipline and Reinforcement

Reinforcement is a consequence of a behavior that causes it to increase in frequency. Thus because eating when we are hungry brings us a sense of satisfaction, food is very reinforcing when we are hungry. We watch a television program because the consequence of this action is pleasure or satisfaction, which reinforces our action of watching the program. Similarly, we work in part to receive a paycheck, which brings a kind of satisfaction and thus reinforces our working.

The term *reward* is often used to refer to a reinforcement, but what is considered rewarding by one person may not be rewarding to another. By definition, a reinforcement is always rewarding, so reinforcement is a more precise and useful term than reward when examining the relation between behavior and its consequences.

Discipline is very important for a child's development and is best instilled through reinforcement, not punishment.

The relation between reinforcement and discipline is very clear: If a behavior is followed by a reinforcer, the incidence of that behavior will increase. Thus behavior is both established and maintained by reinforcement. Initially it may be necessary for reinforcement to follow every instance of the behavior, but after a time a pattern of behavior is established, and reinforcement need occur only occasionally.

Various complications can occur when reinforcement is used to modify behavior. A reinforcer may vary in effectiveness from one time to another, or something a parent perceives to be a reinforcer may not be so perceived by a child. Some behaviors may be established by a single reinforcement, whereas other behaviors may require a long pattern of reinforcement. Despite these complications, any mistake made regarding the use of reinforcement can be easily corrected or modified. Parents do not run the risk of damaging or destroying the parent-child bond by using reinforcers. Providing the positive reinforcement of acceptance and approval whenever a desired behavior is observed is a very effective — and safe — socializing device for children.

Reinforcement can be combined with *modeling*, in which the parent acts as an example (or model) to be imitated. When children base their behavior on that of a parent and the parent responds with approval, a powerful reinforcer is operating. Thus modeling is often combined with reinforcement in bringing about desired behavior in children.

Discipline and Love

Experience has shown that depriving children of love is a very poor way of disciplining them. Perhaps worst of all is making the provision of love conditional on good behavior or using love as a bargaining chip, for these methods may injure the parent-child bond. When love is made conditional on desired behavior (that is, is withheld unless desired behavior occurs), a descending spiral often follows: The unwanted behavior continues, which leads to increased withholding of love, which is followed by an increased incidence of unwanted behavior. This unhappy pattern leads to frustration and unhappiness for parent and child alike and, once established, is very difficult to stop. It is much simpler to avoid the pattern in the first place.

Another basic principle regarding the relation between discipline and love is that a child should never be allowed to feel that parental discipline is a rejection. A parent should criticize or correct the behavior, not the child, saying in effect, "I love you, but that was a naughty thing to do." Parents should not say, "You are a naughty child; I do not love you when you do that." In short, instilling disciplined behavior should never be accompanied by a withdrawal of nurturance, love, or affection; these should be considered a child's right and should be freely and warmly provided.

At the base of all socialization must be a foundation of love and respect. A child whose needs for attention, affection, and love are fulfilled is generally a happy, good-natured, cooperative, productive, and well-disciplined child.

Discipline and Setting Limits

One aspect of discipline is setting limits on behavior. The question, of course, is where exactly these limits should be set. As we have seen, children cannot be permitted to behave in ways that are dangerous; they cannot be allowed to ride their tricycles on the freeway, for example. And children should also be stopped from behaving in ways that infringe on the rights or freedoms of others.

A good rule of thumb is for parents to ask themselves whether the limit being set is really necessary. If it seems so at the moment, the parent should set it but be sure the child is offered another, equally attractive activity and that the interaction does not cause feelings of rejection or resentment. When behavioral limits set by a

parent are realistic and consistently enforced, children usually accept them, although they will occasionally test these limits.

Allowing children to experience things for themselves is a very effective method of socialization (Mazur 1986). Thus a child who is allowed to eat a piece of soap is likely to learn not to repeat the experience, but a child obviously cannot be allowed to eat poison to learn by experience. In other words, limits should be as few as possible, and children should be permitted as much freedom as is practical within these limits. Because community organizations (such as schools) that handle children in large groups often tend to enforce uniformity, it is important for parents to permit as much freedom as possible at home. The more freedom children are allowed within the limits that are set, the greater will be their potential for development as emotionally secure, competent, and creative individuals (Mazur 1986).

Children understand and accept occasional unreasonableness in their parents and are not harmed by it if they feel generally accepted, respected, and wanted; if they have enough activities that they can perform; and if they feel that most of the limits imposed on them are consistent, realistic, and reasonable. Accordingly, children may write on paper but not on the wall, may cut out patterns but not curtains, and may kick a ball but not the baby.

In summary, the principles regarding the setting of limits on children's behavior are as follows:

- Children should not be allowed behavior that is dangerous to themselves or to others.

- Children should not be allowed behavior that infringes on the rights and freedoms of other people.

- The limits set on behavior should be realistic and should be as few as possible. Within these limits, children should be allowed as much freedom as is practical.

- The limits on behavior should be expanded as quickly as possible; that is, children should be allowed increased freedom of movement and access to potentially dangerous objects and activities as soon as their developmental level is appropriate and they can be responsible for their actions.

Discipline and Punishment

Punishment is the deliberate infliction of deprivation, discomfort, pain, or suffering. Discipline and punishment are not the same thing, and punishment is not another word for discipline. However, punishment and discipline can be related, for under certain circumstances punishment may help bring about discipline.

When punishment is effective, it will stop an unwanted behavior; that is, if a behavior is followed by the consequence of punishment, the behavior may be discontinued (Skinner 1974). Examples of this principle are very clear in the physical world. For example, we do not eat rocks because the immediate physical consequences (discomfort) are automatically punishing. There are people who persist in behaviors whose consequences are physically punishing, but such people are regarded as abnormal and are usually institutionalized so they can be protected from the consequences of their own actions (Baron and Byrne 1991).

It is significant that punishment applied deliberately by a social agency (such as a parent) does not necessarily have the same effect as punishment received automatically from the environment. In fact, when punishment is deliberately applied by a social agent, it may paradoxically have an effect opposite to that desired, making the unwanted behavior more likely to occur.

There are many possible reasons for this paradoxical effect of punishment. Punishment may be resented, and a child (or adult, for that matter) may then continue or even increase the incidence of the behavior as a way of showing this resentment. A child may feel that the punishment is unjust and may continue the behavior as a gesture of defiance and an assertion of independence and personal integrity. The motivation for a punished behavior may be so strong that the behavior continues despite the punishment. Or a behavior may be caused by anxiety or tension and may increase simply because punishment increases the anxiety, as is likely the case in stuttering.

If a behavior is genetically programmed, of course, punishment is futile. One interesting example is the small puppy who urinates on the rug and is slapped with a folded newspaper by his master, who is under the impression that the consequence of slapping will be that the puppy stops urinating on the rug. The problem is that the puppy is genetically programmed to demonstrate his acceptance of the dominance of the leader of the pack by urinating. (The leader of the pack is, of course, his master.) Thus slapping the puppy with the newspaper elicits in the puppy an acceptance of this act of dominance, which involves rolling on his back and then urinating. The slapping simply elicits further urination, bringing about an effect exactly opposite of that desired.

Of course, punishment deliberately applied by a social agent sometimes works, and when it does it is often the most effective and economical way to stop an undesired behavior (Axelrod and Apsche 1983). An intriguing and practical question is "Under what circumstances will punishment work?" Conversely, when will it be ineffective or, worse yet, actually increase the frequency of the unwanted behavior (as in the case of the urinating puppy)?

Upon examination of the relationship between discipline and punishment, it becomes clear that punishment by parents will be effective in stopping an unwanted behavior in a child only when the following four conditions are present (Baron and Byrne 1991; Watson 1992; Axelrod and Apsche 1983):

- There must be no significant emotional involvement on the child's part with the punishment. If there is, punishment may cause resentment, which may then result in the continuation (or even an increased frequency) of the punished behavior. Moreover, if the punishment is resented, it may cause a breach in the essential bond of closeness between parent and child and may bring about self-devaluation in the child. (When punishment occurs naturally as a function of physical reality, it is not usually resented.)
- There must be no strong motivation for the behavior. If such motivation is strong and persistent, punishment applied by a parent usually will not stop the behavior. In the face of strong motivation, punishment is ineffective.
- An alternate course of action must be available. A child must be able to avoid the punishment by engaging in an alternate course of action or by behaving in some other, acceptable way. It is important, in other words, to provide an "out" — an alternate behavior that is equally satisfying (for example, in disallowing coloring on the wall, provide instead a coloring book).
- The punishment must be informative. A child must be able to relate the punishment to the behavior. This usually means that punishment must immediately follow the behavior. Punishing a child for an unwanted behavior long after it has occurred will probably be ineffective in stopping future occurrences unless the punishment is clearly informative.

Authoritative, Authoritarian, and Permissive Parents

In her classic studies investigating the relationship between a child's behavioral patterns and parental attitudes, Baumrind (1968, 1979) studied three types of parents: (1) *authoritative* parents, who are the most responsive and nurturant, even though they set limits on a child's behavior; (2) *authoritarian* parents, who rigidly shape and control a child's behavior; and (3) *permissive* parents, who are nonpunishing and accepting of a child's behavior.

Baumrind found that authoritative parents tend to have the most socially competent children. These parents expect mature, independent behavior that is appropriate to a child's developmental level. Children of authoritarian parents tend to have less self-esteem and to be less happy and outgoing; are often depressed, moody, and hostile; and have less coping ability. Children of permissive parents tend to be impulsive and aggressive and are often disliked by their peers.

Recent research exploring the effects of parenting styles on peer relations supports Baumrind's findings. Authoritative parents who show their children respect, include them in family discussions, and encourage independence while remaining in charge are more likely to raise emotionally healthy children than are parents who are authoritarian or permissive (Conger 1992).

The Effects of a Child's Personality on the Family

Although providing children the components for healthy development maximizes the chances that a child's full potential will be attained, children have quite variable abilities, temperaments, and personalities at birth. A child's innate (genetically programmed) disposition inevitably affects the parent-child interaction, for the parent's attitude and behavior is influenced to some degree by the child's attitude and behavior (Kagan 1992).

The parent-child interaction does not proceed in one direction only — that is, from parent to child. A child's personality and characteristic patterns of behavior from birth on will affect the parents' behavior toward the child. The relationship between parent and child is very much an interaction, with each affecting the other and being affected in turn. Thus the cooing and smiling of a contented baby can soothe the most harassed parent, whereas the howls of the chronically cranky and irritable baby are likely to cause even the most patient parent to become self-pitying and angry (Kagan and Snidman 1991; Chess and Thomas 1987).

Children tend to fall into three groups in terms of inborn temperament: the "easy" child, the "difficult" child, and the "slow-to-warm-up" child. The easy child is a pleasure to have around most of the time and is the least likely to develop psychological, social, or intellectual problems. These children respond with interest to new situations, have no eating problems, enjoy strange new foods, and are generally happy, cheerful, and responsive (Chess and Thomas 1987).

At the other extreme is the difficult child, whose troublesome behavior can drain even the most generous supply of patience, disturb emotional equilibrium, and irritate the calmest parent. These children either withdraw when exposed to new situations or else protest vigorously. They reject new people and new foods, are reluctant to learn new games or take part in new activities, and often display temper tantrums, violence, and hostility (Chess and Thomas 1987).

Between these two extremes are slow-to-warm-up children, who neither actively withdraw nor vigorously protest new situations, foods, or people but are passive in their responses. When given a new food as babies, they may simply let it dribble out of their mouths. They might remain on the sidelines for several weeks in nursery school or kindergarten and quietly try to escape when urged to take part in some activity. Throughout childhood they tend to respond passively to new situations, and they adapt to new experiences slowly (Chess and Thomas 1987).

Each of these three basic types of children can have a great deal of influence on parental behavior and therefore on a child's subsequent development. If a child is easy and rewarding to relate to, the mother is more likely to provide the child with affection, warmth, security, and love. Mothers of easy children tend to stay closer to them and to look at, socialize, and play with them more. As a result, the social and intellectual development of the easy child is enhanced; these children tend to score significantly higher than other children on IQ tests given at age thirty months (Sameroff 1974).

In contrast, mothers of difficult children tend to leave them alone more, look at them less, and socialize and play with them less. Put another way, mothers are less likely to provide the stimulation and care that lead to the child's maximal socialization and intellectual development. Children rated as having been difficult at the age of four months are most likely to score lowest of the three categories of children on an intelligence test given at age thirty months (Sameroff 1974). Apparently the child's temperament at four months of age influences how the mother relates to the child, and this in turn influences the child's intellectual development.

Researchers have found that one key difference among babies that provokes different reactive patterns from parents is babies' sleep patterns. Some babies slip into solid and predictable patterns of sleep, lifting a tired mother's spirits in the process. Other babies never seem to be able to drop off easily or to stay asleep when they do; such children can readily cause the very same mother to feel bitter and resentful: "[A mother may view] her child's erratic sleep habits as a sign of failure in childrearing. . . . Tears and runaway anger are an understandable response to a child whose fractured sleep spells for the mother fatigue, frustration, and guilt" (Segal and Yahraes 1978, p. 93).

Another key difference among babies is their ability to make eye contact, which has been found to be important in bonding and in the development of parental attachment (Segal and Yahraes 1978).

A baby's predisposition for gurgling, smiling, and making other expressions of contentment is another key difference. An alert, contented, responsive baby has a very positive effect on the parents' self-concept and, consequently, on the parents' ability to develop skills in relating to the baby. A baby who has the personality characteristics of the easy child helps the parent-infant relationship get on the right track quickly and helps the parents feel optimistic and confident about their ability to relate effectively to the baby (Chess and Thomas 1987). Moreover, a baby's smile "is social behavior. . . . The smile generates favorable and favoring behaviors on the part of interested adults" (Lipsitt 1992, p. 4).

Some babies have the capacity not only to discourage warmly nurturant behavior but to evoke even outright abuse. Such children violate the common parental expectation that babies will be attractive and lovable, for they are neither. They impose almost impossible demands for patience, time, and nurturance. They sleep less, cry more, and are more irritable, and feeding disturbances are common. Progress in muscular development, speech, and social interaction is much slower than expected during the first two years, and periods of developmental readiness are delayed. In consequence, parents often develop feelings of guilt, inadequacy, and anger toward such children (Sameroff 1974).

Often only one child in a family is singled out as a target of abuse, and some abused children continue to be victimized in a succession of foster homes in which no other child has met a similar fate (Segal and Yahraes 1978). Even though child battering is an unspeakable act that can never be justified—it leaves indelible scars on a child's mind and body—researchers have still wondered whether the victims play any role in evoking parental violence. The evidence increasingly indicates that in fact they do:

> Clinical interviews with abusive parents suggest that certain characteristics of the newborn can help push parents beyond their threshold of violence. Newborns who fret a great deal appear to run a greater risk of harm than those who are placid and easily soothed. The abused child is typically the one who is irritable, colicky, fretful, and difficult to feed, satisfy, or diaper. Parents of such children develop feelings of inadequacy, guilt, and anger; nothing about the baby's behavior makes them feel good about being parents. For adults with a low flash point, such an infant can soon precipitate vicious attacks. (Segal and Yahraes 1978, p. 96)

Babies in different racial-ethnic groups seem to have predictably different temperaments at birth. Although this finding suggests that racial-ethnic differences may play a more important role than was hitherto suspected, it does not necessarily mean that such differences are based on genetic factors; because these groups have different cultures, observed differences in temperament could be based on cultural factors. Whatever the basis, racial-ethnic differences among infants are present from birth on (see Box 10-2).

In summary, the child-parent relation is an interaction in which each affects the other. The

BOX 10-2

Racial-Ethnic Differences in Babies

Research has not only found that babies have significantly different temperaments at birth; it also suggests that characteristic ethnic differences show up only a few hours, days, or weeks after birth. For example, on average white babies cry more easily and are more difficult to console than Chinese babies. When being undressed for an examination, Chinese and white babies start to cry at about the same time, but Chinese babies stop sooner. When picked up and cuddled, Chinese babies usually stop crying immediately, whereas the crying of white babies only gradually subsides. White babies tend to turn their faces to one side when they are placed face down in their cribs, whereas Chinese babies tend to keep their faces buried in sheets (Freedman 1979).

Navajo babies are very similar to Chinese babies, even outdoing them in calmness and adaptability. On the other hand, Japanese babies are more sensitive and irritable than either Chinese or Navaho babies, though not as irritable as the typical white baby. Studies indicate that such differences in temperament among these and other racial-ethnic groups may have some biological (genetic) basis, although the evidence is as yet far from conclusive (Freedman 1979).

These studies promise to open up intriguing new areas of speculation about characteristic differences in ethnic temperaments and may increase our understanding of different personality traits in infants.

---

parent shapes the child's behavior, but the parent's behavior is also shaped by the child. Everything the child does affects the parent, and these effects are transmitted back to the child.

Two possible spirals may therefore result: Babies who at birth have responsive, lovable characteristics are loved more, become increasingly lovable, consequently receive even more love, and thus become even more lovable. This is an ascending spiral, and the parent-child interaction is rewarding and pleasurable. On the other hand, babies who at birth are cranky, colicky, passive, or unresponsive to a parent's overtures generally are less lovable, receive less love, become even less lovable, and in consequence receive even less love. This is a descending spiral in which frustration and difficulty bring increased dissatisfaction and irritation to both the child and the parents. The problem, of course, is breaking the descending spiral.

In short, it is easy to love a lovable baby and more difficult to love a baby who is not immediately lovable. Ironically, it is the unlovable baby (or child) who most needs attention, affection, and love—and is most often deprived of them.

During the first month following birth (a period of extraordinarily rapid change and development), the baby is called a neonate. From the moment of birth on, individual differences among babies are apparent: Some neonates are lively and active, whereas others are passive and relatively unresponsive. It is not yet known whether these differences are genetic, are acquired during the first nine months of life in the uterus, or (more probably) result from a combination of both factors.

The brain is virtually complete in size and mass at birth, with 90 percent of all the neurons a person will ever have already in place. Cell division of neurons is thought to stop completely at about twelve months after birth. Prenatal nutrition is therefore very important, for it provides the materials the fetus will use to construct the brain. If these materials are not available — if the fetus is undernourished — the neonate will have about 20 percent fewer brain cells than normal at birth, and there is no second chance for brain development.

The second stage of brain development occurs during infancy, from the second to about the fifteenth month following birth. During this time the neurons grow in size and establish an interconnected neural network. This final stage of brain development, when connections are formed between neurons, is thought to be virtually complete by the time a child is about two years old.

The importance of adequate nutrition for the fetus, the neonate, and the infant thus cannot be overemphasized. Not only will an undernourished fetus have about 20 percent fewer neurons at birth, but an undernourished infant will fail to develop normally and cell division of neurons in the brain will be slowed down by another 20 percent during the first six months following birth. If both the fetus and the infant are undernourished, the brain will have only about 60 percent of the number of neurons a normal brain has.

The first few hours after birth are a critical period in which bonding begins to take place. Bonding is the close, intimate regard and attachment established between mother and child. Mothers who have early physical contact with their babies fondle them more, spend more time soothing them when they cry, and maintain more eye contact during feedings. These babies smile and laugh more, cry less, and gain weight faster. At five years of age, children of such mothers have significantly higher IQs and higher scores on language tests than do children of other mothers.

Children will also bond with fathers as well as they do with mothers, if the father spends enough time with them and gives them enough nurturing and attention. The father may thus act as a crucial force in the social, emotional, and physical development of his children and may be an important source of family cohesion and harmony.

Infancy begins with the second month after birth and ends when the baby is walking and beginning to talk, usually at about twelve to fifteen months. Infants first laugh when they are about four months old and can usually sit up without support when they are about six months old. By seven months, they usually begin to creep for short distances, and by eight months they can crawl.

Children are usually walking, running, climbing stairs, eating with a spoon, and speaking with a vocabulary of about twenty-five words by the time they are two years old. By the time they are five years old, most children are usually toilet trained, can dress themselves completely except for tying and lacing, can play in the immediate neighborhood unattended, and can participate in unsupervised group games with their age-mates and older children.

A critical period for meeting a child's need for emotional security seems to be from birth to about five years of age. Children whose needs for emotional security are fulfilled during this time normally develop a sense of basic trust and establish a sense of autonomy, or self-reliance, that makes it possible for them to develop to their full potential. They will also have self-esteem, which is central to the development of a fully functioning, creative, productive, socially skilled, optimistic, and contented person. Children with self-esteem expect to succeed, which increases the likelihood that they will succeed; this is a self-fulfilling prophecy. On the other hand, children who are characterized by self-doubt anticipate difficulties everywhere, which virtually guarantees failure and confirms their poor opinion of themselves—another self-fulfilling prophecy.

It is also important to provide for the development of mastery skills during this time by giving children tools and information in accordance with their developmental readiness. Success experiences, as opposed to failure experiences, breed confidence, optimism, and a sense that the world is ultimately manageable. It is important that parents maximize the probability for success experiences and minimize the probability for failure experiences.

It is also in the first five years that children acquire a sense of values. Values are standards by which people measure the relative worth of everything from material objects to philosophical ideals. The values held by a family and transmitted to children have important influences on the type and extent of the information and skills children acquire.

The friendships children have, from about age three on, are very important, for it is in these friendships that the complexities of cooperation and competition are first practiced and intimacy in social interaction is first achieved. The vertical relationships children have with their parents (or other care givers) consist chiefly of submission of children and provision of nurturance and control by parents. On the other hand, the horizontal relationships children have with their peers are characterized by mutual exchanges that are egalitarian and cooperative. Children who don't have friends may fail to develop the attitudes and skills necessary for social interactions and may therefore be handicapped in this regard throughout their lives.

Discipline is conduct that sets limits on behavior and induces desired behavior. Discipline is essential for people's happiness, security, accomplishment, and contentment. Because behavior is established and maintained by reinforcement, the most effective way to bring about discipline is by reinforcing desired behavior.

Punishment is the deliberate infliction of deprivation, discomfort, or pain. Punishment is often confused with discipline, and this confusion of concepts can cause trouble if the distinction between them is not clarified. Punishment may stop an unwanted behavior (which is why it is often confused with discipline), but it will only do so if there is no significant emotional involvement with the behavior or with the punishment, or if there is no strong motivation to continue the behavior. Moreover, an alternate course of action must be made available, and the punishment must be informative (that is, the child must be able to relate the punishment to the behavior).

Styles of parenting may be authoritarian, authoritative, or permissive. Children develop best with authoritative parenting; children with authoritarian parents tend to have less self-esteem and to be depressed, moody, or hostile, whereas children with permissive parents tend to be more impulsive and aggressive.

Parents are inevitably affected by a child's disposition and temperament, and children have different temperaments from birth on. The parent-child relationship does not proceed in one direction only — from parent to child — but is an interaction, with each one affecting and being affected by the other. Some children have temperaments that are immediately rewarding for parents; these children are easy to care for and facilitate good parenting. Other children have temperaments that do not provide these rewards, even for conscientious parents, and these children are more likely to be relatively neglected by parents. Neglected children are apt to develop personality characteristics that make them even more difficult to relate to, creating a descending spiral. Pleasant children who are easy to love become even more pleasant — an ascending spiral. Children tend to fall into three categories in terms of inborn temperament: the "easy child," the "difficult" child, and the "slow-to-warm-up" child.

KEY TERMS

The following is a list of key terms in this chapter.
These terms are defined in context within the chapter, and many may also be found in the Glossary.

authoritarian parents	genetically programmed	provider role
authoritative parents	horizontal relationships	reality testing
autonomy	hormonal balance	reciprocity
basic trust	immunizing agent	reinforcement
bonding	independency	relational skills
conceptualized self	intellectual potential	REM
coping ability	interdependency	reward
dependency	manipulative skills	rooting reflex
developmental process	manipulatory skills	self-centeredness
developmental readiness	mastery skills	self-esteem
developmental sequence	modeling	self-fulfilling prophecy
differential development	molding	self-reliance
discipline	motivation	setting limits
emotional deprivation	neonate	socialization
emotional security	neurons	societal expectation
ethnic temperaments	nurture	spoiling
failure experiences	pattern of values	success experiences
fontanels	peers	synapses
frame of reference	perceptual skills	vertical relationships
fully functioning	permissive parents	work ethic
genetic potential	primary care giver	

QUESTIONS

1. Discuss the importance of nutrition for brain development during the fetal stage, the neonate stage, and the infant stage.

2. Discuss the importance of early bonding for the mother and for the child. How does this bonding occur?

3. Discuss the importance of emotional security for children.

4. Discuss the importance of self-esteem in children's development.

5. What is meant by a success experience? Discuss the importance of success experiences in infancy and childhood.

6. What is a vertical relationship? A horizontal relationship? What is the importance of each, and what are their characteristic differences? Give examples of each.

7. Define the concept of discipline. Give an example.

8. Define the concept of reinforcement. Give an example.

9. Define the concept of punishment. What four circumstances must be present before punishment is likely to stop an unwanted behavior?

10. It is obvious that parents have a significant effect on the development of a child, but it is also true that a child's personality has a significant effect on parents. Discuss this parent-child interaction and its effects on family life.

11. Babies have different temperaments at birth. What are the three types of temperamental differences in babies? What effect can these characteristics have on parents?

SUGGESTIONS FOR FURTHER READING

Brazelton, T. Berry. *The Earliest Relationship: Parents, Infants, and the Drama of Early Attachment.* Reading, Mass.: Addison-Wesley, 1990.

Brooks, J. B. *The Process of Parenting,* 3d ed. Mountain View, Calif.: Mayfield, 1991.

Bronstein, Phyllis, and Cowan, Carolyn P., eds. *Fatherhood Today.* New York: Wiley, 1988.

Cable, Mary. *The Little Darlings: A History of Child Rearing in America.* New York: Scribner, 1975.

Cole, M., and Cole, S. R. *The Development of Children.* New York: Scientific American Books, 1989.

Damon, William. *The Moral Child — Nurturing Children's Natural Moral Growth.* New York: Free Press, 1988.

Elkin, Frederick, and Handel, Gerald. *The Child and Society: The Process of Socialization,* 5th ed. New York: Random House, 1989.

Kubey, R., and Csikszentmihalyi, M. *Television and the Quality of Life: How Viewing Shapes Everyday Experience.* Hillsdale, N.J.: Erlbaum, 1990.

La Rossa, Ralph. *Becoming a Parent.* Beverly Hills, Calif.: Sage, 1986.

Lewis, Charles, and O'Brien, Margaret, eds. *Reassessing Fatherhood: New Observations on Fathers and the Modern Family.* Newbury Park, Calif.: Sage, 1987.

Phinney, Jean, and Rotheram, Mary Jane, eds. *Children's Ethnic Socialization*. Newbury Park, Calif.: Sage, 1987.

Spock, Benjamin, and Rothenberg, Michael. *Baby and Child Care*, 6th ed. New York: Pocket Books, 1991.

Steinberg, Laurence. *You and Your Adolescent*. New York: Harper Perennial, 1991.

Conflict, Divorce, and Remarriage

CHAPTER 11

Couples in Conflict: Problems of Communication

The most exhausting thing in life,
I have discovered, is being insincere.

Anne Morrow Lindbergh, "Gift from the Sea"

The Nature of Conflict

The Destructive Consequences of Conflict

Examples of Ineffective Communication

The Constructive Resolution of Conflict

What Do You Know?

Some of the following statements are true and some are false.
Can you tell which are which?

T/F   1. Playing a psychological game usually has the effect of bringing a couple closer together.

T/F   2. Most couples play psychological games.

T/F   3. "Mind reading" is an example of effective communication because it makes an open discussion of a conflict possible.

T/F   4. An example of effective communication is a double message because it makes the intention of the speaker clear.

T/F   5. In a conflict, sentences that start with "You" usually further effective communication because they focus on the other person.

T/F   6. In a conflict, questions that begin with "Why" are usually productive because they encourage the other person to express his or her views.

T/F   7. Rejection by a person who is trusted is usually perceived as betrayal.

T/F   8. Leveling with others is an example of ineffective communication because it reduces the other person's self-esteem.

T/F   9. It is not possible for a couple to avoid conflicts.

T/F 10. The average married couple today who do not divorce can expect to be married for about twenty years longer than the average couple of a century ago.

arital interaction can be harmonious and can provide pleasure and satisfaction for each member of the couple, or it can be disruptive and bring dissatisfaction, disappointment, and pain to one or both.

About half of those marrying in this decade will find the interaction so disruptive that they will end it in divorce, usually within two or three years of marriage. The difficulties often start almost immediately and then escalate during the first year. The couple may separate, then reconcile, then separate again and may finally end their relationship with divorce (see Chapter 12).

About half of contemporary marriages do not end in divorce, however. Moreover, the average couple who do not divorce have the actuarial expectation of remaining married some twenty years longer than the average couple of a century ago because of longer life expectancy today.[1]

What are the differences between successful relationships and those that end in separation or divorce? Are the successful relationships free of conflict, or does conflict occur but is handled differently? Are there significant differences in the nature of the communication of couples who have satisfying and long-lasting relationships compared with those who do not? In this chapter we will examine the nature of conflict and the qualities of effective and ineffective communication in relationships.

The Nature of Conflict

Conflict occurs when something that means satisfaction for one person means deprivation for the other. Thus if one person wants the window open and the other wants it closed, opening the window provides satisfaction for one but deprivation for the other.

A conflict between two people in a couple may occur in a very simple and obvious form (such as the open-window/closed-window example), or it may be extraordinarily complex and involve many interrelated needs so that the initial problem spreads, becomes multidimensional, and colors almost every aspect of the couple's interaction. Thus before one person acts on a need or seizes his or her own satisfaction in a conflict, it is important for that person to see the action as clearly as possible in terms of the deprivation it may cause for the other person.

As Shakespeare noted in *A Midsummer Night's Dream*, "The course of true love never did run smooth" (act 1, scene 1), and conflict within a couple is inevitable. It is simply unrealistic to expect that both people will always want the same thing at the same time. It is inevitable that there will be times when one will want something that the other does not.

The challenge is to avoid as many conflicts as possible, to diminish their number, and to resolve them once they occur. If conflicts occur too frequently or are allowed to persist, grow in strength, and encompass greater and greater areas of dissension, they can be ruinous to the couple's relationship, for all harmony, pleasure, contentment, wonder, and delight will be replaced by bitterness and enmity.

Although any conflict means by definition that satisfaction for one person brings deprivation for the other, it is not always clear what form these satisfactions and deprivations will take or who will experience which and to what degree. Moreover, reprisals made by the deprived person are often made unconsciously and are often not clearly acknowledged by either person.

Conflicts that occur within an intimate couple are, ironically, more likely to escalate than are conflicts that occur within simple social interactions or commercial exchanges. This is

[1]U.S. National Center for Health Statistics, "Expectations of Life and Expected Deaths, by Race, Sex, and Age: 1988" (1991).

because one's rights and expectations are usually precisely spelled out in most social and business transactions so that it is clear what constitutes a violation and what constitutes an appropriate reprisal for such a violation. Thus a secretary who is rude to his or her boss over a conflict regarding continual tardiness will probably be forced to look for a new job, and the shopper who walks out of the supermarket without paying for a bag of groceries after a conflict with the checker will probably be in serious difficulty with the law. In contrast, many of the rights and expectations of individuals within couples are usually left unstated, which leaves the couple much more prone to misunderstanding, disagreement, and continuing conflict.

The Inevitability of Conflict in Marriage

Conflict in marriage is inevitable and unavoidable, for given the amount of enforced interaction characteristic of marriage, it is inevitable that one will want something that the other does not want at that time (see Box 11-1). Conflicts are more frequent in marriage than they are in dating because if two people who are dating find that they do not want the same thing at the same time *most* of the time, they are likely to simply stop dating. Once a couple decide to marry, however, they are held together by bonds that are not present in dating (see Chapter 7). Because it is more difficult to end a marriage than to stop dating, they are forced to confront the conflict within the relationship and to deal with it—one way or another.

The Complexity of Conflict in Marriage

Conflict is sometimes very simple and obvious, as the open-window/closed-window example

previously described would seem to indicate. But let's reconsider this conflict in greater detail, identifying as we proceed each of the couple's behaviors or motives (whether used consciously or not). Suppose, for example, that the husband insists that the window be open (authoritarian resolution) and that he has his way ("wins") in this conflict. In response the wife may then be disinclined to make love (permissive acceptance, placating, displacement, displaced aggression) and in so doing establishes a "win" in *this* area of their relationship (psychological game playing). Is it then worth it for the husband to have the window open, even though his "win" in this situation will cause a disintegration of another aspect of their relationship? The answer to this question is very complex, but it is important that he recognize that the window controversy, rather than being an isolated one, is interrelated with almost every other aspect of their life together. With this clarity of perspective, he is more likely to resolve the conflict in a way that is mutually harmonious, rather than destructive, to the relationship.

Defense-Oriented and Reality-Oriented Responses to Conflict

A person will usually respond to conflict with either reality-oriented behavior or defense-oriented behavior. Behavior that is directed toward obtaining the satisfaction that one is being denied is called *reality-oriented* behavior. Behavior that is not directed toward obtaining this satisfaction but instead either lowers tension related to dissatisfaction or lowers tension by acting to obtain a substitute satisfaction is called *defense-oriented* behavior. (For examples and clarification of this concept, see Box 11-2.)

Behaving in a reality-oriented way in marriage requires first trying to obtain a clear perspective of the initial conflict and then attacking

this problem — rather than attacking the other person (which might score a "win" but undermines the overall harmony of the relationship, and so is counterproductive in the long run). If, for example, the husband arrives home late without phoning and the wife is angry and says that she is angry, and if they both agree that coming home late in this way creates a problem, then they are both reacting with reality-oriented behavior. If, however, she refuses to speak (withdrawal), gets a headache (psychosomatic ail-ment), punishes the children (displacement), or feels no interest in a formerly enjoyable activity (apathy), or if he claims that he "couldn't get to a phone" (rationalization), these would be examples of defense-oriented behavior. Such patterns of behavior are called *defense mechanisms* and are used by all of us from time to time. However, if one or more of these defense mechanisms becomes a chronic, patterned response to conflict and replaces reality-oriented behavior, they are counterproductive and will lead to a worsening

BOX 11-2

Defense-Oriented and Reality-Oriented Behavior

Even though defense-oriented behavior does not satisfy a need, it lowers the tension created by the need. Defense-oriented behavior is thus reinforced, and is likely to be repeated, even though it is illogical, counterproductive, and ultimately self-defeating. Reality-oriented behavior, on the other hand, is a persistent attempt to satisfy the need.

Defense-oriented behavior is rarely used when a physical need is involved. For example, if you are deprived of water, you become increasingly motivated to find some. If the deprivation continues, the search for water will absorb more and more of your attention until it becomes a major part of your awareness. You might use defense-oriented behavior temporarily to alleviate the tension associated with your inability to satisfy your need for water, imagining, for example, cool, beaded glasses of icy-cold pure spring water. This temporary use of a defense mechanism (fantasy, in this case) does not usually interfere for long with your attempts to resolve the underlying need—obtaining water.

Defense-oriented behavior is often used to replace reality-oriented behavior when

the need is social instead of physical. For example, suppose your need is for companionship. Instead of searching for companions (reality-oriented behavior in this case), you might resolve the immediate tension caused by loneliness by watching television (a defense mechanism called "substitution"). Because this lowers the immediate tension caused by loneliness, you might put off indefinitely an attempt to find companionship.

Because defense-oriented behavior brings the rewards of lowered tension and immediate satisfaction, it is reinforced. And because reinforced behavior tends to be repeated, one may develop a pattern of defense-oriented behavior that temporarily resolves the tension associated with the deprivation of a social need but never satisfies the need. Such a pattern of defense-oriented behavior may then become an integral part of one's life-style.

Although defense-oriented behavior is ultimately self-defeating, it may be very difficult to change. The immediate reduction of tension is a powerful inducement to repeat (or continue) the behavior.

of the couple's relationship, as the mutually satisfying characteristics of their interaction — the satisfactions that each provides for the other — are persistently eroded away.[2]

An outsider (a disinterested observer) may watch someone's defense-oriented behavior with astonishment. Why should anyone persist in a behavior that is obviously self-defeating, that is not satisfying any fundamental need? The answer is twofold. In the first place, it is very easy to spot a defensive behavior in someone else but difficult to recognize in oneself. Second, needs do not occur in isolation, so a person may act to satisfy an immediate need ("Close the window!") and lose sight of the overall, interrelated, long-term consequences of that act.

Extrapunitive, Intrapunitive, and Impunitive Responses to Conflict

A person tends to react to a conflict in one of three patterned responses, termed *extrapunitive, intrapunitive,* and *impunitive.*

Extrapunitive people tend to *act out* aggressively, attacking others verbally or even physically while insisting on having their own way in a conflict. Extrapunitive people tend to shout, blame others, establish dominance, and direct their actions not only against other people but against inanimate objects (by slamming doors, kicking furniture, or breaking dishes).

Intrapunitive people tend to direct inward the energy aroused by an unresolved conflict, blaming and unconsciously punishing themselves for their perceived failure by developing a headache, backache, or stomach ache.

Impunitive people tend to direct the energy aroused by the failure to resolve a conflict neither outward against the environment nor inward against themselves, but instead focus their attention on the issue at hand by trying to resolve the conflict without blaming either others or themselves.

A person is not always extrapunitive, intrapunitive, or impunitive in all situations, but instead may respond with one mode of action at one time and another at another time. In general, however, most people tend to follow a characteristic pattern, and are usually an extrapunitive, intrapunitive, or impunitive person in most situations. Personality tends to be relatively consistent in this regard (Coleman 1984).

Common Patterns of Attack and Defense in Conflicts

The ways people attack the other person in a conflict, rather than attacking the source of the conflict, tend to follow certain patterns, depending on the personality of the individual. Some people, for example, tend to be authoritarian, whereas others tend to be passive or evasive. Thus patterns of attack and defense tend to fall into categories that can be described as authoritarian resolution, permissive acceptance, passive aggression, evasion, blaming, placating, distracting, and computing. We will examine each of these in turn in the sections that follow.

Authoritarian Resolution Probably the most obvious, and certainly the most common, method of resolving a conflict is *authoritarian resolution* — "I win, you lose." In this method, one person simply dictates the "solution" and insists that the other yield to his or her decision in the matter.

This method can be very effective when used with subordinates; in positions in which power is assigned, such as police officers or judges; when the other person is smaller and

---

[2]For a fascinating description the use of defense mechanisms, see Coleman (1984).

"Brad, we've got to talk."

weaker or much younger; or with animals. However, it is not usually an effective way to resolve a conflict with a colleague, a companion, a friend, or a spouse because authoritarian resolution creates a winner and a loser with respect to the conflict. If the person who loses is a colleague, companion, friend, husband, or wife, he or she is likely to feel deprived and to resent this deprivation. Moreover, if the relationship is based on friendship, trust, respect, intimacy, or love, the person who wins may feel ashamed or guilty. The resultant tension created by the establishment of a winner and a loser often leads to further conflict over the issue in question and to additional conflicts involving other issues unrelated to the original conflict.

Permissive Acceptance   Resolving a conflict by *permissive acceptance* simply involves giving in and accepting the needs of the other person as having priority over one's own. If a person genuinely feels this way and yields to the other because it brings pleasure to do so, then there is no conflict. (A conflict occurs only if satisfaction for one brings deprivation to the other, and deprivation occurs if the person who yields finds no satisfaction in doing so.)

If a conflict is resolved by accepting the domination of the other person, a winner and a loser are created as surely as they are with authoritarian resolution. For this reason, permissive acceptance must be considered nearly as destructive as authoritarian resolution. A person who continually accepts deprivation in this way, so that the other person always experiences greater satisfaction, will very likely experience a sense of growing resentment, which will result in a reduction of admiration, respect, and trust and will eventually drive a wedge between the two people.

Permissive acceptance sows the seeds for subsequent conflict, resentment, and bitterness.

Moreover, it very often becomes a move in a psychological game, setting the stage for another move intended to inflict a defeat on the other person and reverse the positions of winner and loser.

Passive Aggression   A method of resolving a conflict that resembles permissive acceptance, but is actually very aggressive, is called *passive aggression*. In this type of conflict resolution a person apparently gives in but ultimately has his or her own way. Because the aggression is indirect (covert rather than overt), it can be very difficult to handle.

The passive-aggressive person finds ways not to do what the other person expects when a conflict occurs but never openly takes a stand or states a refusal. Rather, the passive-aggressive person will covertly sabotage the expectation of the other by pointedly ignoring a request, making careless (or intentional) errors, putting something important off, or simply dawdling. Thus a husband who is left to care for a toddler while his wife is out may spill baby powder all over the floor, pin the diapers on inside out, and even "forget" to feed the child, yet he can plead that he was doing his best. (This is a commonly played version of the psychological game called "Look How Hard I Was Trying.")

The person who is faced with passive aggression on the part of another must either endure the oppressive atmosphere and lack of performance or yield to the other's tactical maneuvering. (What is actually happening is that the passive-aggressive moves are a form of attrition in a psychological game.) Because the purpose of the maneuvers in a psychological game is usually not acknowledged, the atmosphere can become very oppressive unless the passive aggressor has his or her own way.

Getting a passive-aggressive person to budge in a conflict is like trying to move a ton of feathers. Often the person faced with passive aggression ultimately accepts the deprivation and becomes the loser. As with authoritarian resolution and permissive acceptance, intimacy, trust, and mutual satisfaction progressively disintegrate, even though there is never any overt attack.

Passive-aggressive people often appear to be easygoing, pliant, and good-natured. They tend to have troubled marriages, however, characterized by an undercurrent of resentment, hostility, and frustration.

Evasion   A pattern of coping with conflict that is similar to passive aggression is *evasion*. Evasion often amounts to passive aggression but lacks the underlying hostility. People who engage in evasion simply avoid a confrontation, putting off a resolution of the conflict. Like passive aggression, evasion also has the appearance of permissive acceptance. The difference is that whereas permissive acceptance provides an apparent solution, evasion precludes any solution because the person simply withdraws into silence, reads a newspaper, watches television, or refuses to address the issue at hand. Some evaders may even physically remove themselves from a situation by getting up and walking out of the room or out of the house (Satir 1972).

This absence of effective communication is, of course, a type of communication in itself because it is sending a message — the message that "things will go my way or they won't go at all." The conflict remains, however, and can be very oppressive, creating pressure for the other person to yield.

Blaming   Blamers act like petty dictators. Their voices are often hard, tight, shrill, or loud. Blamers have an internal feeling of tightness in the muscles and chest; their eyes may bulge, tendons in their necks may stand out, and their nostrils may flare. Blamers fail to listen or to try to understand what other people are attempting to express. They also are likely to ride roughshod over other people's feelings. Their attitude tends to be that the best defense is a good attack. Blamers tend to use authoritarian resolution to resolve a conflict (Satir 1972).

Placating   Placaters are the opposite of blamers; they try to ingratiate, please, or apologize, and they never disagree no matter how great the provocation. Placaters' voices tend to be whiny or squeaky. Placaters never achieve what they really want because they say "yes" to every proposal despite their true thoughts or feelings. As a result, there is little possibility of a satisfying mutual interaction within a couple when one is a consistent placater. Placaters tend to use permissive acceptance or passive aggression to resolve conflicts (Satir 1972).

Distracting   Distracters never make simple straightforward responses; instead they either say something irrelevant to what the other person is saying (a non sequitur) or ignore what is being said by doing something like failing to reply, walking away, or turning to speak to a pet. (Being totally ignored by a person who is talking to a parakeet lowers one's self-esteem very effectively.)

Distracters often win an argument by simply shifting the discussion to a new topic. A perfect example of this strategy can be found in the comic strip "Peanuts": After Charlie Brown effectively disputed Lucy's statement that "the number of stars in the sky is the same as the number of leaves on a tree," Lucy looked at Charlie very intently and said, "You sure have a funny-shaped head." Distracters tend to use evasion to resolve conflicts (Satir 1972).

Computing   Computers are very reasonable, logical, and rational, with completely controlled emotions and correct demeanor. Computers' voices are often dry monotones as they coolly analyze a situation and express their convictions in abstract terms and concepts. Computers think it is important to say the right words, to show no feelings, and to avoid any emotional reaction. They fail to come to grips with a conflict by ignoring the feelings of the other person and by not listening to the total meaning of what is being communicated. They reduce any discussion to an abstract analysis, leaving the other person frustrated and angry, defeated and helpless — and with the sense that somehow or other the real point has been missed (Satir 1972).

The Destructive Consequences of Conflict

Having a conflict remain unresolved is usually very damaging to a couple's relationship, for it results in feelings of frustration, rejection, and betrayal and in lowered self-esteem. The issues surrounding the original conflict are then often *displaced* to other issues involving less important conflicts, the outcomes of which will not be so damaging to the self-esteem of the person who feels betrayed. A pattern of psychological game playing between the two people may then emerge, followed by a breakdown of effective communication. In the sections that follow we will examine five destructive consequences of conflict: frustration, rejection and betrayal, lowered self-esteem, displacement, and psychological games.

Frustration

Frustration is the emotion that is experienced when an important need is being blocked or when an important satisfaction is being denied. The most obvious result of a conflict within a couple is the frustration experienced by both people in the relationship (but felt especially keenly by the person who feels most deprived in the situation). Of course, if a conflict is not resolved satisfactorily, both people may feel deprived by some aspect of the situation.

One example of a situation that can cause frustration occurs when one person wishes to have sex and the other person refuses. Although the person who has been denied sex may feel frustrated, the other person may also feel frustrated for different reasons. Suppose a woman is denying sexual satisfaction to a man. Perhaps she wants affection or companionship but not sex, or perhaps she simply wants to read, watch television, or go to sleep. If she does respond sexually to his entreaties, then *her* needs will be frustrated. Human interaction is very complex, and two people may perceive the same situation quite differently. In this situation, the man in effect is saying, "I need sex and you are denying me," while the woman is saying, "What about my needs? Aren't they just as important as yours?"

This, of course, is a classic conflict. If the needs of both people coincide — if both want sex at the same time or both want to go to sleep or watch television at the same time — then there is no conflict.

An excellent illustration of the development of this type of situation occurs in a very perceptive passage in John Updike's novel *Rabbit, Run* (1960). A young husband wants to have sex with his wife and has been waiting to do so with increasing tension (and deprivation) throughout a long Sunday afternoon:

> His wish to make love to Janice is like a small angel to which all afternoon tiny lead weights are attached. . . . He has come home from church carrying something precious for Janice and keeps being screened from giving it to her. . . . [T]hey blunder about restlessly through the wreckage of the Sunday paper. . . . Rabbit, hoping to possess her eventually, hovers near her like a miser near treasure. His lust glues them together. When they are finally in bed together she refuses his advances.
>
> "Harry, don't you know I want to go to sleep?"
>
> "Well, why didn't you tell me before?"
>
> "I didn't know. I didn't know."
>
> "You didn't know what?"
>
> "I didn't know what you were doing. I thought you were just being nice."
>
> "So this isn't nice."
>
> "Well, it's not nice when I can't *do* anything."
>
> "You can do *something*."
>
> "No I can't. Even if I wasn't all tired and confused from Rebecca's crying all day I can't. Not for six weeks. You know that."
>
> "Yeah, I know, but I thought . . ." He's terribly embarrassed.
>
> "*What* did you think?"
>
> "I thought you might love me anyway."
>
> After a pause she says, "I *do* love you."[3]

Janice's lack of understanding and awareness, or her deliberate misinterpretation of his need, leaves Rabbit with overwhelming feelings of vulnerability and frustration; he used the word "love" as a code for "have sex with" — she chooses to interpret it literally as "love."

From Janice's point of view, she is still recovering from a pregnancy and childbirth, and the baby's crying and fussing have left her tired and confused. She is physically and emotionally exhausted and is certainly not in the mood for sex. She is being frustrated in her need for understanding, for peace, and for not being pressured. Rabbit, of course, understands this but

---

[3]John Updike. *Rabbit, Run*. New York: Knopf, 1960. Reprinted by permission of the publisher, Alfred A. Knopf, Inc.

feels deeply rejected because his wife will not respond to his sexual advances.

With such basic forces involved — powerful, primitive forces that a couple deny at their peril — conflicts can lead to disintegration of the relationship unless successfully resolved. (Updike's Rabbit and Janice separated.)

Rejection and Betrayal

A significant aspect of Rabbit's feelings is his perception of being rejected or betrayed. In a couple's intimate interactions, a conflict involving a basic need is often followed by feelings of *rejection*, and because emotional involvement with another person usually involves lowering the defenses we normally keep in place, rejection by the other person is often perceived as *betrayal*. We drop our defenses and leave ourselves vulnerable because we trust the other person not to reject us; if rejection then takes place, we feel that our trust has been betrayed. In fact, rejection by an intimate we trust and on whom we rely is the ultimate betrayal: "the most unkindest cut of all" (Shakespeare, *Julius Caesar*, act 3, scene 2).

A person who feels rejected will then usually either counterattack or withdraw. The rejected person who counterattacks, whether verbally or physically, is attacking the source of the pain (the other person). Or the rejected person may simply withdraw, either physically (such as leaving the house) or psychologically (such as withdrawing into apathy or dejection). Often, of course, a person may do both, counterattacking and then withdrawing, or withdrawing first and then returning to attack.

Lowered Self-Esteem

A perceived attack or rejection by a person we trust also has the very significant effect of low-

ering our self-esteem. One's self-esteem is especially vulnerable to an attack or rejection by the other person in a couple. When one person in a couple lowers the self-esteem of the other in this way, the effects on the couple's relationship are often devastating.

In any couple, almost everything one person says or does either raises or lowers the self-esteem of the other. Any attack or perceived rejection or indifference on the part of one person in a couple will lower the other person's self-esteem. A response that interrupts the other person or serves as a way of ignoring something the other person has said will lower self-esteem, as will responses that miss the point, reject the statement, or contradict the other person. In addition, a *non*response, such as walking away or starting a noisy task (such as running the dishwasher, the vacuum cleaner, or a power drill), may also be perceived as an attack and may lower the other person's self-esteem. On the other hand, responses that are understanding, accepting, sympathetic, and perceptive help to enhance self-esteem, promote harmony within the couple, and bring closeness and increased intimacy.

In a successful couple, each person supports and raises the self-esteem of the other most of the time. When one person's self-esteem is injured during a quarrel, the other will usually attempt to repair the damage as soon as possible. After the initial anger or dejection has worn off, each person will try to put the relationship back on a mutually supportive basis. When they do not do this, the couple's relationship may be seriously threatened.

Displacement

When the frustration that arises from an unresolved conflict lowers our self-esteem, we may unconsciously *displace* our feelings from the real cause of the deprivation (the genuine or underlying conflict) to a more convenient or safer disagreement. Suppose, for example, that a conflict arises over which television program to watch. One person wants to watch "Nightline," but the other wants to watch "The Arsenio Hall Show." If either insists on tuning the television to the program he or she prefers, the other will be frustrated and may even become verbally abusive. A quarrel may then ensue that escalates and spreads to other grievances ("Why do you always . . . ?"). It is quite possible that the real source of the frustration is not the conflict over which television program to watch, but rather a conflict in which one person or the other is experiencing, say, sexual frustration. As we have seen, such conflicts are very complex and are often displaced to "safer" conflicts. The danger of putting one's vulnerable self-image at risk is thus minimized or avoided — as is the threat of significant rejection — if the conflict is displaced to the relatively minor disagreement over choice of a television program.

Displacement very often explains the surprising emotionalism that two people can exhibit in quarrels that are in and of themselves of little consequence. When displacement occurs, the couple often cannot remember the reason for their quarrel a day or two later because the apparent reason was not the real reason for the conflict.

Psychological Games

When one person in a conflict seeks to inflict a loss on the other — to establish a "winner" and a "loser" — the couple has entered a pattern of interaction that may be considered a psychological game (Berne 1967). A *psychological game* is an interaction in which each person in a conflict attacks the other — attempts to score a "win" — instead of confronting the underlying conflict. It

is called a *psychological* game because, unlike a normal game, the fact that a game is being played is not acknowledged. A psychological game is covert (hidden) and devious (not honest) and is thus a perversion of the openness and honesty of a traditional game, in which the competition, the rules of play, and the methods of scoring a win or inflicting a loss are frankly acknowledged. Much of the satisfaction of a traditional game lies in this open acknowledgement of competition channeled into a culturally acceptable and limited form.

When two friends, companions, or intimates find themselves in a situation in which deprivation for one means satisfaction for the other and are unable to resolve this conflict in a way that provides satisfaction for both, they may unconsciously begin to attack each other as an expression of frustration. This is a psychological game.

Put another way, a psychological game occurs when one person feels resentment toward someone else, is unable to express the resentment openly, and tries to restore his or her feelings of control by making a "move" that tends to demean or "defeat" the other person. The reason psychological games occur is that open aggression in competing for a limited resource is not culturally acceptable among friends, companions, or intimates. The psychological game is a disguised form of such competition.

The results of a psychological game can be very destructive. Because the "players" lose sight of the conflict that originated the psychological game, the possibility of resolving this conflict is virtually destroyed. In addition, playing a psychological game tends to drive people apart rather than bringing them together. The ostensible "winner" in the game may obtain a sense of satisfaction by achieving "victory" in the exchange of charges and countercharges that constitutes the moves of the game, but he or she loses the satisfaction derived from the mutual caring that characterizes a harmonious, non-game-playing interaction. The "loser," of course, is left with no satisfaction and is thus often bitter, resentful, and vengeful; the strength of these negative emotions is in proportion to the significance of the satisfaction at stake in the underlying conflict.

A psychological game may take the form of a direct attack, but never one over the issue under discussion. (One person might, for example, shift the focus of the discussion from the issue at hand to the personality of the other and then make a direct attack.) However, a move in a psychological game is more often an act of *attrition* (or withholding a satisfaction from the other) instead of a direct attack.

Acts of attrition are often accompanied by a plea for understanding, so that not only is satisfaction withheld, but sympathy is demanded as well. If the person being denied satisfaction is impatient, hostile, or abrupt, he or she may then be accused of callousness or selfishness ("You don't care how *I* feel; you just want your own way"). The deprived person is thus caught in a no-win situation.

Although withholding a satisfaction from another person is a common practice in a psychological game, it is a very dangerous move. If attrition becomes a patterned response, the erosion of intimacy is often irreversible.

As long as game playing remains peripheral to the main interaction of a couple, it may not be seriously damaging; it is, perhaps, even inevitable. The danger, however, is that the couple may move further and further into a pattern of game-playing interaction, until the chief preoccupation of each becomes the struggle for dominance and the covert scoring of "points" in the unconscious game that they are playing.

In short, a psychological game almost completely disregards the goal of *solving* the problem underlying a conflict. Instead, it emphasizes continuing competition to defeat or demean the other person. Not only is the basic conflict unacknowledged (and therefore unresolvable), but the game-playing strategy itself erodes trust, honesty, and intimacy. Psychological game playing is thus especially counterproductive. An intimate relationship cannot be happy and rewarding if the two people involved characteristically play psychological games with each other.

It seems very clear, then, that it is extremely important to understand the pattern of game playing. If you know you are playing a game, you can stop it. You can detect that you are playing a psychological game if you sense that something is less than candid. You may then ask yourself, "What is it that I am trying to accomplish?" "Is my activity honestly involved with achieving a solution to a problem?" "What is the real problem?" "Am I trying to defeat the other person rather than trying to find a mutually acceptable solution to the conflict?"

Asking such questions may provide sufficient insight to allow you to simply stop playing the psychological game. You are then restored to a measure of freedom that will allow candid and open examination of the problem: What really is the conflict? Who is being deprived, and of what exactly? Who is being satisfied, and in what way? How can the conflict be resolved to the mutual benefit of each person — without creating a "winner" and a "loser"?

Berne (1967) points out that all of us attack one another instead of attacking the conflict. Becoming aware of this increases the likelihood that we instead can relate to others openly, honestly, and candidly more of the time and can attack problems instead of other people. Obviously, the more often our behavior is characterized by attacking problems and achieving goals instead of playing psychological games, the richer and the more rewarding our relationships will become.

Examples of Ineffective Communication

Psychological game playing is almost inevitably accompanied by a breakdown of effective communication. Ironically, this breakdown often occurs at the very time that effective communication is most important (see Box 11-3).

A major purpose of communication is to achieve mutual understanding of each other's point of view so that a conflict can be resolved. A breakdown of communication furthers misunderstanding rather than understanding, so that the conflict is worsened rather than resolved, and the faulty communication becomes counterproductive instead of productive, increasing the couple's differences instead of resolving them.

If an ineffective pattern of communication can be identified and acknowledged, the likelihood is increased that it can be interrupted and perhaps stopped. Once stopped, the chances are then improved that the pattern of ineffective communication can be replaced by a pattern of effective and productive communication.

There are, of course, innumerable patterns of ineffective, counterproductive communication. In the following sections we will examine some of the most commonly used and most pernicious types of ineffective communication.

Mind Reading

Mind reading is an especially maddening form of ineffective communication because it makes an open discussion of a conflict virtually impossible. "Mind readers" assume they know what the other person is thinking and feeling, and they respond only to these assumptions rather than to what the other person really thinks and feels. An inveterate mind reader believes that he or she knows more about the other person's innermost feelings, thoughts, and intentions than the other person does. Chronic mind readers are so unshakable in this conviction that it is not unusual for them to contradict a statement made by the other person about his or her own feelings ("I know you don't really feel that way"). As long as a person continues mind reading, rather than trying to hear, understand, accept, and respond to what the other person is actually saying, it is virtually impossible to establish good communication.

Sending Double Messages

When two people in a couple no longer communicate openly and directly with each other, double messages often emerge. A *double message* is one that is contradictory or has two meanings that contradict each other. Double messages put the receiver in a "double bind," for he or she does not know which meaning to respond to and thus feels confused, uncomfortable, and irritated and is likely to respond defensively or aggressively.

Sarcasm, for example, often puts out a double message by attacking the other person in an ostensibly friendly way that seems to send a supportive message. Thus a person is sending a double message if he or she says, "You were really the life of the party tonight" in a sarcastic tone of voice. The other person may resent the critical aspect of the message and may respond by asking, "Why do you say that?" The reply, asked with apparent innocence, might well be something like, "What did I say?" Then the stage is set for a series of charges and countercharges in which communication becomes progressively ineffective.

Another way of sending a double message is to contradict a verbal statement with body language — for example, saying, "That's very interesting" while yawning, or saying, "Please

BOX 11-3

Seven Easy Steps to Total Misery

It is easy to have a conflict-ridden, unhappy family characterized by poor communication and the playing of psychological games. Little (1977) has formulated the following seven steps, which, when faithfully followed, are guaranteed to transform a relatively straightforward and readily resolvable conflict into one of monumental proportions, producing in the process a household filled with distress, unhappiness, and even anguish.

- *Snowballing.* One excellent technique for creating problems is to let them snowball. The best snowballers practice a simple rule: When it is past time to do something about a problem, wait a little longer. In marriage, for example, refuse to acknowledge a conflict and bury the resultant feelings of frustration and annoyance until they build up enough pressure to blow your marriage apart. After all, facing a conflict when it first appears and taking realistic steps to resolve it is usually successful. But if you let the conflict become firmly established, it can become a part of your life-style.

- *Negative Focus.* To become an expert in this technique, simply dwell on the times when you were treated unfairly or when someone spoke unkindly to you. Say to yourself, "I am always misunderstood and mistreated by everyone." Beware the intrusion of happy thoughts; if you should think something good about yourself, quickly recall a corresponding weakness and focus on it. You can quickly and reliably transform happiness into anxiety and depression by the skillful use of negative thinking.

- *The I-Told-Me-So Syndrome.* This syndrome simply formalizes the concept that if you expect bad things to happen, they are much more likely to happen. For example, if you are about to join your spouse for dinner, predict that it will be a terrible meal. If you are going to a party together, predict that you will have a miserable time. At the party, remain aloof from others, and complain on the way home that no one would have anything to do with you.

- *Dream the Impossible Dream.* If you want to be truly frustrated, set your goals way beyond your reach and then blame yourself for your failure to achieve them. Never be satisfied; be an "underacceptant overachiever." Then, whatever successes may come your way will be tinged with sadness and overtones of frustration. For example, if you live in a comfortable three-bedroom house, tell yourself that you won't be satisfied until you have a six-bedroom house with a gourmet kitchen, a walk-in pantry, a living room with two fireplaces, a billiards room, and an indoor-outdoor Olympic-size swimming pool — all set on at least three acres of wooded land overlooking a beach.

- *The Fool's Golden Rule.* It is easy to practice the fool's golden rule. Simply reverse the Golden Rule — do unto others as you would have them do unto you — and take advantage of others whenever possible. Treat them as contemptible, craven incompetents. Then take the important step of applying this rule to yourself. Say, "I'm no good. I have no value." Once you have lowered your self-esteem sufficiently, rejection, loneliness, and misery will soon follow. This is truly an excellent technique that can't be recommended too highly.

- *Barrier Building.* If you find that your familial interaction has been producing increasing understanding, harmony, satisfaction, and contentment, then two general principles, consistently applied, will soon restore virtually impenetrable barriers to effective communication. First, avoid all encouraging remarks, and never compliment others. Second, increase the criticism: nag, complain, and belittle. Tell the children that "As long as you live under my roof and eat my food, you will do as I say." Their resentment will soon build into a satisfying generation gap.

- *Martyrdom.* No program of problem production would be complete without the crowning achievement of martyrdom. This puts the final touch on a towering edifice of conflict, strife, and discontent, with everyone working at cross-purposes. Say "No one really cares about me. As far as my family is concerned I'm just a slave. I work my fingers to the bone without any appreciation. I never have any time for myself. Everyone uses me." Chronic, progressive martyrdom is not only useful in generating bad feelings about yourself; it also disgusts the people around you, which enables you to feel even worse.

These seven steps, especially used in conjunction, will lower your self-image, drive away your friends, and quickly achieve a total collapse of your marriage (Little 1977).

tell me more about that" while starting a noisy appliance.

Gunnysacking

Gunnysacking is a term for storing past grievances and bringing them up for review while trying to resolve a present conflict (Bach and Wyden 1970). Gunnysacking not only fails to focus on the specific issue underlying the conflict (thus preventing it from being resolved), but it also tends to feed on itself by creating new grievances that are then stored as well. In consequence, the gunnysack bulges with so many past grievances and lingering grudges that the two people become immersed in a morass of ancient resentments and current conflicts. As each new confrontation is crammed into the gunnysack to be subsequently retrieved and reviewed along with all its predecessors, the satisfactions that each person provides for the other are increasingly diminished while the pleasures that each initially enjoyed may become faded memories that are only occasionally recalled with nostalgia.

Stereotyping

Stereotyping avoids the issue that underlies a conflict by placing the other person in a category or assigning him or her a label. A stereotyper then deals with the category or the label, never with the real person. This behavior not only avoids the basic issue of the conflict but also dehumanizes the other person. Stereotyping focuses on preconceived ideas rather than on the reality of the present interaction, especially when it is combined — as it often is — with mind reading.

For example, the charge "You're a very cruel person" is a nonproductive use of a label. The person so categorized is liable to either retaliate aggressively or to withdraw, thus enlarging the conflict while the initial issue of the conflict

becomes blurred, obscured, and perhaps completely lost.

Using "You" Statements

Sentences that start with "You" are perfectly acceptable in most situations ("You look very beautiful tonight"). However, when two people are discussing a conflict, a "you" statement is almost always analytical, critical, or hostile and may be counted on to provoke a hostile or defensive response. "You always want to have your own way" and "You never listen to what I have to say" are examples of statements often heard in arguments. These "you" statements are also examples of stereotyping and gunnysacking that are virtually guaranteed to bring about either a defensive response or an attack while the basic conflict is left unresolved and the two people expand the extent of their misunderstanding and hostility.

A statement that focuses on the issue at hand, rather than on the personality of the other person, is much more likely to lead to effective communication.

Using "Why" Questions

In a nonconflict situation, questions that begin with "Why" are perfectly acceptable and may lead to intriguing speculation and creative thought. However, like "you" statements, "why" questions are almost invariably counterproductive when the discussion involves a conflict.

"Why" questions not only challenge the other person — and so are likely to provoke either a defensive or a hostile response — but are counterproductive in that they move the discussion into an artificial analysis rather than dealing with the immediacy of present feelings. For example, the question "Why do you always act like I'm the one to blame?" is an invitation for gunnysacking and mind reading and lays the groundwork for round after round of charges and countercharges.

Thus the question "Why did you burn the toast?" is much more likely to bring a defensive response than the simple statement "This toast is burned" or the polite question "May I have another piece of toast?" Openly expressing one's feelings, wants, and desires enables the other person to deal with them nondefensively, candidly, and specifically.

Using "Yes, but" Sentences

In a conflict situation, any sentence that begins with "Yes, but" is likely to be perceived as argumentative and produce either a defensive or an attacking response from the other person. Like "you" statements and "why" questions, "Yes, but" sentences are a tip-off that the confrontation is disintegrating from good communication to a pattern of defense, attack, and counterattack.

Because no one consciously or deliberately wishes to engage in counterproductive, ineffective communication, being aware of one's choice of words can be very helpful. If you hear yourself saying, "Yes, but . . ." and know what it means, you can remind yourself to question your own motives and intentions: Is what you are about to say going to be a productive step in confronting the problem underlying the conflict? Or will it simply move the discussion further in the direction of attacking the other person while justifying your own actions?

The Constructive Resolution of Conflicts

Happily, there is more than one way of responding to a conflict. It is possible for a response to a conflict to be constructive. A constructive resolution to a conflict does not establish a winner or a loser, does not demean or lower one or the other's self-esteem, and does not destroy effective or productive communication. On the contrary, a constructive resolution of a conflict increases the couple's understanding and builds a more harmonious relationship that increasingly yields mutual and reciprocal satisfaction to each of them. In the following sections we will examine some of the key concepts involved both in maintaining effective communication and constructively resolving the conflicts that inevitably come up with couples.

Attacking the Conflict

A conflict cannot be resolved productively until each person in the relationship acknowledges its existence, identifies it precisely, and actively cooperates in trying to resolve it without creating a winner and a loser.

It is important to attack the conflict itself, not the other person, because scoring a "win" over the other will not only fail to resolve a conflict productively but will also sow the seeds of further conflict. In an intimate relationship the winner is likely to wear the laurels of victory uneasily (because the "win" is over someone who is cared for) while the loser is likely to resent being put down by someone who was trusted.

In order to attack the conflict itself, it is necessary to be able to state precisely what the conflict is about. What is the source of the conflict? Who is dissatisfied or deprived in the conflict, and who is being satisfied? What mutually satisfying solutions might be explored? The issues explored by these questions are the topics of the next three sections.

Identifying the Source of Conflict   To identify the real source of the conflict, the couple must address the questions "What are we really quarreling about?" and "What is the real source of our disagreement?" When couples do not address or cannot answer these questions, the quarrel is often displaced to another topic ("And another thing: Why do you always . . . ?").

It is essential that each person put into words the true basis of the conflict. It is also essential that once the conflict has been clearly identified, the couple focus on this one issue and refrain from trying to deal with more than one conflict at a time. Although in actual practice it is often difficult for couples to avoid bringing in other issues, it is essential to isolate the conflict in order to identify any instances of displacement and postpone resolving them until a later time.

Identifying Satisfaction and Deprivation A conflict cannot be clearly identified until both people can state with mutual agreement who is receiving what satisfaction and who is being deprived of what satisfaction. These statements should include the precise nature of the satisfaction and the deprivation being experienced. Once the precise natures of satisfactions and deprivations have been identified, it becomes possible to seek solutions.

Identifying Mutually Satisfactory Solutions The ideal solution to any conflict, of course, is one that brings satisfaction to both people and leaves no one deprived at the expense of the other.

Usually a compromise solution can be found, one that to some acceptable degree satisfies each of the couple. Occasionally a compromise is not possible, and the couple may simply have to agree to disagree. However, if each is clear about what they are disagreeing about, they will probably be able to accept occasional disagreements without jeopardizing the overall harmony of their relationship.

Using Divergent Feedback

Feedback is information we receive about the effects of our behavior. *Convergent feedback* is in-

formation that indicates that our behavior is bringing the desired effect; *divergent feedback* is information that indicates that our behavior is *not* bringing the desired effect (see Box 11-4).

Consider what happens, for example, when you jump into a swimming pool on a hot day: The water feels good. The information that it is "good" to jump into a swimming pool on a hot day is received by (is fed back to) your brain as convergent feedback. Thus you might continue to jump into swimming pools on hot days to continue receiving this convergent feedback of feeling good.

On the other hand, if you had tried to jump into a swimming pool when the water had been drained out, you would have received a painful shock, and the information that it is "bad" to jump into empty swimming pools would be received by (fed back to) your brain as divergent feedback. No matter how much you wanted to cool off, you would probably not jump into such a pool again (because you prefer to avoid the divergent feedback of pain). Similarly, you learn to eat nuts (an action followed by convergent feedback) but not to eat rocks (an action followed by divergent feedback).

People's responses to physical feedback are usually reasonable, rational, and sensible, so that they shape their actions to avoid or limit divergent feedback and to obtain convergent feedback. People's responses to social feedback (responses from other people) are often paradoxical, however. Thus upon receiving divergent feedback about something you have done, instead of simply using the divergent feedback as information you may become angry, upset, and resentful or depressed, sad, and withdrawn.

Social feedback, of course, is often incomplete, difficult to interpret, or delayed, whereas physical feedback is usually clear and often immediate. Moreover, physical objects can usually be depended on not to change. A typist knows to expect the convergent feedback of a correctly typed page if he or she strikes the correct keys. In relationships, however, a person may at different times get either convergent or divergent feedback from exactly the same behavior. A sexual advance, for example, may be warmly received at one time but impatiently rebuffed at another.

Even though interpreting social feedback is often more difficult than interpreting physical feedback, the same basic principles apply. Moreover, the problems a couple may encounter if they do not use divergent feedback effectively may lead to serious difficulties in resolving conflicts and may eventually contribute to creating an unhappy and disharmonious relationship. On the other hand, when used effectively divergent feedback can be an enormously effective tool in resolving conflict.

Instead of responding to divergent feedback by becoming angry or hurt and then either attacking the other person or withdrawing (so that the conflict is left unresolved), it is logical to change your behavior so that it will bring convergent feedback. People will often respond negatively if they feel overwhelmed by frustration, rejection, self-devaluation, or betrayal. Then instead of making attempts to obtain convergent feedback, which might help resolve the conflict, an explosion of anger or withdrawal into sullen silence may simply bring about more divergent feedback. If this feedback is interpreted as further evidence that the other person is being unreasonable, then resentment, a sense of betrayal, and feelings of rejection may increase so that the couple are caught in a descending spiral that steadily worsens their relationship.

In such a disintegrating relationship, each of the couple usually becomes progressively less willing to use divergent feedback effectively, and in consequence the intimacy of the couple is persistently eroded away.

If one person (Jack) attempts to obtain convergent feedback by making an overture of recon-ciliation, the other person (Jill) may not accept it. Although the dynamics involved in refusing to accept such an approach are very complex, Jill is in effect saying something like, "I'm not ready to make up yet. I'm not through being hurt. I still feel wronged and I feel that you are not being contrite enough or haven't been punished enough for injuring me." Jack may feel rejected in turn and thus may refuse Jill's approach to reconciliation when she is ready to offer one. Again, the dynamics involved are very complex, but Jack's refusal is in effect saying, "When I offered to make up, you weren't ready. Now that you are ready, you think that makes everything all right. Well, have I got news for you!"

This scenario of alternating approach and rejection might be replayed several times: The first person makes an overture, the second person rejects it; then the second person makes an overture and the first person rejects it. This pattern may continue for hours or even days; it will not be interrupted until both people are ready to seek convergent feedback (or reconciliation) at the same time. They are then ready to seek a solution that will resolve the conflict to their mutual satisfaction.

This pattern of alternating approach and rejection is characteristic of all couples, whether dating, cohabiting, or married, but it usually doesn't persist long in dating couples because they are likely either to seek mutual reconciliation relatively quickly or simply stop dating. Cohabiting and married couples are bound together by more ties than are dating couples and so are likely willing to endure more and longer periods of alternating approach and rejection.

Practicing Leveling with Others

The opposite of playing a psychological game is to level with the other person. *Leveling* is defined by Virginia Satir (1972) as saying, to the best of your ability, what you think, what you mean, and

BOX 11-4

Physical and Social Feedback

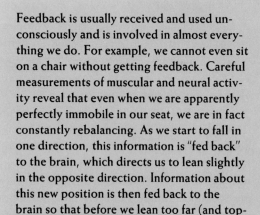

Feedback is usually received and used unconsciously and is involved in almost everything we do. For example, we cannot even sit on a chair without getting feedback. Careful measurements of muscular and neural activity reveal that even when we are apparently perfectly immobile in our seat, we are in fact constantly rebalancing. As we start to fall in one direction, this information is "fed back" to the brain, which directs us to lean slightly in the opposite direction. Information about this new position is then fed back to the brain so that before we lean too far (and topple over) we may again correct the balance and lean back toward the first position. As a result of this constant feedback and rebal-

ancing we are able to remain seated upright on the chair. A golfer hitting a golf ball also uses feedback in the same way, in this case to correct her stroke so that she can hit the ball down the center of the fairway. With practice at modifying her swing, the ball will fly straight and true toward the pin. These are both examples of the use of *physical* feedback.

When we relate to another person, we are using *social* feedback. We use social feedback for the same purpose as we use physical feedback: to adjust to a changing situation. However, social feedback is more difficult to interpret, and our emotions more often get in the way of using feedback effec-

how you feel. When the inevitable conflict occurs, levelers try to be aware of the real nature of the conflict—who is receiving satisfaction and who is being deprived of it. They neither withdraw from the situation nor attack the other person; instead, they address the underlying conflict without becoming defensive or hostile. They relate to each other in an open, nondefensive, and nonhostile way. Because levelers are usually able to recognize and address the issues underlying a conflict, they are much more likely to resolve it. And because they are more likely to resolve each conflict as it occurs, their relationship has a very good chance of remaining essentially harmonious.

Levelers also avoid falling into a pattern of nonproductive or counterproductive communication and avoid psychological game playing by being open and honest and acting with integrity. According to Satir's research, leveling is the only type of communication that makes it possible for a couple to relate to each other with harmony and mutual self-enhancement.

Practicing Active Listening

Another important ingredient of relating honestly and effectively to another person is to *listen actively* to what the other person is saying—listening with your whole attention focused on

tively. (Although we may get angry at the golf ball or the golf club if the ball's flight is disappointing, we are more likely to become angry with a person who does not respond as we wish.) Moreover, physical feedback is usually consistent (unchanging), whereas social feedback is not. A person may be inconsistent — may react quite differently to the same behavior at different times.

In addition to varying from time to time and from place to place, social feedback may be ambiguous or difficult to interpret, whereas physical feedback is usually clear. Feedback that is consistent and unambiguous (clear) is called *free feedback*. Feedback that is inconsistent and ambiguous and is therefore difficult to interpret is called *limited feedback*.

Feedback may also be *immediate* or *delayed*. A gardener who steps on the tines of a rake so that the handle swings up and hits her in the face is receiving immediate feedback that is also consistent and clear. She may easily use this physical feedback to avoid being hit in the face in this way again; she simply avoids stepping on the rake the next time one is lying in her path.

In the physical world, feedback is usually free and immediate. (Physical feedback is not always free and immediate, of course; thus it is difficult to drive in a heavy fog.) However, in the social world of relating to other people, feedback is usually limited and is often delayed (while we wait for a letter or for a phone call to be returned). Thus, a husband who perceived himself as being very witty at the party may find on the way home that he has been misinterpreting his wife's smile. Upon her delayed explosion of impatience on the drive home, he is at last able to accurately process the information (feedback) that, in her perception, he was making a fool of himself.

trying to hear and understand what the other person is trying to say:

> Listen with hungry earnest attention to every word. In the intensity of your attention, make little nods of agreement, little sounds of approval. You can't fake it. You have to really listen. . . . A good listener is far more rare than an adequate lover. (MacDonald 1964, p. 25)

Active listeners listen wholly, completely, and fully. They do not think about what they are going to say in rebuttal while the other person is talking, they do not wait impatiently for a chance to present their own views and argu-

ments, and they do not interrupt. Active listeners respond nondefensively and nonaggressively to what the other person is saying. They have a distinctive ability to make the other person feel especially valued and to feel that what he or she is saying is of significance and concern. By listening actively — intent on every word and gesture and wholly absorbed in what is being said — active listeners help build the speaker's self-esteem enormously.

Active listeners are also attentive to *nonverbal* communication. Nonverbal communication, or "body language," is often a very important part of a speaker's message. In fact, researchers have found that when people are expressing emotions, more than 90 percent of the information is communicated by tone of voice, facial expression, eye contact, gestures, body attitudes, and other nonverbal factors (Mehrabian 1971).

People who are listened to actively are more likely to become active listeners themselves. A good conversation consists of two active listeners alternately responding to each other and trying to understand what each is conveying. When this happens, the conversation builds; each person alternately contributes to and is then drawn along by the conversation. Ideas that were only dimly perceived emerge into a full clarity of expression during this conversational interaction. When leveling is combined with active listening, the two together embody the fundamentals of good communication (see Figure 11-1).

Role Taking

A very effective (yet relatively simple) technique for resolving a conflict—even a very serious one—is called *role taking*. Not only is role taking extraordinarily effective in clearing up patterns of ineffective communication and resolving conflicts, but it also helps to increase each person's understanding of both himself or herself and the other person.

In role taking, each person agrees to cooperate with the other in identifying, mutually acknowledging, and then attempting to resolve the conflict in question without creating a winner and a loser. Role taking consists of the following four steps:

1. Jill (in this case) states her point of view as fully and completely as she can, identifying the conflict as she sees it, exploring both its emotional content (her feelings of rage, frustration, helplessness, or whatever) and its logical and rational content. She must be allowed to continue without being interrupted and must stick to the point of this specific conflict (to avoid the problem of gunnysacking; any topic not specifically related to the current problem must be declared out of bounds, immediately dropped, and deferred until a later time, when it can be the subject of a different role-taking discussion). While Jill is talking, Jack (in this case) must listen and try to understand her point of view. He must not interrupt, except to ask for clarification ("Is this what you are saying?"). Jill should continue until she feels that her feelings and thoughts regarding the conflict have been stated to her complete satisfaction.

2. Jack then must restate what Jill has said, identifying with her feelings as fully as possible. If he misinterprets or misses the point about something that she said, Jill must politely interrupt and say, "No, that's not what I meant," and then restate what she meant. This second step continues until Jack has stated her feelings and thoughts about the conflict to her satisfaction. With practice, a person can become more and more skilled in listening without interrupting and in learning to understand precisely what a situation means to the other person.

3. Jack now has his turn in expressing his thoughts and feelings about the specific conflict under question. The rules stated in step 1 apply here as well.

4. Jill then restates, to Jack's satisfaction, what he has said, according to the rules in step 2.

This process is extraordinarily effective in helping a couple understand each other. Each

Leveling + Active Listening ⟶ Good Communication

FIGURE 11-1
The fundamentals of good communication.

PART IV ✤ CONFLICT, DIVORCE, AND REMARRIAGE

TABLE 11-1

A List of Items That Are Important to Couples for Use in Rating Their Levels of Satisfaction

The following is a list of ten important ingredients of a successful marriage. Each of the items may be rated on a scale from 0 to 10, with 0 representing a very low rating and 10 representing a very high, or ideal, rating.

If each person rates the items independently, the couple may compare their ratings and discover areas of dissatisfaction.

1. common goals and values
2. commitment to growth
3. communication skills
4. creative use of conflict
5. appreciation and affection

6. agreement on gender roles
7. cooperation and teamwork
8. sexual fulfillment
9. money management
10. parental effectiveness

Source: Adapted from Mace and Mace (1978).

will have a much clearer understanding of both's points of view. Moreover, relating in this way is an extremely effective exercise in building understanding and intimacy—the opposite of trying to dominate the other person or trying to lower the other's self-esteem. The couple can now reexamine the conflict to see what points of agreement (if any) are present. (Given the understanding of each other's point of view, they can usually find many points of agreement.) Any remaining disagreements are now isolated and can be examined to see whether these problems can be resolved to the couple's mutual satisfaction. If they can't, the couple can agree to disagree over this specific issue, leaving other areas of their relationship untouched by the potentially corrosive influence of a single conflict. Once a couple becomes skilled in the process of role taking, they may often relate to each other in this way habitually, settling minor conflicts and disagreements as they arise and before they can escalate or be displaced.

Comparing Mutual Goals

Another technique that couples can use to resolve conflict is rating their levels of satisfaction (Mace and Mace 1978). This method consists of two steps.

In the first step, each of the couple separately makes a list of ten areas that are important to their relationship. They then compare their lists and agree on a final list of ten items that together they consider to be crucial. (For an example of the items such a list might contain, see Table 11-1.)

Each person then independently rates each item on the list on a scale of 0 (very low) to 10 (very high, or ideal) to represent his or her feelings about that item, taking as long as necessary. A rating of 0, 1, or 2 for "appreciation and affection," for example, would mean that the person feels a great lack of appreciation and is hungry for demonstrations of affection, whereas a rating of 8, 9, or 10 would mean that the person feels that the other rarely misses an opportunity to communicate feelings of affection, tenderness, and love, or to lavish warmth and praise.

In the second step, the ratings on each list are totaled. If each has a high total rating (80–90), the couple have a remarkably idyllic relationship. If one of the couple has a high total rating while the other has a low total rating, the dissatisfactions of the person with the lower rating can be brought into the open, where they can be discussed and perhaps resolved. Even if both have relatively high total ratings, one or the other may have given one or more items a relatively low rating, revealing a low satisfaction level in this specific area. Such comparisons can be very helpful in revealing areas of difficulty. Once such difficulties have been pinpointed and acknowledged, they may be addressed, perhaps using the technique of role taking previously described. Greater understanding of each other's feelings is an important step in maintaining or reestablishing harmony in a relationship.

SUMMARY

A couple is in conflict when one person wants something that the other person does not; that is, the basis for conflict exists when one person's ability to obtain satisfaction means that the other will experience deprivation.

Conflict is inevitable in any relationship because it is simply not possible for two people always to want the same thing at the same time. The most frequent and most serious conflicts that cohabiting and married couples have are over money, work, and sex. These conflicts may either have destructive consequences that can destroy the couple's relationship or they may be handled constructively.

A persistent conflict can have very destructive consequences to a relationship, including feelings of frustration, rejection, betrayal, and lowered self-esteem. Issues surrounding the conflict are often displaced to other issues related to less important conflicts that will not be as damaging to the self-esteem of the person whose needs are not being met.

A couple involved in a persistent conflict will often play psychological games, overtly attacking each other instead of attacking the problem. Psychological games occur when one person feels resentment toward the other and tries to restore a feeling of control by attempting to "win" the game. The results of psychological games can be very destructive because each person may lose sight of the original conflict and become involved only in the attempt to defeat the other. Psychological games may take the form of a direct attack on the other person (but never over the issue under discussion) or the form of withholding satisfaction from the other person.

Psychological game playing is usually followed by a breakdown of effective communication. Typical examples of ineffective communication include mind reading, sending double messages, gunnysacking, stereotyping, using "You" statements, using "Why" questions, and using "Yes, but" sentences.

Common patterns of attack and defense used by a couple in a conflict are authoritarian resolution, permissive acceptance, passive aggression, and evasion. Ineffective communicators tend to use blaming, placating, distracting, or computing.

Conflicts can often be resolved constructively by practicing leveling with others instead of playing psychological games; by trying to communicate directly, honestly, openly, and nondefensively; and by listening and trying to understand what the other person is saying. Using leveling and active listening form the basis of good communication within a couple.

Instead of playing psychological games, it is important that a couple identify the source of the conflict and discover who is satisfied and who is deprived, so that they can then look for a mutually satisfying solution that will create neither a winner nor a loser. In doing this, it is important to use divergent feedback constructively rather than becoming angry or defensive.

One very effective technique for resolving a conflict is to listen to the grievances of the other person and then restate them to the other person's satisfaction. Once both the people in the conflict have done this, the process can be used to help them identify areas of agreement upon which they may build a resolution or compromise. Sometimes, however, couples have to agree to disagree on a particular issue.

Another effective technique is to have both people rate important areas of the relationship in terms of their level of satisfaction. Then the couple can compare their lists and use the results to identify specific problem areas in their relationship.

KEY TERMS

The following is a list of key terms in this chapter.
They are defined in context within the chapter, and many may also be found in the Glossary.

active listening

ambiguous

authoritarian resolution

barrier building

betrayal

blaming

body language

compromise

computing (in a conflict)

convergent feedback

coping ability

counterproductive

defense mechanism

defense-oriented behavior

deprivation

displaced aggression

displacement

distracting

divergent feedback

double messages

effective communication

evasion

extrapunitive behavior

fantasy

frustration

gunnysacking

impunitive behavior

individuation

ineffective communication

intrapunitive behavior

leveling (in interpersonal relations)

lowered self-esteem

martyrdom

mind reading (in a conflict)

negative focus

nonverbal communication

paradox

parameter

passive aggression

patterned response

permissive acceptance

psychological games

rationalization

reality-oriented behavior

reconciliation

rejection

role taking

self-fulfilling prophecy

snowballing

stereotyping

substitution

syndrome

withdrawal (in a conflict)

QUESTIONS

1. What is the basic definition of conflict within a couple?

2. What is meant by frustration? Describe an example of frustration stemming from a couple's conflict.

3. What is a psychological game? Describe a psychological game that a couple may play as a result of a conflict.

4. What is meant by mind reading? By gunny-sacking? By stereotyping?

5. What is meant by authoritarian resolution? By permissive acceptance? By passive aggression? By evasion?

6. What are the characteristics of the blamer? The placater? The distracter? The computer?

7. What is meant by leveling? By active listening?

8. Discuss the importance of using divergent feedback to resolve a conflict.

9. Describe the technique of role taking as a method of resolving a conflict.

10. Describe the technique of comparing mutual goals as a method of resolving a conflict.

SUGGESTIONS FOR FURTHER READING

Baron, R. *Understanding Human Relations*. Boston: Allyn & Bacon, 1992.

Brehm, S. *Intimate Relationships*, 2d ed. New York: Random House, 1990.

Carlson, J. G., and Hatfield, E. *The Psychology of Emotion*. New York: Harcourt Brace Jovanovich, 1991.

Fitzpatrick, Mary Anne. *Between Husbands and Wives: Communication in Marriage*. Newbury Park, Calif.: Sage, 1988.

Maltz, Daniel N., and Borker, Ruth A. "A Cultural Approach to Male-Female Miscommunication." In John J. Gumperz (ed.), *Language and Social Identity*, pp. 196–216. Cambridge: Cambridge University Press, 1982.

Nunnally, Elam W.; Chilman, Catherine S.; and Cox, Fred M., eds. *Troubled Relationships*. Newbury Park, Calif.: Sage, 1988.

Tannen, Deborah. *You Just Don't Understand*. New York: Morrow, 1990.

CHAPTER 12

The Broken Marriage:
The History, Nature, and
Effects of Divorce in America

There are two ways to catch any knife that fate may throw at you —
by the blade or by the handle.

Sicilian proverb

The Contributions of Christianity to
Our Views on Ending Marriages

The Effects of No-Fault Divorce

The Nature of Divorce in America

The Effects of Divorce on Adults

The Effects of Divorce on Children

What Do You Know?

Some of the following statements are true and some are false.
Can you tell which are which?

T/F   1. Children of an annulled marriage are generally considered by the court to be illegitimate.

T/F   2. Roman Catholics have a lower divorce rate than non-Catholics.

T/F   3. The average ex-husband's standard of living usually rises significantly following a no-fault divorce.

T/F   4. More than half of divorced fathers do not pay court-awarded child support payments.

T/F   5. The disruption rate for remarriages is significantly lower than it is for first marriages.

T/F   6. Those who marry for the first time in their teens have about twice the rate of divorce as those who marry after age twenty.

T/F   7. Women who marry for the first time after age thirty have a higher divorce rate than women who marry in their twenties.

T/F   8. The divorce rate is higher for whites than it is for blacks or Hispanics.

T/F   9. Children of divorced parents are themselves more likely to divorce.

Even though most societies throughout the world (and most religions as well) expect marriages to be permanent, they nevertheless also include provision for divorce. Although the permissible causes for divorce vary, the most common causes are failure to provide the necessities of life, mistreatment, adultery, and sterility. In societies that make use of a dowry or a bride price, the payment must usually be returned when a marriage is terminated.

In societies (usually preindustrial) whose courtship system emphasizes parental selection, marriage customarily involves extensive social, economic, political, or religious ties, and these societies usually have relatively low divorce rates. In societies whose courtship system emphasizes mutual choice, marriage is seen chiefly as a means of personal fulfillment (see Chapter 7); these societies usually have relatively high divorce rates.

Among Western civilizations, divorce was forbidden under Christian doctrine in the fourth century A.D. (Divorce had been possible in the Roman Empire.) The Protestant Reformation in the sixteenth century reinstated the concept of civil divorce, but this remains unacceptable to the Roman Catholic Church.

As recently as 1960, divorce had gained neither public nor institutional acceptance as a respectable alternative to a successful marriage. Sociologists and marriage counselors alike viewed divorce as a social problem. By the mid-1960s, however, professional and public opinion had begun to shift so that divorce came to be considered an acceptable solution to a problem rather than a problem in itself (Davis 1972; Bernard 1971). "Gradually, the standard shifted from one which required a couple to remain married even if they were not in love, to one that virtually demanded divorces unless they remained in love" (Furstenberg 1990, p. 380). In 1970, states began to enact no-fault divorce laws, making divorce easily accessible.

The current attitude in our society is that if a marriage fails to satisfy a person's needs for emotional security, understanding, acceptance, affection, and love, he or she is justified in ending that marriage (and perhaps exchanging it for another), even when children are involved.

The Contributions of Christianity to Our Views on Ending Marriages

Today's emphasis on personal happiness in marriage is quite a departure from the earlier view of marriage as an institution that provided an essential stabilizing base for society and protected the property and inheritance rights of women and children.[1] It is a greater departure from the even earlier view of marriage as a sacrament, an institution of divine significance not to be tampered with by humans.

From the fourth century A.D. to the sixteenth century, Christian doctrine has held that valid, consummated marriages between baptized people cannot be dissolved by any human agency. Once the Protestant Reformation split Christianity in the sixteenth century, divorce became recognized as an acceptable way to end a marriage.

---

[1]Men held property rights with or without marriage, and a man could abandon a woman with whom he had been cohabiting and he could abandon their illegitimate children (bastards). However, a husband could not legally abandon his wife and their legitimate children. Thus marriage protected the property and inheritance rights of married women and their children (although they could be disinherited for cause).

The Roman Catholic View
of Marriage Dissolution

The Roman Catholic view of marriage did not change with the Protestant Reformation; divorce is still prohibited. Roman Catholic doctrine holds that a married couple is joined together by God. Divorce — dissolution of a marriage by a human act — is not consistent with this doctrine (see Chapter 7). The early Christian concept of marriage as divine — that the couple was joined together until the marriage was involuntarily dissolved by death — is still the Roman Catholic position. (The Roman Catholic Church does permit annulment, however, as we will see.)

A Roman Catholic who obtains a civil divorce is divorced in the eyes of the state but remains married in the eyes of the church. Although the "divorced" person is permitted by the state to remarry, in the eyes of the church he or she is still in the original marriage. Thus, a "remarriage" is considered invalid.

Before 1977, any Roman Catholic who obtained a civil divorce and then remarried was excommunicated. In that year, Pope Paul VI ruled that remarriage following a civil divorce should no longer be grounds for excommunication. This was a significant ruling, for excommunication is a severe penalty. A person who is excommunicated is separated from the community of the church, is forbidden to receive the sacraments, and is excluded from public prayers.

Divorced and remarried Roman Catholics are no longer excommunicated, but they are forbidden full communion. To be eligible for full communion, divorced and remarried Roman Catholics must obtain a special dispensation, which is not an easy task (Sciolino 1984).

Even though the lifting of the excommunication penalty does not change the church's traditional teaching that sacramental marriages cannot be dissolved, the papal action is considered important as a gesture of conciliation to the growing number of divorced and remarried Roman Catholics. There are an estimated eight million divorced Roman Catholics in the United States, and the divorce rate is the same for Catholics as it is for non-Catholics (Sciolino 1984).

The Concept of Limited Divorce   Although divorce was not possible under Christian doctrine before the sixteenth century, two ways to end an intolerable marriage existed. The first was a *limited divorce*, which permitted a married couple to live apart but prohibited either from remarrying. A modern version of a limited divorce is *legal separation*.

A legal separation, which is permitted today in most states, does not terminate the marriage but limits the privileges of the spouses. Legal separation provides for separate maintenance — the couple may not cohabit under penalty of law — but the husband is still responsible for the financial well-being of his wife and family.

A couple may find it impossible to live together but may feel the need to retain their marital status. In such a case a couple may prefer a legal separation to a divorce for social, religious, or professional reasons. Not surprisingly, legal separation appeals to only a few people: The incidence of legal separation is only about 3 percent of the incidence of divorce.[2]

Annulment   A second possibility for ending an intolerable marriage is to have it annulled — to be formally and legally declared never to have existed. Annulment was originally conceived to ensure that a male European sovereign whose wife was barren could remarry, thus providing him a second chance to produce an heir to the throne. In the paragraphs that follow we

---

[2]U.S. National Center for Health Statistics, "Legal Separation" (1980).

will consider both church annulment and civil annulment.

Roman Catholic dogma regards annulment as an acceptable way to dissolve a marriage. Because the marriage is considered to never have taken place, the problem of dissolving a sacramental union is avoided.

According to the pronouncement of Pope Paul VI (1970), the grounds for a church annulment include incestuous marriage, impotence, nonconsummation of the marriage, intent by a spouse not to have children, marriage under duress, and marriage under age fourteen for a girl or age sixteen for a boy. In 1977 lack of love (*ex defecto amoris*) was also admitted to the grounds for church annulment.

The new canonical law permits couples to get an annulment after both a favorable decision by one local church court and ratification, without trial, by another. The length of time for this procedure is estimated to be about seven months. Under the old law this procedure could involve three to seven years of heavy expenses and perhaps even a trip to Rome. The new law also grants bishops of dioceses the right to annul a marriage under certain circumstances.

The number of church annulments in the United States increased after the new Roman Catholic regulations went into effect in 1977. In 1967, only 700 church annulments were granted in the United States (Sciolino 1984); by 1985 this figure had jumped to nearly 60,000 (Young and Griffith 1985).

Civil annulment in this country, like most U.S. statutes, developed from English common law, and because English common law long ago adopted the Roman Catholic concept of annulment, nearly all U.S. states today grant annulments as well as divorces. Because an annulment voids the marriage, all rights and obligations may be dissolved, and children may be declared illegitimate. (Even though the laws regarding annulment differ from state to state, in the absence of specific statutes to the contrary the courts generally consider children of an annulled marriage to be illegitimate.) Civil annulments, which are usually sought in our society only when divorce is not legally obtainable, represent about 4 percent of the nationwide total of marital dissolutions.[3]

In civil annulments, the court usually recognizes different grounds from those applicable to divorce. The grounds for annulment generally precede the marriage, whereas the grounds for divorce usually follow it. Typical grounds for annulment include existence of a previous marriage, misrepresentation with intent to defraud, sanguinity (too close a blood tie, such as a half sibling), or proof (to the court's satisfaction) that at the time of the marriage one of the couple did not intend to have children.

The Roman Catholic Church does not recognize a civil annulment. Catholics must have a marriage annulled by the church if they are to be free to remarry — and wish to have the remarriage recognized by the church. A Catholic must get a civil divorce before obtaining a church annulment. The Catholic is then free to enter a new marriage that is acceptable in the eyes of both the state and the church (Brunsman 1985).

The Effects of the Protestant Reformation on Marriage Dissolution Today

In the sixteenth century the Protestant Reformation repudiated many aspects of Roman Catholic dogma, including that prohibiting divorce.

---

[3]U.S. National Center for Health Statistics, "Divorces and Annulments — Rate and Percent Distribution, by Age and Sex: 1987" (1991).

This development opened the way for civil divorce legislation to be enacted.

Divorce by Legislative Action   Although the Protestant Reformation made divorce theoretically available, from a practical point of view a divorce was still almost impossible to obtain in England. Divorce could be granted only through passage of a special act of Parliament (a "Bill of Divorcement"), a very difficult process that could be accomplished only by a wealthy and powerful person. The early reformers felt that the grounds for divorce should be very serious — namely, adultery, cruelty, or desertion. Moreover, they felt that these grounds should be clearly demonstrable before Parliament, which might then choose to enact special legislation granting a divorce.

Divorce by Court Action   The American colonies had initially adopted the British pattern of granting legislative divorce. However, at the beginning of the nineteenth century the United States shifted authority to the courts, and England followed suit in the mid-nineteenth century. Thus, by the twentieth century the concept of courts granting divorce was well established.

Initially, a divorce by court action was regarded as a *contest* between a plaintiff and a defendant. The plaintiff would bring charges against the defendant and would have to prove the charges using points of evidence, which were argued by opposing counsel. The court would grant a divorce only if the defendant were judged guilty as charged. It was not possible, under the law, for a divorce to be granted if there was no contest — that is, if both the husband and the wife wanted the divorce. Cooperation between the couple to obtain a divorce was termed *collusion* and was a felony offense. If the judge so much as suspected collusion, the court would summarily deny the divorce. If a divorce had been granted and collusion was later suspected,

the court could revoke the divorce (Rheinstein 1972).

Most contested divorces were granted on two grounds: cruelty and desertion. The most common of all grounds was cruelty, which was used in about 60 percent of all American divorce suits. Cruelty could be defined by the court in various ways, including psychological stress and physical abuse. Several jurisdictions specifically defined cruelty as the infliction of mental suffering. Desertion was used as grounds in about a fourth of contested divorce suits (Bell 1983; Carter and Glick 1976).

Some two decades ago a truly revolutionary change in divorce laws appeared in our society: no-fault divorce, the next topic in our discussion.

The Effects of No-Fault Divorce

The first no-fault divorce legislation was adopted in California in 1970. Today most states have abandoned the concept of divorce as a legal contest and have replaced it with the concept of no-fault divorce, which means that a divorce can be granted simply because the couple wants it. Many states even stopped using the term *divorce* and substituted the term *dissolution of marriage*. By the 1980s, couples in virtually every state could legally dissolve their marriage simply by agreeing that their differences were irreconcilable. Because there is no legal contest, there is no plaintiff and no defendant, and the law against collusion no longer applies. The intent of no-fault divorce legislation was to reduce the acrimony and deceit in divorce actions.

No-fault divorce law provides that either the husband or the wife can be required to support the other (by alimony payments) after the marriage is dissolved and that either or both can be required to support their minor children, depending on the court's judgment. With the dissolution of the marriage, each member of the couple is free to remarry, responsibility for the care and support for children is assigned, and the property is divided.

After a divorce is granted, about one-third of the states issue a temporary decree, called an *interlocutory decree*, which may then become a final divorce decree after a period of time that varies from one month to a year. This interlocutory decree allows time for the couple to reconsider before the divorce is finalized.

Effects on Ex-Wives and Ex-Husbands

Although legislators did not plan it this way and the consequences were certainly not foreseen, the average ex-wife with the custody of minor children usually experiences a drop in economic well-being that can range from an estimated 30 percent (Hoffman and Duncan 1988) to an estimated 73 percent (Weitzman 1985). Meanwhile, after a no-fault divorce the average ex-husband's standard of living rises significantly, anywhere from an estimated 15 percent (Hoffman and Duncan 1988) to an estimated 42 percent (Weitzman 1985). (Note that these figures are averages; in any particular case the consequences of divorce may be quite different — either much worse or much better.)

Under the contest divorce system, the husband's standard of living usually dropped because the wife usually got the house (if she was granted custody of the children) as well as alimony and child support. Under the new laws, the ex-husband is not required to contribute equally to the support of his children or to share his salary with his former wife. She usually must get an outside job in order to survive, but because of the income gap she will probably earn much lower pay than her ex-husband. In addition to working, she usually must look after the children (Hoffman 1987). Ironically, the intent of no-fault divorce laws was to achieve equality for

women. Although no one is proposing a return to the past contest system, the results of no-fault divorce have acted to women's disadvantage, and social workers, lawyers, women's rights advocates, and legislators are searching for ways to rectify this situation (Hoffman 1987; Weitzman 1985).

Effects of Property Settlements

Before the advent of no-fault divorce, the family home was usually awarded to the wife, especially if she was granted custody of minor children. Under no-fault divorce laws, however, the court usually divides the couple's property equally; in order to do this, the court often orders the family home sold, so that the proceeds may be divided (Weitzman 1985). As a result,

> [t]he loss of the family home, and the subsequent residential moves it necessitates, disrupt the children's school, neighborhood, and friendship ties, and create additional dislocations for children (and mothers) at the very point at which they need continuity and stability. (Weitzman 1985, p. xii)

Moreover, under the no-fault rules for dividing marital property, the courts systematically omit such assets as pensions, medical insurance, the goodwill value of a business or profession, future earning power, the potential value of an education or a professional license, and the major earner's salary. "Thus the courts allow the major wage earner, typically the husband, to keep the family's most valuable assets" (Weitzman 1985, p. xiii).

An equal division of property rarely solves the couple's economic problems. The vast majority of divorcing couples, particularly young couples with small children, own few assets. One study found that the average value of marital property at the time of divorce was only $4,650; half of this sum is not enough to provide much security for a mother with custody of small children (Hewlett 1991).

Nationwide, the proportion of women who receive any property settlement at all following a divorce has been dropping steadily. In 1979, some 45 percent of divorced women received a property settlement; in 1988, only 32 percent received any property following a divorce.[4]

Reduction in Alimony Awards

In early English common law, a divorced man continued to be responsible for his ex-wife's economic welfare. Because he had automatically gained control of his wife's property and income upon marriage, it was deemed appropriate that if he retained control of all property after a divorce, he should continue to support her after the divorce as well. Employment opportunities for the ex-wife were almost nonexistent, so these payments, termed *alimony*, were in fact necessary for her survival—unless she and her children were to become public charges (Weitzman 1985). Thus "alimony simply represented a continuation of the marital responsibility for support" (Oster 1987, p. 81). Marriage laws in the United States are based largely on English common law and have followed the same principle of alimony.

Before the advent of no-fault divorce, women had a valid marriage contract, unless it was broken through adultery, abandonment, or cruelty. "If her husband wanted out of the marriage, she could strike an economic bargain with him—you support me and I'll give you a divorce" (Hewlett 1991, p. 22).

As no-fault divorce was adopted by state after state, the incidence of alimony awards dropped precipitously. Alimony was awarded to only 7 percent of women divorced in 1987, and the average (mean) award was only $4,000 per year. Moreover, one-third of the women awarded alimony did not receive their payments from errant ex-husbands.[5]

Increasingly, judges instruct divorcing women to support themselves by their own labor. "The new litany tends to read: Any woman who wants to can get a job and be self-supporting; she therefore doesn't need alimony or any other long-term support to her income" (Hewlett 1991, p. 109).

Today, most judges appear to view the law's goal of equality as a mandate for placing an equal burden of support on men and women. Most women, however, are not financially equipped to bear an equal burden, and the typical divorced woman does not benefit by this equal treatment. If they are an older displaced homemaker, or if they have the responsibility for young children, they are severely handicapped in a job market that already discriminates against women (Hewlett 1991; Weitzman and Dixon 1980).

Occasionally, of course, an ex-wife receives a very large alimony settlement in a well-publicized divorce. These highly visible divorce actions lead to the mistaken public perception that alimony payments are larger and occur more frequently than they in fact are (Weitzman 1985).

Court-Awarded Spousal Support

The court may award the divorced woman spousal support from her ex-husband for a short time (usually one to three years) to allow her an opportunity to acquire the education or training needed for her to enter the job market or to get a higher-paying position. If the ex-wife is an

---

[4]U.S. Bureau of the Census, "Property Settlement Following Divorce—Selected Characteristics of Women: 1979 and 1988" (1991).

[5]U.S. Bureau of the Census, "Child Support and Alimony—Selected Characteristics of Women: 1987" (1991).

older woman with many years invested in the marriage, the court may award more spousal support and order the ex-husband to extend the payments.

Court-Awarded Child Support

In virtually all divorce actions involving children, the custodial parent—the mother 90 percent of the time (Spanier and Thompson 1987)—is awarded child support payments, which are to be made by the noncustodial parent (usually the father). The current legal theory underlying most divorce actions is that although the ex-husband is not responsible for his ex-wife's economic well-being for more than a short interval following the divorce, he is *partially* responsible for his children's economic care as long as they are minors. The court must specify the meaning of "partially" in terms of dollars per month. If the child support award is too large, the father may not be able to pay it and still provide for his own economic needs; if the award is too small, the children may suffer deprivation of essential goods—food, clothes, shelter, and medical and dental care (Spanier and Thompson 1987).

Since the advent of no-fault divorce in 1970, courts usually take a "father-first" rather than "child-first" approach to assessing the amount of child support payments. The award must leave the father sufficient funds to meet his own needs and to maintain his continuing ability to earn. Few courts allot more than one-third of the father's income to child support, and often the amount is much less than this figure. Nationwide, child support awards averaged 13 percent of the average male's income in 1981 (Weitzman 1985).

Fathers do not usually provide a fair share of child support for children who are in a mother's custody (Furstenberg 1990; Fletcher 1989; Garfinkel and Oellerich 1989). Many absent fathers do not pay any child support at all, and of those who do, many make irregular, partial payments (Peterson and Nord 1990). Fathers who do pay usually pay less than the amount the court has ordered; more than half of divorced fathers do not pay the full amount of child support they owe. In consequence, more than 3.5 million divorced women live in poverty with five million children,[6] for marital disruption is the greatest cause of poverty among women and children (McLanahan and Booth 1991).

Court-Awarded Child Custody

The mother is the parent most often awarded the custody of the children today, but this was not always the case. Under English common law, children were regarded as belonging to the father, and if separation occurred he automatically obtained custody. It was not until the nineteenth century that English courts began to modify what had been an automatic right of fathers.

In the late nineteenth century, courts in the United States began to follow suit by granting custody to the mother, especially if the children were of "tender" age (less than seven years old). This new trend—which assumed that the mother, not the father, was the "natural" and "proper" caretaker of her children — was increasingly accepted by the courts and by divorcing couples (Weitzman 1981; Halem 1980). By the early twentieth century, it had become a well-established principle that it was not in the children's best interests to be separated from their mother unless she could be shown to be unfit (Weitzman 1985).

When no-fault divorce laws were first passed it was assumed that increasing numbers of

---

[6]U.S. Bureau of the Census, "Child Support-Award and Recipiency Status of Women: 1981 to 1987" (1991).

husbands would sue for, and be granted, custody of their children. However, no increase in the percentage of fathers requesting or being awarded physical or legal custody of their children has occurred (Weitzman 1985).

In 1980, California became the first state to enact legislation favoring *joint custody*. The concept of awarding the children to both parents jointly—rather than establishing a custodial parent and a visiting parent—spread rapidly, and by 1985 thirty states had passed some form of joint custody law. Then, in 1983, California law added the distinction between joint *legal* custody and joint *physical* custody; the court may award one without awarding the other. Most commonly, joint *legal* custody may be awarded to both the father and the mother, whereas the mother is usually awarded physical custody (Weitzman 1985).

In her careful research of California custodial awards, Weitzman (1985) found little evidence that either joint physical or joint legal custody are necessarily beneficial for children or parents. If the parents are able to cooperate without hostility, joint legal custody may have some advantages; joint physical custody, however, can be disadvantageous and may be anxiety-provoking for children. Steinman (1981) gives the following example:

> Nine-year-old Josh, who lived one month with his mother and one month with his father, indicated that he felt many things in his life were in disarray, that he was preoccupied with loss and anxious about his ability to keep track of things. He was not working up to his potential at school, and there was a discrepancy between his considerable abilities and his low self-concept. When Josh was contacted about our interviews, he immediately volunteered that "the big problem with joint custody is that you

have to remember where the spoons are." His worry about the spoons reflected all the other worries he has, and an overall level of instability. (p. 410)

Although joint physical custody was initially regarded with enthusiasm, experience has shown that it is an especially unstable arrangement, and it is now adopted by only a small minority of divorced couples (Furstenberg 1990; Emery 1988). When joint legal custody is awarded, fathers typically see less and less of their children over time, leaving women with the major responsibility for child care (Albiston, Maccoby, and Mnookin 1990). Sole custody is often informally renegotiated by the parents, however, with older children especially likely to shift residence. This may be done without the involvement of lawyers and courts; for example, an adolescent may simply go live with her or his father for a time (Furstenberg 1990).

Visitation Rights

As we have seen, in most divorce actions both legal and physical custody are awarded to one parent (usually the mother), and visitation rights are awarded to the noncustodial parent (usually the father). The vast majority of visitation rights orders are for "reasonable" visitation, which leaves the couple to work out the precise details of when visitation occurs. Only 5 percent of court orders limit visitation rights by precisely spelling them out (Weitzman 1985).

Visits from the noncustodial parent are often emotional and difficult. Wallerstein and Kelly (1980) found that 80 percent of fathers felt some stress regarding visits during the first year following the divorce. One-half of part-time fathers were afraid of being rejected by their children and were uneasy about the children's hostility and disapproval of the divorce. One-third of visiting fathers brought expensive gifts to allay their own discomfort and to win the children's favor.

Two-thirds of custodial mothers experienced various degrees of stress regarding the father's visits during the first year, whether passively accepting the visitation with mixed feelings or resenting the father's excessive gift-giving and his "freedom from domestic responsibility." One-third of the children were consistently exposed to intense anger regarding the visits, and one-fifth of the mothers actively tried to sabotage the visits by "sending the children away just before the father's arrival" or by saying that "the child was ill or had homework to do" and could not see the father. However, some of the mothers helped facilitate contact between the father and his children (Wallerstein and Kelly 1980, pp. 121, 124–25).

Once they are no longer living in the same household, most noncustodial fathers actually see very little of their children after divorce and take very little responsibility for them. Remarrying accelerates this process of disengagement because new family responsibilities and increased economic demands are often a part of remarriage. The circumstances of a remarriage usually cause even further erosion of the already tenuous bonds between a noncustodial father and his children (Furstenberg 1990; Seltzer and Bianchi 1988; Furstenberg and Nord 1985).

Black fathers are much more likely to see their noncustodial children than are white fathers. More than one-fourth of black children under age four who do not live with their father see him almost every day, and another one-fourth see him at least once a week, which is three times the rate of white children (Riche 1991a).

A noncustodial father who does maintain regular visits and responsibility for his children often adopts a pattern of *parallel parenting*. With parallel parenting the parents rarely see each other and instead communicate — when necessary — through their children (Furstenberg 1990). Although parallel parenting does reduce conflict between the parents, it creates two separate family systems for the child (Emery 1988; Johnson 1988). The difficulties this presents for the child will be discussed in Chapter 13.

The Nature of Divorce in America

Only twenty-nine states report divorce statistics, and these statistics differ in the information reported. For example, some states do not include race or the number of people remarried in their divorce statistics (Price and McKenry 1988). The divorce rate in the United States is, therefore, of necessity an estimate. Demographers use different methods to make this estimate, using the raw data available (see Box 12-1).

The National Divorce Rate

The divorce rate in the United States (by all estimates) has been steadily accelerating since the latter part of the nineteenth century (see Figure 12-1). Before then, divorce was so rare that the Census Bureau did not think it worthwhile to keep divorce records. When records regarding the incidence of divorce first began to be kept in 1860, only 3.5 percent of marriages begun each year ended in divorce rather than death (Jacobson 1969). By 1974, for the first time, more marriages were ending in divorce than in death (Jacobson 1969). By 1980, one in two, or about 50 percent, of all marriages in the United States were ending in divorce rather than death. (Glick 1988; Furstenberg and Spanier 1987;

BOX 12-1

Estimating the Extent of Divorce

Demographers use many methods to estimate how widespread divorce is from raw data that are necessarily incomplete because not all states report marriage and divorce statistics, and those that do report them in different ways. We will cite three of the methods most commonly used.

One index to the extent of divorce is the ratio of the divorce rate to the marriage rate. Demographers estimated the divorce rate as 4.80 per 1,000 people in 1987, and the marriage rate as 9.79.[a] The ratio of divorces to marriages was thus 4.80/9.79 = 0.49, or just about half the marriage rate. If this ratio were applied to the population as a whole, then about half of all marriages would be ex-

---

[a]U.S. National Center for Health Statistics, "Marriages and Divorces: 1960 to 1987" (1991).

pected to eventually end in divorce. An objection to using this method is that the couples getting divorced in any one year are not necessarily the same couples as those getting married. Therefore, it is not statistically sound to treat them as though they were directly comparable.

A second method is to examine the refined divorce rate for any given year or period of years; the *refined divorce rate* is defined as the number of divorces in a given year per 1,000 existing marriages. This is a very useful method for comparing the incidence of divorce in any two years, decades, or other periods of time. However, to use the refined divorce rate to estimate the probability of a marriage ending in divorce, it is necessary to multiply the incidence of divorce each year by the number of years the aver-

---

Spanier and Thompson 1987; Glick 1984). The United States now has the highest divorce rate of any industrialized nation (Lye 1988), an occurrence that according to Furstenberg and Spanier (1987) is unexpected:

> Divorce and remarriage trends have taken America by surprise. . . . Who would have predicted a generation ago that more than half of all marriages contracted in the latter part of the twentieth century would end in divorce? (p. 11)

Consider the following statistics concerning divorce in America:

- Some demographers estimate that about 56 percent of recent first marriages end in divorce and that another 6 percent end in separation without a divorce. Thus the total disruption rate for first marriages (contracted between 1980 and 1985) is estimated at about 62 percent (Castro-Martin and Bumpass 1989).

- The disruption rate for remarriages is higher than it is for first marriages. Remar-

PART IV ❖ CONFLICT, DIVORCE, AND REMARRIAGE

age marriage lasts. For example, the average refined divorce rate from 1950 to 1970 was about 10. This means that during this twenty-year period, 10 per 1,000, or 1 percent of all marriages, ended in divorce each year. Since the average marriage lasted about 31.5 years during this twenty-year period,[b] the total number of marriages ending in divorce was about 31.5 percent (1 percent each year for 31.5 years). This is the figure commonly accepted as the divorce rate from 1950 to 1970 (Davis 1972). Since the average duration of marriage from 1970 to 1990 is not readily available, it is difficult to use this method to update the estimate of the probability that any given marriage would end in divorce during this period. However, the refined divorce rate in 1960 was 9.2, in 1970 it was 14.9, and in 1987 (the latest data currently available) it was 20.8.[c] This is consistent with other estimates of the ratio of

divorce to marriage, showing a doubling of the divorce rate during this period.

A third method that avoids the statistical problems of the other methods is simply to compare the percentage of marital dissolutions caused by divorce each year (or other period of time) with those caused by death during the same period. The rationale for this method is that all marriages must eventually end one way or another — either in divorce or in death (Davis 1972). This ratio of divorce to death is currently estimated at about one in two (one out of two marriages end in divorce rather than death). Or, put another way, this places the demographic probability for divorce at about 50 percent for all marriages in the United States. Demographers estimate that for all recent marriages the probability for divorce is about 56 percent (Castro-Martin and Bumpass 1989).

There are, however, great individual differences among cohorts and categories of marriage, so that the overall demographic probability for divorce does not apply to all marriages — some have a much higher and some a much lower probability of failure.

---

[b]U.S. Bureau of the Census, *Statistical Abstracts of the United States,* 92nd ed., 1971.

[c]U.S. Bureau of the Census. "Marriages and Divorces: 1960 to 1987" (1991).

---

riages in the first half of the 1980s had a 25 percent higher rate of divorce than first marriages (Castro-Martin and Bumpass 1989). (See Chapter 13.)

- More than 1.1 million divorces and annulments occur in the United States annually[7] (see Figure 12-2).

- The median age at which divorce occurs

has been rising for both men and women. In 1970, the median ages for men and women were thirty-three and thirty, respectively; in 1987 they were thirty-five and thirty-three, respectively.[8]

- The data suggest that the adoption of no-fault divorce by all but two states has had no

---

[7]U.S. National Center for Health Statistics, "Marriages and Divorces: 1960 to 1987."

[8]U.S. National Center for Health Statistics, "Divorces and Annulments — Median Duration of Marriage, Median Age at Divorce, and Children Involved: 1970 to 1987" (1991).

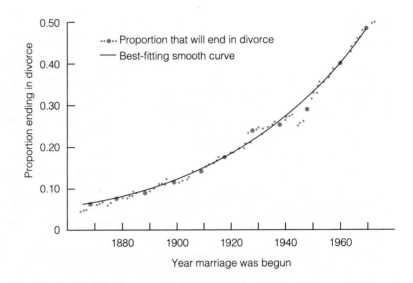

FIGURE 12-1

Proportion of marriages begun each year that end in divorce, 1867–1973.

Source: Adapted from Cherlin (1981), Figure 1.1.

effect on divorce rates. It has, however, decreased the time necessary to obtain a divorce (Kitson and Morgan 1991).

- The peak period for divorce is one to four years into the marriage. About one-third of divorces occur within four years of marriage, and half occur within seven years.

- That most divorces occur relatively early in the marriage is also apparent by the young ages at which people divorce. More than half of all recent divorces occurred before age thirty, and about a third occurred before age twenty-five (Bumpass, Sweet, and Castro-Martin 1990).

- The average (median) duration of all marriages that end in divorce is about seven years.[9]

Although seven years is the median duration of all marriages that end in divorce, this figure includes marriages that have lasted thirty years or longer. Moreover, many divorces that occur after several years of marriage may follow separations that took place in the few years of the marriage (Price and McKenry 1988). Because the decision to divorce is usually made only after a series of separations and reconciliations, it is likely that many of these marriages had serious difficulties from the early years on (Spanier and Thompson 1987).

Although the divorce rate seems to have stabilized in the late 1980s, demographers Castro-Martin and Bumpass (1989) suggest that the drop in divorces between 1980 and 1987[10] may be misleading and does not indicate a true reversal of the trend. The drop may be occurring because

[9]An additional 25 percent occur after ten to nineteen years of marriage, and 12 percent occur after twenty years or more. U.S. National Center for Health Statistics, "Percent of All

Divorces by Duration of Marriage" (1988). Only 15 percent of recent divorces involved women over the age of forty (Bumpass, Sweet, and Castro-Martin 1990).

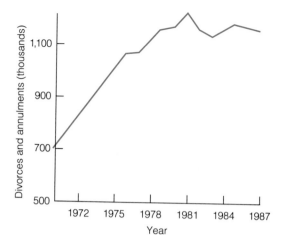

FIGURE 12-2

Number of divorces and annulments, in thousands: 1970–1987.

Source: U.S. National Center for Health Statistics, "Marriages and Divorces: 1960 to 1987." *Vital Statistics of the United States,* annual (1991).

a large part of the "baby boom" generation (born 1946–1960) had passed the most likely age for divorce by the start of the 1980s. If this interpretation is correct, the divorce rate may resume its rise after what would turn out to be a temporary decline. Other demographers point out that the recent decline in divorce rate might reflect the drop in marriage rates (from 10.6 in 1982 to 9.9 in 1987), which means that fewer couples in the pool of married people are in the early stages of marriage that have the highest risks of divorce (Furstenberg 1990).[11] These and other demographers project that the long-term acceleration of the divorce rate will resume in the near future (Castro-Martin and Bumpass 1989; Glick 1988; Furstenberg and Spanier 1987).

---

[10]Census data show divorce rates of 2.5 per 1,000 population in 1965, 3.6 in 1970, 4.8 in 1975, 5.2 in 1980, and 4.8 in 1987. "Marriages and Divorces: 1960 to 1987."

[11]"Marriages and Divorces: 1960 to 1987."

Other analysts examining the same data suggest that the drop in the divorce rate in the late 1980s (from the record high rates of the 1970s) might indicate the beginning of a new trend. These demographers project that only about 40 percent of first marriages will end in divorce in the next decade, compared with the 50 percent rate observed during the 1970s and early 1980s (Norton and Miller 1991).

Falling divorce rates, a leveling-off at the current rate, or a continuing acceleration of the incidence of divorce in our society—which of these projections will prove correct? Only the future will tell.

Individual Factors That Affect Divorce Rates

The probability that a marriage will end in divorce is correlated with many individual factors, including: (1) age at first marriage, (2) level of education, (3) occupation and income, (4) race-ethnicity, (5) religion, (6) presence of children, (7) compatibility of the couple, (8) geographic area, (9) marital history of one's parents, (10) history of cohabitation before marriage, (11) premarital childbearing, and (12) whether the marriage is a remarriage for one or both of the couple. Next we will examine each of these factors in turn.

Age at First Marriage This is one of the most crucial factors determining the probability for divorce; it is in fact the strongest predictor of divorce in the first five years of marriage (Castro-Martin and Bumpass 1989; Teachman 1986). Those who marry for the first time in their teens have two to three times the incidence of divorce as those who marry after age twenty (Norton and Moorman 1987). Men who marry before age twenty have twice the divorce rate of men who marry between the ages of twenty and twenty-four, and more than twice the divorce rate of men who marry between the ages of twenty-five and twenty-nine. Women who marry under age seventeen are twice as likely to divorce as women who marry at age eighteen or nineteen, and they have three times the divorce rate of women who marry between the ages of twenty and twenty-four (Glick 1984).

Early marriages have a much higher divorce rate than other marriages, for several reasons. Individuals are usually less mature — intellectually, emotionally, and experientially — in their teenage years than when older, and thus they are probably less likely to make sound marital choices. It has been suggested that many teenage marriages end in divorce because the partners are too young to make the important decision of whom to marry. Also, teenage marriages are chiefly a lower-class phenomenon, and a higher incidence of divorce occurs in this class for many reasons: Lower social classes generally have more financial pressure, lower job status, lower educational level, and more premarital pregnancy — all of which are correlated with a higher divorce rate (Castro-Martin and Bumpass 1989; Price and McKenry 1988; Thorton and Rodgers 1987).

Level of Education   The relation between level of education and likelihood of divorce is complex (Norton and Moorman 1987; Glick 1984; Glenn and Supancic 1984). High school dropouts have twice the rate of divorce as people with some college education (Castro-Martin and Bumpass 1989). The likelihood of divorce rises for both men and women who have some college education but falls sharply for college graduates. The likelihood of divorce again rises significantly for women with more than five years of college, but for men it rises only slightly (Glick 1984).

Age at marriage exerts a greater influence on the divorce rate than does education level. Thus regardless of their education, women who marry

youngest are most likely to separate or divorce (Glick 1984).

Occupation and Income   Men and women in different occupations have different divorce rates. For men, the lower the occupational status, the higher the likelihood of divorce. For women this pattern is reversed: The higher the occupational status, the higher the incidence of divorce (Bumpass, Sweet, and Castro-Martin 1990).

Similar relations hold true for income, gender, and probability of divorce. For men, incidence of divorce and income are negatively correlated: As one goes up, the other goes down. Thus the lower the income, the higher the incidence of divorce. For women, the likelihood of divorce is positively correlated with income: The higher the income, the greater the likelihood of divorce (Glick and Norton 1977; Carter and Glick 1976).

It is not clear why the divorce rate increases for women at the upper end of the economic and job status scale. It can be speculated that the financial and social independence of these high-income women gives them more freedom to opt for divorce if their standards or expectations for personal happiness are not fulfilled. One study found that for husbands, income was the most important predictor of satisfaction with the quality of their lives. For wives, income was the second most important predictor; the most important was satisfaction with their husband (Berry and Williams 1987).

Race-Ethnicity   The divorce rate for women today is much higher among blacks and slightly lower among Hispanics than it is among whites (see Figure 12-3).

Although the marital failure rate declines for both races as income increases, blacks in all income brackets have much higher divorce rates than whites (Teachman 1986; Norton 1983b). In fact, the difference between the rates of divorce

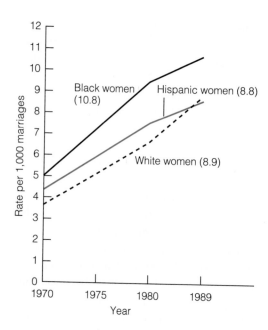

FIGURE 12-3

Rates of divorce per 1,000 marriages of black, white, and Hispanic women ages eighteen and older, 1970–1989.

Note: The figures for men in each of these groups run roughly parallel to these shown for women.

Source: Data from U.S. Bureau of the Census. "Marital Status of the Population, by Sex, Race, and Hispanic Origin: 1970 to 1989." *Current Population Reports*, series P-20, No. 445 and earlier reports. Washington, D.C.: Government Printing Office, 1991.

for blacks and whites is actually greater among high-income groups than it is among low-income groups. Although the divorce rate goes down for both groups as income increases, the ratio of divorce rates for blacks to divorce rates for whites increases.

Similarly, as education level increases, divorce rates drop for both races, but the difference in divorce rates between the races is higher at the upper education levels than it is at the lower levels, a pattern similar to that of income and divorce:

At nearly all levels of education, black persons thirty-five to forty-four years of age had a higher proportion ever divorced than did their white counterparts. Moreover, there was a definite tendency for this discrepancy to increase at the higher education levels. Evidently the mechanisms of social control that tend to inhibit divorce among better educated whites must operate to a lesser degree among black persons with a similar amount of education. (Carter and Glick 1976, p. 436)

Age at marriage among blacks has a similar pattern. Although marriages between younger people are more prone to divorce for both races, in every age-at-marriage category, black divorce rates are significantly higher than those of whites (Norton 1983b).

Studies find that the marital disruption rate of blacks is directly related to their relative lack of economic well-being. "[Divorced] blacks are the least educated, most vulnerable to unemployment, have the most unstable work histories, and have the lowest incomes" (Edwards and Demo 1991, p. 351).

Since 1970, the number of blacks who live below the poverty line has grown by 70 percent. "There has been a frightening disintegration of lifestyles at the bottom of the economic scale, with those who are desperately poor slipping even further downward in health, jobs, and housing." In the late 1960s, for example, poor blacks were paying 25 percent of their income for housing; in 1992 this percentage had risen to between 50 and 60 percent (Currie 1992, p. 22).

Although a small percentage of educated middle-class blacks have moved up on the socioeconomic scale, the income gap is widening; the net wealth of black households is only one-tenth that of whites (Owens 1992).

All of these hardships contribute to stress in black marriages. If current rates continue, an estimated two out of three black marriages will end in divorce (Edwards and Demo 1991).

Although many of these same characteristics are also true for Hispanics, their marital disruption rates are close to those of whites, perhaps because most Hispanics are Catholic and strongly oppose divorce (Edwards and Demo 1991).

Because divorce records are incomplete, it is not possible to estimate the incidence of divorce among Asian Americans, Native Americans, or other racial or ethnic groups (Price and McKenry 1988).

Religion   Despite the papal ban on divorce, Roman Catholics have about the same divorce rate as Protestants in the United States.[12] However, Jews have a lower divorce rate than either Roman Catholics or Protestants.[13]

Interestingly, conservative and fundamentalist Protestants have a higher rate of divorce than mainstream Protestants (Price and McKenry 1988; Raschke 1987). Frequency of church attendance is negatively correlated with divorce: Less frequent churchgoers have higher divorce rates (Teachman 1983).

Presence of Children   The data indicate that higher divorce rates and a faster divorce process occur with child-free marriages (Wineberg 1988; White, Booth, and Edwards 1986). The risk

of divorce is reduced by about one-third if a couple have children, and by 10 percent more if they have a son (Morgan, Lye, and Condran 1988). A couple are least likely to divorce if they have three or more children (Norton 1983a; Spanier and Glick 1981). An exception to this pattern occurs if a couple have children very early in the marriage. These couples are at greater risk of divorce than are child-free couples (Morgan, Lye, and Condran 1988).

The higher divorce rates for child-free marriages seem to contradict the observation discussed in Chapter 8 that children often lower the perceived happiness of a marriage. A possible explanation might be that it is easier for a couple to reach the decision to divorce if they do not have responsibility for any children. Put another way, even though the arrival of children may lower the perceived happiness in a marriage, a couple may tend to resist the idea of divorce when they must care for children. Moreover, happiness is relative; even though a couple may be less happy after children arrive, they may believe that they would be even less happy if they were to divorce.

Compatibility of the Couple   Various idiosyncratic factors may make a couple's interactions so painful that they are driven apart. For reasons not always clear to the couple, disillusionment, discouragement, and disappointment can increasingly replace the joy, anticipation, and delight of dating and courtship. The partners are said to be *incompatible*—a catch-all term that means they are no longer capable of living together with any sort of harmony or mutual satisfaction (see Chapter 11).

Geographic Area   Divorce rates also vary by geographic area, being lowest in the Northeast and the Midwest and highest in the South and the West (Price and McKenry 1988; Glenn and Supancic 1984).

---

[12]Acceptance of divorce among the 500 or so denominations of Protestants in the United States diverges widely. Some Protestant denominations are more rigorously opposed to divorce than are Roman Catholics, whereas other denominations are quite accepting. Nevertheless, the Census Bureau lumps all divorce statistics regarding Protestants into one category.

[13]The three denominations of Jews—Orthodox, Conservative, and Reformed—have significantly different attitudes toward divorce. Nevertheless, as with Protestants, the Census Bureau lumps all Jews together into one category.

Divorce rates are higher in urban areas, which contain more heterogeneous communities that foster more casual, fragmented, and anonymous relationships. It is easier for women in urban areas to be economically and socially independent, which makes it easier for them to leave an unsatisfactory marriage. Divorce is less common in rural areas, where more people usually know one another and greater social pressure to not divorce exists (Eshleman 1991).

Parental Marital History   A growing body of evidence suggests that divorce of parents increases the likelihood of divorce for their children (White 1990; McLanahan and Bumpass 1988; Greenberg and Nay 1982). One study found that the incidence of divorce was nearly 60 percent higher for white couples whose parents had divorced, as compared to divorce rates for couples whose parents had not divorced (Glenn and Kramer 1987). Data from the National Survey of Family Growth found that white women aged fourteen or younger at the time of their parents' divorce were nearly 70 percent more likely to divorce than were women from intact families; black women in this cohort were 25 percent more likely to divorce (London, Kahn, and Pratt 1988). Among the various reasons these researchers propose to explain the higher divorce rates among children of divorced parents are: (1) The stigma associated with divorce might be less for children of divorced parents, (2) the parents' divorce is an example of an option in an unhappy marriage, and (3) the children of divorced parents had role models of parents who solved their marital problems with divorce.

History of Cohabitation   Numerous studies in the United States and Canada conclude that cohabiting couples have a higher probability of divorce should they marry (Booth and Johnson 1988; Bennett, Blanc, and Bloom 1988; and

White 1987). (See the discussion in Chapter 6 for speculation regarding the possible reasons for this.)

Premarital Childbearing   Available data suggest that premarital childbearing increases the probability of divorce in a subsequent marriage, which may be a "shotgun wedding." However, premarital *pregnancy* is *not* correlated with a higher probability of divorce in a subsequent marriage. The likelihood for divorce is higher only if the woman gives birth to the child before the wedding (see White 1990; Castro-Martin and Bumpass 1989; Wineberg 1988; and Billy, Landale, and McLaughlin 1986).

Remarriage   As we have seen, remarriages have a significantly higher divorce rate than first marriages; during the early 1980s, the incidence of divorce of remarriages was 25 percent higher than that of first marriages (Castro-Martin and Bumpass 1989). Researchers find that all the factors predictive of marital failure in a first marriage also apply to remarriage, including early age at marriage, lower level of education, and lower income (White 1990; Castro-Martin and Bumpass 1989; White and Booth 1985). Remarriages also have additional stresses that first marriages do not have, such as economic pressures unique to remarriage, problems with an ex-spouse, and problems with stepchildren, issues that will be explored in Chapter 13.

The Effects of Divorce on Adults

Divorce is *not* a single event, the mere handing down of a divorce decree. In a larger sense, the process of divorce starts with the first, early stirrings of discontent within the marriage, escalates toward the decision to divorce, and lasts for years following the moment the divorce becomes a legal actuality.

"Then one day he said, 'It's either me or the damned cat!'"

Divorced people have higher rates of psychological distress, a higher incidence of physiological illness, and higher death rates than the married, the never-married single, and the widowed in the United States and other societies.[14]

Making the decision to divorce, and then following through on this decision, are very important steps that irrevocably change a person's entire life. Sometimes the change is for the better—and sometimes it is *much* better—but the odds are that it will be for the worse, as we will see.

Making the Decision to Divorce

Threats of divorce usually precede the decision to actually file for divorce. These threats are often made in an attempt to shock the other spouse into making a serious effort to resolve the marital difficulties. It is not unusual for one spouse to threaten divorce and then reconcile with the other spouse several times before actually seeing a lawyer. It is not unusual for a couple to have a series of reconciliations *after* seeing a lawyer, before subsequently allowing the divorce action to run its course (Bohannon 1985).

Recognizing a Failing Relationship The warning signs of impending divorce may occur when the couple's relationship begins to be increasingly fraught with difficulties and conflicts they cannot seem to resolve. Affection, respect, and trust are replaced by feelings of annoyance, resentment, and distrust. Liking becomes disliking; commitment becomes virtually nonexistent. Sexual desire may remain for at least one of the couple, but rarely with the same intensity. Most aspects of love vanish, until not enough interper-

---

[14]See Kitson and Morgan (1990); Trovato and Lauris (1989); Smith, Mercy, and Conn (1988); and U.S. National Center for Health Statistics, "Current Estimates from the National Health Interview Survey: United States, 1987" (1988).

sonal fulfillment remains to hold the couple together (see Chapter 3). Mutually provided satisfactions become increasingly rare while disappointments and misunderstandings increase. As resentments multiply, each spouse grows more and more dissatisfied with the other and with the marriage. As disillusion increases, the pain of remaining in the situation becomes greater than the potential pain of separation. Indeed, separation and divorce may even be seen as relief from the pain of marriage.

One spouse usually becomes disillusioned with the marriage before the other does. Satisfactions may be deliberately withheld by this person, perhaps out of frustration or perhaps out of a desire to get even. The relationship enters a stage of accelerating decline until the couple are on the brink of an open break — physical separation and legal divorce proceedings. The spouse who is the most dissatisfied is usually the one who takes the first step toward legally terminating the marriage by filing for divorce (Bohannon 1985).

Seeing a Marriage Counselor Before taking the step of seeing a lawyer and legally filing for divorce, the couple may seek the help of a professional marriage counselor. This step is often taken only in a last-ditch effort to save the marriage. The couple are usually confused and feel reluctant to make any significant, irrevocable decisions.

Although the methods marriage counselors use vary widely, they rarely tell clients what to do. In general, most counselors avoid giving specific advice, mediating differences, or providing ready-made solutions to conflicts.[15] Instead, counselors are trained to help the couple explore their differences from their own points of view, sorting out the problems and conflicts of their marriage and seeing their difficulties in perspective, so that they are more aware of how they feel and are better able to make choices about what they want to do given the available options. The couple may decide in counseling that their differences are irreconcilable and that divorce is the best solution for them. Successful marriage counseling does not always lead to reconciliation.

Some states regulate the use of the title "marriage counselor," but many do not; in these states anyone can assume the title and can practice without any training, skill, or expertise. Such unqualified counselors may actually harm the couple's relationship. The American Association of Marriage and Family Therapists is a national organization that rigorously screens its members and promotes ethical practices in marriage counseling in all states.

Telling Family and Friends Reactions of a family to word of the breakup of a marriage and the impending divorce vary from solicitous and sympathetic, to gently condemning, to severely condemning, or to angry or detached. Parents can usually understand and accept a separation caused by infidelity, drunkenness, or brutality but are often puzzled (and sometimes impatient) with respect to incompatibility issues that grow out of a desire for change or for something different out of life. Parents may be bewildered, exasperated, and critical of a son or daughter who ends a marriage for reasons they believe to be frivolous, and they may urge a reconciliation (Weiss 1975).

When friends are told of the divorce, they may feel burdened by the heavy claims on their sympathies, or they may feel frightened, "as though the separation were a communicable disease," and react to the divorce as a warning to

---

[15]An exception to this approach usually occurs only if a marital difficulty rests on factual ignorance, such as lack of information about sexual anatomy and physiology. In this situation, the counselor may either provide the information or recommend a source.

themselves, a realization that their own marriage might be vulnerable. Others may be sympathetic, understanding, and supportive. Whatever the reaction, friends recognize that the divorced person is now different and that adjustments in the friendship must be made, often resulting in mutual withdrawal (Weiss 1975, pp. 158–60). There is no explicit ending of the friendship, although once in a while the separated person or a member of a married couple may express disapproval of or disappointment in the other. Rather, the friendship is allowed to fade, as neither the separated individual nor the married friends call to arrange a visit (Weiss 1975, p. 161). One study (Halem 1982) reported that 63 percent of women and 42 percent of men felt that the breakup of old friendships and the making of new ones was one of the major problems of divorce.

Using Divorce Mediation A decade or so ago, divorce mediation was heralded as the wave of the future that would soon replace expensive litigation proceedings in a courtroom. However, these predictions have not been fulfilled; relatively few couples are using mediation instead of litigation (Brannagan 1990).

Many divorce attorneys believe that most mediators are improperly qualified (for example, ignorant of complex tax laws that have long-term consequences). Mediation has also received little support from women's rights groups, who believe that women are at a bargaining disadvantage. They point out that divorcing parties typically have no advocates, which gives the husband an advantage because he is likely to be more accustomed to dealing in business affairs — even though mediators try to give each person an equal chance. Moreover, divorcing couples often choose to battle in the courts because this gives them an opportunity to vent their anger and pain. These couples don't use mediation be-

cause they want justification and revenge (Brannagan 1990).

Approximately 70 percent of couples who have used mediation are satisfied with it. Moreover, mediation is cheaper than divorce attorney fees (Brannagan 1990).

Although mediation is relatively rare in the private sector, it is more widely used in the public realm of social services. As court dockets are clogged with family disputes, the impetus for public sponsored mediation is growing. By late 1988, for example, more than a hundred mediation programs were playing at least a small role in divorce courts in thirty-six states. In some states, such as Maine and California, mediation is a mandatory first step for couples with children. If mediation fails, they may then resort to litigation (Brannagan 1990). In California, mandatory mediation has achieved a settlement rate of between 55 and 85 percent, depending on whether the dispute was over custody, visitation rights, or both (Wallerstein 1988).

The First Three Years of Divorce

After the issues of property settlement, alimony, spousal support, child support, child custody, and visitation rights have been settled — whichever apply — and the divorce decree has been issued, the person is once again single. A divorced single is not the same as a never-married single, however, for responsibilities and emotional ties are not erased by the divorce. Although the divorce decree is a single event marking the legal end of the marriage, a divorce is a long process that is destined to have a long sequel: The aftermath of divorce may continue for years (see Box 12-2).

Francke (1983) found that the first twelve to eighteen months following a divorce typically include high levels of anxiety. However, she found that it is not unusual for the first few

BOX 12·2

The Stages of Divorce

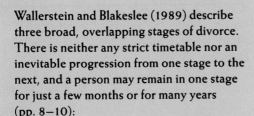

Wallerstein and Blakeslee (1989) describe three broad, overlapping stages of divorce. There is neither any strict timetable nor an inevitable progression from one stage to the next, and a person may remain in one stage for just a few months or for many years (pp. 8–10):

- The first, or acute, stage begins before the decision to divorce is made. It starts with a growing sense of unease and disappointment with the marriage, rises to a peak at the decision to divorce, and usually lasts between several months and a year or two following the divorce (or sometimes longer). This stage is characterized by anger, depression, disorganization, and unhappiness. It typically includes dramatic reversals of mood in which people experience sudden changes from optimism and exhilaration to sadness and immobility, or from being un-

derstanding and forgiving to feeling hostile and vengeful.

- The second, or transitional, stage of divorce is characterized by attempts to establish a new life-style. Adults may return to school, form a new relationship, move to a new community, or renew ties with old acquaintances. Children may move to a new neighborhood, enter a new school, make new friends, and discover new interests. Many families are uprooted and move many times during this stage, which can last several years.

- The third stage is characterized by the attainment of a sense of stability. The family — whatever its form — is reestablished as a secure, functioning unit. Visiting patterns and child-support patterns become stable, and living arrangements and schooling become settled.

months of this period to be characterized by feelings of well-being. The decision has been made, the die is cast, the marriage is over, and the future looks bright. This short period of euphoria is usually followed by feelings of chronic dejection, loneliness, and stress:

The novelty of the first flush of single's freedom fades and loneliness begins to set in. "This is not the sort of loneliness that comes

with an evening's boredom, or the loneliness of having no one to share a sunset with, but loneliness that feeds on the panic that there never, ever will be anyone to share anything with again." (Francke 1983, pp. 25–26)

Research indicates that men and women alike often experience a high incidence of casual sexual adventures during the year following a divorce. It is not uncommon among ex-husbands

A divorced man has a better chance of finding a partner than a divorced woman has.

remain dedicated bachelors for long; most ex-husbands find that they can create a satisfying life-style only within a long-term relationship. Hetherington found that an intense preoccupation with recreational sex tends to diminish for both men and women during the second post-divorce year, when they become increasingly preoccupied with developing a long-term loving relationship. By the second year, most men have reverted to predivorce modes of dress and behavior, and most women are less concerned about losing weight (Hetherington, cited in Doherty 1989).

Francke (1983) found that the second and third years often include a continuation of post-divorce problems, with women usually experiencing more economic problems than men do. As loneliness increases, both ex-husbands and ex-wives often plunge into a frenzy of activity during the second year. No project seems too banal for the person who cannot face another evening alone:

> Suddenly, there is a burning need to learn to make jewelry, throw clay pots, take creative writing courses — anything to get out of the house. Men . . . often go on a social tear and seek companionship, however temporary, in bars, at clubs, and at parties they never would have dreamed of going to while they were still married. Loneliness becomes a malignant enemy, held at bay by a schedule filled to the absurd. (Francke 1983, p. 32)

The Long-Term Effects of Divorce

Research by Wallerstein and Blakeslee (1989) is the first study of its kind to track the long-term effects of divorce. In 1971, when Wallerstein began her study, she agreed with most professionals that divorce was a relatively temporary crisis that would pass in one to three years as people

accustomed to wearing a three-piece suit to shift to more casual attire or to trade in the family sedan or station wagon for a sports car or even a motorcycle. Ex-wives may either devote extra attention to their appearance or become more unkempt during this first postdivorce year, either taking up jogging and aerobic exercises and losing the weight they had long planned to lose or becoming depressed and inactive and gaining weight they don't need. The average weight loss or gain during this period is fifteen pounds, a weight change not found in the control group (Hetherington, cited in Doherty 1989). Wallerstein and Blakeslee (1989) found that although many ex-husbands are preoccupied with having adventurous flings with young women during the first year or so following the divorce, few

PART IV ❖ CONFLICT, DIVORCE, AND REMARRIAGE

started their lives afresh.[16] As her study proceeded, however, she found that divorce is deceptive and that its aftermath is much more persistent than previously thought. Follow-up interviews conducted at five, ten, and fifteen years revealed that divorce is a psychological and social process or chain—sometimes a never-ending chain—of events and responsibilities and shifting relationships that persist much longer than had been previously thought.[17]

Adults in Wallerstein's studies did not easily put their divorces behind them. Ten years after a divorce, half the women and one-third of the men still felt an intense anger toward their former spouses, anger that poisoned their lives and pervaded their relationships with their children.

For most of the couples studied, the divorce benefited one of the couple more than the other. The dominant pattern was for one of the divorcing couple to have an improved life-style and to find happiness in a second marriage but for the other person to have a second and sometimes a third divorce or never remarry at all. One tends to become a winner, the other a loser — economically, psychologically, and socially. Usually the person who wanted the divorce was the one doing well, whereas the one who opposed it was doing less well. In only about 10 percent of couples had both the man and woman constructed happier, fuller lives ten years following the divorce.

Wallerstein found that the children of divorce were rarely among the winners. When parents end a troubled marriage, the children lose a family structure that is fundamental to their healthy development. Most children in the studies described their lives as consumed by their parents' divorce. Even if the children survived the initial years relatively unscathed, buried problems and resentments often surfaced in young adulthood. The studies found that these children usually entered adulthood as underachieving, self-deprecating, angry young men and women. Ten and fifteen years after the divorce, typical problems that surfaced among these young adults were high levels of social difficulties, trouble with the law, alcoholism, and promiscuous behavior. Moreover, as adults these children of divorce were typically unable to form long-lasting intimate relationships because they feared betrayal. (See the section "The Effects of Divorce on Children" in this chapter.)

The Effects of Divorce on Men

Well-established men who are in their thirties and forties at the time of the divorce tend to be the happiest, the most content, and have the highest level of self-esteem ten years after the divorce. Men who divorce in their thirties have usually improved their standard of living since the divorce. They are economically secure, have remarried, and often have their children living with them (Wallerstein and Blakeslee 1989).

A divorced man has a better chance of finding someone who will meet his needs and expectations than a divorced woman does. He also has more opportunities to remarry than a divorced

---

[16] This prevailing view began to change in the late 1970s as researchers began to find that the aftermath of divorce lasted longer than one to three years; see Wallerstein and Kelly (1980); Hetherington, Cox, and Cox (1978); Hoffman and Reiss (1978); and Kalter (1977).

[17] It should be noted that Wallerstein's studies suffer from one obvious weakness: There is no control group. Without a control group, there is no way of knowing whether the same problems would not also occur with the same frequency in families that do not divorce. Furthermore, the sample studied by Wallerstein consisted of well-educated, financially secure, white, middle-class couples who lived in the San Francisco Bay Area; it is not known whether the same results would be found in other socioeconomic groups in other areas. However, compared with other groups, the sample studied by Wallerstein would presumably have the most resources to handle the experience of divorce.

woman has. Many men remarry during the first year following the divorce, and most who remarry do so within three years. A divorced man who remarries usually chooses a woman whom he perceives as being sexier, less critical, more responsive, and more giving than his first wife (Wallerstein and Blakeslee 1989).

A successful second marriage is the single most important ingredient for a divorced man's sense of well-being and happiness. Men who have a successful second marriage are usually content with their lives, are likely to have friends, are happy with their work, and are active in community affairs (Wallerstein and Blakeslee 1989).

Ten years following the divorce, however, only about half of the men who had remarried had succeeded in this remarriage. As we will see in Chapter 13, the divorce rate for remarriage is significantly higher than it is for a first marriage.

Half the men over age forty at the time of a divorce have not remarried ten years later. These men are usually intensely lonely, isolated, and feel socially deprived. Many have no life outside their work; have trouble relating to their children; are uninterested in clubs, churches, political organizations, or community associations; and are worse off than divorced women. One-fourth of the men who were over age forty at the time of a divorce remained isolated from family, friends, and community ten years after the divorce (Wallerstein and Blakeslee 1989).

The Effects of Divorce on Women

Compared with men, the women studied by Wallerstein and Blakeslee (1989) were often physically and psychologically transformed ten years following a divorce. Wallerstein suggests that this may occur, at least in part, because women tend to separate work and family roles, so that a major part of a woman's life is changed

when the family is disrupted. Men's social roles, on the other hand, tend to be defined by employment, and because a man's job and contacts are relatively unchanged, a major part of his life remains stable following a divorce.

Fully half the women who did not remarry experienced noticeable deterioration of their physical well-being: "They have more bodily complaints, including colds, headaches, backaches, constipation, migraines, colitis, high blood pressure, and jaw pain." These physical changes were characteristic of divorced women of all ages. Remarried women did not report this wide range of symptoms (Wallerstein and Blakeslee 1989, p. 53).

Wallerstein's results agree with Weitzman's (1985) finding that the ex-wife's standard of living usually drops sharply, whereas the ex-husband's standard of living rises. As we have seen, women usually obtain custody of the children and receive no alimony and inadequate child support:

> Women with young children, especially if they are driven into poverty after divorce, face a Herculean struggle to survive emotionally and physically. The stress of being a single parent with small children, working day shift and night shift without medical insurance or other backup, is unimaginable to people who have not experienced it. (Wallerstein and Blakeslee 1989, p. 301)

Although successful, relatively affluent ex-husbands do pay child support, many do not continue to provide financial assistance for their children after they reach age eighteen. For example, these men rarely help their children through college (Wallerstein and Blakeslee 1989).

About one-half of divorced women over age forty — those who had sought the divorce — had no regrets ten years later. They were relieved to be free of a marriage in which they felt belittled, bullied, and demeaned. The other half of divorced women of this age—those who had not sought the divorce—found it very difficult to establish a new identity. They said that they had loved their husbands, their homes, their children, and their place in the community and had enjoyed their stable situation. They had, on the whole, been relatively happy with their lives, even though they had not had a good personal relationship with their husbands and had not had a happy sex life.

Ten years after the divorce these women remained intensely lonely. Even though they had become involved in hobby groups, church groups, and community activities that brought them into contact with other women and with friends, they found diminishing opportunities for play and recreation, for sex, and for rewarding work. They felt that they were facing old age— with its increasing infirmity, illnesses, and eventual death—without the support of a loving, intact family structure. Comparing their current situation with their lives ten years ago, they expressed a terrible feeling of loss. Even though their marriage had been flawed, divorce had come as a destructive blow to their self-esteem, their identity, and their entire way of life (Wallerstein and Blakeslee 1989).

As we have seen, the chances of a woman remarrying after age forty are relatively small; only about one in ten ever remarry.

The Effects of Divorce on Children

As difficult as divorce is for adults, it is usually devastating for their children. Children are especially affected by divorce because it occurs during their formative years. What they experience during these years becomes a part of their inner world, their view of themselves, and their

view of society (Wallerstein and Blakeslee 1989). In the sections that follow we will consider how many children are touched by divorce and its effects on them.

The Number of Children Involved in Divorce

Even though the birth rate has declined since 1964, the total number of children involved in divorce has continued to soar—from 0.5 million in 1960, to 0.8 million in 1970, to over a million in 1987.[18] Nearly 38 percent of white children and 75 percent of black children born to married parents in the 1980s will have their families disrupted by divorce before age sixteen (Bumpass 1984a). Three in five couples who divorce have at least one child under age eighteen (Spanier and Thompson 1987). On the average, two children are involved in each divorce decree.[19]

Children's Experience of Divorce

Few children studied by Wallerstein and Blakeslee (1989) believed that their parents would divorce. They thought instead that disagreements would be worked out. Moreover, almost none of the children understood why their parents wished to divorce, even though the parents themselves believed it was obvious. Although it is rare for both parents to want a divorce—usually one wants it while the other does not—they usually agree that the relationship is seriously flawed.

---

[18]"Marriages and Divorces: 1960 to 1987"; U.S. National Center for Health Statistics, "Divorces and Annulments . . . 1970 to 1987."

[19]National Center for Health Statistics, "Divorces and Annulments . . . 1970 to 1987."

Children, however, can be unaware of the depth of their parents' marital problems. Only one child in ten in the study experienced relief when their parents divorced, and these were mostly older children in families in which there had been violence and in which the children feared injury, either for themselves or for their parents.

For adults—or at least for the one who wishes to end the marriage—divorce can mean freedom. It can mean an opportunity for excitement and adventure, for a new and more rewarding life, or for a new romantic relationship. For children, however, divorce usually means a premonition of a serious loss of something that is fundamental to their development—the family structure.

Data from a 1988 national survey on children under age eighteen indicate that children who did not live with both biological parents had poorer health and did not do as well in school as other children. The survey also found that, compared with children living with both biological parents, children of divorce have a higher risk of accidental injury (Dawson 1991). Other researchers have found that children who do not live with both biological parents experience higher levels of fear, loneliness, anxiety, chronic depression, and stress; they are also more likely to be angrier and more aggressive than other children (Zill 1988; Emery, Hetherington, and DiLalla 1985; Hetherington, Cox, and Cox 1982).

Research on long-term adverse effects of divorce on children indicates that children of divorce usually wind up with less education, and with lower-quality education, than children from intact families (Krein and Beller 1988). Growing up with limited resources, attending poor-quality schools, and having fewer opportunities for gaining access to desirable higher education and good jobs limits the future for many children of divorce (Furstenberg 1990).

Next we will examine the most common emotions that children of divorce experience.

Fear More than three-fourths of the children studied by Wallerstein and Blakeslee (1989) were frightened. They were worried about what would happen to them and who would care for them in such fundamental ways as feeding and protecting them. After all, they thought, if the marriage of the mother and father could end so that they were no longer a family living together, couldn't the parent-child relationship end as well? The fragility of their situation became apparent to them with sudden and unexpected force. What stability existed in the world if their most fundamental source of safety—their family—could dissolve?

Loneliness A second pervasive experience of children of divorce is profound, painful loneliness. The only children not extraordinarily lonely were a few adolescents who felt that they still had their father's continuing interest and support, who had a social support system of close, understanding, and sympathetic friends, and who were preoccupied with sports, social, or school activities and interests. (Wallerstein and Blakeslee 1989).

Conflicting Loyalties Most children also experienced a problem that may contribute to loneliness: conflicting loyalties—of being pulled in opposite directions by their divorced parents, two-thirds of whom openly compete for their children's allegiance. This puts the children in a serious dilemma that is impossible to resolve: If they act in such a way as to please one parent, they betray the other. Children who express loyalty by aligning themselves with one parent against the other pay the price with debilitating tension and anxiety. On the other hand, children who do not take sides often feel disloyal to *both* parents. These children may be especially lonely,

PART IV ❖ CONFLICT, DIVORCE, AND REMARRIAGE

for they have no place to turn for comfort because both parents tend to react with anger. Each parent may regard the child's refusal to take sides against the other as a personal betrayal (Wallerstein and Blakeslee 1989).

Anger   A fourth pervasive theme in children's experience of divorce is anger. Although some children keep their anger hidden for fear of retaliation and punishment, others express it spontaneously with temper tantrums, hitting, and screaming. About one child in four directs violent, explosive anger toward one or both parents. These children are resentful and bitter toward their parents for violating an unwritten rule of parenthood: Parents are supposed to make sacrifices for children, not the other way around. This anger often spills over into other areas of the children's lives (Wallerstein and Blakeslee 1989).

The nature of a child's reactions at the time of a divorce does not necessarily predict what the child's later feelings will be. Many children who are initially the most obviously angry at the time of the divorce make an excellent recovery. Others, who are initially calm and apparently untroubled, are bitter, angry, and resentful ten to fifteen years after the divorce. As adults they feel angry that they have suffered because of their parents' mistakes. As we have seen, almost all the children studied by Wallerstein and Blakeslee (1989) felt that their childhood and adolescence had been overshadowed by the divorce.

Young Boys' Typical Reactions to Divorce

Boys who are six to eight years old at the time of the divorce have a particularly difficult time adjusting to the changes in their lives. Many of these boys are unable to concentrate at school, and many either withdraw from friends or are belligerent, hostile, and aggressive. They often expect to fail, not only academically but socially,

and they feel they would be rejected, abandoned, or betrayed by anyone they might trust (Wallerstein and Blakeslee 1989). Hetherington (1987) found that boys may take longer than girls to adjust to changes in the family.

Furstenberg (1990) suggests that the hazards of divorce may not be greater for boys than for girls, but rather that the reaction may be different. Boys "act out" more than girls in response to the trauma of divorce, and they often respond more quickly and openly to marital conflict.

Boys ages nine to nineteen at the time of the divorce make a better immediate recovery than younger boys, but about half of these older boys are "unhappy and lonely" ten years later. As young adults, they typically have difficulties in relating to women (Wallerstein and Blakeslee 1989, p. 67).

Young Girls' Typical Reactions to Divorce

Unlike boys, who often immediately reveal difficulties in reacting to divorce, girls are often well adjusted socially, academically, and emotionally, both immediately after the divorce and throughout adolescence. Much of the research on the effects of divorce on children emphasizes the good recoveries of girls compared with the more troubled experiences of boys. On the other hand, studies have found that a mother's remarrying often causes distress and anxiety for girls, who may be uncomfortable about sexuality (Furstenberg 1990; Zaslow 1987).

Wallerstein and Blakeslee's (1989) longitudinal research revealed an unexpected finding. In the long run—ten to fifteen years following a divorce—girls begin to manifest the same difficulties that boys manifested earlier. Because of this pattern in which feelings remain latent and unsuspected for years, only to assume significant proportions in adulthood, Wallerstein calls it the "sleeper effect" (pp. 56–62).

As young women, these children of divorce, who seemed so untroubled earlier, begin to have difficulty in sustaining intimate, personal relationships with young men. After a few months in a relationship they tend to grow increasingly uncomfortable and distrustful and then break it off. Typically, these adult children of divorce will begin a new liaison, become distrustful, and end it again, perpetuating this pattern repeatedly. These young women struggle with feelings of anxiety and guilt, and with the expectation of rejection and betrayal. Often, attempts to change this pattern by marrying end in early divorce (Wallerstein and Blakeslee 1989).

Although the sleeper effect had been observed by other researchers as well,[20] it has earned special attention since Wallerstein and Blakeslee's research (1989). Because girls *apparently* adjusted to divorce much better than did boys, most studies of the effects of divorce on children have focused on the troubled experience of boys, who were obviously disturbed. The results of Wallerstein and Blakeslee's (1989) research may change our perception that boys suffer from the effects of divorce more than girls;

---

[20]See Furstenberg (1990) and McLanahan and Bumpass (1988) for other independent observations of the sleeper effect.

"perhaps the risk is equalized over the long term" (p. 63).

Older Children's Reactions to Divorce

Children who are about to enter adolescence at the time of the divorce are especially affected by the failure of their parents' marriage. As young adults they tend to fear rejection, betrayal, abandonment, and infidelity in a love relationship. Many feel that all intimate relationships have a high likelihood of failure—that such relationships are inherently unsound, unstable, and untrustworthy and that loss is highly probable. All of the adult children in the Wallerstein and Blakeslee (1989) study—without exception—were afraid of repeating their parents' failure to maintain a loving relationship.

These adult children of divorce wanted a loving relationship, but they were wary and distrustful in their search for it. Every one of these young adults felt an undercurrent of despair and anxiety as they searched for what they feared they would never find. They all feared treachery—that if they ventured to love, their love would be betrayed. All came to adulthood eager for love and marriage, but they feared both marriage and divorce (Wallerstein and Blakeslee 1989).

SUMMARY

Divorce was forbidden in Western civilizations until the early sixteenth century. In extreme cases, marriages could be annulled. From the sixteenth until the mid-nineteenth century in England, a divorce could be obtained, but only through a special act of Parliament (a "Bill of Divorcement"), which was a difficult and expensive procedure that was only rarely used. It

wasn't until the middle of the nineteenth century that England shifted from legislative to judicial divorces. The American colonies initially adopted the British pattern of legislative divorce but shifted to divorce through court action in the beginning of the nineteenth century.

Our divorce system was initially a contest, with a plaintiff and a defendant; and collusion—

when both members of the couple cooperated to obtain a divorce — was a crime. During the 1970s, states began to adopt the concept of no-fault divorce, which involved no plaintiff, no defendant, and no law against collusion, and by the 1980s almost every state had adopted some form of no-fault divorce.

The average ex-wife with the custody of minor children usually experiences a severe drop in her economic well-being following a no-fault divorce, whereas the average ex-husband's standard of living rises significantly. Under the new laws, the ex-husband is not required to contribute equally to the support of his children or to share his salary with his former wife, consequences that were certainly not anticipated, and women's rights advocates, legislators, and members of the judiciary are searching for solutions.

Very few divorce settlements award alimony, but spousal support may be awarded for a limited period, and child support is always awarded when children are involved; however, fewer than half of all ex-husbands pay the amount ordered by the court. After about a year, one ex-husband in four never sees the children again; after five years, one-half to three-fourths of ex-husbands never see the children, leaving the entire responsibility for their care to the custodial mother.

The divorce rate in the United States is necessarily an estimate because not all states report divorce statistics and those that do differ in the information reported. By all estimates, however, the divorce rate has been steadily rising since the latter part of the nineteenth century, and by 1974 about half of all marriages in the United States were ending in divorce. Some demographers estimate that 56 percent of recent marriages will end in divorce and that another 6 percent will end in separation without divorce, yielding a disruption rate of about 62 percent. The divorce rate for remarriages is significantly higher than it is for first marriages.

The national divorce rates tell us very little about the likelihood that any individual will divorce, however. The single most critical factor for the individual is age at marriage; those who marry in their teens have two to three times the incidence of divorce as those who marry after age twenty. Women who marry under age seventeen have three times the divorce rate of women who marry between the ages of twenty and twenty-four. For men in general, the lower the occupational status and the lower the income, the higher the incidence of divorce. This pattern is reversed for women, however: The higher the occupational status and the higher the income, the greater the likelihood of divorce.

The divorce rate is much higher among blacks than it is among whites. Despite the papal ban on divorce, Roman Catholics have about the same divorce rate as Protestants, and Jews have a relatively lower divorce rate than either Roman Catholics or Protestants. Couples are most likely to divorce if they have no children and least likely to divorce if they have three or more children. People whose parents were separated or divorced are themselves more likely to become divorced.

The decision to divorce is usually made after a series of separations and reconciliations. Before taking the final step of filing for divorce, some couples seek marriage counseling, which does not always lead to reconciliation but may help the couple put their difficulties in perspective so that they are more able to make up their minds about how to proceed.

A marriage is legally ended with a divorce, but the aftermath of divorce is never really over. The first stage, which usually lasts for a year or two but may last much longer, is marked by anger, depression, disorganization, and unhappiness. The second stage, characterized by attempts to establish a new life-style, may last for several years. The third stage is distinguished by the attainment of a sense of stability, with the family — whether its head is a single parent or a married couple — becoming reestablished as a secure functioning unit.

Ten years after the divorce, half the women and one-third of the men still felt intense anger toward their former spouses — anger that poisoned their lives and pervaded their relationships with their children.

About half of divorced people feel that their life is improved following the divorce; the other half do not. Usually the person who wanted the divorce is the one who is doing well five, ten, or fifteen years later, whereas the one who opposed it is doing less well. In general, women have more psychological, physical, and financial problems following a divorce than do men. In only a small minority of couples (perhaps one in ten) are both the ex-husband and ex-wife doing well ten years following the divorce.

The remarriage rate for women depends on their age at the time of the divorce. Forty percent of those who are in their twenties remarry, as do 33 percent of those who are in their thirties; however, only 11 percent of those in their forties, and only 3 percent of those in their fifties, remarry.

The remarriage rate for men is much higher than it is for women, although about one-half of men over age forty have not remarried ten years later and are usually intensely lonely, feeling that they have no life outside their work. The most important influence on an older man's sense of well-being and happiness following a divorce is a successful second marriage. Remarried men are much more content with their lives than are men who do not remarry.

Well-established men who are in their thirties and forties at the time of the divorce tend to be the happiest and most content ten years later. Many remarry during the first year following the divorce, and most who remarry do so within three years.

Nearly 38 percent of white children and 75 percent of black children will have their families disrupted by divorce before age sixteen. As difficult as divorce is for adults, it is usually devastating for children. Major themes in children's experiences of divorce are fear, loneliness, conflicting loyalties, and anger. One-third of children are significantly worse off after the divorce, and only one in ten expresses relief; these are mostly older children in families in which there has been open violence and thus the children fear injury either for themselves or for their parents. Ten to fifteen years after a divorce, the majority of children are still intensely angry at their parents for giving a higher priority to adult needs than to children's needs.

Boys who are six, seven, and eight years old at the time of the divorce have a particularly difficult time adjusting and often either withdraw into apathy or become very belligerent, hostile, and aggressive. Ten years later, many of these boys are awkward in relating to women and feel uncomfortable with even casual dating; as a result they tend to live inhibited, emotionally constricted lives, are chronically unhappy and lonely, and have few lasting relationships with young women.

Unlike boys, girls often appear to make a good adjustment — socially, academically, and emotionally — immediately after a divorce and throughout adolescence. In the long run, however — ten to fifteen years later — girls often begin to manifest the same difficulties seen immediately in boys. This "sleeper effect" is quite pronounced, and these young women have great difficulty in sustaining an intimate personal relationship for more than a few months because they anticipate rejection and betrayal. Often, attempts to break this pattern by marrying end in early divorce.

KEY TERMS

The following is a list of key terms in this chapter.
These terms are defined in context within the chapter, and many may also be found in the Glossary.

adultery	cohabitation	legal custody	sleeper effect
alimony	collusion	legal separation	sole custody
"Bill of Divorcement"	compatibility	limited divorce	spousal support
child custody	custodial parent	noncustodial parent	visitation rights
child support	incestuous marriage	no-fault divorce	
church annulment	interlocutory decree	physical custody	
civil annulment	joint legal custody	sacrament	

QUESTIONS

1. Write a paragraph summarizing the history of divorce in Western civilization from the sixteenth century to the present.

2. Compare the concept of divorce as a contest between a plaintiff and a defendant with the concept of no-fault divorce.

3. Why is the national divorce rate necessarily an estimate? Name and describe four methods demographers use to estimate the national divorce rate.

4. How does an individual's likelihood of divorce vary with age at first marriage, education, occupation and income, race-ethnicity, religion, and geographic area?

5. Discuss the effects of divorce on each member of the couple five, ten, and fifteen years later.

6. Discuss the effects of divorce on children — immediately and five, ten, and fifteen years later. What the major themes in children's experiences of divorce?

7. Define and discuss the sleeper effect in divorce.

SUGGESTIONS FOR FURTHER READING

Ahrons, Constance R., and Rodgers, Roy H. *Divorced Families: A Multidisciplinary View.* New York: Norton, 1987.

Arendell, Terry. *Mothers and Divorce: Legal, Economic, and Social Dilemmas.* Berkeley: University of California Press, 1986.

Chesler, Phyllis. *Mothers on Trial: The Battle for Children and Custody.* New York: McGraw-Hill, 1986.

Cherlin, Andrew J. *Marriage, Divorce, Remarriage,* rev. ed. Cambridge, Mass.: Harvard University Press, 1990.

Halem, Lynne. *Separated and Divorced Women.* Westport, Conn.: Greenwood Press, 1982.

Kressel, Kenneth. *The Process of Divorce: How Professionals and Couples Negotiate Settlements.* New York: Basic Books, 1985.

Price, Sharon J., and McHenry, Patrick C. *Divorce.* Newbury Park, Calif.: Sage, 1988.

Riessman, Catherine Kohler. *Divorce Talk: Women and Men Make Sense of Personal Relationships.* New Brunswick, N.J.: Rutgers University Press, 1990.

Spanier, Graham B., and Thompson, Linda. *Parting: The Aftermath of Separation and Divorce.* Beverly Hills, Calif.: Sage, 1984.

Stone, L. *Road to Divorce.* New York: Oxford University Press, 1990.

Walker, Glynnis. *Solomon's Children: Exploding the Myths of Divorce.* New York: Arbor House, 1986.

CHAPTER 13

Remarriage: Stepparents and Stepchildren

When I was twenty, I wanted to meet somebody who was perfect.
Now that I'm past forty, I just wonder if anyone is normal.

Scott Turow, "The Burden of Proof"

Who Remarries?

Remarriage Without Stepchildren

Remarriage with Stepchildren: Stepfamilies

What Do You Know?

Some of the following statements are true and some are false.
Can you tell which are which?

T/F   1. In more than half of all recent marriages, it is a remarriage for at least one of the couple.

T/F   2. The likelihood that a divorced woman will remarry is higher than the likelihood that a woman of the same age will marry for the first time.

T/F   3. Remarriages have a somewhat lower divorce rate than first marriages.

T/F   4. Middle-income or affluent women have a higher rate of remarriage than women with relatively low incomes.

T/F   5. There is usually more commitment in a remarriage than there is in a first marriage.

T/F   6. Ineffective communication is more likely to occur in a remarriage than in a first marriage.

T/F   7. When asked the question "Who do you include in your family?" nearly a third of children did not include a resident stepmother or stepfather.

T/F   8. Stepmothers usually have higher levels of stress than biological mothers, biological fathers, or stepfathers.

Answers: 1-T, 2-T, 3-F, 4-F, 5-F, 6-T, 7-T, 8-T.

emarriages and stepfamilies are not particularly new in America; they have been common since our colonial period. Until the early 1970s, however, a person normally remarried only after a husband or wife's death. Currently, remarriage normally follows a divorce rather than a death (Coleman and Ganong 1990).

As we have seen, most recent first marriages (perhaps more than 60 percent) are disrupted by separation, annulment, or divorce (see Chapter 12). A person who goes through the trauma of divorce is not usually disillusioned with marriage, however, and usually marries again — within about two years;[1] in fact, nearly one-fourth remarry within one year (Spanier and Thompson 1987). Consider the following statistics concerning remarriage:

- The Census Bureau estimates that fully 80 percent of divorced men and 75 percent of divorced women remarry (Wallerstein and Blakeslee 1989).

- More that half of all recent marriages is a remarriage for at least one of the couple, and one recent marriage in four is a remarriage for *both* the bride and the groom (Bumpass, Sweet, and Castro-Martin 1990).

- More than three-fourths of all remarriages involve stepchildren (Pasley and Ihinger-Tallman 1988; Glick 1984).

- Women who do not remarry usually suffer significant economic deprivation; if they have custody of children, this deprivation is likely to be severe both for them and for their children (Bumpass, Sweet, and Castro-Martin 1990).

- Several studies have found that remarriage restores a divorced woman's economic status to its predivorce level (Jacobs and Furstenberg 1986; Duncan and Hoffman 1985).

- Men who do not remarry are not usually as economically deprived as women, but they suffer greater social isolation and poorer health than women who remain unmarried (Wilson 1991).

- The incidence of divorce is about 25 percent higher for remarriages than it is for first marriages; for marriages that are a remarriage for both members of the couple, the divorce rate is 50 percent higher (Wilson 1991; Norton and Moorman 1987).

- About half the children whose parents divorce and remarry will experience a second parental divorce (Bumpass 1984b).

- Remarried couples who divorce usually do so about two years sooner than couples who are in a first marriage (Glick 1984; Spanier and Glick 1981).

- The higher divorce rate of remarriages and the shorter interval of time between a remarriage and a divorce indicate that there are significant differences between a first marriage and a remarriage and that these differences make a remarriage much more fragile than a first marriage.

In this chapter we will see who remarries and who does not, examine the critical differences between a first marriage and a remarriage, and investigate what it means to be a stepfather, stepmother, or stepchild in a reconstituted family.

Who Remarries?

As we have noted, men are slightly more likely to remarry than are women (80 percent versus 75 percent). The likelihood that a divorced person will remarry is higher, at all ages, than the

---

[1] The median time between divorce and remarriage is nearly two years; U.S. National Center for Health Statistics, "Marriage Rates and Median Age of Bride and Groom, by Previous Marital Status: 1970 to 1987" (1991).

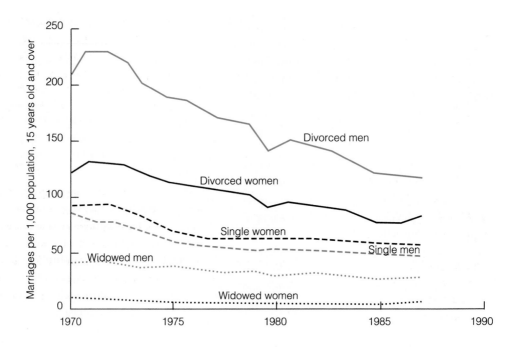

FIGURE 13-1

Marriage rates, by previous marital status: 1970–1987.

Source: U.S. National Center for Health Statistics, "Marriage Rates and Median Age of Bride and Groom, by Previous Marital Status: 1970 to 1987." In *Statistical Abstract of the United States*, 111th ed., p. 87. Washington, D.C.: Government Printing Office, 1991.

likelihood that a person will marry for the first time (see Figure 13-1).

White women are more likely to remarry than are black women; fewer than half of all divorced black women remarry, compared with 75 percent of whites. Hispanics are even less likely to remarry; their remarriage rates are only about one-half those of whites (Bumpass, Sweet, and Castro-Martin 1990).

Except for race, age is the single most important determinant of the likelihood of remarriage (Bumpass, Sweet, and Castro-Martin 1990). Although 75 percent of divorced women remarry, this figures include women who are eighteen to twenty years old. Only about 40 percent of divorced women ages twenty to thirty remarry, as do about a third of women in their thirties, about

10 percent of women in their forties, and about 3 percent of women in their fifties (Wallerstein and Blakeslee 1989). Each year that passes reduces the likelihood that a divorced woman will remarry (Glick and Lin 1987). For middle-aged and elderly women, the likelihood of remarriage drops sharply because of the shorter life span of men and because of the dating differential (see Chapter 5). Thus there is a growing population of unmarried women in their fifties, sixties, and older.[2]

---

[2]For every 100 unmarried women ages forty-five to sixty-four there are only fifty-four available men of that age; U.S. National Center for Health Statistics, "Percent Distribution of Marriages, by Age, Sex, and Previous Marital Status: 1980 to 1987" (1991).

PART IV ❖ CONFLICT, DIVORCE, AND REMARRIAGE

"It's better than my mother's cooking but not as good as my first wife's."

Widows and widowers have lower likelihoods of remarriage than people who are divorced. The probability that a widower will remarry within a given number of years is about half the probability that a divorced man will remarry within the same period. For widows, the probability for remarriage is even less: They have only about one-seventh the likelihood of remarrying that a divorced woman has.[3]

The rate of remarriage for women is negatively correlated with their income: As their income goes up, the rate of remarriage goes down. Either high-income women are choosier, or it is difficult for them to find suitable prospects. On the other hand, middle-income or high-income men have higher rates of remarriage than men

with low incomes (Glick 1980). The rate of remarriage for women is also negatively correlated with their level of education: The higher their level of education, the lower their likelihood of remarrying (Ihinger-Tallman and Pasley 1987). Among black and white women alike, the lower the level of education, the higher the likelihood of remarriage (Teachman 1986).

Divorced women with the custody of children have a lower rate of remarriage than divorced women without children. About 40 percent of divorced women with custody of three or more children will never remarry (Bumpass, Sweet, and Castro-Martin 1990).

Given the overall high rate of remarriage, it is important to note that the expected norms that operate in dating and courtship before remarriage differ considerably from those that occur before a first marriage, especially if one (or both) of the couple have custody of children. Children

---

[3]U.S. National Center for Health Statistics, "Marriage Rates and Median Age of Bride and Groom . . . 1970 to 1987."

often leave a parent little time to pursue a romantic relationship. Moreover, even if a prospective partner is willing to assume the responsibilities of a stepparent, the children may not be willing to accept the person in this role. In addition, a previously married person is often haunted by past mistakes and is usually more cautious in courting (Teachman and Heckert 1985).

Among couples in which one or both members have been formerly married, about six out of ten couples test their relationship by cohabiting first to see how things work out before making the formal commitment of marriage (Bumpass, Sweet, and Castro-Martin 1990; Buunk and van Driel 1989).

Remarriage Without Stepchildren

There are two types of remarriage without stepchildren:

1. Remarriages in which the couple have no children. In this type of child-free marriage (see Chapter 8) at least one member of the couple has been married before.
2. Remarriages in which neither member of the couple has children from a first marriage, but they have their own children after they marry.

Very little research has been conducted on either of these two types of remarriage. The limited research that is currently available does indicate, however, that significant differences exist between a first marriage and remarriage, even when no stepchildren are involved:

- People who remarry are more experienced and may be expected to bring different expectations to the remarriage than they did to their first marriage.

- A person in a first marriage will perceive the marriage from the perspective of previous singlehood, whereas a previously married person will perceive a remarriage from the perspective of the first, disrupted marriage.

- A remarried person has an ex-spouse and ex-in-laws that were factors in the first marriage. Emotional, social, and financial ties may remain following the divorce; for example, a husband in a remarriage might be paying alimony to his ex-wife (Ihinger-Tallman and Pasley 1987; Kressel 1985; Furstenberg and Spanier 1984).

Remarriage with Stepchildren: Stepfamilies

Most remarriages (about three-fourths) involve stepchildren, as we have seen. Much research is available regarding stepfamilies.

The most common form of the stepfamily consists of a biological mother and a resident stepfather; about 90 percent of stepfamilies are of this form. Studies indicate that these stepfamilies have a lower level of education and significantly less income than is average for all married couples with children (Miller 1990). The opposite is true for stepfamilies in which the stepchildren live with their biological father and a resident stepmother. In these stepfamilies, both the level of education and income is higher than is average for all married couples with children (Miller 1990).

For remarried couples to have their own children together is a common occurrence. About half of all stepfamilies have at least one child born to or adopted by both parents after the remarriage (Miller 1990; Wineberg 1990). One preschool-age stepchild in four (25 percent) has a half-sibling in the first eighteen months following a remarriage; the figure is 58 percent if their mother is under age twenty-five (Bumpass 1984b).

Many studies have found that remarriages with stepchildren have a significantly higher divorce rate than do remarriages without stepchildren. This difference in divorce rates would seem to indicate that conflict with stepchildren is often a serious source of dissension (Ihinger-Tallman and Pasley 1987; White and Booth 1985; Knaub, Hanna, and Stinnet 1984).

The Structure and Dynamics of a Stepfamily

The structure and dynamics of a family are a function of the many ways the members relate to one another—the day-to-day family interaction. In a stepfamily this interaction is quite different from that of a first family. There is widespread agreement that stepfamilies have distinctive features that alter family processes (Johnson 1988; Bohannon 1985). For example, whereas the power hierarchy is normally well established in a first family, it is usually less clear in a stepfamily. A stepparent is in the position of parent but is not really a parent. Stepchildren often refuse to acknowledge a stepparent's power. ("You can't tell me what do! You're not my father!") Situations in which a stepparent does not have the power normally granted a parent can lead to severe disruption in the family structure (Ihinger-Tallman and Pasley 1987).

Stepchildren often have two sets of authority figures: a biological mother and a resident stepfather in one household, and a biological father and a stepmother in another household. The new and unfamiliar lines of family power and politics can be bewildering and distressing to parents, stepparents, children, and stepchildren alike (Ihinger-Tallman and Pasley 1987).

"Few children come to view their stepparents as indistinguishable from a biological parent," and few stepparents treat their stepchildren in the same way that they treat their own children. Consequently, it is not surprising that children's ties to stepparents are not usually as close as ties to biological parents (Furstenberg 1990, p. 396). It is informative to note that stepchildren often greet a stepparent differently from the way they greet a parent. They may avoid addressing the stepparent directly, for example, feeling uncomfortable in using "Mom" or "Dad" and equally uncomfortable in using a first name. Some children do form close, personal ties with a stepparent, however. The younger the child, the greater the likelihood of this happening, but it may also occur with adolescents and even young adults (Furstenberg 1990).

In distinguishing first families from stepfamilies, Visher and Visher (1979) cited six structural and dynamic characteristics, all of which could lead to potential difficulties:

1. Displacement of anger and hostility onto the new stepparent when children feel the loss of the nonresidential parent.

2. Ongoing power struggles between custodial and nonresidential parents.

3. Jealousy of children toward the new stepparent, who is seen as an interloper into the household.

4. Different rules and regulations that pertain to children, who suddenly become members of two different households.

5. Unclear stepparenting role.

6. Unclear grandparenting role; children often now have more than two sets.

Successful stepfamilies learn to be adaptive. Their members develop a capacity for understanding and tolerating family differences, and they learn to accept both the special bonds that preexist between biological parent and child and the complex role the stepparent tries to fulfill (Pill 1990).

Four Keys to Stepfamily Interaction

Research on group interaction has identified four factors that must be present before any small group can function effectively, and a stepfamily can certainly be considered a type of small group (Tallman 1976). Accordingly, in order to function effectively a stepfamily must have and maintain the following characteristics:

- commitment
- cohesion
- effective communication
- boundary maintenance

One or more of these four essentials for group stability is more likely to be absent in a stepfamily than in a first family (Ihinger-Tallman and Pasley 1987). In the following sections we will examine each essential in turn.

Commitment The essential element of commitment is stability — the desire to maintain relationships and to make the effort necessary to implement this desire. The higher rate of divorce among remarriages indicates that there may be less commitment in remarriages than in first marriages. Three reasons have been suggested why this is so.

First, the *incomplete institution* hypothesis suggests that remarriages are more fragile because there are fewer norms to guide behavior. Roles and patterns of behavior are not always clear in a remarriage but are instead ill-defined or ambiguous. Thus it is often not possible simply to rely either on customary behavior, on interactions that may be taken for granted, or on norms that are generally accepted (Ihinger-Tallman and Pasley 1987; White and Booth 1985; Cherlin 1978).

Second, the *predisposition* hypothesis suggests that remarriages are more fragile because they are contracted by people who are predisposed to see divorce as a solution to marital unhappiness. At least one person in a remarriage has already ended a marriage with divorce, and this person is thus part of a group (the divorced) that may be inclined to solve the problems of an unhappy marriage by ending it (Furstenberg and Spanier 1984; Halliday 1980).

Third, the *psychopathology* hypothesis proposes that divorced and remarried people are more likely to have behavioral problems or personality disorders (such as alcoholism or a violent temper) that lower the caliber of remarriages. Put another way, previously divorced people in remarriages may represent a population of less stable individuals than people who have never divorced. If these unstable qualities become an issue, the other partner's commitment to the marriage may be reduced, and the marriage itself may be brought into question (Brody, Neubaum, and Forehand 1988; Ihinger-Tallman and Pasley 987; White and Booth 1985).

Researchers have found some support for the first two hypotheses but have yet to obtain evidence that supports the third one (Coleman and Ganong 1990).

Cohesion Cohesion is a sense of unity, a feeling of closeness with other family members and of pride in belonging to or being part of the family (Ihinger-Tallman and Pasley 1987; Giles-Sims 1984).

Cohesion is almost automatic in a first family; although a member of a nuclear family may sometimes feel like an outsider, this is relatively rare. Cohesion is not automatic in a stepfamily, however, and it may not develop for three to five years, or it may never develop. Cohesion is present in the new household when everyone feels comfortable with one another and with the relationships with former spouses, former in-laws, and friends from the first marriage (Ihinger-Tallman and Pasley 1987; Asmundsson et al. 1983).

Effective Communication Effective communication is essential to any good relationship, as we have seen in Chapter 11. Communication may break down and become ineffective in a first marriage, and when it does it often leads to divorce. However, communication is even more likely to break down in a remarriage, for many reasons.

Children of a first marriage have known their parents, and have been known by them, since infancy. In a remarriage, a new family is created suddenly, and some members of this new family — the stepchildren and stepparent — do not know each other very well and are likely to misperceive and misunderstand one another. When stepparent-stepchild communication breaks down (or fails to be established in the first place), difficulties of communication between the married couple usually follow as well (Ihinger-Tallman and Pasley 1987; Koren et al. 1983).

Boundary Maintenance It is essential for the success of any small group that boundaries be established, recognized, and maintained. Three types of boundaries are especially significant in a stepfamily: external boundaries, intergenerational boundaries, and interhousehold boundaries (Ihinger-Tallman and Pasley 1987; Boss and Greenberg 1984; Hunter and Schuman 1980).

External boundaries separate the family from the world at large — from friends, neighbors, social workers, police, and strangers. Such family boundaries can be too rigid, leaving the family too isolated, or they can be too loose. An ideal family boundary is one that protects the family from outside interference, yet is open enough to encourage healthy interactions with nonfamily people (Ihinger-Tallman and Pasley 1987).

Intergenerational boundaries separate the parents' generation from the children's generation. If this

boundary breaks down or is inoperative, serious family disruption usually follows, as when a child becomes beyond parental control or a parent has an incestuous relationship with a child.

Interhousehold boundaries define who is, and who is not, a member of the family. Are nonresident biological parents considered part of the family? Are resident stepparents considered part of the family? Are resident stepchildren?

Surprisingly, researchers have found that almost a third (31 percent) of stepchildren do not include a resident stepfather or stepmother as part of the family when asked the question "Who do you include in your family?" Furthermore, about 15 percent of stepparents do not include stepchildren who live in the household as part of the family. Moreover, 7 percent of children excluded their biological mothers who were not in residence, and 9 percent of children excluded nonresident biological fathers. Clearly, a stepfamily's identity and sense of unity may suffer if members cannot agree on who is and is not a member of the family (Furstenberg et al. 1983).

A family's identity may be threatened if an ex-spouse exerts pressure to open the family boundaries more than the family wishes:

> The process of developing commitment and cohesion among family members who may not like each other, or may not want another member to be considered "in the family," clearly makes it more difficult to establish a cohesive unit. . . . And determining how open or closed the family should be to outside people and pressures is a formidable task. (Ihinger-Tallman and Pasley 1987, p. 50)

Financial Pressures in a Stepfamily

For all but a relatively few families there is never enough money, and economic stress is a major source of problems (see Chapter 14). Financial problems are an invariable and inevitable accompaniment to most marriages, whether a first marriage or a remarriage. Married couples have more arguments over money than over any other issue (see Chapter 14), and economic stress is a major cause of marriage failure. A person who has been through a divorce and is now remarried is certainly no stranger to economic problems, which may have been one of the reasons the first marriage ended.

There is, however, at least one financial problem in a stepfamily that does not occur in a first marriage: the expenses of supporting stepchildren, which may be a serious consideration even if the ex-husband (the children's father) actually pays court-ordered child support.

As we have seen in Chapter 12, more than half (53 percent) of ex-husbands do not send custodial mothers the child support payments ordered by the court, and even fewer ex-husbands send child support money after the custodial mother remarries. By the third year after the remarriage, the rate of nonpayment is 60 percent, and by the fifth year it is 70 to 80 percent (Kressel 1985). More than two-thirds of remarried women receive no financial support at all from their ex-husbands (Furstenberg and Spanier 1987; Ihinger-Tallman and Pasley 1987). Mothers who do receive some support payments receive only a small amount (about $2,000 a year on average), as we have seen (Chapter 12). Failure to send child support payments is frequently a source of continuing conflict between the custodial mother and her ex-husband.

Although the custodial mother usually works to help support the family, her financial contribution is generally much less than that of the children's stepfather (her husband in the remarriage). The children's stepfather must usually assume the chief financial responsibility for his stepchildren (Troph 1984).

Noncustodial fathers who have remarried and have children to support in the remarriage have their own financial difficulties, of course. A second wife may resent her husband's turning over money to his first wife for his first children, feeling that his primary responsibility is to his current family. Does he pay for the braces on his daughter's teeth in his second marriage, or does he send the money to his first wife to pay for orthodontia needed by his noncustodial daughter?

If his second wife has custody of children from her first marriage (to whom he is a stepfather), the situation is even more complicated. Does he send the money to his noncustodial daughter, who is living in another household with her mother and new stepfather, or use it to support his stepdaughter who is living with him in his remarriage?

Relationships with Ex-Spouses

Ahrons and Wallisch (1986) note that although the stereotype of a divorced couple fighting over child support payments and other issues regarding their children is quite common, it is characteristic of only about half of all divorced couples; the other half maintains at least cordial relationships. Of the 50 percent of divorced couples who continue to maintain a cordial relationship, about one out of four are "perfect pals"; the other three out of four are "cooperative colleagues."

Ex-Spouses as Perfect Pals   One out of every eight divorced couples are perfect pals who genuinely like each other. They had a "friendly" divorce and remain good friends. They have fond memories of their early closeness and intimacy and continue to trust each other. They continue to feel responsible for their children and often put the children's welfare ahead of their own. Each perceives the other as a caring and responsible parent, and their parenting is very similar to the way it was during the marriage. They continue to enjoy mutual association with their children at such family events as holiday and birthday celebrations, graduations, weddings, and Little League games. They are not only present at these events but share in their planning and in anticipation of them (Ahrons and Rodgers 1987).

Ex-Spouses as Cooperative Colleagues Three out of eight divorced couples are "cooperative colleagues" who remain friendly but are not as cordial and cooperative as perfect pals. Cooperative colleagues continue to share an interest in their children's welfare and are mutually concerned with the need to be responsible parents. They worry about the children's problems, are happy with their accomplishments, and tend to deal with the normal stresses of child rearing in much the same way as they did while they were married. They attempt to minimize for the children the difficulties inherent in a divorce and the breakup of the family. Unlike the perfect pals, however, arrangements for visitation and other plans for the children must be explicitly and formally defined by the court. Fortunately, cooperative colleagues usually do not have to depend on the court to settle differences that arise because of situational changes, such as new working hours for the ex-husband or a change in scheduled ice-skating or ballet lessons. When such differences arise, cooperative colleagues are able to work out mutually agreeable arrangements between themselves. They celebrate the children's major life events together but with less shared warmth and pleasure than the perfect pals; thus, for example, both may attend an event but will sit separately (Ahrons and Rodgers 1987; Ahrons and Wallisch 1986).

Ex-Spouses as Angry Associates About one-fourth of divorced couples are "angry associates" who have bitter and resentful feelings about their former marriage and about the divorce. The divorce proceedings typically were marked by acrimonious disputes about money, property, child custody, child support payments, and visitation rights for the noncustodial parent, and the anger each feels for the other remains a central aspect of their continuing troubled relationship (Ahrons and Wallisch 1986).

Conflicts and power struggles persist, with the custodial mother using her control over the children as a weapon for withholding visitation rights or altering visitation schedules, while the ex-husband attempts to assert control by withholding or delaying support payments. Ahrons and Rodgers (1987) cite the following example:

> Dad is scheduled to pick Jamie up at noon on Saturday. At 11:00 Mom calls Dad and says Jamie has some chores she must finish before she goes with Dad so she can't leave until 2:00. Dad arrives at 2:00, angry about the change in plans and Mother's control over his relationship with Jamie, and is met at the door by Mother, who announces that Jamie is not quite ready. She uses that time while Jamie is anxiously getting herself together in the next room to argue with Dad about his irresponsibility about child support and the increasing financial needs of Jamie. A fight follows and Jamie and Dad leave in anger, with Mother reminding them to be home precisely at 8:00 that night. At 8:00 Mother is watching at the window waiting for Dad and Jamie to arrive and growing increasingly angry as Dad and Jamie arrive an hour later. Jamie runs into her room after hugging Mom while her parents continue the fight started earlier in the day. Next month Dad sends half the child support or sends it a couple of weeks late. (p. 127)

Rather than being considered opportunities for celebration, major life events are experienced as times of major stress that require delicate and special negotiations: "There is a general quality of tiptoeing through a minefield for all of the participants" (p. 127).

Ex-Spouses as Fiery Foes About one-fourth of divorced couples are "fiery foes" whose divorces were hotly contested legal battles in which each fought over the division of property, child custody, visitation rights, and custody payments, and the memory of this conflict still rankles them. The custody agreement continues to remain a sore point, with the ex-husband's access to the children a persistent source of conflict and disagreement. As with the angry associates, support payments are either not paid at all or are underpaid or delayed. Each parent's ability to accept the other's parenting rights is virtually nonexistent, and each of them continues to focus, with destructive bitterness, on the grievances endured and the wrongs suffered at the hands of the other. They retain no fond memories either of each other or of happy times during their marriage. Major events in the children's life usually set the stage for a power struggle that may be so acrimonious that it destroys the celebratory mood for everyone involved (Ahrons and Rodgers 1987; Ahrons and Wallisch 1986).

Ahron's four categories of divorced couples may be illustrated by the following description of a high school graduation ceremony (Ahrons and Rodgers 1987, pp. 127–29):

- Perfect pals (one out of every eight divorced couples) might plan festivities to celebrate the graduation as a family unit. They might plan a lunch or dinner together, might sit together at the ceremony, and might even give their son or daughter one gift.
- Cooperative colleagues (three out of every eight divorced couples) would be less likely to plan the festivities together but might both attend and might sit together. The mother might plan a dinner and invite her ex-husband to join them.

- Angry associates (two out of every eight divorced couples) would observe the graduation but would do so separately. Perhaps one parent would take the graduate out to dinner the night before, whereas the other would celebrate at a lunch after the ceremony. At the graduation ceremony itself, the parents would sit separately, avoiding each other and any mutual interaction with the graduate.
- Fiery foes (two out of every eight divorced couples) would likely seize the occasion as an opportunity for conflict. The custodial mother might make a point of not inviting her ex-husband to the ceremony and would exclude him from all related events. He, of course, would be aware of the graduation ceremonies and would feel angry and hurt about being left out.

Being a Stepparent

Clearly, the role of stepparent is more difficult and less clearly defined than that of parent (Furstenberg 1987; Giles-Sims 1984). Researchers find that problems regarding discipline and handling of stepchildren are cited by more than one-third of those in a remarriage as a primary cause of stress for both the remarried couple and the stepchildren. Stepparents relatively consistently perceive the stepchildren as the source of persistent problems (Knaub, Hanna, and Stinnet 1984; Lutz 1983). If the stepchildren are teenagers, one-half of remarried couples report difficulties with discipline (Connecticut Remarriage Research Group 1983).

Children usually have very little to say about the remarriage in the first place, but once it has taken place they have the power to break it up. "Stepchildren have the power to pit parent against stepparent, siblings against parents, and stepsiblings against siblings." Stepchildren can create an uncomfortable atmosphere that can put great strain on the remarriage by making derogatory and unfavorable comparisons between it and the previous marriage (Ihinger-Tallman and Pasley 1987, p. 94).

The Resident Stepfather Because the mother becomes the custodial parent in nine out of ten divorce actions, the usual stepfamily household consists of the mother, her children, and her second husband, who is the stepfather of her children (Furstenberg and Spanier 1987). A custodial mother often encourages a stepfather to take an active role as a father figure, and most stepfathers do so. However, entry into this role is usually not easy, often involving uncertainty and anxiety for both the new stepfather and the stepchildren. Stepfathers may tend to feel inadequate in establishing a feeling of closeness with their stepchildren. In general, stepfathers have more difficulty relating to girls than to boys (Ihinger-Tallman and Pasley 1987; Clingempeel, Ievoli, and Brand 1984; Santrock et al. 1982).

Most stepfathers are afraid of not being accepted by the children and are particularly concerned about being compared with the children's biological father. Stepfathers feel more satisfaction in relating to their stepchildren when they have no children of their own or if their own children are not living in the household (Weingarten 1980; Hafkin 1981).

Stepfathers are usually more successful at forming affectionate bonds with stepchildren under eight years of age than with older stepchildren. Stepfathers usually find girls of this age especially responsive to their overtures of warmth and admiration (Wallerstein and Kelly 1980). It is easier for a stepfather to bond with young stepchildren because they are usually more responsive to conciliatory overtures than older children are. Moreover, a stepfather may feel more paternal and protective toward a five-year-old than toward a fifteen-year-old (Wallerstein and Blakeslee 1989).

Stepfathers usually try to make instant friends of their stepchildren, instead of proceeding slowly, with gradual progressive steps, as the children's readiness for intimacy develops. Stepfathers are rarely sensitive to and aware of their stepchildren's needs in this regard. Because of the children's wariness, and perhaps because of their own anxiety, most stepfathers react by becoming overtly authoritative and assuming the role of disciplinarian. A stepfather who does this may only succeed in driving a wedge between the stepchildren and himself (Wallerstein and Kelly 1980).

Even though a stepfather may have significant influence on his stepchildren, he does not usually replace the departed father in their affections. Children usually have no difficulty in both maintaining an affectionate relationship with their noncustodial father and ultimately accepting a stepfather. If the noncustodial father has been visiting the children regularly before the remarriage, he usually continues these visits, and the pattern of visiting seems to remain relatively unaffected (Wallerstein and Kelly 1980).

The Resident Stepmother Because nine out of ten divorce settlements award custody of the children to the mother, relatively few stepfamilies consist of the custodial father, his children, and a resident stepmother. In general, these families have more problems than families that include a stepfather. Studies show that stepmothers have higher stress levels and more dissatisfaction with their lot than do stepfathers, who have higher stress levels than either biological fathers or biological mothers (Jacobson 1987; Santrock and Sitterle 1987; Ahrons and Wallisch 1986).

Several reasons have been suggested to explain why the resident stepmother's role is more difficult than the resident stepfather's. In the first place, because the custody of children is usually awarded to the mother, a woman marrying a divorced man with children from a former marriage may not have anticipated being thrust into the role of stepmother and may feel unprepared and uncomfortable with it. Moreover, our societal expectation is that the mother is the parent who will nurture and care for the children; when this responsibility falls on a stepmother, she may feel ill prepared to fulfill this role (Pasley and Ihinger-Tallman 1988).

A stepmother is usually more discontented and dissatisfied with stepdaughters than she is with stepsons. It is apparently more difficult for stepmothers to relate to girls than to boys (Pasley and Ihinger-Tallman 1988; Clingempeel, Ievoli, and Brand 1984).

The stepmother's role is quite demanding under the best of circumstances. She must not only typically regulate all household tasks but must also nurture, discipline, and provide affection, concern, and care for her stepchildren. While doing this she must usually also work outside the house to earn money to help support the family. Moreover, stepchildren may resent their "rightful" mother's place being usurped by a stepmother no matter what she does to try to win their acceptance. When children have frequent contact with their mother, difficulties with a stepmother tend to increase (Furstenberg 1987; Ihinger-Tallman and Pasley 1987; Furstenberg and Nord 1985).

Being a stepmother in a household in which the father is the custodial parent of children from his first marriage is often a no-win situation, and it calls for an extraordinary amount of tact, patience, and understanding. Francke (1983) quotes a stepmother who describes her situation:

Basically, I'm a mother at heart. But it's turned out to be an extremely disappointing situation for me. The whole experience of being a stepparent has just beaten down my self-confidence about being a parent myself. . . . I've done all the things that I am supposed to do, the right things, and the kids don't love me. . . . Do this all over again? Hell, no. I love my husband dearly and I wish that things could have been easier for us. . . . I would say that over 95 percent of our fights are over the kids' situation. One on one, we're very well matched, we're very compatible, we have a good time together, but when they're around, the fur flies. I could have a much better marriage if it weren't for the kids. (pp. 203–15)

On the other hand, it is possible for a stepmother to have a very rewarding relationship with her stepchildren, especially if the children are very young at the time of the remarriage. She may fill a huge void in the children's lives, providing them with the nurturing, care, love, and discipline they lacked.

Some women thrive on the stepmother's role despite its problems and complications. It is especially possible for deep, enduring friendships to develop between a stepmother and a stepdaughter. And if the stepmother has a baby of her own, stepdaughters can take great pleasure and pride in helping care for the child through infancy and childhood (Wallerstein and Blakeslee 1989; Wallerstein and Kelly 1980).

Unlike the stepmother whose stepchildren live with her, the role of a stepmother of visiting stepchildren is quite limited. Her chief importance as a stepparent lies in her ability to influence her husband's relationship with the children of his first marriage, and her attitude is a very significant factor in this regard. If she resents the attention, the time, or the presents her husband gives the children of his earlier marriage, she can easily discourage him from relating to them. She can, in this way, gradually disengage him from his paternal obligations. If, on the other hand, she encourages him to continue an active relationship with his children, he is more likely to do so. Most stepmothers of nonresident children encourage their husbands to maintain an active relationship with them (Wallerstein and Kelly 1980).

Three Stepmother Roles

Stepmothers usually relate to their stepchildren in one of three roles: as the "other mother," as the primary mother, or as a friend (Draughon 1975). We will examine each of these roles in turn.

The Stepmother as the "Other Mother" Although the role of "other mother" is both the most difficult and the least rewarding role and appears to have few advantages over either of the other two roles, it is the one most stepmothers adopt. Perhaps these women believe that it gives them the respect, status, and responsibility that go with the role of mother (Draughon 1975).

In such stepfamilies the children in effect have two mothers, the biological mother and the "other mother." This type of stepmother typically does not like the children to call her by her first name, so the children call both mothers "Mother" or "Mom" (Draughon 1975).

Unless the two women are consistent about their expectations for the children's behavior, the children may be pulled in different directions and become confused and frustrated. As a result, the children may often play one mother against the other and may sometimes call on their father to act as arbiter. This maneuver can cause serious discord between the father and his new wife (Draughon 1975).

The Stepmother as the Primary Mother The stepmother who acts as a primary mother attempts to replace the biological mother as much as possible. She too does not usually want the children to call her by her first name but prefers instead to be called "Mother" or "Mom." She assumes full responsibility for both the children's discipline and their physical and emotional welfare. When the children are very young (under age five) at the time of the remarriage, they may respond gratefully to the nurturance and love of such a stepmother (Draughon 1975).

The stepmother who assumes the role of the primary mother is rarely able to do this effectively unless the children's biological mother is absent from the scene and is rarely (or never) involved with the children. In fact, a stepmother may successfully act as the primary mother only if the biological mother is either dead or has ceased all contact with the children (so that she is in effect "dead" in their perception). Because a living mother is unlikely to be perceived as dead in this sense, children may have thoughts and fantasies about her even if she is not physically available; they may still perceive her as a primary source of warmth and love despite all evidence to the contrary. These children may not want a new mother, however much they might need one, and may well reject any attempts to replace their "real" mother. "Under these conditions it seems wiser for the stepmother to attempt to be a friend" (Draughon 1975, pp. 187–88).

The Stepmother as a Friend The stepmother who relates to her stepchildren as a friend does not try to become another mother or to replace the children's mother as primary mother. Rather, she concentrates mainly on attempting to win her stepchildren's affection and approval. She is accepting and nonjudgmental, and she hopes to become a trusted confidant of her stepchildren — someone to whom they can come with their problems and ask advice, and with whom they can share intimacies. She hopes that they will relate to her as an older, trusted friend. Accordingly, she prefers that the children call her by her first name rather than "Mother" or "Mom." She is not primarily a disciplinarian (Draughon 1975).

Being a Stepchild

As we have seen, divorce and remarriage are becoming the norm in the United States, and most divorces and remarriages involve children. A vast number of children now go through the experience of their parents' divorce and the remarriage of the custodial parent. In 1987 there were approximately six million stepchildren in the United States (Glick 1987).

Many studies have found that stepchildren experience a higher level of stress than children in first families. Stepchildren have more difficulties in school and a higher rate of delinquency than other children (Furstenberg 1987; Peterson and Zill 1986).

Children in remarriages seem to display the same inclination toward early family formation as do children of divorce — they commence sexual relations earlier than children in nuclear families, and are more likely to leave home earlier (Goldscheider and Goldscheider 1988; White and Booth 1985). They cohabit more often, marry at a younger age, and begin having children sooner (McLanahan and Booth 1989; McLanahan and Bumpass 1988). "Whether these results can be traced to lingering effects of divorce or to experiences of residing in stepfamilies has not been resolved by empirical investigation" (Furstenberg 1990, pp. 396–97).

According to data from a nationally representative sample of more than 17,000 children under age eighteen, children living with mothers and stepfathers were more likely to have repeated a grade in school, to have been expelled, and to have been treated for emotional or behavioral problems in the year preceding the interview than children living with both biological parents (Dawson 1991).

Until the publication of the Wallerstein and Blakeslee study (1989), no information was available about the long-term effect of divorce on children. It is now known, however, that children continue to react to a divorce five, ten, and fifteen years later, as we have seen in Chapter 12. As young men and women, a shockingly high proportion of these children of divorce are still angry at their parents, are severely impaired in their emotional and social relationships, and are obsessed with the fear that they will be betrayed and abandoned if they allow themselves to trust another person in an intimate relationship. They are unable to form lasting, loving relationships in dating, in cohabitation, or in marriage (see Chapter 12).

In the following sections we will focus specifically on what is now known about being a stepchild in a remarriage.

Relating to a Stepparent   About a third of stepchildren find that disciplinary actions of a stepparent are a primary source of stress (Knaub, Hanna, and Stinnet 1984; Lutz 1983). With older stepchildren the situation is even worse; fully one-half of teenage stepchildren experience disciplinary action by a stepparent as a primary source of stress (Connecticut Remarriage Research Group 1983). However, because these studies lack a control group, we must wonder what percentage of children who are not living in a stepfamily also experience stress with discipline.

Girls nine years of age or older have more difficulty in relating to a stepfather than boys of this age do (Ihinger-Tallman and Pasley 1987; Clingempeel, Ievoli, and Brand 1984; Santrock et al. 1982). A girl who is eight years of age or younger finds it easier to relate to a new stepfather (Wallerstein and Kelly 1980).

As we have seen, stepchildren are usually distrustful of a stepfather's overtures of friendliness and affection, typically withholding acceptance of the stepfather for a time. Children ordinarily feel betrayed by the divorce and are wary of leaving themselves open for yet another betrayal. They are often disturbed by a stepfather's expectation for instant acceptance and are uneasy about being pushed for immediate compliance. Children may feel that their emotions are being manipulated, for following the trauma of divorce children are extremely vulnerable and sensitive to having their trust betrayed. Stepchildren are more likely to respond with trust and approval if the stepfather is patient, gentle, respectful of their feelings, sensitive, aware, and empathetic. They are much more likely to accept him if he is willing to wait for them to gradually accept him in his role as the father figure in the household (Wallerstein and Kelly 1980).

Unfortunately, it is a rare stepfather who is able to wait patiently for his stepchildren's acceptance. He often needs their ready acceptance because he needs the children's approval to bolster his own feelings of insecurity (Wallerstein and Kelly 1980).

A further complication in children's emotional life is the quite common belief that responding to their stepfather's overtures would be a betrayal of their noncustodial father. Stepchildren commonly believe that a stepfather is trying to replace the noncustodial father in their affections. Children resent this perceived attempt and respond by noncompliance. Stepchildren can maintain a sense of dignity, self-worth, and control by saying "No." In this situation they are in effect saying "No, I'm not so easily bought" (Wallerstein and Kelly 1980).

Many of the stepfathers in Wallerstein's studies had lived in the household as the mother's lover before the marriage. During this time they tended to be casual and friendly with the children. After the marriage, however—once the live-in lover became a stepfather—he abruptly replaced his casual, friendly behavior toward his new stepchildren with authoritarian discipline. Many stepchildren's perception of this change is illustrated by the words of a typical stepdaughter, Christina, aged ten, in referring to her stepfather of several years:

> I really don't like him. He was nice and kind before the marriage, and we did lots of things together. Since they got married he is mean and strict and not at all loving. (Wallerstein and Kelly 1980, p. 288)

In short, in the first stage of their relationship with their stepfathers, stepchildren are usually wary and distant while the stepfather may try too hard to win their trust, approval, and affection too quickly. In the second stage, stepfathers may become impatient and overly strict disciplinarians, and stepchildren typically describe them as stern and unaffectionate.

Relating to the Noncustodial Parent Although children living with their custodial parent (usually the mother) and a stepparent feel that it is important to see their absent parent as often as possible, relatively few divorced fathers maintain contact with their children (Pasley and Ihinger-Tallman 1988). As we have seen, nearly one-fourth (23 percent) of divorced fathers do not see their children at all after a divorce (Weitzman 1985). Five years after a divorce, one-half to three-quarters of noncustodial fathers do not see their children at all (Furstenberg 1987; Jacobson 1987). Of those absent fathers who do see their children occasionally, one-fifth had not seen them during the previous year (Furstenberg and Spanier 1987), and 40 percent had had no contact during the previous five years (Furstenberg and Nord 1982).

Men typically view marriage and child care as inseparable (Furstenberg 1990). Many men sever ties with their children in order to distance themselves from their ex-wives. If a man remarries, new family responsibilities and increased economic demands exacerbate the erosion of bonds with his noncustodial children. Nonresident fathers often report bewilderment, anxiety, depression, guilt, and uncertainty about how to behave and how to stay involved (Arditti 1990). These feelings contribute to the disappearance of a growing number of divorced fathers, who cease having any contact with their children. This pattern persists with middle-aged or elderly nonresident fathers, who continue to have much less contact with their children and subsequent grandchildren than married fathers do (Cooney and Uhlenberg 1990; White, Brinkerhoff, and Booth 1985). On the other hand, noncustodial fathers who continue to see their children do so quite often, averaging thirteen to twenty-one hours per week (Jacobson 1987).

Continuing conflict and resentment between a noncustodial father and a custodial mother may discourage his attempts to see his children (Fox 1985). If a custodial mother makes his visits with the children difficult, uncomfortable, and unpleasant, it is likely that the frequency of his visits will decrease (Ihinger-Tallman and Pasley 1987).

Noncustodial mothers are more likely to keep in touch with their children than are noncustodial fathers (Furstenberg and Spanier 1987; Ihinger-Tallman and Pasley 1987). About 86 percent of children living with a custodial father and a stepmother have had some contact with their mothers during the previous year. About one-third of noncustodial mothers see their children at least once a week (Furstenberg and Spanier 1987).

Relating to Stepsiblings   It is estimated that two-thirds of children in a remarriage have stepsiblings (Bumpass 1984b). Children may be confused and bewildered by their mother's and stepfather's often unrealistic expectations that they form instant relationships with these stepsiblings. Francke (1983) describes a situation in

which a custodial mother told her two daughters, ages eight and ten, that she was going to get remarried and that their new family was coming to visit in an hour:

> "We were dumbfounded," recalls one of the daughters. "We had only met the guy once and never even knew he had any children. It turned out he had four. When they arrived outside our house in a big brown station wagon, his kids refused to get out of the car and we refused to come out of the house. There we were, peering out of the windows and them peering out of theirs. Our parents stood in the middle of the sidewalk, each frantically waving at their own kids to come out. We finally did." (p. 191)

It is not surprising that new stepsiblings may be wary of one another at first. Almost overnight, everything has changed: A child who has always been the youngest may suddenly have a new younger stepbrother or stepsister; valued toys may seem threatened; a private room is suddenly invaded by a stepsibling (Francke 1983). The initial family may have watched television and permitted soft drinks at dinner, whereas the new family does not, and suddenly both sets of children are together at the same dinner table (Francke 1983).

Despite these problems, after the initial shock most stepsibling interactions seem to work out fairly well. After an adjustment period that usually lasts for about a year, many children even come to enjoy the new situation. If the mother and stepfather do not push them too fast and are fair in arbitrating differences, some children may even feel that the pain of the divorce has been alleviated (to some extent) by the acquisition of new stepsiblings. Rivalries are keen, as in any family, but there are also opportunities for valued friendships to develop (Wallerstein and Kelly 1980).

A stepparent's preferential treatment that favors a biological child over a stepchild may bring the stepsiblings closer together if the one receiving the favored treatment supports the one who is being treated unfairly. Consider the following typical example of a biological daughter (Stephanie) supporting a stepsister (Michelle) who is being treated unfairly:

> By the time the girls were in the seventh grade . . . Stephanie began sticking up for Michelle and taking her stepsister's side in disputes when her mother made demands on Michelle, expecting her to do things Stephanie did not have to do. According to Michelle, their common interest and the discriminatory treatment by her stepmother brought them closer together. (Ihinger-Tallman and Pasley 1987, p. 106)

It is possible for romantic and erotic interests to develop between teenaged stepsiblings. When an adolescent boy finds an attractive teenage girl living in the same household with him, it would not be surprising if he found her romantically and sexually exciting, and she might well return these feelings. This mutual affinity might develop into a potentially explosive situation because stepsiblings are not restrained by the taboos of a blood relation. To date, however, very little is known about the extent of romantic and sexual interaction between adolescent stepsiblings living in the same household (Baptiste 1986).

SUMMARY

More than half of all recent marriages are a remarriage for at least one of the couple, and one in four is a remarriage for both the bride and the groom. A little more than three-fourths of remarriages involve stepchildren. The incidence of divorce is significantly higher in remarriages than it is in first marriages, and the length of time between the remarriage and the divorce is about two years shorter than it was for the first marriage.

The division of labor, norms of behavior, roles for family members, and the power hierarchy are usually different in a remarriage. Four elements must be present before any small group, including families, can function effectively: commitment, cohesion, communication, and maintenance of the group's boundaries. These elements are usually quite different in a remarriage: There is usually less commitment, less cohesion, and more communications problems, and there is often a lack of agreement about the group's boundaries.

Because nine out of ten divorce actions grant child custody to the mother, the usual stepfamily household is composed of the custodial mother, her children, and her second husband (the stepfather of her children). Only about one-tenth of stepfamilies consist of the custodial father, his children, and his second wife (the stepmother).

Fewer than half of all ex-husbands send custodial mothers the child support payments ordered by the court; the mother usually must work outside the household to help support the family. Also, stepfathers are expected to assume financial responsibility for their stepchildren. The noncustodial father usually is also remarried, and his second wife may resent his sending money for child support to his former wife and the children from his first marriage, feeling that any available funds should go to support her children.

Relatively few noncustodial fathers keep in touch with the children of their first marriage; five years after the divorce, one-half to three-quarters of noncustodial fathers do not see their children at all. Noncustodial mothers are much more likely to keep in touch with their children, with virtually all having some contact and about one-third seeing their children at least once a week.

The stepparent's role is more difficult and less clearly defined than the parent's role, and problems regarding the discipline and handling of stepchildren commonly cause significant levels of stress in the stepfamily. Studies indicate that stepchildren are the single most important source of conflict in a remarriage, and remarriages involving stepchildren have a higher incidence of divorce than those not involving stepchildren. Families in which stepchildren are teenagers have the highest incidence of difficulty. Although children usually have very little to say about the remarriage in the first place, they do have considerable power to break it up.

Many resident stepfathers feel inadequate in their role, are afraid of not being accepted by the children, and are concerned about being compared with the children's biological father. It is easier for a stepfather to build a bond with a child under eight years of age than with an older child. Many children come to see their stepfathers as unsympathetic, stern, and demanding. Resident stepmothers are usually even more dissatisfied with their role than are stepfathers and experience more stress. Stepmothers' discontent and dissatisfaction are usually greater with stepdaughters than with stepsons.

Unlike the resident stepmother, whose stepchildren live with her, the second wife who is a stepmother to nonresident children is limited in her role. Her chief importance as a parent lies in her ability to influence her husband's relationship with his children.

Stepmothers chiefly relate to their stepchildren in one of three role models: the other mother, the friend, or the primary mother. Although the role of the other mother is the most difficult and the least rewarding of these roles, it is the one most often adopted. The primary mother role may not be open if the biological mother is available, and the role of friend may not be appropriate for young children.

Studies have found that stepchildren usually have greater emotional and psychological problems, do more poorly in school, and leave home earlier than children in first families. The one longitudinal study available found that the ill effects of divorce on children are long lasting. Ten to fifteen years after the divorce, many children were still angry at their parents, had a high incidence of social problems, and were unable to function effectively in a trusting, close, personal relationship.

Stepsiblings seem to get along fairly well once they have settled into their new relationship. If the stepsiblings are teenagers, romantic and erotic interests may develop; however, the incidence of such attraction between adolescent siblings living in the same household is not known. Stepsiblings may marry in most states because they are not blood relations.

About one-half of all divorced couples fight over child support payments and other issues regarding their children, whereas the other half retain at least a cordial relationship. About one in eight still like and trust each other and continue to enjoy a mutual association with their children at family events. About three in eight continue to share an interest in the children's welfare and cooperate for the children's best interests but are not warm or friendly. About one-half of divorced couples have bitter and resentful feelings about their former marriage, remain angry toward each other, and have conflicts and power struggles over control of the children.

KEY TERMS

The following is a list of key terms in this chapter.
These terms are defined in context within the chapter, and many may also be found in the Glossary.

boundary maintenance   resident stepparent   stepsibling

noncustodial parent   stepfamily

QUESTIONS

1. What are the characteristic differences between a first marriage and a remarriage without stepchildren?

2. What are the four elements that must be present before any small group, such as a family, can function effectively? Give an example of each.

3. Why are financial pressures usually more severe in a remarriage than in a first marriage?

4. What special problems and challenges does a stepfather face in a remarriage?

5. What special problems and challenges does a stepmother face in a remarriage?

6. What are the three characteristic ways stepmothers relate to their stepchildren? Give examples of each. Which of these role models do stepmothers usually use?

7. What is the long-term effect of divorce on children?

8. Discuss the relationship of stepsiblings.

9. Discuss four ways that ex-spouses may relate to each other.

SUGGESTIONS FOR FURTHER READING

Dornbusch, Sanford M., and Strober, Myra H. *Feminism, Children, and the New Families.* New York: Guilford Press, 1988.

Furstenberg, Frank F., Jr., and Spanier, Graham B. *Recycling the Family: Remarriage After Divorce.* Beverly Hills, Calif.: Sage, 1984.

Hetherington, E. M., and Arasteh, J. D., eds. *Impact of Divorce, Single Parenting, and Stepparenting on Children*, pp. 169–95. Hillsdale, N.J.: Erlbaum, 1988.

Maglin, Nan Bauer, and Schniedewind, Nancy, eds. *Women and Stepfamilies: Voices of Anger and Love.* Philadelphia: Temple University Press, 1989.

Pasley, Kay, and Ihinger-Tallman, Marilyn, eds. *Remarriage and Stepparenting: Current Research and Theory.* New York: Guilford Press, 1987.

Spanier, Graham, B., and Furstenberg, Frank F., Jr. "Remarriage and Reconstituted Families." In Marvin B. Sussman and Suzanne K. Steinmetz (eds.), *Handbook of Marriage and the Family*, pp. 416–34. New York: Plenum Press, 1987.

Money and Economic Reality

CHAPTER 14

Uses and Abuses of Money

Getting money is like digging with a needle;
spending it is like water soaking in the sand.

Japanese proverb

Directing Cash Flow

Using Credit Wisely

Getting Your Money's Worth

Investing Regularly

What Do You Know?

Some of the following statements are true and some are false.
Can you tell which are which?

T/F   1. Experts on personal finance usually frown on including a personal allowance in your budget.

T/F   2. A tight, detailed budget that keeps track of every penny spent is important for good personal finance.

T/F   3. Experts on personal finance classify saving as deferred spending.

T/F   4. When buying furniture, it is usually most economical to buy top-quality items.

T/F   5. It is a good idea to get a service contract when you buy an appliance such as a color television set.

T/F   6. In general, you are regarded as a good credit risk if you have always paid cash for everything you have bought.

T/F   7. Credit installment contracts are usually a very good way to buy anything because they have relatively low finance costs.

T/F   8. It is usually a very poor idea to get credit from the dealer who is selling an item.

T/F   9. Home improvement contracts are often written so that if the buyer fails to make a payment, the contractor may take over the house with no foreclosure proceedings necessary.

T/F   10. It is absolutely imperative that you get a copy of any contract you sign.

Answers: 1-F, 2-F, 3-T, 4-T, 5-F, 6-F, 7-F, 8-T, 9-T, 10-T.

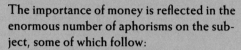
The importance of money is reflected in the enormous number of aphorisms on the subject, some of which follow:

- A heavy purse makes a light heart. (Sixteenth-century English proverb)

- It's a kind of spiritual snobbery that makes people think they can be happy without money. (Albert Camus)

- Money is like a sixth sense without which you cannot make the most of the other five. (Somerset Maugham)

- Wine maketh merry but money answereth all things. (Ecclesiastes 10:19)

- There are three faithful friends—an old wife, an old dog, and ready money. (Benjamin Franklin)

- Lack of money is the root of all evil. (George Bernard Shaw)

- Certainly there are lots of things in life that money won't buy, but it's very funny—Have you ever tried to buy them without money? (Ogden Nash)

Despite its importance in marriage and in the family, the subject of money is often cloaked in mystery. The average person today is as ignorant of the basic concepts of money management as Victorian women were about their sexuality.

The subjects of money and sex are twin areas of ignorance and ineptness in American life. The average person today probably knows less about money than about sex. Contributing to this void of knowledge is the curious but inescapable fact that both subjects are sometimes considered distasteful or repugnant.

Because money is one of three major sources of conflict within couples, it is of central importance to any study of marriage and the family. Moreover, of these three sources of conflict— money, work, and sex — the one that is the most frequently discussed and argued about is money.

We have looked at problems involving sexuality and we have touched on money problems pertaining to working mothers and wives. In this chapter we will focus specifically on problems involving money itself: directing cash flow, using credit wisely, getting a dollar's value for a dollar spent, and investing for retirement. (See Box 14-1.)

Directing Cash Flow

Cash flow means the movement of money through your hands. Money comes in from different sources (such as wages) and then flows out when channeled into various expenditures, such as groceries, clothes, utilities, garbage collection, and telephone service. Directing this cash flow is something that everyone must do. However, few people know what their cash flow is. They simply spend money when they have it and use credit when they don't, with little awareness of what is really happening to them financially.

The Budget

A budget lays out your cash flow very simply and precisely in a brief page or two, allowing you to see your financial options clearly. A budget makes it possible for you to direct your cash flow into those channels that will bring the most satisfaction. The alternative to keeping a budget is for you to let your money seep away without getting the things you most want—and then wondering where the money went.

A budget is *not* a financial straitjacket designed to force you to keep track of every penny you spend. This is a common misconception, however, and probably explains why many people dislike the idea of a budget and refuse to keep one.

Following the Principle of Forced Alternate Choice One of the most useful aspects of a budget is that it clarifies the principle of forced alternate choice: that almost everything a person does involves a choice between available alternatives, so that choosing one usually eliminates the possibility of getting the other; that is, if you choose A, you most likely will not get B as well.

In the realm of personal finance, this means that as long as your available income is limited, you cannot buy everything you would like. Diverting funds to one channel (buying A) automatically diverts them away from another channel (buying B). A budget makes it possible to see these options or alternatives very clearly. You can make the choice you most want to make—the one that will bring you the greatest satisfaction with the least cost.

Developing a Budget The first step in setting up a budget is to list all monthly assets: your spendable or take-home income per month from whatever sources (see Table 14-1).

The second step is to list all monthly fixed (or nondiscretionary) expenses. These nondiscretionary expenses are expenditures over which you have little or no control: essential transportation costs, utility payments, insurance premiums, taxes, mortgage payments, and rent.[1]

The third step is to list all monthly variable (or discretionary) expenses. Discretionary expenses are the costs of buying things over which you do have control. For example, you may buy either a steak or a hamburger—you have the choice.

It is important that your total monthly expenses—discretionary plus nondiscretionary expenses—do not exceed your monthly income. If your expenses exceed your income, you must lower your discretionary expenses. The reason is obvious: If you make up the difference between your income and your expenditures by borrowing or by buying on credit, the following month's nondiscretionary expenses will be increased by the amount necessary to repay the debt. Eventually, this kind of creeping indebtedness can so swell your nondiscretionary expenses with debt repayments that there will not be enough money to pay them. At this point, you are face to face with financial disaster—with collection agencies, repossessions, evictions, and lawsuits. Moreover, if you are married or cohabiting, long before this financial crisis is reached the relationship is usually undermined by the tensions, anxieties, and frustrations associated with insoluble financial pressures. The number-one rule for proper credit management is to never overextend yourself (Porter, S., 1990).

---

[1] Sylvia Porter (1987) suggests that your monthly mortgage or rent payment be no higher than your weekly gross pay, or a week-and-a-half's take-home pay. Taxes usually take between a fifth and a third of your gross income.

TABLE 14-1

Sample Budget Form

Monthly Income

Source   Amount

_____   _____

_____   _____

_____   _____

_____   _____

Monthly Fixed Expenses   Total: _____

Source   Amount

_____   _____

_____   _____

_____   _____

_____   _____

_____   _____

_____   _____

                                          Total: _____

                        Available for discretionary expenses _____
                                 (difference between total income
                                      and total fixed expenses)

Monthly Discretionary Expenses

Source   Amount

_____   _____

_____   _____

_____   _____

_____   _____

_____   _____

                                          Total: _____

The amount spent for discretionary expenses must not exceed the amount available for discretionary expenses. If it does, you are going into debt, and the interest on the debt as well as part of the principal must be added to next month's fixed expenses, leaving you even less for discretionary expenses and pushing you further into debt. This descending spiral can lead to financial ruin.

"You kids looking for an apartment?"

A 1989 report provided by the U.S. Census Bureau and the Conference Board (a New York nonprofit organization) indicated that more than 70 percent of American households had no money available for discretionary expenses. For the nearly 30 percent that did have money available for discretionary expenses, the average annual amount was $12,300. Households most likely to have extra money were households headed by a person with five or more years of college, dual-income households, or households in which the occupants were ages fifty-five to fifty-nine.[2]

Budgeting for a Personal Allowance One important item in the budget should be a personal allowance—a fixed sum of money that does not have to be accounted for. This personal allowance in the budget gives a person a sense of economic freedom. Although the size of the allowance must be scaled to the overall budget, it should be generous enough so that you don't have the feeling of being in some sort of financial straitjacket. Experience has shown that a tight, overly detailed budget that demands accounting for every penny spent does not work. If you feel like a cheat or a miser every time you contemplate buying something, you will soon abandon the budget—with more relief than guilt.

Budgeting for Savings There is a good deal of confusion regarding the concept of saving. You do not remove "saved" money from spendable income. Instead, you hold this money temporarily, regarding it as deferred (temporarily delayed) spending. Thus when you save money, you will use it relatively soon to buy something without finance charges. Saving also increases your discretionary funds by the amount of interest the savings earn and by the bargains you can take advantage of by having cash at hand. Saving also provides funds for unexpected emergencies.

[2]U.S. Bureau of the Census and the Conference Board, *A Marketer's Guide to Discretionary Income, 1989* (1991).

424 PART V ❖ MONEY AND ECONOMIC REALITY

The penalty for not having such cash reserves for deferred purchases or emergencies can be substantial.

Budgeting for Investment You are investing when you put away a portion of your income for a long-term program of growth. You do not plan to spend invested money; you plan to leave it undisturbed. Invested money eventually provides income without touching the principal, or the amount originally invested. Experts in personal finance agree that it is very important to budget a regular sum for investment. The goal of investing is to remove money from spendable resources and allow it to grow (see the section "Investing Regularly").

Major Budgetary Problems in a Family's Life Cycle

As a family goes through its life cycle — from the newlywed and childless years to rearing growing children, to putting children through college, and finally to preparing for retirement — financial responsibilities change significantly. The first stage — from the wedding until the first child is born — is the most financially carefree stage, although it rarely seems so at the time. Even though the young couple face much financial uncertainty and have limited resources and few belongings, they have no one to look after but themselves and usually have a dual income with which to do it.

Most couples feel financially oppressed when they are first married because there are so many things they want: a house (or at least a better apartment), furniture, appliances, sports and hobby equipment, and travel. However, during this period a couple spends more money on personal items, on pleasure, and on leisure activities than they ever will again — unless they become relatively affluent by middle age. In fact, the double income and the relatively low expenses dur-

ing this period often give the couple a false sense of financial security. The nondiscretionary expenses often seem comparatively low until they enter the second stage of their marriage, when they take on responsibility for children at the same time that the one spouse's (typically the wife's) earnings cease (at least for a while).

With the addition of children, the costs of maintaining a family begin to soar; medical care, food, clothing, babysitters, the need for larger living quarters and more furniture and appliances contribute to continually swelling expenditures. Economists estimated in 1989 that expenses for a child for just the first year are about $6,000[3] in moderately expensive locales (Cutler 1989). Not surprisingly, during this period — when the couple plunge from relative prosperity into financial difficulties — money often becomes a leading cause of disagreement.

Prudent newlywed couples have the foresight to live in a modestly furnished apartment during the child-free period and avoid spending beyond their means for entertainment, eating out, recreation, clothes, and vacations. In so doing they are able to save a substantial amount for this second stage and continue their comfortable life-style without becoming embroiled in debt. Entering the second stage with no savings and a backlog of debts is not only foolish but potentially disastrous.

With the costs of raising children continually rising and with so many variables involved — including the rate of inflation; the family's economic circumstances, educational level, and type of employment; and the geographic area in which a family lives — it is difficult to put a figure on how much money it takes to rear a child (see Figure 14-1).

---

[3]In 1958, *Life* magazine calculated the expenses for a baby's first year to be just $800 — which is about $2,900 in today's dollars (*San Francisco Chronicle*, December 19, 1989, p. B-5).

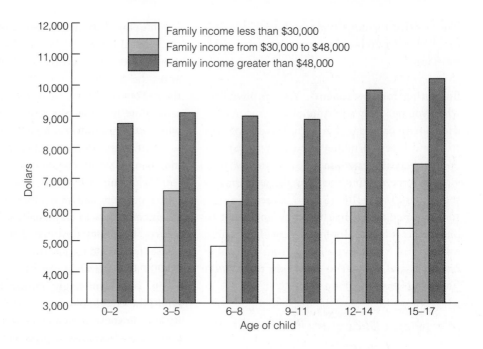

FIGURE 14-1

Average annual cost of raising children, by family income and age of child: 1990.

Source: Mark Lino, U.S. Department of Agriculture Report on Cost of Raising Children: 1990. *Family Economics Review*, July 1991.

Economists estimated that as of 1990, it costs a middle-income family $100,000 to raise one child from birth to eighteen years of age. This figure does not include costs for child care but instead assumes that one parent will stay at home with the child (Loeb 1992). If the loss of income for the stay-at-home parent is factored in, the figure is estimated at about $200,000 (Lino 1991). Economists also estimate that it costs a single parent 5 percent more to raise children than it costs a married couple (Lino 1991).

College costs vary widely, of course, with private institutions costing more than public institutions and with high-prestige colleges costing more than those with lower rankings. In the 1987–1988 academic year, the average annual cost of a college education—including tuition, books, and room and board—ranged from $10,200 annually for public schools to $15,500 at private schools.[4] Tuition and fees at two-year community colleges average about half those at state universities.

Using census data on family income, economists estimate that only 18 percent of children age eighteen or younger live in families that can

---

[4]U.S. Department of Education, "Institutions of Higher Education—Finances: 1975 to 1988" (1991). Costs continue to rise. For example, the cost for the 1992–1993 school year at Stanford University was $22,850 for tuition, room and board, books, supplies, and lab fees, excluding other costs and personal expenses (Workman 1992).

If children's allowances are scaled properly, they will learn sound principles of money management. Children should also be encouraged to earn their own money through such means as delivering newspapers and baby-sitting.

tional norm are in the running for a scholarship. It may be a mistake not to apply to a prestigious university simply because you think you cannot afford it, for many of the top universities have the best financial aid programs. Stanford University, for example, has a long-standing policy guaranteeing tuition and campus housing to any undergraduate who gains admission. More than 60 percent of Stanford students receive financial aid through a combination of scholarships, grants, loans, and campus jobs (Workman 1991). On the other hand, financial aid is sometimes available to students whose families earn more than $100,000 per year (Loeb 1992). Information regarding scholarships can be obtained from a college's financial aid officer, a school guidance counselor, or the state department of education; another excellent source for finding financial aid is Oreon Keesler's *Financial Aids for Higher Education* (1992).

In addition to applying for financial aid, many students work. Nearly nine out of ten of the 1.3 million part-time college students enrolled in the fall of 1989 were working, and another 4 percent were looking for work; of the nearly seven million full-time college students, 46 percent had jobs and 7 percent were looking for them.[5]

The need to work while going to college is making the four-year degree a thing of the past, except for those attending the most expensive private colleges (Porter, O., 1990). Of all students who graduated from the University of California's eight campuses in 1988, for example, less than one-third (30 percent) finished their degree requirements in four years; about 40 percent took six years. Nearly 60 percent of all University

afford a college education at a public school, and fewer than 6 percent live in families that can afford a four-year private school (Mortenson 1989). Since 1980 the cost of a private college education has risen about 85 percent (Loeb 1992). It is a good idea for parents to start saving for college expenses as soon as a child is born (see Table 14.2).

It is possible for students to receive financial aid. Many colleges have recently changed their scholarship programs to make their institution available to students regardless of their financial resources. All students who have at least a B average and College Board scores above the na-

---

[5]U.S. Bureau of Labor Statistics report on working college students, compiled by the staff of *American Demographics Magazine* (1990).

TABLE 14-2

College Savings Calculator

How much parents need to put aside each month to meet the projected cost of college when their child is ready to attend*

Years Until Child Begins College	Projected Four-Year Cost		Monthly Investment	
	Public	Private	Public	Private
1	$27,923	$59,200	$2,228	$4,724
2	29,877	63,344	1,144	2,426
3	31,969	67,778	783	1,661
4	34,207	72,522	603	1,278
5	36,601	77,599	495	1,049
6	39,163	83,031	423	896
7	41,904	88,843	371	787
8	44,838	95,062	333	705
9	47,976	101,716	303	642
10	51,335	108,837	279	591
11	54,928	116,455	259	549
12	58,773	124,607	243	515
13	62,887	133,329	229	485
14	67,289	142,663	217	460
15	72,000	152,649	207	438
16	77,040	163,334	198	419
17	82,432	174,768	190	402
18	88,203	187,002	183	387

Source: T. Rowe Price Associates in Ellen F. Schultz, "College Advice to Parents: Start Saving Money Now." *The Wall Street Journal,* May 17, 1990, p. C-1.

*Four-year costs include tuition, fees, room and board, books and transportation. Table assumes 7% annual increases of college costs and 8% annual pre-tax return on investments. Based on College Board Annual Survey of Colleges, 1989. Table assumes no additional investments, and no additional earnings on balance invested, once child starts school.

of California students worked as well as attending classes (Sewart 1990).

Despite the time, effort, and money required to get a college degree, it pays off. From a purely practical (economic) point of view, there is no better investment. Federal studies indicate that, on the average, people with a four-year college degree or better earn at least 70 percent more than those with just a high-school education, and this disparity may increase during the 1990s (McLeod 1992).

A third period of potential financial difficulty for the family occurs during the couple's middle years, when they must prepare for retirement and old age. If they are able to invest sufficiently during this time, they may have a graceful, dignified old age; if not, they may experience old age as another financial crisis — this time without the advantages of youthful resilience and promise.[6]

One problem that may emerge at this time is the need to assist aging parents. Most custodial care is not covered by insurance, and costs for caring for an invalid parent can exceed $40,000 per year.[7]

Using Credit Wisely

Properly used, credit (buying now and paying later) can make a person's life richer and fuller; improperly used, it can bring ruin. To take advantage of the good uses of credit (and to avoid pitfalls), it is essential to know its various forms,

to understand how each works, and then to handle it — as one would any useful but potentially dangerous tool — with caution and respect.

It is important to understand that there are two main types of credit: *open credit* and *financed credit*. We will examine these categories of credit in detail in the sections that follow.

Open Credit

Open credit is the term used for credit advanced with no finance charges. A merchant who keeps an account of the items a customer bought during the month and then allows the customer to settle the bill when payday comes is extending open credit. Today, open credit opportunities are offered by dairy and bread delivery companies, diaper services, telephone companies, utility providers, newspaper subscription departments, cable television services, doctors and dentists, and many other businesses, stores, and professions that have the facilities for sending monthly statements to their customers and are willing to provide their products or services in advance of payment. Department stores and gasoline companies also extend open credit if the cardholder pays the bill in full at the end of the billing cycle (usually thirty days). Multipurpose bank credit cards (MasterCard, Visa, and so on) usually have an annual charge for the use of the card but extend open credit if the bill is paid in full at the end of the billing cycle.

Used properly, open credit is not only a great convenience but a real bargain. It also provides a cost-free way to build up credit references that are essential if you need to borrow money for major purchases. People often have the mistaken idea that they will be regarded as a good credit risk if they have always paid cash for everything. This is not true. You are regarded as a good credit risk only if you have borrowed money (used credit) and demonstrated your ability to

---

[6]An excellent source of information regarding retirement planning is T. Rowe Price's *Retirement Planning Kit*, which is available at no cost (ph: 1-800-638-5660).

[7]For information regarding ways to help aging parents financially with such legal mechanisms as intervivos trusts, reverse mortgages, and possible tax deductions, see Sylvia Porter's *Your Finances in the 1990s* (1990) and Marshall Loeb's *1992 Money Guide* (1992).

repay it. Always paying cash for everything can actually create unnecessary hardships when you need to make a major purchase (a car, a house, or a major appliance, for example) that requires credit financing.

Financed Credit

Once a person with a charge account or a credit card does not pay in full at the end of the billing cycle, the account is now financed, or charged with interest. This interest charge is usually at least 1.5 percent per month on the unpaid balance, which is 18 percent in true annual interest. Some merchants with charge account systems compute their interest charges from a different base than the monthly unpaid balance, so that the actual true interest rate is higher than 18 percent. For example, many department stores charge 1.5 percent interest on the previous month's balance rather than on the current unpaid balance (which may work out to a true annual interest rate of more than 18 percent, depending on the size of the current payment in relation to the unpaid balance). Other stores charge interest on the original purchase price rather than on the unpaid balance; applied in this way, the 1.5 percent per month is a true annual rate of 36 percent. Interest is often computed this way by car dealers.

The loss of a credit card can be expensive. Until the loss is reported, the credit card holder is responsible for anything charged on it. After it is reported lost or stolen, the holder's responsibility is limited to a maximum of $50 per card (Porter, S., 1990) (see Box 14-2).

The loss of an automatic teller card can also be expensive. A person who does not notify the bank of a card's loss within two working days can lose up to $500. A person who fails to report a loss for sixty days can be liable for the full amount lost — which can be the balance in the

account plus any cash advance privileges (Porter, S., 1990).

Profit-Making Financed Credit *Profit-making credit* — financed loans or credit purchases that promise a financial return — is a sound use of credit *if* the consumers will eventually earn more profit from the use of the borrowed money or credit purchase than they will pay in finance charges. An example of a good use of profit-making credit is borrowing for an education or for vocational training, thereby acquiring the knowledge or skills that will enable the borrower to earn more. Other good uses of profit-making credit might be borrowing to buy tools that are needed to produce income or to save money (a sewing machine, for example), to buy or maintain a car that is needed to get to work or school, to buy work clothes or rent office space, or to make an investment that will bring in income in excess of the costs of the credit. This use of credit is the basis of all commerce.

Non-Profit-Making Financed Credit *Non-profit-making credit* falls into that shadowy region of potential financial difficulty in which you borrow money or make a financed credit purchase to satisfy an immediate need, the satisfaction of which you value more than the cost of the finance charges. This use of credit requires the greatest exercise of judgment; the borrower must weigh the subjective value of the satisfaction against the costs of the finance charges and the decrease of subsequent monthly discretionary funds as a result of these charges. This is not only a "buy now and pay later" plan but also a "buy now, pay more, and buy less later" plan. If you make too many purchases in this way — because each purchase reduces the amount available for future spending by the amount you will be paying for credit — you may eventually severely reduce your standard of living and find

BOX 14-2

Credit Card Scams

It is important to report immediately to the proper authorities any missing or stolen credit cards, bank cards, or checks. Carry only as much personal information as you would need in an emergency, and only the credit card(s) you will be using that day. In addition, be wary of the following four common credit card scams (Pallock 1991a):

- The Sleepy Scam. You receive a phone call late at night from a caller claiming to represent the security department of a bank that issued you a credit card. The caller asks which credit card you are currently using and for your birth date and social security number. With this information, the scam artist can apply for credit cards in your name and can run up thousands of dollars in charges.

- The Stolen Wallet Scam. Your purse or wallet is stolen, and then you receive a phone call from someone claiming to have found it and your credit cards and assuring you that they are safe. You gratefully arrange to retrieve them at a mutually agreed on place and time, and as a result you do not report that your credit cards have been stolen. In the meantime, purchases for which you are responsible are being made on your cards.

- The PIN (personal identification number) Scam. After your purse or wallet is stolen, you receive a phone call from someone claiming to be a representative of your bank. The caller says that your ATM card has been inserted into the machine at the bank, and thus the caller needs your personal identification number in order to retrieve it for you. You tell this scam artist the PIN number, and cash is withdrawn from your account.

- The Scram Scam. Do not give out any personal information — your name, social security number, credit card number, birth date, or PIN — to *anyone* who solicits you without verifying who the caller is. Get the caller's name, title or position, and phone number; then call back to check whether the information is correct. (Is the caller employed at that institution? Does the caller have the title or occupy the position claimed? Is the request for information valid?) Remember, anyone who obtains your name, social security number, and credit card number can make charges to your account.

yourself embroiled in financial stress. It is generally far wiser to follow a deferred spending (saving) plan.

An example of a sound use of non-profit-making credit might be buying a refrigerator that provides more convenience in storing larger amounts of food, thus making it possible to shop less often. Or this form of credit might be used wisely in buying a vacuum cleaner that shortens housecleaning time, or in buying a camera that will provide a great amount of pleasure and capture moments that never return. Countless examples could be given. The important point is that a person needs to know what the costs of the credit are and needs to weigh the relative values carefully (see Table 14-3).

Special Pitfalls of Installment Contracts The use of installment contracts (rather than revolving charge accounts or credit cards) is often required by stores and dealers when they sell what they call "big-ticket" items, such as major appliances, large pieces of furniture, carpeting, and automobiles. An installment contract is a legal agreement between the consumer and the dealer for the financed purchase of a specific item. It provides for delayed payment for the item on a weekly or monthly basis for a specified period, at the end of which the contract is fulfilled.

Credit installment contracts usually involve higher interest rates than almost any other source of financing. Dealers often charge rates as high as 4 percent per month on the unpaid balance of installment contracts, which is a true annual interest rate of 48 percent. In addition to interest costs, service charges (credit investigation, accounting expenses, and so on) and insurance are often tacked on, so that the actual cost for the installment contract may range as high as 80 percent in true annual interest.

The most costly way to make a purchase is to get credit from the dealer who is selling the item. The rule is simple: When buying a "big-ticket" item, borrow the money elsewhere and then pay cash for the purchase. (Be wary of the store that boasts, "We carry our own credit.")

In addition to the high cost of an installment purchase, another pitfall is that the contract usually specifies that the item purchased may be repossessed by the seller if the buyer fails to keep up the payments. If repossession occurs, the item may then be resold by the merchant, with the proceeds from the second sale used to cover the expenses of repossession and the resale and the remaining indebtedness on the item. If the proceeds from the resale fail to pay everything off, the original buyer owes the remainder, even though he or she no longer possesses the item. Thus a credit installment plan is not only costly but may be risky — especially if the item purchased in this way depreciates (loses monetary value) rapidly, as does furniture, any major appliance, and cars.

In addition to the repossession clause in installment plan contracts, many of these contracts have an *add-on clause* — a device by which all the items purchased by a buyer from one dealer over a long period of time are written on the same installment contract, with payments and charges prorated and divided among all outstanding debts and the repossession clause applicable to all items. For example, suppose you buy a television on the installment plan, make regular payments, and then, when the TV is within one month of being paid off, you buy a refrigerator from the same dealer. Suppose that when the refrigerator is within a month of being paid off, you buy an electric range. Then, suppose that when you have made all but the final payment on the electric range you buy a vacuum cleaner, and two months later you are laid off and cannot make the installment payments. You must now return the vacuum cleaner — and the electric range, and the refrigerator, and the television set

T A B L E 1 4 - 3

The Effective Use of Credit

Type	Cost	Risk	Use or Purpose	Advisability	Sources
Open	Free (that is, cost buried in the purchase price, whether or not the credit is used).	Safe — if monthly bills are paid in full.	Any purchase that a person wants, can use, and can afford.	Good — if the item satisfies the test of forced alternate choice.	Revolving charge accounts, credit cards, medical and dental bills.
Profit-making	Financed, but cost is temporary (that is, cost is free in the long run because cost of the credit is repaid by the use to which the credit is put).	Safe — if the income realized from the use of credit will ultimately repay the cost of the credit.	Any purchase that can increase a person's income or reduce living costs — for example, education, car, clothing, or tools for work, investments.	Good — if the item satisfies the test of forced alternate choice.	Any of the above, plus cash loans. If cash loans, finance charges should be kept low by shopping for money as one would for any other commodity.
Non-profit-making	Full finance charges.	Risky — is the cost of the credit worth the need satisfaction? Costs can lead to reduced standard of living, continual financial difficulties and tensions, and repossession if payments are not kept up.	Anything a person would like to have but cannot immediately afford — for example, hobby or sports equipment, recreation and pleasure, travel, new furniture, clothes, or car.	Questionable — even if the item satisfies the test of forced alternate choice. May be good, however, if used with exceptional caution and with available alternates and all possible consequences clearly in mind.	Any of the above.

as well. According to the add-on clause that was a part of the contract you signed, all the payments you had been making were prorated among all items, so that *none* was paid off and *all* are subject to repossession.

Still another device found in installment contracts is the *balloon payment clause*, which requires a very large final installment payment on the contract. Such a clause is often added to a contract to make the monthly payments for an expensive item small enough to be within the current means of the buyer. Then, with the final balloon payment, the buyer must make up the difference between the sum of the small monthly payments already made and the total cost (principal plus finance charges) of the item. A buyer who is careless about preparing for this final balloon payment must either refinance the loan (at still further cost) or have the item repossessed — losing not only the item but also the money already paid.

Another pitfall of an installment contract is the *default judgment*, which can result when a merchant prepares a legal notice stating that the buyer is being sued for nonpayment of a debt. If an unscrupulous process server hired to deliver the notice files a false affidavit claiming that the notice has been delivered or that the buyer was never at home, the buyer — not knowing that he or she was being sued — fails to show up in court and automatically loses by default. Default judgments are among the most serious traps for installment buyers, particularly those in lower income brackets or in neighborhoods in which this is a common technique creditors use to force payments (Porter 1987). The goods and services involved may range from dancing lessons and vocational courses by mail to burglar alarm systems, but any default judgment automatically leaves the buyer vulnerable to repossession of the property — on which he or she is still required to make installment payments.

Home improvement contracts are often written so that if the purchaser fails to make a payment, the contractor may take over the house, with no foreclosure procedure necessary. Suppose, for example, that you live in a $130,000 house and sign a contract to have a $5,000 air-conditioning unit installed. The contract may have a clause (often in fine print) stipulating that if you miss even a single monthly payment of $300 on the air-conditioning unit, your house is automatically forfeited without even obtaining a court judgment. The contractor then sells your house to recover the balance of the contract. Although this may seem unscrupulous, it is a perfectly legal procedure, as many unwary buyers have found to their surprise and dismay (see Box 14-3).

Sources of Loans

You should shop for money as carefully as you would shop for any other commodity. The charge for money is called *interest*, and interest rates vary considerably from one lender to another. (Moreover, other charges are often tacked on.) For example, pawnbrokers are usually very poor sources of money because their charge for using money generally ranges from 36 to 50 percent in true annual interest. Small-loan companies are poor sources of money because their charges usually range from 30 to 36 percent in true annual interest and are often even higher. In 1990, bank credit cards such as Visa and MasterCard charged about 24 percent in true annual interest to borrow cash.

The interest rates quoted on credit card statements are not an accurate reflection of the real interest rates many cardholders are actually paying. The small type on the back of the statement states that if the bill is paid on or before a certain date of receipt by the credit card company, the customer pays no interest. But if pay-

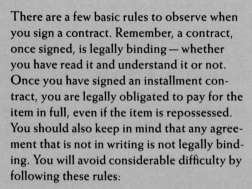
ment of the bill is received after that date — even by one day — then the customer pays interest on the month's entire outstanding balance. In addition, the charge for the next whole month is not only based on the previous balance for which the customer is paying late, but also on any charges incurred during the next month. (This basis for charges is called the "average daily balance.") As a result, the true rate paid by the cardholder depends on the date the payment is made and may be far in excess of the stated rate (Chickering 1992).

Shopping around for credit cards pays off. If you pay your account in full each month the cheapest card would be one with no annual fee. If you do not pay the balance in full each month and incur interest charges, the cheapest card

would be the one with the lowest rate. It is possible to write for a list of low-rate, low-fee, local, regional, and national credit cards.[8]

A good source of convenient credit from a bank is a balance-plus type of account, which is automatically credited to your checking account and usually costs 15 to 18 percent in true annual interest, or a prime line type of account, which is automatically scaled to be about two points above the prime rate. Interest rates, of course, vary, being fixed by such factors as the prime

---

[8]Send $5.00 to *CardTrak*, RAM Research, Box 1700, Frederick, MD 21702. Also, twice a year Bankcard Holders of America updates its lists of credit cards with no annual fees and credit cards with low interest rates. Each list is available for $1.50 from BHA, 560 Herndon Parkway, Herndon, VA 22070.

rate (which is the interest rate banks charge their best corporate customers) and scaled up from there. The prime rate has varied all the way from 6 percent to 15 percent during the past two decades. If the prime rate is high, all personal loans are even higher; if it is low, the rates for personal loans are scaled down accordingly.

If you had a good credit rating and qualified, many major banks were charging 11 to 12 percent interest in 1991 for personal loans that were secured by collateral such as a savings account, CDs, stocks, or bonds. For unsecured loans, which are often available if you have a good credit rating, major banks were charging 16.5 to 20 percent. The best place to start looking for a loan is where you keep your checking or savings account; regular customers are often charged as much as two percentage points less for loans (Loeb 1992).

If you need money for only a short period of time — a bridge loan — you may borrow from your IRA (Individual Retirement Account) without penalty, at a relatively lower rate of interest than a bank loan, *if* you repay the loan within sixty days.

Credit unions are a good source of loans for those who are eligible to become members. Personal loans are available on the member's signature and with no collateral, up to a maximum amount fixed by the policies of the union. Interest rates vary but are usually somewhat lower than comparable bank rates.

Borrowing against the equity in your home is one way to secure relatively low interest rates, especially because interest on such loans is deductible from your income tax. (Beginning in 1991, interest on other loans — such as installment contracts and credit cards — is no longer deductible from your income tax.) Securing low interest rates can be done by using home equity accounts or second mortgage accounts or by refinancing the first mortgage. Home equity accounts are usually the least expensive method,

averaging slightly more than 10 percent in 1991. You can usually borrow up to 80 percent of the value of your home, minus the balance on your mortgage (Loeb 1992).

The downside? You may have to pay closing costs, just as you did when you first got your mortgage. Some banks promote no-fee home equity loans, but check the interest rate. If it's higher than at other banks, you may not save anything. Moreover, since your home is the bank's security for the loan, study agreements carefully. Some stipulate that the bank can seize your property if you miss just one payment or are late with three. This can make a home equity loan potentially very dangerous (Englander 1992).

Credit Ratings

The Federal Fair Credit Reporting Act (which took effect in 1971) assures that anyone refused either credit, a loan, insurance, or a job — and who has reason to believe that the refusal stems from a bad credit rating — has the option to do something about it. Whoever turns down a person's request for credit must give the person the name of the credit agency that made the negative report. This agency must, in turn, allow the person to see exactly what its files contain. If the information is inaccurate or includes data that cannot be verified, the credit agency must promptly delete such data from the file. Moreover, any information that is disputed must be checked again for accuracy. Finally, the person has a right to enter an explanatory statement in the file about any entries that might be misleading, such as a record of late payment for a bill that the person deliberately held up because the merchandise received was unsatisfactory (Porter, S., 1990).

Even if damaging information is accurate, it cannot stay in the file indefinitely. For example, information on bankruptcy must be deleted after ten years. A person who experiences financial loss or embarrassment if the agency does not delete this information may sue the credit agency (Porter, S., 1990).

Copies of your credit report may be obtained by retailers, financial institutions, leasing companies, insurance companies, employers, landlords, credit-card companies, and anyone with an authorized interest in your financial history (Porter, S., 1990). In addition to your financial history, a credit report also lists other companies who have requested a copy. Creditors rate their customers on "the Three C's": (1) Character — are debts paid on time and does the customer live within his/her income? (2) Capacity — will income and other expenses allow the customer to pay off a new debt? and (3) Capital — does the customer have collateral that may be used to secure a new debt? (Porter, S., 1990).

If you are turned down in your application for credit, the Equal Credit Opportunity Act (1975) provides that the creditor must inform you why in writing. In addition, you have the right to know which credit report was used and to obtain a copy of it from the credit bureau. You may be able to take steps either to reapply or apply to another creditor who might evaluate the Three C's differently, or there may have been an error in your report. If the lender insists that you have credit insurance, try another lender; this insurance is usually a bad buy, and you should avoid it if possible (Porter, S., 1990).

Experts advise getting a copy of your credit report early if you plan to take out a big loan, such as a home mortgage or a loan to finance a new car. Credit bureaus are listed in the yellow pages (Jasen 1990a).

Women's Credit Rights

Before the passage of the 1975 Equal Credit Opportunity Act, it was not possible for a married woman to obtain credit in her own name (for example, as Mary Smith). She could get credit only in the name of an employed husband (as Mrs. John Smith), and she would thus be left without a credit rating if she were to become separated, divorced, or widowed. It is now illegal for a bank or other lender to deny a woman personal or commercial credit on the basis of gender or marital status. This legislation was but one significant step in establishing equal opportunity and equal rights for women.

It is important to note that a separated, divorced, or widowed woman will have a credit rating only if she established credit in her own name (as Mary Smith, not Mrs. John Smith) during the marriage. Given the high incidence of separation and divorce and the statistical probability that women who remain married will outlive their husbands, the value to a married woman of obtaining credit in her own name is considerable.

Getting Your Money's Worth

The decisions of whether to make a purchase and then whether to pay for it with credit or cash are the first steps to sound personal finance. The next step is getting the greatest return for each dollar spent. Wise consumers get more for their money by not wasting it on things that will not last or work or that simply do not give full value in relation to their cost.[9] Prudent shoppers know

---

[9] An immensely valuable source of consumer information is *Consumer Reports* magazine. The professional shoppers and evaluators on its staff carefully compare and evaluate a wide variety of consumer goods for durability, safety, effectiveness, and price. *Consumer Reports*, published monthly by the Consumers' Union, a nonprofit organization located at 256 Washington Street, Mount Vernon, New York, may be obtained by subscription, on newsstands, or in the public library. Consumers' Union also publishes an annual digest, *Buying Guide*, which covers the most popular consumer items.

not only the value and comparative prices of items but also how to distinguish quality merchandise from shoddy goods.

The prices for the same or equivalent items often differ widely, depending on the store, the neighborhood, the season, and even the type of sale in which the item is offered. Wise consumers recognize misrepresented merchandise, inflated prices, phony markdowns, and fictitious discounts. Careful consumers read the fine print on guarantees and warranties and know precisely what they are entitled to if something should go wrong with the product.

Wise consumers rarely pay cash for an item. Whenever possible they get the item, try it out, and then pay for it before it is subject to an interest charge. This use of open credit puts consumers at an enormous advantage. If something is wrong with the item, they are in a much stronger position regarding exchanges or returns if they have not yet paid for it (unless, of course, an installment contract has been signed).

Buying Daily Essentials

Getting your money's worth for frequent expenditures for food and clothing is very important; a good rule to remember is the principle of forced alternate choice.

Food Food has many values, of course, and the pleasure it brings may be of such importance to you that it is worth budgeting a relatively high proportion of discretionary funds for it. This is perfectly sensible, as long as you have weighed the relative values and options. To use your shopping dollar wisely, you should buy food that meets both your psychological and nutritional needs at the best possible price. The average person spends about 15 percent of income on food (Loeb 1992).

When buying a large amount of groceries, you should shop from a list that has been based in part on preplanned menus. Supermarkets make a science of inducing shoppers to buy more than they want or need. Packaging, lighting, displays, and other psychological lures are carefully designed by specialists in consumer practices to encourage shoppers to fill their carts. People who wander about the market picking up anything that looks good — especially people who do this when they are hungry — wind up with things that may be overpriced or that they do not really want.

It is also important for you to compare prices and to read labels so that you are aware of what and how much you are getting and how much you are paying for it. Foodstuffs that carry the private label of the market or chain are usually of the same quality as nationally known brands but are significantly cheaper. Most fresh fruits and vegetables have a season of the year when they are in most plentiful supply and are therefore relatively cheap. Buying at the small corner store or late-night market is justified only by convenience, for prices are inevitably higher than in large supermarkets.

Clothing As with food, clothing fulfills psychological as well as practical needs. Again, you should know costs, weigh alternatives, and then try to get the most for your money. You should decide what you want before you shop so you can resist subtle pressures of skilled salespersons, clever displays, and phony (or even legitimate) sales. You should comparison shop and be certain that an item is worth what you pay for it.

One important point to consider in choosing clothes is how many times they can be properly laundered before they need to be mended or thrown out. Another important point to consider is that price is not always a dependable guide when buying clothing; a low price does not necessarily mean lower quality in terms of such important considerations as durable fabric, good seams and thread, and washability. Neither does a high price guarantee high quality and long life.

Clothing expenses can be cut substantially by planning ahead and taking advantage of seasonal reductions. Even during these seasonal sales, however, you must always beware of phony markdowns and closeouts and the substitution of lower-quality and shoddy sale merchandise for the store's regular fare. Most important, you should buy only what you would buy anyway, even if it were not on sale; buying at a sale price something that will not be used or is not needed is certainly no bargain, no matter how cheap it is.

Seasonal markdowns in retail stores began to start earlier and last longer in the 1990s than they did in previous years. Stores need to turn over their merchandise more quickly because it is very expensive to carry slow-moving items. Retailers estimate that customers pay the original price for only 20 to 25 percent of the total sales of high-fashion clothes in department stores — 75 to 80 percent of purchases are at a discounted price. However, all stores make buying errors and carry some inferior-quality goods, so examine a sale item just as carefully as you would if you were paying the full price (Loeb 1992).

Buying "Big-Ticket" Items

As we have seen, "big-ticket" items include the large pieces of furniture and expensive appliances needed to furnish an apartment or house. Salespeople will often advise you to buy a service contract when you buy an expensive appliance such as a microwave oven or a large color television console. This is a bad buy. For average use, for example, the cost of a service contract for a color television set is ten times the probable cost of repairs; for refrigerators it is sixteen times the probable cost of repairs (Loeb 1992).

Furniture is one item for which buying top quality is both the most economical and the most aesthetically satisfying way to go. Poor-quality furniture very quickly loses its appeal and is a constant source of irritation and expense when it breaks down or wears out and needs repair or replacement. Good-quality furniture remains a continuing pleasure and will, with proper care, last a lifetime. If well chosen, its value may even increase. There is generally no particular urgency in selecting furniture, so shoppers can take their time, choose carefully, and watch for bargains. It is possible, for example, to save 15 to 30 percent on quality furniture sales, usually in June or September.

Unless you are unusually knowledgeable about furniture standards and prices, it is risky to shop for it in cut-rate stores, discount houses, or stores featuring distress sales. There are legitimate discount houses and distress sales that offer bargains on furniture, but it is important to be very sure that the furniture (or appliance) is a standard item and that the price is genuinely a bargain. Again, comparison shopping is important.

Do not overlook bargains on unfinished furniture and do-it-yourself kits, which are good ways to acquire simple chairs, desks, bookcases, and tables. Assembling and finishing a piece of furniture yourself saves up to 40 percent of the total cost and gives you the satisfaction of creating the final product.

Used furniture can also be a very good bargain. Quality pieces can sometimes be picked up for next to nothing in thrift shops, at auctions, or through the classified ads in a newspaper. But again, the shopper must be wary, especially with regard to classified ads. There are people who make a good living by buying junk from second-hand stores and disposing of it through want ads. Be skeptical and compare values carefully.

One furniture merchandising swindle that every consumer should be aware of is the type of store known as a "borax store." Such stores specialize in selling furniture by the room. An ad typically reads something like "three rooms of furniture for $198." People responding to such an ad typically are shown the advertised furniture stacked in a dark, dusty corner. Then the salesperson leads them to a different area with better lighting and displays — and higher prices. (This is called the "bait and switch" technique.) The store counts on the fact that many people are unable to resist the need to show the salesperson that they can afford the better merchandise, which is either standard quality merchandise that is outrageously overpriced or highly priced junk.[10] (The store profits even if customers insist on buying the low-quality merchandise for the advertised price.)

The electronics, jewelry, and appliance businesses, frozen food and freezer "bargain" plans, and carpeting dealers also have their share of borax stores and swindles. Carpeting seems to lend itself particularly well to the borax store racket, and the Sunday paper and late night television programs are filled with ads for bargain carpeting "for your whole house." Area rugs are actually much more economical than carpeting, but if you do decide on carpeting you must be wary of misrepresentation and outright rackets. There is an enormous range of carpeting grades, and the unwary consumer can easily be sold an overpriced and inferior grade that stretches,

fades, and wears quickly. Some retailers also advertise "free" installation, when actually the cost of installation is made up by the profit in foisting an inferior grade of carpet on a gullible buyer. It is especially important with carpeting to deal only with reputable stores. The buyer should also take advantage of legitimate sales (usually in January and February) but should expect to save no more than about 20 percent. (With a discontinued mill end, the savings could go as high as 50 percent.)

There is no reason a consumer should be swindled by buying cheap or faulty merchandise at inflated prices. Unfortunately, however, most consumers are willing to cooperate in their own exploitation. They are victimized not so much because they are gullible — although that certainly helps — but because they try to impress the hustler with their shrewdness in realizing a once-in-a-lifetime bargain.

Here are some general principles for any kind of buying:

- Don't be misled by a dealer who lures you into his or her place of business with an attractive ad and then tries to talk you into buying a higher-priced article.

- Don't be blinded by "bargains" offered at impossible-to-believe prices. A deal that seems "too good to be true" is probably neither good nor true.

- Don't be fooled by phony markdowns of overpriced items or by the substitution of poorer-quality merchandise during special sales.

- Don't be rushed into making a decision by a salesperson who talks about "the last chance to get in on a good thing" or the "golden opportunity" you might miss by not acting immediately.

- Don't permit door-to-door salespeople to leave merchandise with you "on approval."

---

[10]Borax stores charge two to five times the usual price for ordinary household furniture and appliances. In one investigation, Florence Rice, consumer education director of the League of Autonomous Bronx Organizations, cited a case in which a customer was sold a Philco washer for $479, including finance charges. The same washer would have cost $250 at a standard price and with legitimate financing. Rice cites another typical example of a customer who was sold a double mattress and box spring for $500; the same item was available in reputable stores in the same area for less than $100! Comparison shoppers in the government-sponsored Project Money-Wise found that people paid $170 to $280 in a borax store for a standard brand television that could be bought in any legitimate store in the same area for $105 to $140 (Miller 1987).

PART V ❖ MONEY AND ECONOMIC REALITY

You may find that you are obligated to pay whether you keep the merchandise or not.

- Never sign a contract that you do not understand or that has not been completely filled in.

Buying from Discount Stores

Shoppers are usually able to find bargains at discount stores. Most of these stores are located in suburban outlet malls[11] and are quite different from the bargain basements of the past. Most of these new stores are attractively decorated, have quality merchandise, and are owned and operated by manufacturers who clear out (for a profit) surplus designer and brand-name clothing, luggage, linens, housewares, electronic goods, and even furniture and offer them to the public at steep discounts (Loeb 1992).

Appliances and furniture can also be purchased at special warehouses or major retail stores such as Macy's, Penney's, or Sears in or near large cities (Loeb 1992). K-Mart, Wal-Mart, and Target stores all compete by offering more and bigger bargains for shoppers.

Membership warehouse clubs, such as Price Club and Costco, are also excellent places to shop. Membership to these huge warehouses is restricted to those who own their own businesses or belong to groups such as credit unions, labor unions, hospitals, banks, savings and loan associations, and local governments. The yearly membership fee is low, usually about $25.00. The floors of the building are usually concrete; most merchandise stays in the suppliers' cartons; and customers wheel around large shopping carts and must find their own goods. Payment is with cash or check. The secret for the success of these unadorned shopping places is the huge volume they sell (Loeb 1992).

The more affluent middle class are the chief beneficiaries of the discount stores, outlet malls, and warehouse clubs that are more and more a part of suburbia. Inner-city neighborhoods are bypassed — being a consumer in the inner city means having fewer selections and paying higher prices. Retailers shy away from the higher costs for insurance and security and the larger theft losses they have to contend with in the inner-city stores; and the gap between the prices paid by the rich and the poor appears to be widening (Schwadel 1992).

Buying a Car

Paying cash is the cheapest way to buy a car; however, if you must finance the purchase, you may be better off leasing rather than buying, unless you plan to keep the car more than four years. Remember, the interest you pay on a car loan is no longer deductible from your income tax (Loeb 1992).

Because most cars depreciate very rapidly, it is much more economical to buy a used car than a new car. Typical used car purchase prices range from 20 to 80 percent below the prices of comparable new cars. In general, the older the car, the greater the savings. Also, your taxes, insurance, and interest are much lower for a lower-priced car (Loeb 1992).

Although it is cheaper to buy a used car than a new car, upkeep costs climb as a car ages. Thus the most economical way to buy a car is to buy one that is a few years old and keep it until the maintenance costs are higher than the costs of buying another car. The precise point at which this happens varies, depending on the individual, the amount and type of driving done, and the

---

[11]Between 200 and 300 of these outlet malls exist across the nation; see the directory *The Joy of Outlet Shopping*, published by the Outlet Marketing Company, St. Petersburg, FL 33737. For discount stores and warehouses, see *The Underground Shopper* by Sue Goldstein (1992).

car. Drivers who follow the maintenance instructions in their owner's manual can usually put 100,000 miles on the car before it begins to need costly repairs.

A good way to find a good auto mechanic is to choose a service station or garage approved by AAA (the American Automobile Association), whose inspectors apply rigorous standards. Look for the AAA's red-white-and-blue sign with the inscription "Approved Auto Repair"; you don't have to join the association to obtain service (Loeb 1992).

If you are seriously interested in a car, you should haggle with the dealer over the price. The sticker price on the window of a car is there because the law says it must be, but only a naive buyer accepts the sticker price as anything but a starting point for negotiations. Shop around, shop carefully, and never pay the asking price (Loeb 1992).

You can easily learn the dealer's cost for a new car (invoice price) by buying an inexpensive guide entitled *Edmund's New Car Prices*, available at bookstores and newsstands. Total the dealer's cost (including options), and then offer $125 to $200 above this cost. You should aim to settle for no more than $200 to $500 over the dealer's cost for an American car, or $500 over for a foreign car (Loeb 1992).

Automobile brokers (listed in the yellow pages) will order a car for you through a network of dealers at prices as low as $150 over invoice; the broker's fee is an additional $100 to $300.

If you buy a car at a dealership, a good time to close a deal is often late Sunday night (or the last night of the week the dealer is open) or at the end of the month. (Many dealerships offer bonuses to the salesperson who has the best sales record at the end of the week or month.) It is good to deal directly with the sales manager or assistant manager because this person is authorized to agree on a price (Loeb 1992).

When you have settled on the car you want and have agreed with the salesperson on a price, you should have the dealer put the agreement in writing before you make a deposit. The order form for this agreement should include a statement of the precise car being bought, the accessories agreed on (if any), the sales tax, registration fee, and the value of the trade-in (if any). In addition, an officer of the firm must sign the order form or it has no legal value. A salesperson's signature means nothing; you may find that when the time comes to close the deal, you have been either low-balled (promised a better deal than you are actually able to get) or high-balled (offered more on your trade-in than you will actually get). A person might be both high-balled and low-balled during the course of the negotiations; both practices are very common among car dealers (Loeb 1992).

In arranging for money to buy a car, it is usually better (as with all "big-ticket" items) to shop for the money elsewhere and pay cash to the dealer. Similarly, auto insurance should be shopped for as carefully as the car itself. Insurance is one of the most costly items of automobile operations; without some comparison shopping, a car owner can spend a lot of money unnecessarily (see Box 14-4).

A good source of information on car buying is the year-end issue of *Consumer Reports*, which contains invaluable and detailed information on the precise steps to take in buying a new or used car. Another useful resource for buyers of used cars is an electronic diagnostic center, which for about $30 may identify the faults in the car and itemize the costs of repair.

In addition to their function of providing transportation, cars hold great psychological value for many people. In making such a purchase it is important to understand and have a clear view of your options — applying the principle of forced alternate choice. If you choose to

buy an uneconomical car for its psychological satisfaction, be sure that you are aware of the other things you will not be able to buy as a consequence. If the car, in your perception, is worth it, then it may be a good buy for you.

Buying a House

Owning a home has long been a "prime ingredient of the American family ideal" (Huttman 1991, p. 155). However, home ownership in the United States dropped during the 1980s for the first time since the 1930s, with young and middle-aged people being the hardest hit (see Table 14-4).

The Census Bureau reported that as of 1991, only 43 percent of all families, only about one-fourth of black and Hispanic families, and only about 13 percent of single-parent families could afford to buy a home in their area.[12]

---

[12]U.S. Bureau of the Census Report on Home Affordability (1991).

TABLE 14-4

U.S. Home Ownership by Age Group: 1980–1990

Home ownership dropped for every age group below sixty during the 1980s. The age group with the highest rate of home ownership jumped in the past decade from people in their late fifties to those in their late sixties.

Age	1980	1990
Under 25	21.3%	15.7%
25–29	43.3	35.2
30–34	61.1	51.8
35–39	70.9	63.0
40–44	74.2	69.9
45–49	76.8	73.9
50–54	78.5	76.8
55–59	79.6	78.8
60–64	78.8	79.8
65–69	77.3	80.0
70–74	72.7	78.4
75+	67.8	72.3
Average	64.4	64.2

Source: U.S. National Association of Home-builders, 1990 Census data (1991).

A house is the single most expensive item you will ever buy, unless you are in that very small minority that has enormous sums available for luxury items such as yachts, jewelry, or art. The first rule in buying a house is that the purchase price should not exceed two and one half times your gross annual income (Connolly 1985). You will normally need 20 percent of the purchase price as a down payment, plus about 2 percent for closing costs. Your total annual expenses for mortgage, taxes, and insurance should not exceed 28 percent of your annual income.[13]

Using these figures as a guideline, you can afford to buy a $75,000 house if you earn $30,000 per year. You can afford to buy a $130,000 house (the median price in the United States) if you earn $52,000 a year.[14]

In many parts of the United States, high costs have pushed the American dream of home ownership out of reach for increasing numbers of our population. The rise in housing costs may be among the most important reasons for the growth in the number of two-earner families (see Chapter 8). A national survey found that 88 percent of first-time buyers were two-earner families, and among all buyers, 80 percent were two-earner families (Chicago Title Insurance Company National Survey, "Recent Home Buyers—General Characteristics: 1976 to 1989," 1991). The most difficult part for the first-time homeowner is getting the down payment together (Rosen 1989).

Middle-class families who are no longer able to buy their own homes are renting—which drives up the cost of renting for working-class families, who are finding it more and more difficult to find adequate housing. According to U.S. Housing Reports, the cost of renting a home rose one-third from 1985 to 1990 (Carter 1990).

If you have the necessary down payment and are earning enough to afford to buy a house, you

[13]U.S. Bureau of the Census Report on Home Affordability. The 1990 census data found, however, that 20 percent of homeowners and 40 percent of renters were spending more than 30 percent of their incomes for housing costs (Shreiner 1992).

[14]In mid-1990, the National Association of Realtors (NAR) found that the nationwide median price for a previously occupied three-bedroom, two-bath house was about $130,000, ranging from about $55,000 in Oklahoma City to nearly $264,000 in the San Francisco Bay Area (Loeb 1992).

should carefully investigate the many pitfalls of home buying. Key points to watch for are size (three-bedroom, two-bath houses have the best resale value), age (it is better to buy a new home because it appreciates faster), proximity to reputable schools, and location.[15] Excellent sources of information regarding the things to explore when buying a home are Marshall Loeb's *Money Guide* (1992), Jane Bryant Quinn's *Making the Most of Your Money* (1991), and Sylvia Porter's *Your Financial Security* (1987).

If you expect to keep the house no longer than three years (before selling or trading up), an ARM (adjustable rate mortgage) might be your best bet. If you plan to keep the house longer, a fixed-rate mortgage won't give you any surprises. No one can predict what will become of interest rates in the future (Loeb 1992).

You should shop for a mortgage as carefully as you shop for a house. Compare the rates of local lenders and look for a real estate broker who uses a computerized service, which makes such comparison shopping easier and faster (Loeb 1992). If, after you buy a house, the mortgage rates drop 2 percent, it will pay you to refinance at the lower rate if you plan to keep the house for at least three years. That is usually the break-even point when the monthly difference between the original payment and the lower payment has repaid the costs of refinancing; after that you begin to come out ahead. The longer you keep the house, the greater your gains will be.

Buying Health Insurance

Although experts on personal finance emphasize that health insurance is absolutely essential and should be budgeted for, as of 1991 more than thirty-three million Americans had no health insurance coverage at all (Sullivan 1991).

Not only should you have basic coverage for health insurance; you should also have a supplemental major medical policy from Blue Cross, Blue Shield, or one of the other large insurance companies that will pick up the charges where the basic plan leaves off. A good supplemental health plan pays all costs above $25,000 up to a maximum of one million dollars. The average premium for a family of four was $430 annually in 1992 for such a plan. The Health Insurance Association of America recommends that each person in a family be covered for at least one million dollars (Loeb 1992). If you can join a group policy through your employer, this is your best bet. However, most group plans stop regular coverage at age sixty-five, offering supplemental coverage only after this age.

People who are eligible for Medicare have the responsibility for notifying the nearest social security office within three months of becoming age sixty-five, in order to receive Medicare coverage. People should not depend on Medicare to cover their medical expenses, however. Americans over age sixty-five are spending more than twice as much on health care as they were before the government established Medicare in 1965. In 1991, the rising costs of services not covered by Medicare — as well as the more costly premiums, higher deductibles, and copayments of the Medicare program — have increased the average elderly family's annual out-of-pocket medical expenses to over $3,000 per year. By contrast, in 1961 medical costs were just over $300 per year for a similar family (Pollack 1992).

Health care costs have been rising for everyone in the population, not just the elderly. Physician's fees, hospital room charges, and other medical care services have skyrocketed since 1970, rising some 500 to 600 percent (see Figure 14-2).

---

[15]A real estate aphorism states that the three most important considerations in buying a home are (1) location, (2) location, and (3) location.

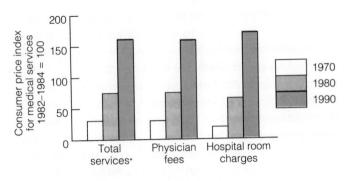

FIGURE 14-2

The rising cost of health care: 1970–90.

Source: U.S. Bureau of Labor Statistics, "Indexes of Medical Care Prices: 1970 to 1990" (1991).

Unfortunately, the nation's deepening health insurance crisis is breeding a new and growing problem: group policies that prove worthless because of fraud or mismanagement. This is a problem of huge proportions, with several million policy holders at risk. These people think they have coverage, but they don't (Meier 1992).

To avoid worthless health insurance schemes, federal and state regulators suggest taking the following steps (Meier 1992):

- Ask state regulators what they know about the provider and its underwriter. Ask whether there have been many complaints about unpaid claims.

- Because most problem plans tend to fail in the first eighteen months, look for a plan that has been in business for three years or more.

- If a small provider says that its policies are backed by a large insurance company, call the company and ask for information about the relationship and how much protection it guarantees.

Buying Life Insurance

You should use life insurance only to protect dependents, not as an investment. The basic purpose of life insurance is to provide income protection for survivors of the deceased. For a relatively modest sum, term insurance (straight protection without any cash value) will provide such income protection. The survivors are left with an "instant estate," and this may be the only substantial amount of money most people are able to leave to their survivors. There can be no question about the value and the importance of insurance coverage—as long as you have someone to protect. In a marriage, for example, both husband and wife should be insured for as substantial a sum as is appropriate to their income and budget (Loeb 1992).

There are two different kinds of life insurance policies with important differences. One, which provides protection only and is a good buy, is called a term insurance policy; the other provides for investment as well as protection and is a bad buy. Insurance-plus-investment policies are called by various names, such as ordinary life, straight life, mortgage insurance, and twenty-pay life.[16]

Although very bad buys, most insurance policies sold are of the insurance-plus-investment type. Most agents will not even discuss term insurance with a prospective client because these policies pay such small commissions. If you want term insurance, you must usually go directly to the company to get it, unless such insurance is part of a group insurance plan.

An insurance agent can make a very convincing argument in pushing an insurance-plus-investment type of policy because these policies have the following features that can be made to sound very attractive:

- The cash surrender value increases during the life of the policy.

- The policy holder may borrow on this cash value at a relatively low interest rate.

- The premiums (payments per month) do not increase periodically, as they do with a term insurance policy, but are fixed for the duration of the policy.

- The face value of the policy (the amount paid out in the event of the policy holder's death) does not drop periodically as it does with a term insurance policy.

- The policy will not be canceled when the insured reaches age sixty-five, whereas a term insurance policy will be canceled right at the time when presumably it is needed the most.

---

[16] Twenty-pay life is an example of a limited-payment insurance-plus-investment policy, with the insurance paid up after a specified time (or sometimes at a specified age). With this type of policy, the insurance company calculates the premiums the insured would pay if he or she lived to age 100 and then collects them over a shorter period of time (such as twenty years). The annual premium payment for this type of policy is much higher than the premium for other types of policies, and it is an especially bad buy.

These certainly sound like very good arguments for purchasing an insurance-plus-investment type of policy, but they don't hold up to close scrutiny. Let us see precisely why an insurance-plus-investment policy is such a bad buy.

The monthly premiums you pay for the insurance-plus-investment policy are divided into two parts. One part of your premium goes to buy a term insurance policy for you (you could buy it for yourself at a much lower premium); the other part of your premium is an investment, for which the insurance company pays you a very small rate of interest—as low as 2.5 percent (compounded annually). This constitutes the cash surrender value of your policy.

If you withdraw this cash surrender value, the term insurance part of your policy is immediately canceled, and you have lost all the premiums that went into this part of your policy.

If you borrow (instead of withdraw) this cash surrender value of your policy, you will have to pay interest on the loan until the money is repaid. (This is ironic because you are paying to borrow your own money.) Moreover, if you die before the loan is repaid, the face value of your policy is reduced by the amount of the loan, and your beneficiaries will get that much less.

If you neither cash in your policy nor borrow on it but keep the face value intact, and if you pay your premiums regularly until you die or reach age sixty-five, then your beneficiary collects the face value of the policy. However, the insurance company keeps the cash surrender value (the total of all the premiums that have gone into the investment part of your policy, plus accumulated interest)!

In other words, if your beneficiaries collect the face value of the policy, they have lost the cash surrender value; if you withdraw the cash surrender value, you lose the premium payments that have gone into the term insurance part of your policy when your policy is canceled. Whatever you do, you are going to lose one or the other — the premium payments you have made for the term insurance part or those you have made for the investment part of the policy. Not a very good deal for you, but an excellent one for the insurance company.

The solution is simple: Buy term insurance and invest the difference between the premium of the term insurance policy and the premium of the insurance-plus-investment policy. This difference is considerable. With the amount of money you save invested at 5 percent interest (which is the average you can probably count on over the years), you will have saved (by age sixty-five) more than the face value of the insurance-plus-investment policy (see Table 14-5). Moreover, although the face value of the term insurance policy will drop periodically, this decline will be more than offset by the accumulated savings, so that you are protected until you reach age sixty-five. In addition, the value of your investment continues to grow (at compound interest) *after* you reach age sixty-five, instead of being fixed at face value as it is in an insurance-plus-investment policy. Thus, if you reach age seventy, eighty, or beyond, the value of your investment continues to grow significantly at compound interest, which is a very important consideration given the erosive effect of inflation. Finally, your investment (which is called the cash surrender value in an insurance-plus-investment policy) is freely available to you at any time without canceling the policy. If you wish, you can borrow it (from yourself) without paying interest.

If you find the foregoing discussion rather difficult to comprehend, you are not alone. Most people in our society have difficulty with such matters and so are easy prey for an agent intent on selling them an insurance-plus-investment type of policy.

It should be clear that such a "buy term insurance and invest the difference" plan, assuming a return of 5 percent in the long run, provides substantially greater protection for your survivors from the outset until age sixty-five and a much higher protection if you live beyond this age. For example, at age seventy-five you will have $70,840 in your savings account, and this sum will continue to grow substantially.

In summary, you should purchase life insurance because it provides an "instant estate" for someone you wish to protect if you should die. For this reason, term insurance should be considered essential and should be budgeted for. You should buy term insurance, invest the difference between the premium for this policy and the premium for an insurance-plus-investment type of policy, and let this investment accumulate at the highest rate of interest consistent with safety.

Experts in personal finance suggest that you look around for an insurance firm that provides special discounts for nonsmokers and for people who exercise regularly, if these apply to you. Nonsmokers may get up to a 30 percent discount on their insurance premium because they have a longer life expectancy. For example, as of 1992, Allstate Insurance's ten-year term life policies were 15 to 30 percent cheaper for nonsmokers who said that they exercised three to five times a week, used seat belts when driving, and avoided excessive salt in their diets (Loeb 1992).

If you have hypertension, you can reduce your life insurance premiums by as much as 50 percent by lowering your blood pressure. For example, a thirty-year-old man with moderately high blood pressure will pay $285 per year for a $100,000 renewable term life policy with Allstate. His premiums will be cut nearly in half to $152 per year if he reduces his blood pressure to normal (Loeb 1992).

Paying Taxes

The average American family spent nearly 40 percent of its income on federal, state, local, and social security taxes in 1990 — about twice as

TABLE 14-5

The "Buy Term Insurance and Invest the Difference" Plan

Age	Annual Premium for Ordinary Life Policy with $50,000 Face Value	Annual Premium for Renewable Term Policy (five-year period)	Amount Saved per Year	Accumulated Savings at End of Five-Year Period at 5% Interest Compounded	Face Value of Renewable Term Policy at End of Five-Year Period	Total Face Value of Renewable Term Insurance Policy Plus Accumulated Savings at End of Each Five-Year Period
30–35	$750	$192	$558	$ 3,083	$50,000	$53,083
35–40	750	202	548	6,962	47,000	53,962
40–45	750	240	510	11,703	43,000	54,703
45–50	750	298	452	17,434	38,000	55,434
50–55	750	359	391	24,410	31,000	55,410
55–60	750	421	329	32,972	24,000	56,972
60–65	750	495	255	43,490	15,000	58,490
65–70	—	—	—	55,505	—	55,505
70–75	—	—	—	70,840	—	70,840

much as it would have paid in 1960 (*Statistical Abstract of the U.S.*, 1991, pp. 452, 454).

Tax laws are not only very complicated, but they change from year to year. It is therefore difficult for people to figure their own income tax and take advantage of all the legal deductions to which they are entitled. They will probably pay lower taxes if they get professional help; a tax consultant is likely to find enough deductions to offset his or her fee.

A tax consultant must have something to work with, however, so you should save and then sort into categories all sales receipts, canceled checks, and records of unreceipted deductible expenditures for the year. The tax consultant will make good use of these data.

Before taking your form and records to the professional, you should first try to compute the tax yourself. You will then be much more knowledgeable about discussing deductions and problems with the consultant, and you will also be aware of just how much the consultant has saved you. In making this initial and informational attempt, you will need a tax guide. A good inexpensive manual is the government's *Your Federal Income Tax* (which can be ordered from the U.S. Superintendent of Documents, Washington, DC 20402). Lasser's annual *Income Tax Guide* is another good source of information available at libraries and bookstores.

A curious provision of the tax law is the "marriage penalty," which provides that if two fully employed people are married and file a joint return, they will pay a higher tax than if they are simply living together (without being married) and file individual returns. Married people who both have incomes cannot legally file individual returns but must file jointly (Cohan 1992). This discriminatory tax law can be quite substantial for two-earner couples in the higher tax brackets (Jasen 1990b). Some couples who are living together have decided not to marry to avoid having to pay the higher tax. Still others who have been living together and filing individual returns have received profound shocks when, in ignorance of the tax law, they marry and file a joint return. Other couples have decided to divorce while maintaining a common residence and telling no one but their tax accountant. This is, of course, illegal; a couple who divorce for tax reasons only can be required to refile their tax returns as if they were married and may be liable for additional taxes, interest, and penalties (Jasen 1990b).

Everyone eligible should take advantage of the opportunity to shelter taxable income through IRA accounts.[17] An IRA is one of the more valuable tax shelters ever devised for individual taxpayers. If eligible, you may deposit up to $2,000 into an account of your choice (for example, a certificate of deposit in a bank). The $2,000 may then be partially or totally deducted from your income that year, so that you do not pay taxes on this amount (thus the term *tax shelter*). Moreover, the interest earned on the investment is also free from income tax until you withdraw the money. After you reach age fifty-nine and a half you may withdraw all your funds in a lump sum via a ten-year averaging tax computation; or, if you prefer, you may let the fund build up tax free until you reach age seventy and a half. (You may continue to contribute to the fund during this time.) At that age, you may either use the lump-sum ten-year averaging option, or you can withdraw the amount as a pension over your life expectancy (or, if you are married, over the joint lives of yourself and your spouse).

---

[17]IRA is an acronym for Individual Retirement Account, which was an option made available to eligible taxpayers by Congress in 1982. Important tax-saving features were eliminated for many people in the 1986 tax revision; however, an IRA can still be a valuable device both for reducing taxes and for saving. Anyone who is not covered by an employee pension plan can still deduct the full IRA deposit from taxable income (Loeb 1992).

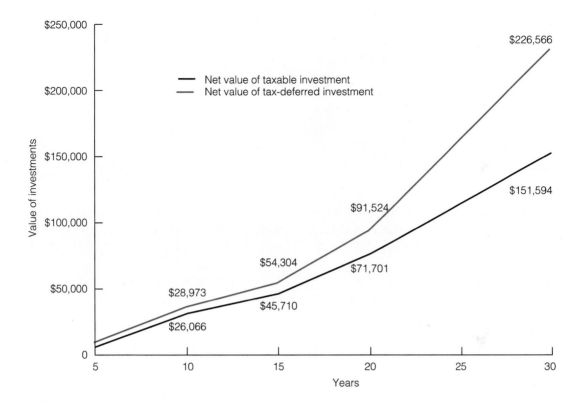

FIGURE 14-3

The value of tax-deferred investing.

Source: Donald Mosby Rembert, *Schwab Report*, Vol. 3, Issue 4, Spring 1992.

*Assumes earnings are taxed at 28% marginal federal tax rate; chart does not include the impact of state and local taxes.

IRA deposits build up surprisingly fast because of the effect of tax-free compound interest. For example, a contribution of $2,000 per year, compounded at 8 percent annually, would grow to $31,300 after ten years, $98,800 after twenty years, $244,700 after thirty years, and $559,600 after forty years (Loeb 1992). (See Figure 14-3.)

Both the Keogh plan and the SEP (Simplified Employee Pension) plan are similar to the IRA. However, if eligible, you can put much more money into either a Keogh or an SEP than you can put into an IRA plan, and you can deduct all

of this money from your taxable income (Loeb 1992). Unfortunately, many people who are eligible for one of these plans fail to take advantage of this opportunity to receive a large tax shelter because they don't realize they are eligible. If you are self-employed full-time or part-time, or if you work at one job for an employer and are self-employed at a second job, you are eligible to contribute to a Keogh or SEP. You can contribute about 18.5 percent of your self-employment income to a Keogh or about 12 percent to an SEP. The maximum contribution is $30,000 per year. If both spouses are self-employed, both

If an investment does not keep pace with inflation, it will lose value in terms of purchasing power and be worth less when it is withdrawn than when it was put in.

can contribute the maximum amount (Loeb 1992).

Investing Regularly

As we have seen, the goal of investing is not deferred spending (which is properly called saving) but rather removing the invested money from spendable resources and allowing it to grow. Eventually, withdrawals may be made, but only from dividends or interest and never (at least ideally) from the principal, which should always be left undisturbed.

A good investment balances three factors: safety, yield, and growth. If an investment is safe but provides a yield less than the rate of inflation and no growth at all, it is obviously a poor investment. If the investment provides safety and a relatively high yield but fails to grow with the

economy, it is also a poor investment. Finally, if growth is phenomenal and yield outstanding but the risks are great, it is obviously a poor investment; in fact, this is properly called speculating rather than investing.

One important concept that should be understood is compound interest. This refers to interest on interest; that is, if the interest that is earned on an investment is itself reinvested each month, this reinvestment will itself earn interest. At compound rates, money will increase in this way, with the doubling time depending on the rate of interest. For example, money will double in twenty-five years at 3 percent interest or in twelve years at 6 percent interest. At 20 percent interest, it will double in just four years.[18]

---

[18]The *rule of 72* is a useful method to calculate doubling time. Simply divide 72 by the annual percentage change to get the

Suppose you could invest $100 per month at 10 percent compound interest. Then, after eight years, suppose you began to withdraw $100 per month (making no further deposits). How long could you continue such withdrawals before exhausting the principal? Eight years? Sixteen years? Twenty-four years? Forever? The answer is forever. This is because the doubling time at 10 percent compound interest is eight years. Therefore, for every $100 you put in you would have $200 eight years later. You could withdraw this $100 each month forever, leaving the principal untouched.

Effects of Inflation on Investments

A point that is especially important to consider in making an investment is the long-range trend of inflation. If your investment does not keep pace with inflation, your funds will lose value in terms of purchasing power, or what they can buy when they are withdrawn. The CPI (Consumer Price Index), a commonly used measure of inflation,[19] has risen at an average annual rate of 6 percent compounded for the past twenty years (Dorfman 1989). At this rate, prices double every twelve years. If this average rate of inflation were to continue, an investment would have to earn at least 6 percent (after taxes) just to keep even with inflation. In other words, if you are in the 28 percent tax bracket, you would have to earn nearly 9 percent on your investment just for your

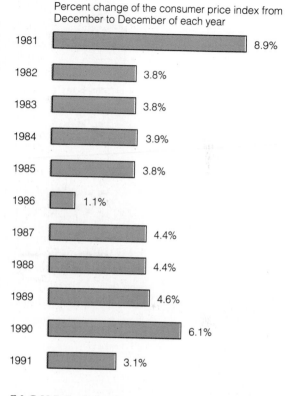

Percent change of the consumer price index from December to December of each year

Year	Percent
1981	8.9%
1982	3.8%
1983	3.8%
1984	3.9%
1985	3.8%
1986	1.1%
1987	4.4%
1988	4.4%
1989	4.6%
1990	6.1%
1991	3.1%

FIGURE 14-4

Inflation rates: 1981–1991.

Source: U.S. Bureau of Labor Statistics, Monthly data in U.S. Bureau of Economic Analysis, *Survey of Current Business,* December 1991.

doubling time at that percentage, compounded. For example, if the annual change is 5 percent, $72 \div 5 = 14.4$ years. Similarly, the doubling time at 10 percent, compounded, is a little over seven years.

[19]The CPI is a measure of the average change in prices over time in a fixed "market basket" of goods and services. The current CPI is based on prices of food, clothing, shelter, fuels, transportation, and medical costs (*Statistical Abstract of the United States* 1991).

money to be worth the same when you withdraw it as it was worth when you invested it.

All societies have experienced a steady, long-term inflation (interrupted by short periods of deflation) from earliest recorded history. In the United States, for example, the rate of inflation for the past sixty-seven years has averaged about 4 percent annually (Rembert 1992). Inflation rates for the past decade have continued this pattern (see Figure 14-4). The doubling time at 4 percent is about eighteen years.

It is not possible to predict the rate of future inflation; regardless, if an investment

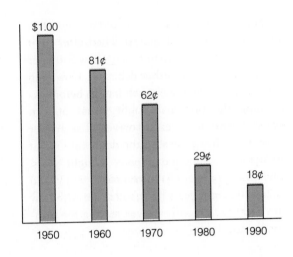

FIGURE 14-5

Purchasing power of the dollar, 1950–1990. In the period from 1950 to 1990 the dollar lost more than 80 percent of its purchasing power. In other words, a 1990 dollar was worth only eighteen cents compared with a 1950 dollar..

Source: Data from U.S. Bureau of Labor Statistics, "Purchasing Power of the Dollar: 1950 to 1990" (1991).

does not keep up with inflation, yielding as much as the dollar is depreciating, the value of your capital will fall (see Figure 14-5). For example, putting $100 in a sugar bowl and hiding it on the top shelf would be a very poor investment because there would be no yield and no growth (and only moderate safety). If inflation were 6 percent per year (the average rate for the past twenty years), the value of the $100 would depreciate by 6 percent each year, compounded. After twelve years, it would be worth only $50 in purchasing power. If you put the $100 into a savings account that paid 6 percent annually, compounded, this investment would keep up with the inflation, so that the $100 would still be worth $100 in purchasing power twelve years later. However, this still does not allow for taxes. If your tax bracket is 28 percent, then more than

one-fourth of the 6 percent would go for taxes, leaving only a little more than 4 percent appreciation. Thus the $100 would, after taxes, actually depreciate nearly 2 percent each year in purchasing power.

Bonds, Stocks, and Other Investments

A classic investment is bonds, which pay a fixed rate over their lifetime. The drawback to bonds, however, is that this fixed rate might look good at the time of purchase but may not be adequate in a time of rapid inflation. During a period of very rapid inflation (such as in Germany in 1923), fixed-value instruments such as bonds or cash (either in the bank or in something similar to a money market fund) become virtually worthless. (See Max Shapiro's *The Penniless Billionaires* [1980] for a fascinating discussion of the impact of inflation.)

Common stocks are another traditional investment vehicle. Investment experts agree that no matter how good a stock looks, it is impossible to predict its movement with certainty. Therefore, they advise that no more than 4 to 5 percent of one's investment funds should be put into any single stock (Zweig 1986). However, it is difficult for the nonprofessional to keep track of a great number of stocks. One solution to this problem is to let a professional money manager make the decisions about the type of stock and the timing of its purchase and sale. This can be done by buying shares in a mutual fund (rather than an individual stock). A mutual fund is an investment company that pays a professional money manager to buy stock in anticipation of its rising value, sell it when it appears to be near its peak value, and withdraw from the market (holding assets in cash) when this seems to be indicated. When you buy a share in a mutual fund, you buy a share in the entire portfolio of stocks the fund owns. Some funds are much better than others, of course.

How do you select a fund that will appreciate? The best answer seems to be to rely on the past performance of the fund over at least ten years. If it has a record of steady appreciation during both up (*bull*) and down (*bear*) markets, the presumption would be that the fund's management is skilled in making investment decisions. *Forbes* magazine puts out annual ratings (in the August issue) of the performance records of all the mutual funds in the United States. Other publications also analyze the performance of mutual funds. For example, *Barrons* and *Money Magazine* publish mutual fund ratings on a periodic basis. The *Weisenberger Report*, published annually, tracks the record of each existing fund for periods up to twenty years. (It is expensive but is available in libraries.) The *Wall Street Journal* often has articles on mutual funds, and its back issues may be consulted in the library.

Mutual funds are typically either *no-load* or *load*. No-load funds charge no investment fee; load funds charge about 8 percent. There are also low-load funds, which usually charge about 3 percent. The charge is usually a "front-end" load, payable when shares in the fund are purchased.

Shares in mutual funds are usually purchased by mail, although some funds may be bought over the telephone through some brokers (for example, Charles Schwab and Company). A phone call or a letter to a mutual fund asking for their prospectus will get you a description of the fund, its track record, and an application form.

Other traditional investments are commodities such as artwork by old masters, Chinese ceramics, coins, diamonds, bonds, U.S. treasury bills, housing, U.S. farmland, oil, foreign exchange, gold, and silver. Whether these appreciate or depreciate depends on many variables. A study by Salomon Brothers (Dorfman 1989) shows that while the consumer price index has risen at the rate of 6 percent per year, compounded, for the past twenty years, stocks have advanced an average of 10 percent per year, compounded. The other commodities mentioned have advanced from 4 percent (foreign exchange) to 17 percent (coins) during this time (see Table 14-6).

What, then, is a good investment? The answer varies with the time and situation, depending on the inflation rate, the condition of the national economy, and the individual asset. Deal with a trusted firm, beware of get-rich-quick schemes, and remember the three cardinal principles of investing: safety, yield, and growth—with safety of paramount importance. Finally, begin your investment program as early as possible to take advantage of the growth-on-growth feature of compound interest.

TABLE 14-6

Rates of Investment Return

Thirteen asset categories are ranked by the twelve-month return through June 1, 1989.

Type of Asset	Rates of Return*			
	1 Year	5 Years	10 Years	20 Years
Old masters	51%	18%	10%	11%
Chinese ceramics	40	12	9	13
Coins	30	15	13	17
Stocks	25	20	17	10
Diamonds	16	11	8	10
Bonds	11	18	11	9
Treasury bills	8	7	10	9
Housing	7	5	6	8
U.S. farmland	6	−5	0	6
Oil	3	−11	1	8
Foreign exchange	−13	7	1	4
Gold	−20	−2	3	12
Silver	−23	−11	−5	6
Consumer price index	5	4	6	6

*Compound annual rates, rounded to nearest whole number. Figures don't include taxes or transaction costs.

Source: Data from Salomon Brothers, reported in Dorfman (1989, p. C-1).

SUMMARY

One of the greatest difficulties in striking out on your own is facing the hard economic reality of making a living and meeting expenses. Yet, despite its importance, personal finance is one of the least understood and most neglected areas of many people's lives. Acquiring even a modicum of financial expertise will bring rich rewards.

Most people do not have enough money to buy everything they want and so must choose between alternatives — not an easy task if the alternatives are unclear. A budget can help clarify these choices and put them in perspective and can help you direct your spendable income where you most want it to go.

Although credit, wisely used, will enhance your life-style, it is a potentially dangerous tool. There are two major forms of credit: (1) open credit, which is not financed and is therefore "free" and a great convenience, and (2) financed credit, which may be either profit-making or non-profit-making. Each of these forms of credit can be used effectively, but all carry inherent risks that are important to recognize, understand, and evaluate.

Credit installment buying of "big-ticket" items is expensive, risky, and usually unwise. It is generally better to borrow the money elsewhere and pay cash for the item. Shop for the loan as carefully as you would shop for any other commodity, looking for the best "buy" — that is, the lowest interest rate.

Never sign an installment contract (or any other contract) that you have not read carefully, that is not completely filled in, or that you do not fully understand. Once you have signed a contract, it is a legally binding instrument.

When you buy appliances such as a microwave oven or a large television, a service contract is a particularly bad buy, costing up to ten times as much as the probable cost of repairs for the average owner.

When buying furniture, it is usually most economical to buy top quality. Although there are legitimate discount houses, it is usually risky to shop for furniture in cut-rate stores or stores featuring distress sales. Be especially leery of "borax stores" that sell furniture by the room and often use a "bait and switch" technique to trap unwary customers. Carpeting seems to lend itself particularly well to the borax store racket. Be especially skeptical of classified ads in a newspaper, and compare values very carefully. In contrast, used and unfinished furniture can be exceptionally good bargains, if shopped for carefully.

Getting your money's worth involves comparison shopping, recognizing overpriced or shoddy merchandise and faulty contracts, distinguishing legitimate from phony sales, handling salespeople who use high-pressure methods, and recognizing and avoiding borax stores. It is not possible to get something for nothing, and offers of "free services" or unbelievable bargains should be regarded with skepticism and suspicion.

Because cars depreciate rapidly, it is much more economical to buy a used car than a new car. Typical used-car prices range from 20 to 80 percent below the prices of comparable new cars. You should never pay the asking price for a car but should haggle with the dealer over the price. When you have settled on a price, have the dealer put the agreement in writing before making a deposit. An officer of the firm must sign the agreement (or order form); the salesperson's signature means nothing. As with all "big-ticket" items, it is generally better to shop for the loan elsewhere and pay cash to the car dealer. Insurance for the car should be shopped for as carefully as the car itself.

In buying a house, you should not pay more than two and one half times your gross annual income. The best investment is a three-bedroom, two-bath house in a good location that is close to schools. You should shop for the mortgage as carefully as you shop for the house.

Life insurance provides an "instant estate" for someone you want to protect in the event of your death. There are two types of life insurance, and only one is a good buy. A renewable term insurance policy is a good buy; the many kinds of insurance-plus-investment policies (ordinary life, straight life, twenty-pay life, mortgage insurance) are all bad buys. You should buy a renewable term insurance policy and invest the difference between the cost of its premium and the cost of an insurance-plus-investment policy premium. The advantage is considerable.

It is well worth paying a tax consultant to figure your income tax. The amount you save in taxes will probably be much more than the cost of the consultant's fee. An IRA account, a Keogh plan, or an SEP plan are all excellent ways to lower your income tax and invest for your future.

A regular program of investing accumulates assets surprisingly fast because of the action of compound interest. For example, the doubling time of money invested at 6 percent compounded annually is about twelve years.

It is important to start an investment program such as an IRA as early as possible and to invest in this program regularly. There are three cardinal factors of a good investment: safety, yield, and growth. Of these, safety is of paramount importance, but an investment that doesn't yield as much as the rate of inflation will drop in purchasing power over the years.

KEY TERMS

The following is a list of key terms in this chapter.
They are defined in context within the chapter, and many may also be found in the Glossary.

adjustable rate mortgage (ARM)

assets

bait and switch

borax stores

budget

bull and bear stock markets

capital

cash flow

cash surrender value

compound interest

Consumer Price Index (CPI)

deferred spending

discount store

financed credit

high-balled

Individual Retirement Account (IRA)

inflation

installment contract

insurance-plus-investment policy

Keogh plan

low-balled

money market fund

open credit

principle of forced alternate choice

purchasing power (of the dollar)

rule of 72

SEP plan

simple interest

speculating

tax shelter

tax-deferred investment

term insurance policy

yield (of investment)

QUESTIONS

1. Discuss the benefits of keeping a budget.

2. What is meant by the principle of forced alternate choice? Discuss the reasons why this principle is important to sound money management.

3. What are nondiscretionary expenses? Discretionary expenses? Give examples of each.

4. Discuss the importance of a personal allowance.

5. Discuss the sound uses of credit. Give examples.

6. Discuss the economics of buying a car, whether new or used.

7. What is the basic purpose of life insurance? Discuss the various types of life insurance policies. What does the phrase "Buy term insurance and invest the difference" mean to you? Give an example that justifies your answer.

8. What is meant by the growth-on-growth feature of compound interest? Give an example.

9. If the population of a country increases 6 percent annually, how long will it take for the population to double? (Use the rule of 72 to calculate the answer.)

10. What three key factors should be evaluated in any investment? Why is each important? Give examples.

SUGGESTIONS FOR FURTHER READING

Edelman, Marian Wright. *Families in Peril: An Agenda for Social Change.* Cambridge, Mass.: Harvard University Press, 1987.

Loeb, Marshall. *Marshall Loeb's 1992 Money Guide.* Boston: Little, Brown, 1992.

Matthews, Arlene Modica. *If I Think About Money So Much, Why Can't I Figure It Out? Understanding and Overcoming Your Money Complex.* New York: Summit Books, 1991.

Porter, Sylvia. *Sylvia Porter's Your Finances in the 1990s.* New York: Prentice-Hall, 1990.

Quinn, Jane Bryant. *Making the Most of Your Money.* New York: Simon & Schuster, 1991.

Thaler, Richard. *The Winner's Curse: Paradoxes and Anomalies of Economic Life.* New York: Free Press, 1992.

Voydanoff, Patricia, and Majka, Linda C., eds. *Families and Economic Distress: Coping Strategies and Social Policy.* Newbury Park, Calif.: Sage, 1988.

APPENDIX A

Sexually Transmitted Diseases: STDs

AIDS: Acquired
Immunodeficiency Syndrome

Hepatitis B

Gonorrhea

Syphilis

Chlamydia

Genital Herpes

Trichomoniasis

Genital Warts

Although there are cures for many STDs,[1] the consequences of STD infection can be very serious, and, in the case of AIDS, hepatitis B, and syphilis, can be fatal. The Centers for Disease Control reports a nationwide annual increase in the rate of AIDS, hepatitis B, and infectious syphilis, a growing number of penicillin-resistant strains of gonorrhea, a high prevalence of chlamydial infection, genital herpes, trichomoniasis, and genital warts among people of all socioeconomic groups, and a greater proportion of *heterosexual* transmission of AIDS (Reinisch et al. 1992).

The Centers for Disease Control estimates that two-thirds of the twelve million Americans infected with an STD are under age 25.[2] Those most vulnerable include the more than thirteen million college and university students in the United States (Reinisch et al. 1992). The risk of acquiring an STD is correlated with age at first sexual intercourse and number of sexual partners. Studies of the sexual behavior of college and university students between 1973 and 1988 indicate that 75–80 percent of males and 60–70 percent of females have had sexual intercourse (MacDonald et al. 1990).

Inherent in any sexual interaction is the possibility of acquiring an STD, unless the interaction is limited to a monogamous relationship in which neither person is infected.

Health experts agree that the incidence and the severity of STDs are increasing at an alarming rate (see Figure A-1). The largest increase of STDs is occurring in our inner cities, where public health diagnostic and treatment centers are

often underfunded and are simply unable to deal adequately with the rapid spread of these diseases, especially among blacks and Hispanics (Aral and Holmes 1991).

As prevalent as STDs are in our society, most of our population is unfamiliar with the basic facts regarding acquisition and prevention of these diseases and usually seeks help only after it is too late — when their bodies have suffered irreversible damage (Hatcher et al. 1990).

Of the twenty-five or so diseases now known to be spread through sexual contact, the most serious and most common STDs in the United States are AIDS, hepatitis B, syphilis, gonorrhea, PID (pelvic inflammatory disease, which can be caused by many agents), chlamydia, genital herpes, trichomoniasis, and genital warts (Hatcher et al. 1990). We will examine each.

AIDS: Acquired Immunodeficiency Syndrome

Although its incidence in the United States is still well below that of other STDs (see Figure A-1), AIDS is the most dangerous because of its rapid spread and because its victims die within one to five years of contracting the disease. There is no effective treatment and no cure for AIDS, although some drugs (such as AZT) have limited effectiveness and prolong survival, especially when administered before symptoms of AIDS have developed (Hatcher et al. 1990).

Incidence of AIDS

AIDS was first recognized as a new disease in the United States in 1979, when a single case occurred in San Francisco.[3] By 1992, little more than a decade later, an estimated 1.5 million peo-

---

[1]The term *sexually transmitted disease* (STD) has largely replaced the term *venereal disease*, although both terms are still commonly used.

[2]U.S. Centers for Disease Control. Division of STD/HIV Prevention, *Sexually Transmitted Disease Surveillance*, 1990 (1991).

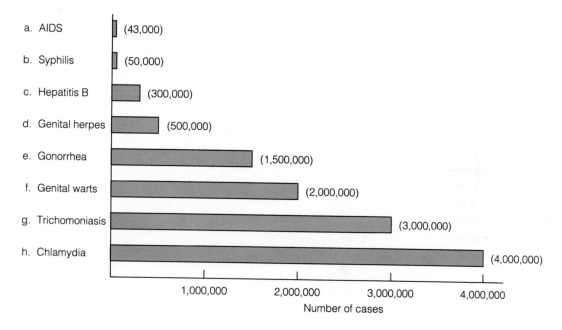

FIGURE A-1

One year's new cases of STDs in the United States: 1990.

a. U.S. Centers for Disease Control, "AIDS Cases Reported, by Patient Characteristics: 1981 to 1990" (1991).

b, d, g, h. U.S. Centers for Disease Control, "1990 Division of STD/HIV Prevention Annual Report" (1991).

c, f. Aral and Holmes, "STDs in the AIDS Era," *Scientific American* 264 (February 1991): 66.

e. Hatcher et al. 1990.

ple in the United States had been infected with HIV (human immunodeficiency virus), the causative agent of AIDS; 218,000 had developed AIDS (see Figure A-2) and more than 141,000 had died of the disease. To put this figure of 141,000 deaths into perspective, it is more than double the number of American soldiers killed

(58,000) during more than a decade of combat in Vietnam.

- An international team of AIDS experts (the Global AIDS Policy Coalition at Harvard University) estimates that fifteen to twenty million adults worldwide will be infected with HIV by 1995 and that an additional five million will have AIDS (Mann 1992).

- AIDS is already the leading cause of death for both adults and children in some cities in Africa (Anderson and May 1992).

- Worldwide, 71 percent of HIV infections are acquired through heterosexual contact (14 percent are through homosexual

[3]A tantalizing medical mystery is the question of the origin of AIDS. Evidence suggests that it originated in Africa, where it may have been slowly spreading for 100 to 200 years or longer, until its sudden explosion in the 1980s (Anderson and May 1992). For an interesting study of the possible origins and rapid spread of AIDS in the United States, see Randy Shilts, *And the Band Played On,* St. Martin's Press, 1987.

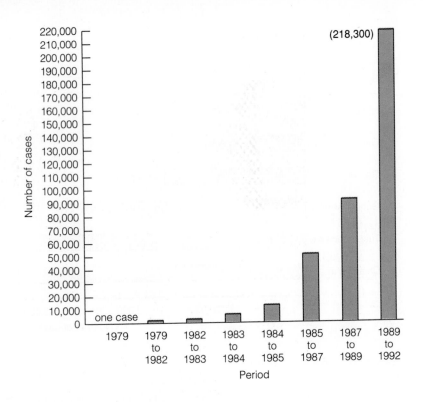

FIGURE A-2

Diagnosed AIDS cases in the United States, 1979–1992.

Sources: Data from U.S. Centers for Disease Control. "Update: Acquired Immunodeficiency Syndrome — United States, 1981–1990." *Morbidity and Mortality Weekly Reports,* June 1991 and 1992. Data for 1979–1980 in "Coolfont Report: A PHS Plan for Prevention and Control of AIDS and the AIDS Virus." *U.S. Public Health Report* 101 (1986): 341–348.

contact, 7 percent through IV drug abuse, 5 percent through blood contact, and 2 percent are unknown).

- The Global AIDS Policy Coalition projects that by the year 2000, nearly 90 percent of all HIV infections will be transmitted heterosexually (Mann 1992; Aral and Holmes 1991).

In the United States, most cases of AIDS have been acquired by men. Only about 12 percent of AIDS cases in the United States have

been women.[4] Worldwide, however, women are just as likely to be affected as men; since January 1992, close to one-half of the one million newly infected adults have been women. Moreover, women's rising infection rates have been accompanied by a corresponding rise in the number of children infected with HIV at birth (Merson 1992). For women in their twenties and thirties,

[4]U.S. Centers for Disease Control, "AIDS Cases Reported, by Patient Characteristic: 1981 to 1990" (1991).

APPENDIX A ❖ SEXUALLY TRANSMITTED DISEASES: STDs

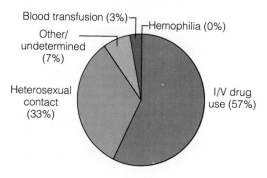

Black females

Blood transfusion (3%)
Other/undetermined (7%)
Heterosexual contact (33%)
Hemophilia (0%)
I/V drug use (57%)

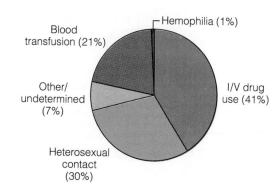

White females

Blood transfusion (21%)
Other/undetermined (7%)
Heterosexual contact (30%)
Hemophilia (1%)
I/V drug use (41%)

FIGURE A-3

Transmission of AIDS cases in the United States by race, women: 1991.

Source: U.S. Centers for Disease Control. Division of STD/HIV Prevention, *Sexually Transmitted Disease Surveillance*, 1990 and cumulative through July 1991.

AIDS now is the leading cause of death in major cities in the Americas, Western Europe, and sub-Saharan Africa (Chin 1990). A woman is much more likely to acquire AIDS from a man than a man is to acquire it from a woman (Padian, Shiboski, and Jewell 1991). In the United States, 70 percent of women contracting AIDS are black or Hispanic, and about 80 percent are of childbearing age (Guinan and Hardy 1987).

In the United States, most male AIDS victims have acquired the disease through homosexual contacts (80 percent of white males and 44 percent of blacks). Among females, most AIDS victims have contracted the disease through IV (intravenous) drug use (41 percent of whites and 57 percent of blacks). The incidence of AIDS acquired through heterosexual contact is increasing, however, especially among females: 30 percent of white females and 33 percent of black females acquired AIDS through heterosexual contact in 1990 and 1991 (see Figure A-3). Among males, the figures were 7 percent of blacks and 1 percent of whites (see Figure A-4).

Although in the United States most cases of AIDS have been acquired through homosexual contact or IV drug use, transmission through heterosexual contact has been disproportionately high among urban racial-ethnic groups. Incidence of heterosexually acquired AIDS is ten times greater for blacks and four times greater for Hispanics than it is for whites. Researchers believe that this can be traced to prostitution, which is endemic among inner-city populations. Blacks and Hispanics also have a higher incidence of other STDs, and this increases their susceptibility to AIDS; other STDs and AIDS interact to promote the spread of each (Aral and Holmes 1991). Moreover, adolescents and young adults are the cohort that is most at risk of contracting AIDS (or other STDs), and blacks and Hispanics have a relatively higher proportion of adolescents and young adults in their populations compared with whites; black and Hispanic populations in the United States have an age pyramid that closely resembles those of developing countries (Aral and Holmes 1991).

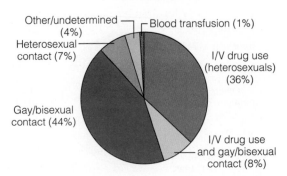

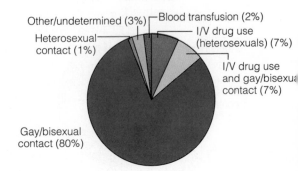

FIGURE A-4

Transmission of AIDS cases in the United States by race, men: 1991.

Source: U.S. Centers for Disease Control. Division of STD/HIV Prevention, *Sexually Transmitted Disease Surveillance,* 1990 and cumulative through July 1991.

One-fourth to one-half of babies born to HIV-infected women develop AIDS (Curran et al. 1988). These babies have easily recognizable physical characteristics called HTLV-3 embryopathy: a prominent, boxlike forehead; slightly slanted eyes set far apart; a short, broad, flat nose; large, loosely shaped lips; and a smaller head circumference than those of normal babies (Marion et al. 1986). These babies rarely live beyond age five, with mortality highest in the first year of life (Scott et al. 1989; Curran et al. 1988).

Our Immune System

To understand AIDS and the virus that causes it, we must understand the nature and importance of our immune system — a highly efficient network, including many different types of cells — that normally functions so automatically that we are not even aware of it.

One type of cell in our immune system specializes in identifying an invading organism. Other cells, called *killer cells,* specialize in attacking and destroying foreign invaders. Our im-

mune system is constantly at work — patrolling our body, ranging throughout the network of veins, capillaries, and lymph vessels and nodes, searching for invading organisms, and identifying and destroying them before they can cause disease. If an invading organism does gain a foothold, our immune system normally responds quickly by dispatching messenger cells that cause killer cells to multiply; these killer cells are then immediately dispatched to the source of the invasion, where they attack the foreign organisms. If the killer cells succeed in destroying the foreign organisms, we recover from the illness; if they fail, we can die (Emini 1992; Waldholz 1992b).

HIV: The AIDS Virus

HIV (human immunodeficiency virus) is the virus that causes AIDS by invading the immune system and multiplying within white blood cells. HIV attacks the immune system that protects us from *all* invading diseases, leaving us vulnerable to any number of disease-causing microorganisms that gain entrance to the body. In addition,

HIV may also attack and destroy other tissues, such as brain cells (Emini 1992; Waldholz 1992b). Moreover, unlike other viruses, HIV produces mutant versions of itself that are resistant to drugs that had been effective in treating the original strain of the virus and slowing its progress. For example, taking the drug AZT is initially successful in slowing the progress of the disease, but the drug accelerates the process of mutation so that AZT-resistant strains of HIV are produced within twelve to eighteen months of treatment (Emini 1992; Waldholz 1992b).

The Incubation Period of AIDS

The average (median) incubation period for AIDS — the time between the initial infection by HIV and the onset of AIDS — is about ten years for adults; this means that half of those who are infected with HIV develop AIDS before ten years and about half develop it after ten years. Researchers project that if a new treatment is not discovered, virtually all of those infected with HIV will eventually develop AIDS (Anderson and May 1992). During the incubation period an infected person has no symptoms of AIDS; the only way to know whether he or she is carrying HIV is to test for evidence of it in the bloodstream.[5] During the incubation period the person is said to be *HIV positive* and is highly infectious to others (DeGruttola 1988).

Symptoms and Diagnosis of AIDS

Symptoms of AIDS may include unexplained fatigue and weight loss, chronic diarrhea, persistent dermatitis, fever, weakness, generalized lymphadenopathy (abnormally enlarged lymph nodes), *Pneumocystis carinii* pneumonia, and Kaposi's sarcoma (skin lesions and discoloration). After these initial symptoms, the patient may acquire numerous serious and incapacitating infections as the body's immune system grows increasingly helpless. Autopsies reveal that AIDS infections devastate virtually every major organ system of the body (Jaffe, Choi, and Thomas 1983). About half of all patients die within eighteen months after AIDS develops, four out of five die within three years, and virtually all die within five years (Hatcher et al. 1990).

Transmission of HIV

HIV is transmitted by contact with blood (including menstrual blood), semen, or vaginal secretions of an infected person. HIV is *not* transmitted by contact with sweat, tears, sputum, nasal secretions, vomitus, urine, or feces — unless these fluids contain visible blood (Hatcher et al. 1990).

In order for HIV to be transmitted from one person to another, the virus must be transferred into the bloodstream of the new host. Our skin is an excellent barrier protecting us from this invasion, but any opening in the skin — any cut or abrasion, however small — can provide entry. HIV may also enter through the permeable tissue of the endometrium (wall of the uterus), vagina, cervix, rectum, and penile urethra without any lesion being present (Peterman and Curran 1986). HIV may also gain entrance to our body through a hypodermic needle, if the needle has been in contact with infected blood (a "dirty" needle), or during a direct transfusion of infected blood.[6]

HIV can be transmitted from the mother to the fetus through the placenta (Van de Perre et

---

[5]A simple blood-screening test that detects the presence of antibodies to HIV in a few drops of blood was approved by the FDA in 1992. The test may be completed within ten minutes (Lehrman 1992).

---

[6]U.S. Centers for Disease Control, "Update: Acquired Immunodeficiency Syndrome — United States, 1981–1990" (1991).

al. 1991). For this reason, a caesarean section does not protect the newborn against exposure to AIDS if the mother is carrying the virus. HIV may be transmitted to an infant by the mother's milk (Van de Perre et al. 1991).

There have been *no* cases of AIDS transmitted by shaking hands, hugging, dancing, or playing sports. There is no evidence of transmission through sneezing, coughing, hot tubs, swimming pools, towels, dishes, doorknobs, or toilet seats. There is no evidence of transmission by food or water, glasses, dishes, utensils, or napkins. There is no evidence of transmission from one family member to another living within the same household with no sexual interaction — other than between mother and infant, as mentioned. There is no evidence of transmission by insects — even insects such as mosquitoes that draw blood from one person and then insert their proboscis into another person (Lifson 1988; Curran et al. 1988; Friedland and Klein 1987).

Because the incubation period of AIDS is an average of ten years and may be much longer, the only way to be sure a person is not infected is to have a test that will detect evidence of the presence of HIV. Latex condoms provide significant protection, so vaginal copulation with a condom is safer than copulation without a condom. Anal intercourse is regarded as exceedingly dangerous even with a condom.[7] The only safe sex is in a monogamous relationship with someone who is not infected with HIV.

Hepatitis B

Until it was overshadowed by AIDS, hepatitis B was the biggest health problem faced by homosexuals in America. Like HIV, HBV is transmitted by contact with contaminated blood (Hatcher et al. 1990).

- Hepatitis B is 100 times more contagious than HIV.
- Hepatitis B is one of the world's leading killers; in 1992 there were an estimated 300 million chronically infected carriers of the hepatitis B virus.
- An estimated 300,000 Americans are infected with the hepatitis B virus each year (Hammers 1992).

Although an effective vaccine is available,[8] once hepatitis B is contracted there is no effective treatment. A person may be infected with HBV without being aware of it because most infections have no symptoms. If symptoms do occur, they may include skin eruptions, fatigue, loss of appetite, nausea and vomiting, dark urine, jaundice, and moderate liver enlargement and tenderness. Potential complications include chronic hepatitis, cirrhosis, kidney failure, and death (Hatcher et al. 1990). The Centers for Disease Control estimates that 10 percent of people who have contracted hepatitis B are chronically infected and that one in five will die of cirrhosis of the liver or liver cancer (Margolin 1991).

Hepatitis B from heterosexual transmission is most common among the lower class — with drug abusers who share needles at greatest risk (Aral and Holmes 1991).

Gonorrhea

The incidence of gonorrhea increased rapidly in the United States in the late 1960s. In the early 1980s the increase slowed and remained rela-

---

[7]U.S. Centers for Disease Control. STD/HIV Prevention.

[8]Hepatitis B is preventable with a three-dose series of vaccine injections. Babies may be given the first injection at birth and the second and third injections when they are one and five months of age (Taylor 1992).

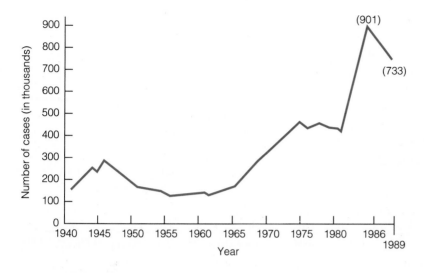

1941–1946 fiscal years (twelve-month period ending June 30 of the
  years specified)
1947–1989 calendar years
An estimated 1.5 million cases occur every year when unreported cases
  are included (Hatcher et al. 1990)

FIGURE A-5

Gonorrhea: Reported cases per 100,000 population, United States, 1941–1989.

Sources: *Historical Statistics of the United States, Colonial Times to 1970,* series B 291–303 (1970); U.S. Centers
for Disease Control, "Specified Reportable Diseases — Cases Reported: 1970 to 1989" (1991).

---

tively steady. However, gonorrhea is nearly twice as prevalent today as it was ten years ago and nearly four times as prevalent as it was in 1950 (see Figure A-5).

- More than 700,000 cases of gonorrhea were reported in the United States in 1989; however, researchers estimate that 1.5 million cases occur every year if unreported cases are included (Hatcher et al. 1990; see Figure A-1).

- People under twenty-five run the greatest risk of contracting gonorrhea; 38 percent of all cases occur among those twenty to twenty-four years old, and another 25 percent occurs among teenagers between fifteen and nineteen years old.

- The highest risk for males is for those twenty to twenty-one years of age; for females it is fifteen to twenty-four years of age.[9] Reported cases of gonorrhea in the United States are higher among men and blacks (see Figure A-6).

Gonorrhea is one of the most widespread of all human diseases and has occurred throughout the history of Western civilization; its origin is unknown. Gonorrhea is one of the few diseases that does not infect laboratory animals, so medical research on it is very limited, and a blood

---

[9] U.S. Centers for Disease Control, "STDs," *MMWR*, December 30, 1984.

APPENDIX A ✤ SEXUALLY TRANSMITTED DISEASES: STDs

469

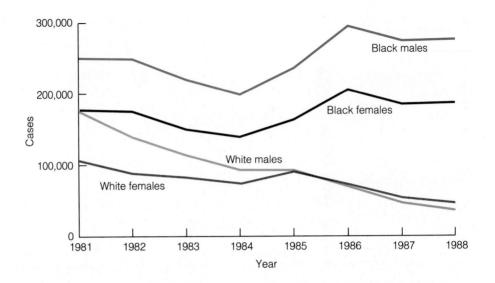

FIGURE A-6

Gonorrhea cases by race and sex: 1981 to 1988.

Source: Aral, Sevgi O., and Holmes, King K. "Sexually Transmitted Diseases in the AIDS Era." *Scientific American* 264 (February 1991):62.

test cannot detect it. Gonorrhea is caused by a bacterium (*Neisseria gonorrhoeae*) that usually infects the mucous membrane in the urethral or rectal tissue.[10]

Although often self-limiting — clearing up without treatment — in about three weeks, gonorrheal infection may go deeper into the tissue of the prostate, epididymis, or testicles of the male, causing pain and swelling of the scrotum,

or into the fallopian tubes of the female, causing pain and swelling in the lower abdomen (Berkow et al. 1987). Gonorrhea may be asymptomatic — that is, may not manifest any symptoms. If symptoms do occur, men usually have painful urination and yellow discharge. Women may have abnormal vaginal discharge or menstruation, painful urination, and/or acute PID — pelvic inflammatory disease (Hatcher et al. 1990; Berkow et al. 1987; see Box A-1).

Gonococcal invasion of the blood may occur in both males and females, with the disease spreading throughout the body to cause infection of nongenital tissue. Joints are the most frequent sites of such infection, and painful arthritis may occur within one to three weeks after the initial contact. Other infections may cause inflammation of a tendon and its sheath (*tenosynovitis*), skin lesions, or inflammation of the membrane of the spinal cord and brain (*meningitis*) (Berkow et al. 1987).

---

[10]A person may also acquire a gonorrheal infection of the eye (gonococcal ophthalmia) if the eye comes in direct contact with an infectious gonorrheal discharge. Newborn babies are especially subject to this form of the disease in passing through the cervix of a gonorrhea-infected mother. Until about 1950, more blindness (10 percent) in the United States was caused by congenital gonococcal ophthalmia than by any other single cause. Now the eyes of newborn infants are routinely treated with erythromycin, tetracycline, or silver nitrate solution, and this precaution has virtually eliminated this form of the disease (U.S. Centers for Disease Control, "STDs").

BOX A-1

Pelvic Inflammatory Disease (PID)

Because PID affects many more women than previously thought, the Centers for Disease Control now believes that PID is the second-most damaging STD affecting women, second only to AIDS. Pelvic inflammatory disease (PID), a complication of STDs, is an infection in a woman's pelvic area, usually her fallopian tubes or uterus. PID is taking a huge toll in pain, infertility, and death. As of 1990, about one American woman in seven has had PID; 500,000 to one million women will develop it each year, and about half of all adult women will have had PID by the end of the 1990s (Washington and Katz 1991).

PID has been called the "invisible disease"; many cases go untreated because no symptoms are evident, and a diagnosis is not made until scar tissue caused by acute or chronic infection has destroyed the fallopian tubes (Washington and Katz 1991).

More than 200,000 victims of PID are hospitalized in the United States each year, and half require surgery. At least a quarter of the million women who contract the disease suffer long-term complications, including chronic pelvic pain, urethral stricture, pelvic abscess, sterility, and ectopic pregnancy (in which a fertilized egg implants itself in a fallopian tube or elsewhere outside the uterus). Ectopic pregnancies are a significant cause of

hemorrhage and death during pregnancy. One-half of all ectopic pregnancies are the result of PID (Washington and Katz 1991).

PID is usually caused by gonorrheal or chlamydial infections, and one-half to two-thirds are transmitted sexually. How other cases of PID are transmitted is unknown; nor is it certain what organisms are involved. PID may be caused by several different strains of bacteria. For this reason a combination of antibiotic drugs is recommended in all cases of PID (Washington and Katz 1991). Sexual partners of women with PID should be treated also, and sexual intercourse should be avoided until both partners are cured; latex condoms should be used to avoid further infection (Washington, Cates, and Wasserheit 1991).

PID occurs most often among sexually active women younger than twenty-five; those who have contracted PID through gonorrhea are concentrated among the poor, whereas those who have contracted it through chlamydia may be of any social class or income (Washington and Katz 1991). The percentage of women with PID who are under age twenty-four and who are white is increasing (Washington, Cates, and Wasserheit 1991).

Gonorrhea is almost always contracted through genital, anal, or oral sexual activity. Infection through contaminated objects (towels, drinking glasses, toilet seats, doorknobs) is theoretically possible but highly unlikely because gonococci usually live for only a few minutes outside a host's tissue (Berkow et al. 1987).

In men, the incubation period is from two to fourteen days. Gonorrheal infection of the urethra is usually unmistakable: urination is accompanied by a sharp burning pain and a yellowish-green discharge of pus, which is highly contagious. If asymptomatic, men are nevertheless highly contagious carriers and may infect their sex partners (Berkow et al. 1987).

In women, symptoms usually begin within one to three weeks after infection; the cervix and reproductive organs are the sites most frequently infected, and an inflamed cervix and purulent discharge (pus) often occur (Berkow et al. 1987).

In many women, however, gonorrheal infections are free of symptoms. There is no pain or burning sensation; any discharge may be so slight that it may pass unnoticed or be attributed to other sources of vaginal irritation (such as a yeast infection), to nervousness or fatigue, or to ovulation (with its increased mucous flow). (Vaginal yeast infections, which are common among women taking contraceptive pills or certain antibiotics, often mask gonorrheal infection.) Spot-checks of all women seen by physicians for any purpose find that 7 percent to 25 percent of women are carriers of gonorrhea, although routine tests do not reveal these carriers. The gonococcus can be found only if the physician makes a smear and/or takes a culture sample from the cervix and, in suspicious cases, from the anus and the throat as well (Schwarcz et al. 1990).[11] As with men, symptom-free women are highly contagious and may infect their sex partners. The complex folds of the vagina's lining may harbor the gonococci for months. Rectal gonorrheal infections in both men and women are common and may also be symptom-free, although some discomfort and mucous discharge may develop if the infection persists. Severe rectal infection is more common in homosexual men. Gonococcal pharyngitis from oral-genital contact is now seen more frequently, although often there are no symptoms. In female infants and prepubertal girls, irritation and swelling of the vulva, purulent vaginal discharge, and painful urination can occur (Berkow et al. 1987).

Because a blood test for gonorrhea has not yet been developed, diagnosis must rely on a microscopic examination of a penile, vaginal, endocervical, or rectal smear for the presence of gonococci or on a culture growth from these areas. For the male, these tests are quite reliable, and in 90 percent of cases the smear test alone, which takes just two or three minutes, is sufficient for diagnosis. In the female, however, fully 60 percent of tests for gonorrhea are inconclusive because the gonococci quickly migrate into the fallopian tubes (Burns et al. 1983).

No case of gonorrhea in a woman should be considered cured until three successive normal smears from the cervix are obtained, at least two of which should be examined immediately after a menstrual period (Thomas 1989). Even then the patient may still have the infection. One of the greatest problems of gonorrhea is that it usually remains undetected in women (and sometimes in men) while such carriers continue to spread the infection.

Until 1976, all cases of gonorrhea could be cured by penicillin. Since then resistant strains have spread globally, involving 5 percent of all the cases reported in the United States in 1989 (Aral and Holmes 1991). Researchers now conclude that the common, inexpensive ways of

---

[11] U.S. Centers for Disease Control, "Sentinel Surveillance System for Antimicrobial Resistance in Clinical Isolates of *Neisseria gonorrhoeae*" (1987).

treating gonorrhea (penicillin and tetracycline) should be abandoned and have published new guidelines for treating gonorrhea, recommending *ceftriaxone* — the only treatment to which all of the strains of gonorrhea have been found to be susceptible (Schwarcz et al. 1990).

About one-fourth of men and two-fifths of women with gonococcal infections also have chlamydial infections at the same time, and both diseases must be treated (Hatcher et al. 1990).

A person who contracts gonorrhea may have been exposed to syphilis at the same time. Because the clinical signs and symptoms of gonorrhea develop several weeks before those of syphilis, treatment of the patient for gonorrhea may mask or delay the onset of signs of syphilis. When this occurs, syphilis may develop unnoticed. It is therefore of vital importance either to treat each case of gonorrhea as if syphilis has also been contracted or to test the patient for serologic (blood-borne) evidence of syphilis each month for at least four months following treatment of gonorrhea (Thomas 1989).

Syphilis

Syphilis first appeared in the Western world in Spain among sailors who had returned from the New World in 1493. From there it spread rapidly throughout Europe, known as the "Neapolitan disease" and the "French pox." Through the Renaissance, the Reformation, and the advent of industrialization, syphilis crippled, blinded, and killed unknown numbers of victims.

Syphilis, a very complex disease, goes through five phases (see Figure A-7). Its symptoms mimic many other diseases, so it is often misdiagnosed. It can be dormant and unsuspected for years and may have no recognized symptoms at all during the primary and secondary stages, when it is highly infectious. It may not be revealed by any symptoms at all until it reaches its final phase — the tertiary stage, years after contraction — when it may suddenly explode into serious and crippling forms (Thomas 1989).

Syphilis is caused by *Treponema pallidum* spirochetes. It is contracted when the spirochetes from the serum of an infectious lesion (a sore containing spirochetes) invades the bloodstream of a new host. This invasion usually occurs though a mucous membrane but may occur through broken skin on any part of the body (even a tiny nick or scratch). The mucous membranes of the penile glans and the vagina are the most frequent sites of infection, but other mucous membranes, such as those of the labia, rectum, tongue, or lining of the mouth may also provide entry for the spirochetes. The infectious lesion is most often on the genitalia, so syphilis is usually acquired through sexual contact.

Syphilis can be contracted only from the serum of an infectious lesion, from the blood (or blood plasma) of an infected person (during a blood transfusion, for example), or by a fetus directly from the bloodstream of a pregnant woman.[12]

Because the spirochetes are fragile and can live for only a short time outside a host's body, it is highly unlikely for syphilis to be transmitted through such objects as drinking glasses, soiled towels, doorknobs, toilet seats, or bathtubs, although this is theoretically possible. (Survival of the spirochetes outside a host's body is usually limited to a few minutes and never exceeds an hour or two, even under ideal conditions of warmth and dampness.)

---

[12]A fetus acquires congenital syphilis directly from the mother's bloodstream when the spirochetes penetrate the placental defenses. This invasion of the placental defenses occurs only after the fourth month of pregnancy (Martin and Reeder 1991). Because congenital syphilis may be prevented if the syphilitic mother is diagnosed and cured before this time, prenatal blood tests are required in forty-five of the fifty U.S. states.

Phase	Symptoms	Infectious	Detection	Duration
Incubation period	No signs or symptoms	Not infectious	Cannot be detected by blood test	10–60 days (usually 4–6 weeks)
Primary stage	Fifty percent chance of infectious lesion at site of infection	Highly infectious if chancre (infectious lesion) is present	Can be detected by blood test	2–6 months
Secondary stage	Infectious lesions may occur on any area of body but are usually on mucous membranes or on warm, damp skin	Highly infectious if lesions are present	Can be detected by blood test	Usually 4–6 weeks (may recur as long as 2 years)
Latent period	No signs or symptoms	Not infectious because lesions are not present	Can be detected by blood test	Usually 10–30 years (may extend for 50 years)
Tertiary stage	Many illnesses that may be quite serious, debilitating, or crippling, causing blindness, heart trouble, insanity, and even death	Not infectious because lesions are not present	Blood test is not applicable because the disease is obvious	Chronic illness may last for years until death

FIGURE A-7

The five phases of syphilis.

An incubation period follows the invasion of the bloodstream of the new host; during this period there are no signs or symptoms of the disease, and it is not infectious. It also cannot be detected by a blood test during the incubation period, which usually lasts from four to six weeks but may be as short as ten days or as long as sixty days (Hatcher et al. 1990).

The primary stage follows the incubation period and may last from two to six months. In about half of all cases, the primary stage is signaled by the appearance of an infectious lesion (chancre). The site of this lesion is the point where the spirochetes entered the body of the new host. Chancres have no typical appearance; they may resemble acne, a cold sore, a blister, or a simple abrasion. Moreover, lesions often occur inside the vagina or the rectum, where they may easily escape detection even during a medical examination. They usually clear up within a few weeks with no treatment (Berkow et al. 1987).

In the 50 percent of cases in which lesions do not occur, the primary stage of syphilis is not infectious because all other physiological secretions—saliva, seminal fluid, vaginal fluids—are not infectious (Hatcher et al. 1990).

During the secondary stage of syphilis, highly infectious lesions may occur intermittently on almost any area of the body (especially where the skin is warm and moist), although they usually appear on a mucous membrane. These lesions may take almost any form: a crack on the corner of the mouth or nostril, a small pimple or ulcer, acnelike abrasions, or cold sores. These lesions are painless, do not itch, and may easily go unnoticed or unrecognized. They usually clear up without treatment in four to six weeks but may recur for as long as two years.

In slightly less than half the cases, the secondary stage of syphilis is also signaled by the appearance of a rash almost anywhere on the body. When this rash occurs, it may appear on the palms of the hands or soles of the feet; the genital areas; the face, abdomen, or legs; or inside the mouth, vagina, or rectum. Because it is neither itchy nor painful, it may easily be mistaken for a heat or drug-reaction rash and usually clears up quickly without treatment. Also in slightly less than half the cases, the secondary stage of syphilis may be accompanied by such symptoms as a slight feeling of illness, a mild fever, a headache, a sore throat, swelling of the lymph glands, or hair falling out in patches. In secondary syphilis, patients have a strongly reactive STS (a serological test for syphilis); primary and secondary syphilis are definitively diagnosed with microscopic examination of material from a chancre, lymph node, or other lesion (Hatcher et al. 1990).

The latent period follows the secondary stage of syphilis. There are no signs or symptoms during the latent period; the person has no indication that he or she has the disease and is not infectious. During this period, the spirochetes tend to leave the bloodstream and lodge in various tissues of the host—the nervous system, blood vessels, and all major organs. The latent period may last from two to fifty years, although the usual duration is ten to thirty years. During the latent period, patients have serologic evidence of untreated syphilis without clinical signs (Hatcher et al. 1990).

The fifth and final phase of syphilis is the tertiary stage, which starts when the disease suddenly breaks into the open after lying dormant

and unsuspected for years during the latent period. It explodes in any number of forms and seriously incapacitates one out of three victims through insanity (general paresis), blindness, paralysis, heart trouble, severe crippling of the joints, or other illness. One in ten dies of the effects of the disease during this stage (Keith, Schink, and Berger 1985).

The U.S. Centers for Disease Control has reported an increase in the incidence of syphilis in the past few years. In 1990, there were over 50,000 cases of syphilis in the United States—a 9 percent increase over the previous year and a 75 percent increase since 1985.[13] The incidence is rising chiefly among black and Hispanic heterosexuals in inner cities, probably because of the use of crack and the subsequent increase in prostitution (Aral and Holmes 1991).

Prompt treatment is now effective for this insidious disease that has plagued humanity for so long. Syphilis may be halted by adequate doses of penicillin (or other antibiotics such as tetracycline), and the infection usually clears up within eight to ten days. Length of therapy depends on estimated duration of infection: If less than a year, treatment is given for fifteen days; otherwise, it continues for thirty days (Hatcher et al. 1990). A cure cannot definitely be considered to have occurred, however, until the reaction to a blood test, such as the Wassermann, is consistently normal for several years (Rein 1981).[14] Syphilis that is treated before it reaches the tertiary (late) stage can be cured with little

---

[13]U.S. Centers for Disease Control. Division of Sexually Transmitted Diseases, *MMWR*, March 16, 1991.

[14]A *Wassermann reaction* is a general term loosely applied to almost any serological test for syphilis (Thomas 1989). The results are designated as 1, 2, 3, and 4 plus—with the intensity corresponding to the severity of the infection; a negative reaction can mean the infection still exists. The patient must return for follow-up serologies three, six, twelve, and twenty-four months after therapy (Hatcher et al. 1990).

or no permanent damage. In untreated cases, about one-third of those infected develop tertiary syphilis. This may not occur for many years after the initial infection (Berkow et al. 1987).

Chlamydia

Perhaps the fastest growing STD and most common sexually transmitted disease is chlamydia. Chlamydia is the common name for infections caused by *Chlamydia trachomatis*. Genital chlamydia infections are the most common bacterial STDs in the United States. Although originally considered viruses because they multiply in host cells, they are more closely related to bacteria since they contain both DNA and RNA[15] (Hatcher et al. 1990; Berkow et al. 1987). No one knows the true extent of chlamydia infections, but the Centers for Disease Control estimates that four million infections occur annually in the United States and that nearly half of sexually active teenagers may have become infected.[16] Congenital infection by CMV (*cytomegalovirus*, a DNA virus of the herpes virus group) is estimated to occur in 0.5 to 2.0 percent of pregnancies in the United States, affecting about 50,000 infants each year (Hatcher et al. 1990).[17]

The symptoms of chlamydia are very similar to those of gonorrhea, and one reason for the rapid rise in the incidence of chlamydia is that a physician may incorrectly diagnose the symptoms as gonorrhea and prescribe penicillin, which does not clear up the disease; thus, the infected person continues to be a carrier and can infect all others with whom he or she has sexual contact (Hatcher et al. 1990).

A woman infected with chlamydia may have symptoms similar to a man, or she may be symptom-free. Untreated chlamydia usually moves into the uterine lining and fallopian tubes, causing PID. Of those women whose infertility is caused by tubal blockage, more than half have had chlamydia infections (Washington, Cates, and Wasserheit, 1991).

Genital Herpes

Ever since the Roman emperor Tiberius tried to halt an epidemic nearly 2,000 years ago by prohibiting kissing at public ceremonies, people have attempted unsuccessfully to control the infection known as *herpes*. Although there are many types of herpes infections caused by this versatile family of viruses, two types are especially widespread. Type I (the concern of Tiberius) has inflicted cold sores on an estimated 90 percent of the U.S. population. Type II is characterized by painful blisters that resemble cold sores that can form anywhere on the genitalia, but more often on the tip of the penis or on the scrotum and on the inside of the vagina or on the cervix. It is also possible for type I herpes to lodge in the genitalia and for type II herpes to cause cold sores on the lips or mouth.

Health authorities estimate that thirty million Americans are infected with genital herpes (Hatcher et al. 1990). Because physicians are not required to report cases of genital herpes to federal authorities, no one knows for sure how widespread the disease is.

The initial invasion of the herpes virus often goes unnoticed. The virus may be introduced

---

[15]RNA, or ribonucleic acid, determines the functions of proteins and thereby of cells.

[16]U.S. Centers for Disease Control. "1990 Division of STD/HIV Prevention Annual Report" (1991).

[17]A pregnant woman infected with the disease can be treated safely with erythromycin; this also protects the unborn baby (Berkow et al. 1987).

into the system without causing any clear symptoms, or the first blister may form where it is undetected — at the back of the mouth or inside the vagina. Thousands of the viruses formed from the original invader are then carried by the bloodstream to other parts of the body to penetrate nerve cells. Instead of attacking the host cell, however, the herpes virus merely waits there dormant — sometimes for years (Lafferty et al. 1987; Gerson et al. 1984).

Any of several events that lower the person's resistance to infection can trigger the virus's release: physical or emotional stress, hormonal changes coincident with menstruation, the biochemical upheaval of puberty, or other infections. When the virus leaves the nerve cell nucleus in which it has been lodged, it enters the skin or a mucous membrane of the host, where it produces a tingling, burning sensation and, a day or two later, a blister (the familiar cold sore).

The fluid-filled blisters that characterize the first stage of herpes usually break down within twenty-four hours, leaving painful shallow ulcers that may take several days to heal. During this time fresh blisters may appear, so the disease may perpetuate itself for one to four weeks before clearing up without treatment. The first occurrence of genital herpes is termed the initial infection and lasts an average of twelve days; recurrent or subsequent infections are usually milder and last an average of five days (Hatcher et al. 1990). Recurrences are common.

Potential complications for both men and women include neuralgia, meningitis, myelitis (inflammation of the spinal cord or of the bone marrow), urethral strictures, and lymphatic infections. Research indicates that genital herpes may be linked to cervical cancer, and annual Pap smears are recommended for women with any history of herpes (Hatcher et al. 1990).

A man infected with genital herpes may have no symptoms and yet may transmit the virus to anyone with whom he has sexual contact (Gibbs and Mead 1992).

A woman infected with genital herpes may transmit the disease to her baby during vaginal delivery, which may have serious, even fatal, consequences. Public health officials estimate that 2,000 American babies die each year of genital herpes acquired at birth (Gibbs and Mead 1992). Many obstetricians now prefer to perform a caesarean section rather than risk a normal delivery if there is a possibility of herpes infection (Hatcher et al. 1990).

Tiberius's ban on kissing was only the first of many attempts to stop herpes, for no cure has yet been discovered. However, outbreaks of the blisters may be limited and their duration shortened by application of *acyclovir*, an antiviral drug used in injection and ointment form (Reinisch 1992).

Trichomoniasis

Trichomoniasis is a vaginitis (inflammation) caused by a species of *Trichomonas* (a protozoan parasite) in secretions of the vagina. This parasite is able to survive for twenty-four hours in tap water, three hours in urine, and nearly one hour on a toilet seat or towel, and so it may be transmitted very easily from an infected person. The incubation period for trichomoniasis is about one week (Fiumara 1986). Symptoms in women include persistent burning and itching of the vulva, profuse white frothy discharge, and a burning sensation while urinating; about one-fourth of infected women have no symptoms. Men usually have no symptoms, but when *Trichomonas vaginalis* is found in the male urethra, both sex partners must be treated to prevent reinfection (Thomas 1989). Treatment consists of a single dose (2.0 grams) of *metronidazole* or 500 mg of *clindamycin* twice a day for one week (Hatcher et al. 1990).

Genital Warts

Genital warts is another STD that has reached epidemic proportions. An estimated two million new cases are diagnosed annually (see Figure A-1), an increase from 169,000 new cases in 1966 (Aral and Holmes 1991).

Genital warts have been increasingly linked with malignancies and premalignant conditions affecting the cervix, vagina, vulva, penis, and anus (Aral and Holmes 1991).

Because genital warts are caused by the human papilloma virus (HPV), they cannot be cured by antibiotics. Recommended treatment for genital warts includes cryotherapy (the therapeutic use of cold) with liquid nitrogen, cauterization, surgical removal or CO_2 vaporization with laser surgery, and topical agents such as podophyllin in tincture of benzoin, although this treatment should not be used during pregnancy or with cervical, urethral, oral, or anorectal warts (Hatcher et al. 1990).

A P P E N D I X   B

Birth Control and Abortion

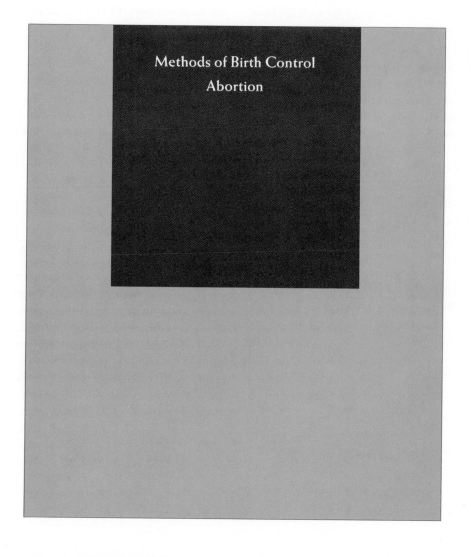

Methods of Birth Control
Abortion

P eople may control the size of their families by birth control or by abortion.

Birth control usually refers to measures used (1) to prevent conception in the first place, properly called *contraception;* (2) to prevent the implantation of the blastocyst in the uterine wall after conception (see Appendix C); or (3) to terminate a pregnancy during the embryonic period (the first two weeks of gestation following conception). Terminating a pregnancy after the embryonic period, or more than two weeks following conception, is usually called *abortion.*

These terms are very flexible, however. For example, all of the following are often (incorrectly) called "contraception": (1) preventing the implantation of the blastocyst by an IUD, by a progestin pill, or by progestin implants; (2) taking a "morning after" pill so that if conception has occurred, the zygote (or blastocyst) is swept away by the menstrual flow; (3) surgically vacuuming out (aspirating) the endometrium (wall of the uterus) together with the blastocyst if one has been implanted (a process called "menstrual extraction" or "menstrual regulation"), which may be done up to three weeks following a possible conception. On the other hand, many right-to-life groups would call any procedure that interrupts the process of gestation an "abortion" whatever the stage following conception — zygote, blastocyst, embryo, or fetus.

In the following sections, we will examine the various methods of birth control now customarily used in our society both before and after conception, and the methods commonly recognized as abortion.

Methods of Birth Control

Methods of birth control used in our society range from "organic" ("natural") methods to surgical sterilization. Some methods of birth control are more effective than others. The rhythm method; withdrawal; the diaphragm and cervical cap (used with spermicide); and spermicidal creams, jellies, foams, and vaginal suppositories all have failure rates of about 18 to 21 percent. Condoms used alone have a failure rate of about 12 percent but when used with a spermicide have virtually a zero failure rate. Birth-control pills also have a very low failure rate, as do progestin implants and injectable progestins. The failure rate of tubal ligation and vasectomy is virtually zero (see Table B-1).

In the United States, the most popular methods of birth control are female sterilization and oral contraceptive pills, with male sterilization and condoms next (Hatcher et al. 1990; Forrest and Fordyce 1988).

Among about one-third of married couples who use some form of birth control, the wife nevertheless is pregnant within five years. Specialists in fertility control believe that the chief reason for this relatively high incidence of pregnancy among couples who use various methods of birth control is carelessness (Hatcher et al. 1990).

"Organic" Methods of Contraception, or "Natural" Family Planning

The Rhythm Method   Natural family planning, which follows the rhythmic cycles of ovulation, is called the "rhythm method" of birth control; it depends on successfully predicting a woman's fertile days and then not copulating during these days. The rhythm method is the only method of birth control currently approved by the Roman Catholic Church (except for total abstinence). Catholic doctrine considers reproduction the primary function of marriage and forbids the use of any "artificial" birth control procedure or device.

TABLE B-1

Typical Failure Rates of Birth-Control Methods in the United States

Method	Percent of Women Experiencing a Pregnancy During One Year of Use
Progestin implant (*Norplant*)	0.04
Vasectomy	0.15
Injectable progestin (*Depo-Provera*)	0.25
Tubal ligation	0.40
Condom with spermicide	1.00
Combination birth-control pill	3.00
IUD (medicated)	3.00
Condom (without spermicides)	12.00
Contraceptive sponge	16.00
Withdrawal (*coitus interruptus*)	18.00
Diaphragm (with spermicidal cream or jelly)	18.00
Cervical cap (with spermicidal cream or jelly)	18.00
Rhythm method	20.00
Spermicides (foams, creams, jellies, and vaginal suppositories)	21.00
Chance — no birth control	85.00

Adapted from Hatcher et al. 1990; Trussell et al. 1990.

A woman can become pregnant for only twenty-four hours in each menstrual cycle — the time during which an egg is in the fallopian tube. Three days must be added to this time when an egg is in the fallopian tube because sperm may live in the tube for as long as three days before ovulation occurs. Thus there are four days during each menstrual cycle when a woman may become pregnant if she copulates. Two additional days are usually added to be on the safe side in case sperm live longer than three days. Thus, the rhythm method rules out copulation for six days of each menstrual cycle. The problem is to determine precisely which six days.

To determine the "safe" period — the days when a woman can copulate without the possibility of becoming pregnant, it is necessary to accurately determine the time of ovulation. Because this is difficult, the rhythm method has a high failure rate estimated to be about 20 percent (Trussell et al. 1990).

A refinement of the rhythm method involves determining the woman's basal body temperature and then watching for a slight rise indicating ovulation. The basal body temperature is the lowest body temperature of a healthy person during waking hours and is usually determined by the woman by taking her temperature at the same time each morning before rising. Usually, the basal body temperature rises slightly (two-fifths of a degree Fahrenheit) following ovulation and stays high until menstruation begins, at which time it falls to its normal level. Using this method a woman may determine her time of ovulation after she has recorded her temperature daily on a chart for three to four successive months (Hatcher et al. 1990).

The basal body temperature method does not predict ovulation in advance, however, and if ovulation occurs unexpectedly early and the woman has copulated within the preceding three days, she may conceive. A further difficulty is that her temperature does not rise during a cycle if ovulation fails to occur. Thus, when no increase is recorded, she cannot be sure whether she is having delayed ovulation or a cycle with no ovulation. In addition, a fever due to infection may lead her to think she has ovulated when she in fact has not (Hatcher et al. 1990).

Using the basal body temperature method does not improve the failure rate of the rhythm method; it is still 20 percent (Trussell et al. 1990).

Prolonged Breast-Feeding

Another organic (or natural) method that is often used in developing nations is prolonged or on-demand breast-feeding. Research has indicated that frequency of breast-feeding is the best predictor of hormone levels, and that among people for whom breast-feeding is an infant's only source of nutrition the pregnancy rate is substantially reduced (Kennedy, Rivera, and McNeilly 1989). Breast-feeding usually delays the onset of the ovulatory cycle after childbirth from two to eighteen months.

Breast-feeding is a reliable method of birth control only during the first six months after delivery, however, and only if the woman does not ovulate during this time. Onset of ovulation in women who breast-feed their babies varies from one month after delivery to twenty-four months; if birth control is not used, about one in ten women will become pregnant while still not menstruating.

Most American couples resume sexual intercourse within one to two months following delivery, and few rely on breast-feeding for contraception (Hatcher et al. 1990).

Withdrawal

Withdrawal (*coitus interruptus*) as a method of birth control is based on the premise that withdrawing the penis from the vagina before ejaculation, and ejaculating extravaginally, will prevent conception. There are two problems with this method: The first is that the premise is wrong; pre-ejaculatory fluid may contain sufficient sperm to effect conception, even in the absence of ejaculation within the vagina. The second is that using withdrawal as a consistent method of contraception frustrates the physical and psychological satisfactions of ejaculating inside the vagina, which is a significant part of the pleasure of copulation; it is unrealistic to expect a man to invariably withdraw just as the intensely pleasurable moment of ejaculation is imminent. Withdrawal is one of the least popular methods of contraception in our society; it is used as a chief method of birth control by only one couple in fifty (Hatcher et al. 1990).

Couples who use withdrawal as their sole method of birth control have a typical failure rate of 18 percent (Trussell et al. 1990).

Coitus Reservatus

It is possible to copulate indefinitely without ejaculating (*coitus reservatus*), and this method of contraception has been an important part of the culture of other societies (such as India); however, it is so rare in the United States that there are no figures regarding its use or its effectiveness as a birth-control method.[1]

The Post-Coital Douche

Although a post-coital douche is often used with the intent of contraception, it has very little contraceptive effect even if a spermicide is used in the douching solution. No matter how soon after copulation a woman douches it is not soon enough; within fifteen seconds of ejaculation millions of sperm have entered the cervical canal and are beyond the reach of vaginal douching (Hatcher et al. 1990).[2]

In the United States, a douche is usually administered with a syringe or nozzle connected to a douche bag. (An impromptu post-coital douche may be achieved by shaking the contents of a soft-drink bottle and then using it to flush the vagina after copulation; this is notoriously ineffective.) The *bidet*, a low basin especially designed for douching, is standard equipment in most European hotels and private homes but is rarely found in American homes, possibly because it is an admission that something sexual is going on in the house.

It should be noted that internal areas of the vagina need no cleansing and that douching is inadvisable as a hygienic measure because it washes away protective levels of residual acidity in the vagina, making it more vulnerable to infection. Moreover, douching has been associated with an increased risk for PID and ectopic pregnancy (Washington and Katz 1991).[3] The vulva and adjacent external areas may be washed with no harmful effects, however, just as one would wash any other area of the body simply in the interests of cleanliness.

Spermicides: Chemical Control

A spermicide is a chemical contraceptive that kills sperm on contact. Nonoxynol-9 is the active chemical agent used in the United States. Most spermicidal preparations contain two ingredients: an inert base (foam, cream, or jelly) and a chemical that kills the sperm (Hatcher et al. 1990).

Formulas for vaginal spermicides appear in early writings as far back as the nineteenth century B.C., and modern chemists think they must have been fairly effective, although even modern-day foam, cream, jelly, or vaginal suppositories are relatively ineffective when used alone. The ancients discovered that environments that were either strongly acid or strongly alkaline were hostile to sperm. In the fourth century B.C., Aristotle suggested a solution prepared with oil of cedar and frankincense in olive oil. Cleopatra and other prosperous Egyptians used a vaginal paste mixed from honey, sodium carbonate, and

---

[1] *Coitus reservatus* as a technique of birth control is well known among historians in the United States as part of the doctrine of the Oneida Perfectionists, a nineteenth-century community in New York State led by John Humphrey Noyes. Adolescent males were taught sexual skills, including the art of *coitus reservatus*, by women of the community.

[2] A folk method related to the post-coital douche is a practice of urinating immediately after copulation in the belief that this will flush out the vagina. This method is based on faulty knowledge of anatomy; the vagina is a separate structure from the urethra, so urination can serve no flushing function whatsoever. The assumption that urinating will flush out the vagina probably comes from regarding the vagina as the homologue of the penis, which does conduct both urine and semen; urinating will flush out the semen. As we have seen, the homologue of the penis is the clitoris, although it does not conduct urine (see Chapter 4).

[3] An ectopic pregnancy occurs when the blastocyst embeds itself in the wall of the fallopian tube or elsewhere, rather than in the wall of the uterus. The blastocyst contains the germinal disc, which will normally develop into an embryo and then a fetus after implantation in the uterine wall (see Appendix C).

dried crocodile dung. In Europe, a sponge moistened with diluted lemon juice has been a popular contraceptive device since biblical times. Salt in an 8 percent solution is deadly to sperm, and eighth-century Indian writers described the use of rock salt dipped in oil or honey. By the twelfth century, Muslims had also developed suppositories or tampons based on these ingredients. The nineteenth-century English feminist Annie Bessant advocated the use of a sponge soaked in quinine solution (Tannahill 1980).

In addition to their contraceptive effect, spermicides provide considerable protection against gonorrhea, genital herpes, and trichomoniasis (Sherris, Moore, and Fox 1984) as well as against cervical, ovarian, and endometrial cancer (Kost, Forrest, and Harlap 1991). Vaginal spermicides have a typical failure rate of 21 percent when used alone (Trussell et al. 1990).

The Condom

The condom consists of a thin sheath of rubber or animal tissue that is rolled over the erect penis before copulation to contain the ejaculate;[4] it is a barrier method of contraception, a mechanical device designed to provide a barrier between the egg and the sperm. The condom is the second most widely used temporary contraceptive in the United States, second only to the pill (Hatcher et al. 1990).

The modern condom was devised in 1564 by an Italian anatomist (Fallopius) who described the use of linen sheaths, and by the eighteenth century the condom had come into widespread use, usually made of lamb membranes. With the development of the vulcanization of rubber in 1849, rubber condoms became available and were popularly known as "rubbers" (Hatcher et al. 1990).

In addition to acting as a contraceptive, the condom provides significant protection against STDs (see Appendix A). Because of the fear of AIDS and other STDs, an estimated 40 to 50 percent of condoms sold in the United States are purchased by women (Hatcher et al. 1990).

The condom may fail, of course (either as a contraceptive device or as protection against STDs), if it has even a microscopic hole. However, quality control in their manufacture is so high that imperfections are rare. The condom may also fail if it slips off the penis after ejaculation, so care must be taken in withdrawal. Moreover, if a couple copulate for a time before rolling the condom over the penis, the pre-ejaculatory fluid may contain sufficient sperm for conception to take place. As with all contraceptive devices, most failures of the condom occur because of carelessness (Hatcher et al. 1990).

A good-quality condom used as directed, but not with foam, cream, or jelly, has a typical failure rate of about 12 percent (Trussell et al. 1990). When used with a spermicidal foam, cream, or jelly, the condom provides virtually 100 percent effectiveness, especially when the condom itself contains an added spermicide, such as those with the trade names Ramses Extra and Sheik Extra.

The Diaphragm

The diaphragm is a barrier method of contraception used by women. Vaginal diaphragms in combination with spermicidal pastes or jellies were invented in the early 1880s. Prior to this, various devices were used to block the entrance to the cervix in conjunction with various spermicides. A small sponge saturated with soapy water is a popular device still used in many parts of the world. Casanova, for his many conquests, devised the use of half a lemon as a kind of

---

[4]A condom worn by women is available, primarily designed to improve protection against STDs. This soft polyurethane vaginal liner has a ring at each end. The end against the cervix is closed, and the outer ring covers the labia, thus preventing direct contact between partners' genitalia.

diaphragm, with the citric acid acting as a spermicide (Finch and Green 1963).

The modern diaphragm consists of a circular piece of thin rubber with a stiffened but flexible rim. It is designed to lie along the roof of the vagina, between its back wall and the pubic bone, so that it covers the cervix, and it must be carefully fitted by a physician, nurse, or paramedic from the various models and sizes available. A woman should have the fit checked at least once a year and may need a larger size after childbirth, an abortion, or pelvic surgery (Hatcher et al. 1990).

It is dangerous to leave the diaphragm in place for more than twenty-four hours because of the possibility of toxic shock syndrome (TSS).[5] For the same reason, it is inadvisable to use the diaphragm during menstruation (Hatcher et al. 1990).

Reasons not to use the diaphragm include allergic reaction to latex or spermicides, cystitis, vaginal anatomical abnormalities resulting in incorrect fit, inability to learn how and when to insert the diaphragm, and pelvic pain. The diaphragm should not be used for at least twelve weeks after giving birth (Hatcher et al. 1990).

The diaphragm by itself is not an effective contraceptive device; instead, it works best by holding spermicidal jelly in the position most likely to encounter sperm. The diaphragm must be left in place for at least six hours after copulation to allow the spermicide to kill all the sperm. If a woman copulates again during this time, she must insert more cream or jelly into her vagina, leaving the diaphragm in place (Hatcher et al. 1990).

Researchers find that the typical failure rate of the diaphragm is about 18 percent (Trussell et al. 1990). As with other contraceptives, the main reason for failure is probably carelessness (Hatcher et al. 1990).

The Cervical Cap

The cervical cap is a vaginal barrier designed to cover only the cervix; it has been available for thousands of years. In ancient Sumatra, for example, women molded opium into caplike devices to cover their cervixes (Finch and Green 1963). The modern cervical cap was perfected in 1838 and became popular in Europe; it has been available in the United States only since 1988.

The cervical cap fits tightly over the woman's cervix and is held in place by suction. Unlike the diaphragm, which is fitted only approximately to the diameter of the vagina near the cervical opening, the cervical cap is fitted exactly to the cervix. A small amount of spermicide is used inside the cap to kill any sperm that might break through the suction seal (Hatcher et al. 1990). It can be worn for forty-eight hours, but some researchers recommend limiting wear to twenty-four hours to avoid the risk of toxic shock syndrome. Contraindications for using the cervical cap are the same as for the diaphragm (Hatcher et al. 1990). The typical failure rate of the cervical cap used with spermicidal cream or jelly is 18 percent (Trussell et al. 1990).

The Contraceptive Sponge

The vaginal contraceptive sponge (made of polyurethane) is available without prescription and comes in one size—two and one-quarter inches in diameter and three-quarters of an inch thick. It contains a gram of spermicide

<hr>

[5]Although toxic shock syndrome (TSS) is usually associated with the use of tampons, several cases have been reported with the use of a diaphragm, contraceptive sponge, or cervical cap (Radetsky 1985). Only a small number of women have developed TSS, but a few of them have died. TSS is probably caused by a strain of bacteria (*Staphylococcus aureus*) that infects some part of the body, often the vagina, and produces toxins that go into the bloodstream. Early symptoms of TSS include fever (101 degrees Fahrenheit or more), diarrhea, vomiting, muscle aches, and sunburnlike rash (Hatcher et al. 1990).

(nonoxynol-9) that is released slowly (Hatcher et al. 1990).

The contraceptive sponge has a dimple in the center and should be inserted into the vagina so that the dimple covers the cervix. Once in place, it expands into the space around the cervix, blocking the opening, so an exact fit is not essential (as it is with the cervical cap). After the sponge is inserted, copulation may occur any number of times without having to add more spermicide; the sponge provides continuous protection for twenty-four hours. It must be left in place, however, for at least six hours after copulation and can be left in the vagina for up to twenty-four hours. The contraceptive sponge has a loop of tape attached to it and is removed simply by pulling on the tape (Hatcher et al. 1990).

To avoid the risk of toxic shock syndrome, the contraceptive sponge should *not* be used during menstruation.[6]

Benefits of the contraceptive sponge include significant protection against chlamydia and gonorrhea, reducing infection rates by one-third and two-thirds, respectively (Rosenberg et al. 1987).

Preliminary reports indicate an actual failure rate of about 16 percent. First-year failure rates range from 17 to 24 percent, with women not previously pregnant twice as likely to conceive (Trussell et al. 1990).

The Pill: Hormonal Control

The most commonly used contraceptive pill is a "combination" pill composed of *estrogen* (the female sex hormone) and *progestin*, which is a synthetic substance chemically similar to *progesterone*, a hormone produced in the ovaries. This pill controls a woman's reproductive physiology by introducing hormones that mimic those of pregnancy and thus "fool" the body into stopping ovulation.

A second type of birth control pill contains only progestin. This progestin-only pill is not really a contraceptive since it does not inhibit ovulation; instead, when taken every day, it causes the cervical mucus to become denser and impedes the thickening of the uterine lining so that the blastocyst is much less likely to implant should conception occur. Progestin-only pills are not as effective in preventing pregnancy as the combination pills, except for women ages forty or older, who have a failure rate of just 0.3 percent. This is important because an older woman may not want to take the combination pill because of the associated cardiovascular risks (Hatcher et al. 1990).

The popularity of either form of the pill is not difficult to understand — both are very effective methods of birth control. Moreover, the pill is very simple to use, requires no special preparation, and causes no interruption of copulation. Some 13.8 million women in the United States currently use the pill. It is the method of choice for nearly 30 percent of American women who practice birth control, most of whom are under age thirty (Williams-Deane and Potter 1992).

Usually, however, no more than 50 to 75 percent of women who start on the pill are still using it after one year. Most women who stop taking the pill do so for nonmedical reasons — that is, they have not developed a complication or major side effect but instead are simply dissatisfied; no particular reasons are given (Hatcher et al. 1990). Researchers generally agree that there is very little risk of side effects for women using the pill if they are young, healthy, and do not smoke (Kost, Forrest, and Harlap 1991; Colditz et al. 1988).

---

[6]Because the schedule of ovulation is not always consistent, it is possible for a woman to become pregnant while she is menstruating. Because of the danger of toxic shock syndrome, a condom is the best contraceptive method for a woman during menstruation.

The birth-control pill neutralizes normal vaginal acids and increases vaginal carbohydrates, which encourage bacterial growth, thus making women who use it more susceptible to vaginal infections. STDs and other infections, such as common vaginitis, are twice as common among pill users compared with other women. Birth-control pills do not protect against STDs, and researchers advise women who have different sex partners to use condoms as well as birth-control pills (Hatcher et al. 1990).

Low-dose, low-potency pills have significantly reduced risks formerly associated with use of the pill, and as a result there appear to be fewer risks for young, healthy women. Those most at risk of developing side effects from the pill are those who smoke, are over thirty-five years old, have a history of diabetes or hypertension, or have a family history of heart attack. Researchers agree that women who smoke should not take the pill because of increased risks of cardiovascular diseases such as heart attacks and strokes (Kost, Forrest, and Harlap 1991).

It is commonly thought that although pregnancy may be dangerous for some women, the pill is even more dangerous. This is simply not true. Studies have shown that the risk of death from pregnancy itself is greater than the risk from the pill (Hatcher et al. 1990). The typical failure rate of the combination pill is 3 percent — probably due to carelessness or inconsistent use (Trussell et al. 1990).

Progestin Implants: Norplant

Norplant is the trade name for flexible silicone rubber capsules that act to control pregnancy when they are implanted subdermally (under the skin). Insertion of Norplant implants is a minor surgical procedure that takes from ten to fifteen minutes under local anesthesia, with no stitches required. Five implants are usually placed in a fan-shaped pattern under the skin on the inside of a woman's upper arm. Once implanted, they steadily release a synthetic form of progestin, maintaining blood hormone levels that suppress ovulation and thicken the cervical mucus, thus providing protection from pregnancy. The capsules are no longer effective after about five years and should be replaced at this time. The implants may be removed whenever the woman wishes; her fertility will be restored with her next menstrual cycle following the removal (Population Council 1991).

Side effects of Norplants are minimal, usually consisting of an irregular menstrual cycle for at least six months of the first year after insertion. Norplants are not recommended for women who are already pregnant or have acute liver disease, heart disease, breast cancer, or blood clots (Hatcher et al. 1990). In 1990, half a million women in seventeen countries had Norplant implants (Population Council 1991). Norplants are 99.96 percent effective as a method of birth control (see Table B-1).

Injectable Progestin: Depo-Provera

Depo-Provera is the trade name for a long-acting injectable progestin product that prevents implantation of the blastocyst. Depo-Provera is designed to be injected at three-month intervals; it is marketed in more than ninety countries and is used by an estimated thirty million women worldwide. A woman who wishes to regain her fertility may discontinue Depo-Provera at any time, but fertility may not return for six to twelve months. Although definitive long-term studies on the side effects of Depo-Provera are not yet available, the only problem that has shown up so far is excessive endometrial bleeding; this is the most frequent reason given for discontinuing the injections (Hatcher et al. 1990). Depo-Provera is highly effective; only about one out of every four hundred women who use it for one year will become pregnant (see Table B-1).

The Intrauterine Device (IUD)

The intrauterine device (IUD) does not prevent conception but, like progestin, is designed to prevent implantation of the blastocyst in the uterine wall. The IUD is a small, inert plastic object (which may have a copper component) that is inserted in the uterus through the vagina. The IUD has a nylon string attached to it that aids in removal and allows the woman to check for the presence of the IUD by feeling the string at the cervix. A woman using an IUD should check for its presence before each copulation because of the possibility of spontaneous expulsion. Five to 10 percent of users expel their IUD within the first year. If the woman does not notice the expulsion, she could become pregnant. About one-third of IUD-related pregnancies result from undetected partial or complete expulsion (Hatcher et al. 1990).

The use of IUDs in the United States has dropped markedly because of adverse publicity regarding pelvic infections resulting from their use. Because of the danger of pelvic infection with IUDs, they come with a consent form, which the provider and the user are required to sign in acknowledgment of the risk in using IUDs. Because of the risk of infection if the IUD is left in place too long, it should be replaced at least every twelve months. No IUD wearer should ever ignore a pain in her abdomen, especially in the first few days and weeks following insertion. If she cannot find the device, she should go to a physician for X rays. Women using an IUD are thought to have up to a fivefold greater risk of getting PID than are women using other forms of birth control (Hatcher et al. 1990).

The only IUDs currently marketed in the United States are those with the trade names Copper-T and Progesterone-T. Both have a typical failure rate of about 3 percent (Trussell et al. 1990).

Sterilization

Contraceptive sterilization has become the most widely used method of family planning in the world (Hatcher et al. 1989). One spouse is sterilized in about one-third of American couples who use some method of birth control (Berkow et al. 1987). These figures are not surprising because sterilization is a safe, economical, and effective method of contraception. Before 1975, more vasectomies (male sterilization) than tubectomies (female sterilization) were performed in the United States; however, throughout the 1980s tubectomies outnumbered vasectomies by a ratio of two to one (Hatcher et al. 1990).

Female Sterilization   Sterilization operations on women (tubectomies) involve surgically blocking each fallopian tube to prevent the sperm and egg from uniting. Blocking the tubes can be accomplished by ligation, electrocoagulation, or mechanical occlusion with clips or rings. The tubes can be approached in two ways: through the abdomen or through the vagina. The vaginal approach has been largely discontinued because of risk of infection and failure; the fallopian tubes are usually reached through the abdomen using a *laparoscopy* or a *minilaparotomy*. Tubal sterilization is a relatively safe procedure, posing far less threat to the life and health of women than do oral contraceptives or a pregnancy that is carried to full term (Hatcher et al. 1990).

With laparoscopy, an instrument called a *laparoscope* is inserted through a tiny incision in the navel, while Teflon-coated forceps are inserted through a one-inch incision further down the abdomen; the forceps carries high-intensity radio waves that cauterize and destroy small sections of the fallopian tubes. The laparoscope contains a lens surrounded by microscopic glass rods that are capable of transferring light but not heat; the lens enables the physician to look into the depths of the woman's abdomen without opening it up. The laparoscope is also used to place rings or to apply clips to effect blockage. A laparoscopy is performed under local or general anesthesia (Hatcher et al. 1990).

A *minilaparotomy* involves making an abdominal incision about an inch long just above the pubic hairline, through which the fallopian tubes can be reached; plastic rings or clips are then put in place to block the fallopian tubes. The procedure is usually performed under local anesthesia (Hatcher et al. 1990).

Sterilization procedures have no effect on a woman's sex life, except for the psychological benefit of no longer having to worry about the possibility of conception. She continues to ovulate, her hormone system remains undisturbed, and the menstrual cycle goes on. The only change is that sperm cannot travel up the fallopian tubes to reach an egg.

Reversal of these operations is difficult because the structures involved are very tiny and are therefore difficult to realign; less than 30 percent of reversal operations are successful (Hatcher et al. 1990).

Because there is no difficulty for the physician in identifying the fallopian tubes and because spontaneous regeneration and realignment are unlikely, the probability of conception after a sterilization is less than one-half of 1 percent (see Table B-1).

Male Sterilization *Vasectomy,* the male sterilization operation, is a simple and inexpensive procedure in which both *vas deferens,* the tubes through which sperm pass from the testicles to the seminal vesicles, are cut and tied off or cauterized. The vas deferens are close to the surface and can be reached through a small incision in the scrotum that is then closed with a suture or two. The procedure can be performed in a physician's office under local anesthesia in fifteen to twenty minutes (Hatcher et al. 1990). The hor-

mone system is undisturbed by the operation (Nikkanen and Punnonen 1982), and erection and ejaculation occur exactly as before (Dias 1983). Sperm cells continue to form, but they never complete their journey up the vas deferens. Instead, they are generally attacked by antibodies, which defend the body against foreign intruders, and are carried away by white blood cells (Berkow et al. 1987).

During ejaculation, the same amount of fluid is released, the sensations and pulsations are the same, and the ejaculate looks and feels as it did before. But examination of the semen under the microscope reveals that the sperm are missing. A vasectomy does not interfere with the male's sex life in any way, except to make him sterile. Research on psychological aspects of male sterilization indicates that the incidence of regret is very low (Hatcher et al. 1990).

A man may copulate immediately after the operation, but because sperm may remain in the male genital system for several weeks, pregnancy may occur. It takes about twenty ejaculations to empty a male's reservoirs and bring his sperm count to zero. To be absolutely certain that no sperm are present, a postoperative microscopic examination of the ejaculate is necessary (Hatcher et al. 1990).

A vasectomy can be reversed only an estimated 50 percent of the time, so it should be used as a contraceptive measure only after a man is certain that he does not want additional children (Hatcher et al. 1990). The incidence of failure with vasectomy is close to zero (see Table B-1) because conception can occur only if the vasectomized male copulates too soon after the operation.[7]

---

[7]Conception can also occur if the physician severs the wrong tube, or if a severed tube spontaneously regenerates and realigns, or if the man has an undiscovered extra vas deferens that continues to function — all of which are exceedingly unlikely.

The "Morning-After" Pill

There are three successful types of "morning-after" pills. Two of these, both used in the United States, are (1) a combination of synthetic estrogen and progesterone (trade name Ovral) and (2) high doses of birth control pills. Either of these treatments will usually interrupt gestation if taken within seventy-two hours (and preferably within twelve to twenty-four hours) after possible conception. The treatment will usually cause the woman to begin menstruating, and if conception has occurred, the zygote (or blastocyst) will be swept away in the menstrual flow. Failure rates are low, and few side effects have been reported with Ovral; however, nausea and vomiting can be side effects of high doses of birth control pills (Glasier et al. 1992; Hatcher et al. 1990).

Preventing a successful implantation of the blastocyst in this way is viewed by some people as a type of abortion and by others as a means of reducing abortions; hence use of the morning-after pill is a delicate issue. In the United States, the morning-after pill has been used in the past decade primarily for rape victims (Hatcher et al. 1990).

The third, and most effective, type of morning-after pill is RU-486, which is available in Europe but as of 1992 was not legally available in the United States. RU-486 not only is more effective in interrupting pregnancy than high doses of birth control pills if taken within 72 hours of possible conception but also causes far less nausea and vomiting. Medical experts and women who favor the availability of abortion want RU-486 to be marketed in our society because it provides an alternative to surgical abortions early in pregnancy. Many opponents of abortion want the drug kept out of the United States because they believe a treatment that prevents the blastocyst from implanting in the uterus is no different from an abortion, which dislodges an embryo or fetus, and that morning-after pills are thus the moral equivalent of abortion. Opponents also point out that if RU-486 is admitted to the United States as a morning-after pill, doctors would be able to use it for abortions when pregnancy is farther advanced (Glasier et al. 1992).

Menstrual Extraction

Menstrual extraction (also called *menstrual regulation*) is a surgical procedure used to terminate a pregnancy; it is effective for up to three weeks following conception or two weeks following a missed menstrual period (Hatcher et al. 1990).

During the first week after conception, the zygote is being propelled down the fallopian tube. During the second week, the blastocyst is embedding itself in the uterine wall, and at the end of this week the embryonic stage begins (see Appendix C). At any time during this period the endometrium (lining of the uterus) may be aspirated (sucked out with a vacuum device) with no dilation of the cervix necessary and with no need for anesthesia or other medication. This procedure brings about menstruation, and the zygote, blastocyst, or embryo (depending on the stage of development) is discharged with the menstrual flow (Hatcher et al. 1990).

Abortion

There are two types of abortion: spontaneous abortion and induced abortion.

Spontaneous Abortion

If the blastocyst, embryo, or fetus is expelled from the uterus through natural processes of a woman's body, this is called a *spontaneous abortion* or *miscarriage.* Spontaneous abortion is the body's way of eliminating a malformed or malfunctioning organism and occurs much more often than is generally realized: Nearly one-third of all pregnancies terminate in spontaneous abortion. Three-fourths of these occur before the sixteenth week of gestation — sometimes with the woman never realizing that she was pregnant (Wilcox et al. 1988). Spontaneous abortion may also occur in the fetal stage of development; 60 percent of spontaneously aborted fetuses are grossly abnormal (Krupp, Chatton, and Werdegar 1985).

Induced Abortion

An *induced abortion* is deliberately caused by interrupting the pregnancy either medically or surgically. Induced abortions performed only for the sake of the mother's health are called therapeutic abortions. Induced abortions are usually simply called "abortions," however. (For a brief discussion of the history of abortion in our society and its controversial position today, see Chapter 9.)

There are two surgical procedures for inducing abortion during the first sixteen weeks (or first trimester) of pregnancy: vacuum curettage and dilation and curettage (D & C).

Vacuum Curettage Vacuum curettage is a simple technique for completely emptying the uterus. The procedure takes little time, requires only local anesthesia, and can be done in a physician's office. Vacuum curettage requires only a small cervical dilation through which a flexible plastic tube is inserted to suck out the endometrium (lining) of the uterus. It is currently the most widely used abortion procedure in the United States (Hatcher et al. 1990).

Dilation and Curettage (D & C) Dilation and curettage (D & C) involves dilating (stretching) the cervix and scraping away the lining of the uterus, together with the embryo or fetus, with a sharp instrument (curette); the procedure is done under general anesthesia and requires hospitalization. Complications may occur with bleeding and with incomplete evacuation. Once the most common method for first-trimester abortions, D & C has virtually been replaced by vacuum curettage (Hatcher et al. 1990).

Abortions After the First Trimester Abortions after the first trimester are relatively rare. Abortion becomes a more difficult procedure after this time, and the risks to the woman increase. The cavity of the uterus is pretty well filled with the developing fetus by the thirteenth week, making it more difficult for the physician to insert instruments without perforating the uterine wall. Also, the placenta has begun to form a large blood supply, so that bleeding is more likely to occur. Fetal bones have begun to form that may perforate the wall of the uterus during removal. And it is difficult to dilate the cervix enough to remove the fetus because of the latter's size. At the end of the first trimester the fetus is normally a little more than three inches long and weighs almost one ounce (Martin and Reeder 1991).

Despite these difficulties, there are both medical and surgical techniques available to perform an abortion after the first trimester. The longer the pregnancy continues after this time, the more difficult and dangerous the abortion becomes (Hatcher et al. 1990).

APPENDIX C

Conception, Gestation, and Childbirth

Conception

Gestation

Diagnostic Prenatal Procedures
Used in Genetic Counseling

Childbirth

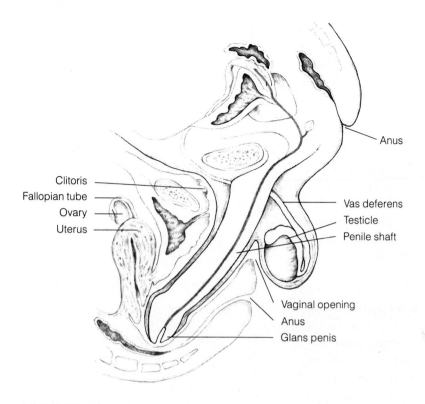

Clitoris

Fallopian tube

Ovary

Uterus

Anus

Vas deferens

Testicle

Penile shaft

Vaginal opening

Anus

Glans penis

FIGURE C-1
Cross section of the penis in the vagina.

Conception

When an egg cell (ovum) unites with a sperm cell, a new organism — the fertilized egg — comes into being. This union is called *fertilization;* in human beings, it is called *conception.*

At ovulation, a mature egg is released from one of the thousands of egg sacs (follicles) that line the walls of the ovaries. The egg then moves from the ovary to the mouth of a fallopian tube. The fallopian tubes are between two and four inches long and are extremely narrow; at their ovarian ends, their diameter is about that of a whisker. The outer walls of the fallopian tube contain muscles that contract and relax rhythmically, creating a wavelike motion called *peris-*

talsis that helps move the egg along. Aiding this peristaltic movement are cilia, hairlike structures that line the inner walls of the tube. Their constant undulation creates a current that moves the egg in the direction of the uterus.

During copulation the vagina receives the erect penis, which ejaculates against the cervix (see Figure C-1). The sperm then make their way into the cervix, through the uterus, and into the fallopian tubes, lashing their tails in a swimming motion, traveling about an inch a minute.

Unless sperm are able to make their way from the vagina, through the cervix, and into a woman's fallopian tubes, they die almost immediately after they are ejaculated. Once sperm reach a fallopian tube, they may survive for two, three, or possibly as long as five days. If an egg is released from an ovary into the fallopian tube during this time (while the sperm are still viable in the tube), the woman may become pregnant (Hatcher et al. 1990).

If a penis ejaculates on a woman's abdomen or thighs, it is possible that sperm may reach her vagina, penetrate the cervix, and reach a fallopian tube. If enough sperm do this, she may become pregnant, even though the penis never entered her vagina. (Only one sperm cell fertilizes an egg, but several hundred million sperm must start the journey from the vagina, and at least fifty must reach the egg in order for a single fertilization to occur.) She may then carry the pregnancy to full term and give birth to a baby even though, technically, she is still a virgin (Hatcher et al. 1990).[1]

Conception takes place when a sperm cell fuses with the egg to form a fertilized egg, normally in a fallopian tube. This usually occurs when the egg is about one-third of the distance from the ovary to the uterus. If conception does not occur, the egg usually disintegrates before reaching the uterus and is discharged during menstruation.

If more than one egg are released from the ovary, or if the fertilized egg divides into two, then a multiple birth may occur. The likelihood of a multiple birth rises with the mother's age, the number of children she has borne, and whether she used fertility drugs[2] (Martin and Reeder 1991). (See Box C-1.)

The fallopian tube serves several functions in reproduction. Initially it is responsible for the transfer of the egg from the rupturing follicle and for providing a hospitable environment for the egg and sperm in which fertilization (conception) is likely to occur. It then provides a favorable environment for the fertilized egg, which begins to divide almost immediately and continues to divide during the seven to eight days that it takes to make the journey through the fallopian tube to the uterus.

Gestation

Gestation is the period from conception to birth (see Box C-2).

The Germinal Period: The First Two Weeks

The germinal period begins when the sperm fertilizes the egg. As soon as the fertilized egg begins to divide, it is called a *zygote*. As the zygote, it is transported down the fallopian tube toward the uterus, and the initial cell divides into two cells, then four, eight, sixteen, and so on. Although the fertilized egg divides rapidly, doubling in the number of cells with each division, it does not grow in size. When it reaches the uterus it is still the size it was initially (Guyton 1989).

Meanwhile, the uterine wall has thickened and become enriched with blood and a supply of nutrients in response to hormones triggered

---

[1]It is not possible, however, for a woman to become pregnant in a swimming pool (or hot tub) if a man ejaculates in the water near her; there is no evidence that such a pregnancy has ever occurred.

[2]Scientists agree that as a woman ages and bears more children, she releases more than one egg each month during ovulation. More fertilized eggs are surviving with healthier mothers, and women who become pregnant soon after going off the pill

have an increased chance of bearing twins. Those who choose in-vitro fertilization, in which several fertilized eggs are implanted in the uterus, also have a higher chance of having twins. The majority of twins are fraternal. About 10 percent of women who get pregnant while taking Clomid, the most widely prescribed fertility drug, also experience multiple births (Keith 1992).

BOX C-1

Multiple Births

Normally the ovary releases only one egg, but occasionally two or more are released, and the result may be a multiple birth. Twins produced by the fertilization of two separate eggs are called *fraternal twins*. Because they are the product of separate eggs, separate sperm, and separate sets of genes, fraternal twins are no more closely related genetically than are any other siblings; they simply happen to be born at the same time.

More rarely, a single egg separates with the first division, with each separate cell then dividing again, so that two zygotes are formed. Twins produced by these two genetically identical zygotes are called *identical twins*. Because they are the product of a single egg and a single sperm, identical twins are genetically indistinguishable, although environmental factors may cause differences in their physical and psychological develop-

ment. About 33 percent of twins are identical (Martin and Reeder 1991; Creasy and Resnik 1989).

Twins of both types occur approximately once every ninety-three white births and once every seventy-three nonwhite births. Some families have a higher incidence of twins than others do, and the incidence varies with race, unknown environmental factors, and age of the mother. Women past age thirty-five are more likely to conceive fraternal twins and are also more likely to have taken fertility drugs, the use of which is correlated with multiple births. The number of twins in the United States rose 33 percent from 1975 to 1988; the number of triplets rose 101 percent while single pregnancies rose only 17 percent during this time (Keith 1992).

by ovulation. The fertilized egg has now become a multicellular hollow sphere called a *blastocyst*. Inside the blastocyst is a cluster of cells containing the *germinal disc*, which will develop into a human being—together with other tissue that provides a protective nutrient environment for the developing germinal disc (Guyton 1989).

The blastocyst secretes enzymes that help carve out a cavity in the uterine wall, into which it may embed. Tiny tendrils (*chorionic villi*) begin

to extend from the blastocyst into the uterine wall, marking the end of the germinal period and the beginning of the embryonic period (Guyton 1989). (See Figure C-2.)

The Embryonic Period: Two to Six Weeks After Conception

About two weeks after conception, the germinal disc (the part of the blastocyst that will develop

BOX C-2

The Periods of Pregnancy

- As soon as the fertilized egg begins to divide, it is called a *zygote*.

- About seven to eight days after conception, the zygote has been propelled through the fallopian tube to the uterus, where it begins to embed itself in the uterine wall. It is now called a *blastocyst*.

- The first two weeks after conception — from the time the egg is fertilized until the blastocyst is firmly embedded in the uterine wall — are called the *germinal period*.

- The next four weeks are called the *embryonic period*.

- The time from the sixth week after conception until labor begins (about nine months after conception) is called the *fetal period*.

- The time from conception until childbirth is called *gestation*.

into a human being) is firmly embedded in the uterine wall and is about one-twelfth of an inch long. It begins to assume an animal shape and is now called an *embryo* (Guyton 1989).

The chorionic villi burrow into the blood-filled uterine tissue, absorbing nutrients, oxygen, and antibodies from the mother and passing back into her bloodstream carbon dioxide and other waste products. However, the blood itself is never mixed between the developing embryo (or later, the fetus) and the mother; all embryonic (or fetal) blood originates within the embryo (or fetus) itself (Creasy and Resnik 1989).

The villi are connected to the embryo by a *body stalk*, which develops from the inner cluster of cells containing the germinal disc. The cluster of cells that develops into the body stalk also

develops into the *amnion,* a sac filled with amniotic fluid in which the embryo (and later the fetus) floats — separated from the uterine wall, cushioned against injury and temperature change, and free to move and shift about (Creasy and Resnik 1989).

By the end of the third week, the embryo has grown to about one-seventh of an inch in length and has a clearly distinguishable head and spinal cord and the buds of arms and legs. Lenses are forming in the eye areas, the location of ears has been marked off, a few isolated nerves have appeared, and various other glands and organs are taking rudimentary shape (Guyton 1989).

About the fourth week the woman becomes aware of the possibility that she is pregnant (see Figure C-3). Her menstrual period is now about

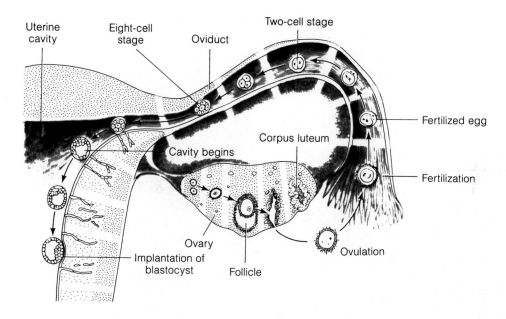

FIGURE C-2
Ovulation, fertilization, and the germinal period of pregnancy.

Labels in figure:
Uterine cavity — Eight-cell stage — Oviduct — Two-cell stage — Fertilized egg — Corpus luteum — Cavity begins — Fertilization — Ovulation — Ovary — Implantation of blastocyst — Follicle

two weeks overdue, and she may have noticed a heaviness and fullness in her breasts and an enlargement and darkening of her areolae and nipples (which may exude a secretion when pressed). She may also need to urinate more often than usual because of the pressure on the bladder from the expanding uterus; in the early weeks of pregnancy she may experience morning sickness (Martin and Reeder 1991).[3]

By the fifth week the body stalk has developed into the *umbilical cord*, which contains blood vessels that link the circulatory system of the embryo (and later the fetus) to the uterine wall.

It is a rubbery, transparent tube containing two arteries and one vein. The rush of blood (about four miles an hour) through the cord keeps it relatively stiff and prevents it from entangling (or strangling) the embryo or fetus. At full term, the umbilical cord is about twenty inches long and about three-quarters of an inch in diameter (Creasy and Resnik 1989).

Several early signs of pregnancy that can be detected at this time are changes in the shape of the abdomen, darkened color of the vaginal area, softening of the cervix and the area between the cervix and the uterus, and enlargement of the uterus. However, in these early (germinal disc and embryonic) stages of pregnancy, only specific tests can determine without doubt whether a woman is pregnant. Pregnancy can be diagnosed about six weeks after the last menstrual period by using two-minute urine tests and earlier by using serum tests (Hatcher et al. 1990).

[3]All these symptoms can occur in "false pregnancy," a psychosomatic response to various psychological stimuli (including fear of pregnancy). False pregnancy may even simulate the gradual swelling of the abdomen for a full nine months (Martin and Reeder 1991).

1. About 15 days after fertilization.

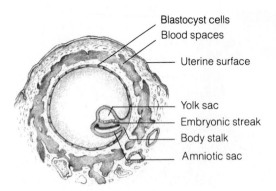

Blastocyst cells
Blood spaces
Uterine surface
Yolk sac
Embryonic streak
Body stalk
Amniotic sac

2. Buildup of placental villi, about two and a half weeks after fertilization.

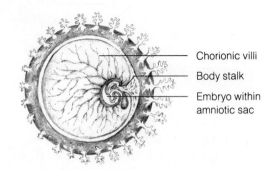

Chorionic villi
Body stalk
Embryo within amniotic sac

3. Dwindling of yolk sac; embryo about three weeks old. Umbilical vessels are forming.

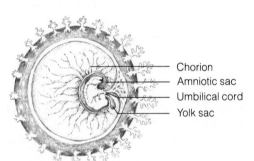

Chorion
Amniotic sac
Umbilical cord
Yolk sac

4. Embryo at about four weeks. Embryo and placenta well formed.

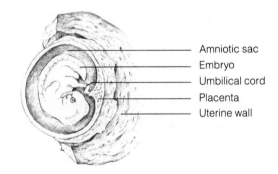

Amniotic sac
Embryo
Umbilical cord
Placenta
Uterine wall

FIGURE C-3
The development of the embryo.

The Fetal Period: Six Weeks After Conception Until Birth

During the fetal period, which begins about six weeks after conception, the organs and structural systems that budded during the embryonic period are further developed and refined. Moreover, the primitive gonadal tissue now begins to secrete hormones that direct the differentiation of tissue into male (if there is an XY chromosomal structure) or female (if the chromosomal structure is XX). At this time the sex of the fetus can be discovered using the technique of *amniocentesis*. (See the section "Diagnostic Prenatal Procedures Used in Genetic Counseling.")

By the tenth week following conception the fetus begins to make breathing movements and reflex movements of the lips resembling sucking.

The external genitalia are now differentiated into male or female forms if development is proceeding normally (Creasy and Resnik 1989).

During the third month following conception the fetus reaches a length of about three inches. The features of the face become more differentiated; the lips take shape, the nose begins to stand out, and the eyelids are formed, although they remain fused. The fingers and toes are well developed, and fingernails and toenails are forming. The primitive kidneys begin to excrete small amounts of urine. The fetal heart can be heard by the twelfth week with an ultrasonic stethoscope (Guyton 1989).

By the fourteenth week a stethoscope can detect spontaneous movements of the fetus. However, the first fetal movements of which the woman herself is aware do not occur until about the seventeenth week (Creasy and Resnik 1989). The fetal movements that are detected by the mother are called *quickening* and have great historical and theological significance; St. Augustine thought they indicated the entrance of the soul into the unborn child and the moment when the fetus may be considered a human being.

By the fourth month the chorionic villi have disappeared, except for those that are functioning in direct contact with the uterine wall and the umbilical cord. These villi, together with the portion of uterine tissue in which they are embedded, become the *placenta*. The placenta holds the fetus in place in the uterus while continuing and increasing the nurturing functions that the villi served. On the side connected to the uterine lining, the placenta is a spongy mass of blood vessels; on the other side, to which the fetus is connected by the umbilical cord, the placenta is smooth. At full term, the placenta weighs about a pound and is about eight inches in diameter and one inch thick (Creasy and Resnik 1989).

In the fourth month, the fetus grows to about six inches and weighs about four ounces. Most of its bones have been formed, although they are still cartilage and will not be completely hardened into bone (a process called ossification) until many years after birth.

The fetus begins to develop increasingly complex functions during the fourth month, with hormonal secretion becoming greater, the liver beginning to secrete bile, and digestion starting to take place (Guyton 1989).

In the fifth month, quickening becomes apparent to the woman, first as a mild fluttering and later as solid kicks against the inside of her abdomen. Any nausea she may have had is probably gone, and she is now in the most comfortable period of pregnancy (Martin and Reeder 1991).

During the sixth month the fetus grows to a foot in length and about twenty ounces in weight. The eyelids are now separated and may be opened and closed. Eyelashes and eyebrows begin to appear. The fetus now makes slight, but regular, breathing movements. However, a fetus of this age is not just a smaller version of a full-term infant. If the baby is born at this time, the chances of survival are very slim (Creasy and Resnik 1989).

By seven months, the fetus is about fifteen inches long and weighs about two and a half pounds or more. If the baby is born now there is a good chance for survival with the aid of specialized attention and equipment.[4]

A baby born in the eighth month of pregnancy has a "very good" chance of survival because development is virtually complete. In the eighth and ninth months, changes consist mainly of a very rapid gain in weight—an average of nearly half a pound a week (Creasy and Resnik 1989). (See Figure C-4.)

---

[4]Until a few years ago, the mortality rate for premature neonates weighing under thirty-five ounces at birth was 80 to 85 percent. Because of advances in their care, the mortality rate has dropped to 15 to 20 percent (Creasy and Resnik 1989).

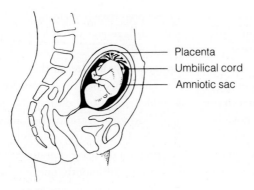

Placenta
Umbilical cord
Amniotic sac

Fifth month

Fetus measures about 10 to 12 inches and weighs ½ to 1 pound.

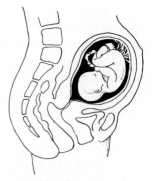

Sixth month

Fetus measures 11 to 14 inches and weighs 1¼ to 1½ pounds.

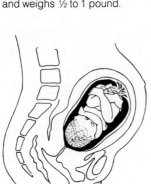

Seventh month

Fetus measures 14 to 17 inches and weighs 2½ to 3 pounds.

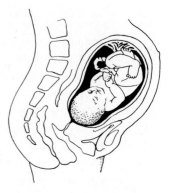

Eighth month

Fetus is 16½ to 18 inches long and weighs 5 to 8 pounds.

FIGURE C-4
The development of the fetus.

During the final months of pregnancy the woman probably feels generally healthy but is likely to be uncomfortable because of the crowding of her organs by her expanding uterus and because the increasing weight of the fetus causes some problems in her movement and her equilibrium. Many women feel awkward and cumbersome in these months and look forward to childbirth as liberation. Many others, however, report that the later stages of pregnancy are a time of unparalleled physical and mental well-being (Kitzinger 1978).

Prenatal Influences

It has long been known that biological factors affecting the woman's body may also affect the embryo and fetus and development of the baby.

One of the most obvious of these factors is nutrition, and we have seen its effect on the development of the brain of the fetus and infant (Chapter 10). However, a pregnant woman's nutrition affects not just the brain, but the entire body of the fetus. A woman's diet must enable her body to supply the fetus with an adequate supply of building materials necessary for its normal development, or irreparable harm will be done (Lozoff 1989; Krupp, Chatton, and Werdegar 1985). For example, if the mother's diet contains too little calcium or vitamin A, the fetus will not develop properly, and no amount of postnatal care will repair the damage. On the other hand, excessive amounts of vitamin A may cause severe malformations in the developing fetus (Cook, Petersen, and Moore 1990). Data indicate that pregnant women who take the vitamin *folic acid* (part of the B vitamin complex) from the onset of their pregnancy greatly reduce the risk of the baby being born with neural tube defects, such a spina bifida (open spine), a potentially paralyzing condition (Wald et al. 1991).

Other physical factors that may have a significant effect on the developing fetus are maternal X rays, drugs, diseases, and the Rh factor. We will examine these factors in the following sections.

X Rays and Pregnancy X rays and other forms of radiation are damaging to the embryo or fetus, and a pregnant woman should avoid them if possible. (It has become routine in many hospitals to administer a pregnancy test before taking X rays of a woman of childbearing age.) A study conducted at Johns Hopkins Hospital showed that the incidence of children with Down's syndrome[5] born to older women was closely re-

lated to the number of diagnostic and therapeutic medical and dental X rays to which the women had been exposed during their lifetimes (Reeder et al. 1987).

Drugs and Pregnancy Almost any drug women take during pregnancy may affect the offspring. Apparently the only safe procedure for a pregnant woman is to avoid all drugs, except those prescribed by a physician when absolutely necessary. During gestation, all drugs cross the placenta and enter the bloodstream of the developing embryo and fetus, where they may cause irreversible damage.

Many interacting genetic factors in the unborn baby and in the mother, as well as the amount and type of drug and the stage of pregnancy, affect the vulnerability of the embryo or fetus. Drug use during the fourth to the eighth week following conception is more likely to cause spontaneous abortion or physical abnormalities in the newborn than use later in the pregnancy. After the eighth week, drugs are more likely to cause growth retardation, neurological damage, and premature birth. Prematurity and low birth weight are related to many serious problems in babies, including respiratory distress, infections, and developmental delays (Cook, Petersen, and Moore 1990).

Perhaps the most common substance pregnant women use that may damage the fetus is caffeine. Research has linked caffeine (contained in coffee, cocoa, tea, and cola drinks) to birth defects (Krupp, Chatton, and Werdegar 1985).

---

[5] The incidence of Down's syndrome (mental retardation, retarded physical growth, facial disfiguration), which once accounted for a third of all birth defects, dropped by 25 percent

in the early 1980s, apparently because of prenatal detection (using amniocentesis) and abortion (U.S. Centers for Disease Control, "Congenital Malformations," 1984). Down's syndrome still affects 1 percent to 2 percent of newborns, with the risk increasing as women get older. Currently, diagnostic *ultrasonic scanning* (the use of sound waves to produce a picture of the fetus) looks for short thigh bones and an extra roll of skin at the back of the neck to help diagnose this syndrome (Benacerraf et al. 1987).

Another common substance that pregnant women use is nicotine (and other substances) in cigarettes. Smoking cigarettes during pregnancy is correlated with an increased incidence of bleeding and premature rupturing of the membranes with early (pre-term) delivery (Cook, Petersen, and Moore 1990). There is also direct correlation between the amount of smoking during pregnancy and the frequency of spontaneous abortion and fetal death. Smoking is also significantly correlated to low birth weight, and babies with a low birth weight have a much higher incidence of illness and a higher mortality rate than babies of normal weight. Data indicate that firstborn babies of mothers who smoked less than a pack a day were 25 percent more likely to die within their first year than babies of nonsmoking mothers. Smoking by mothers (regardless of the number of cigarettes smoked per day) increased the rate of infant death among babies subsequent to the firstborn by 30 percent, primarily because of respiratory difficulties and SIDS (Sudden Infant Death Syndrome). SIDS is the leading cause of death in babies during their first year. As they grow older, children of mothers who smoked while they were pregnant are more likely to have impaired intellectual and physical development and are more likely to have such behavior problems as hyperactivity, irritability, and disinterest than children of nonsmoking mothers (Cook, Petersen, and Moore 1990).

Cigarette smoking by the father can apparently cause genetic damage in offspring, presumably because a male who smokes cigarettes produces more abnormal sperm than nonsmokers. An increased rate of prenatal deaths and birth defects has been found among the offspring of men who smoke (Hulka et al. 1986). Moreover, cigarette smoking by the father (or anyone else in the environment) causes damage from passive smoking, which can damage a pregnant woman's health and so indirectly injure the embryo or fetus she is carrying. The harmful effects of passive smoking continue after a baby is born and represent an unacceptable health risk for both the mother and her offspring. Children who live with smokers have higher rates of bronchitis, pneumonia, chronic cough, and middle-ear infections, and their blood cholesterol levels are higher than average (Spock and Rothenberg 1991).

Alcohol is an exceedingly dangerous drug for a pregnant woman because it is likely to cause significant damage to an embryo or fetus in what is called *fetal alcohol syndrome*. Studies indicate that alcohol interferes with the transfer of maternal nutrients to the developing embryo and fetus, impairs the oxygen supply, and alters cellular functions, causing fetal abnormalities. Maternal alcoholism is associated with a high incidence of spontaneous abortion and stillbirth. Pregnant women who have one or two ounces of alcohol per day are twice as likely to have low birth-weight babies who are at risk for respiratory problems, serious infections, and long-term developmental problems (Cook, Petersen, and Moore 1990).

Fetal alcohol syndrome is characterized by abnormal facial features, growth deficiencies, central nervous system disorders, and mental retardation. Medical authorities generally recommend that pregnant women avoid alcohol entirely because no "safe" amount has been established, and some fetuses may be particularly susceptible. Fetal alcohol syndrome is now the leading cause of mental retardation (Cook, Petersen, and Moore 1990).

The effects of alcohol on the newborn continue if the mother nurses her infant. Alcohol reaches the same concentration in a mother's breast milk as in blood. A baby oxidizes alcohol more slowly than an adult, so that nursing babies whose mothers consume alcohol may be irritable, drowsy, and have abnormal weight gain. The effects of alcohol on the nursing infant are intensified if the woman smokes because nicotine is also transmitted in breast milk (Cook, Petersen, and Moore 1990).

Studies find that drug abuse (other than such commonly used substances as caffeine, tobacco, and alcohol) affects an astonishingly high number of babies and is a growing concern for American children (see Chapter 9). Abuse of cocaine by pregnant women is especially alarming. Fetuses become addicted to cocaine when it passes from the mother's bloodstream through the umbilical cord and into the baby's bloodstream. Of the babies born in inner-city hospitals in 1989, 25 percent were addicted to cocaine (Brazelton 1990). Babies whose mothers use crack may be born fourteen weeks premature and weigh one-and-a-half to two pounds. These tiny babies usually have severe brain damage. They also have severe respiratory distress (cannot breathe) and cannot eat, so that they must be fed through a tube run through their umbilical cord and must be hooked up to a respirator. Other common symptoms are tremors and severe irritability. In addition, they may have other birth defects and are highly susceptible to infection. When they leave the hospital, these babies are unattractive, not very lovable, and very difficult to care for; in consequence, they are often abused and neglected (Herscher 1989).

In addition to caffeine, cigarettes, alcohol, and crack, the U.S. Department of Health and Human Services cites the following commonly used drugs as having unacceptable risks for pregnant women (Cook, Petersen, and Moore 1990, pp. 44–46):

- *Accutane.* An anti-acne vitamin A derivative associated with major abnormalities such as severe retardation.

- *Hormones.* Estrogens contained in birth-control pills increase the risk of congenital abnormalities.

- *Tranquilizers.* All the minor tranquilizers have

been associated with increased reproductive risks, including lethargic newborns with poor muscle tone, cleft palates, and other malfunctions of the heart, arteries, and joints. The risk of these congenital defects appears to increase with smoking and alcohol use.

- *Sedatives.* Associated with increased birth defects and infant withdrawal symptoms.

- *Anti-migraine medications.* May cause reactions in nursing babies such as vomiting, diarrhea, and weak pulse.

- *Salicylates.* Includes Bufferin, Anacin, Empirin, and other aspirin-containing medications. When taken in therapeutic doses by pregnant women close to term, they may cause bleeding in the mother, fetus, or newborn.

- *Antibiotics.* For example, tetracycline used during the second half of pregnancy may cause permanent discoloration of a child's teeth.

Diseases During Pregnancy A number of diseases may be particularly dangerous during pregnancy, and a woman is well advised to consult a physician about any illness she contracts. Infections that she may pass on to the embryo or fetus include HIV, syphilis, hepatitis B, chlamydia, herpes II, other STDs, typhoid, influenza, diphtheria, and rubella (German measles). We will briefly examine the effects of HIV, hepatitis B, chlamydia, herpes II, and rubella on the embryo or fetus.

More than 70 percent of women with AIDS are black or Hispanic, and more than 80 percent are of childbearing age (Hatcher et al. 1990, Guinan and Hardy 1987).

As noted in Appendix A, although HIV infected mainly men initially, women and children are fast becoming the major victims. An estimated one-fourth to one-half of babies born to mothers infected with HIV will themselves be infected (Curran et al. 1988).

Because the hepatitis B virus is occurring more frequently in pregnant women, the Centers for Disease Control now advises a screening test for the disease by the thirty-fourth week of pregnancy for all pregnant women. Mothers who are carrying the virus pass it to their babies at birth. Maternal-infant transmission of hepatitis B usually occurs during infant contact with infectious material (secretions or blood in the birth canal) rather than through placental transmission, and only rarely through breast milk (Berkow et al. 1987). Screening for the infection and immediate vaccination of babies born to infected women will keep an estimated 2 percent of newborns (some 4,000 each year) from getting the disease. Children born infected with hepatitis B are not only at risk of severe illness at birth but also may be chronic carriers, harboring infection all their lives, and they often die early (Arevalo and Washington 1988).

During vaginal delivery, babies of mothers infected with chlamydia also have a 60 to 70 percent chance of becoming infected. Conjunctivitis, pneumonia, middle-ear infections, and gastrointestinal and rectal infections may also result from the newborn's exposure to chlamydia. Neonatal chlamydia infections are preventable through diagnostic screening of pregnant women (Gause 1987).

Neonates infected with either herpes I or herpes II often become seriously ill and may die. One-third of newborns infected with either of the herpes viruses die from the illness, and one-fourth of those who survive the infection suffer brain damage (Berkow et al. 1987). For this reason, physicians recommend that pregnant women should always be examined for herpes. The neonatal exposure to the disease occurs at the time of vaginal delivery if the mother has had an active herpes episode within a few days of the baby's birth. A caesarean section may be advised to avoid the risk of infection during a vaginal delivery (Prober et al. 1988).

German measles contracted during pregnancy, or during the three months prior to pregnancy, causes congenital heart disease, brain damage, deafness, or blindness in the embryo or fetus. The use of rubella vaccine has greatly reduced the number of victims born with congenital rubella in the United States, and only 20 cases were reported in 1983. Since 1989, however, increases in the disease have been reported every year, and the Centers for Disease Control now recommends that all women of childbearing age, and all children under age fifteen months, be vaccinated against rubella.[6]

Diagnostic Prenatal Procedures Used in Genetic Counseling

Each year, 280,000 babies are born with birth defects (Martin and Reeder 1991). Often these defects are caused by genetic disorders. To address this problem and provide information to pregnant women and their husbands about the health of the fetus, genetic counseling centers have been established at all medical schools and in many private institutions in the United States and Canada. These centers provide diagnostic prenatal testing procedures such as amniocentesis, ultrasonic scanning, alpha-fetoprotein (AFP) measurements, chorionic villi sampling, and gene probes. They also provide testing for the Rh factor, which is not a genetic disorder of the fetus but has important consequences for the baby's health (Berkow et al. 1987). We will examine these procedures briefly in the following sections.

---

[6]U.S. Centers for Disease Control. "Recommendations for Rubella Vaccinations" (1992).

Amniocentesis

Amniocentesis is a procedure in which a slender, hollow needle is inserted through the pregnant woman's abdomen into the uterus, and a small amount of amniotic fluid is drawn off. This amniotic fluid contains cells from the fetus's skin, eyes, and digestive tract. After the cells are cultured in a nutrient broth, the chromosomes are examined for abnormality. The cells cultured must first multiply to about 1,000 cells, and this process takes from three to four weeks. The procedure is performed during the twelfth to sixteenth week of pregnancy.

Amniocentesis is especially important in determining such serious abnormalities as Down's syndrome and sickle-cell anemia, neurological defects such as spina bifida (protrusion of the spinal cord), encephaly (absent brain), and Tay-Sachs disease.[7]

Amniocentesis cannot be performed until the second trimester, which means prolonged uncertainty and, in positive diagnosis, the possible physical and emotional trauma of a second-trimester abortion (Krupp, Chatton, and Werdegar 1985). Moreover, amniocentesis carries a small (0.5 percent) risk of causing a miscarriage (Benacerraf et al. 1987). For these reasons, ultrasonic scanning is largely replacing amniocentesis as a prenatal diagnostic procedure.

Ultrasonic Scanning

With *ultrasonic scanning*, acoustic pulses (sound waves) in the range of 20,000 to ten million cycles per second are sent through the pregnant woman's body from a probe applied to her abdominal skin. A computer analyzes the pulses that are reflected back to the probe, revealing structures as small as the pupil of an eye of a second-trimester fetus (Miller 1985).

Ultrasonic scanning provides a direct observation of the fetus and placenta in a painless procedure that carries no known risk for the fetus. Ultrasonic scanning not only provides information about the size, age, growth, and well-being of the fetus but is now accurate enough to replace amniocentesis in checking the fetus for spinal abnormalities and some other severe birth defects (Nadel et al. 1990).

Alpha-Fetoprotein (AFP) Measurements

A simple, inexpensive test called *alpha-fetoprotein* (AFP) may also detect the existence of fetal defects and is now a routine preliminary test for pregnant women. (AFP is a blood protein the fetus produces during pregnancy.) High levels of this fetal blood protein detected in the mother's blood indicates a possible problem with the fetus. Other procedures such as amniocentesis and ultrasonic scanning may then be used to confirm the diagnosis (Nadel et al. 1990).

Chorionic Villus Sampling (CVS)

Another method used to test for genetic defects in fetuses during the first trimester is called *chorionic villus sampling*. In this procedure, a thin flexible tube threaded into the uterus from the vagina is used to remove a small piece of tissue from the developing placenta. This procedure is done at eight to ten weeks of gestation, which is two months earlier than amniocentesis can be done, and results are available within hours or days rather than weeks (Berkow et al. 1987). Chorionic villus sampling thus gives the woman the option of choosing to have an abortion in

---

[7] The victims of Tay-Sachs disease appear normal until about six months of age, but they invariably die before age five. There is no known cure. Tay-Sachs disease is thought to have originated in a Jewish community in Europe in the Middle Ages and is more prevalent among Jews of Northeastern European origin than among the general population (Krupp, Chatton, and Werdegar 1985).

the first trimester if the test reveals serious fetal defects. The procedure carries a 4 percent incidence of complications (Rhoads et al. 1989) and causes a miscarriage rate of between 2 and 6 percent; data are as yet incomplete regarding the chance of causing harm to a fetus that goes to full term after CVS (Berkow et al. 1987).

Gene Probes

Gene probes, or genetic marker tests, offer great promise as a diagnostic and treatment procedure. This approach focuses on the genes that cause specific diseases, such as hemophilia, sickle-cell anemia, cystic fibrosis, and muscular dystrophy. Someday genetic engineering may provide effective countermeasures for these diseases.

The Rh Factor

As we have noted, the Rh factor is not a genetic disorder of the fetus; determining the Rh factor in a pregnant woman's blood is an important diagnostic procedure, however. If the woman has Rh-negative blood, this can be very dangerous for a fetus with Rh-positive blood; maternal Rh-negative antibodies cross the placental barrier into the fetus's bloodstream and then attack and destroy its red blood cells. This creates serious anemia and various organ malfunctions in the fetus (Berkow et al. 1987).

Testing for the Rh factor is now a simple procedure, and a medical treatment (RhoGAM) is available that prevents the mother's immune system from producing the Rh-negative antibodies that attack the red blood cells of the fetus. Before the introduction of this treatment, an estimated 10,000 infants died from Rh complications every year in the United States, with another 20,000 suffering major birth defects (Reeder et al. 1987).

Childbirth

Toward the end of pregnancy the fetus usually changes its position so that the head is in the lower part of the uterus. This may occur as early as four weeks before birth, or it may not occur until the onset of labor — the process whereby a baby is expelled from the mother's body.

Labor

Labor consists of rhythmic, progressive contractions of the uterine and abdominal muscles and relaxation of the sphincter muscles of the cervix; the process allows the baby to be gradually squeezed out of the uterus, through the cervix, into the vagina, and then into the outside world. Initially, uterine contractions occur at regular intervals of about fifteen to twenty minutes and are rather mild. As labor progresses, the contractions become more intense and the time between them shortens, eventually to about two or three minutes (Berkow et al. 1987).

During the last weeks of pregnancy, uterine contractions may become frequent without signaling the beginning of labor. These "false labor" contractions may be mistaken for true labor, and the woman may enter the hospital prematurely. Several signs help distinguish true labor from false labor. One sign is an increase in the intensity and frequency of the contractions as well as a continuing regularity. By itself, however, this sign does not necessarily indicate that labor has begun. A second sign (called "show") is the discharge of a small plug of mucus, often spotted with blood, from the cervix. This mucus plug helps prevent infection from entering the uterus through the cervix during pregnancy, and it is released in the early hours of labor as the cervix begins to relax and dilate. The release of the plug is followed by various amounts of bloody discharge — the nearer the onset of labor, the greater the amount of discharge. Another sign is the release of amniotic fluid when the amniotic sac ruptures. When this occurs, the onset of labor is usually imminent. Occasionally, the amniotic sac ruptures before labor begins, and amniotic fluid leaks through the cervix and vagina. If this happens, the woman should immediately inform her physician, as there is risk of infection should she not go into labor within twenty-four hours. The only certain indication that true labor is actually commencing is the dilation of the cervix (Berkow et al. 1987).

In a first pregnancy, true labor generally lasts from twelve to fourteen hours; successive labors average six to eight hours (Berkow et al. 1987).

The Three Stages of Labor

Obstetricians recognize three stages of labor. The first stage begins with the initial contractions of the uterus and lasts until the cervix reaches a dilation of about ten centimeters. The second stage begins with complete dilation of the cervix and ends with delivery of the baby. The third stage consists of the expulsion of the afterbirth — the placenta, the amniotic sac, the chorionic membranes, and the remainder of the umbilical cord. We will examine each of these stages briefly in the following sections.

The First Stage of Labor   The first stage — and the longest — begins with the onset of back pain and lower abdominal and uterine contractions. The rhythmic contractions become progressively better coordinated, and the cervix softens and begins to dilate. This stage lasts for an average of thirteen hours for first births and seven hours for subsequent births. In our society, when uterine contractions become very regular and are five to ten minutes apart, the woman is usually taken to a hospital, where an obstetrician or obstetrical nurse examines her vaginally to as-

certain the extent of the cervical dilation. It is important that the woman be observed carefully and frequently; maternal heart rate and fetal heart tones should be checked every fifteen to thirty minutes during the first stage of labor (Berkow et al. 1987). When the cervical dilation reaches a diameter of about ten centimeters, the woman is usually moved to the delivery room, and the first stage of labor merges into the second.[8] Fluid from the leaking or rupturing of the amniotic sac and the cervical mucous plug may be discharged at this time.

The Second Stage of Labor   The second stage of labor lasts about an hour for women having their first baby and about fifteen minutes for women having successive births (Berkow et al. 1987). It begins when the cervix is completely dilated and ends with the delivery of the baby.

The woman should be attended constantly during the second stage. Fetal tone should be checked after every contraction or every three minutes (Berkow et al. 1987). Uterine contractions of the mother and the heart rate of the fetus are routinely monitored through electronic sensors applied to the woman's abdomen; these sensors record the uterine contractions and the fetal heart rate and provide information that is important in evaluating and managing difficulties before they become critical (Berkow et al. 1987).

The woman can speed the birth process during the second stage of labor by tightening her diaphragm and her abdominal and back muscles to aid the uterine muscles in pushing the baby through the cervix. The woman's active participation at this point also seems to help reduce her discomfort. Sitting up during the delivery helps

---

[8]If the woman has elected to deliver in an *alternative birth center,* she remains in the same room throughout her labor and delivery and postpartum care. See the later section on such birth centers.

the mother use gravity to expel the baby, making the birth easier for both.

The physician may use drugs to relieve pain, but because drugs always have some harmful effect on the baby, it is advisable to limit their use (Berkow et al. 1987). All medications pass the placental barrier and reach significant levels in the fetus; thus a newborn is affected longer than the mother when medication is given to the woman to ease her pain during labor and delivery. The sedative effects of this level of medication are noticeable in the baby for a few days to a week after delivery (Brazelton 1990).

Taking sedatives during delivery can also affect the degree of bonding between the mother and her baby. Research indicates that when mothers and babies are alert and responsive to each other at delivery, bonding is significantly increased. The lasting effects of this initial bonding persist into childhood (Brazelton 1990; Klaus and Kennell 1982).

When anesthesia is used, regional (localized) anesthesia, such as epidural or spinal anesthesia, is much preferred to general anesthesia, which is now normally used only in complicated deliveries. With regional anesthesia, which is effective in both vaginal and caesarean deliveries, the woman stays awake and is able to participate actively in the birth of her baby (Brazelton 1990).

About 70 percent of women request some relief from pain during labor, whereas about 30 percent choose "natural childbirth" with no anesthetic.[9]

If uterine contractions weaken or stop during labor, the obstetrician may choose to assist the delivery by the use of forceps — tongs that fit around the baby's head. In the vast majority of cases, however, forceps are used only when the baby's head is visible or almost so (*low forceps*). If the head is not yet through the cervix, the procedure is known as *high forceps*, which is extremely dangerous for both mother (hemorrhage and infection) and baby (disfiguration and brain damage) and is used only when absolutely necessary (Reeder et al. 1987). Many more male babies than females have difficulty during birth, and their deliveries usually take an average of one hour longer than those of female babies (Jacklin 1989).

When the baby appears at the vaginal opening, the head turns so that the back of the skull emerges first. If it seems likely that the emerging head will tear the vaginal tissues, the obstetrician may make an incision (*episiotomy*) at the top of the perineum to enlarge the opening. However, a study of 1,000 births in Canada reported in 1992 that although episiotomy is performed in about 80 percent of all births in Canada and the United States, the operation produces no benefit in the prevention of injury or tearing of the birth canal; the study recommended that the routine use of episiotomy be abandoned (McGill University 1992).

Once the back of the skull has been squeezed out, the rest of the head quickly follows. The baby's body rotates so that the shoulders follow next. Because the head and shoulders of the baby are the largest part of the body, once they have passed through the vagina the torso and legs slip out quickly and easily, followed by the umbilical cord, which is still attached to the placenta.

Nearly 95 percent of births involve the normal *vertex presentation*, in which the baby's head emerges first. The remaining 5 percent are more difficult deliveries because the baby's buttocks (*breech presentation*), shoulders (*shoulder presentation*), foot (*incomplete breech*), or face (*brow presentation*) emerge first (Martin and Reeder 1991).

Median birth weights for newborns in 1988 were seven pounds nine ounces for whites and seven pounds for blacks; their average length was

---

[9]The American Society of Anesthesiologists and the American College of Obstetricians and Gynecologists survey, 1986.

about twenty inches, with females generally shorter than males and often lighter in weight.[10]

Immediately after the delivery, the baby's nose, mouth, and pharynx are aspirated with a bulb syringe to remove mucus and fluids that could obstruct breathing by being inhaled (Berkow et al. 1987). The obstetrician then places the baby on the mother's abdomen, where its weight helps in the later expulsion of the afterbirth. As the baby lies on the mother's abdomen, the obstetrician holds the umbilical cord, feeling for the pulsations of its blood vessels to stop. After the pulsations in the cord stop and the baby has taken its first breaths, the cord is clamped and cut (Berkow et al. 1987).

As soon as the cord is cut, antibiotic ophthalmic ointment or one drop of silver nitrate solution is applied to each of the baby's eyes to prevent *ophthalmia neonatorum*—a severe eye disease that can occur if the baby picks up an infection while passing through the birth canal. (The infection is frequently gonococcal.) This treatment is so important that it is mandatory by law in all fifty states (Berkow et al. 1987).

Before the baby leaves the delivery room, identifying bands are fastened around the wrists and ankles. Usually the baby's footprint is placed on the same identifying card as the mother's thumb print. The baby is then washed, wrapped in a warming blanket, placed in a crib, and taken to the nursery to be observed carefully, or the baby may be kept in a crib at the mother's side until she leaves the delivery room (Martin and Reeder 1991).

The Third Stage of Labor The third stage of labor occurs from two to twenty minutes after delivery of the baby and involves the expulsion of the *afterbirth*, which consists of the placenta, the amniotic sac, the chorionic membranes, and the remainder of the umbilical cord (see Figure C-5). The afterbirth is carefully examined for signs of abnormality and to make certain that all of it has been expelled; fragments left in the uterus can cause delayed hemorrhage (Berkow et al. 1987). While this is going on, the mother is usually given hormone injections to hasten the shrinkage of her uterus and to stimulate her milk production. If she does not wish to nurse her baby, she is given medication that will help dry up her milk. (See Box C-3.)

In the United States, the average hospital stay for a woman having a baby with vaginal delivery is two to three days (Martin and Reeder 1991). Physician and hospital fees for an uncomplicated delivery and immediate postpartum care averaged just over $4,000 in 1990 (Hewlett 1991).

The Caesarean Section

If the baby is too large to pass between the bones of the mother's pelvic arch or if the mother's or baby's physical condition makes the stress of childbirth dangerous, the baby is delivered by *caesarean section*, an operation in which delivery occurs through an incision in the mother's abdominal and uterine walls. (The name comes from the legend that Julius Caesar was born this way.)

The American College of Obstetricians and Gynecologists recommends that most women who had caesarean sections opt for vaginal deliveries in subsequent births, as all surgical procedures carry risks, and 50 to 80 percent of women who have had caesarean sections can later have successful vaginal deliveries (O'Sullivan 1988). Nearly one million babies born in the United States in 1990 were delivered by caesarean section; this is about 24 percent of all births, up from about 5 percent in 1970 (Wolfe 1992).

---

[10] U.S. National Center for Health Statistics, "Live Births, by Place of Delivery; Median and Low-Birth Weight; and Prenatal Care: 1960 to 1988" (1991).

BOX C-3

The Importance of Breast-Feeding

Nutritional needs of species vary widely, and substances in breast milk have been genetically developed through millions of years of evolution so that the milk is closely tailored to the offspring's needs; as a result, there is no ideal substitute for mother's milk. With human beings, for example, forty different substances in breast milk have been identified that are different from breast milk in other species. Research indicates that these substances stimulate human cells to grow, differentiate, and otherwise function normally; they also stimulate the immune system to provide protection against various allergies, stomach disorders, and inflammatory bowel diseases that may develop in infants and recur in adulthood (Koldovsky 1991). Thus, breast-fed babies have a higher resistance to infections than bottle-fed babies and a lower risk of contracting almost all common childhood diseases (Eibl 1988).

In addition to being more healthy physically, children who were breast-fed as infants are more advanced mentally than those who were bottle-fed, and psychologists believe that this added intelligence persists into adulthood. A study that compared children ages seven to eight who had been breast-fed with a matched group of children who had been bottle-fed found that the breast-fed group had an average IQ (Intelligence Quotient) of 104, as compared with an average IQ of 93 for children who had been bottle-fed as infants. This eleven-point difference in IQ is considered to be statistically significant because it is almost one-half a standard deviation (Lucus et al. 1992; Watson 1992; Coleman 1984).

Studies also indicate that breast-feeding encourages optimal development of the dental arch, making the need for future orthodontia much less likely (Hatcher et al. 1990). Finally, research finds that breast-feeding is more psychologically satisfying and fulfills more emotional needs than bottle feeding — for both the mother and the infant — facilitating closer bonding (Brazelton 1990; Hatcher et al. 1990).

The Apgar Score

One minute after delivery and again five minutes after delivery, the baby is rated on an evaluation scale called the *Apgar* scoring system, a useful and precise way of assessing the newborn's condition at birth. In this assessment, the newborn is given a rating of 0, 1, or 2 in each of the following five indexes: heart rate, respiratory effort, muscle tone, reflex irritability, and color. The optimum Apgar is 10. A score of below 7 suggests that the baby is having difficulty, and a score under 4 indicates that the baby's condition is critical (Berkow et al. 1987).

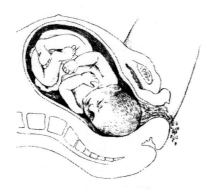

Uterine contractions, rupturing or leaking of the amniotic sac, and dilation of cervix

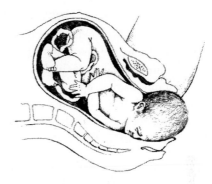

Baby's head seen at vaginal opening

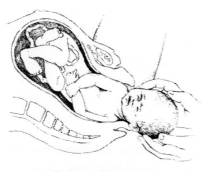

Delivery of the head

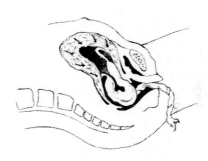

Expulsion of afterbirth

FIGURE C-5
Childbirth.

About half of all American infants receive high one-minute Apgar scores, and almost nine in ten receive high five-minute scores. However, black infants are twice as likely to receive low Apgar scores at one and five minutes after delivery, according to natality statistics.[11]

Following the delivery, the mother is transferred to a postpartum unit and is closely ob-served to make sure that the uterus is contracting and that no excessive bleeding is occurring.

Bonding

There is apparently an especially important time immediately following delivery during which "bonding" will occur if the mother and baby have

[11]Mothers of black babies were less likely than those of white babies to have received prenatal care during pregnancy, and this shows up clearly in the birth weights of black and white babies. Thirteen percent of black babies have a low birth weight, compared to 5.6 percent of white babies. U.S. National Center for Health Statistics, "Live Births, by Place of Delivery; Median and Low-Birth Weight; and Prenatal Care: 1960 to 1988" (1991).

sufficient close tactile (skin-to-skin) contact (see Chapter 10). Mothers who have extended contact with their babies during the first hours after birth demonstrate a higher quality of child care, a greater capacity for mothering, and a stronger commitment to the child than do mothers who do not have this early contact (Trevathan 1987; Spezzano and Waterman 1977; Klaus and Kennell 1976).

Premature Babies

A baby who is born before the thirty-seventh week of gestation is considered to be premature, regardless of birth weight (the normal time of gestation is forty weeks). More than 250,000 babies are born prematurely each year in the United States (Gross 1990).

Premature babies require special care and treatment if they are to survive, although the closer they are to full term, the healthier they are likely to be. Each week is important, so physicians try to keep the pregnancy going as long as possible. When the baby must be delivered, either because of fetal or maternal distress, the baby must be given special care immediately after delivery (Martin and Reeder 1991).

Although the physical and mental development of these babies is initially retarded, they may achieve normal physical and mental development by the second or third year if they are provided with optimal care (Gross 1990). Premature babies gain weight faster and leave the hospital sooner when they are frequently held by their mothers (and fathers) while hospitalized. Medical researchers report that a program of frequent holding and cuddling that begins immediately after birth quickly improves both physical and mental development of these infants. These discoveries are reversing the practice in many hospitals of prolonged separation of premature babies and their mothers (Gross 1990).

Participation of Fathers

Studies indicate that a major source of support for the woman in labor is the presence of the baby's father or a supportive companion. Fathers who wish to be present during labor and delivery are usually required to take childbirth education classes along with the woman toward the end of her pregnancy. Taking these classes together not only helps the woman through her labor and delivery but also promotes a strong bond between the prospective parents (Brazelton 1990).

Doulas

It is not always practicable for the father to be present during labor; he may not be available, or may not wish to participate, or the hospital may be too crowded and may not have the space to accommodate the father. Because the value of a supportive companion for the woman cannot be overestimated, many hospitals are engaging *doulas*, experienced women who assist the mother through labor and then through the initial stages of caring for the newborn infant. Studies indicate that women attended by a doula — from the admission stage through delivery — were less likely than other patients to request anesthesia and had shorter periods of labor than other patients (Kennell et al. 1991). Length of labor is negatively correlated with later problems with babies and children; the longer the labor, the greater the problems (Kraemer et al. 1985).

The Alternative Birth Center

A woman who is not in a high-risk category[12] may choose to deliver her baby in an *alternative birth center* — a special area of the maternity unit

---

[12]A woman is put in a high-risk category (and has the sophisticated resources of modern medicine available to her) if prenatal screening identifies such hazards as prematurity, a breech

in a hospital. The alternative birth center is a special area of the maternity unit in the hospital where labor, delivery, postpartum, and nursery care all take place in the same room, making it possible for the father and one other support person (often her labor coach) to spend as much time with her as she wishes during her hospital stay.

Although the alternative birth center is in a hospital setting, it nevertheless allows the mother to become actively involved with the baby almost immediately after birth and lets the father share the experience, thus enabling the newborn to have more attention and care than are provided in the communal nursery.

Hospitals began to make alternative birth centers available to their patients during the 1970s in response to protest movements directed against the depersonalization of the birth process. Protesters objected to the regimentation imposed by physicians and hospitals and emphasized that childbirth was a natural process, not an illness. The alternative birth centers in hospitals were designed to simplify delivery and strengthen the family unit (Kerner 1992). They have accomplished their purpose so well that they are now commonplace in the United States and Canada (Ryan 1988).

Nonhospital Birth Centers

Nonhospital birth centers began to be developed to parallel the emergence of alternative birth centers in hospitals. The nonhospital birth center provides an alternative for women who want to avoid a hospital setting entirely when they give birth to their babies. The first nonhospital ("free-standing") birth centers were developed to serve rural communities. Then, in 1975, the first urban nonhospital birth centers were established in New York City. These centers have apparently met a long-felt need and their popularity has grown rapidly; by 1989 there were 132 nonhospital birth centers in the United States. Most states require licenses for these centers, and patient costs are covered by most health insurance plans. The centers are more cost-effective than hospitals, with total charges for a delivery only one-third to one-half the usual hospital charge. About 20,000 babies are delivered each year in nonhospital birth centers (Rooks et al. 1989).

Certified Nurse-Midwives

Many large hospitals are now using certified nurse-midwives[13] for uncomplicated deliveries, freeing physicians to work with high-risk pregnancies (Russell 1992). According to the National Center for Health Statistics, nurse-midwives attended 123,000 births in 1989 — fully six times the number in 1975 (Russell 1992).

Infant Mortality Rates

As discussed in Chapter 9, infant mortality rates in the United States are among the highest in the industrialized world.[14] Infant mortality rates are correlated with low birth rates, the incidence of which has been climbing (see Chapter 9). Low birth weight is, in turn, correlated with level of education, smoking, alcohol and drug use, and race. Studies indicate that even when social

---

[13]In order to be certified, registered nurses must also complete at least a year of midwifery training in a program accredited by the American College of Nurse-Midwives (Russell 1992).

[14]U.S. National Center for Health Statistics, "Infant, Maternal, and Neonatal Mortality Rates, and Fetal Mortality Ratios, by Race: 1950 to 1989" (1992).

---

or transverse position of the baby, multiple births, an Rh problem, a too-small pelvis, diabetes, high blood pressure, or an active herpes infection (Berkow et al. 1987).

factors such as income, maternal education, marital status, maternal smoking, alcohol use, and health insurance have been controlled for, racial disparities in infant mortality persist (Wise and Pursley 1992). Researchers find that the mortality rate is significantly higher for black infants, even when they have college-educated parents; death is invariably related to low and very low birth weight (Schoendorf et al. 1992; Navarro 1990; Gould and LeRoy 1988). Why these racial disparities persist even when social variables are taken into account is a complex and puzzling issue (Wise and Pursley 1992).

Poor prenatal care is also a significant factor in the high rate of infant death. Since 1979 about 25 percent of all pregnant women in the United States have received late or no prenatal care (Sullivan 1992; Koop 1988).

GLOSSARY

abortifacient Usually defined as a drug that interrupts gestation during the embryo or fetal stage; may be defined as a drug or device that interrupts gestation earlier or prevents implantation of the blastocyst, although this is usually classified as *birth control.* (See also *germinal period, embryo, fetus.*)

abortion *Spontaneous abortion* is the interruption of gestation by a woman's own bodily processes; also called "miscarriage." *Induced abortion* is usually defined as the interruption of gestation two weeks or more after conception (after the germinal period) by the use of drugs or surgery. (See also *birth control.*)

acquaintance rape See *date rape.*

active listening Involves listening fully, completely, and intently — attempting to understand what the other person is saying without interrupting, arguing, or changing the subject.

adultery Copulation by a married person with someone other than his or her spouse.

agape A self-sacrificing, undemanding, "spiritual" love; satisfaction that a person feels when providing for the other.

AIDS (Acquired Immunodeficiency Syndrome) An STD caused by HIV infection; transmitted by contact with infected blood, semen, or vaginal secretions; incubation period an average of ten years; treatment may delay symptoms but there is no cure and no vaccine; death usually occurs within three years; now a worldwide pandemic. (See also *HIV.*)

altruistic love Characterized by giving and providing; the emotional satisfaction a person receives for nurturing another person. (See also *agape.*)

amniocentesis An important prenatal diagnostic procedure used in the second trimester of pregnancy; a hollow needle is inserted through the woman's abdomen and into the amniotic sac, and a sample of the amniotic fluid is drawn off; this fluid contains sloughed-off cells from the fetus that may be examined microscopically for signs of disease or genetic defects.

anabolism The building of tissue and heightened functioning of the immune system; associated with feelings of well-being.

androgen Often called the "male sex hormone," it is active in many ways, such as directing the differentiation of embryonic tissue into male genitalia, the differentiation of prenatal brain tissue that governs various male physiological functions, and the development of secondary gender characteristics at puberty; produced in the male's testicles and adrenal cortex and, to a lesser extent, in the female's ovaries and adrenal cortex.

annulment Invalidates or nullifies a marriage, in effect declaring that it never took place.

attachment The aspect of love that brings feelings of warmth, comfort, and security when the other is present or felt to be accessible.

birth control Avoiding conception or interrupting gestation during the first two weeks following a possible conception. (See also *abortifacient, abortion, contraception, menstrual regulation.*)

bisexual A person who is erotically attracted to a person of either gender. (See also *episodic homosexual.*)

blastocyst The organism that develops from the zygote and that contains the germinal disc; about two weeks after conception, the blastocyst is normally implanted in the uterine wall where the germinal disc normally develops into an embryo and then a fetus.

bonding Forming a close personal relationship, as between a mother and a child, between lovers, or between friends.

bride price Money or goods paid to the family of the bride by the family of the groom. (See also *dowry.*)

cash flow The relation between income and expenditures.

catabolism The breakdown of tissue and reduced functioning of the immune system; associated with a drop in general feelings of well-being.

cerebral erection Penile erection caused by psychological stimuli.

chlamydia A bacterial infection of the uterine lining and fallopian tubes; often causes a very dangerous pelvic inflammatory disease (PID) in women; usually less serious in men, causing difficult or painful urination, although the intensity of the symptoms varies; if the infection goes deeper it can affect the male sperm ducts and cause sterility. Now the most common STD in the United States.

chorionic villus sampling Medical procedure to test for genetic defects in fetuses during the first trimester.

clitoris The chief organ of erotic response in females, homologue of the male penis; consists of shaft and glans; extends with erotic arousal.

cohort A group sharing a statistical factor such as age, marital status, social class, or race.

coitus Copulation.

coitus reservatus Copulation without ejaculation; a method of contraception; notoriously ineffective.

commitment Stability, duration, dependability, and consistency in a relationship.

companionate love Emphasizes the trust and tolerance aspects of love; has strong overtones of liking, admiration, respect, and affection.

compound interest Interest that itself earns interest.

conflict A situation in which the needs of a couple are opposed, so that satisfaction for one person means deprivation for the other.

congenital An aberrant condition present at birth that is not caused by heredity.

contraception Literally means "against conception"; a procedure, device, or chemical designed to prevent fertilization of the ovum by the sperm. (See also *abortifacient, birth control.*)

convergent feedback Information that a behavior is bringing about a desired result; receiving a desired response to a behavior. (See also *divergent feedback.*)

copulation Insertion of the erect penis into the vagina; a significant source of intimacy and communication as well as erotic pleasure and satisfaction; the basis for reproduction.

courtly love Began in the twelfth century; embodied the devotion of a knight errant who swore eternal fidelity to his lady; the origin of the concept of romantic love.

crystallization A characteristic of limerence that exaggerates attractive qualities in the admired person while minimizing the unattractive ones.

culture The way that persons in a society or subsociety customarily behave and the implements, artifacts, institutions, and concepts that they characteristically use in their behavior.

cultural conditioning See *socialization.*

cunnilingus Oral stimulation of the clitoris, labia, and vagina.

date rape Rape that occurs with a date rather than with a stranger.

dating The basis for marital choice by mutual selection in our society but rare in most societies; also provides adventure, excitement, romance, and other sociosexual satisfactions; originated in the late nineteenth and early twentieth centuries; became generally accepted about 1920.

dating differential The tendency of a man to prefer women who are smaller, younger, somewhat less intelligent and less educated, and of somewhat lower status than himself and the tendency of women to prefer men who have the converse of these qualities. This cultural phenomenon results in a residue of relatively high-status women and low-status men who have difficulty in dating and marrying.

defense-oriented behavior Behavior directed toward alleviation of the stress and self-devaluation associated with the failure to achieve a basic need, rather than toward resolution of the basic need itself.

demography Study of statistical characteristics of people and populations.

developmental readiness The optimal periods in infants' and children's development; describes the neuromotor maturity necessary for learning a particular skill. If the child is not developmentally ready, the skill cannot be learned, whereas if the period of developmental readiness has passed, the learning of the skill is not challenging.

developmental sequence A pattern that children follow in proceeding from dependency to independence and from self-centeredness to other-centeredness.

dilemma A predicament in which a person must choose between two alternate behaviors, each of which interferes with fulfilling the other; often resolved by trying to do both.

discipline Setting limits on behavior and inducing wanted behavior that eventually becomes self-perpetuating.

displacement A defense mechanism that involves moving (or displacing) the actual cause of a frustration to another, more acceptable or safer cause.

divergent feedback Information that a behavior is not bringing about a desired result; receiving an unwanted response to a behavior; enables one to modify the behavior in order to obtain convergent feedback. (See also *convergent feedback*.)

DNA molecules (deoxyribonucleic acid) Contained within each gene, these complex, chainlike, double-helix structures encode the information of heredity in molecular form and direct all cell activities.

dowry Money or goods paid to the bridegroom or his family by the family of the bride.

dyspeurnia Painful copulation.

economic determinism The doctrine that many important cultural patterns — as well as individual behavior — stem from economic forces.

economic well-being Access to goods and services by both paid and unpaid work plus access to leisure time.

ejaculate Seminal fluid.

ejaculation The discharge of seminal fluid from the penis.

ejaculatory control The ability to delay ejaculation while maintaining an erection and perhaps experiencing one or more orgasms.

embryo The developing organism from the second to the sixth week of pregnancy. (See also *fetus*.)

endogamy The inclination or the necessity to marry within a particular group.

episiotomy A surgical incision made in the mother's perineum during childbirth to prevent tearing of the tissues of the birth canal; no longer recommended as a routine procedure.

episodic homosexual A person who has occasional homosexual experiences or episodes but is primarily heterosexual. (See also *obligatative homosexual*, *bisexual*.)

erection The penis, engorged with blood, becomes stiff and hard, and projects out from the body. (See also *cerebral erection*, *reflex erection*.)

erogenous zones Areas of the body that are erotically responsive to tactile stimuli.

eros A passionate, sensual, sexual love.

erotic Pertaining to sexual stimulation and pleasure.

erotic response The result of appropriate and sustained erotic stimuli; has four phases: excitement, plateau, orgasm, and resolution.

erotophile Someone who enjoys erotic stimulation. (See also *hyperphilia*.)

erotophobe Someone who dislikes or is bored by erotic stimulation. (See also *hypophilia*.)

estrogen Often called the "female sex hormone"; active in many ways such as directing the differentiation of embryonic tissue into female genitalia, governing various female physiological functions, and directing the development of female secondary gender characteristics at puberty. Produced chiefly in the ovaries and adrenal cortex of the female and, to a lesser extent, in the testicles and adrenal cortex of the male.

ethnic group A subsociety that shares the same customs, language, social views, and cultural origins and that is embedded in a larger and ethnically different society.

ethnicity Common customs, language, social views, and cultural origins.

euphoria A sense of extreme well-being.

exogamy The inclination or the necessity to marry outside a particular group.

extended family Nuclear family plus the couple's kin.

extrinsic Derived externally or from without. (See also *intrinsic*.)

family process Four essential processes that must be present before any group (such as a family) can function effectively: commitment, cohesion, communication, and maintenance of the group's boundaries.

family system Consists of some form of courtship, some form of marriage, and some form of the family; universally found in all human societies.

feedback Information received by a person about the effects of his or her behavior. (See also *convergent feedback*, *divergent feedback*.)

fellatio Oral stimulation of the penis.

fetal alcohol syndrome (FAS) An affliction of babies whose mothers drink heavily during pregnancy; characterized by abnormal facial features, central nervous system disorders, and mental retardation.

fetish An object (such as a shoe) that is necessary for a person (fetishist) to experience sexual arousal; an erotic fixation upon a particular aspect of another person (such as a foot).

fetus The developing organism from six weeks after conception to birth. (See also *embryo*.)

forced alternate choice The concept that using money to buy one item eliminates the possibility of buying another item; an important principle in the management of cash flow and the basis for making a budget.

foreskin Extension of the loose skin of the penile shaft that covers the glans.

frenum The area of the glans just below the meatus where the foreskin is attached; normally the most erotically sensitive area of a man's body.

frigid A woman who is nonorgasmic or sexually aversive; usually a hypophiliac or erotophobe. The term *preorgasmic* is replacing the term *frigid*.

frustration Being blocked in obtaining an important satisfaction; also, the feelings of depression or anger that occur with significant deprivation; often combined with feelings of self-devaluation.

gamete The germ cell; either the sperm in the male or the egg (ovum) in the female.

gender Maleness and femaleness; comprised of the physical characteristics, social behavior, and gender identity associated with one's maleness or femaleness; physical, psychological, behavioral, societal, and cultural characteristics that differentiate boys from girls and men from women in a society.

gender identity Core of a person's self-image as a male or female; begins to take definite form at about age three and is usually well established by about age five.

gender role Behavior that a society regards as more appropriate for one gender than the other; universally found in all human societies.

gender-role revolution The changing of gender roles from the 1960s to the 1990s with "men's work" and "women's work" redefined, the percentage of women in paid employment rising, the birthrate dropping, the marriage rate dropping, the divorce rate rising, and the proportion of women not marrying rising. Economically, women's and children's well-being has declined.

gender-role socialization The indoctrination of the individual into a pattern of gender-linked behaviors, expectations, and attitudes characteristic of the society.

genes The subcellular structures within the chromosomes in the cell nucleus that are built of DNA molecules; determine the behavior of all cells and thus program much of the behavior of the individual (genetic programming).

genetically programmed behavior Behavior that originates from genetic factors rather than from experience.

germinal disc The part of the blastocyst that will develop into a human being.

germinal period The first two weeks of pregnancy from the formation of the zygote in the fallopian tube to the embedding of the blastocyst in the uterine wall.

gestation The period between conception and birth. (See *embryo, fetus, germinal period*.)

glans The cone-shaped head of the penis; about one-fourth of the penile length; a primary erogenous zone.

glass ceiling The concept that most women are limited in the advancement they can make in a business or professional career.

gonads The organs that produce the gametes (sperm or egg); testicles in the male and ovaries in the female.

gonococcus The microorganism that causes gonorrhea.

gonorrhea An STD caused by gonococci; usually localized in the genitalia and is self-limiting, although it may persist and cause serious and permanent damage, including sterility. Symptoms are easily identified in men, but the disease is often asymptomatic (without symptoms) in women and difficult to detect.

G-spot An area between the vagina and the abdominal wall that is erotically sensitive in some women; not verified by anatomists.

Hepatitis B A disease that may cause severe liver damage; transmitted by infected blood; vaccine effective before it is contracted, thereafter not effective and there is no adequate treatment; most infections have no symptoms but carrier is highly infectious to others; second most deadly STD among men (after AIDS).

hermaphrodite A person who has both male and female organs or organs that are indeterminate (such as a clitoris that resembles a penis).

Herpes II Genital herpes; an STD that has been spreading rapidly throughout the world; difficult to treat and incurable; highly contagious; a baby may be infected by the mother at birth with serious, even fatal, consequences.

heterogamy The mutual attraction of people with opposite traits such as dominance-submission or nurturance-dependence ("opposites attract"); although widely believed to exist, research has failed to verify.

heterosexual A person who is erotically attracted to people of the opposite gender. (See also *homosexual*.)

HIV (Human Immunodeficiency Virus) The virus that causes AIDS by invading the immune system and then multiplying within white blood cells.

homogamy Mutual attraction of people who share similar characteristics, such as race, religion, ethnic group, intelligence, education, social class, age, interests, and skills.

homologue Developed from the same prenatal tissue. For example, the same tissue will develop into a penis or a clitoris depending on the prenatal hormone mix present, which in turn depends on the presence (or absence) of sex chromosomes (XX in the female, XY in the male).

homosexual A person who is erotically attracted to people of the same gender.

hormones Chemical messengers secreted into the bloodstream by endocrine glands to help regulate the body's physiological processes.

hymen A membrane that partially covers the vaginal opening; ruptured by initial copulation or by sports or other activities; absent in some females.

hyperphilia A very strong sex drive or interest in erotic stimulation.

hyperphiliac A person characterized by hyperphilia; an erotophile.

hypophilia A very low sex drive or disinterest in or aversion to erotic stimulation.

hypophiliac A person characterized by hypophilia; an erotophobe.

immune system Highly efficient network of many different types of cells that attack and destroy invaders that enter the body.

impotence The inability of a man to experience erection; caused by either physical or psychological factors and usually temporary.

incest Copulation between blood relatives; the degree of closeness that is considered incestuous varies from state to state, but all states define copulation between children and parents, children and grandparents, and brother and sister as incest.

infancy The period from the second month after birth to the time when a baby is walking and beginning to talk (usually about twelve to fifteen months).

installment contract Legal agreement between the purchasers and the dealer for the financed (delayed payment) purchase of a specific item.

intimacy Experiencing the essence of one's self in intense physical, intellectual, and emotional communion with another; while all three factors are always present, the physical aspect may be emphasized by some intimates, whereas with others the intellectual or the emotional aspects may be more important.

intrinsic Derived internally or from within. (See also *extrinsic*.)

isolates People who have very little social interaction.

jealousy Emotion we feel when a satisfaction that we have been receiving from someone is withdrawn from us and given to someone else.

labia majora The larger outer lips of the vulva.

labia minora The smaller inner lips of the vulva.

lactation Producing milk in the mammary glands after giving birth.

laparoscopy A simple female sterilization procedure that does not require major abdominal surgery.

"latch-key" children Children who are unsupervised for part of the day.

lesbianism Female homosexuality.

leveling Speaking openly, honestly, and undefensively to another person; when combined with active listening, this produces good communication.

limerence An aspect of love that is characterized by a compulsive attachment to another person; thoughts of the other may occupy up to 90 percent of the limerent person's consciousness; accompanied by feelings of extreme joy when reciprocated and of extreme pain when it is not.

love Very complex emotion whose many components make it very difficult to define; usually understood to encompass bonding, intimacy, and commitment.

love map An idealized version of the type of person one is mentally "programmed" to be erotically attracted to or fall in love with.

ludus Playful, flirtatious love.

masochist A person who experiences pain as erotically arousing.

mass society An industrialized and urbanized society that is characterized by massive production, massive consumption, widespread manipulation of taste, highly specialized institutional and individual roles, a relative decline of primary relationships, and a proliferation of secondary relationships.

mastery skills Ability to manipulate objects; to build and construct things.

masturbation Stimulation of an erogenous zone by one's self; typically involves tactile stimulation of the penis in the male and the clitoris and adjoining areas in the female; may or may not include orgasm; may include orgasm but not ejaculation in the male. (See also *ejaculatory control*.)

meatus The opening in the tip of the glans through which urine, pre-ejaculatory fluid, and semen are discharged; a primary erogenous zone.

menarche The beginning of ovulation and the menstrual cycle in women.

menopause The end of ovulation, menstruation, and fertility in women; usually occurs between ages forty-five and fifty in our society.

menstrual cycle The monthly cycle of ovulation, engorgement of the uterine wall with blood and nutrients, and expulsion of this material through the vagina — called menstruation — when the ovum is not fertilized; ceases with menopause.

menstrual regulation Aspirating (vacuuming out) the endometrium (lining) of the uterus during the first two weeks following a possible conception; also called *vacuum curettage*. (See also *germinal period*.)

mons The fleshy mound just above the vulva; a primary erogenous zone in some women.

neonate The newborn during the first month after birth.

no-fault divorce Replaces concept of divorce as a contest with divorce by mutual agreement; has made divorce easier to obtain; intended to reduce deception in divorce and unfair alimony; it has had the unintended result of economic deprivation for women and children; first enacted in California in 1970 and now available, in some form, in all states.

noncustodial parent The parent in a divorce action who is not granted physical custody of the children.

normophilia Sexual acts that are regarded as normal; this judgment varies from person to person, time to time, and subculture to subculture. (See also *hyperphilia, hypophilia, paraphilia*.)

nymphomania Hyperphilia in a woman.

obligative homosexual Someone who is erotically aroused only by a member of the same gender. (See also *episodic homosexual*.)

orgasm A sudden release of sexual tension, usually accompanied by pronounced physiological changes, by ejaculation in the postpubertal male, and by a profound sense of well-being, in part because of heightened levels of testosterone and oxytocin in the bloodstream. (See also *oxytocin*.)

ovary The female gonad; produces egg cells (ovulation).

ovulation The rupture of an ovarian follicle and release of a mature ovum; part of the menstrual cycle.

ovum Egg cell.

oxytocin The "pleasure hormone"; heightened levels in the bloodstream are associated with anabolism and feelings of well-being; relatively low levels in the bloodstream are associated with catabolism and lowered feelings of well-being. (See also *anabolism, catabolism*.)

paired bond A couple who have formed a bond. (See also *bonding*.)

paraphilia Abnormal sexual behavior; perversion. (See also *hyperphilia, hypophilia, normophilia*.)

pedophile Someone who sexually abuses a child.

pedophilia Sexual abuse of a child; a type of paraphilia.

penis A male sex organ; usually flaccid, is engorged with blood during the excitement phase of erotic response and becomes erect and hard; during copulation may ejaculate semen containing sperm cells into the vagina; a primary erogenous zone. (See also *glans, shaft of the penis*.)

perineum The area between the anus and the scrotum in men and the anus and the vulva in women; a primary erogenous zone for many people.

philos A type of love characterized by deep, enduring friendship.

phobia An illogical compulsive fear.

photoplethysmograph A device placed just inside the entrance of the vagina to measure degree of vasocongestion, and thus the erotic response in a woman.

PID (Pelvic Inflammatory Disease) Infection of the pelvic area, mainly the fallopian tubes and uterus; caused by gonorrhea, chlamydia, and other infections; the second most dangerous STD for women (after AIDS).

placenta The organ, developing from the chorionic villi, that joins the fetus to the uterine tissue; serves as the medium for the metabolic exchange between the pregnant woman and the fetus.

PMS (premenstrual syndrome) Feeling ill, irritable, or depressed just before the onset of menstruation.

polyandry A form of marriage in which a woman has more than one husband; very rare in the world's societies.

polygamy Multiple marriage, either polyandry or polygyny.

polygyny A form of marriage in which a man has more than one wife; approved in most of the world's societies.

position A sociological term for a socially defined relationship carrying a prescribed role, such as "boyfriend," "girlfriend," "wife," "husband." (See also *role*.)

post-coital depression Feelings of dejection or sadness following copulation instead of the normal elation; usually related to guilt or shame regarding erotic activity.

postpartum After birth.

preejaculatory fluid A clear, viscous fluid that the erect penis may secrete during the excitement and plateau phases of erotic arousal; begins to appear about two years before puberty; after puberty may contain enough sperm cells to impregnate a woman during copulation without ejaculation.

preintimates People who have a low need for intimacy, prefer privacy and independence, and thus may live and work alone by choice. (See also *isolates, pseudointimates.*)

prenatal Before birth.

prepubertal orgasm An orgasm before puberty; not accompanied by ejaculation.

primary gender characteristics The biological characteristics of men and women directly related to reproduction; sperm production and ejaculation in men and ovulation, menstruation, and lactation in women.

primary relationship A relationship characterized by affection, respect, informality, immediacy, spontaneity, and intimacy. (See also *secondary relationship.*)

progesterone A female hormone (known as the pregnancy hormone) produced in the corpus luteum; its function is to prepare the uterus for the reception and development of a fertilized ovum.

progestin A synthetic hormone related in chemical structure to the male hormone androgen; a component of the birth-control pill.

propinquity Closely related in time and space.

pseudointimates People who appear to be in an intimate relationship but really are not; they have social interactions but these are superficial. (See also *isolates, preintimates.*)

puberty The beginning of sperm production and ejaculation in the male and ovulation and menstruation in the female.

psychoendocrine The effect of hormones upon emotions and behavior as well as upon physiological responses.

punishment Deliberate infliction of deprivation, discomfort, pain, or suffering; may stop a behavior if applied immediately following the behavior if the punishment is informative (the person understands why the punishment was applied), if there is no strong motivation to continue the behavior, and if there is no emotional involvement with the punishment such as feelings of resentment or betrayal.

quickening The first fetal movements that the pregnant woman can feel, usually at about the seventeenth week following conception.

quid pro quo Latin term meaning "something for something."

race Anthropologists do not agree on the definition of race; the U.S. Census Bureau recognizes four races: (1) white, (2) black, (3) American Indian, Aleut, and Eskimo, and (4) Asian and Pacific Islander.

rape Forcible copulation by the use of force or the threat of force; copulation without mutual desire; copulation without the consent of the person being assaulted, male or female. (See also *date rape.*)

reflex erection Penile erection caused by tactile stimulation.

refractory period Characteristics of the resolution phase of erotic response in the male during which he is physiologically incapable of responding to erotic stimulation; may last from a few minutes to several hours, or a day or more, depending on such factors as age, nutrition, fatigue, and erotic interest.

reinforcement Consequence of behavior that causes the behavior to happen more often.

role Expected behavior of a person in a socially recognized position. (See also *position.*)

role function Purpose the role behavior serves; usually measured in terms of goods or services provided.

role interaction Reciprocal behavior between two people relating to one another in mutually accepted positions; each is performing behavior expected by the other in a relationship. (See also *position.*)

role taking Effective technique for resolving a conflict so that no one wins or loses; each person describes the other's role to the other's satisfaction, verbally assuming or "taking" the other's role.

romantic love Tender and idealistic love, idyllic, imaginative, and adventurous.

sadist A person who derives erotic pleasure from inflicting pain or suffering on another person.

salpingectomy Major abdominal surgery in which the fallopian tubes are surgically cut and tied off to prevent conception.

satyriasis Hyperphilia in a man.

scrotum The sac that holds the testicles.

secondary gender characteristics The physical characteristics that emerge at puberty as a function of the sex hormones, such as physical size and strength, breast development, hair distribution, skin thickness, fat distribution; great individual variation. (See also *primary gender characteristics.*)

secondary relationship A relationship that is formal, impersonal, highly structured, and functional.

self Complex and difficult to define precisely; in general, what we mean when we say *I, me,* or *mine;* essential qualities of a person that tend to be enduring and provide perceptual continuity.

self-esteem Respect for and confidence in oneself; central to the development of a fully functioning, productive, creative, contented child or adult.

self-image One's perception of one's self as a unique individual.

separation distress Painful emotion that occurs when a person to whom one is attached is not present or felt to be accessible; often characterized by profound feelings of devastation, insecurity, and loneliness.

sex hormones Hormones secreted by the gonads; responsible for the development of the primary and secondary gender characteristics.

sexual harassment Unwanted physical or psychological sexual aggression; may be illegal in some situations, for example if the aggressor is taking advantage of a position of authority.

sexual love Love with a strong erotic component; passionate love.

shaft of the penis A cylindrical body composed chiefly of erectile tissue surrounding the urethra; makes up about three-fourths of the penile length; a primary erogenous zone. (See also *glans.*)

social class Convenient but imperfect index of a person's position in the social hierarchy; based on amount and source of income, occupation, level of education, and nature and location of residence.

socialization The process of learning (from parents, siblings, peers, social institutions, and other sources) the information, knowledge, skills, and patterns of behavior characteristic of a society.

society Difficult to define precisely; in general, an aggregate of people in an association that has some measure of permanence and has a common culture.

spectatoring A problem with copulation caused by being self-consciously aware of one's performance and focusing on it rather than upon the feelings and sensations of the moment.

sperm cells The male cell of reproduction.

spermicides Chemical substances that kill or immobilize sperm; used as contraceptives.

spirochete A spiral-shaped microorganism that causes syphilis.

stepfamily Family that has a stepparent and stepchildren.

storge Calm, companionate love.

subculture The culture of a subsociety.

subsociety The larger society is usually composed of a number of smaller groupings, each with its own distinctive subculture.

sudden infant death syndrome (SIDS) Respiratory distress for no apparent reason; leading cause of death in babies during their first year; more common among babies whose mothers smoked during pregnancy.

syphilis Major STD caused by spirochetes; goes through four stages, each with separate and distinct characteristics; can involve every part of the body; transmitted by contact of mucous membrane or broken skin with an infectious syphilitic lesion.

tactile Pertaining to the sense of touch.

testicle The male gonad; produces sperm cells and testosterone.

testosterone An important component of the male sex hormone androgen; responsible for inducing and maintaining male secondary gender characteristics from puberty throughout adulthood; level of testosterone in the bloodstream is positively correlated with anabolism, effective functioning of the immune system, and feelings of well-being. (See also *anabolism, catabolism.*)

transsexual A person who feels trapped in the body of the wrong gender; occurs when a person's gender identity is not in accordance with his or her biology and gender-role socialization.

transvestite Someone who periodically feels compelled to wear clothes of the opposite gender (cross-dress) and to be accepted in a social situation as a member of the opposite gender (pass).

trimester The three-month periods of pregnancy.

uterus The thick-walled, expandable female organ that contains, protects, and nurtures the developing blastocyst, embryo, and fetus.

vagina The elastic sex organ of a female that extends from the lips of the erotically sensitive external genitalia to the cervix, the opening to the uterus; receives the erect penis during copulation; relatively insensitive with few nerve endings, therefore not a major organ for erotic response. (See also *clitoris.*)

vaginismus Spontaneous contraction of the vagina; may be associated with dyspeurnia.

value Measure of how much something (an object, activity, information, wealth, power, or love) is wanted or prized; one will do something to obtain a valued object, situation, or experience and nothing to avoid it; the higher the value, the more energy one will expend to attain it.

vasocongestion The flow of blood into veins and capillaries causing the tissue to become engorged and, in the case of an erogenous zone, to become erotically sensitive and responsive.

voyeurism A paraphilia in which a person (voyeur) may only be sexually aroused and then satisfied by viewing nudity or erotic activities.

vulva External genitalia of the female, consisting of the labia majora, labia minora, clitoris, and opening of the vagina.

withdrawal Withdrawing the penis from the vagina before ejaculating as a method of contraception; notoriously ineffective; also called *coitus interruptus*.

womb The uterus.

X chromosome Chromosome that determines female traits; all eggs and slightly fewer than one-half of all sperm carry an X chromosome.

Y chromosome Chromosome that determines male traits; slightly more than one-half of all sperm carry a Y chromosome.

zygote Fertilized egg after it has begun to divide.

BIBLIOGRAPHY

Abrahamse, A. F.; Morrison, P. A.; and Waite, L. J. *Beyond Stereotypes: Who Becomes a Single Mother?* Santa Monica, CA: Rand Corporation, 1988.

Abramson, Jill. "Image of Anita Hill, Brighter in Hindsight, Galvanizes Campaigns." *Wall Street Journal,* October 5, 1992, pp. A-1, A-4.

Achenbach, T. M., and Edelbrock, C. S. "Behavioral Problems and Competencies Reported by Parents of Normal and Disturbed Children Aged 4 through 16." *Monographs of the Society for Research in Child Development* 46 (1981): 1.

Adams, Bert N. and Adams, Diane. "Child Care and the Family." In 2001: *Preparing Families for the Future,* pp. 18–19. Minneapolis, MN: National Council of Family Relations Presidential Report, 1990.

Ahrons, Constance R., "The Binuclear Family: Two Households, One Family." *Alternative Lifestyles* 2 (1979): 499–515.

Ahrons, Constance R., and Rodgers, R. *Divorced Families.* New York: W. W. Norton, 1987.

Ahrons, Constance R., and Wallisch, L. "The Close Relationship between Former Spouses." In S. Duck and D. Perlman (eds.), *Close Relationships: Development, Dynamics, and Deterioration,* pp. 269–96. Beverly Hills, CA: Sage, 1986.

Agnew, R., and Huguley, S. "Adolescent Violence Towards Parents." *Journal of Marriage and the Family* 51 (1989): 699–711.

Albiston, C. R.; Maccoby, E. E.; and Mnookin, R. H. "Joint Legal Custody." *Stanford Law Policy Review* 1 (1990): 101–115.

Allen, Laura, and Gorski, Roger. "Evidence of Differences in Brains of Gay Men." Published in the Proceedings of *The National Academy of Sciences.* Washington, DC: August, 1, 1992.

American Humane Association. "Child Maltreatment Cases Reported—Summary: 1976 to 1986." *National Study on Child Neglect and Abuse Reporting,* annual. Denver, CO, 1991.

American Jewish Yearbook. "Estimates of the Number of Jews Holding Membership in Synagogues or Temples of the Branches of Judaism." New York, 1991.

American Society of Anesthesiologists and the American College of Obstetricians and Gynecologists. "Survey of Analgesia Given During Labor: 1986." *San Francisco Chronicle,* September 22, 1988, p. A-6.

Anderson, Bernice; Mead, Nancy; and Sullivan, Susan. "Television: What Do National Assessment Results Tell Us?" Princeton, NJ: National Assessment of Educational Progress, December 1986.

Anderson, Roy M., and May, Robert M. "Understanding the AIDS Pandemic." *Scientific American* 266 (May 1992): 58–66.

Anderson, S. "The Adult Incest Survivor: Protocol for the Treatment of Rape and Other Sexual Assault." *Nurseweek/California Nursing* (March/April 1992): 20–21.

Andrews, Bernice, and Brewin, Chris R. "Attributes of Blame for Marital Violence: A Study of Antecedents and Consequences." *Journal of Marriage and the Family* 52 (August 1990): 757–67.

Andrews, Bernice, and Brown, G. W. "Marital Violence in the Community: A Biographical Approach." *British Journal of Psychiatry* 153 (1988): 305–312.

Angelo, Bonnie. Interview with Toni Morrison, "The Pain of Being Black." *Time,* May 22, 1989, pp. 120–22.

Angier, Natalie. "Pleasure Hormone Reveals New Facets." *San Francisco Chronicle,* January 22, 1991, p. A-2.

Angyal, A. *Neurosis and Treatment: A Holistic Theory.* New York: John Wiley, 1965.

Arevalo, Jose A., and Washington, A. Eugene. "Cost-effectiveness of Prenatal Screening and Immunization for Hepatitis B Virus." *Journal of the American Medical Association* 259 (1988): 365–69.

Aral, Sevgi O., and Holmes, King K. "Sexually Transmitted Diseases in the AIDS Era." *Scientific American* 264 (February 1991): 62–69.

Arditti, Joyce. "Noncustodial Fathers: An Overview of Policy and Resources." *Family Relations* 39 (October 1990): 460–65.

Ariès, Phillipe. *Centuries of Childhood.* New York: Vintage, 1965.

Aronoff, Joel, and Krano, William D. "A Reexamination of the Cross-Cultural Principles of Task Segregation and Sex-Role Differentiation in the Family." *American Sociological Review* 40 (February 1975): 12–20.

Asimov, Nanette. "How Schools Shortchange Girls." Adapted from American Association of University Women Report. *San Francisco Chronicle,* February 12, 1992, pp. A-1, A-12.

Asmundsson, R., et al. "Life in Remarriage Families." Paper presented at the annual meeting of the American Association for Marriage and Family Therapy, Washington, DC, 1983.

Astin, Alexander W.; Green, Kenneth C.; and Korn, William S. *The American Freshman: Twenty Years of Trends.* Los Angeles: Higher Education Institute, 1987, p. 23.

Auchnicloss, Douglas. "The Gay Crowd." In Joe David Brown (ed.), *Sex and the Sixties,* pp. 65–75. New York: Time-Life Books, 1968.

Avery, Caryl S. "How Do You Build Intimacy in an Age of Divorce?" *Psychology Today* 23 (May 1989): 27–31.

Axelrod, S., and Apsche, J., eds. *The Effects of Punishment on Human Behavior.* New York: Academic Press, 1983.

Azadzoi, Kazem M., et al. "Endothelium-derived Nitric Oxide and Cyclooxygenase Products Modulate Corpus Cavernosum Smooth Muscle Tone." *Journal of Urology* 147 (January 1992): 220–25.

Bach, George R., and Wyden, Peter. *The Intimate Enemy: How to Fight Fair in Love and Marriage.* New York: Avon, 1970.

Baldwin, Wendy, and Nord, Christine. "Delayed Childbearing in the U.S.: Facts and Fictions." *Population Bulletin*, Population Reference Bureau, Inc., Vol. 39, No. 4. Washington, DC: Government Printing Office, November 1984.

Baptiste, David A. "How Parents Intensify Sexual Feelings Between Stepsiblings." *Remarriage* 3 (1986): pp. 5–6.

Bardwick, Judith M. *Psychology of Women.* New York: Harper College Books, 1971.

Barinaga, Marcia. "Is Homosexuality Biological?" *Science* 253 (August 30, 1991): 956–57.

Barlow, Brent A. "Notes on Mormon Interfaith Marriages." *The Family Coordinator* 26 (April 1977): 143–50.

Baron, R. A., and Byrne, D. *Social Psychology.* 6th ed. Boston: Allyn & Bacon, 1991.

Basow, Susan A. *Gender Stereotypes: Traditions and Alternatives.* Belmont, CA: Wadsworth, 1986.

Baumeister, Roy F. "The Optimal Margin of Illusion." *Journal of Social and Clinical Psychology* 8 (1989): 176–89.

Baumrind, Diana. "Authoritarian Versus Authoritative Parental Control." *Adolescence* 3 (1968): 255–72.

———. "Current Patterns of Parental Authority." *Developmental Psychology Monographs* 41 (1979): 255–41.

Beecher, Catherine E. *A Treatise on Domestic Economy, 1841.* New York: Schocken, 1977.

Behrman, R., and Vaughan, V. *Nelson Textbook of Pediatrics.* 13th ed. Philadelphia: W. B. Saunders, 1987.

Bell, Robert R. *Marriage and Family Interaction.* 6th ed. Homewood, IL: Dorsey, 1983.

Bell, Robert R., and Coughey, Kathleen. "Premarital Sexual Experience Among College Females, 1958, 1968, and 1978." *Family Relations* 29 (July 1980): 353–56.

Bellah, Robert N.; Madsen, Richard; Sullivan, William M.; Swidler, Ann; and Tipton, Steven M. *Habits of the Heart: Individualism and Commitment in American Life.* Berkeley and Los Angeles: University of California Press, 1985.

Bellanti, J., et al. "Immunology of the Fetus and Newborn." In G. Avery, *Neonatology: Pathophysiology and Management of the Newborn*, 3rd ed. Philadelphia: Lippincott, 1987.

Belle, Deborah. "Poverty and Women's Mental Health." *American Psychologist* 45 (March 1990): 385–89.

Benacerraf, Beryl R.; Gelman, Rebecca; and Frigoletto, D. "Sonographic Identification of Second-Trimester Fetuses with Down's Syndrome." *New England Journal of Medicine* 317 (1987): 1371–76.

Benderly, Beryl Lieff. *The Myth of Two Minds: What Gender Means and Doesn't Mean.* New York: Doubleday, 1987.

Bengston, Vern L. "Aging, the Family, and the Future." In M. Bergener (ed.), *Perspectives on Aging: The 1986 Sandoz Lectures in Gerontology.* New York: Academic Press, 1986.

Bennett, Neil G.; Blanc, Ann Klimas; and Bloom, David E. "Commitment and the Modern Union: Assessing the Link Between Premarital Cohabitation and Subsequent Marital Stability." *American Sociological Review* 53 (1988): 127–38.

Berger, P., and Kellner, H. "Marriage and the Construction of Reality." In H. P. Dreitzel (ed.), *Recent Sociology*, Vol. 2. New York: Macmillan, 1970.

Berk, R.; Newton, P.; and Berk, S. F. "What a Difference a Day Makes: An Empirical Study of the Impact of Shelters for Battered Women." *Journal of Marriage and the Family* 48 (1986): 481–90.

Berk, S. F. *The Gender Factory: The Apportionment of Work in American Households.* New York: Plenum Press, 1985.

Berkow, Robert, et al., eds. *The Merck Manual of Diagnosis and Therapy.* 15th ed. Rathway, NJ: Merck, 1987.

Berliner, Lucy. "Deciding Whether a Child Has Been Sexually Abused." In E. B. Nicholson and J. Bulkley, *Sexual Abuse Allegations in Custody and Visitation Cases.* Washington, DC: American Bar Association, 1988.

Bernard, Jessie. *Remarriage: A Study of Marriage.* New York: Russell, 1971.

Berne, Eric. *Games People Play.* New York: Grove Press, 1967.

Berry, Ruth E., and Williams, Flora L. "Assessing the Relationship Between Quality of Life and Marital and Income Satisfaction: A Path Analytic Approach." *Journal of Marriage and the Family* 49 (February 1987): 107–16.

Berscheid, Ellen, and Peplau, Letitia Ann. "The Emerging Science of Relationships." In Harold H. Kelley et al. (eds.), *Close Relationships*, pp. 1–19. New York: W. H. Freeman, 1983.

Berscheid, Ellen; Walster, Elaine; and Bohrnstedt, G. "Body Image." *Psychology Today* 6 (1972): 57–66.

Bieber, Irving, et al. *Homosexuality: A Psychoanalytic Study.* New York: Basic Books, 1962.

Biegel, H. G. "Romantic Love." *American Sociological Review* 16 (1951): 326–34.

Billy, John; Landale, Nancy; and McLaughlin, Steven. "The Effect of Marital Status at First Birth on Marital Dissolution Among Adolescent Mothers." *Demography* 23 (1986): 329–49.

Blankenhorn, David, and Sacks, Ivan A. "How the Child Care Market Works: An Economic Analysis." Working Paper Publication No. WPI. New York: Institute for American Values, March 1989.

Blood, Robert O., and Wolfe, Donald W. *Husbands and Wives: The Dynamics of Married Living.* New York: Free Press, 1960.

Blumstein, Philip, and Schwartz, Pepper. *American Couples.* New York: Pocket Books/Simon & Schuster, 1983.

Bodovitz, Kathy. "Black America." *American Demographics Desk Reference* 1 (July 1991a): 8, 10.

———. "Hispanic America." *American Demographics Desk Reference* 1 (July 1991b): 14–15.

Bodowitz, Kathy, and Edmonson, Brad. "Asian America." *American Demographics Desk Reference* 1 (July 1991): 16, 18.

Bohannon, Paul. *All the Happy Families.* New York: McGraw-Hill, 1985.

Booth, Alan, and Johnson, David. "Premarital Cohabitation and Marital Success." *Journal of Family Issues* 9 (1988): 255–72.

Bootzin, Richard R., et al. *Psychology Today.* 6th ed. New York: Random House, 1986.

Boss, P., and Greenberg, J. "Family Boundary Ambiguity: A New Variable in Family Stress Theory." *Family Process* 23 (1984): 535–46.

Bowlby, John. *Attachment and Loss.* Vols. 1–2. New York: Basic Books, 1973.

Boyer, Debra, and Fine, David. "Sexual Abuse as a Factor in Adolescent Pregnancy and Child Maltreatment." *Family Planning Perspectives* 24 (January/February 1992): 4–11, 19.

Bradley, Robert H. "Fathers and the School-Age Child." In Shirley M. H. Hansen and Frederick W. Bozett (eds.), *Dimensions of Fatherhood.* Beverly Hills, CA: Sage, 1985.

Brannigan, Martha. "Warring Couples Shun Divorce Mediators and Opt to Battle It Out in Court Instead." *Wall Street Journal,* March 27, 1990, pp. B-1, B-9.

Brauer, Alan, and Brauer, Donna. "ESO (Extended Sexual Orgasm)." *Playboy,* July 1984, p. 40.

Brazelton, T. Berry. *What Every Baby Knows.* New York: Ballantine Books, 1987.

———. *The Earliest Relationship: Parents, Infants, and the Drama of Early Attachment.* Reading, MA: Addison-Wesley, 1990.

Brecher, Edward M., and Brecher, Ruth, eds. *An Analysis of Human Sexual Response.* Boston: Little, Brown, 1966.

Brecher, Edward M. (and the Editors of Consumer Reports Books). *Love, Sex, and Aging: A Consumer's Union Report.* Boston: Little, Brown, 1984.

Brock, Connie. "Menopause." *Human Behavior* 8 (April 1979): 38–46.

Brody, Gene; Neubaum, E.; and Forehand, R. "Serial Marriage: A Heuristic Analysis of an Emerging Family Form." *Psychological Bulletin* 103 (1988): 211–22.

Bronowski, J. *The Ascent of Man.* Boston: Little, Brown, 1973.

Bronstein, Phyllis. "Sex Roles Remain." *Science News* 124 (1983): 172.

Brown, Ina. *Understanding Other Cultures.* Englewood Cliffs, NJ: Prentice-Hall, 1963.

Brown, Judith K. "A Note on the Division of Labor, by Sex." *American Anthropologist* 72 (1970): 1073–78.

Brown, Roger. *Social Psychology: The Second Edition.* New York: Free Press, 1986.

Brunsman, B. *New Hope for Divorced Catholics.* San Francisco: Harper & Row, 1985.

Bucuvalas, J., and Ballistreri, W. "The Neonatal Gastrointestinal Tract: Development." In A. Fanaroff and R. Martin (eds.), *Neonatal-Perinatal Medicine,* 4th ed. St. Louis: C. V. Mosby, 1987.

Bumpass, Larry L. "Children and Marital Disruption: A Replication and Update." *Demography* 21 (1984a): 71–82.

———. "Demographic Aspects of Children's Second Family Experience." *American Journal of Sociology* 90 (1984b): 608–23.

———. Panel discussion on the results of a 1987 cohabitation survey by Larry L. Bumpuss, James A. Sweet, and Andrew Cherlin. Annual meeting of the Population Association of America, San Francisco, March 30, 1989.

———. "What's Happening to the Family? Interactions between Demographic and Institutional Change." Presidential Address, annual meeting of the Population Association of America. *Demography* 27 (1990): 483–98.

Bumpass, Larry L., and Sweet, James A. "Children's Experience in Single-parent Families: Implications of Cohabitation and Marital Transitions." National Survey of Families and Households Working Paper No. 3, Center for Demography and Ecology, University of Wisconsin, 1989a.

———. "Differentials in Marital Stability, 1970." *American Sociological Review* 37 (1972): 754–66.

———. "National Estimates of Cohabitation." *Demography* 26 (1989b): 615–25.

Bumpass, Larry L.; Sweet, James A.; and Castro-Martin, Teresa. "Changing Patterns of Remarriage." *Journal of Marriage and the Family* 52 (1990): 747–56.

Bumpass, Larry L.; Sweet, James A.; and Cherlin, Andrew. "The Role of Cohabitation in Declining Rates of Marriage." *Journal of Marriage and the Family* 53 (1991): 913–27.

Burns, David. *Intimate Connections.* New York: Signet, 1986.

Burns, Mark, et al. "A Preliminary Evaluation of the Gonozyme Test." *Sexually Transmitted Diseases: Journal of the American Venereal Disease Association* 10 (October–December 1983): 180–83.

Burt, M. "Estimating the Public Costs of Teenage Childbearing." *Family Planning Perspectives* 18 (1986): 221–226.

Buss, David M. "Human Mate Selection." *American Scientist* 73 (1985): 47–51.

———. "Toward an Evolutionary Psychology of Human Mating." *Behavioral and Brain Sciences* 12 (March 1989): 39.

Buss, David M., and Barnes, Michael. "Preferences in Human Mate Selection." *Journal of Personality and Social Psychology* 50 (1986): 559–70.

Butler, Robert. *Why Survive? Being Old in America.* New York: Harper & Row, 1985.

Buunk, Bram P. "Strategies of Jealousy: Styles of Coping with Extramarital Involvement of the Spouse." *Family Relations* 31 (1982): 13–18.

Buunk, Bram P., and van Driel, Barry. *Variant Lifestyles and Relationships.* Newbury Park, CA: Sage, 1989.

Byrne, Donn. "A Pregnant Pause in the Sexual Revolution." *Psychology Today* 11 (July 1977): 67–68.

Callan, Victor J. "Voluntary Childlessness: Early and Late Deciders." *Journal of Biosocial Science* 16 (1984): 501–9.

Campbell, A. "The Roots of Aggression." In A. Campbell (ed.), *The Opposite Sex,* pp. 64–69. Topsfield, MA: Salem House, 1989.

Campbell, A.; Converse, P. E.; and Rodgers, W. L. *The Quality of American Life.* New York: Russell Sage Foundation, 1976.

Canter, R. J., and Ageton, S. S. "The Epidemiology of Adolescent Sex-Role Attitudes." *Sex Roles* 11 (1984): 657–76.

Carlson, B. E. "Dating Violence: A Research Review and Comparison with Spouse Abuse." *Social Casework* 68 (1987): 16–23.

Carter, Hodding. "Housing Costs Create a New Privileged Class: Home Buyer." *Wall Street Journal,* December 13, 1990, p. A-13.

Carter, Hugh, and Glick, Paul C. *Marriage and Divorce: A Social and Eco-*

nomic Study. Rev. ed. Cambridge, MA: Harvard University Press, 1976.

Case, Robert B.; Moss, A. J.; Case, N.; and McDermott, M. "Living Alone After Myocardial Infarction: Impact on Prognosis." *Journal of the American Medical Association* 267 (January 22/29, 1992): 515–19.

Cash, Thomas F., and Janda, Louis H. "The Eye of the Beholder." *Psychology Today* 18 (December 1984): 46–52.

Castro-Martin, Teresa, and Bumpass, Larry L. "Recent Trends and Differentials in Marital Disruption." *Demography* 26 (1989): 37–51.

Cazenave, Noel A. "Race, Socioeconomic Status, and Age: The Social Context of American Masculinity." *Sex Roles* 11 (1984): 639–56.

Cazenave, Noel A., and Straus, Murray A. "Race, Class, Network Embeddedness, and Family Violence: A Search for Potential Support Systems." *Journal of Comparative Family Systems* 10 (1979): 281–300.

Cernea, M. *Changing Society and Family Change: The Impact of the Cooperative Farm on the Peasant Family*. Stanford, CA: Center for Advanced Study in Behavioral Sciences, 1970.

Charles, Andrew V. "Physically Abused Parents." *Journal of Family Violence* 4 (1986): 343–55.

Cherlin, Andrew J. "Remarriage as an Incomplete Institution." *American Journal of Sociology* 84 (1978): 634–50.

———. *Marriage, Divorce, Remarriage*. Cambridge, MA: Harvard University Press, 1981.

———. "Marriage, Divorce, Remarriage: From the 1950s to the 1980s." Paper presented at the American Sociological Association, San Francisco, August 11, 1989.

———. *Marriage, Divorce, Remarriage*. Rev. ed. Cambridge, MA: Harvard University Press, 1990.

Cherlin, Andrew J., and Furstenberg, F. F., Jr. *The New American Grandparent: A Place in the Family, A Life Apart*. New York: Basic Books, 1986.

Chess, S., and Thomas, A. "Inherent Bonding: Mystique and Reality." *American Journal of Orthopsychiatry* 52 (1982): 213–22.

Chess, Stella, and Thomas, Alexander. *Know Your Child*. New York: Basic Books, 1987.

Chicago Title Insurance Company National Survey. "Recent Home Buyers — General Characteristics: 1976–1989." In *Statistical Abstract of the United States*, 111th ed., p. 732. Washington, DC: Government Printing Office, 1991.

Chickering, A. Lawrence. "A Matter of Extra Interest: Pay Heed to the Credit Card Statement's Fine Print — or Pay More." *San Francisco Chronicle*, March 24, 1992, p. A-6.

Children's Defense Fund. *A Vision for America's Future, An Agenda for the 1990s: A Children's Defense Budget*. Washington, DC: 1989, pp. 16–17.

Chin, James. "Current Dimensions of the HIV/AIDS Virus Pandemic in Women and Children." *Lancet* 336 (July 28, 1990): 221–24.

Clanton, Gordon, and Smith, Lynn G., eds. *Jealousy*. Englewood Cliffs, NJ: Prentice-Hall, 1977.

Clement, U.; Schmidt, G.; and Kruse, M. "Changes in Sex Differences in Sexual Behavior: A Replication of a Study on West German Students, 1966–1981." *Archives of Sexual Behavior* 13 (1984): 99.

Clingempeel, W. G.; Ievoli, R.; and Brand, E. "Structured Complexity and the Quality of Stepfather-Stepchild Relationships." *Family Process* 23 (1984): 547–60.

Cohan, Henry. "Marriage Penalty Unfair to Taxpayers." *San Francisco Chronicle*, March 2, 1992, p. B-5.

Coie, J. D.; Dodge, K. A.; and Kupersmidt, J. "Peer Group Behavior and Social Status." In S. Asher and J. Coie (eds.), *The Rejected Child*. New York: Cambridge University Press, 1988.

Colditz, Graham A., et al. "Cigarette Smoking and Risk of Stroke in Middle-Aged Women." *New England Journal of Medicine* 318 (April 14, 1988): 937–41.

Coleman, James C. *Contemporary Psychology and Effective Behavior*. 4th ed. Glenview, IL: Scott, Foresman, 1979.

———. *Abnormal Psychology and Modern Life*. 7th ed. Glenview, IL: Scott, Foresman, 1984.

Coleman, Marilyn, and Ganong, Lawrence H. "Remarriage and Stepfamily Research in the 1980s: Increased Interest in an Old Family Form." *Journal of Marriage and the Family* 52 (1990): 925–40.

Coleman, Marion Tolbert. "The Division of Household Labor." In Rae Lesser Blumberg (ed.), *Gender, Family, and Economy*. Newbury Park, CA: Sage, 1991.

Collins, Randall, and Coltrane, Scott. *Sociology of Marriage and the Family*. 3rd ed. Chicago, IL: Nelson-Hall, 1991.

Coltrane, Scott, and Ishii-Kuntz, Masako. "Men's Housework and Child Care: A Life Course Perspective." Paper presented at the annual meeting of the American Sociological Association, Washington, DC, August 1990.

Comfort, Alex. *The New Joy of Sex: A Gourmet Guide to Lovemaking for the Nineties*. New York: Crown, 1991.

Conger, John. Lecture Series, Smithsonian Institution, Fall 1991. Reported by Nina Youngstrom in the *APA Monitor* 23 (March 1992): 4.

Connecticut Remarriage Research Group. "Life in Remarriage Families." Paper presented at the meeting of the American Association for Marriage and Family Therapy, Washington, DC, 1983.

Connolly, William G. *The New York Times Guide to Buying or Building a Home*. New York: Times Books, 1985.

Conrad, P., and Schneider, J. W. *Deviance and Medicalization: From Badness to Sickness*. St. Louis, MO: C. V. Mosby, 1980.

Coolfont Report: A PHS Plan for Prevention and Control of AIDs and the AIDS Virus. *U.S. Public Health Report* 101 (1986): 341–48.

Cook, Paddy Shannon; Petersen, Robert C.; and Moore, Dorothy Tuell. *Alcohol, Tobacco, and Other Drugs May Harm the Unborn*. DHHS, Publication No. (ADM) 90-1711. Rockville, MD: Public Health Service, 1990.

Cooney, Teresa, and Uhlenberg, Peter. "The Role of Divorce in Men's Relation with Their Adult Children After Mid-Life." *Journal of Marriage and the Family* 52 (August 1990): 677–88.

Coombs, Robert H., and Landsverk, John. "Parenting Styles and Substance Use During Childhood and Adolescence." *Journal of Marriage and the Family* 50 (1988): 473–82.

Cornell, C. P., and Gelles, R. J. "Adolescent to Parent Violence." *Urban Social Change Review* 15 (1982): 8–14.

Corsaro, William A., and Eder, Donna. "Children's Peer Cultures." *Annual Review of Sociology* 16 (1990): 197–220.

Corzine, William L. "The Phenomenon of Jealousy: A Theoretical and Empirical Analysis." Ph.D. dissertation, United States International University, San Diego, 1974.

"Cost of Caring for Drug Babies." Memorandum to Van McMurtry, staff director, Senate Finance Committee, from Senator Lloyd Bentsen, November 15, 1989, p. 1.

Cowan, Carolyn Pope, and Cowan, Philip A. "Fatherhood in Transition." *Science News* 124 (1983): 172.

Crawley, Lawrence; Malfetti, James L.; Stewart, Earnest I., Jr.; and Vas Dias, Nini. *Reproduction, Sex, and Preparations for Marriage.* 2nd ed. Englewood Cliffs, NJ: Prentice-Hall, 1973.

Creasy, R., and Resnik, R., eds. *Maternal-Fetal Medicine: Principles and Practice.* 2nd ed. Philadelphia: W. B. Saunders, 1989.

"Crisis in Adolescent Health." Report by the Office of Technology Assessment, Washington, DC, April 22, 1991.

Crispell, Diane. "How to Avoid Big Mistakes." *American Demographics* 13 (March 1991a): 48–50.

———. "Blurred Boundaries." In Marketing Tools Alert, news supplement to *American Demographics* 15 (August 1991b): 1.

———. "Immigrant Impact Grows on U.S. Population." *Wall Street Journal*, March 16, 1992, p. B-1.

Cromie, William J. "Everyone's Private Bubble." *Enterprise Science News*, January 8, 1978.

Culp, R. E.; Cook, A. S.; and Housley, P. C. "A Comparison of Observed and Reported Adult-Infant Interactions: Effects of Perceived Sex." *Sex Roles* 9 (1983): 475–479.

Cunningham, Ann Marie. "The Pill Turns 30." *San Francisco Chronicle*, "This World," July 15, 1990, pp. 15–16.

Cunningham, F., et al. *William's Obstetrics.* 18th ed. Norwalk, CT: Appleton & Lange, 1989.

Curran, J. W.; Jaffe, H. W.; Hardy, A. M.; et al. "The Epidemiology of HIV Infection and AIDS in the United States." *Science* 239 (1988): 610–16.

Currie, Elliott, University of California at Berkeley. Quoted in Clarence Johnson and William Carlson's "Economic Despair Among Blacks," *San Francisco Chronicle*, May 2, 1992, p. A-22.

Cutler, Blayne. Senior Editor, *Demographic Magazine.* Quoted in *San Francisco Chronicle*, September 19, 1989, p. B-5.

Cutright, Phillips, and Polanto, Karen. "Areal Structure and Rates of Childlessness Among American Wives in 1970." *Social Biology* 24 (Summer 1977): 52–61.

Danzinger, Sheldon, and Stern, Jonathan. "The Causes and Consequences of Child Poverty in the United States." UNICEF, International Child Development Center, Project on Child Poverty and Deprivation in Industrialized Countries, 1990.

Davis, Rabbi David, Chairman Judaic Studies, University of San Francisco. Private correspondence, February 28, 1992.

Davis, Keith E. "Near and Dear: Friendship and Love Compared." *Psychology Today* 19 (February 1985): 22–30.

Davis, Kingsley. "The American Family in Relation to Demographic Change." In Charles F. Westoff and Robert Parke, Jr. (eds.), *Demographic and Social Aspects of Population Growth*, pp. 235–65. Commission on Population Growth and the American Future. Washington, DC: Government Printing Office, 1972.

Dawson, Deborah. "Family Structure and Children's Health and Well-Being: Data from the 1988 National Health Interview Survey on Child Health." *Journal of Marriage and the Family* 53 (1991): 573–84.

DeBuono, Barbara A.; Zinner, Stephen H.; Daamen, Maxim; and McCormak, William M. "Sexual Behavior of College Women, in 1985, 1986, and 1989." *The New England Journal of Medicine* 322 (March 22, 1990): 821–25.

DeGruttola, Victor. "Latency Period of AIDS." Paper presented at the International Symposium on AIDS, San Francisco, September 23, 1988.

Demos, J. *A Little Commonwealth: Family Life in Plymouth Colony.* London: Oxford University Press, 1970.

Devereux, George. "A Typological Study of Abortion in 350 Primitive, Ancient, and Preindustrial Societies." In Harold Rosen (ed.), *Abortion in America.* Boston: Beacon Press, 1967.

deVita, Carol, and Bouvier, Leon. "The Baby Boom — Entering Midlife." Washington, DC: Population Reference Bureau, January 3, 1992.

Dewitt, Paula M. "All the Lonely People." *American Demographics* 14 (April 1992): 44–48.

Dias, P. L. R. "The Effects of Vasectomy on Testicular Volume." *British Journal of Urology* 55 (1983): 83–84.

Dick, Everett. *The Sawed House Frontier: 1854–1890.* Lincoln, NE: Johnsen, 1954.

Dickens, Charles. *A Tale of Two Cities.* New York: Oxford University Press, 1926.

Doherty, William J. "New Information on Post-Divorce." *Family Therapy News* 20 (January–February 1989): 1–2.

Dolnick, Edward. "The Mystery of Superwoman." *San Francisco Chronicle*, July 16, 1991, pp. D-3, D-4.

Doress, Paula Brown, et al. "Women Growing Older." In *The New Our Bodies, Ourselves* by the Boston Women's Health Collective, pp. 435–72. New York: Simon & Schuster, 1984.

Dorfman, John R. "Which Assets Have Performed Best?" *Wall Street Journal*, June 6, 1989, p. C-1.

Douglas, John H., and Miller, Julie Ann. "Record Breaking Women." *Science News* 112 (September 10, 1977): 172–74.

Downey, Kirsten. "Typical Buyer: A Vanishing Breed." *Washington Post*, February 10, 1990, p. E-1.

Draughon, M. "Stepmother's Model of Identification in Relation to Mourning in the Child." *Psychological Reports* 36 (1975): 183–89.

Dryfoos, J. "School-Based Health Clinics: A New Approach to Preventing Adolescent Pregnancy." *Family Planning Perspectives* 17 (1985): 70–75.

Dullea, Georgia. "Men Asking More in Premarital Pacts." *San Francisco Chronicle*, July 8, 1988.

Duncan, Greg J., and Hoffman, Saul D. "A Reconsideration of the Economic Consequences of Marital Dissolution." *Demography* 22 (November 1985): 485–97.

Dunnigan, Phillip. Lieutenant of police, San Francisco. Private discussion, February 20, 1992.

Dutton, D. G. *The Domestic Assault of Women: Psychological and Criminal Justice Perspectives.* Toronto: Allyn & Bacon, 1988.

Eastman, Peggy. "Empty Nest Zest." *AARP Bulletin* 33 (January 1992): 2.

Edwards, John N., and Demo, David H., eds. *Marriage and Family in Transition.* Boston, MA: Allyn & Bacon, 1991.

Egeland, Byron. Study of Children Born to High-Risk Families. Paper presented to the annual meeting of the American Association for the Advancement of Science, San Francisco, January 18, 1989.

Egeland, Byron; Jacobvitz, Deborah; and Stroufe, L. Alan. "Breaking the Cycle of Abuse." *Child Development* 59 (1988): 1080–88.

Eggebeen, David, and Uhlenberg, Peter. "Changes in the Organization of Men's Lives: 1960–1980." *Family Relations* 34 (April 1985): 255.

Ehrlich, Ryan L., and Finnegan, L. "Cocaine Abuse in Pregnancy: Effects on the Fetus and Newborn." *Neurotoxicology and Teratology* 9 (1988): 315–19.

Eibl, Martha M., et al. "Prevention of Necrotizing Enterocolitis in Low-Birth Weight Infants by IgA-IgG Feeding." *New England Journal of Medicine* 319 (July 7, 1988): 1–7.

Ellwood, David T., and Crane, Jonathan. "Family Change Among Black Americans: What Do We Know?" *Journal of Economic Perspectives* 4 (1990): 65–84.

Elster, A., and Lamb, M. *Adolescent Fatherhood.* Hillsdale, NJ: Lawrence Erlbaum Associates, 1986.

Emery, Robert E. *Marriage, Divorce, and Children's Adjustment.* Beverly Hills, CA: Sage, 1988.

Emery, Robert E.; Hetherington, E. Mavis; and DiLalla, L. F. "Divorce, Children, and Social Policy." In H. W. Stevenson and A. E. Siegel (eds.), *Child Development Research and Social Policy.* Chicago: University of Chicago Press, 1985.

Emini, Emilio, Director of Merck's basic AIDS research. Quoted in "New Discoveries Dim Drug Maker's Hopes for Quick AIDS Cure," reported by Michael Waldholtz in *Wall Street Journal,* May 26, 1992, p. A-11.

Emslie, G. J., and Rosenfeld, A. "Incest Reported by Children and Adolescents Hospitalized for Severe Psychiatric Disorder." *American Journal of Psychiatry* 140 (1983): 708–11.

Englander, Debra Wishik. "How to Get the Best Loan." *Redbook,* February, 1992, pp. 46–52.

Erikson, Erik H. *Childhood and Society.* 2nd ed. New York: W. W. Norton, 1963.

Eshleman, J. R. *The Family: An Introduction.* 6th ed. Boston: Allyn & Bacon, 1991.

Exter, Thomas G. "Birthrate Debate." *American Demographics* 13 (September 1991): 55.

"Fact Sheet" prepared for hearing before the Select Committee on Children, Youth and Families, U.S. House of Representatives, "Caring for New Mothers: Pressing Problems, New Solutions," October 24, 1989.

Fagan, J. A.; Stewart, D. K.; and Stewart, K. W. "Situational Correlates of Domestic and Extra-domestic Violence." In D. Finkelhor, R. Gelles, G. Totaling, and M. Straus (eds.), *The Dark Side of Families: Current Family Violence Research,* pp. 49–67. Beverly Hills, CA: Sage, 1983.

Faller, Kathleen Coulborn. *Child Sexual Abuse: An Interdisciplinary Manual for Diagnosis, Case Management, and Treatment.* New York: Columbia University Press, 1988.

———. *Understanding Child Sexual Maltreatment.* Newbury Park, CA: Sage, 1990.

Farley, Reynolds, and Allen, Walter R. *The Color Line and the Quality of Life in America.* New York: The Russell Sage Foundation, 1987.

Fathalla, Mahmoud. "Reproductive Health, A Key to a Brighter Future." Report from the World Health Organization (WHO). Geneva, June 24, 1992.

Feinman, S. "A Status Theory of the Evaluation of Sex-Role and Age-Role Behavior." *Sex Roles* 10 (1984): 445–56.

Festinger, Leon. "Architecture and Group Membership." *Journal of Social Issues* I (1951): 152–63.

Finch, B. F., and Green, Hugh. *Contraception Through the Ages.* Springfield, IL: C. C. Thomas, 1963.

Fiumara, N. J. "Trichomoniasis." *Medical Aspects of Human Sexuality* 20 (1986): 33, 36.

Flax, Carol. "Columbia University Survey on Sex, Eroticism, and Sensuality." *San Francisco Chronicle,* October 25, 1984, p. 10.

Fletcher, Cynthia Needles. "A Comparison of Incomes and Expenditures of Male-Headed Households Paying Child Support and Female-Headed Households Receiving Child Support." *Family Relations* 38 (1989): 412–17.

Force, Elizabeth S. "Aging and Family Life." In *2001: Preparing Families for the Future.* Minneapolis, MN: National Council on Family Relations Presidential Report, 1990, pp. 20–21.

Ford, C. S., and Beach, F. A. *Patterns of Sexual Behavior.* New York: Harper & Row, 1970.

Forgas, J. P., and Dobosz, B. "Dimensions of Romantic Involvement: Towards a Taxonomy of Heterosexual Relationships." *Social Psychology Quarterly* 43 (1980): 290–300.

Forrest, J. D., and Fordyce, R. R. "U.S. Women's Contraceptive Attitudes and Practice: How Have They Changed in the 1980s?" *Family Planning Perspectives* 20 (1988): 112.

Forrest, J. D., and Singh, Susheela. "The Sexual and Reproductive Behavior of American Women, 1982–1988." *Family Planning Perspectives* 22 (September/October 1990): 206–14.

Forsyth, C. J., and Fournet, L. "A Typology of Office Harlots: Mistresses, Party Girls, and Career Climbers." *Deviant Behavior* 8 (1987): 319.

Fraker, Susan. "Why Women Aren't Getting to the Top." *Fortune,* April 16, 1984, pp. 40–45.

Francke, Linda Bird. *Growing Up Divorced.* New York: Fawcett Crest, 1983.

Freedman, Daniel G. "Ethnic Differences in Babies." *Human Nature* 2 (January 1979): 36–43.

Freeman, Ruth, and Klaus, Patricia. "Blessed or Not? The New Spinster in England and the United States in the Late Nineteenth and Twentieth Centuries." *Journal of Family History* 9 (Winter 1984): 394–414.

Freud, Sigmund. *The Basic Writings of Sigmund Freud.* Edited by A. A. Brill. New York: Modern Library, 1938.

Friedan, Betty. *The Feminine Mystique.* New York: Norton, 1963.

Friedland, G. H., and Klein, R. S. "Transmission of Human Immunodeficiency Virus." *New England Journal of Medicine* 317 (1987): 1125–35.

Fries, James F. *Aging Well*. New York: Addison-Wesley, 1989.

Fromm, Erich. *The Art of Loving*. New York: Bantam, 1970.

Fuchs, Victor R. *Women's Quest for Economic Equality*. Cambridge, MA: Harvard University Press, 1988.

Fuchs, Victor R., and Reklis, Diane M. "America's Children: Economic Perspectives and Policy Options." *Science* 255 (January 3, 1992): 41–46.

Furillo, Andy. "Writer's Aspiring to Passionate Prose." *San Francisco Examiner*, July 29, 1990, p. 18.

Furstenberg, Frank F., Jr. "Child Care After Divorce and Remarriage." In E. M. Hetherington and J. Arasteh (eds.), *The Impact of Divorce, Single Parenting and Stepparenting on Children*. Hillsdale, NJ: Erlbaum, 1988.

——. "Divorce and the American Family." *Annual Review of Sociology* 16 (1990): 379–403.

Furstenberg, Frank F. Jr.; Brooks-Gunn, Jeann; and Chase-Landsdale, Lindsay. "Teenaged Pregnancy and Childbearing." *American Psychologist* 44 (February 1989): 313–20.

Furstenberg, Frank F. Jr., and Cherlin, Andrew J. *Divided Families*. Cambridge, MA: Harvard University Press, 1991.

Furstenberg, Frank F., Jr., and Harris, Kathleen Mullan. "The Disappearance of the American Father? Divorce and Waning Significance of Biological Parenthood." Draft, Department of Sociology, University of Pennsylvania, March 1990, p. 4.

Furstenberg, Frank F. Jr.; Morgan, Philip; and Allison, Paul. "Paternal Participation and Children's Well-Being After Marital Disruption." *American Sociological Review* 52 (1986): 695–701.

Furstenberg, Frank F. Jr., and Nord, C. W. "The Life Course of Children of Divorce: Marital Disruption and Parental Contact." Paper presented at the annual meeting of the Population Association of America, San Diego, April 29– May 1, 1982.

——. "Parenting Apart: Patterns of Childrearing After Marital Disruption." *Journal of Marriage and the Family* 47 (1985): 893–904.

Furstenberg, Frank F. Jr.; Nord, C. W.; Peterson, J. L.; and Zill, N. "The Life Course of Children and Divorce: Marital Disruption and Pa-

rental Conflict." *American Sociology Review* 48 (1983): 656–88.

Furstenberg, Frank F. Jr., and Spanier, Graham B. *Recycling the Family: Remarriage After Divorce*. Updated ed. Newbury Park, CA: Sage, 1987.

Gallup, George Jr. "Good Family Life Tops Priority List." Gallup Poll. *San Francisco Chronicle*, February 27, 1989a, p. B-6.

——. "Intolerance Is on the Rise in U.S." Gallup Poll. *San Francisco Chronicle*, March 6, 1989b, p. A-12.

Gallup Organization. "Religious Preference, Church Membership, and Attendance: 1957 to 1989." *Statistical Abstract of the United States*, 111th ed. Washington, DC: Government Printing Office, 1991, p. 55.

Garbarino, James. *The Psychologically Battered Child: Strategies for Identification, Assessment, & Intervention*. San Francisco: Jossey-Bass, 1986.

Garfinkel, Irwin, and Oellerich, Donald. "Noncustodial Fathers' Ability to Pay Child Support." *Demography* 26 (1989): 219–33.

Gause, Ralph W. "Sexually Transmitted Diseases, Part I." *American Baby* 49 (November 1987): 64, 69.

Gelinas, D. J. "The Persisting Negative Effects of Incest." *Psychiatry* 46 (1983): 312–32.

Gelles, Richard. "Abused Wives: Why Do They Stay?" *Journal of Marriage and the Family* 33 (1976): 659–68.

Gelles, Richard J., and Cornell, Claire Pedrick. *Intimate Violence in Families*. 2nd ed. Newbury Park, CA: Sage, 1990.

Gelles, Richard J., and Straus, Murray A. *Intimate Violence*. New York: Simon & Schuster, 1988.

Gerson, Marvin; Portnoy, Joseph; and Hammelin, Claude. "Reliable Identification of Herpes Simplex Viruses by DNA Restriction Endonuclease Analysis with ECORI." *Sexually Transmitted Diseases: Journal of the American Venereal Disease Association* 2 (April–June 1984): 85–90.

Gibbs, Nancy. "How America Has Run Out of Time." *Time*, April 24, 1989, p. 58.

Gibbs, R. S., and Mead, P. B. "Preventing Neonatal Herpes — Current Strategies." *New England Journal of Medicine* 326 (April 2, 1992): 946–47.

Giles-Sims, Jean. "The Stepparent Role: Expectations, Behavior, Sanctions." *Journal of Family Issues* 5 (1984): 116–30.

Glasier, Anna, et al. "RU-486 Effective as Contraceptive." *San Francisco Chronicle*, October 8, 1992, p. A-3.

Glass, Shirley P., and Wright, Thomas L. "The Relationship of Extramarital Sex, Length of Marriage, and Sex Differences on Marital Satisfaction and Romanticism: Athanasiou's Data Reanalyzed." *Journal of Marriage and the Family* 39 (November 1977): 692.

Glenn, Norval D. "Interreligious Marriage in the United States: Patterns and Recent Trends." *Journal of Marriage and the Family* 44 (1982): 555–68.

——. "The Family Values of Americans." Paper prepared for the Wingspread Commission on the Family in America, Institute for American Values Working Paper No. WP7, 1991.

Glenn, Norval D., and Kramer, Kathryn B. "The Marriages and Divorces of the Children of Divorce." *Journal of Marriage and the Family* 49 (1987): 563–76.

Glenn, Norval D., and Supancic, Michael. "The Social and Demographic Correlates of Divorce and Separation in the United States: An Update and Reconsideration." *Journal of Marriage and the Family* 46 (1984): 563–75.

Glick, Paul C. "Remarriage: Some Recent Changes and Variations." *Journal of Marriage and Family Issues* 1 (1980): 455–79.

——. "Marriage, Divorce, and Living Arrangements." *Journal of Family Issues* 5 (1984): 7–26.

——. "Remarried Families, Stepfamilies, and Stepchildren." Paper presented at the Wingspread Conference on the Remarried Family, Racine, WI, 1987.

——. "Fifty Years of Family Demography: A Record of Social Change." *Journal of Marriage and the Family* 50 (November 1988): 861–73.

——. "Marriages and Family Trends." In *2001: Preparing Families for the Future*. Minneapolis, MN: National Council on Family Relations Presidential Report, 1990, pp. 2–3.

——. Quoted in Jan Larsen, "Understanding Stepfamilies" in *American Demographics* 14 (July 1992): 36.

Glick, Paul C., and Lin, Sung-Ling. "Remarriage After Divorce: Recent Changes and Demographic Variations." *Sociological Perspectives* 30 (1987): 162–79.

Glick, Paul C., and Norton, Arthur J. "Marrying, Divorcing, and Living Together in the United States Today." *Population Bulletin* Vol. 32, No. 5. Washington, DC: Population Reference Bureau, 1977.

Goedert, James J. National Cancer Institute. Letter to the Editor, *New England Journal of Medicine* 317 (November 5, 1987): 1223.

Goldberg, S. "Parent-Infant Bonding: Another Look." *Child Development* 54 (1983): 1355–82.

Goldin, Claudia. "The Economic Status of Women in the Early Republic: Quantitative Evidence." *Journal of Interdisciplinary History* 16 (Winter 1986): 375–404.

Goldscheider, F. K., and Goldscheider, C. "Leaving Home and Family Structure: Nestleaving Expectations in Step- and Single-Parent Families." Paper presented at the annual meeting of the Population Association of America, New Orleans, April 29, 1988.

Goldstein, Sue. *The Underground Shopper, 1992,* Dallas/Forth Worth Edition. Dallas, TX: Great Buys, 1992.

Gordon, Michael. *The American Family: Past, Present, and Future.* New York: Random House, 1978.

Gordon, Michael, ed. *The American Family in Social-Historical Perspective.* New York: St. Martin's Press, 1983.

Gorer, Geoffrey. *Himalayan Village: An Account of the Lepchas of Sikkim.* 2nd ed. New York: Basic Books, 1967.

Gortmaker, Steven L.; Dietz, William H., Jr.; Sobol, Arthur M.; and Wehler, Cheryl A. "Increasing Pediatric Obesity in the United States." *American Journal of Diseases of Children* 141 (May 1987): 535–40.

Gottschalk, Helmuth. *Problems of Jealousy.* Copenhagen: Fremad, 1936.

Gough, Kathleen E. "The Origins of the Family." *Journal of Marriage and the Family* 33 (1971): 760–71.

Gould, J. B., and LeRoy, S. "Socioeconomic Status and Low Birth Weight: A Racial Comparison." *Pediatrics* 82 (1988): 896–904.

Grady, Denise. "The Brains of Gay Men." *Discover* 13 (January 1992): 29.

Grafton, Sue. *H Is for Homicide.* New York: Henry Holt and Co., 1991.

Gray, Madeline. *Margaret Sanger.* New York: Marek, 1979.

Graziano, William, et al. "Eye to Eye Appeal: Taller Isn't Better." *Human Behavior* 7 (October 1978): 41.

Greaves, L.; Heapy, N.; and Wylie, A. "Reassessing the Profile and Needs of Battered Women." *Canadian Journal of Community Mental Health* 7 (1988): 39–51.

Greeley, A. M.; Michael, R. T.; and Smith, T. W. "A Most Monogamous People: Americans and Their Sexual Partners." *Society* 27 (1990): 36.

Green, Jonathan; Bax, Martin; and Tsitsikes, Helen. "Neonatal Behavior and Early Temperament: A Longitudinal Study of the First Six Months of Life." *American Journal of Orthopsychiatry* 59 (January 1989): 82–93.

Greenberg, Ellen F., and Nay, Robert W. "The Intergenerational Transmission of Marital Instability Reconsidered." *Journal of Marriage and the Family* 44 (1982): 335–47.

Greenfeld, Mark. "Incest: How to Recognize the Warning Signs." *Nurse Week/California Nursing* (March/April 1992): 20–21.

Griffith, W. "Environmental Effects on Interpersonal Affective Behavior: Ambient Effective Temperature and Attraction." *Journal of Personality and Social Psychology* 15 (1970): 240–44.

Gross, Ruth T. Stanford University Study Citing Benefits of Early Education and Parent Training to Help Raise IQs of Preemies. Interview reported by David Perlman in *San Francisco Chronicle,* June 13, 1990, p. A-1.

Guinan, M. E., and Hardy, A. "Epidemiology of AIDS in Women in the United States, 1981 Through 1986." *Journal of the American Medical Association* 257 (1987): 2039–42.

Gutmann, Stephanie. "Date Rape: Does Anyone Really Know What It Is?" *Playboy* 37 (October 1990): 48–51.

Guyton, A. *Textbook of Medical Physiology.* 7th ed. Philadelphia: W. B. Saunders, 1989.

Hafkin, Mark I. "Association Factors for Stepfathers' Integration Within the Blended Family." *Dissertation Abstracts International* 42 (1981): 4578.

Haire, Doris. "Research on Drugs Used in Pregnancy and Obstetrics." Paper presented to the Subcommittee on Investigations and Oversights of the House Committee on Science

and Technology, Washington, DC, July 30, 1981.

Halem, L. C. *Divorce Reform.* New York: Free Press, 1980.

———. *Separated and Divorced Women.* New York: Greenwood, 1982.

Hall, Edward T. *The Silent Language.* New York: Anchor Press, 1973.

———. *Beyond Culture.* New York: Anchor Press, 1976.

Halliday, T. C. "Remarriage: The More Complete Institution." *American Journal of Sociology* 86 (1980): 630–35.

Hammers, Maryann. "Hepatitis B Vaccination Program." *Nurse Week,* October 5, 1992, pp. 1, 8.

Hammond, Dorothy, and Jablow, Alta. "Women: Their Familial Roles in Traditional Societies." Menlo Park, CA: Benjamin/Cummings, 1975.

Hansen, G. L. "Dating Jealousy Among College Students." *Sex Roles* 12 (1985): 717.

Hanson, Shirley M. H., and Bozett, Frederick W., eds. *The Dimensions of Fatherhood.* Beverly Hills, CA: Sage, 1985.

Harris, Marvin. "Why It's Not the Same Old America." *Psychology Today* 15 (August 1981): 23–51.

Harry, J. "Gay Male and Lesbian Relationships." In E. D. Macklin and R. H. Rubin (eds.), *Contemporary Families and Alternative Lifestyles.* Beverly Hills, CA: Sage, 1983.

Hartmann, Heidi. "Capitalism, Patriarchy, and Job Segregation by Sex." In Martha Blaxall and Barbara Reagan (eds.), *Women and the Work Place.* Chicago: University of Chicago Press, 1976.

Hartup, Willard W. "Social Relationships and Their Developmental Significance." *American Psychologist* 44 (February 1989): 120–26.

Harvey, Dennis. "The Psychologist Who Changed Our Minds." *San Francisco Chronicle,* Datebook, June 14, 1992, pp. 31–32.

Hatcher, Robert A., et al. *Contraceptive Technology 1990–1992.* 15th rev. ed. New York: Irvington Publishers, 1990.

Hatcher, Robert A.; Kowal, D.; and Guest, F.; et al. *Contraceptive Technology: International Edition.* Atlanta: Printed Matter, 1989.

Hatfield, Elaine, and Sprecher, Susan. *Mirror, Mirror: The Importance of Looks in Everyday Life.* Albany: State University of New York Press, 1986.

Heaton, Tim B. "Religious Homogamy and Marital Satisfaction Reconsidered." *Journal of Marriage and the Family* 46 (August 1984): 729–33.

Heiman, Julia R. "The Physiology of Erotica: Women's Sexual Arousal." *Psychology Today* 8 (1975): 91–94.

Henig, Robin Marantz. "Perils of Painless Childbirth." *Human Behavior* 7 (October 1978): 50–51.

Henshaw, Stanley K., and Van Vort, Jennifer. "Teenage Abortion, Birth, and Pregnancy Statistics: An Update." *Family Planning Perspectives* 21 (March–April 1989): 85–88.

Herbert, Tracy Bennett; Silver, Roxane Cohen; and Ellard, John H. "Coping with an Abusive Relationship: How and Why Do Women Stay?" *Journal of Marriage and the Family* 53 (1991): 311–25.

Herscher, Elaine. "Special Report: The Cost of Crack." *San Francisco Chronicle*, February 21, 1989, p. A-13.

Hess, E. H. "The Role of Pupil Size in Communication." *Scientific American* 233 (1975): 110–19.

Hetherington, E. M. "Family Relations Six Years After Divorce." In K. Pasley and M. Ihinger-Tallman (eds.), *Remarriage and Stepparenting Today: Current Research and Theory*, pp. 185–205. New York: Guilford, 1987.

Hetherington, E. M.; Cox, Martha; and Cox, Roger. "The Aftermath of Divorce." In J. H. Stevens and M. Matthews (eds.), *Mother-Child, Father-Child Relationships*, pp. 149–75. Washington, DC: National Association for the Education of Young Children, 1978.

Hewlett, Sylvia Ann. *A Lesser Life: The Myth of Women's Liberation in America.* New York: Morrow, 1986.

———. *When the Bough Breaks: The Cost of Neglecting Our Children.* New York: Basic Books, 1991.

Higginbotham, E. "Is Marriage a Priority?" In Peter J. Stein (ed.), *Single Life: Unmarried Adults in Social Context*, pp. 259–67. New York: St. Martin's, 1981.

Hill, Charles T.; Rubin, Zick; and Peplau, Letitia. "Breakups Before Marriage: The End of 103 Affairs." *Journal of Social Issues* 32 (1976): 147–68.

Historical Statistics of the United States, Colonial Times to 1970, series B-291-303. Washington, DC: Government Printing Office, 1970.

Hochschild, Arlie. *The Second Shift: Working Parents and the Revolution at Home.* New York: Viking Penguin, 1989.

Hoffman, H., and Reiss, D., eds. *The American Family: Dying or Developing.* New York: Plenum, 1978.

Hoffman, L. W. "Changes in Family Roles, Socialization, and Sex Differences." *American Psychologist* 32 (1977): 644–57.

Hoffman, Saul D. "Divorce and Well-Being: The Effects on Men, Women, and Children." *Delaware Lawyer* (Spring 1987): 18–22.

Hoffman, Saul D., and Duncan, Greg J. "What *Are* the Economic Consequences of Divorce?" *Demography* 25 (November 1988): 641–45.

Hooper, J., and Teresi, D. *The Three-Pound Universe.* New York: Macmillan, 1986.

Horn, Jack C., and Meer, Jeff. "The Pleasure of Their Company." *Psychology Today* 18 (August 1984): 52–58.

Hornung, C.; McCullough, B.; and Sugimoto, T. "Status Relationships in Marriage: Risk Factors in Spouse Abuse." *Journal of Marriage and the Family* 43 (1981): 679–92.

Hotaling, Gerald T., and Sugarman, David B. "An Analysis of Risk Markers in Husband to Wife Violence: The Current State of Knowledge." *Violence and Victims* 1 (1986): 101–124.

Houseknecht, S. K.; Vaughan, S.; and Statham, A. "The Impact of Singlehood on the Career Patterns of Professional Women." *Journal of Marriage and the Family* 49 (1987): 333–66.

Howes, Carollee, University of California at Los Angeles. Quoted in "Childhood Friendship Is No Simple Matter," by Madeline Drexler. *San Francisco Chronicle*, March 2, 1992, pp. D-3, D-5.

Hulka, Barbara, et al. International Study on Passive Smoking, sponsored by the Office of Smoking and Health, Department of Health and Human Services. Washington, DC: Environmental Protection Agency, November 14, 1986.

Humphrey, Michael. "Sex Differences in Attitude to Parenthood." *Human Relations* 30 (August 1977): 737–50.

Hunt, Morton. *The Natural History of Love.* New York: Alfred A. Knopf, 1959.

———. *Sexual Behavior in the 1970s.* Chicago: Playboy Press, 1974.

Hunter, J. E., and Schuman, N. "Chronic Reconstitution as a Family Style." *Social Work* 25 (1980): 446–51.

Huttman, Elizabeth. "A Research Note on Dreams and Aspirations of Black Families." *Journal of Comparative Family Studies* 22 (Summer 1991): 147–55.

Hutton, Mary D. "TB Spreading Among the Homeless." *Morbidity and Mortality Weekly Report.* Centers for Disease Control, Atlanta: December 20, 1991.

Hymowitz, C., and Schellhardt, T. D. "The Glass Ceiling." *Wall Street Journal*, March 24, 1986, pp. D-1, D-4, D-5.

Ihinger-Tallman, Marilyn, and Pasley, Kay. *Remarriage.* Newbury Park, CA: Sage, 1987.

Iverson, T. J., and Segal, M. *Child Abuse and Neglect: An Information and Reference Guide.* New York: Garland Publishing, 1990.

Jacklin, Carol Nagy. "Female and Male: Issues of Gender." *American Psychologist* 44 (February 1989): 127–33.

Jacobs, J., and Furstenberg, Frank F., Jr. "Changing Places: Conjugal Careers and Women's Marital Mobility." *Social Forces* 64 (1986): 711–32.

Jacobson, D. S. "Family Types, Visiting Patterns, and Children's Behavior in the Stepfamily: A Linked Family System." In Kay Pasley and Marilyn Ihinger-Tallman (eds.), *Remarriage and Stepparenting Today: Research & Theory.* New York: Guilford Press, 1987.

Jacobson, Paul H. *American Marriage and Divorce.* New York: Rinehart, 1969.

Jaffe, Harold W.; Choi, K.; Thomas, P. A.; et al. National Case-Control Study of Kaposi's Sarcoma and *Pneumocystis carinii Pneumonia* in Homosexual Men: Part I, Epidemiologic Results. *Annals of Internal Medicine* 99 (1983): 145–51.

James, J. *Women and the Blues: Passions That Hurt, Passions That Heal.* New York: Harper & Row, 1988.

James, P. D. *Unnatural Causes.* New York: Charles Scribner's 1967.

Jane Roe et al. v. Henry Wade, Supreme Court of the United States, Opinion No. 70-40, January 1973.

Jasen, Georgette. "It Can Pay to Peek at Your Credit Report." *Wall Street Journal*, January 9, 1990a, p. C-1.

————. "Marriage Can Tie Knots in Tax Planning." *Wall Street Journal*, November 5, 1990b, C-1.

Jastrow, Robert. *The Enchanted Mind in the Universe*. New York: Simon & Schuster, 1981.

Johnson, C. L. *Ex Familia*. New Brunswick, NJ: Rutgers University Press, 1988.

Johnson, Robert. *Religious Assortative Mating in the United States*. New York: Academic Press, 1980.

Johnson, S. M. "Integrating Marital and Individual Therapy for Incest Survivors: A Case Study." *Psychotherapy* 26 (1989): 96–103.

Jones, E. F., et al. *Teenage Pregnancy in Industrialized Countries*. New Haven, CT: Yale University Press, 1986.

Jones, L. Colette. "Father-Infant Relationships in the First Year of Life." In Shirley M. H. Hanson and Frederick W. Bozett (eds.), *Dimensions of Fatherhood*, pp. 92–114. Beverly Hills, CA: Sage, 1985.

Jones, L. Colette, and Lenz, Elizabeth R. "Father-Newborn Interaction: Effects of Social Competence and Infant State." *Nursing Research* 35 (May–June 1985): 149–53.

Kagan, Jerome. "Inborn Tendency of Shyness." Press release, Harvard University. *San Francisco Chronicle*, March 11, 1991, p. B-5.

————. "Six Forces That Influence Children." Lecture Series, Smithsonian Institution. Reported by Nina Youngstrom in *American Psychological Association Monitor* 23 (March 1992): 4.

Kagan, Jerome, and Snidman, Nancy. "Temperamental Factors in Human Development." *American Psychologist* 46 (August 1991): 856–62.

Kalish, Richard A. *Death, Grief, and Caring Relationships*. Monterey, CA: Brooks/Cole, 1981.

Kalter, Neil. "Children of Divorce in an Outpatient Psychiatric Population." *American Journal of Orthopsychiatry* 47 (1977): 40–51.

Kanin, E. J.; Davidson, K. D.; and Scheck, S. R. "A Research Note on Male-Female Differentials in the Experience of Heterosexual Love." *Journal of Sex Research* 6 (1970): 64–72.

Kaplan, H. S. *PE: How to Overcome Premature Ejaculation*. New York: Brunner/Mazel, 1989.

Karlen, Arno. *Sexuality and Homosexuality*. New York: W. W. Norton, 1971.

Kass, John. "Psychiatrists Get Rich, But Do Patients Profit?" *Chicago Tribune*, May 29, 1989, p. 1.

Katrowitz, Barbara, et al. "Kids and Contraceptives." *Newsweek*, February 16, 1987, pp. 54–65.

Katz, P. "The Development of Female Identity." *Sex Roles* 5 (1979): 115–37.

Keesler, Oreon. *Financial Aids for Higher Education*. 17th ed. Dubuque, IA: William C. Brown, 1992.

Keith, Louis, Northwestern University Medical School, Chicago. Quoted in "Era of the Multiple-Birth Explosion," reported by Elizabeth Rosenthal, *San Francisco Chronicle*, June 7, 1992, p. 3.

Keith, L. G.; Schink, J. C.; and Gerger, G. S. *Physician's Guide to Sexually Transmitted Diseases*. Chicago: Abbott Laboratories, 1985.

Kelley, Harold H., et al. *Close Relationships*. New York: W. H. Freeman, 1983.

Kelly, Rita Mae. *The Gendered Economy*. Newbury Park, CA: Sage, 1991.

Kempe, R., and Kempe, H. *The Common Secret: Sexual Abuse of Children and Adolescents*. New York: W. H. Freeman, 1984.

Kennedy, K. I.; Rivera, R.; and McNeilly, A. S. "Consensus Statement on the Use of Breastfeeding as a Family Planning Method." *Contraception* 39 (1989): 477–96.

Kennell, J., et al. "Continuous Emotional Support During Labor at a U.S. Hospital: A Randomized Controlled Trial." *Journal of the American Medical Association* 265 (1991): 2197.

Kenney, A. "School-Based Clinics: A National Conference." *Family Planning Perspectives* 18 (1986): 44–46.

Kerner, John A. Private correspondence. Mount Zion Medical Center of the University of California, San Francisco, February 18, 1992.

Kessler-Harris, Alice. *Women Have Always Worked*. Old Westbury, NY: Feminist Press, 1981.

Kieffer, Carolynne. "New Depths in Intimacy." In Roger W. Libby and Robert N. Whitehurst (eds.), *Marriage and Alternatives: Exploring Intimate Relationships*, pp. 267–93. Glenview, IL: Scott, Foresman, 1977.

Kilborn, Peter T. "For Many Women, One Job Isn't Enough." *New York Times*, February 15, 1990, p. A-22.

Kilpatrick, James J. "Lost in Geography." *Washington Post*, April 2, 1987, p. A-19.

Kinsey, Alfred C.; Pomeroy, Wardell B.; and Martin, Clyde E. *Sexual Behavior in the Human Male*. Philadelphia: W. B. Saunders, 1948.

Kinsey, Alfred C.; Pomeroy, Wardell B.; Martin, Clyde E.; and Gebhard, Paul H. *Sexual Behavior in the Human Female*. Philadelphia: W. B. Saunders, 1953.

Kirsch, Irwin S., and Jungeblut, Ann. *Literacy: Profiles of America's Young Adults*. Princeton, NJ: Educational Testing Service, 1986.

Kitano, Harry H. L. *Japanese Americans: The Evolution of a Subculture*. Englewood Cliffs, NJ: Prentice-Hall, 1976.

Kitson, Gay C., and Morgan, Leslie A. "The Multiple Consequences of Divorce: A Decade Review." *Journal of Marriage and the Family* 52 (1990): 913–24.

Kitzinger, Sheila. *The Experience of Childbirth*. New York: Penguin Books, 1978.

Klaus, Marshall H., and Kennell, John H. *Maternal-Infant Bonding*. St. Louis, MO: Mosby, 1976.

————. *Parent-Infant Bonding*. 2nd ed. St. Louis, MO: Mosby, 1982.

Knaub, P. K.; Hanna, S. L.; and Stinnet, N. "Strengths of Remarried Families." *Journal of Divorce* 7 (1984): 41–55.

Kobrin, Francis E. "The Fall in Household Size and the Rise of the Primary Individual in the United States." *Demography* 13 (1976): 129.

Kolbe, R., and LaVoie, J. C. "Sex-Role Stereotyping in Preschool Children's Picture Books." *Social Psychology Quarterly* 44 (1981): 369–74.

Koldovsky, Otakar. "Benefits of Breast Milk Extend to Adulthood." Eleventh Annual Bristol-Myers Squibb/Mead Nutrition Research Symposium, Boston, September 9, 1991.

Koop, C. Everett. "Infant Mortality in the U.S." Address to the 57th meeting of the American Academy of Pediatrics. San Francisco, October 17, 1988.

Koren, P. E.; Lahti, J. I.; Sadler, C. S.; and Kimboko, P. J. *The Adjustment of New Stepfamilies: Characteristics and Trends*. Portland OR: Regional Research Institute for Human Services, 1983.

Kosmin, Barry. *1990 National Jewish Population Survey.* New York: Council of Jewish Federations, June 6, 1991.

Koss, Mary P.; Dinero, Thomas; and Seibel, Cynthia. "Stranger and Acquaintance Rape: Are There Differences in the Victim's Experience?" *Psychology of Women Quarterly* 12 (March 1988): 1–24.

Koss, Mary P.; Gidycz, C. A.; and Wisniewski, N. "The Scope of Rape: Incidence and Prevalence of Sexual Aggression and Victimization in a National Sample of Higher Education Students." *Journal of Consulting and Clinical Psychology* 55 (1987): 162–70.

Kost, Kathryn; Forrest, Jacqueline D.; and Harlap, Susan. "Comparing the Health Risks and Benefits of Contraceptive Choices." *Family Planning Perspectives* 23 (March/April 1991): 54–61.

Kotelchuck, M. "The Infant's Relationship to the Father: Experimental Evidence." In Michael E. Lamb (ed.), *The Role of the Father in Child Development.* New York: Wiley, 1976.

Koutsky, L. A.; Galloway, D. A.; and Holmes, K. K. "Epidemiology of Genital Human Papillomavirus Infection." *Epidemiology Review* 10 (1988): 122–63.

Kozell, Jonathan. *Rachel and Her Children: Homeless Families in America.* New York: Crown, 1988.

Kraemer, H. C.; Korner, A. F.; Anders, T.; Jacklin, C. N.; and Dimicelli, S. "Obstetric Drugs and Infant Behavior: A Reevaluation." *Journal of Pediatric Psychology* 10 (1985): 345–53.

Kratcoski, Peter C. "Families Who Kill." *Marriage and Family Review* 12 (1987): 47–70.

Krein, Sheila Fitzgerald, and Beller, Andrea H. "Educational Attainment of Children from Single-Parent Families: Differences by Exposure, Gender and Race." *Demography* 25 (May 1988): 221–33.

Kressel, K. *The Process of Divorce: How Professionals and Couples Negotiate Settlement.* New York: Basic Books, 1985.

Kronhausen, Phyllis, and Kronhausen, Eberhard. *Erotic Fantasies: A Study of the Sexual Imagination.* New York: Grove Press, 1969.

Krupp, Marcus A.; Chatton, Milton J.; and Werdegar, David (eds.). *Current Medical Diagnosis & Treatment.* Los Altos, CA: Lange Medical Publications, 1985.

Kurdek, L. A., and Schmitt, J. P. "Relationship Quality of Partners in Heterosexual Married, Heterosexual Cohabiting, and Gay and Lesbian Relationships." *Journal of Personality and Social Psychology* 51 (1986): 711–20.

Ladas, A. K.; Whipple, B.; and Perry, J. D. *The G Spot and Other Recent Discoveries About Human Sexuality.* New York: Holt, Rinehart & Winston, 1982.

Lafferty, W. E.; Coombs, R. W.; Benedetti, J.; Critchlow, C.; and Corey, L. "Recurrences After Oral and Genital Herpes Simplex Virus Infection: Influence of Site of Infection and Viral Type." *New England Journal of Medicine* 316 (1987): 1444–49.

Lamb, M. *Nontraditional Families: Parenting and Child Development.* Hillsdale, NJ: Lawrence Erlbaum, 1982.

Lambert, Wallace E.; Hammers, Josiane F.; and Frasure-Smith, Nancy. *Child-Rearing Values: A Cross-National Study.* New York: Praeger, 1979.

Lane, K. E., and Gwartney-Gibbs, P. A. "Violence in the Context of Dating and Sex." *Journal of Family Issues* 6 (1985): 45–59.

Lapointe, Archie E. *Survey — The Second International Assessment of Educational Progress.* Princeton, NJ: Educational Testing Service, February 5, 1992.

Lauer, Jeanette C., and Lauer, Robert H. *Till Death Do Us Part: How Couples Stay Together.* New York: Haworth, 1986.

Lee, John Alan. *The Colours of Love.* Toronto: New Press, 1973.

————. "Styles of Loving." *Psychology Today* 8 (1974): 44–51.

Lehrman, Sally. "FDA Approves Quick HIV Test." *San Francisco Examiner,* May 20, 1992, pp. D-1, D-2.

Lenski, Gerhard, and Lenski, Jean. *Human Societies: An Introduction to Macrosociology.* 2nd ed. New York: McGraw-Hill, 1974.

Leonard, K. E., and Jacob, T. "Alcohol, Alcoholism, and Family Violence." In V. B. Van Hasselt, R. L. Morrison, A. S. Bellack, and M. Herson (eds.), *Handbook of Family Violence,* pp. 383–406. New York: Plenum, 1988.

Lester, D.; Deluca, G.; Hellinghausen, W.; and Scribner, D. "Jealousy and Irrationality in Love." *Psychological Reports* 56 (1985): 210.

Lewin, M. "Unwanted Intercourse: The Difficulty of Saying No." *Psychology of Women Quarterly* 9 (1985): 184–92.

Lewin, Tamar. "Study Finds High Turnover in Child Care Workers." *New York Times,* October 18, 1989, p. A-10.

Lewis, I. A. "The *Los Angeles Times* Poll of 3,050 Adults Growing Older, April 1–6, 1989." *San Francisco Chronicle,* May 4, 1989, p. A-30.

Lewis, M., and Weinraub, N. "The Father's Role in the Child's Social Network." In M. Lamb (ed.), *The Role of the Father in Child Development,* pp. 157–84. New York: Wiley, 1976.

Lewis, Robert. "Equity Eludes Women: Earnings Gap Is Greatest After Age 50." *AARP* 32 (November 1991): 1, 11–13.

Liederman, David. Report on Increase in Child Abuse. Washington, DC: Child Welfare League of America, 1991.

Lifson, A. R. "Do Alternate Modes for Transmission of Human Immunodeficiency Virus Exist?" *Journal of the American Medical Association* 259 (1988): 1353–56.

Lightfoot-Klein, Hanny. *Prisoners of Ritual: An Odyssey into Female Genital Circumcision in Africa.* New York: Harrington Park Press, 1989.

Lindenmayer, Jean Pierre; Steinberg, Maurice D.; Bjork, Darla A.; and Pardes, Herbert. "Psychiatric Aspects of Voluntary Sterilization in Young, Childless Women." *Journal of Reproductive Medicine* 19 (August 1977): 87–91.

Lino, Mark, U.S. Department of Agriculture Report on Cost of Raising Children: 1990. Published in *Family Economic Review,* July 1991. Reprinted by Ramon G. McLeod in *San Francisco Chronicle,* July 26, 1991, p. A-2.

Lips, H. M. *Sex and Gender: An Introduction.* Mountain View, CA: Mayfield, 1988.

Lipsitt, Lewis. Brown University Child Study Center. Lecture Series, Smithsonian Institute, reported by Nina Youngstrom in *American Psychological Association Monitor* 23 (March 1992): 4.

Little, Bill L. *This Will Drive You Sane.* Minneapolis, MN: Compcare, 1977.

Lobsenz, Norman M. "Taming the Green-Eyed Monster." In Gordon Clanton and Lynn G. Smith (eds.), *Jealousy*, pp. 26–34. Englewood Cliffs, NJ: Prentice-Hall, 1977.

Lockhart, Lettie L. "A Reexamination of the Effects of Race and Social Class on the Incidence of Marital Violence: A Search for Reliable Differences." *Journal of Marriage and the Family* 49 (August 1987): 603–10.

Lockheed, M. E. "Reshaping the Social Order: The Case of Gender Segregation." *Sex Roles* 14 (1986): 617–28.

Loeb, Marshall. *Marshall Loeb's 1990 Money Guide.* Boston: Little, Brown, 1992.

London, Kathryn; Kahn, Joan; and Pratt, William. "Divorced Parents, Divorced Daughter." *Wall Street Journal*, June 14, 1988, p. B-1.

Long, Lynette, and Long, Thomas. *The Handbook for Latchkey Children and Their Parents.* New York: Arbor House, 1983.

Lopata, Helena Z. *Women as Widows: Support Systems.* New York: Elsevier Press, 1979.

Lopez, Julie Amparano. "Career Women Are Being Helped More, and in New Ways, When Jobs Turn Sour." *Wall Street Journal*, July 3, 1992, p. B-1.

Lott, B. *Women's Lives: Themes and Variations in Gender Learning.* Monterey, CA: Brooks/Cole, 1987.

Lovenheim, Barbara. "Brides at Last." *San Francisco Chronicle* This World, September 13, 1987, pp. 12–14.

Lozoff, Betsy. "Nutrition and Behavior." *American Psychologist* 44 (February 1989): 231–36.

Lucus, Alan, et al. "Breast Milk and IQ." *Lancet* 339 (February 1, 1992): 256.

Lunneborg, Patricia W., and Rosenwood, Linda M. "Need Affiliation and Achievement: Declining Sex Differences." *Psychological Reports* 31 (December 1972): 795–98.

Lutz, P. "The Stepfamily: An Adolescent Perspective." *Family Relations* 32 (1983): 367–75.

Lye, D. N. *The Rise of Divorce in Fifteen Countries: A Comparative Study of Changes in Economic Opportunities and Family Values.* Ph.D. thesis. University of Pennsylvania, 1988.

Lynch, James J. *The Broken Heart: Medical Consequences of Loneliness.* New York: Basic Books, 1977.

McCabe, Michael. "Stanford Surgeon Who Quit over Sexism Returning to Post." *San Francisco Chronicle*, September 5, 1991, p. A-1.

McCall, Cheryl. "The Cruelest Crime." *Life*, December 1984, p. 35.

Maccoby, Eleanor E. "Gender and Relationships: A Developmental Account." *American Psychologist* 45 (April 1990): 513–20.

———. Quoted in "Childhood Friendship Is No Simple Matter," by Madeline Drexler. *San Francisco Chronicle*, March 2, 1992, pp. D-3, D-5.

Maccoby, Eleanor E., and Jacklin, Carol Nagy. *The Psychology of Sex Differences.* Stanford, CA: Stanford University Press, 1974.

———. "Gender Segregation in Childhood." In Hayne Reese (ed.), *Advances in Child Development and Behavior*, Vol. 20. New York: Academic Press, 1987.

McCubbin, Hamilton I. "Ethnic and Mixed-Race Families." In *2001: Preparing Families for the Future*, pp. 38–39. Minneapolis, MN: National Council on Family Relations Presidential Report, 1990.

MacDonald, John D. *Nightmare in Pink.* Greenwich, CT: Fawcett, 1964.

———. "The Random Noise of Love." *Seven.* Greenwich, CT: Fawcett, 1971.

MacDonald, N. E., et al. "High-Risk STD/HIV Behavior Among College Students." *Journal of the American Medical Association* 263 (1990): 3155.

Mace, David, and Mace, Vera. *We Can Have Better Marriages.* Nashville, TN: Abingdon Press, 1974.

MacFarlane, Aidan. *The Psychology of Childbirth.* Cambridge, MA: Harvard University Press, 1977.

McGill University Report on the Overuse of Episiotomy. *San Francisco Chronicle*, July 2, 1992, p. A-8.

McIntosh, Bruce J. "Indulged? Or Just Plain Spoiled?" Interview by Kathy Henderson, St. Vincent's Medical Center, Jacksonville, FL. *Psychology Today* 23 (June 1989): 28.

McKinlay, John. Paper on Menopause and Depression presented at the Society of Behavioral Medicine, Cambridge, MA, May 1988.

McKinney, Kathleen. "Perceptions of Courtship Violence: Gender Difference and Involvement." *Free Inquiry in Creative Sociology* 14 (May 1986): 61–66.

McKnight, Curtis, et al. *The Underachieving Curriculum: Assessing U.S. School Mathematics from an International Perspective.* Champaign, IL: International Association for the Evaluation of Education Achievement, Stipes Publishing, 1987.

McLanahan, Sara, and Booth, Karen. "Mother-Only Families: Problems, Prospects, and Politics." In Alan Booth (ed.), *Contemporary Families: Looking Forward, Looking Back.* Minneapolis, MN: National Council on Family Relations, 1991.

McLanahan, Sara, and Bumpass, Larry L. "Intergenerational Consequences of Family Disruption." *American Journal of Sociology* 94 (1988): 130–52.

McLeod, Ramon G. "How Education and Income Are Linked." *San Francisco Chronicle*, September 1, 1992, p. A-1.

McNally, J. W., and Mosher, W. D. "AIDS-Related Knowledge and Behavior Among Women 15–44 Years of Age: United States, 1988." *Family Planning Perspectives* 23 (September/October 1991): 234–35.

McNeil, Jack. "Income Trends Show Shrinking Middle Class." U.S. Bureau of the Census, *Current Population Reports*, Series P-60, Nos. 166, 168. Washington, DC: Government Printing Office, 1992.

Macklin, Eleanor D. "Heterosexual Couples Who Cohabit Nonmaritally: Some Problems and Issues." In Catherine S. Chilman, Elam W. Nunnally, and Fred M. Cox (eds.), *Variant Family Forms*, pp. 56–72. Newbury Park, CA: Sage, 1988.

Magnuson, Ed. "Child Abuse: The Ultimate Betrayal." *Time*, September 5, 1983, pp. 20–23.

Makepeace, James Michael. "The Birth Control Revolution: Consequences for College Student Life Styles. Ph.D. dissertation, Washington State University, 1975.

Makinson, C. "The Health Consequences of Teenage Fertility." *Family Planning Perspectives* 17 (1985): 83–90.

Malandro, Loretta A., and Barker, Larry. *Nonverbal Communication.* Reading, MA: Addison-Wesley, 1983.

Malson, M. R. "Black Women's Sex Roles: The Social Context for a New Ideology." *Journal of Social Issues* 39 (1983): 101–13.

Maltz, Daniel N., and Borker, Ruth A. "A Cultural Approach to Male-Female Miscommunication." In John J. Gumpertz (ed.), *Language and Social Identity*, pp. 196–216. New York: Cambridge University Press, 1982.

Mancini, Jay A., and Orthner, Dennis K. "Recreational Sexual Preferences Among Middle-Class Husbands and Wives." *Journal of Sex Research* 14 (May 1978): 96–105.

Mann, Jonathan, International AIDS Center, Harvard University. Quoted from report by the Global AIDS Policy Coalition. Washington, DC: June 3, 1992.

Margolin, Harold, U.S. Centers for Disease Control, Hepatitis B Branch. Interview in "Need to Vaccinate Americans Against Hepatitis B," reported by Sabin Russell, *San Francisco Chronicle*, November 5, 1991, p. A-1.

Margolis, Maxine. *Mothers and Such: Views of American Women and Why They Changed*. Berkeley and Los Angeles: University of California Press, 1984.

Marion, Robert, et al. "Human T-Cell Lymphotropic Virus Type III (HTLV-III) Embryopathy." *American Journal of Diseases of Children* 140 (July 1986): 638–40.

Marshall, Donald S. "Too Much in Mangaia." *Psychology Today* 4 (1971): 43–44, 70–79.

Marsiglio, W., and Mott, F. "The Impact of Sex Education on Sexual Activity, Contraceptive Use, and Premarital Pregnancy Among American Teenagers." *Family Planning Perspectives* 18 (April 1986): 151–62.

Martin, Dorothy H. "Fathers and Adolescents." In Shirley M. H. Hansen and Frederick W. Bozett (eds.), *Dimensions of Fatherhood*, pp. 170–95. Beverly Hills, CA: Sage, 1985.

Martin, Leonide L., and Reeder, Sharon. *Essentials of Maternity Nursing*. New York: Lippincott, 1991.

Marvin v. Marvin 18 Cal. 3d. 660, 134 *California Reporter* 815, 557 P.2d106 (1976).

Maslow, Abraham H. *The Farther Reaches of Human Nature*. New York: Viking, 1971.

Maslow, Abraham H., and Mintz, N. L. "Effects of Aesthetic Surroundings: Initial Effects of Three Aesthetic Conditions Upon Perceiving 'Energy' and 'Well-Being' in Faces." *Journal of Psychology* 41 (1956): 247–54.

Massey, Douglas S. "The Settlement Process Among Mexican Migrants to the United States." *American Sociological Review* 51 (1986): 670–84.

Massie, Robert K. *Nicholas and Alexandra*. New York: Atheneum, 1967.

Masters, William H., and Johnson, Virginia E. *Human Sexual Response*. Boston: Little, Brown, 1966.

Masters, William H.; Johnson, Virginia E.; and Kolodny, Robert C. *Masters and Johnson on Sex and Human Loving*. Boston: Little, Brown, 1988.

Mattox, William R., Jr. "The Family Time Famine." *Family Policy* 3 (1990): 2.

Mayer, Egon. *Love and Tradition: Marriage Between Jews and Christians*. New York: Plenum, 1985.

Mazur, J. E. *Learning and Behavior*. Englewood Cliffs, NJ: Prentice-Hall, 1986.

Mead, Margaret. Introduction to *Premarital Dating Behavior*, by Winston Ehrman. New York: Holt, 1959.

Meer, Jeff, "Pet Theories." *Psychology Today* 18 (August 1984): 60.

Mehrabian, Albert. *Silent Messages*. Belmont, CA: Wadsworth, 1971.

Meier, Barry. "Is Your Health Insurance Safe?" *New York Times*, January 4, 1992, p. A-4.

Menaghan, Elizabeth G., and Lieberman, Morton A. "Changes in Depression Following Divorce: A Panel Study." *Journal of Marriage and the Family* 48 (May 1986): 319–28.

Mersky, Helen S., and Swart, G. T. "Family Background and Physical Health of Adolescents Admitted to an Inpatient Psychiatric Unit: I, Principal Caregivers." *Canadian Journal of Psychiatry* 34 (March 1989): 79–83.

Merson, Michael H., World Health Organization's Global AIDS Program. Eighth International Conference on AIDS. Amsterdam, July 19–26, 1992.

Milbank, Dana. "Campus Liberation: Gay Students Enjoy Programs, Protections at Rutgers University." *Wall Street Journal*, February 3, 1992, p. B-1.

Miller, Julie Ann. "Window on the Womb." *Science News* 127 (February 2, 1985): 75, 77.

Miller, Louisa. "Married Couples with Stepchildren." U.S. National Center for Health Statistics report. *Wall Street Journal*, February 20, 1990, p. B-1.

Miller, Roger LeRoy. *Economic Issues for Consumers*. 5th ed. St. Paul, MN: West, 1987.

Minge-Klevana, Wanda. "Does Labor Time Increase with Industrialization? A Survey of Time Allocation Studies." *Current Anthropology* 21 (June 1980): 279–98.

Mohr, James C. *Abortion in America: The Origins and Evolution of National Policy*. New York: Oxford University Press, 1978.

Money, John. *Love and Love Sickness: The Science of Sex, Gender Difference, and Pair Bonding*. Baltimore, MD: Johns Hopkins University Press, 1980.

———. *The Destroying Angel*. Buffalo, NY: Prometheus Books, 1985.

———. *Lovemaps*. New York: Irvington, 1986.

———. *Gay, Straight, and In-Between: The Sexology of Erotic Orientation*. New York: Oxford University Press, 1988.

Money, John, and Tucker, Patricia. *Sexual Signatures: On Being a Man or a Woman*. Boston: Little, Brown, 1975.

Monkkonen, E. H., ed. *Walking to Work: Tramps in America 1790–1935*. Lincoln: University of Nebraska Press, 1984.

Montagu, Ashley. *The Concept of Race*. New York: Free Press, 1964.

Morgan, Barrie S. "A Contribution to the Debate on Homogamy, Propinquity, and Segregation." *Journal of Marriage and the Family* 43 (1981): 909–21.

Morgan, Gwen. *The National State of Child Care Regulations, 1989*. Watertown, MA: Work/Family Directions, 1989.

Morgan, Philip; Lye, Diane; and Condran, Gretchen. "Sons Help a Marriage." *American Journal of Sociology* 93 (February 1988): 60–64.

Morrison, Ann M., and Von Glinow, Mary Ann. "Women and Minorities in Management." *American Psychologist* 45 (February 1990): 200–208.

Morrison, Ann M.; White, Randall P.; and Van Velson, Ellan. *Breaking the Glass Ceiling*. Reading, MA: Addison-Wesley, 1987.

Mortenson, Thomas. "Study of Costs of a College Education." *Wall Street Journal*, May 15, 1989, p. B-1.

Mosher, William D. "Infertility Trends Among U.S. Couples: 1965–1976." *Family Planning Perspectives* 14 (January/February 1982): 22–27.

Moss, M. "One in Eight Female Students is a Victim of Date Rape or a Rape Attempt." *Behavior Today News Letter* 19 (February 1987): 1.

Muehlenhard, Charlene L. "Misinterpreted Dating Behaviors and the Risk of Date Rape." *Journal of Social and Clinical Psychology* 9 (1988): 20–37.

Mullahy, Patrick. *Oedipus, Myth and Complex*. New York: Hermitage, 1952.

Murdock, George. *Social Structure*. New York: Macmillan, 1949.

———. "World Ethnographic Sample." *American Anthropologist* 59 (August 1957): 664–87.

Murstein, Bernard I. *Love, Sex, and Marriage Through the Ages*. New York: Springer, 1974.

Murstein, Bernard I., and Brust, Robert G. "Humor and Interpersonal Attraction." *Journal of Personality Assessment* 49 (1985): 637–40.

Murstein, Bernard I., and Christy, P. "Physical Attractiveness and Marital Adjustment in Middle-Age Couples." *Journal of Personality and Social Psychology* 34 (1976): 537–42.

Nadel, Allan S., et al. "Absence of Need for Amniocentesis in Patients with Elevated Levels of Maternal Serum Alpha-fetoprotein and Normal Ultrasonic Examinations." *New England Journal of Medicine* 323 (August 30, 1990): 557–61.

Navarro, V. "Race or Class vs. Race and Class: Mortality Differentials in the United States." *Lancet* 336 (1990): 1238–40.

Newman, Katherine S. *Falling from Grace: The Experience of Downward Mobility in the American Middle Class*. New York: Free Press, 1988.

Newton, Niles, and Modahl, Charlotte. "Pregnancy: The Closest Human Relationship." *Human Nature* 1 (March 1978): 40–49.

Nielsen Media Research. "1990 Nielsen Report on TV." In Sylvia Ann Hewlett, *When The Bough Breaks: The Cost of Neglecting Our Children*, p. 303. New York: Basic Books, 1991.

Nikkanen, V., and Punnonen, R. "Serum Prolactin FSH, LH, and Testoster-one Before and After Vasectomy in Normal Men." *Archives of Andrology* 8 (1982): 311–13.

Nord, Christine Winquist, and Zill, Nicholas. "American Households in Demographic Perspective." In Institute for American Values Working Paper for the Commission on Families in America. Publication No. WP5. New York: June 1991.

Norton, Arthur J. "Measuring Marital Quality: A Critical Look at the Dependent Variables." *Journal of Marriage and the Family* 45 (February 1983a): 141–51.

———. "Family Life Cycle: 1980." *Journal of Marriage and the Family* 45 (May 1983b): 267–75.

Norton, Arthur J., and Miller, Louisa. "Drop in Early Marriages May Have Lasting Impact." *Wall Street Journal*, November 26, 1991, p. B-1.

Norton, Arthur J., and Moorman, Jeanie. "Current Trends in Marriage and Divorce Among American Women." *Journal of Marriage and the Family* 49 (1987): 3–14.

Norwood, Robin. *Women Who Love Too Much*. New York: Pocket Books/Simon & Schuster, 1985.

Novello, Antonia, Surgeon General of the United States. "The Problem of Domestic Violence." News Conference, Cook County Hospital, Chicago, October 16, 1991.

Offermann, Lynn R., and Gowing, Marilyn K. "Organizations of the Future." *American Psychologist* 45 (February 1990): 95–108.

O'Herlihy, Colm. "Jogging and Suppression of Ovulation." Letter to *The New England Journal of Medicine* 306 (January 7, 1982): 50.

O'Kelly, Charlotte G. *Women and Men in Society*. New York: D. Van Nostrand, 1980.

O'Leary, K. D. "Physical Aggression Between Spouses: A Social Learning Perspective." In V. B. Van Hasselt, R. L. Morrison, A. S. Bellack, and M. Herson (eds.), *Handbook of Family Violence*, pp. 31–55. New York: Plenum, 1988.

O'Neill, Nena. *The Marriage Premise*. New York: Evans, 1977.

O'Reilly, Jane. "Wife Beating: The Silent Crime." *Time*, September 5, 1983, pp. 23–26.

Orlofsky, J. L. "Intimacy Status: Theory and Research." In J. E. Marcia (ed.), *Identity in Adolescence*. Hillsdale, NJ: Erlbaum, 1987.

Osius, Isobel. "A Day Late and a Dollar Short." In Marketing Tools ALERT, a special news supplement to *American Demographics*, September 1991, pp. 4, 6, 8, 16.

Oster, Sharon M. "A Note on the Determinants of Alimony." *Journal of Marriage and the Family* 49 (February 1987): 81–86.

O'Sullivan, Mary Jo. Press release on the American College of Obstetricians and Gynecologists New Guidelines on Repeat Cesarians. *San Francisco Chronicle*, October 28, 1988, p. A-9.

Otten, Alan L. "Part-Time Work Is Fine, If It's What You Want." *Wall Street Journal*, April 23, 1990, p. B-1.

Owens, Russell, Joint Center for Political Studies, Washington, DC. Quoted in Clarence Johnson and William Black, "Economic Despair Among Blacks." *San Francisco Chronicle*, May 2, 1992, p. A-22.

Padian, N. S.; Shiboski, S. C.; and Jewell, N. P. "Female-to-Male Transmission of Human Immunodeficiency Virus." *Journal of the American Medical Association* 266 (September 25, 1991): 1664–67.

Pagelow, Mildred Daley. *Family Violence*. New York: Praeger, 1984.

Pallock, Laurel. "New Credit Card Scams." *San Francisco Chronicle*, January 9, 1991a, pp. Z-5, Z-6.

———. "Auto Insurance Tips." *San Francisco Chronicle*, November 5, 1991b, p. B-5.

Parker, J. G., and Asher, S. R. "Peer Relations and Later Adjustment: Are Low-Accepted Children 'at Risk'?" *Psychological Bulletin* 102 (1987): 357–89.

Parker, Robert B. *The Widening Gyre*. New York: Dell, 1983.

Parrot, Andrea, Cornell University Department of Human Service Studies. Quoted in Stephanie Gutmann, "Date Rape." *Playboy* 37 (October 1990): 48.

Pasley, Kay, and Ihinger-Tallman, Marilyn. "Remarriage and Stepfamilies." In Catherine S. Chilman, Elam W. Nunnally, and Fred M. Cox (eds.), *Variant Family Forms*. Newbury Park, CA: Sage, 1988.

Paul VI, Pope. "An Apostolic Letter Determining Norms for Mixed Marriages." *San Francisco Chronicle*, April 29, 1970, p. 11.

Patzer, Gordon L. *The Physical Attractiveness Phenomena.* New York: Plenum Press, 1985.

Pearlin, Leonard I., and Johnson, Joyce S. "Marital Status, Life Strains, and Depression." In Peter J. Stein (ed.), *Single Life: Unmarried Adults in Social Context,* pp. 165–78. New York: St. Martin's Press, 1981.

Pedersen, Frank A. *The Father-Infant Relationship: Observational Studies in the Family Setting.* New York: Praeger, 1980.

Peek, C. W.; Fischer, J. L.; and Kidwell, J. S. "Teenage Violence Toward Parents: A Neglected Dimension of Family Violence." *Journal of Marriage and the Family* 47 (1985): 1051–58.

Peplau, Anne. "The Meaning of Loneliness." Interview at UCLA. *San Francisco Chronicle,* June 23, 1986, p. 16.

Peplau, L. A., and Amaro, H. "Understanding Lesbian Relationships." In J. Weinreich and W. Paul (eds.), *Homosexuality: Social, Psychological, and Biological Issues.* Beverly Hills, CA: Sage, 1982.

Perlman, Daniel, and Duck, Steve, eds. *Intimate Relationships.* Newbury Park, CA: Sage, 1987.

Perlman, Daniel, and Fehr, Beverley. "The Development of Intimate Relationships." In Daniel Perlman and Steve Duck (eds.), *Intimate Relationships,* pp. 13–42. Newbury Park, CA: Sage, 1987.

Peterman, T. A., and Curran, J. W. "Sexual Transmission of Human Immunodeficiency Virus." *Journal of the American Medical Association* 256 (1986): 2222–26.

Petersen, James R. "The Extended Male Orgasm." *Playboy,* May 1977, pp. 90–92, 232–36.

Petersen, James R., et al. "The Playboy Reader's Sex Survey, Part I." *Playboy,* January 1983, pp. 108, 241–50.

Peterson, J. L., and Nord, C. W. "The Regular Receipts of Child Support: A Multistep Process." *Journal of Marriage and the Family* 52 (1990): 539–51.

Peterson, J. L., and Zill, N. "Marital Disruption, Parent-Child Relations and Behavior Problems in Children." *Journal of Marriage and the Family* 48 (1986): 295–307.

Pettigrew, Thomas F. "The Changing — Not Declining — Significance of Race." In Charles Vert Willie, *Caste and Class Controversy on Race and Pov-*

erty. Dix Hills, NY: General Hall, 1989.

Pietropinto, Anthony. *Not Tonight Dear: How to Reawaken Your Sexual Desire.* New York: Doubleday, 1990.

Pietropinto, Anthony, and Simenauer, Jacqueline. *Beyond the Male Myth.* New York: Times Books, 1977.

Pill, Cynthia. "Stepfamilies: Redefining the Family." *Family Relations* 39 (April 1990): 186–93.

Pines, A., and Aronson, E. "Antecedents, Correlates, and Consequences of Sexual Jealousy." *Journal of Personality* 51 (1983): 108–36.

Pines, Maya. "A Child's Mind Is Shaped Before Age 2." *Life,* 1971, pp. 63, 67–68.

Pollack, Ron. "Health Costs for Persons 65 or Older." *Wall Street Journal,* February 26, 1992, p. B-3.

Pomeroy, Sarah B. *Women in Hellenistic Egypt.* New York: Schocken Books, 1984.

Population Council, Norplant Fact Sheet. New York: Norplant Worldwide, January 1991.

Porter, Oscar, National Institute of Independent Colleges and Universities, Washington, DC. Quoted in "It's Taking Longer to Get a Degree," reported by April Lynch. *San Francisco Chronicle,* September 12, 1990, p. A-1.

Porter, Sylvia. *Your Financial Security.* New York: William Morrow, 1987.

———. *Sylvia Porter's Your Finances in the 1990s.* New York: Prentice-Hall, 1990.

Price, Sharon J., and McKenry, Patrick C. *Divorce.* Newbury Park, CA: Sage, 1988.

Prober, Charles G., et al. "Use of Routine Viral Cultures at Delivery to Identify Neonates Exposed to Herpes Simplex Virus." *New England Journal of Medicine* 318 (April 7, 1988): 887–91.

Proctor, E. B.; Wagner, N. N.; and Butler, Julius C. "The Differences of Male and Female Orgasm: An Experimental Study." In Nathaniel N. Wagner (ed.), *Perspectives on Human Sexuality,* pp. 115–32. New York: Behavioral Publications, 1974.

Quinn, Jane Bryant. *Making the Most of Your Money.* New York: Simon & Schuster, 1991.

Quinn, Thomas C. "Heterosexuals with STDs Face Greater Risk of HIV Infection." *Medical Aspects of Human Sexuality* 23 (April 1989): 101.

Radetsky, Peter. "The Rise and (Maybe Not the) Fall of Toxic Shock Syndrome." *Science 85* (January–February 1985): 73–78.

Rafferty, Yvonne, and Shinn, Marybeth. "The Impact of Homelessness on Children." *American Psychologist* 46 (November 1991): 1170–79.

Rao, V. V. P., and Rao, V. N. "Alternatives in Intimacy, Marriage, and Family Lifestyles: Preferences of Black College Students." *Alternative Lifestyles* 3 (1980): 485–98.

Raschke, H. "Divorce." In M. Sussman and S. Steinmetz (eds.), *Handbook of Marriage and the Family.* New York: Plenum, 1987.

Read, Eileen White. "Birth Cycle: For Poor Teenagers, Pregnancies Become New Rite of Passage." *Wall Street Journal,* 1988, p. 1.

Reeder, Sharon, et al. *Maternity Nursing.* 16th ed. Philadelphia: J. B. Lippincott, 1987.

Reik, Theodore. *Of Love and Lust.* New York: Farrar, Straus, 1949.

Rein, Michael F. "Therapeutic Decisions in the Treatment of Sexually Transmitted Diseases: An Overview." In *Sexually Transmitted Diseases: Journal of the American Venereal Disease Association* 8 (January–March 1981): 93–99.

Reinisch, June M. *The Kinsey Institute New Report on Sex.* New York: St. Martin's Press, 1990.

———. "Learning to Control Arousal." Kinsey Report, *San Francisco Chronicle,* February 25, 1991, p. D-5.

———. "Reducing the Risks of Getting Herpes." Kinsey Report, *San Francisco Chronicle,* June 23, 1992, p. D-5.

Reinisch, June M.; Sanders, Stephanie A.; Hill, Craig A.; and Ziemba-Davis, Mary. "High-Risk Sexual Behavior Among Heterosexual Undergraduates at a Midwestern University." *Family Planning Perspectives* 24 (1992): 116–22.

Reiss, Ira L. *Family Systems in America.* 3rd ed. New York: Holt, Rinehart & Winston, 1980.

———. "A Sociological Journey into Sexuality." *Journal of Marriage and the Family* 48 (May 1986): 233–42.

Reiss, Ira L., and Lee, G. R. *Family Systems in America.* 4th ed. New York: Holt, Rinehart & Winston, 1988.

Rembert, Donald Mosby. "Straight Talk About Planning Your Retirement." *Schwab Report* Vol. 3, Issue 4, Spring 1992.

Renzetti, C. M., and Curran, D. J. *Women, Men, and Society: The Sociology of Gender.* Boston: Allyn & Bacon, 1989.

Rheinstein, Max. *Marriage Stability, Divorce, and the Law.* Chicago: University of Chicago Press, 1972.

Rhoads, George G., et al. "The Safety and Efficiency of Chorionic Villi Sampling for Early Prenatal Diagnosis of Cytogenic Abnormalities." *New England Journal of Medicine* 320 (March 9, 1989): 609–17.

Richardson, J. L., et al. "Substance Use Among Eighth-Grade Students Who Take Care of Themselves After School." *Pediatrics* 84 (September 1989): 556–66.

Richardson, L. *The Dynamics of Sex and Gender: A Sociological Perspective.* 3rd ed. New York: Harper & Row, 1988.

Riche, Martha Farnsworth. "The Second Time Around Becomes More Common." *Wall Street Journal,* March 15, 1991a, p. B-1.

———. "We're All Minorities Now." *American Demographics* 13 (October 1991b): 26–34.

Ricketts, Erol R., and Sawhill, Isabel V. "Defining and Measuring the Underclass." *Journal of Policy Analysis and Management* 7 (1988): 316–24.

Robertson, Ian. *Sociology.* 3rd ed. New York: Worth Publishers, 1987.

Robinson, Ira E., and Jedlicka, Davor. "Change in Sexual Attitudes and Behavior of College Students from 1965 to 1980: A Research Note." *Journal of Marriage and the Family* (February 1982): 237–240.

Rollins, Boyd C., and Feldman, Harold. "Marital Satisfaction over the Life Cycle." *Journal of Marriage and the Family* 32 (1970): 20–28.

Rooks, Judith P., et al. "Outcomes of Care in Birth Centers: The National Birth Center Study." *New England Journal of Medicine* 321 (December 28, 1989): 1804–11.

Roper, William L. "AIDS Deaths Rise." Press Release, National Centers for Disease Control, *San Francisco Chronicle,* January 8, 1992, p. A-3.

Rosen, Kenneth T. "Apartment Dwellers Plan on Staying Put." Reported by Joan Lebow in *Wall Street Journal,* June 2, 1989, p. B-1.

Rosenberg, M. J., et al. "Effect of Contraceptive Sponge on Chlamydial Infection, Gonorrhea, and Candidiasis." *Journal of the American Medical Association* 257 (1987): 2308–12.

Rosenberg, Milton L. Private discussion, Mount Zion Medical Center of the University of California, San Francisco, March 10, 1992.

Rossi, Peter H. "The Old Homeless and the New Homelessness in Historical Perspective." *American Psychologist* 45 (August 1990): 945–59.

Rothman, Ellen K. *Hands and Hearts: A History of Courtship in America.* New York: Basic Books, 1984.

Rubin, Lillian Breslow. *Worlds of Pain.* New York: Basic Books, 1976.

———. *Erotic Wars.* New York: Farrar, Straus & Giroux, 1990.

Rubin, Zick. *Liking and Loving: An Invitation to Social Psychology.* New York: Holt, Rinehart & Winston, 1973.

Russell, Diana H. *The Sexual Trauma: Incest in the Lives of Girls and Women.* New York: Basic Books, 1986.

Russell, Graeme. *The Changing Role of Fathers?* St. Lucia: University of Queensland Press, 1983.

Russell, Sabin. "Midwives Win American Hearts." *San Francisco Chronicle,* July 28, 1992, pp. A-1, A-8.

Ryan, Kenneth J. "Giving Birth in America, 1988." *Family Planning Perspectives* 20 (November–December 1988): 298–301.

Ryder, Norman B. "What Is Going to Happen to American Fertility?" *Population and Development Review* 16 (September 1990): 447–48.

Sachs, P. B.; Layde, P. M.; Rubin, G. L.; and Rochat, R. W. "Reproductive Mortality in the United States." *Journal of the American Medical Association* 247 (1982): 2789–92.

Sadker, Myra, and Sadker, David. "Sexism in the Schoolroom of the '80s." *Psychology Today* 19 (March 1985): 54–57.

Sagan, Carl. *Cosmos.* New York: Random House, 1980.

Sameroff, A. J. "Early Influences on Development: Fact or Fancy?" *Merrill-Palmer Quarterly* 21 (1974): 267–94.

Sandler, B. R. *The Campus Climate Revisited: Chilly for Women Faculty, Administrators, and Graduate Students.* Washington, DC: The Project on the Status and Education of Women, Association of American Colleges, 1986.

Sanford, Linda. "Innovative Treatment Approaches to Child Victims." Panel, National Symposium on Child Victimization, Anaheim, CA, April 1988.

Sanger, Margaret. *An Autobiography.* New York: W. W. Norton, 1937.

Santrock, J. W. "Relation of Type and Onset of Father Absence to Cognitive Development." *Child Development* 43 (1972): 455–69.

Santrock, J.W., and Sitterle, K. "Parent-Child Relationships in Stepmother Families." In K. Pasley and M. Ihinger-Tallman (eds.), *Remarriage and Stepparenting Today: Research and Theory.* New York: Guilford Press, 1987.

Santrock, J. W.; Warshak, R.; Lindbergh, C.; and Meadows, L. "Children's and Parents' Social Behavior in Stepfather Families." *Child Development* 53 (1982): 472–80.

Satir, Virginia. *Peoplemaking.* Palo Alto, CA: Science and Behavior Books, 1972.

Schellenbarger, Sue. "Helping Parents with Latchkey Anxiety." *Wall Street Journal,* November 11, 1991, p. B-1.

Schlegel, Alice, ed. *Sexual Stratification: A Cross-Cultural View.* New York: Columbia University Press, 1977.

Schmidt, Gunter, and Sigusch, Volkman. "Sex Differences in Responses to Psychosexual Stimulation by Films and Slides." *Journal of Sex Research* 6 (1970): 268–83.

Schoendorf, Kenneth C., et al. "Mortality Among Infants of Black as Compared with White College-Educated Parents." *New England Journal of Medicine* 326 (June 4, 1992): 1522–26.

Schreiner, Tim. "Census Figures Show the Cost of Housing Skyrocketed in 1980s." *San Francisco Chronicle,* May 29, 1992, p. A-4.

Schultz, Ellen E. "College Advice to Parents: Start Saving Money Now." *Wall Street Journal,* May 17, 1990, p. C-1.

Schwadel, Francine. "Urban Consumers Pay More and Get Less, and Gap May Widen." *Wall Street Journal,* July 2, 1992, pp. A-1, A-9.

Schwarcz, Sandra K., et al. "National Surveillance of Antimicrobial Resistance in Neisseria Gonorrhoeae." *Journal of the American Medical Association* 264 (September 19, 1990): 1413–17.

Schwartz, Joe, and Waldrop, Judith. "The Growing Importance of Grandparents." *American Demographics* 14 (February 1992): 9–10.

Sciolino, Elaine. "Sex and the Church." *San Francisco Chronicle, This World,* December 16, 1984, pp. 7–8.

Scott, Gwendolyn B., et al. "Survival in Children with Perinatally Acquired Human Immunodeficiency Virus Type I Infection." *New England Journal of Medicine* 321 (December 28, 1989): 1791–96.

Seeley, R.; Stephens T.; and Tate, P. *Anatomy & Physiology.* St. Louis: Times Mirror/Mosby College Publishing, 1989.

Segal, Julius, and Yahraes, Herbert. *A Child's Journey: Forces That Shape the Lives of Our Young.* New York: McGraw-Hill, 1978.

Segraves, Kathleen Blindt. "Extramarital Affairs." *Medical Aspects of Human Sexuality* 23 (April 1989): 99–105.

Select Committee on Children, Youth and Families. "Caring for New Mothers: Pressing Problems, New Solutions." Hearing, U.S. House of Representatives, October 24, 1989.

———. *U.S. Children and Their Families: Current Conditions and Recent Trends, 1989.* Washington, DC: House of Representatives, September 1989.

———. *U.S. Children and Families: Key Trends in the 1980s.* Washington, DC: House of Representatives, 1988.

Selman, R. L. *The Growth of Interpersonal Understanding.* New York: Academic Press, 1980.

Seltzer, J. A., and Bianchi, S. M. "Children's Contact with Absent Parents." *Journal of Marriage and the Family* 50 (1988): 663–77.

Sewart, John, University of California's Office of the President, Berkeley. Quoted in "It's Taking Longer to Get a Degree," reported by April Lynch. *San Francisco Chronicle,* September 12, 1990, p. A-1.

Shapiro, Max. *The Penniless Billionaires.* New York: Times Books, 1980.

Shaver, Phillip, and Freedman, Jonathan. "Your Pursuit of Happiness." *Psychology Today* 10 (August 1976): 26–29.

Sheldon, Amy. "Pickle Fights: Gendered Talk in Preschool Disputes." *Discourse Processes* 13 (1990): 1.

Sheldrake, P.; Cromack, M.; and McGuire, J. "Psychosomatic Illness, Birth Order, and Intellectual Preference: Women." *Journal of Psychosomatic Research* 20 (1976): 45–49.

Sherman, Laurence, and Berk, Richard A. "The Specific Deterrent Effects of Arrest for Domestic Assault." *American Sociological Review* 49 (1984): 261–72.

Sherris, J. D.; Moore, S. H.; and Fox, G. "New Developments in Vaginal Contraception." *Population Reports* H (1984): 7.

Shilts, Randy. *And the Band Played On.* New York: St. Martin's, 1987.

Shorter, Edward. *The Making of the Modern Family.* New York: Basic Books, 1975.

Shortland, R. L. "A Model of the Causes of Date Rape in Developing and Class Relationships." In C. Hendrick (ed.), *Close Relationships,* pp. 246–70. Newbury Park, CA: Sage, 1989.

Silverman, I. "Physical Attractiveness and Courtship." *Sexual Behavior* (September 1971): 22–25.

Simenauer, Jacqueline, and Carroll, David. *Singles: The New Americans.* New York: New American Library, 1982.

Skinner, B. F. *About Behaviorism.* New York: Alfred A. Knopf, 1974.

Skolnick, Arlene S. *The Intimate Environment: Exploring Marriage and the Family.* 4th ed. Boston: Little, Brown, 1987.

———. *Embattled Paradise.* New York: Basic Books, 1991.

Smith, B. "Racism and Women's Studies." In G. Hull, P. Scott, and B. Smith (eds.), *But Some of Us Are Brave,* pp. 48–51. Old Westbury, NY: Feminist Press, 1982.

Smith, Daniel Scott. "Family Limitation, Sexual Control, and Domestic Feminism in Victorian America." In Mary Hartmann and Lois W. Banner (eds.), *Clio's Consciousness Raised,* pp. 119–36. New York: Harper & Row, 1974.

Smith, Jack C.; Mercy, James A.; and Conn, Judith, M. "Marital Status and the Risk of Suicide." *American Journal of Public Health* 78 (1988): 78–80.

Smith, Tom W. "Adult Sexual Behavior in 1989: Number of Partners, Frequency of Intercourse, and Risk of AIDS." *Family Planning Perspectives* 23 (May/June 1991): 102–107.

Sonenstein, Freya L.; Pleck, Joseph H.; and Ku, Leighton C. "Levels of Sexual Activity Among Adolescent Males in the United States." *Family Planning Perspectives* 23 (July/August 1991): 162–67.

Sorensen, G., et al. "Sex Differences in the Relationship Between Work and Health: The Minnesota Heart Survey." *Journal of Health and Social Behavior* 26 (1985): 379–94.

Spanier, Graham B. "Bequeathing Family Continuity." *Journal of Marriage and the Family* 51 (February 1989): 3–13.

Spanier, Graham B., and Glick, Paul C. "Marital Instability in the United States: Some Correlates and Recent Changes." *Family Relations* 30 (1981): 329–39.

Spanier, Graham B.; Lewis, Robert A.; and Cole, Charles L. "Marital Adjustment over the Family Life Cycle: The Issue of Curvilinearity." *Journal of Marriage and the Family* 37 (May 1975): 263–77.

Spanier, Graham B., and Thompson, Linda. *Parting: The Aftermath of Separation and Divorce.* Updated ed. Newbury Park, CA: Sage, 1987.

Spezzano, Charles, and Waterman, Jill. "The First Day of Life." *Psychology Today* 11 (December 1977): 110–16.

Spock, Benjamin, and Rothenberg, Michael. *Baby and Child Care.* 6th ed. New York: Pocket Books, 1991.

Staples, Robert. "Black Singles in America." In Peter J. Stein (ed.), *Single Life: Unmarried Adults in Social Context,* pp. 40–51. New York: St. Martin's, 1981.

Staples, Robert, and Mirande, Alfredo. "Racial and Cultural Variations Among American Families: A Decennial Review of the Literature on Minority Families." *Journal of Marriage and the Family* 33 (1980): 119–35.

Stark, Rodney. *Sociology.* 3rd ed. Belmont, CA: Wadsworth, 1989.

Starr, Bernard D., and Weiner, Marcella Bakur. *Sex and Sexuality in the Mature Years.* New York: Stein & Day, 1981.

Starr, Raymond H., Jr. "Physical Abuse of Children." In Vincent B. Van Hasselt, Randall L. Morrison, Alan S. Bellack, and Michel Herson (eds.), *Handbook of Family Violence,* pp. 119–155. New York: Plenum, 1988.

Starr, Tama. *The Natural 'Inferiority' of Women: Outrageous Pronouncements by Misguided Males.* New York: Poseidon Press, 1991.

Steck, L.; Levitan, D.; Mclane, D.; and Kelley, H. H. "Care, Need, and Conceptions of Love." *Journal of Personal and Social Psychology* 43 (1982): 481–91.

Stein, Peter J. *Single Life: Unmarried Adults in Social Context*. New York: St. Martin's Press, 1981.

———. "Singlehood." In E. Macklin and R. H. Rubin (eds.), *Contemporary Families and Alternative Lifestyles*. Beverly Hills, CA: Sage, 1983.

Steinman, S. "The Experience of Children in a Joint-Custody Arrangement: A Report of a Study." *American Journal of Orthopsychiatry* 51 (1981): 403–14.

Stephens, William N. *The Family in Cross-Cultural Perspective*. Lanham, MD: University Press of America, 1982.

Sternberg, Robert J. "The Measure of Love." *Science Digest* 93 (April 1985): 60, 78–79.

Stevens, Michael J.; Rice, Mary Beth; and Johnson, James J. "Effect of Eye Glaze on Self-Disclosure." *Perceptual and Motor Skills* 62 (1986): 939–42.

Stewart, R. A., and Beatty, M. J. "Jealousy and Self-Esteem." *Perceptual and Motor Skills* 60 (1985): 153–54.

Stoneman, Z.; Brody, G. H.; and MacKinnon, C. E. "Same-Sex and Cross-Sex Siblings: Activity Choices, Roles, Behavior, and Gender Stereotypes." *Sex Roles* 15 (1986): 495–511.

Stratton, Joanna L. *Pioneer Women: Voices from the Kansas Frontier*. New York: Simon & Schuster, 1981.

Straus, Murray A. "Violence Among Unwed Couples." Paper presented at the American Sociological Association Conference, Atlanta, August 25, 1988.

———. "Family Violence." In *2001: Preparing Families for the Future*. Minneapolis, MN: National Council on Family Relations Presidential Report, 1990, pp. 26–27.

Straus, Murray A., and Gelles, Richard J. "Societal Change and Change in Family Violence from 1975 to 1985 as Revealed by Two National Surveys." *Journal of Marriage and the Family* 48 (August 1986): 465–79.

Straus, Murray A.; Gelles, Richard J.; and Steinmetz, Suzanne K. *Behind Closed Doors: Violence in the American Family*. Garden City, NY: Anchor Press/Doubleday, 1980.

Stroufe, L. Alan, and Waters, Everett. "Attachment as an Organizational Construct." *Child Development* 48 (1977): 1184–99.

Struckman-Johnson, C. C. "Forced Sex on Dates: It Happens to Men, Too." *The Journal of Sex Research* 24 (1988): 234–41.

Sue, Stanley, and Okazaki, Sumie, "Asian-American Educational Achievements." *American Psychologist* 45 (August 1990): 913–20.

Sullivan, Louis. Quoted in Speech to the Economic Club of Detroit. *San Francisco Chronicle*, October 3, 1991, p. A-4.

———. Health and Human Services Report on the Increasing Proportion of Low-Birth Weight Births in the U.S. Washington, DC, April 24, 1992.

Svejda, M. J.; Pannabecker, B. J.; and Emde, R. N. "Parent-to-Infant Attachment: A Critique of the Early 'Bonding' Model." In R. N. Emde and R. J. Harmon (eds.), *The Development of Attachment and Affiliative Systems*. New York: Plenum Press, 1982.

Sweet, James A., and Bumpass, Larry L. *American Families and Households*. New York: Russell Sage Foundation, 1987.

Syrzycki, Cindy, and Walsh, Maureen. "Singles are No. 1 Target for New Advertising." *San Francisco Chronicle*, April 30, 1986, p. 24.

Tallman, I. *Passion, Action, and Politics: A Perspective on Social Problems and Social Problem Solving*. San Francisco: W. H. Freeman, 1976.

Tamis-LeMonda, Catherine, and Bornstein, Marc. "Interaction with Infants Is Linked to Later Abilities." Reported by Kathleen Fisher, in *American Psychological Association Monitor* 21 (April 1990): 10.

Tanfer, Koray. "Patterns of Premarital Cohabitation among Never-Married Women in the United States." *Journal of Marriage and the Family* 49 (August 1987): 483–97.

Tannahill, Reay. *Sex in History*. New York: Stein & Day, 1980.

Tannen, Deborah. *You Just Don't Understand*. New York: William Morrow, 1990.

Tavris, Carol, and Sadd, Susan. *The Redbook Report on Female Sexuality*. New York: Redbook, 1977.

Taylor, Frances. "Hepatitis B Vaccine Plan for All San Francisco Newborns." Reported by Russell Sabin, *San Francisco Chronicle*, March 6, 1992, p. A-4.

Taylor, Robert J.; Chatters, Linda M.; Tucker, Belinda M.; and Lewis, Edith. "Developments in Research on Black Families." In Alan Booth (ed.), *Looking Forward, Looking Back*. Minneapolis, MN: National Council on Family Relations, 1991.

Teachman, J. "Early Marriage, Premarital Fertility, and Marital Dissolution: Results for Blacks and Whites." *Journal of Family Issues* 4 (1983): 105–26.

———. "First and Second Marital Dissolution: A Decomposition Exercise for Whites and Blacks." *Sociological Quarterly* 27 (1986): 571–90.

Teachman, J., and Heckert, A. "The Impact of Age and Children on Remarriage." *Journal of Family Issues* 6 (June 1985): 185–203.

Tennov, Dorothy. *Love and Limerence*. New York: Stein & Day, 1979.

Thoits, Peggy. "Multiple Identities: Examining Gender Differences in Distress." *American Sociological Review* 51 (1986): 259–72.

Thomas, Clayton Lay, ed. *Taber's Cyclopedic Medical Dictionary*. 16th ed. Philadelphia: F. A. Davis, 1989.

Thomas, D. A., and Alderfer, C. P. "The Influence of Race on Career Dynamics: Theory and Research on Minority Career Experiences." In M. Arthur, D. Hall, and B. Lawrence (eds.), *Handbook of Career Theory*. Cambridge, England: Cambridge University Press, 1989.

Thompson, Clara. *Psychoanalysis: Evolution and Development*. New York: Hermitage, 1951.

Thorne, B. "Girls and Boys Together . . . but Mostly Apart: Gender Arrangements in Elementary Schools." In W. W. Hartup and Z. Rubin (eds.), *Relationships and Development*, pp. 167–84. Hillsdale, NJ: Erlbaum, 1986.

Thorton, Arland, and Freedman, Deborah. "Changing Attitudes Toward Marriage and the Single Life." *Family Planning Perspectives* 14 (November–December 1982): 32–38.

Thorton, Arland, and Rodgers, Willard. "The Influence of Individual and Historical Time on Marital Dissolution." *Demography* 24 (1987): 1–22.

Tolstoy, Leo. *Diaries.* Edited and translated by R. F. Christian. New York: Scribners, 1986.

———. *War and Peace.* Translated by Constance Garnett. New York: Crowell, 1976.

Trevathan, Wenda R. *Human Birth: An Evolutionary Perspective.* New York: Aldine De Gruyter, 1987.

Troph, W. D. "An Exploratory Examination of the Effects of Remarriage on Child Support and Personal Contact." *Journal of Divorce* 7 (1984): 57–73.

Trost, Cathy. "Women Working: A Special Report." *Wall Street Journal,* May 23, 1989, p. A-1.

Trovato, Frank, and Lauris, Gloria. "Marital Status and Mortality in Canada: 1951–81." *Journal of Marriage and the Family* 51 (1989): 907–22.

Trussell, James. "Teenage Pregnancy in the United States." *Family Planning Perspectives* 20 (November–December 1988): 262–72.

Trussell, James, et al. "Contraceptive Failure in the United States: An Update." *Studies in Family Planning* 21 (January/February 1990): Table 1.

Turner, R. "One-Third of Working Mothers of a School-Age Child Pay for Day Care." *Family Planning Perspectives* 23 (January/February 1991): 46–47.

Uchitelle, Lois. "Women Joining Workforce at Slowest Pace Since '70s." *San Francisco Chronicle,* November 24, 1990, p. 1.

Udry, J. Richard. "Sex and Family Life." *Annals of the American Academy of Political and Social Science* 376 (March 1968): 25–35.

United Nations. "Adolescent Reproductive Behavior: Evidence from Developed Countries." *Population Studies* 109. New York, 1988.

U.S. Bureau of the Census. "Black-White Married Couples: 1970–1989." *Current Population Reports,* Series P-20, No. 445 and earlier reports. Washington, DC: Government Printing Office, 1991.

———. "Changing American Households and Families: 1980–1990." *Current Population Reports,* Series P-20, Nos. 433, 437, and 441; series P-60, No. 162, and forthcoming data. Washington, DC: Government Printing Office, January 1991.

———. "Child Care Arrangements: Winter, 1986–87." *Current Population Reports,* Series P-70, No. 20. Washington, DC: Government Printing Office, 1990.

———. "Children Below the Poverty Line, by Race and Hispanic Origin: 1970–1989." *Current Population Reports,* Series P-60, No. 168, and earlier reports. Washington, DC: Government Printing Office, 1991.

———. "Children Under 18 Years Old, by Presence of Parents: 1970 to 1988." *Current Population Reports,* Series P-20, No. 433. Washington, DC: Government Printing Office, 1990.

———. "Child Support and Alimony — Selected Characteristics of Women: 1987." *Current Population Reports,* Series P-23, No. 167. Washington, DC: Government Printing Office, 1991.

———. "Child Support — Award and Recipiency Status of Women: 1981 to 1987." *Current Population Reports,* Series P-23, No. 167. Washington, DC: Government Printing Office, 1991.

———. *Current Population Reports,* Series P-20, No. 450, March 1990; *Current Population Reports, 1970 revised.* Washington, DC: Government Printing Office, 1991.

———. "Families Below Poverty Level — Selected Characteristics, by Race and Hispanic Origin: 1989." *Current Population Reports,* Series P-60, No. 168. Washington, DC: Government Printing Office, 1991.

———. "Families, by Number of Own Children Under 18 Years Old: 1970 to 1989." *U.S. Census of Population 1970* (PC-2-4A), and *Current Population Reports,* Series P-20, No. 447 and earlier reports. Washington, DC: Government Printing Office, 1991.

———. *Historical Statistics of the United States, Colonial Times to 1970, Parts I and II.* Bicentennial edition. Department of Commerce. Washington, DC: Government Printing Office, 1975.

———. "Household and Family Characteristics: March 1989 and 1990." *Current Population Reports,* Series P-20, Nos. 445, 447. Washington, DC: Government Printing Office, 1990.

———. "Households, Families, Subfamilies, Married Couples, and Unrelated Individuals: 1960 to 1990." *Current Population Reports,* Series P-20, No. 447. Washington, DC: Government Printing Office, 1991.

———. "Marital Status and Living Arrangements: March 1989 and 1990." Prepared by Arlene F. Saluter, *Current Population Reports,* Series P-20, No. 445 (1990); Series P-20, No. 450. Washington, DC: Government Printing Office, 1991.

———. "Marital Status of the Population, by Sex and Age: 1989." *Current Population Reports,* Series P-20, No. 445. Washington, DC: Government Printing Office, 1991.

———. "Marital Status of the Population, by Sex, Race, and Hispanic Origin: 1970 to 1989." *Current Population Reports,* Series P-20, No. 445, and earlier reports. Washington, DC: Government Printing Office, 1991.

———. "Mean Earnings of Husbands and Wives in Married-Couple Families: 1981 and 1987." *Current Population Reports,* Series P-60, Nos. 163 and 165. Washington, DC: Government Printing Office, 1991.

———. "Money Income of Families — Percent Distribution by Income Level, by Race and Hispanic Origin of Householder, and Selected Characteristics: 1988 and 1989." *Current Population Reports,* Series P-60, Nos. 166 and 168, and unpublished data. Washington, DC: Government Printing Office, 1991.

———. "1980 Census Questionnaire on Race." *Statistical Abstract of the United States.* 111th ed. Washington, DC: Government Printing Office, 1991, p. 4.

———. "Persons Living Alone, by Sex and Age: 1970 to 1989." *Current Population Reports,* Series P-20, No. 445 and earlier reports. Washington, DC: Government Printing Office, 1991.

———. "Persons 65 Years and Over — Characteristics, by Sex: 1970 to 1989." *Current Population Reports,* Series P-23, No. 59; and Series P-60, No. 166 and earlier reports. Washington, DC: Government Printing Office, 1991.

———. "Population 65 Years and Over, by Age Group and Sex, 1900 to

1989, and Projections, 2020." *Current Population Reports*, Series P-25, Nos. 519, 917, 1018, 1057, and earlier reports, and unpublished data. Washington, DC: Government Printing Office, 1991.

———. "Projections of the Hispanic Population by Age and Sex: 1989–2010." *Current Population Reports*, Series P-25, Nos. 995 and 1018. Washington, DC: Government Printing Office, 1990.

———. "Projections of the Total Population by Age, Sex, and Race: 1989–2010: *Current Population Reports*, Series P-25, Nos. 1018. Washington, DC: Government Printing Office, 1990.

———. "Property Settlement Following Divorce — Selected Characteristics of Women: 1979 and 1988." *Current Population Reports*, Series P-23, No. 167. Washington, DC: Government Printing Office, 1991.

———. "Ratio of Males to Females, by Age Group: 1940 to 1989." *U.S. Census of Population*: 1940, Vol. II, Part I, and Vol. IV, Part I; 1950, Vol. II, Part I; 1960, Vol. I, Part I; 1970, Vol. I, Part B; and *Current Population Reports*, Series P-25, Nos. 1045 and 1057. Washington, DC: Government Printing Office, 1991.

———. Report on Home Affordability. Press Release, *San Francisco Chronicle*, June 14, 1991, p. A-2.

———. "Resident Population, by Age, Sex, and Race: 1970 to 1989." *Current Population Reports*, Series P-25, Nos. 917, 1045, and 1057. Washington, DC: Government Printing Office, 1991.

———. "Single (Never-Married) Persons as Percent of Total Population, by Sex and Age: 1970 to 1989." *Current Population Reports*, Series P-20, No. 445. Washington, DC: Government Printing Office, 1991.

———. "Social and Economic Aspects of the Hispanic Population: 1989." *Current Population Reports*, Series P-60, and P-20, No. 444. Washington, DC: Government Printing Office, 1991.

———. "Social and Economic Characteristics of Women, 18–44 Years Old, Who Have Had a Child in the Last Year: 1988." *Current Population Reports*, Series P-20, No. 436. Washington, DC: Government Printing Office, 1991.

———. *Statistical Abstract of the United States*, 92nd, 110th, and 111th eds. Washington, DC: Government Printing Office, 1971, 1990, and 1991.

———. "Studies in Marriage and the Family." *Current Population Reports*, Series P-23, No. 162, p. 5. Washington, DC: Government Printing Office, 1989.

———. Tenth Annual Status Report on Minorities in Education. U.S. Department of Education. Washington, DC: Government Printing Office, January 20, 1992.

———. "Total Population, by Sex, Race, and Age: 1989." Series P-25, Nos. 1045 and 1057. Washington, DC: Government Printing Office, 1991.

———. "Unmarried Couples, by Selected Characteristics, 1970 to 1989, and by Marital Status of Partners, 1989." *1970 Census of Population*, Vol. II, Part 4B, and *Current Population Reports*, Series P-20. Washington, DC: Government Printing Office, 1991.

———. "White, Black, and Hispanic Households, by Type: 1970 to 1990." *Census of Population*: 1970, *Persons of Spanish Origin*, PC (2)-1C; and *Current Population Reports*, Series P-20, No. 447. Washington, DC: Government Printing Office, 1991.

U.S. Bureau of the Census and the Conference Board. "A Marketer's Guide to Discretionary Income, 1989." *Statistical Abstract of the United States*, 111th ed., p. 453. Washington, DC: Government Printing Office, 1991.

U.S. Bureau of Labor Statistics. "Employed and Unemployed Workers, by Work Schedules, Sex and Age: 1980 to 1989." Bulletin 2307 and *Employment and Earnings*, monthly. Washington, DC: Government Printing Office, 1991.

———. "Inflation Rates: 1981–1991." Monthly data in U.S. Bureau of Economic Analysis, *Survey of Current Business*, December 1991.

———. "Indexes of Medical Care Prices: 1970 to 1990." *CPI Detailed Report*. Washington, DC: Government Printing Office, January 1991.

———. "Labor Force Participation Rates for Wives, Husband Present, by Age of Own Youngest Child: 1975 to 1989." Bulletin 2340, and

unpublished data. Washington, DC: Government Printing Office, 1991.

———. "Marital and Family Characteristics of the Labor Force, Current Population Survey, March 1990." U.S. Department of Labor. Washington, DC: Government Printing Office, 1991.

———. "Marital Status of Women in the Civilian Labor Force: 1960 to 1989." Bulletin 2307. Washington, DC: Government Printing Office, 1991.

———. "Married, Separated, and Divorced Women — Labor Force Status by Presence and Age of Children: 1960 to 1989." Bulletin 2307. Washington, DC: Government Printing Office, 1991.

———. "Purchasing Power of the Dollar: 1950 to 1990." Monthly data in U.S. Bureau of Economic Analysis, *Survey of Current Business*. Washington, DC: Government Printing Office, 1991.

———. Report on Working College Students, compiled by the staff of *Demographics Magazine. Wall Street Journal*, August 3, 1990, p. B-1.

———. "Workers on Flexible Schedules, by Selected Characteristics: 1989." *Monthly Labor Review*, July 1990. Washington, DC: Government Printing Office, 1991.

U.S. Centers for Disease Control. "AIDS Cases Reported, by Patient Characteristics: 1981 to 1990." Division of Sexually Transmitted Disease, Atlanta: Public Health Service, 1991.

———. "Coronary Heart Disease Attributable to Sedentary Lifestyle — Selected States: 1988." *Journal of the American Medical Association* 264 (September 19, 1990): 1390–92.

———. Division of Sexually Transmitted Diseases. *Morbidity and Mortality Weekly Report*. Atlanta: March 16, 1991.

———. Division of STD/HIV Prevention. *Sexually Transmitted Disease Surveillance, 1990*. Atlanta: November 1991.

———. "1990 Division of STD/HIV Prevention Annual Report." Center for Prevention Services, Atlanta: 1991.

———. "Recommendations for Rubella Vaccinations." *Morbidity and Mortality Weekly Report*. Atlanta: July 2, 1992.

———. "Sentinel Surveillance System for Antimicrobial Resistance in Clinical Isolates of Neisseria Gonorrhoeae." *Morbidity and Mortality Weekly Report*, 36. Atlanta: 1987.

———. "Specified Reportable Diseases—Cases Reported: 1970 to 1989." Summary of Notifiable Diseases, *Morbidity and Mortality Weekly Report*, 38. Atlanta: 1991.

———. "STDs." *Morbidity and Mortality Weekly Report*, 33. Atlanta: December 30, 1984.

———. "Update: Acquired Immunodeficiency Syndrome—United States, 1981–1990." *Morbidity and Mortality Weekly Reports*, Atlanta: June 1991 and 1992.

U.S. Center for Population Options. "Teenage Pregnancy and Too-Early Childbearing: Public Costs, Personal Consequences." Washington, DC: Government Printing Office, 1989.

U.S. Conference of Catholic Bishops. *Human Sexuality: A Catholic Perspective for Education and Lifelong Learning.* Washington, DC: November 14, 1990.

U.S. Conference of Mayors. *The Continued Growth of Hunger, Homelessness, and Poverty in America's Cities.* Washington, DC: December 1991.

U.S. Department of Agriculture, Economic Research Service. "Farm Population and Employment: 1960 to 1986." *Current Population Reports*, Series P-27, No. 60. Washington, DC: Government Printing Office, 1988.

———. *Food Guide Pyramid.* Washington, DC: Government Printing Office, April 25, 1992.

U.S. Department of Education, Center for Education Statistics. "Enrollment in Institutions of Higher Education, by Sex, Age, and Attendance Status, 1970 to 1985, and Projections, 1995." *The Condition of Education*, annual. Washington, DC: Government Printing Office, 1988.

———. "Higher Education—Summary: 1970 to 1988." *Digest of Education Statistics*, annual. Washington, DC: Government Printing Office, 1991.

———. "Institutions of Higher Education—Finances: 1975–1988." *Digest of Education Statistics*, annual. Washington, DC: Government Printing Office, 1991.

U.S. Department of Health and Human Services. *Executive Summary: National Study of the Incidence of Child Abuse and Neglect.* Washington, DC: Government Printing Office, 1981.

———. *Study Findings: Study of the National Incidence and Prevalence of Child Abuse and Neglect.* Washington, DC: Government Printing Office, 1988.

U.S. National Assessment of Educational Progress. *Learning to Be Literate in America.* Princeton, NJ: Educational Testing Service, March 1987.

———. "Twenty-Year Review of Test Results," second report. Washington, DC: National Assessment Governing Board, 1991.

———. *The Writing Report Card, 1984–1988.* Princeton, NJ: Educational Testing Service, January 1990.

U.S. National Association of Homebuilders, 1990 Census data. Special Report. Washington, DC: Government Printing Office, November 29, 1991.

U.S. National Center for Children in Poverty. "Distribution of All Children and of Poor Children, by Family Type and Race: 1987." Washington, DC: Government Printing Office, 1991.

U.S. National Center for Education Statistics. *Digest of Education Statistics: 1989*, p. 20, Table 108. Washington, DC: Department of Education, Office of Educational Research and Improvement, December 1989.

———. *Undergraduate Financing of Postsecondary Education, May 1988.* Washington, DC: Government Printing Office, 1991.

U.S. National Center for Health Statistics. "Advance Report of Final Natality Statistics, 1986." *Monthly Vital Statistics Report* 37, Supplement. Washington, DC: Government Printing Office, July 12, 1988.

———. "Annual Summary of Births, Marriages, Divorces, and Deaths: 1989." *Monthly Vital Statistics Report* 38 (13): 3. DHHS Publication No. PHS 90-1120. Washington, DC: Government Printing Office, 1990.

———. "Babies Born Out-of-Wedlock in the United States, by Race: 1970 to 1988." *Monthly Vital Statistics Report.* Washington, DC: September 1991.

———. "Births to Unmarried Women, by Race and Age of Mother: 1950 to 1981." *Vital Statistics of the United States*, annual. Washington, DC: Government Printing Office, 1985.

———. "Births to Unmarried Women, by Race of Child and Age of Mother: 1970 to 1988." *Vital Statistics of the United States*, annual. Washington, DC: Government Printing Office, 1991.

———. "Current Estimates from the National Health Interview Survey: United States, 1987." *Vital and Health Statistics* 10, No. 166, Public Health Service. Washington, DC: Government Printing Office, 1988.

———. "Death Rates by Selected Causes and Selected Characteristics: 1970 to 1989." *Vital Statistics of the United States*, annual. Washington, DC: Government Printing Office, 1991.

———. "Divorces and Annulments—Median Duration of Marriage, Median Age at Divorce, and Children Involved: 1970 to 1987." *Vital Statistics of the United States*, annual. Washington, DC: Government Printing Office, 1991.

———. "Divorces and Annulments—Rate and Percent Distribution, by Age and Sex: 1987." *Vital Statistics of the United States*, annual. Washington, DC: Government Printing Office, 1991.

———. "Expectation of Life at Birth, 1960 to 1989, and Projections, 1990 to 2010." *Vital Statistics of the United States*, annual. Washington, DC: Government Printing Office, 1991.

———. "Expectation of Life and Expected Deaths, by Race, Sex, and Age: 1988." *Vital Statistics of the United States*, annual. Washington, DC: Government Printing Office, 1991.

———. "Infant Deaths and Infant Mortality Rates by Cause of Death: 1980 to 1988." *Vital Statistics of the United States*, annual. Washington, DC: Government Printing Office, December 1991.

———. "Infant, Maternal, and Neonatal Mortality Rates, and Fetal Mortality Ratios, by Race: 1950 to 1989." *Vital Statistics of the United States*, annual (1991), and *Monthly Vital Statistics Report.* Washington, DC: Government Printing Office, February 1992.

————. "Legal Separation." *Monthly Vital Statistics Report*. Washington, DC: Government Printing Office, December 1980.

————. "Live Births, by Place of Delivery; Median and Low-Birth Weight; and Prenatal Care: 1960 to 1988." *Vital Statistics of the United States*, annual, and unpublished reports. Washington, DC: Government Printing Office, 1991.

————. "Live Births, by Race and Type of Hispanic Origin — Selected Characteristics: 1988." *Vital Statistics of the United States*, annual. Washington, DC: Government Printing Office, 1991.

————. "Live Births per 1,000 Population." *Monthly Vital Statistics Report*. Washington, DC: Government Printing Office, December 1991.

————. "Marriages — Age Differences of Bride and Groom, by Age: 1987." *Vital Statistics of the United States*, annual. Washington, DC: Government Printing Office, 1991.

————. "Marriages and Divorces: 1960 to 1987." *Vital Statistics of the United States*, annual. Washington, DC: Government Printing Office, 1991.

————. "Marriages and Divorces — Number and Rate, by State: 1980 to 1988." *Vital Statistics of the United States*, annual. Washington, DC: Government Printing Office, 1990.

————. "Marriage Rates and Median Age of Bride and Groom, by Previous Marital Status: 1970 to 1987." *Vital Statistics of the United States*, annual. Washington, DC: Government Printing Office, 1991.

————. "Percent of All Divorces by Duration of Marriage." *Vital Statistics of the United States*, annual, and unpublished reports. Washington, DC: Government Printing Office, 1988.

————. "Percent Distribution of Marriages, by Age, Sex, and Previous Marital Status: 1980 to 1987." *Vital Statistics of the United States*, annual. Washington, DC: Government Printing Office, 1991.

————. "Personal Health Practices, by Selected Characteristics: 1985." *Health Promotion and Disease Prevention, United States*. Washington, DC: Government Printing Office, 1990.

————. *Vital and Health Statistics*, Series 10, and *Monthly Vital Statistics Reports*. Washington, DC: Government ment Printing Office, December 1984.

————. "Weddings Performed in Religious Ceremonies." *Vital Statistics of the United States*, annual. Washington, DC: Government Printing Office, 1988.

U.S. National Center for Children in Poverty. "Distribution of All Children and of Poor Children, by Family Type and Race: 1987." Washington, DC: Government Printing Office, 1991.

U.S. National Center for Juvenile Justice. "Delinquency Cases Disposed, by Juvenile Courts: 1975 to 1986." Pittsburg, PA: Juvenile Court Statistics, annual, 1991.

U.S. National Commission to Prevent Infant Mortality. "International Infant Mortality Comparisons: Briefing Paper." Washington, DC: Government Printing Office, February 1, 1988.

————. "Infant Mortality: Care for Our Children, Care for Our Future." Washington, DC: Government Printing Office, August 1988.

————. "Infant Mortality Fact Sheet." Washington, DC: Government Printing Office, January 1990.

U.S. National Commission on the Role of the School and the Community in Improving Adolescent Health. *Code Blue: Uniting for Healthier Youth*, pp. 3–4. Washington, DC: National Association of State Boards of Education and the American Medical Association, 1990.

U.S. National Council of the Churches of Christ. *Yearbook of American and Canadian Churches*, annual, 1991.

U.S. Social Security Administration. "Social Security (OASDI) — Retirement Benefits, by Sex: 1970–1985." *Social Security Bulletin*. Washington, DC: Government Printing Office, 1987.

————. "Social Security (OASDI) — Benefits, by Type of Beneficiary: 1970 to 1989." *Annual Statistical Supplement to the Social Security Bulletin*. Washington, DC: Government Printing Office, 1991.

U.S. Survey of Income and Program Participation (SIIP). *Family Planning Perspectives* 23 (January/February 1991): 46.

Updike, John. *Rabbit, Run*. New York: Alfred A. Knopf, 1960.

————. *Too Far to Go*. New York: Ballantine, 1979.

Valdés, Isabel. "Understanding Hispanic Consumers." *Marketing Tools Alert*, supplement to *American Demographics* 13 (October 1991): 1.

Van de Perre, Phillipe, et al. "Postnatal Transmission of Human Immunodeficiency Virus Type I from Mother to Infant." *The New England Journal of Medicine* 325 (August 29, 1991): 593–98.

Veevers, Jean E. *Childless by Choice*. Toronto: Butterworths, 1980.

————. "Voluntary Childlessness: A Review of Issues and Evidence." *Marriage and Family Review* 2 (1979): 1, 3–20.

Visher, E. B., and Visher, J. *Stepfamilies: A Guide to Working with Stepparents and Stepchildren*. New York: Brunner/Mazel, 1979.

Von Glinow, M. A., and Krzyczowska, Mercer A. "Women in Corporate America: A Caste of Thousands." *New Management* 6 (Summer 1988): 36–42.

Waehler, Charles. "Happiness of Single Men." Paper presented at the annual meeting of the American Psychological Association, San Francisco, August 15, 1991.

Wald, Nicholas. "Prevention of Neural Tube Defects: Results of the Medical Research Council Vitamin Study." *Lancet* 338 (July 20, 1991): 131–37.

Waldholtz, Michael. Report on Federal Survey of Obese Children. *Wall Street Journal*, January 10, 1992a, p. B-1.

————. "New Discoveries Dim Drug Makers' Hopes for Quick AIDS Cure." *Wall Street Journal*, May 26, 1992b, pp. A-1, A-11.

Walker, Lenore E. *The Battered Woman*. New York: Harper & Row, 1979.

Wallerstein, E. *Circumcision: Information, Misinformation, Disinformation*. Corte Madera, CA: National Organization of Circumcision Information, Resource Center, 1986.

Wallerstein, Judith S. "Children of Divorce: The Dilemma of a Decade." In Elam W. Nunnally, Catherine S. Chilman, and Fred M. Cox (eds.), *Troubled Relationships*, pp. 55–73. Newbury Park, CA: Sage, 1988.

————. Quoted in "The Deception of Emotional Child Abuse," by Lisa Klug. *San Francisco Sunday Examiner and Chronicle*, April 19, 1992, p. C-3.

Wallerstein, Judith S., and Blakeslee, Sandra. *Second Chances: Men, Women, and Children a Decade After Divorce.* New York: Ticknor & Fields, 1989.

Wallerstein, Judith S., and Kelly, Joan Berlin. *Surviving the Breakup: How Children and Parents Cope with Divorce.* New York: Basic Books, 1980.

Wallis, Claudia. "Children Having Children." *Time,* December 9, 1985, pp. 78–90.

Walster, Elaine, and Walster, G. William. *A New Look at Love.* Reading, MA: Addison-Wesley, 1978.

Walster, Elaine; Walster, F.; Piliavin, J.; and Schmidt, L. "Playing Hard to Get: Understanding an Elusive Phenomenon." *Journal of Personality and Social Psychology* 26 (1973): 113–21.

Washington, A. Eugene; Cates, Willard, Jr.; and Wasserheit, Judith N. "Preventing Pelvic Inflammatory Disease." *Journal of the American Medical Association* 266 (November 13, 1991): 2574–80.

Washington, A. Eugene, and Katz, Patricia. "Cost and Payment Source for PID: Trends and Projections, 1983 Through 2000." *Journal of the American Medical Association* (November 13, 1991): 2565–69.

Watson, David L. *Psychology.* Belmont, CA: Wadsworth, 1992.

Wehler, Cheryl. "Widespread Hunger of Children Under 12 in the United States." Survey conducted by the *Food Research and Action Center.* Washington, DC: March 1991.

Weingarten, H. R. "Remarriage and Well-Being: National Survey Evidence of Social and Psychological Effects." *Journal of Family Issues* 1 (1980): 533–59.

Weisner, Thomas, and Gallimore, Ronald. "My Brother's Keeper: Child and Sibling Care Taking." *Current Anthropology* 18 (1977): 169–90.

Weiss, Robert S. *Marital Separation.* New York: Basic Books, 1975.

———. "The Study of Loneliness." In Peter J. Stein (ed.), *Unmarried Adults in Social Context,* pp. 152–64. New York: St. Martin's Press, 1981.

Weitzman, Lenore J. *The Marriage Contract.* New York: Free Press, 1981.

———. *The Divorce Revolution: The Unexpected Social and Economic Consequences for Women and Children in America.* New York: Free Press, 1985.

Weitzman, Lenore J., and Dixon, Ruth. "The Alimony Myth: Does No-Fault Divorce Make a Difference?" *Family Law Quarterly* 14 (Fall 1980): 185.

Wernick, Robert. *The Family.* New York: Time-Life Books, 1974.

Westoff, Charles F. "Contraceptive Paths Toward the Reduction of Unintended Pregnancy and Abortion." *Family Planning Perspectives* 20 (1988a): 4.

———. "Unintended Pregnancy in America and Abroad." *Family Planning Perspectives* 20 (1988b): 254–61.

Westoff, Charles F., and Parke, Robert Jr., eds. *Demographic and Social Aspects of Population Growth,* Vol. 1, pp. 39, 593. U.S. Commission on Population Growth and the American Future. Washington, DC: Government Printing Office, 1972.

White, Burton. *The First Three Years of Life.* Englewood Cliffs, NJ: Prentice-Hall, 1975.

———. "Blueprint for Rearing Happy Children." Paper presented at the annual meeting of the American Association for the Advancement of Science, February 19, 1976, Boston.

White, James. "Premarital Cohabitation and Marital Stability in Canada." *Journal of Marriage and the Family* 49 (1987): 641–47.

White, Lynn K. "Determinants of Divorce: A Review of Research in the Eighties." *Journal of Marriage and the Family* 52 (November 1990): 904–12.

White, Lynn K., and Booth, Alan. "The Quality and Stability of Remarriages: The Role of Stepchildren." *American Sociological Review* 50 (1985): 689–98.

White, Lynn K.; Booth, Alan; and Edwards, John. "Children and Marital Happiness: Why the Negative Relationship." *Journal of Family Issues* 7 (1986): 131–48.

White, Lynn K.; Brinkeroff, David; and Booth, Alan. "The Effect of Marital Disruption on Child's Attachment to Parents." *Journal of Family Issues* 6 (1985): 5–22.

White House Conference on Families. *Families and Economic Well-Being.* Washington, DC: Government Printing Office, 1980.

Whitley, B. E., Jr. "The Relationship of Sex-Role Orientation to Heterosexuals' Attitudes Toward Homosexuals." *Sex Roles* 17 (1987): 103–113.

WHO (World Health Organization). Report on AIDS. Geneva, Switzerland, February and May 1992.

Widom, Cathy S. "The Cycle of Violence." *Science* 224 (April 14, 1989): 160–66.

Wilcox, Allen J., et al. "Incidence of Early Loss of Pregnancy." *New England Journal of Medicine* 319 (July 28, 1988): 189–94.

Williams, N. D. *Psychology of Women: Behavior in Biosocial Context.* 3rd ed. New York: Norton, 1987.

Williams-Deane, Martha, and Potter, Linda S. "Current Oral Contraceptive Use Instructions: An Analysis of Patient Package Inserts." *Family Planning Perspectives* 24 (May/June 1992): 111–115.

Wilson, Barbara Foley, "The Marry-Go-Round." *American Demographics* 13 (October 1991): 52–54.

Wilson, Margaret Gibbons. *The American Woman in Transition: The Urban Influence, 1879–1920.* Westport, CT: Greenwood, 1979.

Wilson, William J. *The Truly Disadvantaged: The Inner City, The Underclass and Public Policy.* Chicago: University of Chicago Press, 1987.

Wineberg, Howard. "Duration Between Marriage and First Birth and Marital Stability." *Social Biology* 35 (1988): 91–102.

———. "Childbearing After Remarriage." *Journal of Marriage and the Family* 52 (1990): 31–38.

Winslow, Ron. "Study Raises Issue of Biological Basis of Homosexuality." *Wall Street Journal,* August 30, 1991, p. B-1.

Wise, Paul H., and Pursley, DeWayne M. "Infant Mortality as a Social Mirror." *New England Journal of Medicine* 326 (June 4, 1992): 1558–59.

Wolfe, Sidney. "Caesarean Sections Performed Unnecessarily." *Public Citizen's Health Research Group Report.* Washington, DC, May 12, 1990.

Workman, Bill. "Basic Costs at Stanford Hit $21,262." *San Francisco Chronicle,* February 14, 1991, p. A-6.

———. "Stanford Increases Tuition 9.5 Percent." *San Francisco Chronicle,* February 12, 1992, p. A-13.

WOW (Wider Opportunities for Women) Report. "No Way Out: Working Poor Women in the United States." Washington, DC: National Commission on Working Women in the United States, 1988.

Wyatt, G. E., and Peters, S. D. "Issues in the Definition of Child Abuse in Prevalent Research." *Child Abuse and Neglect* 10 (1986): 231–40.

Wyatt, G. E.; Peters, S. D.; and Guthrie, D. "Kinsey Revisited, Part I: Comparisons of the Sexual Socialization and Sexual Behavior of White Women over 33 Years." *Archives of Sexual Behavior* 17 (1988): 201.

Wyatt, G. E., and Powell, G. J., eds. "Lasting Effects of Child Sexual Abuse." Beverly Hills, CA: Sage, 1988.

Wyden, Barbara. "Growth: 45 Crucial Months." *Life* 25 (1971): 93, 95.

Wynne-Edwards, V. C. "Population Control in Animals." *Scientific American*, August 1964.

Yankelovich, Daniel A. "New Rules in American Life: Searching for Self-Fulfillment in a World Turned Upside Down." *Psychology Today* (April 1981): 35–91.

Young, J. L., and Griffith, E. E. H. "Psychiatric Consultation in Catholic Annulment Proceedings." *Hospital and Community Psychiatry* 36 (1985): 346–347.

Youngblade, Lisa M., and Belsky, Jay. "The Social and Emotional Consequences of Child Maltreatment." In R. Ammerman and Michel Hersen (eds.), *Children at Risk: An Evaluation of Factors Contributing to Child Abuse and Neglect*. New York: Plenum, 1989.

Zabin, L.; Hirsch, M.; Smith, E.; and Hardy, J. "Evaluation of a Pregnancy Prevention Program for Urban Teenagers." *Family Planning Perspectives* 18 (1986): 119–26.

Zajonc, R. B. "Attitudinal Effects of Mere Experience." *Journal of Personality and Social Psychology* 9 (1968): 129.

Zaslow, M. J. *Sex Differences in Children's Responses to Parental Divorce*. Symposium on Sex Differences in Children's Responses to Psychosocial Stress, Woods Hole, MA, 1987.

Zavella, Patricia. *Women's Work and Chicano Families: Cannery Workers of the Santa Clara Valley*. New York: Cornell University Press, 1987.

Zerfoss, Nancy. "School Marm to School Ms." *Changing Education* 6 (1974): 23, 48.

Zigler, Edward F., and Lang, Mary E. *Child Care Choices: Balancing the Needs of Children, Families, and Society*. New York: Free Press, 1991.

Zilbergeld, B. "Pursuit of the Grafenberg Spot." *Psychology Today* 16 (1982): 82–84.

Zill, Nicholas. "Behavior, Achievement, and Health Problems Among Children in Stepfamilies: Findings from a National Survey of Child Health." In E. Mavis Hetherington and Josephine D. Arasteh (eds.), *Impact of Divorce, Single Parenting, and Stepparenting on Children*. Hillsdale, NJ: Lawrence Erlbaum Associates, 1988.

Zimbardo, Philip G. *Shyness*. Reading, MA: Addison-Wesley, 1977.

Zoglin, Richard. "Is TV Ruining Our Children?" *Time*, October 15, 1990, pp. 75–76.

Zuravin, Susan J. "Unplanned Childbearing and Family Size: Their Relationship to Child Neglect and Abuse." *Family Planning Perspectives* 23 (July/August 1991): 155–61.

Zweig, Martin. *Winning on Wall Street*. New York: Warner Books, 1986.

ILLUSTRATION CREDITS

NAME INDEX

Fathalla, Mahoud, 268
Fausto-Sterling, Anne, 50
Fehr, Beverley, 12
Feldman, Harold, 237
Finch,. B. F., 485
Fine, David, 252
Finkelhor, David, 256
Finnegan, L., 288
Fischer, J. L., 253
Fitzpatrick, Mary Anne, 360
Fiumara, N. J., 477
Flax, Carol, 103
Fletcher, Cynthia Needles, 369
Force, Elizabeth S., 254
Ford, C. S., 142
Fordyce, R. R., 480
Forehand, R., 402
Forgas, J. P., 67
Forrest, Jacqueline D., 66, 154, 160, 480, 484, 486–487
Forsyth, C. J., 203
Fournet, L., 203
Fox, G., 484
Fraker, Susan, 276
Francke, Linda Bird, 382–384, 408, 412
Franklin, Benjamin, 241, 421
Freedman, Daniel G., 325
Freedman, Deborah, 169
Freedman, Estelle B., 125
Freedman, Jonathan, 282
Freeman, Ruth, 169 n. 3
Freud, Sigmund, 42 n. 12
Friedan, Betty, 268
Friedland, G. H., 468
Fries, James F., 240, 242, 244
Fromm, Erich, 10 n. 5, 55–56
Fuchs, Victor R., 35, 37–39, 205 also n. 6, 228, 267, 270 n. 10, 272–273, also n. 19, 274, 279, 284, 288–289, 291
Furillo, Andy, 64
Furstenberg, Frank F., Jr., 163, 243, 256, 272, 284, 288, 291, 363, 369–372, 375, 388–390 n. 20, 397, 400–404, 406–408, 410–412, 415
Gallimore, Ronald, 47 n. 15
Gallo, Frank, 256
Gallup, George, Jr., 182, 222
Gandhi, Indira, 48 n. 16
Ganong, Lawrence H., 397, 402
Garbarino, James, 253
Gardella, Peter, 81
Garfinkel, Irwin, 294, 369
Gause, Ralph W., 504
Gelinas, D. J., 251–252
Gelles, Richard J., 246–250, 253–254, 256
Gerson, Marvin, 477
Gibbs, Nancy, 289
Gibbs, R. S., 477
Gibran, Kahlil, 337
Gibson, Charles, 134

Gidycz, C. A., 159
Gilder, George, 217
Giles-Sims, Jean, 402, 406
Glasier, Anna, 490
Glass, Shirley P., 204
Glenn, Norval D., 212–213, 222 also n. 2, 223–224, 376, 378–379
Glick, Paul C., 177, 180, 207, 210, 230, 366, 371–372, 375–378, 397–399, 410
Goldberg, S., 305
Golden, Stephanie, 273, 294
Goldscheider, C., 410
Goldscheider, F. K., 410
Goldstein, Sue, 441 n. 11
Gordon, Michael, 221, 225 n. 7, 226, 265
Gorer, Geoffrey, 73
Gorski, Roger, 121
Gortmaker, Steven L., 289
Gottschalk, Helmuth, 71
Gough, Kathleen E., 27, 47, 259–260 also n. 1, 261
Gould, J. B., 514
Gowing, Marilyn K., 285
Grafenburg, Ernst, 97 n. 12
Grandma Moses, 241
Gray, Madeline, 265, 270
Graziano, William, 142
Greaves, L., 246
Greeley, A. M., 202
Green, Hugh, 485
Green, Jonathan, 299
Green, Kenneth C., 223
Greenberg, Ellen F., 379
Greenberg, J., 403
Greenfeld, Mark, 251–252
Griffith, E. E. H., 365
Griffitt, W., 143
Gross, Ruth T., 512
Guinan, M. E., 465, 503
Guinevere, 62
Gumperz, John J., 360
Guthrie, D., 203
Gutmann, Stephanie, 159
Guyton, A., 494–496, 499
Gwartney-Gibbs, P. A., 159
Hafkin, Mark I., 407
Hagen, Uta, 71
Halem, L. C., 369, 382, 394
Hall, Edward T., 144–146
Hammers, Maryann, 468
Hammond, Dorothy, 48
Handel, Gerald, 329
Hanna, S. L., 401, 406, 410
Hansen, G. L., 72
Hanson, Shirley M. H., 316
Hardy, A., 465, 503
Harlap, Susan, 484, 486–487
Harris, Kathleen Mullan, 284
Harris, Marvin, 267
Harry, J., 116

Hartmann, Heidi, 27, 47
Hartup, Willard W., 208, 305–306, 317–318
Harvey, Dennis, 119
Hatcher, Robert A., 93, 97–98, 107–111, 160–163, 266, 278, 462, 467–470, 473–478, 480–485 also n. 5, 486–491, 494, 497, 503, 510
Hatfield, Elaine, 81, 142, 360
Hayes, Cheryl D., 166
Heapy, N., 246
Heaton, Tim B., 213
Heckert, A., 400
Heiman, Julia, 105–106
Henig, Robin Marantz, 304
Henshaw, Stanley K., 162
Hepburn, Katherine, 241
Herbert, Alan Patrick, 277
Herbert, Tracy Bennett, 247
Herscher, Elaine, 503
Hess, Elizabeth, 81
Hess, E. H., 144–145
Hetherington, E. Mavis, 384, 385 n. 16, 388, 415
Hewlett, Sylvia Ann, 278–279, 284, 288–291, 368, 509
Higginbotham, E., 176
Hill, Anita, 158–159
Hill, Charles T., 66
Hochschild, Arlie, 47, 223, 279–283, 315–317
Hoffman, H., 385 n. 16
Hoffman, L. W., 37
Hoffman, Saul D., 279, 367, 397
Holmes, J. G., 22
Holmes, King K., 462, 464–465, 468, 470, 472, 475, 478
Hooker, Evelyn, 119
Hooper, J., 303
Horn, Jack C., 10
Hornung, C., 248
Hotaling, Gerald T., 248
Houseknecht, S. K., 171
Housley, P. C., 36
Howes, Carollee, 317
Huguley, S., 253
Hulka, Barbara, 502
Hunt, Morton, 63, 115, 116 n. 19, 117, 202
Hunter, J. E., 403
Hutter, Mark, 256
Huttman, Elizabeth, 443
Hutton, Mary D., 224, 291
Hymowitz, C., 274
Ibsen, Henrik, 257
Ievoli, R., 407–408, 410
Ihinger-Tallman, Marilyn, 229, 397, 399–404, 407–408, 410–413, 415
Ishii-Kuntz, Masako, 316
Iverson, T. J., 252
Jablow, Alta, 48
Jacklin, Carol Nagy, 37, 39, 508

SUBJECT INDEX

AAA (American Automobile Association), 442

Abortifacients
IUDs, 480–481, 488
"morning after pill" (Ovral), 480, 490
progestins, 480–481, 487, 488
RU-486, 490

Abortion
after the first trimester, 491
controversy over, 162, 164, 268–269, 480, 490–491
criminalization of, 265–266, 292
defined, 480
hunting and gathering societies and, 260 n. 2
illegal, 265–266
incidence of, 162, 265
methods of surgically induced, 266 also n. 8, 491
mortality rate of medically induced, 266
pro-choice groups, 153, 268–269
right-to-life groups, 164, 268–269, 480
Roe v. Wade, 266 also n. 9, 268–269
self-induced, 265–266 also n. 8
spontaneous (miscarriage), 490–491, 501
teenagers and, 162, 164

Abstinence, 480

Abuse. See Alcohol abuse; Battering; Child abuse; Date rape; Drug abuse; Family violence; Incest; Psychological abuse

Acquaintance rape, 158–159. See also Date rape

Active listening, 151, 354–356, 358–359

Acute stage, of divorce, 383, 391

Acyclovir, 477

Adolescents
adaptation to stepparents, 410–411, 413
alcohol and drug abuse by, 284, 286
contraceptive use and, 160, 163
divorce, effect on, 388–390, 392
friendships, 317
living arrangements of, 176
loneliness, 177, 286, 388, 392
marriage, 376

need for independence, 55
obesity in, 289
psychological problems of, 289, 390
puberty and, 32–33 also n. 9 & 11, 45, 48
romantic love and, 35, 61–66
sexual abuse of, 252–253
sexual behavior of, 18–19, 66 also n. 2, 67, 136, 153–161
shyness, 150–151
STDs and, 462, 465, 471
suicide and, 289
See also Courtship; Dating; Education; Love; Marriage; Primary and Secondary gender characteristics; Teenage pregnancy; Sex hormones

Adoption, 208, 224, 226, 230
kinship rights and, 198

Adult children
increase in single, 170–171
living at home, 176–177
and parental caregiving, 243
and violence, against parents, 253–254

Adultery
attitudes toward, 62–63, 202
consensual, 202–203
and divorce, 202, 363
emotional involvement in, 202, 204
incidence of, 202–204, 215
jealousy and, 70–72
and mistress, 202 n. 5
motivation for, 204–205
open marriage, 203
STD risk, 203
swinging, 203

Adult-infant love, 55–56, 68, 78, 304–306

AFP (alpha-fetoprotein measurements), 505

African Americans. See Blacks

Afterbirth, 509. See also Childbirth

Agape, 53, 68, 78, 80

Age
adultery and, 204
chronological, 240
cohabiting couples, 182
dating differential and, 140–141

divorce predictor and, 19, 375–377, 391
first marriage and, 172, 375–376, 391
first sexual intercourse and, 153–155
living arrangements and, 176–177
marital status and, 373–374
puberty and, 31–32
remarriage and, 398
risk of STDs and, 462, 465, 469, 471, 476
singles and, 170–171, 176
"vital" (biological), 240

Age of child
adaptation to stepparents and, 407, 412, 414
adjustment to divorce and, 387–390, 392
and cost of raising, 425–426

Aging
double standard of, 140–141, 398
effect of, on sexuality, 93–94, 101–102, 239
and health, 242
and income, 240
parents, need to assist, 243, 429 also n. 7
as stage in family life cycle, 237, 240–244, 254–255
and work, 241

Aggression
children of divorced parents and, 388–389, 392
children with permissive parents and, 322, 327
chromosomal anomalies and, 46
gender trait of, 37
jealousy and, 70–71
lower animals and, 36
sexual, 158–160

Agrarian economy, 169, 259–261, 292

Agricultural economy, 261–264, 292

(AIDS) acquired immunodeficiency syndrome
anal copulation and, 468
children with, 464, 466, 503–504
college students and, 462
death and, 462–463, 465–467
diagnosis of, 467
fear of, 111, 155, 157
heterosexuality and, 462–466

556

history of, 462–463 *also* n. 3
homosexuality and, 463, 465–466
immune system and, 466
incidence of, 462–464, 466
incubation period of, 467–468
prevention of, 462, 468
prognosis of, 462, 467
race/ethnicity and, 465–466,
469–470, 503
sexual behavior changes with fear of,
155, 157
symptoms of, 467
transmission of, 462–468
treatment of, 462, 467
women with, 464–466
See also HIV
Alcohol abuse
decreased sexual desire and, 108, 110
family violence related to, 249
fetal alcohol syndrome and, 288
Aleuts, 16
Alimony, 366, 368, 391
Alpha-fetoprotein testing, 505
Alternative birth centers, 305, 507 n. 8,
513
Alternative life-style
cohabitation as, 180–189
homosexuality as, 114–123
singlehood as, 169–180
Altruistic love, 56, 68, 78, 80
American Academy of Pediatrics, 85 n.
2
American Association of Marriage and
Family Therapists, 381
American Psychiatric Association,
118–119
American Psychological Association,
118
Amish, 16 n. 12, 133 n. 1
Amniocentesis, 498, 501 n. 5, 504–505
Amnionic fluid, 496
diagnosis of congenital defects and,
498, 501 n. 5, 504–505
release of, during labor, 502, 507
Anabolism, 92
Anal copulation (sodomy), 86 n. 5,
117–118 *also* n. 21, 157, 251
AIDS and, 467–468
gonorrhea and, 472
Anatomy and physiology, sexual
female, 29–32, 34, 43, 94–102
male, 29–32, 34, 43, 85–94
And the Band Played On (Randy Shilts),
463 n. 3
Androgen, 30, 32, 34
chromosomal anomalies and, 43 n.
13, 46
prenatally androgenized females and,
44
Anger
decreased sexual desire and, 108, 380
of ex-cohabitors, 183

of ex-spouses, 385, 390–392, 405
in family crises, 244, 388–389
jealousy and, 71
latchkey children, 286
of sexually abused children, 253
Annulment, 193–194, 364–365, 373,
397
Anorgasmic, 110
Anus, 87, 97–98, 493
Apgar rating, of neonate, 510–511
Aphodisiacs, 111–112
ARM (adjustable-rate mortgage), 445
Arranged marriage, 63, 131–133, 363
Asian Americans
cultural impact of, 236
divorce and, 236, 378
education and, 236
family life of, 236
gender roles of, 236
increase in U.S. population of, 16,
233, 236
interracial marriage of, 210
median family income of, 236
never-married singles, 173
singlehood and, 173
teenage pregnancy and, 160–161
Associated circumstances, 143–144,
152, 165
Attachment, 305
Attraction, 210
compromises in, 147–148
dating and, 131, 142–153
interracial, 210
limerent, 9, 58–61, 76–77, 150, 152,
165
physical, 142, 150, 152
reciprocal interaction and, 148–150,
165
reward theory of, 151–153, 165
Attraction factor, 150
Authoritarian parent, 322, 327
Authoritarian resolution, to conflict,
339–340, 358
Authoritative parent, 322, 327
Automobile
buying, 441–443, 457
insurance for, 441, 443, 457
maintenance of, 441, 442
Average annual cost of raising children,
426
AZT (zidovudine), 462, 467
"Baby boom" generation, 206, 269–270,
375
Bachelors, 170, 175
Barrier building, in conflict, 349
Balloon payment clause, in installment
contracts, 434
Barrons, 455
Basic needs, 5, 13, 20, 66–67
Basic trust, establishing in children, 301,
306–307

Battering
alcohol abuse and, 249
battered child, 249–251
battered husband, 249
battered parent, 253
battered wife, 246–249, 255
batterer, characteristics of, 247–251
cycle of violence, 246–247
date rape and, 158–159
police intervention, 245, 248–249
shelter movement, 248–249
See also Child abuse; Family violence;
Incest
BBT (basal body temperature), 481–482
Behavior modification, reinforcement
and, 151, 318–319, 327
Beloved (Toni Morrison), 231
Bigamy (polygamy), 195
Bigotry, 211
Big-ticket items, buying, 439–441, 457
"Bill of Divorcement," 366, 390
Binuclear family. *See* Remarriage;
Stepfamily
"Biological clock," 174, 208, 271
Biological imperative, 259–260
Birth. *See* Childbirth; Illegitimate births;
Pregnancy
Birth centers. *See* Alternative birth
centers; Freestanding birth centers
Birth control
attitudes toward, 161–164, 181, 265,
265–267, 270–271, 480
basal body temperature (BBT)
method, 481–482
breast-feeding as, 482
calendar method (rhythm method),
480–482
cervical cap, 480–481, 485 *also* n. 5,
486
clinics, 157, 160, 163–164, 266–267
coitus interruptus (withdrawal), 271,
481–482
coitus reservatus, 482–483 *also* n. 1
condoms, 157, 163, 270, 468, 471,
480–481, 484 *also* n. 4
contraceptive sponge, 481, 484 *also* n.
5, 486
defined, 480
Depo-Provera (injectable progestin),
480–481, 487
diaphragm, 480–481, 484–485 *also*
n. 5
douche, 483 *also* n. 2
education in, 163
failure to use (chance), 160, 162, 481
failure rate of methods, 480–489 *also*
n. 7
history of, 483–485
IUD, 480–481, 488
laparoscopic tubal ligation, 488–489
menstrual extraction, 480, 490
minilaparotomy, 488–489

Birth control (*continued*)
morning-after pill (Ovral), 480, 490
nonoxynol-9, 483, 486
Norplant (progestin implant),
480–481, 487
oral contraceptive pill, 153, 163, 183,
205, 267, 472, 480, 486–487
RU-486, 490
spermacides, 480–481, 483–486
STDs and, 472, 484
vaginal suppositories, 481, 483
vasectomy, 480–481, 488–489 *also* n.
7
See also Abortion; Sterilization; Toxic
shock syndrome
Birth control clinics, 157, 160, 163–164,
266–267
Birth defects
congenital, 470 n. 10, 473 n. 12, 491,
501 *also* n. 5, 502, 504–505
preventable, 287–288, 470 n. 10, 468
n. 8, 473 n. 12, 476 n. 17,
501–503
risks for, 163, 287–288, 501–503
tests to identify, 498, 501 n. 5,
504–506
STDs and, 470 n. 10, 468 n. 8, 473
also n. 12, 476 n. 17
Birth rate, 18, 267
declining, 269–271, 387
replacement level, 205 *also* n 6, 270
also n. 10
Bisexuality, 114–115, 120. *See also*
Episodic homosexual
Blacks
adultery and, 203
AIDS and, 465
cultural impact of, 177, 231, 233–234
divorce and, 19, 234, 376–379, 387,
391
education and, 37, 176, 377
extended family of, 177
family life of, 231, 233–234, 316, 371
gender roles of, 37, 177, 231,
233–234
home affordability for, 377, 443
homogamy in mate selection of, 140
n. 5
homosexuality and, 115, 117, 176
illegitimate births of, 231, 233–234,
278
increase in U.S. population of, 16,
233, 272
infant mortality of, 286, 514
interracial marriage of, 176, 210–211
life expectancy, 29, 176
living arrangements of, 177
marital status of, 233–234, 376–378
marriage odds for women, 172, 176,
234
maternal employment of, 285
median family income of, 236

never-married singles, 172–173, 176
premarital copulation of, 154–155
poverty and, 231, 233–234, 278, 377
separation (marital) of, 234
single-parent families, 177, 231,
233–234
STDs and, 462, 465–466, 469–470,
475
teenage pregnancy and, 160–161,
278
unemployment of, 233–234, 290,
377
violence among, 233
Blastocyst, 97 n. 11, 269, 480, 483 n. 3,
488, 490, 495
Blended family. *See* Remarriage;
Stepfamily
Body language
communication and, 165
conflict and, 144–146, 165, 355
dating and, 144–146
eye contact and, 144
Bogand tribe, of central Africa, 226
Bonding
family, 221, 245, 254
homosexual, 116–118
importance of, 9, 19, 245, 302,
304–305, 316
intimacy and, 10–12, 20–21
neonate and, 9, 302–305, 326, 508,
511–512
See also Attachment; Commitment;
Intimacy; Love; Marriage;
Paired bond; Primary
relationships
Blood tests
fetal defects, 505
HIV, 467 *also* n. 5
pregnancy, 497
Rh factor, 504, 506
syphilis, 196, 475 *also* n. 14
Blue-collar families
divorce in, 20
job insecurity, 290
parenting in, 316
poverty for, 289–290
unemployment and, 289–290
See also Family
Borax stores, 439–440 *also* n. 10, 457
Boundary-maintenance mechanism, 72
Brain
complexity of, 303
of homosexuals, 121
"lateralization of," 121
nutrition and development of,
302–304, 326
prenatal influences on, 121, 302
Breadth of intimacy, 11, 20
Breaking up
gender differences in, 65–66

Breaking the Glass Ceiling (Ann M.
Morrison, Randall P. White, and
Ellan Van Velson), 274
Breast
changes during pregnancy, 497
erotic response of, 87, 89, 97, 99, 107,
118
Breast feeding, 259, 503
advantages of, 510
alcohol and, 502
as method of birth control, 482
smoking and, 502–503
transmission of AIDS through, 468
Breech presentation, 508, 512 n. 12
Bride price, 132–133, 363
Buddhism, 16
Budget
definition of, 422
development of, 422–425, 456
major problems of, in life cycle,
425–429
for personal allowance, 424
principle of forced alternate choice
in, 422, 442
sample, 423
Buying "big-ticket" items, 439–441, 457
Buying daily essentials, principles of,
438–439, 457
Caesarian section
AIDS and, 468
anesthesia and, 508
genital herpes (active) and, 477
incidence of, 509
Caretaker role
of father, 279, 283, 316–317
of grandparent, 177, 231
of mother in traditional family, 35,
188, 224, 228, 259–264, 272,
283, 315
in two-earner family, 279, 282–283,
316–317
Casanova complex, 103
Cash
surrender value, of life insurance
policies, 447–448
when to pay, 438, 441
Cash flow, 421–429, 437. *See also*
Budget; Credit; Income;
Investments; Money; Personal
finance; Savings
Caste system, 14–15
Castration, 33 n. 11, 36
Catabolism, 92
Catholics. *See* Roman Catholics
Celibacy, 20
Cerebral erection, 86
Certified nurse-midwives, 513 *also* n. 13
Cervical cancer
contraceptives and, 484
STDs and, 477
Cervical cap, 480–481, 485 *also* n. 5,
486

Cervix, 497
 dilation in labor, 491, 506–507
 fitting cervical cap, diaphragm, and
  sponge, 485–486
"Change of life," for men, 94
Chicanos. *See* Hispanics; Mexican
 Americans
Child abuse
 age of mother and, 255
 battering, 249–251
 chronically ill children and, 250–251
 cycle of, 246–248
 families at risk for, 246, 249
 incidence of, 250–252
 psychological, 249, 253
 sexual, 249, 251–253, 255
 unreported, 250
 See also Incest
Childbearing, postponement of,
 206–208
Childbirth, 511
 alternative birth centers, 305, 507 n.
  8, 513
 anesthesia/pain relief, 508
 Apgar rating of neonate, 510–511
 appearance of neonate, 299
 cost of, 509
 doulas, role during, 512
 father's role, during, 305, 512
 freestanding birth centers, 513
 high-risk categories, 502–503,
  512–513 n. 12
 labor, stages of, 506–509
 nurse-midwife delivery, 513
 natural, 508
 postpartum period, 511
 premature, 287–288; 499 *also* n. 4,
  501–502, 512
 See also Bonding; Caesarian section;
  Neonate; Pregnancy; Prenatal
  care
Child care
 corporate policies concerning, 285
 day care, types of, 284–285 *also* n. 34
 employed mother and, 283–286, 291,
  293
 ethnic diversity in, 231, 233–234,
  236
 father's participation in, 279, 283,
  292, 315–317
 grandparents' role in, 177
 preschools, 285
 primary responsibility for, 47, 259,
  272–273, 279–283, 291–293,
  315–316, 370, 391
 relatives helping with, 177, 285
 self-care, 284–286, 293
 single fathers and, 231 n. 11
 single mothers and, 19, 160–163, 165,
  214, 231 *also* n. 11, 233–235,
  273, 278–279, 282

traditional, with mother at home, 35,
  188, 224, 228, 259–264, 272,
  283, 315
Child custody, 369–371
Child-free marriage, 205–208,
 214–215, 237, 283, 378, 391
Child rearing
 authoritarian, 322, 327
 authoritative, 322, 327
 developmental process in, 297
 developmental sequence in, 297–314
 differential development in, 301–302
 education, 288–289
 ethnic diversity in, 231, 233–234,
  236, 316
 father's role in, 279, 283–284,
  315–317
 gender-role socialization in, 13, 27,
  34–46, 49, 259–264, 316
 grandparents' role in, 177, 231
 historical perspectives in, 47 also n.
  15
 maternal employment while, 18, 37,
  48, 232–233, 279–286, 291,
  293
 permissive, 322, 327
 as stage in family life cycle, 237–238,
  297–328
Children
 academic performance of, 37, 288,
  388
 anger of, 253, 286, 388–389, 392
 AIDS and, 464, 466
 of annulled marriage, 365
 autonomy and, 301
 average cost of raising, 207, 425 *also*
  n. 3
 basic trust and, 301, 306–307
 in cohabiting families, 19, 182, 186,
  189, 228, 232
 conflicting loyalties of, 388–389
 crying of, 307, 325
 dependency needs of, 55, 78, 297
 deprivation in, 306
 developmental readiness of, 302, 307,
  313–314, 327
 difficulties at school, 286, 288–289,
  389
 discipline of, 318–322
 drug-exposed, 287–288
 economic asset of, 263, 265
 education and, 288–289, 312
 economic liability of, 265, 267
 effect of personality on family,
  322–325, 327–328
 failure experiences of, 313–314, 327
 family values, 221, 254, 302, 314–315
 father's involvement with, 279,
  283–284, 315–317, 326, 407
 father's disinterest in, 284, 316,
  370–371, 391, 404, 413–414
 gender-role identity of, 42–46

genetic potential of, 302–304, 322
genetic programming of, 5, 39, 42,
 302, 312, 321, 323
grandparents and, 177, 231
health problems of, 286–288, 502
homeless, 19, 286
illegitimate, 18–19, 153, 160–164,
 185, 189, 214, 231, 233–234,
 278, 363 n. 1, 365
impact of divorce on, 278–279, 282,
 284, 383, 385, 387–390, 392
importance of early bonding, 302,
 304–305, 316
importance of friends for, 39,
 317–318
importance of nutrition for, 298,
 302–304, 310
independency needs of, 55, 78, 297,
 307
inheritance rights of, 198–199, 363
 also n. 1
intellectual development of, 304,
 310–312, 323, 326
in interracial marriage, 210–211, 216
"latchkey," 284–286, 293
learning to love, 55, 78
legitimization of, 195, 214–215
living arrangement of, 284
living in stepfamily, 19, 228–230,
 400–404, 406–413
loneliness of, 286
long-term effects of divorce on, 284,
 387–390, 392
love and affection for, 55, 306–307,
 323
mastery skills and, 301, 312–314, 327
number of, in families, 263, 269–272
number of, involved in divorce, 387
obesity and, 289 *also* n. 52
parental contact time and, 283–284,
 292–293, 316, 370–371
play of, 35, 38–41, 301
poverty and, 19, 231, 278–279,
 282–283, 367–371, 386
providing emotional security for,
 306–307, 327
providing success experiences for,
 314, 327
psychological problems of, 286–289,
 293
punishment of, 321–322
racial-ethnic differences in
 temperaments of, 325
reinforcement of wanted behavior in,
 318–319, 327
relating to noncustodial parent, 230,
 316, 407, 411–412
replacement rate of, 205 *also* n. 6, 270
 also n. 10
self-esteem and, 308–310, 312, 322,
 327
shyness in, 151

Elderly population. *See* Old age
Electronic fetal monitoring, 507
Embryo, 97 n. 11, 269, 490, 496
    development of, 498
Embryonic period of pregnancy, 32, 45,
    480, 490
Emotion, components of, 53, 152
Emotional maturity, 57, 79
Employment
    affluent women and, 273–274
    cohabitation and, 181
    education and, 38, 273–274, 429
    ethnicity and, 233–234, 290
    gender differences in finding, 274
    independence through, 18, 21, 134,
      171
    maternal, 18, 37, 48, 232–233,
      272–273, 279–286, 291–293
    part-time, 246, 274, 427–428
    pay inequities of, 273 *also* n. 20,
      274–275
    retirement benefits, 274
    two-earner family, 228, 232–233,
      279–283, 292–293
    two jobs, or more, 278
    wage drop, in 1980s–1990s, 290
    work ethic, 315
Empty-nest syndrome, 238
Endogamy, 139–140, 142, 164
Endometrium, 97 n. 11, 490
Engagement, 132–133, 138
Ephebophobia, 113
Episiotomy, 508
Episodic homosexual, 114–115. *See also*
    Homosexuality
Equal Credit Opportunity Act, 437
Equal Pay for Equal Work, 268–269,
    273 *also* n. 20
Equivalent status matching, 146–147,
    152
Erection, penile
    cerebral, 86
    performance anxiety and, 109–111
    tactile, 86, 93, 109–110
    See also Ejaculation; Erotic response,
      male; Orgasm; Penis; Sexual
      dysfunction
Erogenous zones, 86–87, 94, 97–99,
    122–123
Eros, 53, 74–76, 78, 80, 150. *See also*
    Attraction; Limerence; Love
Erotic response
    aging and, 86, 101–102, 239, 243,
      255
    cultural influences on, 85, 104–106,
      108–109, 118–120
    erotophiles, 67, 102–103, 108, 123,
      243
    erotophobes, 67, 102–103, 108–109,
      123, 243
    female, 97–102, 107, 109–111,
      122–123

four phases of, 88–93, 97–101, 122
homosexuality and, 116–118
incompatibility and, 99, 101, 103,
    108–111
male, 86–94, 107, 109–110, 122–123
male-female differences in, 97, 99,
    101, 104, 106–107, 122
male-female similarities in, 88, 92, 97,
    99–100
prepubertal, 89, 99
research on, 88–89, 93, 98, 104–106
See also Homosexuality; Paraphilias;
    Sex drive
Erotophile-erotophobe scale, 67,
    103–104, 108, 123, 179, 186–187,
    200–201, 215
Estrogen, 30–32, 34–35, 43, 108, 110,
    486, 490
Ethnicity
    babies' temperaments and, 325
    bilingualism, 235–236
    child socialization, 37, 316
    defined, 16
    diversity of, 15–16, 19, 21, 234–236
    divorce and, 19, 234, 376–378
    education and, 235–236
    fertility and, 272
    gender roles and, 235–236, 316
    homogamy and, 140, 235
    infant mortality rate and, 287,
      513–514
    premarital copulation and, 154–155
    singlehood and, 172–173, 176, 234
    single-parent family and, 177, 231,
      233–235
    socioeconomic status and, 235–236,
      290
    STDs and, 462, 465–466, 469–470,
      475
    See also Asian Americans; Blacks;
      Hispanics; Race
Excitement phase, of erotic response,
    89–90, 97–99, 122
Exclusivity, 11 *also* n. 5, 58–59
Ex defecto amoris (lack of love), 365
Exercise, importance of, 242
Exhibitionist, 114, 122
Exogamy, 138–139, 142, 164
Extended family, 198, 400
    blacks, 231
    corporate, 225
    monogamy, 104, 195, 225
    parents living in children's household,
      254
    polyandry, 195–196, 215, 227
    polygamy, 195–196, 215, 224–227
    polygyny, 195–196, 215, 226–227
    stem, 226
Extramarital affairs. *See* Adultery
Extrinsic satisfactions. *See* Mass society;
    Secondary relationships
Eye contact, body language and, 144

Failure experiences, 313–314
Fallopian tube, 96, 481, 493
    fertilized egg in, 494
    infertility and, 471
    peristalsis in, 493
    PID and, 471
    prenatal development of, 31
    sterilization and, 488–489
Family
    agrarian, 227 n. 8
    Asian American, 233, 236, 278
    black, 231–234, 272, 290, 316, 371
    changing, 5, 18–21, 48, 224,
      227–236, 254, 280–286,
      289–290
    cohabiting, 19, 182, 185, 228, 232
    defined, 221, 224
    effect of poverty on, 290
    extended, 224–225 *also* n. 7, 226
    group, 226–227
    Hispanic, 234–236, 272, 290
    homeless, 19, 224, 290–291
    impact of industrialization on,
      169–170, 227
    importance of, 20–21, 221–223, 254
    income of, 236
    institution of, 131, 221
    latchkey children in, 284–286
    life cycle of, 221, 237–244, 254–255
    nuclear, 214, 216, 223–225 *also* n. 7,
      22
    nurturance of, 221–222, 280–283
    single-parent, 19, 160–163, 165, 214,
      230–231 *also* n. 11, 233–234
    size of, 225 *also* n. 7, 263, 269–272
    stability of, 254
    traditional, 19, 21, 224–225,
      227–228, 254, 259–264, 279,
      281–282, 292, 315
    two-earner, 19, 228, 232–233, 254,
      269, 279–286
    values, 221, 254, 302, 314–315
    violence in, 221, 244–255
    See also Family violence; Life cycle;
      Marriage; Remarriage;
      Stepfamily
Family cohesion, 316, 236
Family households, types of, 18,
    223–224 *also* n. 4
Family structure, 221, 254
Family system, 131, 164, 214, 254
Family violence
    alcohol abuse and, 249
    battering, 246–251, 253–254
    child abuse, 249–255
    cycle of, 246–248
    divorce and, 388, 392
    elder abuse, 253–254
    husband abuse, 249
    incidence of, 246, 250, 253
    mortality as a result of, 244, 246
    police intervention in, 245, 248–249

Immune system
AIDS and, 466
of neonate, 298
stress and, 244
women and, 31
Impotence, 109, 281
Incest, 197, 251–253
Income
discretionary, 422–424
dual, 232–233, 254, 273, 279–283, 424
education and, 171–172, 426–429
effects of divorce on, 278–279, 282–284, 367–371
marital power structure and, 187
retirement and, 240, 243, 274
single-parent family and, 19–20, 160, 162–163, 165, 231, 273, 278–279
spendable, 422–424
students and, 209, 427, 429
teenage mothers and, 162–163, 278
wage differential and, 273 also n. 20, 274–275
widowhood and, 240
See also Budget; Credit; Inflation; Interest; Investing; Savings; Taxes
Income Tax Guide (J. K. Lasser), 450
Incompatibility
as grounds for divorce, 375, 378
sexual, 99, 101, 103, 108–111, 123, 215
Independency needs, 55–56, 78, 297
Individuation, 5, 7, 20, 27, 298–299, 326
balance between togetherness and, 337
Industrial Revolution
impact on family life, 169–170, 227, 281–293
Infancy
AIDS, 464, 466
attachment to caregiver during, 305–306, 316
brain development in, 302–304, 326
crack cocaine, 287–288, 503
crying in, 299, 325
defined, 299
developmental sequence in, 299–301, 326–327
experiencing self-love in, 55
provision of emotional security during, 306–307, 327
socialization in, 301–302
See also Children; Gender-role socialization; Neonate
Infanticide, 245, 260 n. 2
Infantile love, 55–56
Infant mortality rates, 30, 162–163, 287, 466, 513–514
Infantophilia, 113

Infatuation, 60
Infectious diseases, during pregnancy, 503–504. See also AIDS; STDs
Infertility, 471, 476
Inflation, purchasing power and, 240, 453–454, 458
Inheritance rights, 198–199, 363
In locus parentis, 157
Installment contract, 432–434
Intellectual potential, 302–304, 310–312, 323, 326
Interclass marriage, 140
Interdependency needs, 55–56, 78, 297
Interest rates
"average daily balance," 435
compound, 451–455, 458
true annual, 430, 434–435 also n. 8
Interfaith marriage, 211–213, 216
Interlocutory decree, 367
Intermarriage, 140, 210–213, 216
Interracial marriage, 140, 210 also n. 12, 211, 216
Intimacy
betrayal of, 70, 72, 80, 202, 263
bonding and, 10–12, 20–21
cohabitation and, 183
components of, 11
dating and, 137–138
defined, 11
degree of intensity in, 11–12, 20
fear of, 175
low need for, 12
marriage and, 198
search for, 10–12, 20–21, 40–41, 177–179
self-esteem and, 71
Investing
budgeting for, 425
comparing rates of return on, 455–456
inflation and, 453–454, 458
life insurance and, 448–449, 457
safety, yield, and growth in, 452, 456, 458
versus speculating, 452
stocks and bonds, 454–455
IQ, early bonding and, 510
Intrinsic satisfactions. See Bonding; Commitment; Intimacy; Love; Primary relationships
In-vitro fertilization, 494 n. 2
Involuntary permanent singles, 174–176
Involuntary temporary singles, 174–175
IRA accounts, 436, 450 also n. 17, 451, 457–458
Isolates, 12, 17–18
IUD (intrauterine device), 480–481, 488
I/V drug users, AIDS and, 465, 467
Jealousy
constructive handling of, 73–74
destructive, 73

gender differences in, 71–72, 80
grief and, 69
love and, 69–71, 80
patterns of, 70–71
sexual, 72–73
violence and, 71, 73, 80
Joint custody, 370
Joint tenancy, 198
Judaism
adultery and, 202
Conservative, 211, 213
divorce and, 194 n. 2, 378 also n. 13, 391
incidence of, 16, 211 n. 14
interfaith marriage and, 211–213
Orthodox, 211, 213
Reform, 211, 213
Judeo-Christian heritage, 203, 245
Julius Caesar (William Shakespeare), 344
Kama Sutra, 107
Kaposi's sarcoma, 467
Keogh plan, 451–452, 457
Kinsey Institute for Research in Sex, Gender, and Reproduction, 85 also n. 3
Kinship relations, 198, 400
Labia
anatomy, 30, 32
erotic sensitivity of, 98, 106, 122
fused, 43
Labor
false, 497 n. 3, 506
stages of, in childbirth, 506–509
See also Childbirth
Lactation, 33
See also Breastfeeding
Lady Chatterley's Lover (D. H. Lawrence), 63
Laparoscopy, 488–489
Latchkey children, 284–286
Legal separation, 364
Leisure time, 273, 279–280. See also Second shift
Lesbians, 104, 116–118, 120–122. See also Homosexuality
Leveling, 353–354, 358–359
Life cycle
child-free marriage, 237
child-rearing years, 237–238, 297–328, 425–429
postchild year, 237–240
prechild years, 237, 425
retirement years, 237, 240–244, 254–255
return to singlehood, 237, 244, 255
U-shaped curve of marital satisfaction, 237 also n. 27, 238–239, 244, 254
Life expectancy (actuarial), 29–31, 173 also n. 13, 176, 240
Life insurance
buying, 446–449, 457

Marriage (*continued*)
    sacred aspects of, 193–194, 215
    satisfaction levels in, 357–359, 381
    second shift in, 273, 279–283
    sexual love in, 198–201, 215
    teenage, 376
    trade-offs in, 147–148, 152, 165
    traditional, 214, 216, 223, 237, 254,
        259–264, 279, 281–282
    two-earner, 18, 232–233, 254, 267,
        279–286
    See also Intimacy; Commitment;
        Marital conflict; Marital
        satisfaction; Sex; Two-earner
        family
Marriage broker, 132
Marriage ceremony, 193, 196, 199
Marriage certificate, 196
Marriage contract, 132, 215
Marriage counseling, 381 *also* n. 15, 391
Marriage license, 196–197, 214–215
Marriage odds, 140–143, 171–172, 174
Marriage penalty tax, 184 *also* n. 22
Marriage rates, 18, 272, 375, 398
Masochism, 70, 113, 122
Mass society, 17 *also* n. 13, 20, 196; 222
Mastery skills, 301, 312–314, 327
Masturbation, 89, 99, 104–105, 107,
    117–118
Mate selection. *See* Cohabitation;
    Courtship; Dating; Marital choice
Mattachine Society, 116 n. 19
Maternal employment, 18, 37, 48,
    232–233, 279–286
    economic necessity for, 267, 289
    effect on children, 280–286
    effect on husband, 280–283
    sharing household work, 279–283
    second shift and, 273, 279–283
Mature love, 55–57, 79
Marvin v. Marvin, 185
Mediation. *See* Divorce mediation
Medicare, 445
Men
    abnormal sexual behavior of
        (paraphilias), 107, 112–114
    "breaking up" and, 65–66
    changing role of, 279–282
    child support and, 278–279, 282,
        369, 404, 413
    competitive needs of, 40
    dating prospects for, 140–143, 175
    dominance and power of, 47, 208,
        248–249, 261–262, 280–282
    economic advantages, following
        divorce, 279, 282
    ejaculatory pattern of, 89–91, 94, 101
    erotic response of, 86–94, 107,
        109–110, 122–123, 154,
        200–201
    gender-role socialization of, 13, 27,
        35–47, 49

homosexuality and, 114–117, 175
housework and, 279–282
late-marrying, 174–175
life expectancy of, 29–31, 173 *also*
    n. 13, 240
loneliness of, 178–179
never-married, 171, 175–176
patriarchal authority of, 235–236
provider role of, 35, 224, 228, 272,
    280, 282, 292
sexual dysfunctions of, 93, 109–111,
    123, 281
status needs of, 40–42
stress and, 31, 244
suicide and, 31, 66
as "superdads," 279, 283, 316
and violence, 71, 80
Menarche, 97, 260
Menopause, 96–97, 101–102, 239
Menstrual cycle, 96–97, 107, 481
Menstrual extraction (regulation), 480,
    490
Menstruation, 33 *also* n. 9, 97, 494
    use of contraceptives during, 486
        n. 6
Mexican Americans
    cultural impact of, 234–235
    education of, 235
    employment of, 235
    gender roles of, 235–236
    family income of, 235
    living arrangements of, 177
    marital patterns of, 173
    See also Hispanics; Racial-ethnic
        families
Middle age
    life cycle in, 238–239
    romantic love in, 64
    sexuality in, 94, 102
Minilaparotomy, 488–489
Mid-life crises, 238–239
Midsummer Night's Dream, A (William
    Shakespeare), 335
Miscarriage, 490–491
Mistress, 202 n. 5
Money
    arranged marriages and, 132–133,
        135, 363
    balance of power and, 187
    borrowing, 269, 434–436
    budgeting, 422–425
    buying, general principles for,
        440–441, 457
    cash flow, 421–429
    cohabitation and, 187–188
    conflicts over, 421–422, 425
    dating and, 135
    expenses (discretionary and
        nondiscretionary), 422–425
    investing, 425, 449–455, 457–458
    management of, 223, 421–422 *also*
        n. 1, 456–458

saving, 424–425, 427–428
spending, 425
See also Child support; Credit;
    Income; Inflation; Loans;
    Mortgage loans; Personal
    finance; Spousal support
Money Guide (Marshall Loeb), 445
Money Magazine, 455
Monogamy, 104, 195, 225
    STDs and, 462
Mormons, 196, 211
Morning-after pill, 480, 490
Morphophilia, 113
Mortality rate
    abortion and, 266
    AIDS and, 462–463, 465–466
    birth ratio and, 29
    divorce and, 380
    gender and, 29–31, 240
    infant, 30, 162–163, 287, 466, 477,
        499 n. 4, 513–514
    PID and, 471
Mortgage insurance, 457
Mortgage loans
    adjustable rate (ARM), 445
    eligibility for, 269, 444–445
    fixed rate, 445
    home equity, 436
    payments as percentage of gross
        income, 422 n. 1, 457
    refinancing, 445
Motivation, 53, 78
Multiple births, 43–44 *also* n. 14, 494
    also n. 2, 495
    fertility drugs and, 494 *also* n. 2, 495
Mutual funds, 455
Mutual goals, 357–358
National Committee for Prevention of
    Child Abuse, 253
National Domestic Violence Prevention
    and Treatment Act, 248
National Family Violence Survey, 249
Native Americans (American Indians),
    16, 378
Nature versus nurture, 38–39, 43, 299
Nayar, of Malabar Coast, 227
Necrophilia, 113 *also* n. 16
Neurons, 302–303
Never marrieds, 169 n. 2, 171–176, 188,
    194, 272. *See also* Singles
Neonate
    adjustment to temperature, 297–298
    appearance, 299
    bonding, 9, 302–305, 326, 508,
        511–512
    brain development, 302, 304, 310,
        326
    crying patterns, 298, 325
    defined, 297, 326
    developmental sequence, 297–299,
        310

effects of prenatal nutrition, 302, 310, 326
evaluation of (Apgar rating), 510–511
fontanels of skull, 299
gender assignment of, 34–35, 43–47
HIV and, 288, 466
immune system, 298
inadequate prenatal care and, 162–163, 287, 511 n. 11
low birth weight, 162, 287–288, 501, 511 n. 11
median birth weight, 299, 508
molding of head, 299
postnatal blood circulation, 297
prenatal influences, 287–288, 500–502
providing emotional security for, 306
rooting reflex of, 298 also n. 3
STDs and, 288, 470 n. 10, 468 n. 8, 473 n. 12
uniqueness, 298–299, 326
vision, 298, 305
weight loss (normal), 298 n. 2
See also Breast-feeding; Childbirth
New Joy of Sex (Alex Comfort), 107
No-fault divorce, 363, 366–371, 373, 391
Noncustodial parent, 230, 316
Nondiscretionary expenses, 422–423
Nonfamily households, 176, 223
Nonoxynol-9, 483, 486
Non-profit-making credit, 430, 432–433
Norplant contraceptive, 480–481, 487
Nuclear family, 214, 216, 223, 237, 254, 315
Nucleotides, 28 n. 3
Nurture
    as gender trait, 34–35, 38–39, 316
    See also Altruistic love; Bonding
Nutrition, importance of, 110, 302–304
Obesity, 242, 289 also n. 52
Obligative homosexual, 114, 116–117.
    See also Homosexuality
Old age
    abuse by children in, 253–254
    contact with family and, 243–244
    economic status in, 240, 429
    fulfillment in, 241, 244
    health in, 242, 429
    living arrangements in, 242–243, 255
    loneliness in, 240, 255
    marital status in, 102, 173 also n. 12, 240, 244–245, 255
    number of population in, 240, 254
    sexuality in, 86, 93–94, 101–102, 239
    See also Grandparents; Life cycle
Oneida Perfectionists, 483 n. 1
Open credit, 429–430, 433, 438, 456–457

Open marriage, 203
Openness in intimacy, 11, 20, 72
Oral contraceptive pill, 163, 205
    contraindications for taking, 486–487
    failure rate of, 481, 486–487
    hormones in, 486
    popularity of, 480, 486
    risk of death compared to pregnancy, 487
    smoking and, 486–487
    societal effects of, 153, 205
    STDs and, 487
    vaginitis and, 487
    See also Birth control
Organic methods of birth control, 480–482
Oral-genital sex. See Cunnilingus; Fellatio
Orgasm
    differences in male and female, 97, 99, 106–107, 122–123
    failure to achieve, 109–110
    female pattern of, 97–102, 107, 109–111
    male pattern of, 89–91, 94, 101
    multiple, 97, 101, 105, 107
    pattern set at puberty, for male, 89–91, 94, 101
    prepubertal, 89, 122
    similarities of male and female, 92, 97, 99–100
Orgasm phase, of erotic response, 89–93, 117, 122
Othello (William Shakespeare), 69 n. 4
Ovaries, 31–32, 34, 45, 96, 493
Overlapping distributions, 33–35
Ovral (morning-after pill), 490
Ovulation, 96, 493, 495
    breast-feeding and delay of, 482
    cessation of, 96–97, 101–102, 239, 486
    fertilization and, 481
    menstrual cycle and, 96, 481, 486 n. 6
    onset of, 33, 97, 260
    probable time of, 481–482, 486 n. 6
    See also Contraception; Menopause; Menstrual cycle; Menstruation
Ovum (egg cell), 28, 31, 33 n. 8, 96–97, 493
Oxytocin, 91–92
Paired bond
    animals and, 10
    asexual, 9, 20
    commitment and, 68–69
    dating and, 131
    friendships and, 317–318
    intimacy and, 10–12, 20
    marriage and, 193, 199, 215
    neonate and, 9, 302–305, 316
    sexual, 12, 20–21, 58, 66–67, 80, 116

    See also Bonding; Commitment; Intimacy; Love; Primary relationships
Pap smear, 477
Parallel parenting, 371
Paraphilias, 107, 112–113 also n. 16, 114, 122, 251
Parenthood
    cohabiting families and, 182
    deferred, 206–208
    noncustodial, 230, 316, 371
    at stage in family life cycle, 237–238, 297–328
    singles and, 19, 160–163, 165, 214, 228, 230–231, 233–235, 254, 278–279, 283
    teenage, 18–19, 160–165, 278
    See also Child rearing; Children; Divorce; Neonate; Parenting
Parenting
    cohabitation and, 182
    enjoyment of, 237–238
    father's role in, 163, 279, 283–284, 315–317, 326, 370–371
    parallel, 371
    race/ethnicity and, 231, 233–234, 236, 316, 371
    role strain in, 279–286
    styles of, 322, 327
    stepparents and, 228–230, 400–404, 406–413
    See also Children; Child rearing; Neonate; Parenthood; Single-parent family; Two-earner family
Passion cluster, 58–59, 80
"Passionate Shepherd to His Love, The" (Christopher Marlowe), 167
Passive smoking, 502
Patriarchy, 48 n. 16, 261–262
Pedophilia, 113, 122, 251–252, 255
Penis
    anatomy of, 85–86 also n. 4, 87, 493
    erection of, 86, 89–90, 93, 122
    erotic sensitivity of, 86–87, 122
    prenatal development of, 29–32, 34
    reproductive function of, 96
    size of, 85–86, 106
    surgery to reconstruct, 47
    See also Circumcision; Sexual dysfunction
"Penis envy," 42 n. 12
Penniless Billionaires (Max Shapiro), 455
Perception, 33, 41, 69
Perineum, 87, 97
Permissive parent, 322, 327
Personal finance
    budgeting in, 422–429
    directing cash flow in, 421–429, 437
    getting your money's worth, 437–448

as subcultures of society, 15–16, 21,
  235–236
Rape, 111–112, 158–159
Rationalization (in conflict), 337
Reality-oriented behavior, 336–339
Reciprocal interaction, 148–150
Reconstituted family. *See* Remarriage;
  Stepfamily
Refined divorce rate, 372–373
Refractory period, of erotic response,
  93–94, 101, 122
Reinforcers, behavior, 151, 318–319,
  327
Rejection, 142, 151, 343–344
Relationship-centeredness, 282
Relationship satisfaction, 186–187,
  282–283
Relationships
  balance of nurture provision in, 57,
    282–283
  commitment in, 10–13, 20–21,
    67–69, 317
  continuum in, 8–9, 20, 148
  egalitarian, 201, 208, 282–283, 317
  with ex-spouses, 404–406
  homosexual, 116–118
  horizontal, 317
  intimacy in, 10–12, 20–21
  jealousy in, 69–74
  primary, 6–9, 17, 20
  secondary, 6–9, 17, 20
  vertical, 317
  See also Children; Cohabitation;
    Dating; Family; Friendships;
    Marriage; Paired bond; Singles
Religion
  adultery and, 202
  child abuse and, 251
  childlessness and, 207
  cohabitation and, 180–181, 189
  divorce and, 193–194 *also* n. 2,
    363–365, 375 *also* n. 12 & 13,
    391
  family values and, 254
  homosexuality and, 115, 117–118
  interfaith marriage and, 211–213, 216
  marital commitment and, 198
  as subculture of society, 16
REM (rapid eye movement), 298
Remarriage
  age at, 398
  child free, 207, 400
  child support and, 371
  cohabitation prior to, 400
  in colonial period, 230, 397
  communication in, 403, 413
  conflict with stepchildren in, 401,
    406–408, 414
  demographics of, 173, 244, 397–399,
    413
  differences between a first marriage
    and, 397, 399–400, 413

divorce and, 19, 173, 188, 230, 371,
  379, 386, 391–392, 397 *also* n. 1
financial problems of, 379, 403–404,
  413
incidence of, 18–19, 229–230, 244,
  386, 392, 398
odds for, 244, 385–387, 392, 398 *also*
  n. 2, 399
own children only in, 400
relationships with ex-spouses in,
  404–406
stepchildren in, 228–230, 397,
  400–404, 406–413
success of, 19, 387, 391–392
widows and widowers and, 244, 399
Repossession, 434–435
Reproduction, human. *See* Childbirth;
  Conception; DNA molecule;
  Fertilization; Genes; Gestation;
  Pregnancy; Spermatogenesis; Sex
  chromosomes
Resolution phase, of erotic response, 93,
  101, 122
Resolution of conflict. *See* Conflict
Retirement
  age at, 240
  budgeting for, 240, 429 *also* n. 6
  health and, 242
  income at, 240, 244, 274
  interests at, 241
Reward theory of attraction, 151–153
Rh factor, 506, 512 n. 11
Rhythm method of birth control,
  480–482
Right-to-Life Movement, 164,
  268–269
RNA (ribonucleic acid), 476 n. 15
"Roaring twenties," 134
Roe v. Wade, 266 *also* n. 9, 268–269
Role behavior, 7 *also* n. 3
Role taking
  conflict resolution and, 356–357
  self-assurance, 151
Roman Catholics
  abortion and, 164
  adultery and, 202
  annulment and, 193–194, 364–365
  birth control and, 164, 480
  commitment in marriage, 69
  divorce and, 193–194 *also* n. 2,
    363–365, 378, 391
  excommunication and, 364
  homosexuality and, 115, 117–118
  incidence of, 16, 211
  interfaith marriage and, 211–213, 216
Romantic love, 12, 58, 61–66, 80, 283
Romantic novels, 64
Romeo and Juliet (William Shakespeare),
  85, 150
Rooting reflex, 289 *also* n. 3
RU-486, 490

"Rule of 72," 452–453 n. 18
Sacrament, 193–194, 215
Sadism, 113, 122
SAT (Scholastic Aptitude Test), 37, 288
Saturday Evening Post, 63
Savings, budgeting for, 424–425
Scrotum, 30, 32, 47, 85–86
"Second shift," 273, 279–283, 292
Second Shift, The (Arlie Hochschild), 279
Secondary gender characteristics,
  32–34, 46–48
Secondary relationships, 6–9, 17, 178
Self-assurance, 151, 174
Self-blame, 70, 80, 247, 252
Self-destruction, 70, 252
Self-disclosure, 11, 72, 106
Self-esteem, 72, 110–111, 247,
  308–310, 327, 344, 387
Self-image, 27, 33, 349
Selfishness, 55
Self-love, 55, 78
Self-pity, 70
Semen, 91
SEP (Simplified Employee Pension),
  451–452, 457
Separation distress, 305
Separation, marital, 234, 272, 335, 372,
  374, 381, 397
Service contracts, 439, 457
Setting limits, 308, 318, 320–321
Sex
  abnormal (paraphilias), 112–113 *also*
    n. 16, 114, 122, 251–253
  cohabitation and, 18, 136, 186–187
  cultural attitudes toward, 62–63, 67,
    85, 102–108, 118–120, 153, 157,
    180–183, 189
  extramarital, 62–63, 70–72,
    202–205 *also* n. 5, 215, 363
  marriage and, 198–201, 215
  premarital, 18–19, 66 n. 2, 153–158,
    160
  procreational, 85, 131
  power and, 187, 200–201, 215
  STDs and, 155, 462–477
  See also Copulation; Date rape; Erotic
    response; Homosexuality;
    Incest; Intimacy; Masturbation;
    Paraphilias; Sex hormones
Sex change surgery, 47
Sex chromosomes, 28, 29 *also* n. 4,
  30–31, 34, 43–48, 498
Sex drive
  aging and, 93–94 *also* n. 6 & 7
  chromosomal anomaly and, 46
  effect of menopause on, 101–102
  effect of sterilization on, 489
  individuation of, 20, 67, 77, 89–91,
    99, 101, 104, 106–111, 175, 179,
    186, 215
  lowered, 108–111, 280–281

forms of, 229, 400, 413
incidence of, 19, 230, 413
noncustodial parents and, 407, 411–414
stepfather role in, 407, 410–411, 414
stepmother role in, 407–410, 414
stepsibling role in, 406–407, 412–414
Stepparent
cohabiting family and, 182
difficulty of role for, 406–411, 414
resident, 406–411
stress for, 406–407, 414
Stereotypes of women, 273, 276–275
Sterility, 33
abortion and, 265
chromosomal anomalies and, 46
divorce as a result of, 363
following sterilization, 489
PID and, 171
Sterilization
failure rate of, 489
laparoscopy, 488–489
minilaparotomy, 488–489
popularity of, 480, 488
safety of, 488
vasectomy, 488–489 *also* n. 7
Stock market, 454–455
Stop-start technique of ejaculatory control, 93
Storge love, 12, 59, 74, 76–77, 80
Stress
caring for elderly parent and, 254
death of spouse and, 244
of divorce, 38, 278–279, 283–284, 367, 386
economic, 246, 248, 253, 289–293, 367, 386, 403–404, 413
of homeless, 290–291
parental, 251, 279–283, 292–293, 406–407, 414
psychological, 286–289, 411, 414
role overload, 273, 279–283, 292–293
unemployment and, 246, 249, 251, 289–290
units, 244
violence and, 244–255
virus infections and, 477
Submission, as gender ideology, 280–281
Subsocieties, 13–16, 21
Subsistence farms, 262–264
Suicide
battered wives and, 247
children and, 286
love affairs and, 66, 70
men and, 31, 66
"Superdad," 279, 283, 316
"Supermom," 279, 283
Swinging, 179

Syphilis, 196, 462–463, 473 *also* n. 12, 474–476
Taoism, 16
Tactile stimulation, 86–87, 94–95, 97, 106–107, 109–110, 123
Tale of Two Cities, A, (Charles Dickens), 68
Tax-deferred investment, 451
Taxes
information regarding changes in, 450
"marriage penalty," 450
percent of income spent on, 448–449
tax consultants, 450, 457
tax shelters (IRA, Keogh, SEP), 450 *also* n. 17, 451–452, 457
Taxonomy, 88
Tay-Sachs disease, 505 *also* n. 7
Teenage pregnancy
abortion and, 162
birth defects associated with, 163
contraceptive use and, 160, 162
cost for caring for, 160, 163
ethnicity and, 160–161
infant mortality and, 162–163
illegitimate, 18, 20, 162–163, 286
incidence of, 18–19, 160–161, 165, 278
poverty and, 19–20, 160, 162–163, 165, 278
solutions to curb, 163–164
Teenagers
AIDS and, 462
divorce and, 20, 376, 391
marriage and, 376, 391
pregnancy and, 160–165
premarital pregnancy and, 18–19, 153, 160–164, 278, 286
sex and, 18, 153–157
STDs and, 462, 465, 471
See also Dating; Education; Gender-role socialization; Puberty; Sex hormones; Shyness
Television and children, 288
Temperament, 299, 306–307, 323–325, 327–328
Term insurance, 446–449, 457
Testicles, 30, 34, 45, 85, 87, 93, 493
removal of, 44, 47
Testosterone, 33 n. 10, 87, 108
psychoendocrine aging and, 94
well-being and, 91–92
Tomboyism, 44
Toxic shock syndrome, 485 *also* n. 5, 486 *also* n. 6
Trade-offs, in dating and marriage, 147–148, 152, 165
Transsexualism, 46–47
Transvestism, 47
Trichomoniasis, 462–463, 477, 484
Trimester, 491
Trust, betrayal of, 72, 80, 251–253

Tubal ligation, 488–489. *See also* Sterilization
Twins
fraternal, 494 n. 2, 495
identical, 43–44 *also* n. 14, 494 n. 2, 495
Two-earner family, 232–233, 254, 279–283
child care options, 284–285 *also* n. 34 & 36, 286, 293
division of household labor in, 279–283, 292
financial consequence of divorce in, 282–283
gender-role identity in, 279–283
marital power in, 280–283
marital satisfaction in, 282–283
necessity for, 267, 284, 291, 293
second shift in, 273, 279–283, 292
See also Employment; Income; Work; Stress
Ultrasonic scanning, 501 n. 5
Umbilical cord, 497, 508–509
Unemployment
chronic, 14, 290
coping with, 234
defined, 290 n. 53
ethnicity and, 290, 377
stress of, 246, 248, 251, 289–290
violence and, 246, 249, 251
Unnatural Causes (P. D. James), 147
Urogenital system, female, 96
U-shaped curve, of marital satisfaction, 237 *also* n. 27, 238–239, 244, 254
Uterus, 31, 96–97, 493–497
Vacuum curettage, 491
Vagina, 94–95, 97–99, 106, 111, 122, 493
construction of artificial, 47
lubrication and vasocongestion in, 98–99, 101, 105, 122
prenatal development of, 31–32
Vaginal yeast infections, 472, 487
Vaginismus, 110–111
Values (cultural), 221, 223, 254, 302, 314–315
Vas deferens, 30, 489, 493
Vasectomy, 480–481, 488–489 *also* n. 7
Venereal diseases. *See* AIDS; STDs
Violence. *See* Child abuse; Date rape; Family violence; Homicide; Spousal abuse; Suicide; Wife abuse
Virginity, 66 n. 2, 157, 170
Visitation rights, 370–371, 405
"Vital" (biological) age, 240
Voluntary permanent singles, 174–176
Voluntary temporary singles, 174–175
Voyeurism, 114, 122
Vulva, 94–95, 97–98
Wage differential, 273 *also* n. 20, 274–275, 367
War and Peace (Leo Tolstoy), 148

Wasserman test, for syphilis, 196, 475
also n. 14
Weddings, 132
Weisenberger Report, 455
Well-being, feelings of, 53, 91–92
Widows, 102, 173 *also* n. 12, 240, 244, 255
Widowers, 173, 244, 255
Wife abuse
    battered women, characteristics of, 246–247
    escaping from, 247, 249
    incidence of, 244, 246, 255
    learned helplessness, 247
    remaining in relationship, 246–247
    shelters, 248–249
    suicide and, 247
Withdrawal (coitus interruptus), 271, 481–482
Withdrawal (in conflict), 337
Women
    abused, 158–160, 246–249, 255
    AIDS and, 464–466
    biological clock for, 174, 208, 271
    "breaking up" and, 65–66
    career versus children, 274–275, 283
    career versus marriage, 171–172, 174, 274, 283
    caregiver role of, 35–37, 55, 224, 228, 272, 280–283
    changing role of, 48, 228, 259, 272–273, 279–283
    child care, responsibility for, 47 *also* n. 15, 259–265, 272, 280–283, 291, 293
    cohabiting, 180–189
    connection and intimacy needs of, 40, 42
    credit rights of, 269, 437

discrimination against, 37, 269, 273–275
divorced, 38, 173, 176, 178–179, 188, 272, 278–279, 367–371, 386–387, 391–392
economic productivity of, 37, 47, 259–265, 267, 272–273, 279–283, 291–293
economic and social independence of, 171–172, 196, 283, 292
education of, 37, 134, 171
employment of, 18, 37, 48, 134, 171, 232–233, 272–276, 279–286, 291–292
erotic response of, 97–102, 107, 109–111, 122–123
friendships for, 40–41, 177–178
gender-role socialization of, 13, 27, 35–46, 49, 259–264
homosexuality and, 115, 117–118
idealization of, 62, 80
late-marrying, 174
leisure time for, 273, 279–284, 292
life expectancy of, 29–31, 173 *also* n. 13, 240
loneliness of, 177–180, 240
marital odds for, 140–143, 171–172, 176, 234, 398
never-married, 171–176, 272
options for, 18, 171–172, 268, 283
poverty of, 19–20, 160–165, 231, 240, 273–274, 278–279, 282–283, 292, 368–369
power and, 48 *also* n. 16, 187, 200–201, 215, 316
reproductive rights of, 153, 162, 164, 266–268
second shift for, 273, 279–283, 292

sexuality of, 97–102, 107, 109–111, 116–118, 120–123, 153–157, 179–180, 200–201
single, 170–176, 178–180, 173 *also* n. 12, 240, 244, 278–279, 398
stereotypical views of, 273, 276–277
stress and, 31, 244–249
Women's Liberation Movement, 183, 268
Women Who Love Too Much (Robin Norwood), 64
Work ethic, 315
Workplace
    child care issues, 273, 283–286
    dating opportunities in, 133–134
    glass ceiling, 273–275
    lower income 1980s and 1990s, 290
    pay inequities of, 273 *also* n. 20, 274–275
    sexual harassment in, 158–159, 276
    women's entry into, 134, 171, 188, 228, 267, 272–273
    See also Employment; Income
Working poor, 289–290, 377,444
XX chromosome structure. *See* Sex chromosomes
XY chromosome structure. *See* Sex chromosomes
You Just Don't Understand (Deborah Tannen), 39
Your Federal Income Tax (U.S. Superintendent of Documents), 450
Your Financial Security (Sylvia Porter), 445
Zoophilia, 113
Zygote, 97 n. 11, 269, 480, 490, 494, 496